LIVING BY THE SWORD

KNIGHTHOOD FOR THE MODERN MAN

ERIC DEMSKI

ISBN: 978-1-4907-3607-5 (sc)
ISBN: 978-1-4907-3608-2 (e)

Library of Congress Control Number: 2014908819

Trafford rev. 06/27/2014

www.trafford.com
North America & international
toll-free: 1 888 232 4444 (USA & Canada)
fax: 812 355 4082

This book is dedicated to GOD, as well as my mother and father, who first placed my feet on the honorable path to Chivalry.

Some say that the Age of Chivalry is past, that the spirit of Romance is dead. The Age of Chivalry is never past, so long as there is a wrong left un-redressed on earth.
—Charles Kingsley, *His Letters and Memoirs of His Life*,
vol. II, ch.28

Your first task is to be dissatisfied with yourself, fight sin, and transform yourself into something better. Your second task is to put up with the trials and temptations of this world that will be brought on by the change in your life and to persevere to the very end in the midst of these things.
—Saint Augustine, *Commentary on Psalm 59, 5*

The Christian and the hero are inseparable.
—Samuel Johnson, *Rambler # 44*

For protection of the good, and for the destruction of evil-doers, to make a firm footing for the right, I come into being, age after age.
—*Bhagavad-Gita*, 4, 8

Five Paradoxes of Chivalry

True Strength from Humility
True Courage from Fear of GOD
Everything worthwhile from true Sacrifice
True Faith from doubt of the World
True Obedience from rebellion to the World and the flesh

CONTENTS

An Introduction to Living by the Sword.. xiii

The Mind of the Knight... 1
Strength 46
Strength Chapter Appendix: Some Steps to Strength 134
Courage 143
Sacrifice.. 210
Faith 300
Obedience... 390

Appendix 2: Some Chivalry Codes mentioned in the text 497
Appendix 3: Classifications of Crosses displayed in this book.......... 509
Bibliography... 515

AN INTRODUCTION TO LIVING
BY THE SWORD

Over 25 years ago, surrounded by a circle of older, wiser men, I stood my ground. I had just graduated from high school, and these men confronted me with the inevitable question. What was I going to do with my life?

It was some crowded event, probably a congratulatory dinner after graduation, but to be honest, I don't remember. All I recall are the older men, some bearded, some not, some Christian, some Jewish, some agnostic, but all intent upon my answer. I was very young, around 18, and didn't quite have all the right phrases to express my exact thoughts; but even then I was filled with the vision of quests for GOD's greater glory. "There are warriors out there for GOD." I told these men. "I would like to be one, I think."

"What do you mean?" They asked.

"I would like to be a man who goes on missions for GOD, like a knight in shining armor—you know, going around saving people and saving souls, doing good things, GOD's work."

One man, more cynical and bitter than the rest, snapped with a quick retort: "Knights in shining armor? Like a knight errant? None of them I ever read about fought for anyone but themselves."

Taken aback by his irritated response, I mentioned Galahad. "Ha!" He laughed. "If you're going to talk about him, why not bring up Moses?"

Moses and Galahad? My mind filled with images of daring sword battles and talks with raging flames on tops of mountains. These two great heroes seemed vastly different at first, but didn't they both engage in battles for GOD, and didn't they both fight for the common good, and for Truth? Of course, Moses is considered a historical figure, while Galahad is a literary creation, probably a composite of several knightly examples. Still, these were good men, honorable heroes, who had walked with GOD.

I realized that we were discussing a topic poorly defined. What was a good man? What really makes a good person? How does one recognize such people? How does one embark on a life of honorable action? What is an honorable action? Can such things exist?

In my heart, I knew that history overflowed with examples. How could this man not understand that such things existed? But so surprised was I by this man's nonchalant denial of goodness, I could not articulate any exemplar of true selflessness. I wanted to really amaze him with some glowing story of heroism and GODly glory, but nothing witty or helpful came from my vocal chords.

All I could say was "How can you not believe in powerful knights fighting for GOD?"

Later that night, after all the men had gone, it occurred to me that we never discussed an even more important question: How does one become like Moses, or Galahad? How does one become any good, honorable man? How does one become a hero? How does one become the type of person, like a knight, who would roam the world tirelessly, doing the work of GOD?

As I grew older, I saw that other people seemed plagued by the same questions. They wanted to be good and decent people, but even more than that. The men especially, although sometimes trying to hide it, wished to be honorable, courageous, epic, valiant. Not satisfied with just being a responsible citizen or a good worker, they desperately aspired to be heroic and powerful. They wanted to have the strength to do great things, great adventures, not just for glory, but for a greater cause, an honorable vision. They, like me, wished to be heroes for GOD and truth.

But they, like me, were confused, stunned, and dismayed by the constant distractions, false impressions, and deceptions of the world. They, like me, were constantly inundated by selfish emotions and yearnings that drove in the opposite direction of anything honorable. Their hearts nearly burst with wrath, lust, and ambitions which screamed to be satisfied. They were told again and again by the secular world that to be a "real man" they had to surrender to these desires, and use their strengths to subjugate those around them for selfish pride. So said the materialistic captains of money and position, crime and political power.

Then came the modern "progressives", who shouted down the masculine desires of the flesh, but also taught that manly drives like ambition and responsibility were foolish and archaic. They told men to become more feminine, and any concern about morality and battle, honor and virtue were out-moded ways of thought which would be swallowed up by a new age of androgynous peace. A visit to their political rallies will convince anyone that they are nothing new and certainly have no peace within themselves. Many of these preached forms of Communism, viewed though an impossible lens that denied human nature and GOD, but promised a quasi-religious, blind fanaticism.

True and quiet religious movements abounded, to be sure. But many of these seemed strangely shadowed by a lackluster malaise, hinting at tired, old women rather than knights or saints. Instead of burning with Holy Fire, and swords of the spirit, they spoke of cake sales and soup kitchens. Instead of wrestling with the Devil Himself, they struggled at festivals and car washes. When I asked them for stories of their saints, they gave me pamphlets on costumes for children. When I spoke of the mighty archangel Michael, they thought of cute cherubs with chubby cheeks. When I asked them for weapons of the soul, they gave me cheap knickknacks and plastic beads. They had sold their birthright of glory for a handful of sequins.

Nowhere in this modern world did I hear of the hero I aspired to. No wonder that man I had talked to so long ago did not believe in selfless, honorable knights.

I think most people do give up. Whether it is the press of life, the constant grind of worries, the misleading false philosophies, the little pleasures that eventually rob all strength and time, or the ever-present shadow of terrible evils in the world. Whatever it is, most people gloss over their yearnings for honorable adventure and good deeds, with years and years of toil, chimeras, confusion, and regret.

But I refused to surrender. I knew I was weak and inexperienced, but I promised myself that I would grow as strong as I could, as virtuous as I could, so that I could become a knight, a saint, a holy warrior, a mighty hero, if GOD would allow it.

But how?

Eventually, I found important clues from two sources: St. Augustine and Sir Thomas Malory. Malory, in his 15th century book *Le Morte D'Arthur*, shows King Arthur filling his Round Table with the best warriors in the world. He convinced these rough and brutal men to fight for goodness, Justice, and right, instead of for themselves. Arthur harnessed the aggressive skill in these men to make the world a better place. This example still shines, 1500 years later.

St. Augustine writes in his *Confessions* that, although he knew what was right, he could not find the inner strength to do it. He loved GOD and the Truth with all his heart, but his other desires would get in the way. Totally frustrated by his inability to conquer himself and dedicate his life to GOD, he was stunned when he heard about Roman soldiers and Bedouins being converted to a Christian life by the examples of Simeon Stylites and Antony of Egypt. When the soldiers and nomads, obsessed with strength and courage, beheld the example of spiritual strength Simeon possessed, they exclaimed, "This is true strength! We will become Christians as well!" These men were driven to GOD by their very desire to be strong, Augustine thought, and here my desires only hold me back. It was not long after that he dedicated himself totally to GOD's service.

In these two examples, I had found a great key. There was a way to take the fierce martial fire and desire in every man, his thirst for strength and courage, and aim these traits to fulfill all righteousness. A man could conquer himself and his selfish desires, but also use the energy and drive from these base desires to help him fight for goodness and truth. An earthly, selfish fighter could become a holy, spiritual warrior, if he could harness the power of his desires and turn them to the greater glory of GOD.

The ultimate guide posts on the road to the heroic were Knights and Saints. Honorable warriors and holy men of GOD. Men like Galahad and Moses. Men who could see past the foolishness of the world, spy the true meaning in everything and fight for it. Men who used strength and valor to conquer the stupidity in their own hearts, avoid selfish pitfalls, and beat the Devil himself. Knights and Saints!

I set out to find a book that would teach me how to be more like them; a book that would show me how to be a knight, a saint, a hero. There seemed to be many such books on the market, with self-help titles that demanded attention. Some had a story or two, a quote or two, a tiny piece of advice, and then the rest just platitudes and nice-sounding but empty phrases that gave no direction on how to reach these plateaus. Some had more detailed advice, but based on nothing but hearsay. That seemed rather dangerous to me. Some claimed to be based on historical knighthood, but soon left that path to introduce ideas that would never have occurred to a real knight. Many were based on the image of the Southern Gentleman, and warmed the heart with noble manners, but had little bearing on the warrior code of Medieval Chivalry. All of them told me to be good, but none of them told me *how* to achieve goodness. All of them told me to be honorable, but none of them told me how to acquire honor in my heart and soul.

I am a typical American; I need steps, guidelines, road-maps to help my selfish nature become more heroic and grand, knightly and saintly. All I could find were vague clichés.

Just as bad, many of the books seemed mired in what I began to call "grandma morality". This is a morality that avoids anything with manly passion or violent energy, and instead focuses on ethics routine at an elementary school cupcake party. "Follow your heart" and "hugs" are two catch-phrases of this mushy philosophy. They tend to center around food and feelings, the kitchen and childhood memories. I have nothing against Grandmothers, and certainly loved my own, but I wished for the way to become a true knight, not an effeminate socialite. I did not need a book that taught me to smile or be friendly, how to share or pass the cookies. I wished for the way to defend myself against vice and death, dishonor and Hell.

Finally, I set out to write such a book myself. I decided to write the book that I always wanted to find.

This book is filled with stories of knights and saints. Most of the stories are historical. A few personages are not, such as Lancelot, but the lessons they teach, and the honor they reflect, are painfully real. We sometimes mention fictional and non-fictional accounts at the same time, but this is not a comment on the trueness of the story, but on the profound importance of their message. (The Medieval man, as I do, believed whole-heartedly and sincerely in Bible stories and miracles, but a Modern might doubt them. I and the Medievals might doubt the historical veracity of Lancelot, while some literary historians would believe in his actual existence.) In other words, some of these stories are legendary, but all of their messages are TRUE. St. George and the Dragon, for instance, is a metaphor on how to fight and die for the ultimate cause, against the true horrors of torture, the temptations of the Devil, and the agonizing pain of Martyrdom.

Obviously, these are not bedtime stories, but tales of suffering and death; yet Honor shines in them, with terrifying discipline, and power of soul. Some are familiar, some not, and some real stories so strange you will swear they are more impossible to believe than the fables.

Regardless, the central stories of each chapter are fact.

All the stories have been thoroughly researched, using original, primary sources whenever possible, and we discuss their meanings in detail, so that anyone can use them as guideposts to the lessons they reveal. Many of the stories are archaic, but their lessons have been around so long because they work. They are time-tested, found to be worthy in the fires of experience. Dismiss them at your peril.

These stories center around what I have identified as the five pillars of Honor: Strength, Courage, Faith, Sacrifice, and Obedience. Each pillar is adorned with how to acquire these great virtues. I discuss each virtue carefully, the components necessary to build them, and why they are used. None of these are based on my opinion, but on the battle-tested views of real knights and saints. The book also goes into some detail about how these virtues are used in the modern world. A second book will cover the modern angle more thoroughly, as well as compare Western Chivalry with other Chivalries of the world.

Christian knighthood, Western Chivalry, is the main aim of this book, and reflects the Catholic sentiments of many knights of a by-gone time. I think most Christians will find this book theologically sound, although the stress on spiritual combat may be disturbing. Some heroes listed are not Catholic, and a few not Christian, but they carry with them the same disciplines that all Christians should have.

Some will be scandalized by the violent and martial nature of these stories and pillars. Consider that this world is a battlefield, not only of the body, but also in the heart, mind, and soul. My goal is not to justify violence against any person on this earth, but to use the weapons of the spirit against the true enemies of mankind: evil, greed, envy, prejudice, hate, lust, laziness, arrogance, wrath, stupidity, gluttony, apathy, selfishness, dishonesty, and cowardice. All the wars and battles in this book can be seen as simply metaphors for the struggle that should go on in every heart against the forces of darkness.

And for those of you who think that all men, all knights, throughout history have only fought for themselves, this book is my response.

Eric Demski
2014

Prepare

Not only does this book contain the way to heroism and knighthood, it can help us protect our own immortal souls as well as save mankind. But it contains the most difficult lifestyle imaginable, demanding all our sweat, blood, and effort; an existence so brutal, so painful, and so intolerable that only the bravest, most powerful individuals can maintain it and survive. It will test our greatest courage, our best strength, requiring awesome sacrifice and absolute devotion.

As Christ says, before a man embarks on a great undertaking, he must make sure he is ready and capable; otherwise he will fail and suffer. Likewise, if we dare to engage this particular path, we must steel our minds and souls, armoring our hearts and mortifying our bodies, preparing ourselves to the highest degree. We will need it if we want to be called Knights Errant.

What makes the knight's existence so difficult? Not his religion, for the yoke of Christ is easy and GOD's love illuminates the knight's deepest core. It is what the knight intends to do that constitutes the colossal struggle. The knight's mission is to turn the world and his soul back to GOD.

UNDER ATTACK

The True knight's mission in life is to protect his soul and change the world for the better. But can one person really make a difference in this world? Can an individual stand against the World, the Devil, and the Flesh, holding back the darkness, even for a moment?

We are under siege. Our country and our world are overrun with violence, crime, dishonesty, hatred, rape, ignorance, apathy, indolence, debauchery, and ethical irresponsibility. Murder, gang-related killings, and sexual molestations seem to be everywhere. Cruelty is so commonplace, its occurrence fails to even raise eyebrows anymore. Whole countries fall victim to torture and genocidal warfare. The United States has already lost a generation to hate, death, drugs, and nihilism, and other countries to poverty and mass-murder. We stand on the threshold of losing even more.

Some have told me that things are not as bad as they seem. If that is so, there still exists a battlefield which requires even more work and attention: the battlefield of the heart, mind, and soul. The hollow and bitter core of human nature stands as the most terrible problem of all, and I have seen it in the eyes of my fellow men, and when I looked into my own heart, I saw the abhorrent pit awaiting there, as well. Such is the true conflict, the war with our own natures, our own selfishness, our own self-deceptions, lies, and desires.

These problems, across the world, and within us, are interconnected. They are spiritual, mental, and physical in nature.

The spiritual problems of our age are the least obvious but the most destructive in the long term: Separation from GOD, lack of wholeness, extreme selfishness, arrogance, and the many lusts the world suffers under. This spiritual rot is the root of the other two enemies.

When arrogance and selfishness rule our souls, it's easy to fall for the second form of the problem, the mental. This is using our ever-growing knowledge in science, not to help others or for wisdom, but for material gain, self-worship, and power. As our pseudo-psychologies and theories increase, so does our hateful ability to justify our short-comings and abuses. Modern philosophies are good examples of our convincing knack to justify stupidity.

The physical problems that assail us today, as yesterday, are the most obvious, but perhaps the stickiest to deal with. Words and intentions and philosophies can work well on the mental problems, but no witty phrase can stop the bullet or knife from speeding toward us. Today's crime and violence, especially gang violence and government-sanctioned brutality across the world, make up a fundamental puzzle that no one can ignore with safety.

We have two choices: either fight this tide or die. Not just a death of the body, but destruction of the soul, falling into vicious emptiness and despair.

Modern man has tried just about everything: awareness education and MTV commercials, "boot" camps and charity concerts, police actions and diplomatic intrigues, drugs and feel-good campaigns, but nothing stems the force of moral decadence in America, let alone the problems of other countries. Nothing works, and each "solution" seems to plunge us deeper into decay.

What can we do? How can we defeat these problems? It seems impossible!

A SOLUTION

Far removed from silly movements and attempts, a solution presented itself in ancient times, and is still effective today. The concept is simple and straightforward: in order to help the world, even to save it, an individual begins with himself.

It is an honorable belief, held in many cultures and many places, that an individual, working to make himself a better person, everyday and a little at a time, could in the end, transform the world. Not by coercion or government mandates, not by focus groups or advertisements, not by mass murder or internment camps, but one man, working with himself and in himself, building his relationship with the Divine, and defeating the foes called Sin and Ignorance in one soul at a time, one person at a time. This concept is called Chivalry.

The Middle Ages needed this kind of help. In 476 AD, the Western Roman Empire fell, overwhelmed by hostile Barbarian tribes. For hundreds of years after, civilization faded, devolved, struggled, or else totally collapsed. Kingdoms rose and toppled. Violence and evil flourished seemingly everywhere, just as it does today. For the average person, life was brutish, mean, and short[1]. In many places, the day could be measured often by how many scraps of food one could weasel together or coax out of the soil. At any moment, one could fall victim to barbarian or criminal raids, innumerable wars, and all the plunder and rapine riding forth from the human heart. A person's horizons were crippled by total lack of basic education, and the future, often void of any concept of human dignity or even uniqueness from animal flesh, could only lead to wasted talent and a cold grave. The potential of most lives remained unknown, un-regarded, and unsalvageable from brute selfishness.

Tyrants, instead of using their power and organization to improve humanity's lot, rained down violence and coercion on their subjects. The few just and magnanimous rulers would have to constantly engage in battle simple to stay alive and protect what small respite they had gained.

Gangs roamed the land even in those days, although they used swords and cudgels instead of guns. Either a powerful man would surround himself with loyal conspirators, or one monstrously strong man would lay waste the country-side himself. They were very skilled warriors, battle-proven and hardened, without need of a simple weapon like a gun to wreak unimaginable havoc. This battle ability, along with their armor and horsemanship made them virtually indestructible. They were the equivalent of modern-day tanks, except no one had anti-tank weapons. No one could defeat them!

These barbarous warriors were the ancestors of what we would call knights, the most feared and dangerous force in the land.

They did what they pleased. They fought each other, captured whole towns, burned farms, raped women, butchered men, and basically laid waste the countryside. The poor peasants suffered the most. As in any time, innocent bystanders were caught in the middle and paid the price. But what could anyone do? The land was split up among so many kings and barons, tyrants and bullies, and they refused to cooperate. Even if they did, it was simply impossible to patrol the lands. And how could they defeat human tanks? Often, the barbarian warriors just squashed them and laughed.

But in all this darkness and confusion, there were oases of light, people who wished to walk in the shadow of GOD. Monasteries in hidden places stilled hummed like quiet, ethereal engines. Priests and

---

[1]   As paraphrased from the *Leviathan* of Thomas Hobbes

monks, hermits and nuns still worked hard for GOD's kingdom, but many ordinary people, and even some warriors themselves, also longed for righteousness. Through their efforts, a new way of life began to congeal, partially from the echoes of Roman discipline, but fostered, infused, and enlivened by the Catholic Church. This way of life slowly formed into the spiritual side of Chivalry. All over the world, such things have manifested in many cultures, Europe was no exception. But the Church gave this Chivalry a higher ideal than simply reforming society or the self; it gave Chivalry the imitation of Christ, and the foe of the Devil.

This ideal grew with twin roots. Thousands of stories and legends of knights and saints passed on by writers, poets, and singers of songs blossomed in the entertainment arts. Stirred by brutal passions, the French public loved to hear tales of men like William of Gellone, Roland, and the Paladins of Charlemagne, who chopped and hacked their way through invaders and evil. In Spain, campfires rang with the exploits of the Cid and others like him, raising the spirits of warriors everywhere. Stories of King Arthur and his unbeatable knights arose from Britain, chronicled first by Nennius in the 9th century, William of Malmesbury and Geoffrey of Monmouth in the 12th, and spread like wild fire, joining the songs of France and Spain. Poets like Chretien De Troyes and Wolfram von Eschenbach wove tapestries of these tales in more and more intricate forms, fleshing out the likes of Percival, Gawain, and other famous knights.

Not to be outdone, the Church revisited these stories, reforming them with a more spiritual sheen, as in the anonymous *Quest of the Holy Grail*, written by a monk with an eye for flamboyant battles and spiritual swords.

This way of life, this code of Chivalry, slowly manifested itself within the minds, hearts, and souls of warriors everywhere. Legions of warriors began to see themselves as fighters for GOD and goodness. Soon they began battling the tyrants and oppressors of the poor, defending helpless civilians, respecting and defending women, and upholding the right with their might. No longer would they abuse their power for selfish ends, but instead they harnessed it for the glory of the MOST HIGH. These barbaric, gruff, violent men were changing into something grand, something noble.

Many criminals re-evaluated their actions and themselves, and became heroes, fighting other criminals and righting the wrongs they themselves once perpetrated. Men from all walks of life, from peasants to noblemen (in the early Middle Ages, anyone could be allowed into the ranks of knighthood) dropped their typical, selfish lives and donned their gauntlets and sword-belts for the adventure and glory of fighting evil. Every young man wished to be a knight, because every man wanted to be a hero.

Chivalry worked well because it connected with something already in these men. Chivalry brings out the Honor hidden deep within every man, where it had been asleep, dormant at the center of the soul. Also important to note, unlike many modern programs that seek to stymie natural violent tendencies, Chivalry simply redirects violent energy towards more positive, constructive goals. A knight needs his aggression, his anger, and his righteous fury, to push himself harder in the direction he needs to go. Chivalry helps him use his own animal nature to attack, not the innocent or other knights, but the real enemies: invading hordes and criminals, as well as the evil desires within men, and the Evil One Himself.

These true enemies of Mankind, lead directly or indirectly by the Evil One, come in three-fold form, physical, mental, and spiritual. Chivalry armored the knight in all three areas, making even the rudest and basest of tools, the body, as just one more weapon for good in an eternal struggle waged on every level.

But the Middle Ages were very physical times, and one of the great tests of knighthood came in a decidedly physical way. In the Crusades, the knights fought the enemies of the Church in the form of invading Moslems who had destroyed the Holy Sepulcher in Jerusalem, threatened the Christian Empire of Byzantium, and ravaged unarmed pilgrims to the Holy Land. Christian knights fought the Moslems in this arena continuously for over five hundred years, with various degrees of success.

What might be called the pinnacle of Knighthood sprung from these wars. The Order of the Temple of Solomon, or the Knights Templar, was founded in 1119 to protect and hold Jerusalem as a Christian city. The Order of St. John of Jerusalem, known as the Hospitallers, was first established to take care of recuperating pilgrims and knights before the Crusades, but began fighting after the first Crusade, and became an almost full military order by 1168[2]. A hospital in Acre, started by

---

[2]   (Bradford, 1972) pg. 27

German merchants, adopted the Hospitaller's code and became an independent order called the Teutonic knights in 1198[3]. Blessed by Saint Bernard, these groups brought knighthood to a new level, one of focused spiritually and monk-like devotion to poverty and Christian warrior brotherhood.

Knights themselves wrote Chivalrous guidebooks, showing not only how to fight a physical enemy, but how to guard one's honor and soul against temptation, dishonor, and stupidity. Sirs Ramon Lull and Geoffroi de Charney are two of the most famous of these. By the turn of the 15th century, Sir Thomas Malory set down the myths and legends on King Arthur, and the French addition of Sir Lancelot, in the famous *Le Morte D'Arthur*, which is the culmination of this great movement, giving us tales of knights we recognize today.

Chivalry, through church proclamations, teachings, and a flood of knightly legends and stories, penetrated warriors' minds and souls, and slowly, over decades and centuries, changed the way they saw themselves, the world, and their duties in it.

They were inspired, they bettered themselves, and thus, one man at a time, they bettered their communities. Crime, violence, and cruelty are simply effects, their root is the soul. Change enough individual souls, and you transform the whole world. "Before kingdoms change, men must change", and "this is not a battle for land or gold, but for men's minds, men's souls". Their world became more just, more honorable, more bearable, because they did. Chivalry made the world a better place, because it made the knight a better man. A powerful and transformational force for goodness and hope began to be felt in the land.

They had become new creations. They had become true knights

Chivalry made the world a better place, because it made the knight a better man. A powerful and transformational force for goodness and hope began to be felt in the land.

So, it can be done. We can defeat the rising tide of wickedness and crime in our modern world and within ourselves, with ancient Chivalry.

This is not to say that everything was suddenly reformed into the Garden of Eden because of the ascendance of Chivalry. For the most part, Chivalry made it possible to train and make a man honorable, regardless of his surroundings and limitations. The majority of men are selfish and

---

[3]   (Gies, 1986) pg. 131

un-knightly, but when even a fraction of men are Chivalrous, society improves, and indeed, society is made possible. Men in history who exhibited Chivalry made it more possible for Civilization to restore itself, but this is not the final goal of Chivalry.

The final goal is to aid one's fellow man as much as possible, while keeping one's soul and honor intact. In a word, Chivalry is the individual's road to Heroism.

Many times, a knight's mission aided civilization, and many times it led indirectly to a destabilization of civilization. But if your goal is to make yourself better, sharpen your soul ethically while helping civilization as much as possible, Chivalry is paramount. While protecting ethical societies, it establishes Honor and restores basic humanity to all men.

In the final estimation, this is truly how to save the world. If we wish to make the world a better place, we must make ourselves better. This begins when we make the conscious decision, individually, personally, and very concretely, to become people of honor, men of valor, knights of GOD.

If we have lost the world, it is time to win it back.

THE MIND OF THE KNIGHT

Be noble! And the nobleness that lies in other men, sleeping but never dead, will rise in majesty to meet thine own.

—John Russell Lowell, *Sonnet IV*

The unexamined life is not worth living.

—Plato, *Apology*

All action has its origin in the Mind.

—Samuel Johnson, *The Rambler* #8

What is glory without virtue? A great man without religion is no more than a great beast without a soul.

—Daniel Defoe, *The Instability of Human Glory*

Honour and virtue are the ornaments of the mind, without which the body, though it be so, has no right to pass for beautiful.

—Sir Miguel Cervantes, *Don Quixote De La Mancha*, ch. 14

If we are to go forward, we must go back and rediscover those precious values—that all reality hinges on moral foundations and that all reality has spiritual control.

—Rev. Martin Luther King, Jr., *The Papers of Martin Luther King, Jr: Rediscovering Precious Values*, Feb. 28, 1954

1

Ex umbris et imaginibus in Veritatem.
[From shadows and symbols into the Truth.]
— The epitaph of Cardinal John Newman,
at Edgbaston, 1890

THE KNIGHT'S MENTAL ATTITUDE

Imagine a warrior who treats women with the utmost courtesy, and even his enemies with respect. Imagine the same man who refuses to tell even the smallest lie, but is instead kind and gentle as he speaks the truth. A man who never cheats on his wife, nor covets other people's goods, nor even wants to. A man willing to give his life to save friends, a child, or even a stranger, cheerfully and without regret. A man strong enough to lift a bull over his head, but meek enough to comfort children[4]. Fierce enough to fight demons[5], and kind enough to give his food and his only shelter to a crippled beggar[6]. A man who would strike at Hell itself for a good cause, and yet never ask anyone to do what he himself would not. Brutal and disciplined enough to keep eternal vigilance over his own soul by striking down the darkness within himself, as well as protecting all those around him from the darkness of the world. Imagine this man, who is warrior, saint, hero, and gentleman all at the same time.

Such is the knight[7].

How does one understand such a man, especially in our world of situational, slippery ethics and complacent convenience? What is more, how does one imitate, match, and ultimately become him?

We are what we do, and our deeds come from our thoughts. Honorable and heroic deeds begin with an Honorable and heroic mind. If we wish to understand and ultimately achieve the knight's incredible deeds, we must absorb the knight's thoughts into our own.

To begin, we will examine the stories that molded the very perceptions of how the knight saw himself. The stories he grew up with,

---

[4]   (Loomis, 1951) pg. 287, (Gautier, 1989) pg. 43
[5]   (Malory, 1962), pg. 370, (Matarasso, 1969), pg. 62, said of Galahad
[6]   (Matthews), pg.84
[7]   (Gautier, 1989), pg.23 (Corley, 1989), pg 52

treasured, and emulated[8] with all his heart and considerable ability. These stories become the knight's touch stone, and taught him everything he needed to know about himself, his mission, and his purpose in the world.

An Early Knight Story

One of the first stories of a true knight and warrior for GOD is the story of St. George, the patron saint of Knights. Knights throughout the Middle Ages looked to him as the model of Knightly behavior and demeanor. But two essential stories make up the tale of George, and they seem very different.

The earliest accounts place St. George's birth during the third century, in Nobatia[9], to a leader in the Roman Army, at the time of Emperor Aurelian. He grows up to be an excellent warrior, receiving awards for bravery and conduct in battle.

His commanding officers saw him as one of the strongest, toughest soldiers they had, capable in both attack and defense, ready to withstand any privation without complaint[10]. It is possible that he served under the general Galerius in the Roman wars against the Persians[11]. But then, as all saints and knights in all times, there comes a moment of great decision, when the warrior must choose between GOD and everything else.

This fateful time of decision looms in 298AD, when the Roman Emperor of the time, Diocletian, announces his decree that everyone in the military, without exception, must publicly worship Roman gods[12]. This required a sacrifice before the pagan god Apollo, or Bacchus, perhaps even the emperor himself. It is a customary token, a small, traditional ritual, which most Roman soldiers commit without much thought. But now, this ceremony has taken on considerable weight, for the emperor has become very distrusting of Christians, and has declared any public admission of Christianity in the military ranks as punishable by death[13]. But George is not just any Roman soldier.

---

[8]   (Gies, 1986) pg. 97
[9]   (Morgan, 2006) pg.17
[10] (Lang, 1912) pg.376-7
[11] (Ghezzi, 2000) pg.92
[12] Ibid.
[13] (Morgan, 2006) pg.17

George is a true Christian warrior, worshipping only GOD, for he knows that there is no other. Rather than tarnish his soul with stupidity, he resigns, giving up a very lucrative military career, and drops into obscurity.

In the year 303, Diocletian goes a step further on his plan to eliminate Christianity. He passes a decree that outlaws all Christian assemblies, and commands the destruction of all churches and the burning of all Scripture in the empire[14].

As knights in all times, George cannot bring himself to sit by and allow churches and the holy books destroyed, nor stomach the harassment and torture of his fellow Christians. First, he gives his sizable estate to the poor, preparing himself [15]. He then travels to Nicomedia, and the royal court there, where he may face Roman authority squarely, and testify for the elimination of these harsh decrees. Surely the Roman emperor, an intelligent man, will see the hateful ignorance of these laws.

A curious statement in Eusebius' *History of the Church* describes a prominent man, standing in the public street of Nicomedia, tearing to pieces Diocletian's decree, even while the emperor and his general Galerius are in the city[16]. Many historians believe this man to be Saint George. Other historians place George's passion in Lydda[17].

Here is where the two stories diverge. In the older story, Diocletian, enraged by this public rebuke of his commands, orders George tortured into submission. The saint is forced to wear terrifying iron shoes, spiked within and made red hot by a furnace, but George refuses to relent, and instead seems to be unhurt by this torture, where others have died from the pain[18]. The guards thrust their spears at him while he languishes in his cell, but he avoids them, seemingly with ease, even though his feet should have been crippled. Then they grab him and tie him to a wheel full of sharp knives[19], which should have cut him to pieces. When he doesn't die quickly, he is thrown back into his cell to bleed to death.

---

[14] Ibid. pg.18
[15] (Lang, 1912) pg.377-8
[16] (Williamson, 1965), pg.261
[17] (Ghezzi, 2000) pg.93 and (Morgan, 2006) pg.16-17
[18] (Lang, 1912) pg.377-8
[19] (Morgan, 2006) pg.20 and (Lang, 1912) pg.377-8

The Emperor demands to see the body the next day, so he can present the fate of all Christians that speak out against him. George walks into the meeting apparently unhurt.

"How can this be!" Diocletian demanded.

"My Lord Jesus Christ has sent his angel to cure me"[20]. George said.

Diocletian's wife and daughter, who have become Christians, beg for George's release, but the Emperor will have none of it. In his heart, he is certain other Christians have plotted against him recently[21], and have weakened the empire with their beliefs.

Next, Diocletian calls upon a trusted magician to administer poison, or in some versions, molten iron, to be poured down George's throat. Miraculously, George survives this[22], and when he is called before the Emperor again, George seems completely unharmed.

Diocletian looks at the magician and his other advisors, waiting for some explanation.

"St. Michael himself has come and cured me." George said. "Are you ready to admit the error of your decrees? Stop this evil attack upon the faithful Christians of your empire! They have done nothing against you, o Great Emperor!"

The magician and more of Diocletian's court convert to Christianity[23].

In a blinding rage, the Emperor claps his hands, sending his guards to behead the young soldier. George has escaped certain death 3 times[24]. Now, as he stares down the Emperor, he sees the hardness of the Emperor's heart, and accepts martyrdom. He doesn't move as the guards fall upon him and cleave his head from his shoulders.

The more popular story in the western kingdoms, made famous by *The Golden Legend*, came to be nearly 900 years after the first account. In this more fanciful telling, George travels alone throughout Northern Africa. While trudging through weeds and swampy morasses near the town of Silene[25], George reins his horse at a strange sight.

---

20 (Lang, 1912) pg.377-8
21 (Morgan, 2006) pg.18
22 This event is reminiscent of the Diphtheria cures of the 1800's
23 (Morgan, 2006) pg.20 and (Lang, 1912)
24 Ibid.
25 (Lang, 1912) pg.378-9, (Voragine, The Golden Legend, Readings on the Saints, translated by William Granger Ryan, 2012) pg. 238

A woman, dressed in wedding finery, tied to a post. She is weeping silently, and seems to be awaiting some unseen doom. George looks around, only seeing cane-breaks and wilderness.

"What is this?" asks the knight. "Is this the custom in this land, to affix young ladies to posts and leave them to die?"

The maiden looks up, breathing erratically, obviously shocked and terrified.

"Do not be afraid." George says to her soothingly. "I will release you. But tell me why you are in such a situation."

Even through her tears, the young lady begs him to allow her to face her fate. For many months, a terrible beast has been attacking people and livestock near her town, killing as many as 30 children, and the townspeople had tracked it to a small lake and fountain, the town's source of water. Several soldiers had assailed the thing, but the creature had slaughtered them. The beast guarded the water source with its serpent-like body and huge fangs, claws, and thunderous tail, so that the townspeople could only get near by offering it a sheep or two. Soon they ran out of sheep.

"And now you are to be given up to the beast, in place of sheep?" George spits.

"Our town devised a lottery, and I was chosen." She sighs. "If you free me, the dragon will attack again, and my people will be hunted down, even while they thirst to death."

"Listen," George responds. "I will destroy this beast, this dragon. And then you and your town will be free."

George pulls his mighty sword, Ascalon, to cut the girl's bonds. But behind him, in the cane-breaks, he can hear the oncoming movement of something heavy, and scaled. He turns to face his enemy.

The Dragon is indeed that, a monstrous reptile, with armored skin and claws the size of the saint's misercorde[26], and fangs, like a wild boar's, large enough to skewer his horse. But the thing's tail presents a bigger danger, swinging around with ridges that could saw a man's arm or leg clear through, or knock him down to the ground, incapacitated. Worse yet, as the thing opens its jaws, George can see fumes spilling forth, a poison breath that blackens the cane and weeds around it. The creature

---

[26]   In Medieval times, a special dagger used by knights to administer the final *coup de grace*, about a foot in length.

moves closer, lumbering but quick enough, roaring its anger at the presence of the saint.

George's mind is alive with strategy. How can one kill this thing, obviously heavily armored and armed as it is? He reaches for his long-range weapon, the spear, which presents his only real chance.

"GOD preserve me," he prays as he mounts his horse and gallops full long at the thing, spearing the dragon through its mouth and throat, transfixing its head to the ground.

"Quickly," George says as he cuts the girl's bonds." Give me your belt."

The girl obeys and George ties shut the beast's mouth, while making a kind of leash with the free end. Half-dragging the dragon behind them, he gives the girl a ride on his horse, into the town square.

A crowd forms around him, although they are obviously frightened by the dragon. "What will you give me to kill this thing?" George demands.

"This creature has destroyed many of our people and our livestock." The king of the town comes forth. "We will give you your weight in gold and silver, and my daughter, that young girl you have there, as your wife."

George smiles gently. "I require something far more precious. If all of you will swear to become Christians and save your souls, I will kill the beast."

Once the king and the entire town convert to Christianity, George beheads the dragon and rides off without taking any reward. In most of the old stories, he refuses any payment for his services, giving away any wealth he has earned to the poor of the surrounding areas.

One last message he leaves for the citizens and the king: love the Church, attend Mass, honor the priests, and care for the poor[27].

Both stories have the knight, St. George, living a blameless life for GOD and Honor. Both stress the importance of fighting, whether physically or spiritually, for virtue, for religion, and the welfare of others. Both stories stress the conversion of many after seeing the knight's noble actions and the miraculous events that surround him. Both show the existence of evil as a potent reality, a reality that must be faced with iron resolve, Faith, and courage. Both stories insist that the martial virtues

---

[27] (Morgan, 2006) pg.48

inherent in the knight please GOD and ultimately prove the knight's adoption as a child of GOD.

It is my contention that these two stories, though wildly divergent in detail, one true and one fantasy, are actually the same story, reflecting in each other one central theme. The warrior for GOD, a knight, must use his skills and fight physically and spiritually, and eventually face terrible suffering for his loyalty, even unto death. He must face the dragon, in all its painful forms, and honorably wrestle with it.

The dragon, for the Medieval, traditionally represented the devil, or his temptations. In these stories, the dragon could also represent the hatred in the heart of the Emperor, definitely a terror that ate up people of his realm. To conquer such a creature was to save one's own soul, or to convert others to Christianity and save their souls from the jaws of Hell. George's sword, spear, and equipment represent justice, virtue, and the iron will of Chivalry[28]. The claws, teeth, breath, and tail of the dragon are the weapons of evil temptation, torture, untruth, and hopelessness, hurled at the knight from every corner of the world. The water, guarded by the dragon and denied the people, can be the life-giving faith of Christ. The witnesses to the dragon fight, or the martyr's passion, are potential souls to be won for the greater glory of GOD. The king is converted to Christianity; but the Emperor? His empire, Rome, eventually becomes the central hub of the Catholic Church.

The true knight understands that the thrilling, romantic trappings of fighting a dragon and saving the princess are but a metaphor, pointing to the grisly reality of the true life of honor: wielding knightly virtue against evil in the face of mortal agony. The knight who endures to the end, honorable refusing to surrender before evil, even though he suffers bodily death, will gain glory and Heaven itself[29].

This story, and the others like it shared in this book, expresses the ideals of the knight in startling and violent prose. In Ancient times, anyone who aspired to knighthood, the young or the old, could listen to these knightly stories and discern the demands of Chivalry, the rules of knighthood. We too, even in the cloud of our modern thoughts, can listen to these tales and still discover the spirit of Chivalry and the way of the knight.

---

[28]   (Lull, 2001) pg. 63-75
[29]   Matthew 24:13

This is the first way to understand the mind of the knight: by understanding the messages and lessons within the awesome tales of Chivalry.

The modern may ask, how can this help us? How can such examples of chivalrous violence, sacrifice, faith and martyrdom actually change the world? How can the example of the knight make the world better?

Saint George battled for his soul, and the souls of others, but his example inspires good people from around the world, and soon many powerful leaders and kings take up George's vision.

Constantine the great, who took over as Emperor after Diocletian not long after George's death, set up a church in honor of St. George in Lydda. There, a huge image in bas relief of a man slaying a dragon, may have lent something to the legend of St George's monster[30]. Constantine made Christianity legal across the Roman Empire, and presided over the Council of Nicea in 325, which was to lay the bedrock of Christian Dogma for the centuries to come. Nicea is another name for Nicopolis, the very city of George's martyrdom.

Justinian, a later emperor of Rome, and King Clovis, ancestor of Charlemagne, built churches in George's name in Armenia and France, respectively, and admirers sprang up from all over the world, making George a true, multi-cultural hero[31].

By 1066, in Normandy alone, nearly 70 churches had been built in George's name[32] and by 1095, Saint George's flag, white with a red cross, flew over the English Crusaders. St. George would soon be needed in that war.

By 1098, the Crusaders had conquered Antioch, a strategically essential city, as well as a religiously important one, the first place where the followers of Christ had been called Christians. The siege had been difficult for the Crusaders, low on provisions, but now, as they finally controlled the city, they heard a huge Moslem army was on its way. The Christian warriors could not foresee withstanding such an attack, and many soldiers abandoned the city, fleeing into the surrounding wilderness. The warriors that were left prepared as best they could, eating boiled bark and waiting. The Byzantine Emperor had sent word that he

---

[30] (Morgan, 2006) pg.26, see also Budge's work on *George of Lydda*
[31] (Morgan, 2006) pg.27
[32] Ibid. pg.77

would not come to aid them. Defeat seemed eminent and total. Death awaited them.

A monk named Peter Bartholemew receives a vision, telling him that the spear of Longinus, the spear that pierced the side of Christ, is under the Church of St. Peter in the city. Few believe him, but some of the leaders of the Crusade agree to look for the weapon. After digging all day through the floor of the church, they can find nothing, and they look at Bartholomew askance. He looks back, totally certain of his vision[33].

The Spear is the chosen weapon of the Knight, second only to the sword. It is George's spear that wounds the dragon, and it is Longinus's spear that tests the side of Christ, bringing forth blood and water that defeats all dragons. And when Peter Bartholomew reaches down into the excavation, he pulls forth the iron spear tip[34]!

A cheer rises in the city of Antioch. Although terribly outnumbered, the Crusaders decide to march out of the safety of the walls to meet their enemy head-on in the fields, dying like men, carrying the spear like a flag before them. The Moslem army attacks, nearly surrounding the Christians, and then a sound comes from the nearby hills. Another army suddenly appears, crushing down into the Moslems, slamming them with terrible iron. The besieging army of Moslems panic and flee, totally crushed by what eye-witnesses claim is an spectral army of saints on horseback, led by none other than the great martyr, St. George himself[35].

During the taking of Jerusalem, the knights carried this spear and St. George's relics into battle. Many warriors claimed to have seen St. George fighting beside them, jumping onto the walls from the siege-towers[36]. In another Crusade, a hundred years later, Richard the Lionheart, King of England, had a vision of St. George leading him to victory, as his men stormed Acre, another crucial city of the Middle East[37].

---

[33] (Pernoud, 1963), pg.98, St. Joan will have a similar vision, 300 years later, (Spoto, 2007) pg. 60

[34] (Morgan, 2006) pg.81, also (Stark, 2009), pg. 159

[35] (Morgan, 2006) pg.8—another account credits the discipline of the Crusaders, (Stark, 2009), pg.152

[36] (Voragine, The Golden Legend, Readings on the Saints, translated by William Granger Ryan, 2012) pg. 242

[37] (Morgan, 2006) pg.87

In a far larger Crusade a thousand years hence, hundreds of English solders see St. George in the sky, gesturing to them and fighting for them against the much larger German army at the battle of Mons.

As a true, spiritual warrior for Christ, George's spirit arises in many modern charitable, humanitarian causes. The influence on the International Red Cross organization is unmistakable, with its Red Cross on a white field, of course borrowed directly from George's traditional flag. In America, the organization still holds awards diners in honor of St. George. The symbol is immediately recognizable anywhere in the world as the sign of aid and charity. In 1908, General Robert Baden-Powell decided that boys across England needed an organization that would help them retain strength in their bodies and moral character, and developed the Boy Scouts, basing the group's ideals on the example of St. George. This organization can be found as a symbol of civility and clean living in 100 countries[38].

One man, one knight, even at the point of death, can influence the entire world, and change it for the better. This is Honor. This is Chivalry.

The knight inspires us, through his stories, whether real or imagined, to strive for a better character, a better individual soul[39], and through one person at a time, a better world. His goals, to strive for virtue and justice, become our goals, though we no longer ride horses or chase after villains with swords. By his sacrifice, we wish to be more selfless, by his faith and courage, we wish to push back fear, by his strength and obedience, we wish to be of stronger moral fiber, of stronger spirit, humble yet zealous for GOD.

This encapsulates the entire point of the book, to inspire every reader to be a better, more honorable person, striving for excellence in mind, body, spirit, in charity and respect to others. To use stories of knights, some real and a few not, as they did, to show us a metaphor of more honorable, stronger living, giving greater glory to GOD.

These are the honorable lessons burned into the mind of the knight.

---

38   (Morgan, 2006) pg.112
39   (Barber, 1995) pg.136

The Goals of the Knight

Such stories illustrate, more clearly than any textbook, the goals of the knight. A knight's official goal can be simply stated: "Maintain Christianity". "In all his acts, the knight is bound to propose himself a double aim—the safety of his soul and the honour of the Church of which he is a guardian"[40].

The knight is also the protector of the poor, so that the wealthy and powerful shall never injure them and he is to "sustain the weak, so that the strong shall never oppress them"[41].

Finally, a knight strives to "combat all evil, and defend all good"[42]. He battles forever against the various forces of wickedness that swell in the world, struggles to defend all orphans, widows, the weak, the innocent, and avenges all injustice.

These are mountainous goals, worthy of only the most dedicated, strong, disciplined, and unselfish of people. Indeed, anyone who even sets such goals is courageous far above the norm[43]. Yet the knights of history and legend, from the Knights of Malta to Sir Lancelot, the Templar Knights to Sir Guy of Warwick, King Arthur's Round Table Knights to Rodrigo De Bivar (El Cid), and King Charlemagne's Paladins to Sir Jean de Joinville achieved Honorable and glorious heights. They set their goals and fought for them with courageous and honorable acts that have mystified generations of people for over a thousand years.

How far distant are these goals and deeds from modern pursuits. The knight's mind, the hero's mind, is much removed from our weak, pathetic, modern minds. To bridge the gap between ourselves and the knight, we will continue to look at other lessons of the knight's inner world.

---

40 (Gautier, 1989) pg.39
41 Ibid. pg.44
42 (Gautier, 1989) pg.72
43 (Barber, 1995) pg 137

FOCUS ON GOD

If you were to open the dark, mysterious closed-off box of the knight's mind, you would first find the word "GOD", emblazoned on his brain.

The knight focuses on GOD above all things. He is truly what Novalis said of Spinoza: "a GOD-intoxicated man". From St. Augustine[44] to Godfrey of Bouillon[45], such men are obsessed with GOD. In the morning he awakes, with thoughts of GOD flowing within him, and in the evening he falls asleep to the Music of the words of GOD. The knight rides off to battle, because he believes GOD wishes him to go. Before he even straps on his sword, however, he goes to Mass to make sure his soul is clean and worthy of ascending to Heaven if he should die. And the thing he looks forward to the most, above any reward or fame, is to selflessly fight for GOD's name, without hesitation, reservation, or fear. This is the defining moment of the knight's life: "to march into Hell for a Heavenly cause"[46], to die in terrible battle carrying the knowledge he fights for GOD's sake[47].

Indeed, this is the crowning difference between modern man and medieval knight. One must ask oneself, what is most important, in life and in death? There is a thousand, thousand answers for us, from family to friends, pleasure to comfort, but for the true knight there is only GOD.

GOOD vs. EVIL

The knight sees GOD and all that GOD has made as good. But there is evil in the world.

Many people have pointed out that the St. George story is a classic story of good versus evil. It is not the first such story, nor will it be the last. The story of good versus evil is not one of many stories, however. It is the only story. It is everyone's story, even if some refuse to see that good and evil exist at all.

---

[44] (Deane, 1963) pg. 13

[45] (Gautier, 1989) pg. 115-6

[46] From *The Impossible Dream*, lyrics by Joe Darian, from the musical by Dale Wasserman

[47] As mentioned in St. Ignatius' Prayer of Generosity

The dragon, for the knight of the Western world, is simply a symbol of evil. But what truly is evil? Evil causes unnecessary suffering in the world, and attempts to impede our relationship with the Most High GOD. The knight stands forever against evil and all its effects[48].

The Ultimate Book

If ever there were stories that lead to a more chivalrous and honorable mind, it is the story of GOD and HIS people, the Bible.

Everything a knight does, in one way or the other, corresponds with the Bible. You will find most, if not all, of this book reflected in either a well-known, or little-known part of the Word of GOD.

It is imperative for us, as future knights, to read the entire Bible and ponder it thoroughly day and night.

Even the religious today take the Bible for granted, however. Bibles are sold almost everywhere, and even provided free by the Gideon organization in hotels. But, ironically enough, in this age of mass-information, too many lies are floating around for us not to read the Bible on our own.

St. George only had the word of holy men. The typical person in later Medieval times could not even read. In truly dark times, the Scriptures were suppressed by evil tyrannies. The knights of old usually did not have access to the Holy Writ, and had to rely upon the words of the priest, or memorize some valued section of it.

As a person affected by the misinformation of modern society[49], you may say to yourself: "The Bible is boring", and full of "dry religious sayings that I have heard before". Anyone saying this has not truly read the Bible with the eyes of the knight. There are many strange and valuable notions and gems of truth in the Bible that no one speaks of, and it is brimming with stories and battles of great saints and heroes which can show a true warrior the way to defeating the Evil One Himself. The Bible is only as boring as fighting for your life with a dragon.

---

[48] (Vauchez, 1993) pg.59, and The Knight's Code, circa 1100's
[49] We are all affected in some way by the zeitgeist of our times, but we must be more than creatures of it.

The knight considers both the Old and the New Testaments, and is wary of isolating one reading from the others. The Bible must be taken as a whole, or not at all.

Influence of the Catholic Church

"The Lady of the Lake", as some have called Her[50], is responsible for much of the formation of the knight's religious viewpoint and his powerful soul. In George's time, she was only very young. Before she placed the yoke of Christ on them, warriors and knights tended to be no more than pitiless fighters out for glory and wealth. But She, with her authority over all things spiritual in the Middle Ages, slowly brought knighthood from the snarling animal to a shining example of polished nobility and harnessed brutality[51].

Because of Her influence, and the elevating influence of the mercy of Christ in general, the knight brought his great might to protect who had formally been the victims of his iron hand: women, children, the poor, and the defenseless. The Christian religion itself, as well as the clergy and the very church buildings, also gained this protection. Roman soldiers, as we have seen with St. George and so many others, flocked to her as their true mother.

The Influence of the Saints as "Warriors of GOD"

> ". . . but we cannot all be friars, and GOD brings His children to Heaven by many paths: Chivalry is Religion, and there are sainted knights in Glory."
> —Sir Miguel De Cervantes[52]

Obviously, the lives of the saints stirred the heart of the knight. He constantly revered the saints and saw them as models for life and deed, inspiration to great heroics, and leaders in the battle against evil for the greater glory of GOD. Knights sometimes even became saints.

---

[50] (Boyden, 1923) Note 282 on page 161
[51] (Gautier, 1989) pg. 19, also, (Gies, 1986) pg. 20, 21, 30-32
[52] From his *Don Quixote*, Book II, ch. 8

Many saints counted themselves as knights. The Cistercian monk Gauberto Vagad spoke of saints as "Knights of GOD", in service of "The Eternal Prince, Christ Jesus"[53]. The knight known as Ignatius Loyola began his ascent to sainthood by reading the lives of the saints while suffering from a grievous injury obtained in a battle. Soon, his "desire to be an outstanding knight of Christ replaced his thoughts of chivalrous service to ladies"[54].

Ignatius even fashioned his entrance into saintly life exactly the way a knight would, by standing vigil all night long and praying before the Virgin Mary's statue (a knight before his initiation and dubbing, performs a prayerful vigil of arms throughout the night)[55].

St. George, one of the first Christian martyrs and saints, happened to be a soldier in the army of pagan Rome, and thus, in the mind of the Medieval, he was knighted. As all knights, he is portrayed on his horse, forever running down the devil with his spear. This vision of holy, ancient soldiers or warriors as Medieval knights became a common facet of medieval thought.

In fact, according to the Medievals, any saint who started an order, such as Augustine or Bernard of Clairvaux, became great knights[56], battling dragons of falsehood across a spiritual battlefield. Saint Bernard had a triple connection with knights: raised as a knight, writing the much revered treatise *In Praise of the new Knighthood*, and becoming the model for Sir Galahad. It was Bernard who, as the most respected theologian of the day, secured the creation of the Order of Templar Knights, writing a detailed rule for them[57].

St. Francis of Assisi, at first considered himself not good enough to be a knight, perhaps because he had failed to win the title as he had sorely wished early in his life. As his sense of mission became focused, this changed. "Saint Francis embodied both the poor man and the knight— the two forces that had set out together in olden times along the road to the Holy Land and had retaken Jerusalem. The chivalrous ideal exercised

---

[53] (Caraman, 1990) pg.27
[54] (Ganss, 1992) pg. 16
[55] (Ganss, 1992) pg. 26
[56] (Caraman, 1990) pg.27
[57] (Stark, 2009) pg. 174-5

a great attraction over Saint Francis. He wished to become GOD's *jongleur*, then GOD's knight"[58].

St. Louis holds a special position in history as saint, warrior, and king, with an army of knights to back him up. He believed GOD wished him to free the holy land and he spent his vast fortune and his incredible life striving to make that vision a reality.

St. Joan of Arc, another patron saint of France and all knights, epitomized the life of a knight and a saint at the same time, and died refusing to give up her belief in her visions or her knightly garb.

St. Michael, the holy and victorious arch-angelic warrior against the Evil One, is always portrayed as a knight, complete with armor and sword. Angels, and some writers claim lesser gods, were expected by GOD to fulfill the work of a knight. Psalm 82 shows GOD demanding the heavenly host to "Uphold the cause of the weak and the fatherless, and see the right done to the afflicted and destitute, Rescue the weak and the needy, and save them from the clutches of the wicked." This is almost word for word the duty given to all knights everywhere. St. Michael fulfills these duties well.

In modern times, St. Maximilian Kolbe created the Knights of Mary Immaculate, and when given a chance to sacrifice himself for others in a Nazi concentration camp, he stated "I would like to suffer and die in a knightly way, even to the shedding of the last drop of my blood, to hasten the day of gaining the whole world for the Immaculate Mother of GOD"[59].

Let us not forget that CHRIST HIMSELF was named "GOD HERO"[60].

Saints are indeed knights of GOD, and to be such a saint is the highest form of knighthood. That is why I treat saints as knights in this book, and GOD grant that I may one day be counted in their number, though I am terribly lacking. Many of these knightly saints did not war

---

[58] (Pernoud, 1963) pg.269

[59] (Ellsburg, 2001) pg. 350

[60] Isaiah 9:6, according to the New American Bible, "Mighty Hero" according to the Revised English Bible, and "Mighty GOD", KJV

on evil in a physical sense, but they did not "cease in mental fight"[61] against the Evil One, albeit their weapons were words, sacrifice, and awesome Love.

A Knight's HONOR

The road called Honor, or Chivalry, is the knight's path to GOD. It defines the knight, separates him from other saints and orders, setting him apart.

Even a random skimming of knight stories will offer the word Honor, but that great word has many meanings. The lowest meaning is that of worldly Personal Honor, where a knight battles or suffers for selfish, individual fame or when he feels his ego bruised[62]. This is beneath that of true knighthood, and is often preached against by the Church Fathers[63]. Then there is the honor in serving a gentle woman, considered above the first meaning as heaven is above the earth, since it is unselfish. Then there is the honor of serving king and country. And finally, the truest meaning, for the truest knights, is the honor of serving GOD in all things. In this way, all good people are served, and selfishness is defeated. All real knights, true knights, hold honor in the fourth definition, but many travel through the other three levels to build to the zenith of the fourth, as Sir Thomas Malory and St. Augustine instruct[64].

Honor is not easily defined, and we will explore Honor further in later chapters, but it is basically everything good and decent in the human spirit as placed there by Divine Grace. It is strength and courage, sacrifice and faith, discipline and self-control, respect and love. Honor is all these things, and more. But only by terrible trial, pain and sacrifice, can anyone truly grasp Honor.

A quick, plain definition of Honor, as well as a good rule of thumb could be: Honor can usually be determined by the difficulty and

---

[61] From William Blake's *Jerusalem*

[62] (Deane, 1963) pg. 112

[63] St. Augustine, St. Aquinas, and St. Bernard warn of this type of "honor".

[64] (Malory, 1962) Baines' translation, pg. 458, (Filippo, 2007), (Fife, 1991) pg. 111-112, to become spiritual and unselfish, one may ascend in stages, as on the rungs of a ladder, for love of another teaches one to be more honorable

selflessness of an action. The more difficult, and unselfish, the more Honorable[65].

Ignatius Loyola had another similar way of dictating all his actions; he simply did whatever action brought greater glory or praise to GOD. "What more can I do for Christ", he would ask himself[66]. To him, this was the highest goal and Honor possible[67].

The Way of Chivalry

The Medieval mind understood that the aggressive beast living in the human chest could not be entirely tamed, but it could be focused and aimed, as one might aim an arrow, crossbow bolt, or spear. Chivalry takes the wild energies of the warrior and the blind blaze of testosterone and makes them work for Honor, Truth, and the protection of the good and the innocent[68]. The Catholic Church used Chivalry to reform the feral warrior, making him into a powerful force for good[69]. This is the total philosophy of Chivalry itself.

To ignore these energies and drives, to pretend they do not exist, or to insist they are to be thrown away is to horribly misappropriate a great treasure of energy. Worse, without the taming of these energies, the disciplining of them, men become less than men. What happens when young, virile males have no purpose, goal, or guidance in their lives? They become destructive animals[70]. When effeminate religion refuses to look at aggression, or discipline it into a tool, masses of men leave its ranks or turn to hypocrisy. When mothers giggle at the selfishness of their toddlers, or try to squash or shame their sons into becoming passionless drones, warped feelings and even serial killers result. When cultures give no outlet or aim to aggression, people roam the streets looking for trouble, with furtive meanness in their eyes. Without some sort of channel or focus for these violent energies, any civilization finds itself in danger.

---

[65] (Cummins, 1991) pg. 87 and (Mottola, 1964) pg.17-18
[66] (Mottola, 1964) pg. 18
[67] (Ganss, 1992) pg.11 and (Mottola, 1964) pg. 18
[68] (White, 1958) pg. 237 and (Steinbeck, 1976) pg. 261
[69] (Vauchez, 1993) pg.69 and (Gies, 1986) pg. 20,21, 30-32
[70] (Gerritsen and Melle, 1998) pg. 215

When these young people are given powerful stories, moral guidance, discipline, and strong, healthy role models and GODly goals, they become great workers, warriors, humanitarians, leaders, and what is more important, honorable human beings with mature and full personalities[71].

Goodness is Strength

> "Justice and power must be brought together, so that whatever is just may be powerful, and whatever is powerful may be just."
>
> —Blaise Pascal[72]

Socrates always preached morality over strength (right over might), while cynics and modern philosophers claim that strength is more important than goodness (might over right)[73].

For the knight, to have moral goodness is, by necessity, to be strong (might for right or even right is might)[74].

It is a great good to defend the poor against the excesses of the rich, but the enemies of the poor tend to be very strong as well, so it takes great strength to defeat them. Thus, to do good is to be strong. And it is the greatest good to give glory to GOD, but demonic forces try to stop anyone who does this. For human beings, demons are very strong indeed, so for a knight to defeat the efforts of these demons and give glory to the MOST HIGH takes incredible strength. Thus to be good is, by definition, to be strong.

On the other hand, if a man sinks into the throws of wickedness, he becomes weak. If he rapes a woman for instance, it is because he was too weak to confront his own unclean desires and defeat them. He falls victim to his own baseness[75].

If a man steals, it is usually because his own greed is too powerful for him, and he follows gold and wealth around like a drooling dog. Can such a cur be considered strong in any real sense? Hardly. The man

---

[71] (Green, 1984) pg. 39
[72] from Pascal's *Thoughts on Religion and other subjects,* (1825), pg. 238
[73] (Durant, 1953) pg. 24
[74] (Lull, 2001) pg. 48, 84-90, (White, 1958) pg. 237
[75] (Lull, 2001) pg. 31, 85 and (Deane, 1963) pg. 84

confronted by greed who is strong enough to wield his will like a club against it, such is a strong person[76].

Goodness, and the over-riding desire and discipline to achieve that good, makes a man strong. The wickedness and baseness of men makes them weak. To fight this wickedness in oneself and others is to defend mankind against itself, so to speak. The strongest of men control themselves and do good, the weakest of men are controlled by their base, animal desires and do evil. "He who controls himself is stronger than he who controls cities"[77].

Obviously, physical strength does not necessarily make a man good, nor does good morals necessarily make a man physically strong (only mentally and spiritually strong)[78]. Yet philosophers like Socrates and Epictetus, knightly scholars as Saint Bernard of Clairvaux, Sir Ramon Lull, and Sir Thomas Malory, even modern knightly writers like T.H. White and John Steinbeck, thought it essential for the core of the knight that he use his physical, as well as mental and spiritual strengths, to promote goodness. "Might for the Right"[79]. This is spiritual strength, and this strength lends itself to every other strength, until they converge[80].

Control of Emotions

> "The good man, though a slave, is free; the wicked, though he reigns, is a slave, and not the slave of a single man, but—what is worse—the slave of as many masters as he has vices."
>
> —St. Augustine[81]

---

76 (Lull, 2001) pg. 87 and (Eschenbach, 1980) Hatto's version pg. 231—"Self-denial was his arm against the Devil"

77 Proverbs 16:32

78 (Lull, 2001) pg. 35, 38, 86

79 (White, 1958) pg. 237, 628, (Steinbeck, 1976) pg. 2, (Matthews, 1998)pg. 149, (Gautier, 1989) pg. 7, (Clairvaux, 1977) pg. 129-130

80 Consider Flannery O'Connor's understanding of Teilhard de Chardin's ideas, that the soul must eventually merge with GOD, and thus our strength grows as our selfishness dwindles.

81 From *City of GOD*, IV, 3

For most people, their emotions and feelings influence and even form their beliefs[82]. This is why advertizing agencies, pressure groups, and organizations appeal to the emotions of the masses instead of their intellect. They have been taught by the weak-willed.

For the knight, as St. George, his thoughts and beliefs, channeled through Chivalry, influence his emotions.

He believed in the truth of Christianity, and so his rage burned when he saw Diocletian's attempt to destroy that truth. This righteous fury led him to confront the Emperor, even though it meant a torturous death. George feels pity for the maiden, and in the heat of the dragon's breath, rescues her from certain doom.

Observe this. Most people are instead controlled by their own pleasures, as a puppet is manipulated. Modern men pursue pleasure constantly. It influences nearly everything they do, and obstructs the best efforts of their own spirituality. It used to be that the focus of a man's house lay squarely at the family table, now it is centered on TV, video games and entertainments. Pleasure has become the focus.

Look at a man considering the virtues of celibacy. He thinks about taking the vows as he walks down the street. He may even be on the verge of accepting the whole difficult idea of celibacy when he sees a beautiful girl walking the opposite way.

Suddenly, all thoughts of celibacy drop from his mind and he thinks, "how stupid of me! I wonder if I can get her number".

This is what modern man is reduced to, a slave to his own desires[83].

The knight refuses to be a slave so easily. He considers celibacy as he walks down the street, and sees the same girl as well, but this only gives him a better understanding of the difficulties of celibacy, instead of making it fall from his mind like water[84]. He may be tempted, but his resolve is strong. Sometimes he can become so distracted by the pursuit of Chivalry and Honor that he does not even see the girl.

The mission and the pursuit of Truth is always more important to the knight than his emotions[85].

---

[82]   (Durant, 1953) pg. 20, 22
[83]   (Deane, 1963) pg. 41, (Gleason, 1966) pg. 179, ch.556
[84]   (Lull, 2001) pg. 42, 84-5
[85]   (Lull, 2001) pg. 25, 39

We will discuss how to control emotion in following chapters, but the knight keeps reign over his heart by, once again, focusing on GOD. The "GOD intoxicated" man.

For one thing, most human emotions tend to chase after worldly things, even against or in the face of GOD's rules. But the knight considers "what does it profit a man to gain the whole world, yet lose his soul"[86]? To become a slave to the desires of the world is to have his soul evaporate in a blaze of heat and noise and stupidity. St. George refused to allow his worldly ambitions and possessions to stray him from the right path.

As opposed to this world, the knight remembers that only GOD is permanent. All other things pass away, including family and friends (and enemies), as well as the entire universe. The knight is not much tempted by a beautiful woman passing by, for he knows in a few years she will be dust and bone. The gold of the world does not interest him, for how is he to spend it in the grave? He gets used to the idea that one day, all things must die and disappear, and thus his heart is armored against loss. The whole world can die around him, his flesh can fall away into nothing, but he knows that it was supposed to happen anyway.

St. Augustine reflected on this on his deathbed. Barbarians were slowly destroying the entire civilized world, as Augustine knew it. They were even now breaking through the gates of his city. As Augustine lay dying, his whole universe was crumbling around him.

But he said, "No great man is he, who thinks it a great affair, that bricks and bridges fall, and men die"[87]. This echoes Sir Galahad when he said "Remember how ephemeral is this world"[88].

Fairness

Throughout all knight stories, and thus embedded in the knight psyche, is a sense of fairness; fairness for the poor, fairness for the weak, fairness above all.

---

[86] Mark 8:36, KJV Luke 9:25
[87] (St. Augustine, The Giants of Philosophy, produced by Carmichael and Carmichael, Inc., 1990)
[88] (Malory, 1962) pg. 43

The knight cannot stand the bully beating upon weaker children, or a tyrant whipping innocent peasants. He cannot tolerate the strong monster terrorizing the townspeople, or the rich master squashing down the poor around him. He cannot abide a gang of ruffians robbing and beating on an elderly person. He cannot stomach loud street urchins haranguing the handicapped. Nor can he allow a government to persecute a peaceful religious group.

The knight, strong himself, champions the weak in the face of the strong, throwing his gauntlet at the powerful for the sake of the powerless. He is the voice of the voiceless, the arm of the weaponless, the hope of the hopeless. By the same token, he is the law for those "above the law", the fear of those in high places, the doom of evil kings.

In personal combat also, the knight accepts no unfair advantages beyond ability. If his honorable opponent has no weapon, he tosses his own aside. If his honorable opponent has fallen, he stops the match or waits until the opponent comes to his feet. He will never "gang up" on a lone man (although his enemies usually do this to him). He refuses to become a bully himself, even as he battles them.

The knight knows that to take unfair advantage, to bully the weaker, to scheme treacherous things, is to take the easier path, the weaker path. To be a bully is to be weak; to cheat is to fail. Only the weakest man harasses the small and innocent, only the coward attacks the defenseless.

When St. George happened upon a town and a woman terrorized by a much powerful monster, he did not hesitate. Lancelot also concerned himself to fairness, even when it worked against him. Happening upon a smaller force of men losing before a greater force, Lancelot chose always the losing side, just to even the odds[89]. Such balancing of the field may be the origin of America's love for the underdog.

As a side-note, many in this world have shouted for fairness and equality, when they would like nothing better than to stack odds in their favor, to have fairness as long as it profits them, and especially to have it fair for themselves, but not for others.

Although knights fight for the weak and innocent, a true knight never allows himself to take advantage of the situation or the charges under his care. This generous and selfless duty is opposed to many modern "champions of the oppressed", who seem to have compassion for

---

[89]   (Malory, 1962) pg. 391 and (Matarasso, 1969) pg. 156

the down-trodden, but then twist things to benefit the "champion". The knight is sincere and watches over his motives.

Justice

This is a much used and misused word in today's society, but the knight's understanding was the original and ancient one of Socrates, Plato, and Aristotle. They listed it as one of the four essential qualities of a man, later adopted by the Church as the four cardinal virtues. Similarly, for the knight, Justice was one of the four virtues "essential in the estimation of mankind to the character of the knight in the days of Chivalry"[90].

As with the Greeks, the Knight's idea of Justice was simple and easily said: "To give to each man his due, what he deserves"[91].

When people do well and honorably, they are to be rewarded and admired. When people commit crimes, they are to be punished and chastised. Simple, brutal, and clear.

Compare this to the more complex panorama that stands for Justice in this modern world. People talk of "Social Justice" when they sometimes mean respect and sometimes financial equality and sometimes a free pass. People talk of class and race struggles, the plights of the poor, and the dreams and aspirations of the migrant workers.

For the knight, when it comes to Justice, there is no rich or poor, no class or race, no Capitalist or Communist, no employer and no worker[92]. There is only what a man deserves. If he works hard, he deserves a fair wage and if he doesn't work although he is able, he deserves nothing[93]. If a man acts like a man, he is due the respect of a man; if a man acts like a dog, he deserves the treatment of a dog.

---

[90] (Meller, 2002) pg. 52
[91] (Stalker, 1902) pg. 67-68
[92] Deuteronomy 1:17, Job 34:19, Leviticus 19:15, Acts 26:22
[93] 2 Thessalonians 3:10

Mercy

The other side of the coin is Mercy. Without Mercy, Justice is altogether brutal, and all of mankind would be damned. Without Justice, Mercy is over-sentimental and without meaning or merit. The knight must know, weigh, and have the proper balance of both[94].

The knight shows mercy when he hesitates to kill, allowing his honorable opponent to yield. He shows mercy when he gives to the blind beggar on the street, or the ragged and dirty child in the gutter. He shows mercy when he forgives the calumny and spittle from people who misunderstand him. He shows mercy when he gives water to fallen warriors on the battlefield, friend and foe alike[95]. He shows mercy when he comes to the aid of anyone, even those who would have hated him. The knight knows that Christ is his ultimate model when Mercy is concerned[96].

The knight has the strength and magnanimity of Mercy. Through Mercy, as through Justice, the knight shows his honor[97].

Respect

Much is made of this word, even by modern gang members on the street. They talk of it as if they understand it, and continuously say "I respect only those who respect me." This violates Justice, Fairness, Mercy, and the true meaning of Respect.

Respect flows from the knight because he understands that everything is GOD's creation, and thus GOD's property, and what is more, he respects himself, so he respects all other creatures. The knight knows that respect is not raw fear, as opposed to those who wish to force "respect" on others, but reverence for the Creator through genteelness and courtesy toward the creation.

The knight respects everyone, even his enemy. When St. George came to confront Emperor Diocletian, there were no curses or epithets on his lips. This is how an honorable man is known, how a true Christian man

---

[94] (Lull, 2001) pg. 36, 49
[95] As in the Civil War story of Richard Kirkland, or Clara Barton
[96] Luke 6:36 KJV
[97] (Steinbeck, 1976) pg. 85

can be known as well: he shows respect even to those who do not respect him, and even to those who hate him.

This is the chivalrous version of the Golden Rule. Chivalry, Honor, and Courtesy might as well be the same word[98].

One way a knight shows this respect is by not shouting anyone down, by listening to legitimate concerns, by never being cruel, or vicious, or brash, or prone to name-calling. A knight has the strength of courtesy[99].

Respect also means "expect". A knight expects a man to act like a man, not as a dog, and is disgusted when men do not live up to their potential. To be treated with respect is to be expected to act respectable. A knight respects by openly expecting the best from others, although he must also be prepared for the worst.

We will spend this book discussing expectations of knights. Understand, that the world no longer agrees with this ancient, Chivalrous standard. Consider the title of "Sir", which in the past always meant "knight", marking the dubbed soldier-saint from all other men. The word rang with respect and dignity. But now, such a title is used for any man in a position of authority, whether deserving or not, or even as a title given to worldly entertainers who please the Queen of England. Lately, two famed Rock and Roll performers, both sodded, overweight, and effeminate, have gathered that prefix simply for singing! Can such men be considered true knights?

And what of the expectations for men? In ancient times and the Middle Ages, a man was expected to do the impossible, defeat a dragon, risk his life for a cause and even a promise, uphold an entire country with the work of his hands, always controlling himself and molding a better world. Then, expectations lowered a bit, but still men were required to fight for country, GOD, family, and honor, working hard and steadily.

In this modern time, what is expected of men? Are they expected to fight for honor or GOD, even morality? Are they expected to take care of their families? Are they expected to contain their desires and their loins? Are they even expected to control themselves in small matters, at least? Or is the only expectation placed upon them the lifting of a toilet seat cover, the showing friends a good time, or the running a few errands for their mother?

---

[98] (Gautier, 1989) pg. 109

[99] Alfred, Lord Tennyson, "The greater the man, the greater the courtesy", *the Last Tournament*, v. 638

Beware, men only live up to the expectations placed upon them, and no farther. The knight expects, even demands, the best from himself.

Accountability

One of the most frightening and difficult tasks of a knight, which he takes as a matter of course, is his accountability for his actions. The knight is always responsible for his actions, and can never blame others for his own failures.

Accountability is rarely if ever spoken of in knightly stories, because it is assumed. In the world of the knight, rigors of life, honest mistakes, and even accident are no excuse for sin[100]. Although magic and strange occurrences abound in the story of Balin and Balan, when Balin accidently kills a magical woman, he does not blame anyone else and accepts the curse laid upon him. Sir Gawain does not throw accusations around when he is duped into accepting a supposedly magical belt, but he accepts the punishment as if he were alone in the decision. King Arthur, completely misled by his shape-shifting half-sister, never wasted time looking for excuses. When Nathan pointed out his guilt, King David humbly and readily accepted it[101], as did Lancelot. The knight can never say "The devil made me do it". Humans have free will, but are their own worst enemies.

While we are all, partially at least, products of the time and place where we live, we must continuously strive to be better than ourselves[102]. It is counterproductive and pointless to blame the supposed prejudices of others, or the failings of one's family, or the biases of the world around us. We are ultimately accountable for our mistakes.

Once we accept this with an iron will, it is strange to note that we become happier, stronger, and more as men should be.

Closely aligned with this is the idea of self-sufficiency. The knight enjoys being self-sufficient and looks to make himself thus as much as possible. It bothers him to be beholden to anyone else, for a borrower

---

[100] (White, 1958) pg. 302
[101] 2 Samuel 12:7-13
[102] Paraphrased from William Faulkner, in his Paris Interview, 1956

becomes, in a sense, a slave[103]. The knight, as many men in modern day, comes to realize that to depend on others is to be at their mercy, and this is not a pleasant place to exist, especially as a man-at-arms.

The knight is accountable for his beliefs as well, popular or not. St. George could have pretended to be pagan when Diocletian's persecutions started, but instead, George was true to himself and to his GOD. Accountability is being true to yourself, not because your self is important, but because you aligned yourself with Truth.

Honesty

Truth carries a mighty banner in the minds and hearts of knights, because it is placed there by GOD[104]. A lie is unthinkable, and a knight will not break a promise, even to save his life.

Just as the knight searches for the Truth of GOD, so is the knight an instrument of Truth, a mouthpiece of Truth, a weapon of Truth, crushing lies everywhere. He always speaks the truth, and even his enemies can depend on his frankness.

"My task is to bear witness to the truth. For this I was born, for this I came into the world, and all who are not deaf to truth listen to my voice"[105].

The knight must also be honest with himself. To lie to one's self is the easiest thing in the world, and makes it impossible to be honest with others. The knight must stand watch over his own mind and heart forever.

The Mystic meets the Temporal

Within every man of GOD, and thus within every knight, is a tug of war between the concerns of this world, and the realities of the next. In Medieval times, the priest and the knight often disagreed how best to approach a problem, since they often came from opposite poles of

---

[103] Proverbs 22:7
[104] (Lull, 2001) pg. 42, and (Gautier, 1989) pg. 67-8
[105] John 18:37, the Revised English Bible

perception, the knight from the very near and physical, the priest or monk from the spiritual and aloof. Where can the mystic and the warrior meet?

If a man bends himself only to crushing suffering and evil, only arming himself so as to battle an endless war against cruelty, looking for an earthly paradise of peace, he runs the risk of losing sight of GOD. Like Wolfram von Eschenbach's Parzival, the warrior can become bitter, disillusioned, and overwhelmed by the infinite well-spring of evil in men's hearts and in demonic eyes, for only GOD can defeat all evil and suffering in the world, which He will do in His own time[106].

But if a man totally ignores such battle in the world, filling himself only with a temporal taste of GOD's peace to the ignoring of all suffering, he runs the risk of ignoring the suffering Christ, who is found in the pain of our fellow man. Some accused John Cassian of not caring for the mission of Christ, because this mystic chose communion with GOD through meditation, instead of the soup-kitchens and charity[107].

Both St. Augustine and St. Bernard of Clairvaux suffered terribly because of this natural dichotomy within reality. Both felt caught between their love of divine contemplation and their mission to save souls[108]. As many saints before and since, they found a balance between the silent peace of the contemplative life and the hurried work of helping others, quiet meditation on GOD and winning the world for Christ.

The true knight finds himself both as warrior and monk. The knight must do both, battle and pray, work and think. These two extremes must meet together in the knight's mind, heart and soul. Like the Templar and Hospitaller knights, he must be a priest with a sword, a monk with a mission[109]. He must use GOD's internal peace to fight evil in the external world.

He does this by recognizing the true battle occurs in three arenas, in three "places"—the physical world, the mental plane, and the spiritual reality.

---

[106] (Eschenbach, 1980) pg. 229-235 in Hatto's version

[107] (Holmes, originally 1980, electronically 2002) pg. 46; Such accusations show the two views of Christianity, physical versus spiritual, work vs. pure meditation.

[108] (Tamburello, 2000) pg. 28, (Trape', 1986) pg. 102,131,143-145

[109] (Meller, 2002) pg. 10

CONTINUOUS BATTLE

The very nature of the knight's existence as a protector of Christianity, the defenseless, and his own soul means that he must be in constant warfare against all things evil[110]. This requires battle on three fronts or arenas: the physical, the mental, and the spiritual.

The physical battle is against physical enemies, such as robbers, murderers, rapists, terrorists, and anyone who wishes to inflict cruelty on others. Because of this, the knight is called to have great physical skill, great preparation, and excellent weapons.

The mental battle is against opponents who attack in the world of ideas, such as atheists, new-agers, pagans, heretics, and detractors of Christ. Many of these are skilled in debate and clever in their influence, so the knight must match and exceed them in knowledge, wisdom, and determination. This battle also requires the knight to keep watch over his own thoughts and emotions, so that a wayward inclination does not lead him astray from his Honorable goals.

As Fr. Scupoli says, one should not trust one's self too much[111]. It is too easy to be fooled by our own desires, as well as the glamour of the world. We must be able to question ourselves and be ready to know when we have been wrong. Sometimes the evil is within our own hearts!

By far the most profound is the battle of the Spirit, where the knight engages demons, illusions, and the terrible pitch battle that is his own soul.

All these battles have several features in common.

> ➢ The knight must be prepared and trained to be successful in them.
> ➢ He constantly trains himself to be more effective in each kind of battle.
> ➢ Everything he does must be geared for victory in all and each of them
> ➢ A knight is always looking for effective weapons in these battles, and all things are judged based on their effectiveness in these battles.
> ➢ As long as a battle is not decisive, the knight may learn from a loss in any of them.

---

[110] The Code of Chivalry, numbers V, VI, and X, as well as (Vauchez, 1993) pg. 59, and innumerable others

[111] (Scupoli, 1945 edition) pg. 7-10

> ➤ But loss in any of them may lead to terrible consequences not just for the knight, but for everyone around him, so he considers all battle very seriously.

These battles make up the lion's share of his thoughts and success in them is the driving force behind the majority of his actions. For example, while the rest of the human world spends an enormous amount of time thinking on (and buying) clothing fashions, the knight's view is different. He measures good clothing, as everything else, by how it helps him battle evil. Will this business suit help him in his battles, he asks himself. Perhaps, if it helps him appear more trustworthy and knowledgeable, thus inclining people to listen to his appeal against evil.

While the rest of the world is in constant pursuit of pleasure, even the knight's "hobbies" help him somehow in his pursuit of victory over evil. In this sense they are not hobbies, but small training vehicles by which he prepares himself. Physically he engages in weight training, sparing, martial arts, archery, or the like. Mental "hobbies" may include theology, the study of Christianity and other religions, symbolism, collections of Chivalry codes, research of saints, heroes, and their strategies against evil. Spiritual "hobbies" often include prayer and study of prayer, mortification of the flesh, voluntary isolation in lonely places, and fasting.

This focus, of course, leads the knight away from the "normal" activities and past-times of many humans. He always feels on the "edge of the world" and "in the world but not of the world"[112]. There is always a piece of his mind and soul that is separate from earthly concerns, and removed from worldly emotional attachments. Indeed, the knight keeps a part of his mind and soul locked away from others, so that he may share this place only with GOD, alone with HIM who is alone[113].

Especially Spiritual Battle

In the past, a knight was more trained in physical combat than in any other. Now, the emphasis has changed, largely because of the influence of the Catholic Church and knightly scholars like Ramon Lull. Mental

---

[112] John 15:19, 17:14
[113] (Smith, 1963) pg. 282

and especially spiritual victory is most prized. This is nothing new, and harkens back to the original teachings of Christ, as seen by such as St. Paul and Justin Martyr, who understood the importance of spiritual struggle[114]. A knight might crush the whole world under his heel, but such a victory would not lead people to the Truth, or to Christ, thus such a victory is useless[115]. The knight understands that the battle for the heart and mind and soul is far more important, and far more difficult, and far more glorious[116].

No man or women need fear the knight. A knight does not wish to conquer or kill anyone. If I cut another man down, does that make me a better man? Does it convert him to my cause? If I conquer countries and make them subservient to my views, does that make these countries truly Christian? Can anyone be forced to love GOD and Christ? Indeed, the knight physically defends himself and others against marauders and the cruel, but never uses violence to "convince" or harass anyone.

A knight bends himself to the tireless war against evil[117], but this war is like the one spoken of in the song "Onward Christian Soldiers", or the Buddha's Dharma Conquest, or Sir Galahad's pursuit of the Holy Grail. The true battle is not with people, "but the principalities and powers"[118] of the other world, and the untruths spread by the ignorant, the arrogant, or the Evil One Himself. Let us raise our spiritual swords against greed, lust, wrath, envy, sloth, gluttony, and pride[119]! Let us spit in the face of the Devil, and make his minions fear us!

Throughout this book, you will read of tremendous physical battles, but I hope you see behind and between the lines. These battles, important as they were, are also symbols of the unseen but more ominous battle that rages within every human soul. It is more important to fight St. George's fight, against the "dragon"[120].

---

[114] (Donaldson, 2009)

[115] (Deane, 1963) pg. 139 and (Dales, 2004) pg. 92

[116] Lancelot and Cicero agree, "The more difficult the battle, the greater the glory".—*The Offices*, Book I, section 64; also Thomas Paine, in the first lines of his excellent pamphlet, *The American Crisis*

[117] Code of Chivalry, X, as in (Gautier, 1989)

[118] Ephesians 6:12

[119] (Lull, 2001) pg. 84

[120] Just as St. Michael fights the "dragon" and "the serpent", they being Satan, see St. Michael's Prayer

One day, everyone will realize that they serve one Lord or the Other. Either they Serve Lord Christ, or the Evil One. I beseech you, take my side and let us ride with our Lord and King Christ Jesus. Is there anything more glorious than to battle in His name, for His causes, for His Truth?

Yet The Need For Earthly Battle

This does not detract, however, from the very physical nature of some conflict the knight engages in. Of course, traditionally, the knight hunted his enemies physically and struck at them with deadly force at every possible opportunity[121]. For the most part, the modern knight will no longer be able to do this, because of the nature of modern civilization, warfare, and his own honorable disposition. Yet, whenever the enemy appears and attacks physically, the knight is obligated to strike back with terrifying force. Whenever rapists and child molesters attack, the knight must beat them down until they are unable to harm the innocent. Whenever terrorists or fools seek to kill populations, the knight is required to do everything possible to stop them. Whenever communists and fascists move to slay, or secular humanists and atheists come to destroy believers, the knight must stand up and crush them. War, in this way, helps the world[122] and the good.

The modern knight, just as the medieval knight, cannot afford pacifism and weak-willed politics to open the door to our enemies. When the Saracens attacked Europe, when the Nazis attacked their neighbors, and when the Terrorists attack the world, the only response is to stop them with all three types of battle.

The Church saw that some enemies must be stopped physically and with crushing force. Saint Augustine and Saint Bernard gave the knight the right to fight the Just War[123]. They understood that allowing evil men to burn ideas, grind the innocent, and kill people gives no glory to GOD. Allowing good people to suffer and innocent people to die does not please Jesus Christ. "The only thing necessary for evil to triumph is for good

---

[121] (Lull, 2001) pg. 38
[122] (Gautier, 1989) pg. 10-11
[123] (Doornik, 1953) pg. 412

men to stand by and do nothing"[124]. A knight cannot simply attack those he feels are guilty without iron-clad evidence (Honor and Christian piety demand restraint), but he cannot sit by and do nothing[125].

The Sword and Weaponry

St. George's sword, often paired with the lance as the knight's favorite weapon, represents Chivalry itself, Honor, Justice, and Truth[126], as well as focus on GOD[127]. It is at once a sublime and terrible symbol, but it is known the world over as the ultimate symbol of the Knight, along with the horse and armor. Statues of Justice hold a sword, and Medieval paintings of CHRIST often portray the sword that is said to be HIS word. The almost-worship of the sword in knighthood is owed to ancient Germanic influence, and every knight longed for one of his own to settle in his hand and give its reassuring weight.

The knight is never far from his sword, even when asleep. It was included in every knightly ceremony, including the "watching of the armor" and the "dubbing", and many knights were buried with their weapons. The sword was even used in prayer, often forged in a "cruciform" manner, so that the knight could pray with the sword set before him as a kind of cross. When St. George drew his sword at the sight of the dragon, the text of the Golden Legend suggests the sword, held in front of him, was like crossing himself in the fashion of Catholics[128].

The knights loved their swords so much that they gave them unique names, like St. George's "Ascalon", Roland's "Durandel", Charlemagne's "Joyeuse" and "Flamberge"; and Rodrigo De Bivar's "Tizon" and "Colada". They perceived their weapons as having individuality and even a personality. But whatever name it possessed, the sword embodied the Honor of the knight, and the grim resolve to enforce that Honor.

---

[124] Attributed to Edmund Burke

[125] (Steinbeck, 1976) pg. 261

[126] (Lull, 2001) pg.64, (Williams, 2008)

[127] (Matarasso, 1969) pg. 297

[128] (Voragine, 1275, 1483) In Caxton's version, St. George crosses himself as he takes out his sword, almost as if it is one and the same action.

Adoration of Women

Because of Catholic and ancient Germanic influence[129], as well as input from the French, one of the most terrorized and victimized groups in the history of humanity found a ready protector in the knight: women. St. George's rescue and courtesy towards women, echoing as it does nearly every Chivalrous story, is not simply a personal whim of the knight, nor a character trait of just one saint, it is the ever-present duty of all true knights everywhere.

Some knights went so far as to idolize their women, worshipping them as emissaries of GOD on earth[130]. The woman was seen as the ultimate symbol of manners, courtesy, humanity, gentleness, and kindness. It was no accident that Lancelot, greatest and gentlest earthly knight, was trained in manners by women[131]. To love a woman "from afar" was practice for the more perfect love of and obedience to GOD, as well as a way to reach Honor[132].

Women were not seen as models for everything, however. Effeminate ways, such as the coddling and spoiling of children, were seen as evils so disastrous that the child destined to be a knight was almost always shipped off to be trained by an uncle or other male far removed from the home. Conniving women who plotted against others, spread rumors, wallowed in vanity, and obsessed over trivial matters were said not to deserve the name of "woman"[133].

Mission Driven Vs. the Butterfly of Fate

The knight's heart and mind pulse with the idea of the mission, the quest, the purpose, his meaning in life. He tends to see his life as a series of grand adventures with the final goal being to save others from Evil, save his own soul, and better the world. It is not enough to live a domestic existence of going to work every day and coming home to the family, unless going

---

[129] (Tierney, 1978) pg. 37

[130] Ibid., and (Gies, 1986) pg. 69, 77

[131] (Corley, 1989) pg. 27, 50-59

[132] (Malory, 1962) pg. 458, (Fife, 1991) pg.111-112

[133] (Gautier, 1989) pg. 308, (Gies, 1986) pg. 76, (Steinbeck, 1976) pg. 288, (Barber, 1995) pg. 83, (Hopkins, 1999) pg. 54

to work is a mission against evil, and the family also is an extension of this mission. Full of initiative, the knight is driven and obsessed.

This of course makes it difficult at times to live with a knight, for he is constantly thinking of battle, planning some campaign, and "gallivanting" out on some adventure.

A knightly assumption of this mission obsession is that "one man can make a difference". In the Middle Ages, the idea of a single man, riding into battle and turning the tide seemed very normal and expected[134]. Whole battles of armies were decided sometimes by the duel of only two men[135], similar to the "duel" of David and Goliath in the Bible.

The opposite of this is the modern man, who seems content to live his life as a "butterfly of fate" drifting between the winds of happenstance, accepting any pleasure that flops by, and waiting for something good to come his way. If life is simply a series of ups and downs, why try to improve at all? Why try to be better? People grow cynical and bitter, often assuming that nothing can be done in a defeatist world-view that chokes all personal betterment or advancement.

The knight sneers at such lazy self-indulgence and recognizes it for what it is, an excuse, a slothfulness, a surrender.

To Reach Higher

Related to this mission-obsession is the knight's constant drive to better himself[136]. A capitalist might constantly try to better his lot in life, but a knight constantly seeks to make his actions and thoughts more pure and GOD-like, his mind sharper and more informed and wiser, his body stronger, faster, and more skilled. In the back of his mind, always pushing him, also exhorting him like the strongest habit, the knight cannot feel happy unless he is involved in some endeavor that makes a better man, knight, and saint out of himself.

He is no Pelagian, understanding full well that the final Grace is GOD's, but still that wind is always behind him, that nagging reminder, to strive, to win, to beat the Devil down, to conquer the self, the quest of Excellence! Excelsior! To do better than before. To do one's best, against

---

[134] (Romer, 1988) pg. 91, (Bradford, 1972) pg. 96-7, (Matthews, 1998) pg. 68
[135] For an example of this see (Moncrieff, 1976) pg. 266
[136] (Vauchez, 1993) pg. 61, Philippians 3:12-15, and (Mottola, 1964) pg.18

all odds. To hold Excalibur and to sit in the Siege Perilous, or at least to strive and seek the worthiness of such honors. GOD has done His part, let us now do ours!

This also has an opposite in the modern world. Too many parents are telling their children that they are "perfect just the way they are", that the child needs no improvement, encouraging the child to fall in love with himself, like Narcissus. Narcissus drowned because of his own self-aggrandizement. And if one is so perfect when born, why does one need to be toilet-trained! A child is potential, a great potential of course, but nothing more until he uses his GOD-given tools and talents to polish himself into a brilliant, powerful, GODly adult!

Both the mission-driven spirit and the will to improve come from a very important aspect of the Judeo-Christian Ethic. Unlike the pagan cultures, which saw all of existence as simple cycles within cycles of growth and decay, the Jews beheld GOD's creation as a linear progression, having small cycles within it to be sure, but overall a continuous movement toward the better, if only a man would stay on the right path with GOD. If the people of Abraham would keep to their covenant with GOD, life would become more holy, more fulfilled, and more perfect. The Jews conceived this properly, as an understanding worked out between GOD and man, where man had to rise above himself, and GOD would aid him[137]. Later, the Greeks and Romans would try to force it through politics and war[138].

This idea, that life can be made better, through a proper relationship with GOD, discipline, and hard work, is distinctly Judeo-Christian[139], and a fundamental part of what it is to live in the "Western World". This is why the Western World is more technologically advanced, and enjoys the highest standard of living in the history of Humanity: We have never been satisfied with the ways things were[140].

Such a physical consequence to a philosophical idea is simply a side-effect. The original concept was to become better spiritually, to walk with GOD. St. Matthew and St. Luke remind us that the way to Heaven

---

[137] (Romer, 1988) pg. 61
[138] Ibid. pg. 120
[139] (Romer, 1988) pg. 61
[140] I am told this is the "progressive" view in politics. In this way, even they imitate Chivalry.

is a "narrow gate"[141], a narrow road that is difficult to walk and where we must push ourselves, discipline ourselves, suffer the pain of spiritual growth. The others walk a wide and easy path, comfortable and without the drive to change for the better. But the ultimate destination of the wide and easy path is Perdition.

The Natural World as a Symbol

The knight's mind is close to the Biblical mind, in that it perceives everything in the world, in fact the entire world itself, as a symbol[142].

Since GOD created the natural world, it has HIS mark upon it[143]. Thus, if a man is wise, he can look at the natural world and see signposts that point to GOD. To the knight, the world is a giant symbol, puzzle, or pictogram with GOD as its final solution. In this way, the knight uses the world to see GOD.

Everywhere the knight looks, he sees a finger pointing to GOD[144].

The sun is a symbol of the light Christ sheds upon the whole world, and its rising after the terrors of the night speaks of Christ's glorious resurrection after death.

Animals also are lessons about the Almighty. In Medieval times, scholars believed the pelican shed its own blood to feed its young, just as Christ sheds His blood so that we may be saved[145]. Similarly, that the cubs of the lioness were born dead, and on the third day the father lion comes to breathe life into them, as a striking symbol of GOD rising Christ, the lion of Judah, from the grave[146].

These are not accidental, nor mindless attempts to explain natural phenomena, but a mindset, a particular way of seeing, which calls GOD to mind with every step, every sight, every sound.

In much the same way as the knight uses his interpretations of the sight around him, he also uses the world's tools to fight for GOD. The

---

[141] Matthew 7:13, Luke 13:24
[142] (Vauchez, 1993) pg. 63, (Charbonneau-Lassay, 1991) pg. VIII, and (Copleston, 1952) pg. 77
[143] (Doornik, 1953) pg. 163
[144] (Copleston, 1952) pg. 77
[145] (Charbonneau-Lassay, 1991) pg. 259
[146] Ibid. pg. 10

sword, the pen, even the musical instrument are all tools developed by the world, but all can used to further GOD's glory in the hearts of men, or defend GOD's chosen against those who hate them.

The world does not use the knight, the knight uses the world. He does not love the world for its own sake, but for the sake of the Lord[147].

The World in "Why's"

Similar to Biblical populations, the knight searched for the meaning of everything, and this is one of the major separations between him and the scientific, modern man. The knight sees the "Why", whilst the modern man sees the "How".

This difference can be seen in how a medieval might see a miracle, and a modern might react. Let us say Moses, who thought much like a medieval, and a scientist, who thinks like a modern, both see the same thing: a pillar of fire.

The scientist would ask "How', as in "How is this occurring? How is the light suspended there in the air? Is it from afar-off volcano? How does the fire rise? Does hot steam blow up the magma from the deep in the earth"?

(It is curious to note that when a child asks, "Why does rain fall"? For example, we as moderns always answer in terms of how: "rain falls from the clouds, which makes the rain". This is *how* the rain falls, not *why*).

Moses would look at the fire and say, "This must be a sign of GOD. But why would GOD send such a thing? And curious it comes at the time I am thinking of what to do with the children of Israel".

Moses is not concerned with how the fire got there. It does not matter if it is an apparition, a volcano erupting, or a laser beam from Mars, he only looks for the significance of "Why". Why did it appear this way? Why did GOD's providence allow me to see it? Why did GOD send it at this time and place? This is the proper way to view any miracle.

The scientist ponders the forces of nature and perhaps discovers how steam moves molten rock, but he misses the miracle. Moses goes on to free a nation from slavery. The scientist looks for and sees the glory of creation, but he never looks past it. Moses reads the meaning and catches a glimpse of the mind of the Creator.

---

[147] John 15:19

These two viewpoints illustrate the positive and negative aspects of the world. One, the world can point the way to GOD because it is ultimately good, or it can hamper your search for Truth if you cannot see beyond the world.

The World as a Barrier

Just as a woman can be a road to Honor or a great obstacle, the World can become a barrier instead of a royal road to GOD's door[148]. The knight has a way of handling this too.

Usually what happens is like this: a man becomes too interested in the creation, and begins to lose sight of the Creator. It is like a man becoming too enamored of a woman. Her body, her eyes, her speech, her movements and even her personality distract him from what he must do. Soon he wastes all his energy and strength trying to please her, instead of trying to please He Who created her[149]. The man exhausts himself on what will soon be nothing but bone and dust, instead of investing his time in the glory of the MOST HIGH.

As Dante points out in his *Purgatorio*, most sins are derived from misplaced love; people loving the creation, and forgetting to love the hidden Creator[150].

Although the world was created good, in the above way it can become an evil distraction[151]. When this happens, when the knight finds himself sorely tempted by this world to neglect GODly things, he regards the world as a veil, or blindfold, which must be ignored at times to see GOD[152]. The world is like a porch light, which is good, but is harmful when one wishes to see the greater beauty of the stars. To gaze at the Heavens properly requires switching off the inhibiting lights.

So, instead of loving the world and working for its sake, the knight either uses the world to reach for GOD's hand, or ignores the world's distractions.

---

[148] (Deane, 1963) pg. 60
[149] (Tuoti, 1999) pg. 32
[150] (Bergin, 1955) Canto X, line 2-3, Pg. 30 of Dante's *Purgatorio*, and (Deane, 1963) pg. 61
[151] (Vauchez, 1993) pg. 47, 49, 50-52
[152] (Barron, 2008) pg. 68

Through the rest of this book, I will assume you have to work against the world of men in order to find GOD. For us modern men, the world has become so large and over-powering, that it is almost impossible to look beyond political systems, the towering amounts of consumer goods, even the concerns of family and friends all blend together to distract even a strong soul from pondering on GOD and prayer.

The following chapters will contain pointers on how to ignore the world and see past it.

Opposing Philosophies

Philosophy is everything. The belief systems of people, deep within them, are reflected in their actions, and influence everything they say and see.

Christians believe that GOD made all people, all nations, all worlds, and that GOD commands charity. Mercy is at the heart of the law[153]. Thus, whether they feel like it or not, Christian knights are obliged to help the poor, the weak, the old, the infirm, the innocent, and anyone who cannot help themselves. Even the knights of the Crusades, usually presented as blood-thirsty brutes, were in reality much concerned with the welfare of others, as Godfrey of Bouillon and the Templars, or the Hospitallers, with their gigantic hospital. Thus is the belief system of the Christian, and the knight.

Modern philosophies, with all their talk of charity and compassion, do not have any obligation, since they perceive no final authority but themselves. What they feel is thus what they do; nothing commands otherwise, in their minds and hearts. Beware such un-restraint. Feelings can turn quickly.

In America and Europe, these modern philosophies and organizations have set themselves up as the judges of the world, deciding who does this and who does that, what subjects we are allowed to speak of in schools and public arenas, and who runs the charities and institutions. But the Christians were there first. The fact that there are so many charities is the work of the Christians, and they began the Universities and schools. Now the moderns come in and say "You serve at our pleasure, at our behest". They see themselves as GOD, in the place of GOD.

---

[153] Matthew 9:13, Matthew 23:23, Luke 10:37

Christians, and thus knights, have only one GOD, and HE is not a modern. So exemplifies the difference between knightly philosophy and modern beliefs.

Further Points

Throughout the knight's career, he must guard against feeling too proud of his accomplishments. As soon as they were finished with their latest adventure, Knights from legend constantly pursued greater and more difficult tasks, never satisfied with themselves or their victories[154].

At the same time, a knight should not become too disheartened at his progress in chivalry, or lack thereof. Knightly spiritual growth, from a weak, selfish man, to a shining knight is probably not linear[155]. Becoming a true knight is often like a constant trial and error session, doing the best you can and stumbling through the maze of morality and spirituality and theology, until you come across a sudden insight, a beam of light in the darkness, a sudden burst of Grace from GOD.

Hence this book can only guide you to knighthood, it cannot bestow Chivalry upon you magically. The knights of old did not have textbooks to follow, only the advice of priests, holy men, legends, other knights and an occasional vision from Heaven.

I cannot turn you into knights automatically, through scholarly debate or otherwise. I can only offer actions and thoughts that should trigger certain thoughts and experiences within you. As you attempt any knightly action, even a small one, I hope the spirit of Honor will awaken within you, and the HOLY SPIRIT will alight upon you.

Why Should I continue?

Modern man may look at the life of the knight, with its struggles and pains and woes and say, "What sort of life is this? It is no life"!

For my answer, I quote the monk Bernadin Schellenberger, who was speaking about the life of a pilgrim when he said, "This is no life. But it is not meant to be a life—a safe, solid, certain, cozy condition. That is

---

154 (Deane, 1963) pg. 61, (Vauchez, 1993) pg. 61
155 (Schellenberger, 1981) pg. 52

precisely the burden and the cross of the prophet's calling: not to lead a 'normal', satisfied, quiet life, but to be a wanderer, a fugitive, a pilgrim, a stranger. And this, not only in some deep theological sense, about which one might occasionally hear a clever devotional lecture. No, indeed, it has to be in a palpable, concrete sense, one must be capable of experiencing it day after day"[156].

". . . Strictly speaking, it is an "impossible" life—an open, an exposed, an unfulfilled life—because it is geared to HIM who is to come"[157].

You may ask, as I am sure any modern man might, "Why the heck would I want to do all this"?!

For the knights of old, as for myself, there is no choice. They loved GOD so much, their spirit burned so deep, they could not hold themselves back from adventuring, fighting and dying for GOD. If they tried not to be knights, if they tried to stay at home and do nothing but the normal domestic existence, their hearts would explode[158].

For the knight, the love of GOD and HIS honor are so pure, so fiery, so bright, nothing else will quench the blaze of desire in his heart. It is a towering pyre, a thundering voice, a glowing ambition, a violent crushing thirst. They had to be knights[159]. I HAVE to be a knight!

If yours is not such a love for GOD and honor, then perhaps your desire is to help save the world. Chivalry can certainly secure humanity from its own vices and destructions, one person at a time.

If this is not enough for you, perhaps you wish joy above all things. Yet, as Augustine points out[160], the greatest earthly joy is the fulfillment of goodness in a human being, all other joys or pleasures fade away in a blizzard of pursuit and spent searching. The greatest human goodness is only to be found in honor, and agape love, which are the hallmarks of Chivalry and knighthood.

There is another reason. Something I did not expect when I first started down this road of Knighthood. The knight's way of life raises him above the usual humdrum and shallowness of human existence. NO matter where you are or what you do for a living, knighthood separates

---

[156] Ibid. pg. 29
[157] Ibid. pg. 33
[158] Jeremiah 20:9
[159] (Steinbeck, 1976) pg. 222
[160] (Copleston F., 1962) pg. 96

you from all other men and the typical life. It provides a special meaning to life, above and beyond the experience of most men. There is added danger and pain, but also added weight and significance of everything the knight does.

It gives him a reason to get up in the morning, and the reason to try harder. He is never assailed by nihilism or the seeming meaninglessness of most men's lives. "The mass of men lead lives of quiet desperation"[161], but the knight feels his struggle is special and profound, and thus does not feel despair, but instead a glorious anticipation of battle, regardless of the earthly outcome.

A Final Question

Thomas Merton, the great monk-turned-international philosopher, came up with two questions that have always haunted me, and are very important for the beginning of a true knight's life. "If you want to know who I am, says Merton, then ask me: What are you living for, very concretely, here and today in your everyday life? And: What do you think keeps you from living fully for what you would like to live for?"[162] We always think we have the highest motives, but how often do we truly examine our lives in the light of these great ideals?

Along the same lines, we should ask ourselves: Are we living for GOD, or the world (family, friends, careers, ourselves, comfort, pleasure, security—all of this fitting in the world)? Why do we want to be knights? Is it to serve GOD, or ourselves? And do we live our lives in a proper, knightly way? And if not, what prevents us from doing so? We turn our feet to the Chivalrous road, and break down any obstacle to GOD in our hearts, minds, souls, or bodies[163].

---

161 Quoting Henry David Thoreau, from *Walden*
162 (Schellenberger, 1981) pg. 38
163 See the Chaplet of St. Michael

STRENGTH

It is GOD who girds me with strength and makes my way free from blame, who makes me swift as a hind and sets me secure on the heights, who trains my hands for battle so that my arms can aim a bronzed-tipped bow.

—Psalms 18:32 From the Revised English Bible

Lord, I seek you with all my heart, with all the strength you have given me. I long to understand that which I believe . . . . You created me in order to find you; you gave me strength to seek you. My strength and my weakness are in your hands: preserve my strength and help my weakness.

—St. Augustine, *On the Trinity* XV, 28, 51

Indeed, there are two kinds of strength. The outer strength is obvious, yet it succumbs to sickness and old age. Everyone possesses the inner strength too, although it is indeed much harder to develop. But the inner strength lasts through every heat and every cold, through old age, and beyond.

—Master Kan, from the 1972 movie, *Kung Fu*

Virtue shuns ease as a companion. It demands a rough and thorny path.

—Montaigne, *Essays* II, xi

The means we use must be as pure as the ends we seek.
> —Rev. Martin Luther King, Jr.,
> *Letters from a Birmingham Jail*

This man [The Cid], the scourge of his time, by his appetite for glory, by the prudent steadfastness of his character, and by his heroic bravery, was one of the miracles of GOD.
> —Ibn Bassam, a contemporary and an enemy of the Cid, wrote this in 1099, the year of the Cid's death

Self-reliance, the height and perfection of man, is reliance on GOD.
> —Ralph Waldo Emerson, *The Fugitive Slave Law*

Let us love GOD, but with the strength of our arms, in the sweat of our brows.
> —St. Vincent de Paul, *Documents* Vol.11, pg. 32, no.25

The strength of a man consists in finding out the way GOD is going, and going that way.
> —Henry Ward Beecher, *Beecher, A Volume of Representative Selections* pg. 226

Strength: The first pillar of Honor

In the Medieval mind, the lion is the embodiment of strength and courage. He is the king of beasts, terrifying to behold, with such regal power and might that nothing and no one can stand in his way. Sometimes, people in Biblical and medieval times were so impressed by this strength, they made the lion a symbol of GOD Himself[164].

Once, on a documentary about the Serengeti, a pack of hyenas, nearly 20 or more, bullied and harassed a mother rhino and her baby. The torture went on for over an hour, with the mother desperately trying to

---

[164] (Charbonneau-Lassay, 1991) pg. 6

protect her baby, but the quick and cruel hyenas had cut the poor baby rhino repeatedly, shredding its ears to bloody strips.

There seemed no hope for this baby rhino, just another victim of the unfeeling plain. Then, just as a hyena sunk its teeth into the baby for the deathblow, a roar loud as the world stopped all in their tracks. From a nearby hill, a lion charged into view, coming hard on the hyenas and their prey. The rest scattered in terror, but the one hyena with its teeth in the baby rhino couldn't free itself in time. Suddenly the lion was upon hyena, and the scavenger flipped head-over-heels in its desperation to escape, but it wasn't fast enough. The lion trampled the hyena, and threw it away with a swing of lion's mighty head.

The lion watched in sullen fury as the bullies fled into the night, their yelps and shutters echoing in the lonely sky[165]. At first, I thought the lion meant to save the rhinos for itself, but the king of beasts simply let the fat ones go happily on their way. It was as if the lion had been angry with so many torturing so few.

In modern times, the lion has fallen out of favor. Animals in the wild are not clean symbols, nor is the savagery that takes place in jungles clear moral tales. But if a lion can perform a chivalrous action even once, it sends a powerful message to me. Documentation exists showing lions saving even human children from kidnappers and other criminals[166]. Imagine such power and might focused on the protection of the innocent, the destruction of the cruel, and the righting of wrongs. This is the ultimate potential of true strength, and the image of the knight in his glory.

What Is Strength?

How does one become a lion among men? How does one find the secrets to true strength?

Before one can find strength, one must know what it is.

We should approach carefully the question, "What is strength?" One will certainly encounter the modern world's answer first. Many in this modern world have mistaken physical strength for the only kind of strength, and their definition of such strength is simply force without

---

[165] I originally saw this on TV years ago, probably National Geographic, a similar video is (Talos124, 2008)

[166] (AssociatedPress, 2005-2011)

grace, respect, or noble purpose. Such a definition ignores discipline and scoffs at internal control. Incredibly, they have defined moral and mental weakness as strength and immaturity as power. They mistake cruelty for manliness. They idolize brute force, thinking it is where strength lives. This world is full of crying babies with big muscles, slaves to their own stomachs and loins, animals who have yet to wean themselves from the spoiled double-breast of material prosperity and selfish desire[167]. If you are looking only for this immature, brute power, with no direction or purpose beyond ego, you are in the wrong place, and you will die without ever knowing Knighthood.

The true knight, although not hiding from himself the dangerous and powerful nature of this "strength according to the world", looks beyond it to true strength and power[168]. Instead of building his strength to act out his desires as the modern man would, the knight perfects all kinds of strength[169], and channels them for the good of others and the greater glory of GOD[170]. Might for Right[171].

Traditionally, knights have been physically strong, but a true knight does not and cannot limit himself to only one strength[172]. Indeed, the knight discovers that just as there are three kinds of men[173], so there are three kinds of strength: physical strength, mental strength, and spiritual strength. Physical strength is obvious, although it can be hidden. Mental strength is marked by wisdom, fortitude, discipline, discernment, and internal control. Spiritual strength, the most mysterious, the most difficult, and the most powerful, is marked by humbleness, patience, purity, and righteousness[174].

So, where does one go to learn the secrets of all these strengths? To those men who have shown it consistently in battle and in their lives, who have used great strength for the greater good. Who better than men who have fought for goodness and GOD? True knights. And what better knight than the one who never lost a battle, Rodrigo De Bivar, known as the CID.

---

[167] (James, 1906)
[168] (Lull, 2001) pg. 33
[169] (Pernoud, 1963) pg. 314
[170] (Lull, 2001) pg. 35, 81
[171] (White, 1958) pg. 237
[172] (Lull, 2001) pg. 30
[173] (Pascal, 1966) pg. 82, n.160, also (Colliander, 1982) pg. 15
[174] (Matarasso, 1969) pg. 141-2

The Master of Battle

The year, 1094. A wave of Islamic extremism, in the form of Yusef bin Tashufin and his mighty army, sailed out of Africa. Their mission, to kill every Spanish Christian who would not convert to Islam, and even the Moslems who were not Islamic enough for Yusef's tastes. For this purpose, Yusef had given his heavily trained and skilled army to the capable hands of his nephew Abu Abdullah bin Muhammad, with the added assignment of killing the noted Christian hero, Rodrigo De Bivar, The Cid[175]. This forced, deadly revival would begin with the Cid's home, the beautiful doorway to Spain known as the city of Valencia.

This Islamic army numbered at least 30,000 men, an ocean of warriors from Morocco, Mahgreb, the Sahara, and Senegal[176], chanting the death of the Cid and his followers. Extremely disciplined and well-organized, they rolled out their siege towers to rain flaming arrows upon the Spanish defenders, and stirred their giant elephants to battle fury, every group and motion choreographed by flags and war drums, beating with a gigantic echo that reverberated everywhere, inescapable, against the thundering sea and the looming towers of the city where the Cid waited with his wife and daughters.

His wife, Jimenia, pressed her face against the Cid's mighty chest. "I can't stand those drums." She cried, holding close her young children. "They're monstrous."

"Do not worry," the Cid smiled. "After we win, I will take those drums, show them to you so that you can see that they are only drums, and then they will hang from the walls in the Church of Santa Maria"[177].

This was no idle boast to calm his wife. The Cid had studied his enemy carefully, and after speaking with men like his friend Álvar Háñez de Minaya, who had fought Yuseph before, he constructed a battle plan which would open the possibility of success. He also waited for signs in the sky, for he wished even the weather and terrain, the rivers and the sea to aide him in his fight against this enemy. But the final key to this battle was sheer brutal force of the Cid's inexorable heavy cavalry charge. He

---

[175] (Matthews, 1998) pg. 72
[176] (Gilliam, 2011), Gilliam's numbers are extremely conservative, some say 150, 000
[177] (Merwin, 1959) pg. 152, canto 91

would crush the invaders beneath the hooves of his horse, Babieca, and the blade of his sword, Colada.

That morning, at around 3 AM, with the moon almost full in the sky and the besiegers still sleeping among the siege towers, the great gates of Valencia cracked open. Minaya and 130 men quickly fanned out, armed with specially-made shields and torches. By the time the Moslem besiegers realized what was happened, Minaya and his men had stuffed straw beneath the great siege towers, set them alight, burning the siege engines like tall pyres in the morning air. The besiegers screamed and fired arrow after arrow at Minaya and his men, only to see the missiles thump harmless against Christian shields[178].

Suddenly, the gates of the city sprang open wide and the Cid came forth leading his men astride their great horses, flanked by the flames, as if charging Hell itself. "For GOD and Saint James!" cried the Cid[179].

The enemy cowered, hammered back by the Cid and his men as they thundered through the gate and onto the battlefield. Once Rodrigo waded into the enemy and sent them into panic, he would then lead his men around in a tight circle, trampling any who remained in the way. Some 5000 men were cut, killed, and trampled as the cavalry came around like a force of nature. The Cid himself was covered with blood as he speared his enemies, and then chopped again and again with the terrible sword Colada[180].

But this would not be the end. The Cid drew his men together and they raced, flags flying, to where the other battle would have to be, the field of Cuarte, just four miles away. Here, the main force of Yusef's army waited as reinforcements, some 20,000 men, acres of black tents and supplies, horses and weaponry. Just before the Cid's army arrived, a rain storm of incredible proportions came down upon this area, engulfing the encampment, sending Yusef's men into disarray. The thunder and rain had taken them, now the lightning.

The Cid and his men descended upon them and chased them as they fled flood and foe alike. It was said here that the Cid fought like ten men[181], and the once overwhelming armies of Islamic Africa fell apart.

---

[178] (Gilliam, 2011), (Merwin, 1959) pg. 161, canto 93
[179] (Merwin, 1959) canto 69, (Gilliam, 2011)
[180] Ibid.
[181] (Matthews, 1998) pg. 75, just like Sir Galahad

The Cid, with 4000 soldiers, had captured or killed a force five times their size.

Yusef's army had never been defeated, until that day. In the hours after, the commanding general, Abu Abdullah bin Muhammad, Yusef's nephew, was captured. He and Yusef had come to kill everyone not Moslem or Moslem enough and had left an almost apocalyptic devastation upon the land. Anyone would understand if revenge or hate filled the Cid's heart. But that was not the Cid's way. When Yusef refused to ransom his nephew, leaving him for dead, the Cid, in typical fashion for him, released Mohammed to freedom, unharmed[182].

This was a great battle, but only one. Someone could claim that luck or chance decided the day. Indeed, perhaps anyone could win a single battle. But what about 40 years of war with continuous victory? Such was the Cid's record. If I wish to adopt his prowess as my own, and understand the many keys to true strength, I must study such a man carefully.

The First Kind of Strength

Knights were known for their strength. They could take an iron horseshoe and crumple it with one hand. They carried hundreds of pounds of armor on their back into storming battle, swinging a sword weighing twenty pounds or more. They chopped other men in half, cutting through iron armor, bone and sinew, so that only the trunk still road the horse[183], or from the crown of the head to the waist and into the saddle[184]. And yet, this type of strength is only the smallest manifestation of the knight's true power.

Rodrigo Diaz of Bivar, the Cid, had so much strength and courage that it was said lions followed him as loyal hounds would follow their master, recognizing in him a kindred spirit[185]. Like Charlemagne, Charles Martel, and Jan Sobieski, he was mighty enough to beat back the surging Islamic hordes that threatened his home, and like Lancelot,

---

[182] (Gilliam, 2011)
[183] (Raffel B., 2009) pg. 51-53 canto 1:38
[184] (Gerritsen and Melle, 1998) pg. 126, (Bradford, 1972) pg. 41
[185] (Merwin, 1959) pg. 203, Canto 3:112

powerful enough to treat all enemies with respect. He stood the epitome of physical strength and victory in battle, always taking the field, so that every warrior hailed him *el campeador*, "the Champion" or "the expert warrior"[186], the Master of Battle.

Rodrigo gained this title for the first time in his twenties, acting as the king's champion to King Sancho, then king of Castille and prince of Spain. In deadly hand-to-hand trial by combat, Rodrigo defeated the champion of Navarre and won for his king an entire city. This was only the beginning.

The city of Zaragosa, taking advantage of political situations at the time, decided to rebel against King Sancho by not paying tribute. Rodrigo was dispatched and Zaragosa surrendered, contemporary reports giving much of the credit to Rodrigo[187]. From then on, the king of Zaragosa respected the Cid greatly, and in time his son, Montimid, would became the Cid's friend.

In 1068, civil war broke out in the Christian half of Spain, pitting the two prince brothers, Sancho and Alfonso, against each other over the city of Leon. Again, the Cid led Sancho's forces and totally routed Alfonso, but the prince fled to hide within Leon, and launched further attacks. On the field of combat, Rodrigo rescued Sancho from capture, and brought Alfonso away in chains[188].

Eventually, perhaps through intrigue, Sancho was killed and Alfonso took the throne of Christian Spain. Such fighting had occurred between these two aspirants to the throne, and such fear and bitterness caused by it, that only The Cid was able to assure enough people to help him bury the prince[189]. After the Cid forced Alfonso, in front of the entire court and on sacred relics, to swear no design in Sancho's death, the new king and Rodrigo were polite to each other. As would happen time and again, the Cid remained loyal to the throne of Christian Spain regardless of his personal feelings, in the cause of a greater good: the unity of Spain.

Rodrigo's loyalty to king and friend alike hurled him into webs of difficulties, and the King Alfonso never forgot his forced confession. When a revolt swept through Toledo, perhaps involving Yusef's

---

[186] (Merwin, 1959) pg. x., intro, (Raffel T. B., 2009) pg. ix, intro, (Matthews, 1998) pg. 54

[187] (Merwin, 1959) x.

[188] (Matthews, 1998) pg. 63

[189] Ibid. pg. 64

sympathizers and even some Christian lords, the Cid galloped off to defend Alfonso's holdings. In the battles that followed, Rodrigo secured Toledo, but had built such a large army of followers that his enemies at court accused him of trying to create his own kingdom. The king believed this, and, in effect cutting off his own right arm, sent the Cid into exile[190].

Sad to say, such exile would happen to Rodrigo several times. Good men are always hounded by envious elites, even in modern times. Because of this and his loyalties, huge armies would combine against the Compeador, but were defeated and smashed. In a continuous example, Count Ramon Berengeur of Barcelona tried his numerically superior forces against the Cid several times, even to take Alfonso's protectorates, and every time Rodrigo defeated him soundly, finally holding the count prisoner for five days as punishment for his impudence[191]. Time and again, whenever the Campeador rode onto the field, even greatly out-numbered, he always won the day.

Black-listed but not alone, the Cid continued to defend Alfonso's interests while helping his old friend Montamid, and other Spanish Moor cities. In exchange for this service, he required Montamid's Zaragossa and the other Moslem cities to reassert their allegiance to King Alfonso[192].

This was a habit with Rodrigo: to soundly trounce armies much larger than his own force, but always with his head bowed toward the throne of Christian Spain[193] and a hand to his friends and men[194].

Though separated, Alfonso and the Cid eventually built such an impressive list of successes that many Moslems in Spain called upon a terrible force that was building in Africa. Yusuf bin Tashufin, master of Morocco, the grand emir of Islamic Almoravids, who used disciplined battle tactics and psychological warfare to crush the states of Africa beneath his Islamic foot, answered the call to battle [195]. Invading Spain and with the Cid away in exile, Yusef had inflicted terrible losses on

---

[190] (Matthews, 1998) pg. 65, 84-85, (Raffel B., 2009) pg. xvi-vxii, intro
[191] (Merwin, 1959) pg. xix, intro
[192] (Matthews, 1998) pg. 66
[193] (Raffel T. B., 2009) pg. xvi, intro, (Matthews, 1998) pg.67, 68
[194] (Raffel T. B., 2009) pg.xvii, intro, (Matthews, 1998) pg. 67
[195] (Gilliam, 2011)

King Alfonso's forces at Sagrajas, even piling mountains of Spanish heads "from the top of which his muezzins called the faithful to prayer"[196].

With a large chunk of his kingdom bitten out by this attack, and himself wounded, Alfonso felt the need to call Rodrigo back from exile. Immediately, the Cid began to work to consolidate the pieces of Christian Spain, but also working with several members of Islamic Spain, to rescue all the country, for even the Moslems of Spain realized that Yusef was a threat to everyone[197].

In 1093, Yusef commanded his army to advance, gathering more and more men, moving liked an enormous pack of wolves toward Rodrigo's encampment outside of Valencia[198]. They ravaged the countryside, consuming whole cities, raking the entirety of Islamic Spain, and with Yusef's approval, executing both Moslem and Christian rulers or throwing them in irons, like they did Montamid. Moslem Spain called upon King Alfonzo for help, but even the great king found his forces smashed and destroyed outside of Seville, many of his knights taken prisoner[199]. Now, the Cid stood alone as the only Christian power left.

Yusef's army taunted the Cid with attacks on his periphery, but the Campeador did not cower. Terrible thunderstorms battered him, as well as the knowledge that his enemy vastly outnumbered him and was growing daily, but Rodrigo prepared his men with courage, faith, and strategy.

In October of 1094, like a lion setting his jaws, Rodrigo clenched his fists and prepared for anything. He gathered men from all over Spain to his side, but pro-Yusef forces had consolidated like storm clouds and more of Yusef's troops landed on the coast, so that the Cid knew he was hopelessly outnumbered, and unable to wait for reinforcements. Pro-Yusef forces were coming from seemingly every direction. Still, Rodrigo always held a secret weapon: himself.

Unmoved by the Campeador's awesome reputation and with Abu Beker now leading Yusef's army, the Moslems surrounded Rodrigo and his men with chanting warriors. Undaunted and almost cheerful, Rodrigo roared forward, continuously leading his men in terrifying charges directly into the face of the Yusef's forces, smashing them with brute

---

[196] (Matthews, 1998) pg. 68, (Gilliam, 2011)
[197] (Matthews, 1998) pg. 72, (Gilliam, 2011), (Merwin, 1959) pg. xix
[198] (Merwin, 1959) pg. xviii
[199] (Merwin, 1959) pg. xix

power, heavy swords, and horses hooves. But so many warriors fought for Yusef that these charges seemed like spitting against the sea. On a pre-arranged signal, the Cid and his men backed into retreat. Yusef's hordes rushed forward with joy, thinking to finally destroy the host of the Cid. More of the Campeador's men, hiding in ravines to this moment, suddenly appeared from all around, crushing and routing Yusef's vast forces as if between hammer and anvil. Thousands of Islamic invaders, overwhelmed, abandoned their weapons and fled[200]. The Campeador won again.

This battle occurred not long before the battle of Valencia at the beginning of this chapter.

Time and again, the great Yusef, all his generals and his vast armies, suffered sound defeat by the Campeador, but again he tried to take Spain, this time engaging King Alfonso and Rodrigo's son, Diego, at Consuegra, and giving the young man a mortal wound. Rodrigo, who had been waiting for another attack at Valencia, heard the news and nearly collapsed in a breakdown. "So great was Rodrigo's grief that he was almost paralyzed for several weeks"[201]. Yusef's forces then took the cities of Almanara and Murviedo, and promised to hold them against any force. It was a strategic placement, one threatening all of Spain.

Five decades weighed on Rodrigo's shoulders. His entire life had been spent in battle without rest, and he bore the scars of numerous near fatal wounds, left for dead many times, and now he had lost his only son. A lesser man might have given up, handing over the battle to Fate. But the Champion knew he was needed again, and he could not surrender or retreat. He took up again his swords, Tizon and Colada, marshaling his strength which shown bright and clear as ever. He was 55 years old, but far from defeated.

Rodrigo knew that a siege of such strong cities would take nearly a year or more, but in the summer of 1098, the Champion Rodrigo crushed the enemies of Christ and Spain, and sang with the Mass in the very center of the city of Murviedo.

Totally overpowered, the grand emir Yusef never returned personally to Spain. Yes, he would send various generals to attempt the conquering of the country, but only the Cid had made Spain with room enough for

---

[200] (Merwin, 1959) pg. xxiii
[201] (Matthews, 1998) pg. 76, (Merwin, 1959) pg. xxiv, intro

both Christian and Moslem[202]. For a brief, shining moment, the hero Rodrigo Diaz de Bivar had made Spain a peaceful co-existence of many peoples.

After over forty years of continuous combat, the Cid secured his country against all invaders and galvanizing the splintered kingdom of Spain into a more united whole. Even today, a thousand years later, Rodrigo of the Lion is remembered as Spain's greatest hero, and its most deserving knight[203].

A Hint at another, greater Strength

Rodrigo's physical power was legendary, even in his time[204], but it was only part of his real strength. Throughout the Cid's life, hints at his real worth and strength show through.

Early on in Rodrigo's career, five Moorish kings had attacked Castille, a Christian part of Spain, destroying and plundering many towns. When these five kings returned to commit more damage, The Campeador was waiting for them in the mountains of Oca. With a small army he defeated them and took the five kings prisoner. Other leaders of his time would have slaughtered them or sent them off as hostages, but Rodrigo was different. He was a true knight.

"It is no good to keep kings captive," He said. "In the name of the King, go back to your lands as free men, and no more war with Spain."

The five kings were amazed, and they bowed to him. They swore that no man but a lord among men could show such mercy, magnanimity, and Honor toward his enemies. And so Rodrigo gained the title even greater than his other names, even greater than el Campeador. These five kings, these former foes, called him *El CID*, which means "The Lord"[205].

Such mercy and magnanimity became the mark of the Cid. When he captured Ramon Berenguer after the grueling battle of Tebar, The Cid offered to set him free, as long as he joined the Campeador for one dinner

---

[202] (Matthews, 1998) pg. 72

[203] (Gerritsen and Melle, 1998) pg. 81, 84

[204] (Merwin, 1959) pg. vii, the Song of the Cid was written in the lifetime of people who would have known the Cid

[205] (Matthews, 1998) pg. 82, and (Gerritsen and Melle, 1998) pg. 87

with his friends[206]. Even Mohammed, the nephew of the terrible Yusef bin Tashufin was given freedom without ransom.

This magnanimity separates the knight's strength from that of a mere strong fighter, marking his skill in more than physical battle. Wherever El Cid ventured or battled, he always maintained this respect for others, even his enemies, and gave Honor and help to the down-trodden around him. A knight's true strength is not only found in his sword arm[207], but in his soul: The soul of Honor.

The Soul of Honor

A mighty knight was Rodrigo de Bivar, but his soul was mightier still. He was a man of striking piety and humility[208], visited by angels and saints, always attributing his successes to GOD, praying everywhere he went and before any undertaking. Putting his faith into action throughout Spain, the Cid was known as a merciful, compassionate, and magnanimous man, helping the poor, showing kindness to the oppressed and the outcast, including his enemies[209]. Even in exile, he thought of others before himself, securing others safety before his own. The Cid was a knight of singular moral and spiritual power.

In yet another exile, and yet another lonely place, El Cid came upon a leper, ringing his bell and warning all within ear-shot of the horror that was leprosy. Rodrigo took pity on him, and handed some water for the poor man to quench his terrible thirst.

One story has the leper recognizing the man immediately. "You must be Rodrigo de Bivar, the greatest knight of Spain," the leper said as he drank the water gratefully.

""How did you know?" Rodrigo asked, wary of being recognized.

"Because only the Cid would give someone like me a drink from his own cup."

The official story of this leper, from one of the earlier translations of the *Chronica del Cid*, translated by Robert Southey, tells us very

---

[206] (Bacon, 1919)
[207] (Lull, 2001) pg. 48, 51, 84 and (Barber, 1995) pg. 136
[208] (Raffel, 2009) intro xvi, (Matthews, 1998) pg. 63, 86, 90
[209] (Raffel, 2009) pg. xvi-xvii

specifically how Rodrigo built his spiritual strength through good works[210].

The mighty knight invited the leper to dinner, to the rough dissent of his men. "How can you possible let this unclean man sit at the table with you?" They demanded.

The Cid went further, and even had his own bed made for the leper, which was the custom of the time for honored guests.

In the middle of the night, Rodrigo awoke. He had felt someone's breath upon him. And the breath seemed to have passed through his back and chest. He looked around, but he was alone in the chamber. Suddenly a bright light shone all around him, and St. Lazarus appeared before the knight.

"Know that I was the leper to whom thou didst so much good and so great honour for the love of GOD; and because though didst this for his sake GOD now granted thee a great gift . . ."[211]. The saint tells Rodrigo that he will always be successful against his enemies and will die an honorable death, having done great things against the enemies of GOD, "For GOD has blessed thee" [212].

Spiritual Strength

> "For a tear is an intellectual thing,
> And a sigh is the sword of an Angel King,
> And the bitter groan of the Martyr's woe
> Is an arrow from the Almighty's bow."
> —William Blake, *The Gray Monk*

The Cid was a true knight, a spiritual as well as a physical warrior, and thus he cultivated the greatness of his spirit[213].

The Cid exemplifies what the great philosopher of Chivalry, Sir Ramon Lull, once said, "The knights exercise themselves to arms and thus maintain the order of knighthood . . . All of these things aforesaid

---

[210] (Matthews) pg. 84
[211] Ibid. and (Pernoud, 1963) pg. 314
[212] (Matthews, 1998) pg. 84
[213] (Merwin, 1959) pg. xxv, intro, (Lull, 2001) pg.30, (Clairveaux, 1977) pg 129-130, and (Barber, 1995) pg. 136

pertain to a knight as touching his body; In likewise do Justice, Wisdom, Charity, Loyalty, Verity [Truth], Humility, Strength, Hope, Swiftness and all other virtues touch the soul"[214].

The knight, to be true, must use both sets of weapons, the physical and the spiritual. Morality coupled with mercy, prayer, righteous action, kindness, and charity are beautiful and correct ways of treating humans on Earth, but they are blistering and powerful weapons against the Devil in the realms of the Soul[215]. The knight uses all of these weapons.

How can things like mercy, generosity, prayer, and humility be weapons of the spirit? To understand this as a knight would, we must look at things differently than perhaps we are used to.

In this modern world, and in the modern churches that I visit, Jesus Christ is the epitome of the peaceful man, usually portrayed in art and literature as the Good Shepherd and the King of Peace. These are correct analogies, because Christ's message is one of awesome piety and sincere morality, peace and harmony with one's fellow men, and those who rest in Him know a peace not of this world. Christ is the GOD of peace. But, in the spiritual realms of the Middle Ages, he was also the GOD of Justice[216].

Although Christ preached and practiced love and peace in this world, He was a leader of an army in Heaven[217], the glorious commander of a host of sword-wielding angels who dealt destruction to the forces and regions of Hell[218]. The Medievals called this campaign against the legions of Darkness, the Harrowing of Hell[219], and they envisioned a mounted Christ holding a banner with a red cross, as in the Crusades, and a sword in his mouth[220], symbolizing the power of the Word, leading his angelic armies to victory against Death, Hell, and the Devil himself! The Devil and Hell try to hold back this deluge of absolute power, but soon

---

[214] (Lull, 2001) pg. 30

[215] (Scupoli, 1945 edition) pg. 47, (Matarasso, 1969) pg. 142, (Vauchez, 1993) pg. 44, 48

[216] Isaiah 30:18 Revised English Bible, Psalm 50:6, Job 34:12, Deut. 16:20

[217] John 18:36

[218] (Bonaventure, 1978) pg. 159

[219] (Coss, 1996) pg. 158-161, (Dante) Canto IV of the Inferno, as well as the Apostle's Creed, 1 Peter 3:18

[220] Rev. 19:15

they find themselves, and all the demons of Pandemonium, engulfed in the cleansing and burning power of the Almighty GOD. The spirit captives of a thousand centuries, the Patriarchs and other holy people, are released from Limbo and Christ emerges as the conquering knight[221], the GOD-HERO.

Christ, to Medieval warriors as well as saints, was the spiritual warrior par-excellence, greater even than St. Michael, complete with a fiery sword of Holiness and a mighty right arm that easily smashed all evil, and paved the way for the final victory of GOD's people in the golden age to come.

"The young hero stripped himself then (that was GOD Almighty), strong and resolute. He ascended onto the high gallows, brave in the sight of many, there, [since] he wished to release mankind"[222].

Indeed, there is more than one world, for the knight. The world that we see, and the world unseen[223]. That which happens here in the world of men, has effects, by GOD's Grace, upon that other world, and vice versa. The Spirit World, Heaven and Hell, and the very arenas of each man's soul are the universes of this struggle. Every man's soul is a battlefield[224], and everywhere there are struggles between Good and Evil.

When any man walks in the footsteps of Christ, doing Christ's work and performing great acts of kindness and selflessness on Earth, his soul, in the Spiritual world, stands with the Army of the Lord and beats down the Devil himself. Any man performing acts of morality, even in the tiniest ways, actually fights off demons in the form of temptations, and when a good man, or even a pathetic man prays, more angels step up to battle for his immortal soul[225].

This is what came to the knight's mind when he thought of Spiritual Strength, a kind of moral but ethereal and mysterious power enlivening holy people not only to be kind and good, but also to conquer temptation, wrestle with demons, perform exorcisms, strengthen Faith, call upon miracles, and do the impossible. Many times, the effects of this peculiar kind of might could not be seen by the physical eye, nor be

---

[221] (Coss, 1996) pg. 158-161
[222] (Rambaran-Olm, 2006) Lines 39-41, 104-105
[223] See the Nicean Creed
[224] (Scupoli, 1945 edition) pg. 46
[225] (Bourdon, 1948) pg.9, 12

understood by the worldly mind, but only be known and felt by the hand of the soul.

For the soul to grasp such strength and power, as El Cid did, it had to take hold of Faith, Morality, Virtue, Honor, Purity, Prayer, Piety, Humbleness, Magnanimity, Justice, Sacrifice, and kindness as if these things were weapons of the highest order, for they are swords of the spirit, and the armor of the LORD GOD of HOSTS.

The Perfect Knight

Now we must consider the legendary Sir Galahad: a more precise exemplar of spiritual knighthood, wielding all the weapons of the spirit within one sword, holding all the armor of GOD within one shield.

Galahad was a man, born of woman[226], and the son of Sir Lancelot, but within him burned the perfect and pure spirit of Chivalry placed within him by the Grace of GOD. He stood the perfection of knighthood, the apex and harmony of all things Chivalrous and Pious. Lancelot was the greatest knight on earth, but Galahad was the greatest knight everywhere[227], not just on earth, but in spirit as well. His name became the symbol of spiritual knighthood absolute and complete, and thus he echoes down the centuries as the very reflection of the archetype of CHRIST[228]. His story, created by Christian monks and worthy knights like Sir Malory, demonstrated quintessentially chivalrous, spiritual power.

Galahad came upon a monastery that housed a holy shield, pure white and once carried by angels of GOD. The shield was given to him, with the understanding that before he left, he was to free the place from a demonic force in the monastery graveyard.

The monks warned him that many knights had tried to exorcise the demon on their own, but even the demon's voice could strike a man senseless for days. Sir Galahad marched out to face this demon.

---

[226] (Matarasso, 1969) *The Quest for the Holy Grail* connects Galahad to Christ through literary allusion

[227] (Malory, 1497) pg. 368, 377-8, 390, as well as (Matarasso, 1969) pg. 140-5, 154, and (Steinbeck, 1976) pg. 248

[228] (Barber, 1995) pg. 124

Before he reached the infected tomb, many terrifying sounds and billowings of flame erupted from the place, but Galahad kept walking, fearlessly approaching the tomb of fire. Then a thing in the shape of a man came forth from the tomb. Sir Galahad blessed himself.

"Sir Galahad," Cried the Demon. "I can see you are surrounded by angels on every side, and I cannot touch you. If you proceed, I must depart to where I came from!"[229]

Without hesitation, Galahad gave thanks to GOD and ripped off the cover of the tomb. The demon fled forever.

The greatness of a knight is not just in his ability to defeat foes and fears, but also in the destruction of temptation and suffering. Many times, Galahad's mercy saves the lives of his enemies, but when he draws near to the crippled and shriveled King Mordrain, he accomplishes more. His very touch, imbued with the saving power of GOD, brings Mordrain back to health and vitality. Mordrain says to him, "You are the lily of purity; you are the true rose, the flower of strength and healing with the tint of fire: for the fire of the Holy Ghost burns in you so brightly that my flesh which was withered and dead is now made young and strong again".[230]

Such miracles aside, the greatest moment of the Knight is his own salvation, and the salvation of others. Such salvation is represented, in knightly stories, by a glimpse of Heaven and the achievement of the Holy Grail.

The quest for the Holy Grail is a task too great for any human or knight, except for those willing to make themselves like Galahad, since Galahad made himself like Christ. Percival found himself harangued and buffeted on every side by visions and obstacles, even the Devil himself. The temptations of all the world, including lust, comfort, fame, fortune, and even the Princess of his heart, struggled against him, threatened to lead him from the quest, and thus doom him forever. But "Then after I was joined with Galahad—Cared not for her, nor anything upon Earth".[231] Once Percival and Sir Bors join with Galahad, they are the only knights who win the presence of the Grail. And those who win the Grail, win the Kingdom of Heaven.

---

[229] (Matarasso, 1969) pg. 62—Matarasso's translation of *The Quest for the Holy Grail*

[230] (Matarasso, 1969) ch.15, pg. 269

[231] (Tennyson, 1983) Chapter of The Holy Grail v.610

Hell and the limitations of the flesh stand between any man and the Holy One. Only the man who is pure of heart, unafraid of evil and fears only the Lord, who has no falsehood in his mouth or in his mind, who has only absolute faith, walking consistently and perfectly through all temptation in the Shadow of the Lord, may grasp perfection and see within it the ladder to Heaven. Only the True Knight may achieve the Mystery.

In the past one hundred years, artists and writers have focused on this spiritual strength in many ways. Some artists, in their earnestness to emphasize Galahad's spiritual prowess, diminished his physical stature. G. F. Watts, for instance, portrays Galahad as an almost frail youth clad in armor.

"But what Watts means that fragile figure to indicate is that the mighty things of life are not the physical but the spiritual . . . .

> "My strength is as the strength of ten, because my heart is pure." Cries Sir Galahad with radiant joy, and right at the entrenched forces of evil he hurls himself, fearing GOD and knowing no other fear. And at the flash of his sword the legions of darkness roll back, for no cohorts, however consolidated, can stand against the impetuous rush of those whose hearts are set on fire by GOD, who have seen the Vision, and whose spears are leveled against iniquity. So the Sir Galahad whom Watts with such spiritual insight depicts is youthful and frail, he stand there, no type of massive physical force, but the possessor of a fire within which burns up all fear of wounds or pain or death, and which girds the weakest arm with the might of the irresistible."
> —James Burns, *Sir Galahad: Call to the Heroic*[232]

But Galahad is all the best of knighthood, earthly and spiritually. It was important to medieval writers to show him as being powerful in every way, not just in some otherworldly and abstract sense. To them, his ultimate prowess was reflected on earth as well as in the spirit

---

[232] (Burns, 1915, 2013) pg. 3

world. Watts and Burns show his call to Righteousness, and this is awesomely important, but we must remember Galahad had great physical strength, stamina, and ability. His physical ability is not an enemy of his spirituality; within the knight, they work together to defeat all evil in all worlds.

This is Chivalry, the cooperation of body and soul, force and faith. In the next stories, we see this complimenting of the two strengths.

As Galahad and his friends rode on their quest for the Holy Grail, they came upon a great castle filled with many evil warriors. This was the Earldom of Hernox, a terrible place where evil knights turned against their own vows, raped their own sister and swore to destroy all things good that came near. These false knights killed priests and burned chapels, turning themselves into, as Sir Malory describes "veritable antichrists"[233].

A female servant ran out, begging Galahad and his friends Percival and Bors to turn back. "Within that castle, death awaits!"

"Worry not." Galahad told her. "The Lord will protect us from all evil."

They rode on, and presently ten robber knights hailed them. "Yield or die!" They chanted.

"Our yielding will cost you." Galahad remarked[234].

The ten robber knights attacked, but the three noble knights fought with such skill, daring, and strength, soon they found themselves beating back the larger number and invading the castle itself. Within were even more evil knights, and Galahad and his friends fought ferociously, back to back and back to the wall, until nothing could be seen but flashes of steel and sprays of blood. Soon, the three men found themselves surrounded with gore and dead bodies. They had killed scores of evil men, and the castle of Antichrists was no more.

"I too believe that GOD made us instruments of His wraith, for the strength and power to destroy them all surely did not come from ourselves." Galahad said as he wiped his brow[235].

He constantly pitted this strength against cutthroats, thieves, and robber knights, for he saw beyond his solid foes the movements and markings of Evil. His battles, throughout the Grail story, whether physical or moral, continued to reflect a deep, dual quality.

---

[233] (Malory, 1962) Sir Malory's *L'Morte D'Arthur* pg. 417
[234] (Malory, 1962) pg. 415
[235] (Malory, 1962)pg. 415

Near the end of his journey, Galahad came upon a ship so holy and deadly that none but the man of greatest faith could enter it without ill effect. Within this ship, he found a sword that seemed to be cursed, for any who were not pure and pious could not unsheathe it without terrible things happening to them. This sword could only be unsheathed by the strongest knight, and, a knight of absolute spiritual strength, for the sheath bore this message "Let say that he that draweth me from the sheath must be the hardiest man alive"[236].

The history and meaning of this sword is too long to be recounted here[237], but when Galahad wielded it, the sword could not only cut through any substance, but also heal any wound, including the wounds it caused, and the woes of the Fisher King of legend.

The two-fold strength of this sword[238] reflects the two-fold strength of the true knight and of CHRIST Himself: spiritual and physical power. The true knight must be like Galahad, strong in soul as well as body, powerful in virtue as well as skill, purity in intention as well as perfection in battle[239]. The knight, who wishes to be the strongest on Earth, must also be the strongest spiritually, showing superhuman purity, piety, and obedience to GOD. These are the central pillars of Christ's mission on earth, and the knight's calling.

Mental Strength

Yet another strength is needed to be a true knight[240], for there are many battlefields, many arenas in which we will find ourselves.

While physical battle and even spiritual challenges, as in the stories of Sir Galahad, are seen as knightly domains, the world of mental prowess is often overlooked. Rodrigo knew better than to ignore the vital practice of the mind. The Champion, the Cid, fought in all the arenas, and so must we.

Educated thoroughly in the courts of Spain, able to read both Latin and Arabic, the Cid would pour over the most venerable and ancient

---

[236] (Malory, 1962). pg. 406

[237] More will be discussed of this sword in Book II

[238] (Lull, 2001) pg. 64

[239] (Clairveaux, 1977) pg. 129

[240] (Lull, 2001) pg.34, (Gerritsen and Melle, 1998) pg. 235, (Barber, 1995) pg. 136

books on battle tactics and strategy, including Vegetius's *De re military*[241]. Sometimes he would read pages of these aloud to his men, then hold brainstorming sessions to glean the best way to proceed. This reflected a surprising aspect of the Campeador's mental ability, humility enough to accept the advice and suggestions from even the lowest ranks of his soldiers. All this would come together to give him an almost preternatural talent to discover the weakness of any army that came against him[242]. Such ability would allow him to harness psychological warfare and even enlist the aid of the weather against his enemy, as he did in the Battle of Valencia against Yusef[243].

Remember how The Cid watched for "signs in the sky"[244]? This was not for superstition or astronomy, for Rodrigo waited for the flights of birds that would indicated the coming of expected rainstorms. Yusef's army had no idea that the fields of Cuarte, which presented such a nice place to set up camp, would soon become a raging torrent of water, washing them out to sea, as soon as the seasonal rains came[245]. The Cid's strategies included even the clouds and the birds of the air.

Strategy brings strength, and is worth more than numbers of men[246].

This aspect of mental strength is personified in Charles Martel, the Hammer of GOD, whose strategies also made him undefeatable in battle. Similar to the Cid, Martel studied his opponents, the weather, the landscape, his soldiers' strengths and weaknesses, using his observations in battle plans so thoroughly he might rightly be called the Sun Tzu of the Medieval world[247].

Illustrating another form of mental strength, St. Aquinas revolutionized the philosophical world with his translations of Aristotle in the light of Christian Revelation. Along with Anselm and other Christian thinkers, Aquinas's vision of a reasonable and logical GOD, bolstered by his trust in the truth of Christianity, helped paved the way for the eventual technological superiority of the West[248].

---

[241] (Gilliam, 2011)
[242] (Gilliam, 2011)
[243] Ibid.
[244] In the section called the Master of Battle, in this chapter on pages 50-51
[245] (Gilliam, 2011)
[246] (Lull, 2001) pg.82-83
[247] Sun Tzu, the great Chinese strategist, employed these five aspects to defeat any enemy in his famous book *The Art of War*
[248] (Woods, 2005) pg. 75-81

It is no mistake that most of the greatest discoveries and theories of science and logic were made by men of strong Faith. Names like Louis Pasteur, Alexander Fleming, Nicolas Copernicus, Galileo Galilei, and Rene Decartes were all devout Catholics, and sharp, discerning men who learned by debate and careful observation. Some, like Georges LeMaitre (the big bang theory) and Gregor Mendel (founder of modern genetics), were committed priests, others like Roger Bacon (early proponent of the modern Scientific Method), were pious monks. Johannes Kepler, Blaise Pascal, Sir Isaac Newton, Gottfried Leibniz, and Sir Francis Bacon were extremely religious men, serious about faith and great mental explorers. All were knights of the mind.

Sir Ramon Lull belongs with such holy, logical men, but he wished to use his incredible mental skills to convert the Islamic World. Inspired by St. Francis of Assisi and St. Paul's work among the Greeks, he wished to preach and convert Moslems using, instead of force or Scripture, intellectual argument[249].

He spent ten years studying Islamic philosophy and language, building up a repertoire of solid arguments highly intelligible and attractive to Islamic thought, and the language skills to deliver them directly to his audience. He started one of the first evangelical colleges, designed to train missionaries to proselytize around the world[250].

Then, in one of the most innovative steps of intellectual history, he created an extremely sophisticated system of charts and graphs which intersected various interchangeable and corresponding statements. This portable chart system, resembling a pinwheel construction with 17 concentric layers, literally wheels within wheels[251], could, when used properly, present any Christian theological proof and rebuff any argument, proving logically the nature and existence of GOD, as well as the supremacy of Christian thought[252]. He called this paper device the Ars Magna[253].

Greatly impressed by this creative tour de force of logic, Gottfried Wilhelm Leibniz used Lull's ideas of systematic aligning of concepts, or computation of concept symbols, to help him create a system of computing number symbols, the fore-runner of modern computer binary language.

---

[249] (Zwemer, 1902) pg. 56-57, (Ellsburg, 2001) pg 384-5
[250] (Ellsburg, 2001) pg 384-5
[251] (Zwemer, 1902) pg. 73, Ezekiel 10:10
[252] (Zwemer, 1902) pg. 69, 73, and others
[253] (Gilson, 1938) pg. 30-31,

Before the first calculator had been invented or electricity harnessed, Lull had envisioned a method that would eventually herald the modern computer[254].

As these examples illustrate, knights are not mindless automatons, simply obeying and believing in anything that is said to come from the mouths of the supposedly spiritually wise. Only after long questioning and debate[255], using reason and logic, as well as inspiration and Revelation, has the true knight come to the conclusion that GOD is the greatest thing that can be imagined, that GOD's law must be fulfilled, and that Honor is the only policy. The Modern calls the knight's faith "blind", but his tenacious faith is founded on Reason and Truth[256]. The Church itself stands on the twin pillars of Reason and Revelation[257], for GOD created both[258].

Thus prepared and trained, by mental fire and cerebral combat, the knight naturally is mightily equipped to take on any error and untruth lurking in the world.

Mental Prowess stands a mighty weapon in the arsenal of the true knight[259], at least as important, if not more so, as physical ability.

Where to Begin?

Imagine a battlefield that has no end[260], a battlefield that includes tremendous hand-to-hand combat, and battles on a cerebral plain, bloodless but just as costly in world affairs and philosophies. Then add to all this physical and mental upheaval a spiritual component, where combatants wrestle for neither land, nor ideology, nor even safety, but eternal life itself, a cosmic duel which threatens the death of not only the

---

254 (Crossley, 2013), (Sales, 2013)
255 (Green, 1984) pg. 38-39, (Illingworth, 1903) pg. 202-203
256 Reason used to make sense of Faith, and prove it (Shannon, 1999) pg. 17, 78, 82, (Illingworth, 1903) pg. 2-6
257 (Chesterton, 2008) pg.111
258 (Brighenti, 2003) pg. 376, (Gilson, 1938) pg. 84, (Knowles, 1962) pg.261-262
259 (Lull, 2001) pg. 82, 83
260 (Scupoli) pg.46-47

body, but the soul. In this triple battlefield and against myriad and multi-faceted enemies, what modern warrior is hero enough to engage injustice and evil on all levels, all times, and be victorious?[261]

To be a man that can perform great feats of physical strength is not enough to be a warrior for GOD, just as a fighter is not necessarily a champion[262]. I have known men who have almost boundless physical strength, but who are weak in the will. Such men typically become bullies and end by destroying themselves. Some men have a strong mind, but are weak in the body. They usually find themselves in a tug of war with the physically strong, or they can fall prey to the chaotic wiles that dwell within their own wayward emotions. Then there are the men who are wise in the ways of the spirit; but their plans are many times foiled by the other types of men, and they may find themselves unsure of how to win Glory for GOD against a sea of vigorous earthly foes and political opponents.

The true knight must be able to challenge evil in all three worlds, the physical, mental, and spiritual[263], for in all three of these worlds, the good and the innocent will be attacked. The knight must excel in all kinds of strength and show himself to be like the Cid, possessing strength in body, mind, and spirit.

A knight learns that all strength, no matter the kind, begins with something very mysterious, the well-spring of all strength as well as all virtue in the world. The knight finds this true strength in a very unlikely place. We will begin in that place. We will begin in Humility[264].

The First Lesson

> "True virtue is attainable only by the man who, by GOD's grace, is turned from pride to humility, from love of self to love of GOD. If pride is the root of sin, true humility is the source of all true virtue."
>
> —Herbert A. Deane[265], on the views of St. Augustine

---

[261]   Ibid.

[262]   (Lull, 2001) pg. 30, 84, 97

[263]   (Clairveaux, 1977) pg. 129, (Lull, 2001) pg. 82, 83

[264]   (Augustine, 1986) pg 101, Sermon 69, 2, (Bangley, 2007) pg. 33, and (France, 1997) pg. 39

[265]   (Deane, 1963) pg. 81

"A wise man walks with his head bowed, humble like the dust."

—Said by Master Kan,
Kung Fu, the television series[266]

Rodrigo De Bivar, The Cid, one of the most powerful men who ever lived, knew his place. "Sancho was heard to remark that he was equal to a thousand men while Rodrigo was equal to another hundred. El Cid replied, modestly, that he was only equal to one man at a time, and that as for the rest it was up to GOD"[267]. It may seem strange that a man who could crush whole cities had a truly humble core.

But the most powerful always begin in humbleness.

The three wise men found the King of the Universe, not in a splendid palace, but in a cave fit for the raising of livestock. Were they shocked to have to place their gifts on a dirt floor before a trough where the Master of All Things rested? My guess is that they understood: The Prince of Heaven was to be born, not in a place of gaudy human finery, but in humility[268].

The reign of King Arthur also began with an act of humility. It was small enough and quick enough so that most modern commentators ignore it. Arthur as a boy was unknown, even to himself, and acted as the squire for his foster brother Sir Kay. One day they had left for a joust and Arthur had forgotten his brother's sword. The squire searched everywhere, even in the forest, but was unable to find another to replace it. Then Arthur stumbled across the Sword in the Stone. It is even possible that Arthur had no idea of the significance of this weapon; all he knew was that his brother needed a sword.

The magical sword came out of living stone as if from butter. He rushed over to where his brother was preparing for the tournament and handed over the remarkable blade.

"This is the Sword in the Stone!" Kay exclaimed. "How did you pull it from the rock?"

---

[266] (Thorpe, 1972)
[267] (Matthews, 1998) pg.63
[268] (Alfred, Idylls of the King, edited by J.M. Gray, 1983) *The Holy Grail* lines 445- 454

"I just pulled it out." Arthur said. "I couldn't find your sword, so I supplied you with a better one."

"Do you realize that he who pulls forth the sword and possesses it will be king of all England?" Kay demanded.

At that moment, the father, Sir Ector arrived. "Kay! Did you pull the Sword from the Stone?"

For a moment, temptation set in. "Yes." Sir Kay stumbled, but then he looked at his brother. "No, my father. It was Arthur who freed the Sword from the Stone. It is he who deserves the glory"[269].

Both brothers had acted selflessly for the other, but Sir Kay's humbling of himself made possible the creation of the most honorable and knightly kingdom in the history of the world.

For the rest of his life, King Arthur would always conduct all his affairs in humility, showing respect and courtesy to anyone who arrived in court. He did this because he was a true king,[270] and he always remembered himself as that squire, serving his brother.

This is the first lesson of knighthood, and the most important lesson of strength: humility. It is seen, in one aspect or another, in almost all the knight tales. Even Sir Gawain, who would later be described as wrathful and arrogant, was originally portrayed as powerful enough to exhibit that special aspect of humility: to chastise oneself. When he failed the final test of the green knight, Sir Gawain freely admitted it in saddened tones to the entirety of Arthur's court, and forever wore a green sash to remind himself of his failure. In fact, all the knights followed his example, and wore green sashes as a sign of solidarity with Gawain, understanding their own frailty[271].

To see and speak the truth of oneself, even when such truth is unpleasant, will always be a sign of the greatest strength. To see oneself as a lone and lowly servant before the LORD, is an act of awesome power[272]. To understand this irony is to understand why Arthur began his reign as a squire[273], and Christ, as a swaddled babe in a manger.

---

[269] (Malory, 1497) pg. 25
[270] (Lull, 2001) pg.31
[271] (Borroff, 1967) pg. 52, line 2505-2510
[272] (France, 1997) pg. 40, 39, 80, (Spoto, 2002) pg. 197, (Bangley, 2007) pg. 33, (Bonaventure, 1978) pg. 129
[273] (Lull, 2001) pg.21

Because of Christ, and in imitation of Him, the masters knew humility must always be the first rule of Chivalry. Christ, even though He was perfect, began his earthly life in humility and lived always with humbleness by his side. Not on a horse did he enter Jerusalem, not on a splendid chariot, for that would have indicated the frail human need for splendor; he instead entered his most triumphant day on a donkey. And he committed his last and most glorious deed whipped and scorned and spit upon, stripped naked and lowly as he hung on the cross, the death place for a criminal. The knight remembers his LORD's example, and thus walks always with his head bowed[274].

Among many striking examples of knights who walked with their head bowed was Sir Gareth, the youngest brother of Sir Gawain. His story illustrates the potent mixture of patience and humility that is needed to become a true knight. The natural combination of Christ-like humility and awesome patience is sometimes referred to as the lesson of Sir Gareth.

The Nobody (The Lesson of Sir Gareth)

"Though you denude yourself and insult me, what is that to me? You cannot defile my soul with your outrage."
—Mencius[275]

He could have been anyone, or no one.

Although some records say he was handsome and "well-made", Gareth caused little stir as he entered King Arthur's court. He was the youngest brother of the famous Sir Gawain, one of the most celebrated of all Arthur's knights, but many years had passed since Gawain had left home and even he did not recognize his kin as Gareth walked by. Simply announcing his name upon entering, or making known the name of his mother, would have caused everyone to praise him instantly. All the fame of his brother and family would cloak him in glory. But Gareth remained silent[276].

---

274 (Matarasso, 1969) *The Quest of the Holy Grail* pg. 141, (Thorpe, 1972)
275 (Nitobe, 1969) see chapter 8, *Honor*
276 Isaiah 53:7

True Honor needs no words, no boasts or arrogant claims, but speaks instead with deeds[277]. Gareth hid his identity so that he might earn a fair and rightful place in the court[278] (this echoes the ninth and tenth century egalitarian concept of knighthood, that all men may become knights, regardless of rank in the society[279]).

It was a custom that all new-comers to court petitioned the king for three favors. Gareth humbly waited in line.

"My lord and king," Gareth said. "GOD bless you and your court. I humbly ask you to grant me three favors. They neither are large things, nor will they cause you grief if you promise them to me."

"It is my custom to grant new-comers a boon." Returned the King. "What is it that you wish?"

"For now, my King, only food and lodging for twelve months." The other favors I shall ask for in due course."

The King smiled. "You ask only for food and lodging? My friend, I grant that to everyone who comes to my court, regardless. Surely there is something more you would ask?"

"Only that, for now, my liege," answered Gareth.

"Tell us your name, for you have a noble bearing about you." The king said.

"Please, my lord, allow me to avoid your question for now."

"It is strange, but I will not require you to answer." The king turned to the seneschal, Sir Kay. "My brother, feed this man plenty and take care of him."

"I will surely take care of him!" Sir Kay complained. "Obviously he is not much of a man, for a real man would have asked for armor and a horse! I will put him to work in the kitchens, where he will have all the food he needs!"

For twelve long months, Gareth worked in the hot kitchens under the biting tongue of Sir Kay, who called the young man "beaumains", or "pretty hands". This was on account of Gareth's large and well-formed hands, which no doubt became wrinkled and abused by washing dishes and other kitchen work. The name also seems to suggest Kay's contention that Gareth had the hands of someone who had never known real labor.

---

[277] (Brady, 1983) pg. 116, St. Francis says that he preaches every day, and sometimes even speaks

[278] (Moncrieff, 1976) pg.154

[279] (Gies, 1986) pg. 40

It was a lowly and heavy insult for a fighting man, but Gareth said nothing. He kept working[280].

Sir Lancelot and Sir Gawain treated the young man well and offered him money for his various needs and a place at their honorable tables many an evening, but Gareth always refused[281]. His place was at work, in the kitchens with the servants. Only when the knights jousted or fought in tournaments did the young man emerge to watch. He participated in practice battles as well, always showing himself to be an accomplished fighter. But always he would return to washing dishes and scrubbing the floor.

He was a true strong man, accepting his work humbly, without complaint, and continuously practicing in secret to make himself better and stronger.

For a year he slaved, biding his time, waiting for the chance to prove his worth and honor. His chance finally came.

During the feast of Pentecost[282], as Gareth served the knights at table, a serving girl burst in with dire news. Just as the Disciples, Gareth was about to receive his baptism of fire.

"Please, my lords, help! My lady, the Lady Lioness, is held captive by the most brutal of knights. My great liege, you must help me, or my lady will suffer!" She pleaded. "Please allow even one of your knights to help me free my lady!"

As King Arthur mused over whom to send, Gareth spoke up. "Oh mighty king, remember your oath to grant me two more boons? Now I ask my second favor! Let me ride to the aid of this servant and her lady!" True strength is shown in defense of the right, and the innocent[283].

Everyone was stunned at the servant's request, and more so when the king agreed.

"I also ask to have Sir Lancelot follow me, so that he may knight me when my battles are over. For he alone is peerless among all knights, and it would be an honor for him to knight me."

"But, my lord!" cried the servant girl, Linnet. "How can a mere kitchen boy help me and my lady!"

---

[280] (Moncrieff, 1976) pg.155
[281] Ibid.
[282] (Moncrieff, 1976) pg.155
[283] (Lull, 2001) pg. 35

"I will show you," answered Gareth. "I will save your lady and rid the world of her enemies."

Linnet was livid and shouted insults at him. "You are nothing more than a knight of grease! A warrior of the spit! The court of Arthur insults me and my lady!"

Gareth did not reply, nor did he need to. He held his tongue under her repeated insults, for true strength is control of oneself. True strength is strong enough to withstand insults and vicious words[284].

Angrily, Linnet rode away, forcing Gareth to dress his horse in a rush and race after her. All through the journey to the realm of Lioness, Linnet refused to even look at the man sworn to aid her.

Instead, her mouth was full of insults. "Go home, cockroach! The first obstacle you must face is the black knight. He will easily chop you to bits. Save yourself and rid me of a pest."

Gareth rode behind her in silence, and waited to see what manner of foe awaited him.

A giant of a man waited. The Black Knight, with impressive black armor and an equally impressive black charger, blocked the way forward and guarded the bridge leading to the land of Lioness.

"Lady," the Black Knight shouted with a booming voice from his mighty chest. "Who do you have with you as guardian, a kitchen boy?"

"Yes!" Cried Lady Linnet, "And one who doesn't know when to go home for his own good!"

"He looks like not much of a challenge." The Black Knight laughed. "But I have not had much sport today! Sir Kitchen boy, I think I will take your horse and trappings!"

"You can try." Gareth said. "But you will have to do it with your hands, not your words."

At that, the two knights clashed. The Black Knight's spear shattered against Gareth's shield, but Gareth's spear pierced the Black Knight and gave him such a terrible wound that he finally fell from his saddle, feint from pain and blood loss.

Linnet gave him no credit for the victory, saying it was "Luck", and although each knight Gareth faced after this was larger and more powerful than the last, Linnet insisted upon hurling insults at him.

---

[284] (Lull, 2001) pg. 71, (Moncrieff, 1976) pg.166

"You are unfair." Gareth only said. "But any anger I feel from your words will help me defeat the next obstacle"[285].

A man without strength could not have defeated each of these foes, but Gareth had strength to spare. He dispatched each evil robber with heightening skill and power, until Linnet stood breathless as she watched them. Even Linnet began to recognize the strength in this young man, even though she had missed it all along[286].

Humility and patience create the foundation on which the entire round table of King Arthur is built. "And since neither humility nor patience can be conquered, it was on them that the same fellowship was founded, where chivalry has since derived such vigour from the fraternal love that binds its members that it has shown itself unconquerable"[287].

The first mark of strength is humility, and humbleness itself is the royal road to strength. Without humility, a powerful man is simply a brazen and overbearing brute who will eventually crush himself under the weight of his own ego! And without patience, man cannot find the calm within himself to discover the proper time and place and use of that strength. Nor can a man, who is lacking these things, ever be a true knight in the service of GOD[288].

"He who cast pride out of Heaven, even Jesus Christ, who humbled Lancelot to the point where He stripped him bare. He stripped him of his sins, and Lancelot found he was naked of all the virtues that make a man a Christian, and pleaded for forgiveness. And Our Lord made haste to array him, but in what? In patience and humility . . ."[289].

Not only are these holy and GOD-sent, but also practical virtues. Humility allows a man to understand that he will always have much to learn, and patience will give him the ability to keep learning. Because of his knowledge of his own weakness, he is able to learn how to be stronger, growing in strength and power continuously. The proud man stops learning and growing in strength, and is thus eventually overcome.

---

[285] (Moncrieff, 1976) pg. 166—this is a major idea of Chivalry, to use base emotions to force good actions

[286] (Malory, 1497) pg. 147-8 and (Headon, 1982) pg. 116-119

[287] (Matarasso, 1969) pg. 170

[288] (Lull, 2001) pg. 42-43

[289] (Matarasso, 1969) pg.172

A full cup can never receive more water, but an empty cup can receive eternity[290].

Humility and patience allows a man to learn to control himself. A man who controls himself is stronger than a conqueror of cities, or countries, or worlds[291]! A man who can conquer himself has, in one blow, defeated his greatest enemy, and gained his best friend. "Long-suffering [patience] is like the emerald whose colour never varies. For no temptation, of whatever magnitude, can overpower long-suffering, which always gleams with a green and constant light; and who so strives against it, it wins each time with honour and the palm. For no one can better overcome his enemy than by long-suffering"[292].

Humility and Inner Strength

Humility, simply and completely, is the true knowledge of one's self, with strengths and weaknesses, as compared to GOD Almighty. Humility then, is seeing ourselves truly, the way we really are, in the light of GOD[293].

A man of humility and patience[294] is not assailed by trivial matters. He realizes he is not the universe, but only a small part in a very big world. His ego is not tremendous, and thus it presents a small target. He does not need to worry about insults, because they cannot harm him. He does not fret over small issues, for they cannot disturb him. If someone treats him poorly, what matter? It is simply a way to test oneself and grow stronger[295].

Arrogance demands constant homage and pays more and more attention to smaller and smaller details of that homage until the smallest complaint, the tiniest mishap, brings the ego crashing to the ground! Pride and arrogance are wounded by words or dirty looks, or a turn of

---

[290] (Senzaki, 1985) pg. 19
[291] Proverbs 16:32 as seen in the Revised English Bible
[292] (Matarasso, 1969) pg. 141
[293] (Tamburello, 2000) pg. 61-62, Bernard of Clairvaux follows Augustine's lead with this definition of Humility
[294] Luke 21:19 KJV
[295] (Malory, 1962) pg. 148

the head, or a wag of the tongue, because they are too weak to withstand even the smallest silliness.

Pride and arrogance also spend all their time worrying over such things until their energy is whittled away to nothing. Humility and patience, like wolves, conserve their energy for important matters that concern the code, honor, and GOD, not themselves.

When someone says "All I have left is pride", I wonder why. Is it because their arrogance forced them to sacrifice everything else in an insane attempt to protect it? Arrogance eats all else, destroys all else, burns all the bridges, ruins all the relationships, so that it can kiss its own mirror. Pride, in its attempt to elevate itself above all else, loses what is most important. Those who worship themselves, lose themselves and the universe.

At the end of the day, at the end of time, at the darkest hour, the knight says "All I have left is GOD." And that makes all the difference, for with GOD all things are possible, and all things are freely given.

Humility and the Truth

Humility may seem difficult and tedious, having little to do with strength or victory. But such an attitude is mistaken. True victory is impossible without reality, and reality impossible without truth. Humility allows the knight to search and accept the truth. Without humility, you could never accept that you didn't already have the truth. In fact, many people in history who did not possess humility decided they were the truth, and all the truth encompassed. Without humility, people assume they are GOD.

Even logic and science, the very fruits of Reason, and perhaps the highest of man's achievements, are not safe. These are great tools, but without humility, human reason and science lead to destruction. During the Revolution in France, people believed they could solve everything with the power of their minds, that they had ultimate power and could eventually control the universe. They began to think of themselves as gods. They began to worship the reasoning of men, as if the capacity of man's mind was infinite. They converted churches across France into temples to Human Reason. It was not enough that this "age of Reason" led to the Great Terror, where thousands were beheaded simply for being suspected of a lack of loyalty to the new popular State. By denying the real GOD in favor of themselves as god, they threw out GOD's objective morality and codes of conduct. This in turn led to philosophers like Nietzsche and thus nihilism, which lead to Hitler, Stalin, Mussolini, and Mao Tse Tung[296]. Secular man, in his zeal to forsake GOD and religion, murdered more people in the 20th century than all the religious wars combined.

Once Humility is abandoned, the human mind will drag even Reason down into a selfish universe of suffering, torture, and death.

The key to avoid such horror is obvious: even great intelligence must accept humility. But still, humans without the knowledge of history think they may leave humility behind. They cling to romantic ideas of modern and post-modern ideology instead of the humiliating truth.

Fortitude: The Inner Fortress[297]

"These are the times that try men's souls."
—Thomas Paine, *The American Crisis*
1776

"Heroism, the Caucasian mountaineers say, is endurance for one moment longer."
—George Kennan[298]

Knights often place themselves in positions where all they have left is a hope in GOD's mercy.

St. Louis was in such a position. Standing a saint and king, he led his men in a daring attack against the Moslem holdings in the twelfth century, what is usually called the Seventh Crusade.

The war, while starting in a promising way, soon turned harsh and terrifying for the saint and his men. One of the many horrors besides the

---

[296] (Durant, 1953) pg. 301-2
[297] (Digby, 1829) Book 1, *Godefridus*, "'Where is now your fortress?—Then he laid his hand on his heart and answered 'Here, and one who's strength will laugh a siege to scorn.'"
[298] George Kennan quoted the mountaineers of the Caucasus in a 1921 letter to Henry Munroe Rogers.

shocking battles was the Nile River filling up with bloated bodies of the slain, and the river was the only source of water[299].

At the battle of Mansourah, things grew worse. "In the eight weeks that Louis remained outside Mansourah, one hundred and twelve of his ships were sunk. The army began to starve, and succumbed to dysentery and typhoid. Louis contracted both, but would not leave his men"[300].

Compounding his anemia, which St. Louis had suffered all his life[301], the dysentery was so acute the saint could not stand without assistance. But no matter the pain, no matter the annoyance, the frustration, or even embarrassment, the saint's sheer force of will refused to crumble.

In order to save his men, Louis tried to negotiate a treaty. The Moslems refused. Louis ordered a retreat, but was captured and imprisoned. The Moslem leaders demanded the saint to give over all the crusader castles, and when knight and king refused, they threatened him with a special torture.

> "The bernicles" said de Joinville, "are the most cruel torture you can suffer. They consist of two pliable lengths of wood, armed at the end with teeth. They fit together and are lashed at the end with strong ox-hide thongs. When they wish to put people in them, they lay the victims on their sides and insert their legs between the teeth. They then have a man sit on the planks. The result is that there is not six inches of unbroken bone left in the leg. To make the torture as sever as possible, at the end of three days, when the legs are swollen, they place them in the bernicles again the break them afresh." Even the idea would make most ordinary people give in; but Louis was extraordinary. "To these threats the king answered that he was their prisoner, and that they could do with him as they wished"[302].

The Moslems were taken aback by this response, even frightened, and refrained to torture him further. Seeing everything he had suffered to this

---

[299] (Joinville, 1963) pg. 236-7
[300] (Howarth, 1982) pg. 218, (Pernoud, 1963) pg. 316
[301] (Robinson, 1991) pg. 297
[302] (Howarth, 1982) pg. 219, (Joinville, 1963) pg. 249

point, and watching his incredible force of will—humble, yet completely unyielding—they found themselves deciding he was the strongest man they had even known[303]. Without further adieu, they paid their respects and ransomed him free.

St. Louis's seneschal, Sir Jean of Joinville, had been captured with him and also suffered from the same illness, while carrying the wounds of five arrows[304]. They looked with sadness at the ruins of their army and at the horrible fate that awaited them in this desolate land, surrounded by enemies and without proper supplies or support from home. Disease and death had swept through the army, combining with the horrid battles to wipe out most of the king's men. Out of the two thousand and eight hundred knights in the king's company, only one hundred remained alive.

"I have asked all my advisors if they think we should return home and give up the crusade." The king said. "They say that my kingdom desperately needs me to return, my wife the queen is demanding it, and besides, we have lost most of our men and have no hope of reinforcements. We are all sick and are constantly facing death. What do you say we do?"

"My lord," said Sir Joinville. "If I were you, I would stay and fight. What we do is right, and even if we die trying, we should continue. We cannot return without some victory for GOD and honor."

"If I remain, if I stand and fight," Asked the king, "Will you stay with me?"

"My king," said Sir Joinville, "I will"[305].

This is what the Ancients called Fortitude. Many dictionaries refer to it as a kind of Courage, but Fortitude is more than that, it is strength of character[306]. For the knight, this is the will power and strength to do what is right and good in the face of all resistance, pain, and hardship. Such is doing what is right, no matter what the consequences. Fortitude is a mark of great mental strength, a mighty fortress around the knight's center.

---

[303] (Joinville, 1963) pg. 255
[304] (Pernoud, 1963) pg. 315
[305] (Joinville, 1963) pg. 271
[306] (Brighenti, 2003) pg. 205

Consider Sir Ignatius of Loyola. Before his conversion to sainthood, his leg had been shattered by a canon ball on the field of battle. After setting the bones the first time, his caretakers discovered the bones were not setting right, and needed to be broken again. Ignatius, like a true knight, made no sound and only made a tight fist as his leg was broken and re-set without anesthesia. This did not take well either, jutting a thick bone out of the top of his knee. He was told that, to repair this, the offending bone would have to be sawed with a process much more painful than any previous procedure. Ignatius endured a third operation, with no sound, no calling out, no tears, no exclamation, only the tight fists of a fighter[307]. This silent patience in the face of such pain was expected of any who carried the title of "knight".

Later, Ignatius would carry this hobbled leg throughout his saintly adventures, limping slightly on bare feet. Never did he complain, or draw undue attention to his injury, even as he climbed a hill known as Bismantova, on a 180-mile journey to Bologna. The path along this hill is so treacherous that one is forced to continue on all fours, Ignatius dragging his tortured knee across a place used by Dante to describe the Mountain of Purgatory[308]. Ignatius would not be deterred. He carried the spiritual path to Christ in his soul.

Consider the Christian martyrs throughout history. Fortitude is stamped on each one, along with the Cross. Another word for this Fortitude is Endurance. "The man who endures to the end, will be saved"[309].

All this requires another aspect of true strength, known the world over as Discipline. Discipline is a corner stone of strength for every chivalry on earth.

The Hammer of Discipline

He planned to do the impossible. He planned to do what no one had ever done before. He prepared his men to face and withstand galloping death.

---

[307] (Loyola, 2004) pg. 13
[308] (Caraman, 1990) pg. 97
[309] Matt. 24:13

His name was Charles Martel, meaning Charles, "The Hammer"[310].

Charles Martel trained his soldiers to be unbeatable. He knew the Romans had trained soldiers to act as a squared unit, wielding overlapping shields and spears, forming a line of impenetrable iron called a Phalanx. Developed originally by the Greeks, and made famous in battles like Thermopylae, this design had helped defend and conquer vast countries and worlds.

But even the best Roman design could not withstand a direct heavy Cavalry charge[311]. This led to the whole of a thousand years of strategy to be based on the mounted swordsman, including the original style of knightly battle. Martel, grandfather of Charlemagne, decided to improve the phalanx by heightening the discipline of his men, so they could stand against the direct assault of heavy horses and blood-mad, armored men[312].

Martel's army had remained nigh undefeated against mainly Saxons, with the effective combination of Martel's brilliant strategy and the amazing discipline of his men. But their most important test would come in the form of a gigantic Moslem army, moving from the East to conquer all of Europe.

The Moslem army, under Abder Rahman, rumbled into Eastern Europe like a prolonged storm of hoofs and metal. Numbers of men vary, but they probably outnumbered the Martel's force considerably, with armored cavalry wielding 20-foot spears and more cavalry armed with light bows. Rahman had been given a Fatwa by the emir, the power to use all available manpower and weapons to defeat the Christian enemy.

In accordance with his strategies, Martel strove to choose the battleground and arrive first. His men, composed mainly of infantry and with almost no bowmen, prepared for battle on the high ground, knowing this would force the Moslems to attack uphill, a decidedly important factor, and one typical of Martel. It would be one of the few advantages he could gain.

They must have looked down upon the vast array of their Moslem foes, seeing the heavy armor and terrible 20-foot spears, feeling the thunder of thousands of hoofs. The winter was deepening, and Martel and his men wrapped their traditional wolf-skins around their shoulders.

---

[310] (The New Encyclopedia Britannica in 30 volumes, Micropedia, volume 2, 1982) pg. 765

[311] (Library, 2013), (Hickman, 2013)

[312] (Davis, 1912-1913)

The Moslems were not as used to the cold, but they had tents to sleep in. Martel's men slept in the cold air, under the stars.

In the morning, the battle began. Martel's lines, phalanx after phalanx next to each other, steeled themselves against the coming onslaught of horse flesh and sharp iron charging at full speed, with arrows singing their deadly song from above.

Anyone who has every stood and watched a horse galloping by remembers the echoing thud of each hoof, the heavy presence of the animal, the sheer power of the beast. Imagine this living engine of war bearing down straight on you, with an armored man atop stabbing forward at you with a huge spear, then couple this with thousands of the same massive brutes and men plowing toward you at top speed, and you have an idea of what Martel's men experienced. They calmly but tensely waited behind their shields and the shoulders of their fellows. They kept one idea in their minds: hold the line, and do not break, or it is death.

Bishop Isidore of Beja's *Chronicle* describes it like this:

"And in the shock of the battle the men of the North seemed like a sea that cannot be moved. Firmly they stood, one close to another, forming as it were a bulwark of ice; and with great blows of their swords they hewed down the Arabs. Drawn up in a band around their chief, the people of the Austrasians carried all before them. Their tireless hands drove their swords down to the breasts of the foe" [313].

The line of Martel held. Unbelievably, impossibly, Martel's men withstood the lances and the heavy cavalry—the tons of crushing horse flesh, hooves, and steel—a deed almost unheard of in the ancient world, a feat not even matched by the Legions of Rome[314]. In this way they held all day, until the sun fell and the armies disengaged[315].

According to Islamic sources[316], a few places in Martel's line broke, only a few, but it was enough to allow a group of Moslems to storm into and behind the line of defense. This was enough to place Martel's campaign in jeopardy and Martel himself in grave danger, since he was the major target of the Islamic soldiers.

---

[313] (Davis, 1912-1913)
[314] (Hickman, 2013), (Library, 2013)
[315] (Davis, 1912-1913), (Creasy, 1998)
[316] (Davis, 1912-1913)

But Charles Martel had foreseen this, knowing human nature as he did, and the nature of any defense. He knew his enemy, and the discipline of his enemy as well, and especially the fact that the Islamists had not trained as rigorously as his own men. He knew the Moslems had several glaring weaknesses, cracks and fissures in their own personal discipline. He knew that to win, one must not only have great discipline, but one must have greater discipline than the enemy.

First, Martel's men quickly set up a ring of steel around him, this time with his most trusted men and totally impenetrable. Second, he gave a predetermined signal, and a special force of men, separated from the rest of the line, swung around the battle and entered the Islamic camp, freeing prisoners they found there and exposing the large treasure stores that the Moslems had brought with them, booty from their ravaging of the country[317].

The Islamists panicked. Their greed overcame their ill-prepared discipline, their will-power breaking before their visions of losing their gold. Thousands of Moslem warriors broke away from the front lines and rushed to save whatever they could.

To the Islamic Leader, Abder Rahman, and the other Islamic warriors, this looked like a retreat. Soon, huge chunks of warriors abandoned their positions, creating a real rout. Rahman tried to stop this and rally his men, but found himself surrounded by Martel's forces. They did to him what he had intended to do to Martel[318].

While Martel's men returned to the phalanx line, awaiting a further attack, the Islamic warriors fled the field completely[319].

The other Umayyad leaders, back in their camp, vied to take over the army after Rahman was killed. They could not agree over who should lead. They all were desirous of power and suspicious of each other, and could not rein in their ambitions in order to do what was best for their forces. They could not discipline themselves, nor control their petty differences, nor come together as a solid force.

This lack of discipline, in their leaders as well as in their ranks, spelled defeat for the Umayyad army[320]. Charles Martel and his super disciplined soldiers had won, and had saved Europe and the entire

---

[317] (Creasy, 1998), (Hickman, 2013)
[318] (Library, 2013), (Hickman, 2013)
[319] (Hickman, 2013), (Davis, 1912-1913)
[320] (Creasy, 1998)

Western World from Islamic invasion and complete domination[321]. Martel had earned his name[322].

The hammer of Discipline is the hammer of GOD.

The honorable man and the knight use discipline in every aspect of life, not just in deadly combat.

The Life of Discipline

"The first and best victory is to conquer yourself."

—Plato[323]

A martial artist quietly trains every day until his arms and legs are like swords and spears. A blind mountain climber pushes himself until he reaches the peak of Mount Everest. A student insists upon studying, succeeding in all tests and graduations. The swordsman practices for hours a day until he can defeat three other swordsmen in a single duel. The knightly priest keeps his mind on GOD and refuses the illicit advances of a comely wantonness. The patient man maintains his cool as others lose theirs, and he smiles inwardly while others insult him. A man decides to give up his smoking habit, and never looks at another cigarette again. Another man turns from his pornography addiction, and is able to leave it behind forever.

This invisible but powerful aspect of mental and moral strength is known as self-discipline. It is the awareness and the ability to control one's own actions and thoughts, plus the willingness to do so. It is so subtle, however, it is ignored or missed by many proponents of the modern hero. Yet with self-discipline, all things in this book are possible and much more, but without it, a man is simply a victim and a slave to the forces around him[324], capable of nothing glorious. "With discipline, even a life of a single day can be a triumph; but without it, even a life of a hundred years is a tragedy"[325].

---

[321] (Creasy, 1998), (Hickman, 2013), and (Library, 2013)
[322] (Kurth, 2008), (Davis, 1912-1913)
[323] Quoted in Plato's *Laws*, 6262
[324] (Deane, 1963) pg. 27
[325] Attributed to Confucius

Indeed. Any man who dares face the onslaught of deadly sins in this world will feel like Charles Martel, facing down the enemy charging at him like a legion of armed horsemen.

If a man becomes a disciplined knight, and truly strong, he will have nothing of weakness. But a man who is not disciplined can only follow weakness. Only a weak man gains riches through evil, or rapes a beautiful girl, or strikes in revenge. The acting out of these desires makes him weak, for they are weakness. What does it prove for a strong man to surrender to the weaker side of his nature? "What does it profit a man to gain the whole world, but lose his soul?"[326]

When a man rapes a woman, can it be said that he is strong? It can only be said that he gave in to weak desires[327], and that he proved himself weak against Lust, and that he acted as a bully too weak to conquer himself. Such a man is too weak to be a knight[328]. If a man gives in to weakness, he is only weak.

A man hits a woman, or abuses a child? Is he then considered strong? He beat on someone smaller, and not as skilled as he. Anger overcame him. Let him strike a stronger man than himself, if this can prove him strong. As Lancelot might have said "a superior warrior fights only superior battles"[329].

One man kills another out of anger. Who is the strong one? A man can kill another by chance, even an accident. In the modern world, the gun can slay in the blink of an eye with no skill, nor bravery, nor even consciousness. It is too easy to kill in this way; it proves nothing. The only thing we can say is the killer was too weak to defeat his own anger and lust for blood. He only lashed out like a child. He cannot be a knight[330].

One man spends his entire life, using others and employing crime and lies to gather wealth. He was so weak, he couldn't resist the temptation of gold, and gold cannot even move or speak! Gold can't give him love or friendship or happiness or eternal life. The man was simply too weak to defeat his own greed. He cannot be a knight[331].

---

[326] Mark 8:36
[327] (Deane, 1963) pg. 119
[328] (Lull, 2001), pg.42
[329] (Bangley, 2007) pg. 19
[330] (Lull, 2001) pg. 48, James 1:19
[331] (Lull, 2001) pg. 39, (Deane, 1963) pg. 119

The disciplined man needs to strike no one, nor rape, nor gain wealth through deceit, nor move in any selfish way. He doesn't need to prove anything to anyone. This strongest man, this knight, is master of himself and his desires, and is strong enough to see that the service of GOD is the only thing worthy of a strong man, the only challenge proper for the spiritual Conan. "He who controls himself is stronger than he who controls cities"[332]. "Thus must a knight control himself"[333].

Only the disciplined man can bend his own desires, "to slay his own will" so to speak, before GOD. Who but the strongest man can control the strongest desires? Who but the most disciplined man does what GOD asks, instead of what he himself wants?

The battle between the disciplined man and his base desires occurs inside the mind and soul, and no one sees it. It seems as if the honorable and disciplined man does nothing, even as he saves his brothers and sisters from himself.

All things in this book require discipline. In fact, to be successful in any endeavor requires this special form of determination. Even religious duties are as naught without some sort of self-discipline to bolster them.

Self-discipline simply gives the power to do what is uncomfortable or painful. All training is painful or uncomfortable, sometimes only because it takes time that could be used doing more pleasurable things. It is difficult to go outside and work in the cold, or study when a favorite TV show is on, but self-discipline enables one to do anything necessary to complete a plan or mission. Most religions or causes demand this ability to ignore the desires of the self, flesh, and stomach in order to concentrate on more important things[334]. Without this ability, any path or belief becomes impossible to follow. When a religious person fails, more often than not it is a lack of self-discipline, rather than a loss of faith or knowledge, that causes it. Any and all religions, just as every cause in the world, suffer because some of their followers do not possess and never were trained in the demands of self-discipline.

Some in the modern world have tried to escape this by living a life that displays the trappings of religion or spirit, but which requires nothing extra-ordinary from them. This is many times seen in modern pseudo-religious movements like the New Age movement, which,

---

[332] Proverbs 16:32 in the Revised English Bible
[333] Deschamp's "Code of the Knight" circa 1200
[334] (Underhill, 1990) pg. 156-157

although preaching vague ideas like love, compassion, and peace, requires almost nothing of followers beyond doing what makes them feel good. They live their lives as anyone else, perhaps on purpose choosing a religion or belief that demands nothing more than to follow their own inclinations[335]. There is no challenge. Such a way of life cannot truly be seen as a real religion or faith system, otherwise the animals could be considered to be following a certain religion as well! No, this is simply following the stomach. A true religion or belief system inevitably requires the denial of self somewhere, and thus requires the cultivation of self-discipline.

A true religion or belief system affects one's life and actions, demanding a marked difference from a life without it[336]. This marked difference always requires an act of self-discipline.

My father used to speak of the two sides of Christianity. One side contained the vision of Christ, the other the vision of the Cross[337]. Most people think of them as one and the same, but a difference can be ascertained.

The Christ is usually seen as the vision of forgiveness and kindness in the religion of Christianity. The Cross is a vision of the sacrifice and self-denial required to truly follow Christ[338]. Most Christians are enamored of the vision of the Christ, with His good will towards all men, but the vision of the Cross is frightening. While Christ offers charity and compassion, the Cross offers pain and suffering. Peace is more sought after than Justice, and love more than Sacrifice. Peace is easier than Justice, and love softer than Sacrifice. But what is Peace without Justice? Death, or a farce. And can True Love live without Sacrifice? Most would like to have Christ without the Cross. But both must have the other to be complete. Christ took up the Cross, and so must we all before we can be truly His followers. This requires discipline.

Although they are the same person, it is simply human to admire the Baby Jesus, but it is heroic to admire the Crucified Lord.

---

[335] (Martin, 2010) pg. 47
[336] My father, as well as (Spoto, 2002) pg. 49
[337] (Sheen, Throughout the Year with Fulton Sheen, 2003) pg. 46
[338] (Sheen, Those Mysterious Priests, 2005) pg. 169

"Forgive us that our preferences run to Bethlehem and Joseph's garden, to poinsettias and lilies, and away from Golgotha, with its rusty nails and twisted thorns"[339].

The Battle Within

As one can see from the previous stories of strength, the knight demands that the body, with all its unruly desires and wants, subjugate itself under the iron fist of the knight's iron will. But because the mind and the body are connected in many subtle ways, the knight's mind seems to find itself in a battle with itself, to follow its own orders!

Let us say that you decide to fast for a day in order to test your mental strength and discipline. You will find desires for food popping up in your mind almost immediately, along with images of delectable dishes waiting to be eaten. Your mind pushes down these desires and images, but they come back later, only to be pushed down again.

Two parts of your mind are in battle for dominance. One part, the part that has all those desires and hungers and sees images of food, is what the Ancients referred to as the "desires of the flesh". It is truly a part of the mind, animal instinct as old as the World, but it is simpler to think of it as "the body", or "the flesh", or even "the stomach", talking to the mind.

The other part, the part that endeavors to control and stop those desires and images from taking over, is another part of the mind as well. The Ancients referred to this sometimes as "the spirit", "the Conscience", "the higher self", or simply the "will of the righteous man".

Be careful, because words are very slippery, and these terms can be used in different ways at different times, but the main idea is that there are two parts of your mind at war when you decide to abstain from any action.

There is then a third part of the mind that is aware of itself and is aware of the first two parts warring with each other. This third part can watch the battle of the first two almost as if it is separate from them.

And all these in one being, interconnected yet separate, combined and yet opposed. A knight must learn to combine them into one lightning strike against the Devil.

---

[339] Ernest Campbell, a minister, 1915

The knights of the Middle Ages did not engage in too much self-reflection on these aspects of the mind; they just did their duty as a matter of course. But as modern people, we must be keenly aware of how our mind works, so that we can be in control of it and discipline ourselves.

Control of Emotions

In order to find true strength, be strong, and to use strength as it should be used, one must be in control of one's emotions. This control of emotions is a great aspect of self-discipline.

Emotions make up a large part of the beauty of humankind, but they also mar the face of humanity. While loyalty, fellowship, and courage burned in the breasts of the men who fought in a thousand wars, hatred and prejudice drove them to massacre many hapless people as well. After the battle of the Alamo, Houston's men were aflame with loyalty and righteous fury, so that they could not wait to attack the forces of Santa Anna, although the Mexican forces were superior in number. Soon, San Jacinto fell upon Santa Anna. The battle was one of the quickest in history, and within fifteen minutes, Houston's forces routed the surprised Mexican soldiers. But once the demands of loyalty and friendship were abated, the emotions of revenge and prejudice took over, and many of Houston's men killed unarmed or fleeing soldiers, half stabbing and half drowning hundreds of surrendered men under the marshes and swollen streams of Buffalo Bayou[340].

Sam Houston reportedly said, "Boys, I like your courage, but damn your manners"[341].

A true man and a knight does not strike down surrendered and unarmed people[342]. The heart can lead to the height of Honor, and the depth of moral horror.

The first Crusade saw thousands of knights spurred on by love of GOD and loyalty to the Church. They were horrified and driven to

---

[340] In the Texians' defense, Santa Anna's mission from the beginning was one of extermination, as can be seen at the Alamo, Goliad, and even earlier, at Zacatecas and Coahuila. Santa Anna rarely ever showed mercy.

[341] (Deshields, 1935)

[342] (Malory, 1962) pg. 89, See the Dharma Conquest and other knightly codes of conduct

righteous fury and action when they heard the new-comer Turks had destroyed the Holy Sepulcher, and when Christian pilgrims, unarmed and in holy travel to Jerusalem, were continuously robbed and killed by Islamic bandits. These knights then felt their hearts soar with the knowledge that they would free the Holy Land from the tyranny of the Pagan, as they stormed over the walls of Jerusalem in 1099. But this amazing accomplishment was blackened by the hatred and wrath that followed, when hundreds of Jewish and Islamic men, women, and children, unarmed and terrified, were massacred in the streets of the Holy City, until the alleys flowed up to their knees with blood[343].

Sir Godfrey of Bouillon, as a true knight, alone refrained from this atrocity, stunned as he saw his men awash in civilian gore[344].

The love that a man feels for a woman is a special and awesome thing[345]. For her, he would turn the world on its head, and he is capable of great and mighty things for her affections. I have seen the creations of men deeply smitten: The "Rose Window" in the San Jose Mission, the Taj Mahal in India, Shakespeare's Sonnets, the symphonies of Tchaikovsky. But then the agonizing hate that can be produced by venomous relationships and scandalous happenings. The terrible, animal thing that is a man when he finds his true love has been betrayed by a fickle and cold wantonness.

A man, pushed on by the best intentions at one moment, can find himself falling into the traps of selfishness the next. Emotions can be beautiful, but, more often than not, they cause horror. Base emotions that make up "the flesh" or "the body" or "the stomach" are the cause of nearly every terrible thing on earth, and they have their origin in the animal part of the brain. They are the part of mankind that has fallen from grace. Hatred, wrath, blood lust, concupiscence, greed, prejudice, arrogance, gluttony, and envy could all make a hell out of any paradise.

Perhaps the worst and most insidious of all, a man may not be aware of which it is that compels him, the highest or lowest of drives. Emotions, the good and the evil, mix together in a patchwork that is difficult to interpret or defend against. A man may assume he leads the country for his people, when his greed and arrogance have snuck in without a hint. A woman may think she acts out of kindness, when it might be selfish

---

343 (Robinson, 1991) pg. 18
344 (Spencer, 2005) pg. 136
345 (Malory, 1962) pg. 458

foresight that is truly to blame. Who can trust himself[346]? Beware! As Abelard warns, actions are not the indicator of intention[347]. Intentions and motives, emotions and feelings, are often hidden to the world and even to oneself! Only GOD is the final judge of intentions, actions, and the inner mind and heart[348].

A knight must constantly analyze and keep watch over himself, to forever weed out any vile, prideful, or unrighteous emotion from himself and his reasons. Every thought, every intention, every reason must be scrutinized and sifted, for the knight is a great weapon that cannot be allowed to be used by anything but the greatest and most shining of motives.

Because of the slipperiness of emotion, some have advocated to eliminate all emotion at all times, even the good kind. This is dangerous and I would suggest against it. A true gentleman and knight controls his emotions not by eliminating all emotion within himself, but instead by making them bend to his will. He crushes "uncontrollable" base desires, but any emotion that he can harness, even selfish and base ones, a wise knight will use for the Greater Glory of GOD[349].

How Emotions can Edify

> "My Lady, you are forgiven, and if formerly anger made
> me strong, may joy now make me invincible."
> —So says Sir Gareth, from *L'Morte D'Arthur*[350]

It is a mark of Western Chivalry to use the emotions to fight for GOD and the Church, to use even the base emotions as well-springs of energy to drive the fight of righteousness forward[351], like the fire driving

---

[346] (Scupoli, 1945 edition) Scupoli says that it is absolutely essential to avoid trusting yourself; instead trust GOD
[347] (Copleston, 1961) pg. 51
[348] James 4:12
[349] Traditionally the motto of the Jesuits, (Harcourt, 2007) pg. 226, (Mottola, 1964) pg.18
[350] (Malory, 1962) Keith Baines translation, pg. 148
[351] (Buber, 1969) pg. 20, (Malory,1962) pg. 148, (Barclay, 1975) pg. 68

the steel into red-hot frenzy. A knight does not allow these base emotions in his reasoning or motives, but he uses them in the execution of his plans.

This is because, at the beginning of time, all emotions and human drives were good, proper, and put to their intended purposes[352]. Lust, for instance, that ancient obstacle, was originally meant to help men chase after their spouses and propagate the race. Of course, now it is a drive which encourages all sorts of mayhem. Instead of driving people to beat each other for silly reasons, Anger was originally meant to help defeat wrong by evoking Righteous Fury.

The Fall from Grace, the expulsion from Eden, called Original Sin, twisted all our drives and emotions to serve chaotic and selfish ends, instead of the original purposes they served from GOD[353].

Emotions, even the base type, can still sometimes be used for their original purposes, although imperfectly. The knight bends his emotions as a man bends the string of a bow, aiming all emotion, even the twisted ones, at the target which is Righteousness and Goodness. He sets his Honorable Intention, then focuses and aims his base emotions like an arrow of flame.

Take the well-known stereotype of the knight who goes on a quest to help the fair maiden. Now, the True Knight knows that he is bound to help everyone, regardless of their appearance, but in this case he can use the attractiveness of the maiden to spur him on. It is easier to labor in this situation than perhaps another more mundane mission. He is well aware that his unconscious mind is excited by the hints of winning the maiden, and energy courses through his veins, even though he is aware also that he will deny himself at the end and leave without ever seeing any reward. And, of course, survival instincts drive him to live to the end of the mission. The conscious, Honorable mind of the knight thus harnesses the unconscious libido and base emotions.

And if lust, the lowest of all deadly sins[354], can be harnessed and forced to obey Honor, so can violence and rage! When a knight, even a regular man, sees unjust violence done to an innocent person, especially a woman or child, he is then filled with fury, and he may use it as a

---

[352] (Lull, 2001) pg.15
[353] (Lull, 2001) pg. 15, (Annotated Catechism, 1981) pg. 147
[354] (Deane, 1963) pg. 56

springboard for heroic action. Imagine the rage you would feel if you saw a child molested, or a woman attacked! What manner of dangerous feats would you be capable of to punish the evil doer, impelled by such energy!

What of the emotions that slow a man down, hindering him in his duty? Would it not be easier to be free of all emotion?

Without emotion, one is not assailed by the terrible and embarrassing afflictions such as sadness, emotional pain, depression, anxiety, feelings of loneliness, fear, pity, rejection and abandonment, etc. Being under the control of such powerful emotions would surely make one yearn to be free of them, and even envy those who seem to have none. Such a man, free of these hindrances, would seem to be in complete control of his destiny, without question. In fact, even so-called "tough guys", "macho men", and "gang bangers" try to prove their strength by not showing any of these "softer" emotions. They want to appear totally unaffected by the weight of the world[355]. Many are street-toughs, trying to convince each other that they are strong and without fear or depression, but by never showing sadness, shame, or pity, they are instead showing a particular weakness.

My observation is that humans always have baser instincts and emotions (of the flesh), even if they do not seem to possess the other, softer emotions. Baser emotions like lust and greed are always around, and if not coupled with the emotions of sadness and pity, for instance, a man is only a creature, in tune with only animal instincts, just like a pig or a slug.

Some see themselves as stronger if they follow these selfish, base emotions and are devoid of edifying feelings, but in truth it is a robotic and colorless exercise of fulfilling the stomach and loins, nothing more. A man who feels no sadness at the death of innocence, a friend, or the suffering of good people is not worthy to be called a man. Lust without love becomes simply a biological function, like urinating. Conversation without true friendship becomes an exchange of trite clichés. Debate without dignity simply becomes a howling match between baboons. Such creatures are totally selfish automatons, using all other people and never knowing anything of nobility, virtue, honor, or even edification or joy. Imagine the faces of men who have all the base desires, but feel no pity, nor sadness, nor pangs of conscience. Such faces are the faces of beasts.

---

[355] (Sheen, *The Cross and the Beatitudes*, 2000) pg. 83

Believe it or not, there are many in this world worshiping the image of such non-men.

In truth, a man needs both sets of emotions; one set to make his heart noble, and the other to nobly struggle against or to be used to bolster Honorable intentions. Emotions like shame, sadness, and concern help the Knight share in Christ's passion. But as for the fleshy emotions that cannot be used honorably, a true strong man, and a great knight, understands that without a challenge, where is the Honor? A chaste man, for instance, is only honorable if he must battle lust to be chaste. A courageous man is only honored because he must overcome his fear. If I never suffer internally, how did I struggle for anything? If I do not struggle for victory, how is there glory? If I only felt excitement and fun in an obstacle, is it really a test of my strength?[356] True strength is only demonstrated when used against an actual obstacle or opponent—even if the opponent is within [357].

Therefore, to be a man, and finally a knight, one must have the full range of emotions in order to be fully capable of Honor.

Nowhere do I suggest a knight should succumb to emotion. Most times they should be hidden and controlled[358]. A knight has the full range of emotions that any other human may have, but he reins them in as one might rein in a stubborn horse. For the knight, it is not his emotions, but how those emotions are used that are important—of utmost importance. If they inspire honorable deeds, they are good. If they cause one to make mistakes or act like a pig, they are unacceptable.

Righteous Desire

Some emotions are edifying, some are challenges, but there is one emotion that is absolutely essential. In order to achieve self-discipline, we must have the desire for discipline! How strange it is to hear that word in this place: Desire.

---

[356] (Bangley, 2007) pg. 132-One must know one's weaknesses. Only take on challenges that you are prepared for.

[357] Augustine's *Sermons*, 3, "We make a ladder of our vices, if we trample those same vices underfoot."

[358] (Gracian, 1996) pg. 7, Dostoevsky says something similar in referring to gentlemen

This is not the desire of the flesh, which we are used to speaking about, but righteous desire, spiritual desire, which is a gift from GOD. It is to be touched by the Grace of GOD. GOD's hand promotes the growth of desire for discipline, but the man himself must work with GOD, cultivating his own self-control. This is as a man, borrowing the metals from GOD's mountain and the fire from GOD's sky, forges a sword with the sweat of his brow and a hammer. The fire is righteous desire, the metals are the raw mental strength and talent, the sweat is the effort, and the hammer the necessary focus[359].

The desire drives discipline, and the discipline tempers the desire. The desire causes the search for discipline, and the understanding of discipline causes desire. Desire and discipline become two sides of the same coin. The coin is called Righteousness. Righteousness is the desire for and the power to do the right and honorable thing in the face of all obstacles. Desire fuels the discipline, and the discipline, aided by Grace, brings the power of Righteousness.

The knight must burn with Righteousness. His desire for GOD and the discipline to reach GOD's law rages in him greater than the bonfires of the pagans! Only one with such violent desire may gain Heaven[360].

It is true that an undisciplined person can be brought to love discipline slowly, by forcing them to have discipline. But love of discipline only happens when the Grace of GOD shines in the heart of a man. Although being forced to do something right is better than doing it wrong, such activities cannot save the soul of the forced, nor can it make them honorable, nor does it make them righteous or pleasing in GOD's eyes. Something must happen within each person's heart, to make each life honorable, righteous, and truly holy. They must turn to GOD and Righteousness[361]. They must desire GOD and Righteousness.

There is another emotion connected to righteousness: Righteous Fury. And Righteous fury, as far above revenge as Love is above lust, feeds the sword of Justice.

---

[359]   (Annotated Catechism, 1981), pg.146, art.126
[360]   (Sheen, *The Cross and the Beatitudes*, 2000) pg. 68, Matt. 11:12
[361]   (Annotated Catechism, 1981), pg.146, art.126

The Hand of Justice[362]

> "The magic happened. The Bible and Shakespeare and Pilgrim's Progress belonged to everyone. But this was mine—It was a cut version of the Caxton Morte d'Arthur of Thomas Malory . . . . I think my sense of right and wrong, my feeling of noblesse oblige, and any thought I may have against the oppressor and for the oppressed, came from this secret book."
>
> —John Steinbeck[363]

In the days of King Arthur, there were no policemen. The law was the King's word, and the enforcers of that law were the knights[364]. When a crime was committed, when a wrong was done upon an innocent person, the knights were expected to offer aid. Not only the proverbial damsel in distress, but anyone attacked unfairly, or oppressed by a power greater than themselves, had the right to call upon the knight[365]. Especially the Church could expect physical protection from the knight's shield[366]. The knight stood as the right hand of Justice[367]. The knight represented the force of GOD's righteous fury against all evil everywhere.

When Lancelot encountered an evil knight trying to kill his wife, Lancelot forcibly stopped the man and demanded an explanation.

"She has cheated on her vows to me!" cried the evil knight. "Now, allow me to kill her as is her due!"

"He lies in his jealousy!" cried the woman, desperately hiding behind Lancelot's horse. "I was visiting my family and he thinks I had incestuous affairs with my own cousin! He is so jealous he is blind!"

Lancelot shut them up with a thrust of his hand. "No one will kill today! I know not what has happened, but no woman will be destroyed on my watch!"

---

[362] (Lull, 2001) pg.81

[363] (Steinbeck, 1976) From his introduction to *The Acts of King Arthur and His Noble Knights,* pg. XI

[364] (Barber, 1995) pg. 186

[365] (Lull, 2001) pg.15

[366] (Gautier, 1989) pg. 26, (Corley, 1989) pg. 53

[367] (Barber, 1995) pg. 137, see also Charney's work on Knighthood

He decided to take the evil knight and the lady to King Arthur so that the monarch would decide what to do with both of them. The husband pretended to acquiesce, but on the way, acted in treachery, suddenly jumping upon the woman's horse and sliced off cleanly the woman's head.

Lancelot howled with rage and attacked, raising his awesome sword to behead the man in turn. But the husband cowered and bowed before him. "Do not kill me, for I have only done what was necessary!"

"Get up and fight!" Lancelot growled, aware he could not kill a man on his knees.

"I am no fool to fight a man such as you, especially in your rage." Cried the husband. "I will not get up."

Steinbeck says that at this point, Lancelot acted uncharacteristically cruel, because he had been frightened by the evil knight's trickery. But I think this particular story shows Lancelot's stern sense of Justice. Instead of killing the evil husband, he forced the man to have the head and body of his now-decaying wife strapped to his body and to journey that way to King Arthur's court to ask for forgiveness. Imagine, feeling the slow dissolving of the corpse upon his own skin, in a external, stark sign of his own internal, spiritual ugliness and spoilage[368].

This strange punishment actually caused the evil man to eventually repent his violence and become a hermit, spending his final years in prayer. This is one argument for the use of such "cruel" punishments, for the very definition of punishment to many educators today is an action that causes a change of behavior for the better.

King Arthur himself traveled the country righting wrongs and had originally gathered the strongest knights in the world to effectively create a police force to protect the weak and innocent from evil, as well as create a kingdom where these ideals are possible. We realize, as King Arthur did in a very real and immediate way, that the world at large is a violent and dangerous place, in need of strong people who are capable and willing to defend others and themselves against dictators, evil-doers, and injustice. As Antoine De Riveral once said "The sword of Justice has no scabbard", meaning that the sword must always be ready to defend the just, and cannot safely be put away.

---

[368] (Steinbeck, 1976) pg. 278-80

The belief in justice is so powerful and even when terrible disasters befall knights, they still insist to fight for righteousness and the righting of wrongs, even in disregard for their own revenge or desire.

Mercy and Forgiveness

> "Though they may wound your feelings, these three you have only to forgive, the breeze that scatters your flowers, the cloud that hides your moon, and the man who tries to pick quarrels with you."
> —Inazo Nitobe, from *Bushido, the Soul of Japan*[369]

The heart of the Law is mercy[370].

The modern hero on the silver screen cannot seem to understand mercy, nor are the enemies of such heroes worthy of it. This is **not** a reflection of how the knight views the world. The knight knows that mercy is a mighty symbol of strength.

The knight's world was a harsh battlefield of endless bloodshed and war. With such horrible suffering, one wonders how a knight ever found in his heart the mercy to spare his enemy, but many is the time when Lancelot refused to kill, and many is the time when Galahad stayed the finishing blow. Every knight gives his vanquished foe a chance to yield. This explains the strange epitaph of Lancelot's tomb: "And thou were the kindest man who ever struck with sword"[371].

There is a famous drawing of a knight kneeling before a crucifix, and the Christ carved on the cross leans down to kiss the forehead of the downcast warrior. The caption reads "Of a knight who forgave his enemy when he might have destroyed him, and how the image of Christ kissed him in token that his acts pleased GOD"[372].

The Cid earned his most illustrious title by being forgiving and merciful to his enemies, and even to his floundering king, Alphoso.

---

[369] (Nitobe, 1969) pg.32
[370] Matt. 23:23
[371] (Moncrieff, 1976), pg.105
[372] (Moncrieff, 1976) pg.104

In a legend of French Chivalry, Ogier was a Dane, and thus perhaps not always trusted by many of the other warriors in Charlemagne's court, but on one fateful day of horror and forgiveness, he showed himself to be a most loyal and merciful man[373].

Charlemagne's son, called Charlot in many stories, was not the magnanimous future leader that his father had been, and he was much quicker to rash anger. One day, as he sat losing a chess game to Ogier's son, Baldwin, he lost his temper and grabbed the heavy stone chessboard as a weapon. He thrashed Baldwin's head in before he had realized what he had done.

When Ogier came home and found the still warm body of his son, he lost his mind and raged through the castle, looking for the murderer. He had discovered who the scoundrel had been, and, even though the murderer was the son of the emperor, Ogier would have vengeance!

"I would give anything to undo this horrible thing, to make amends." The king told him with true feeling.

"Nothing will make amends except the blood of the murderer! The death of your son, who killed my son!" And with that, Ogier threw himself at the king, but was held down by everyone in the court.

Ogier was imprisoned for seven years, and had long to think about the proper course of action. Revenge is a path that leads to sure destruction. Before one sets out for revenge, one must dig two graves— one for the object of revenge, and the other for oneself[374]. This desire cost him dearly, for he spent long years in the dungeons of the French king.

At the end of the seventh year, it came to pass that the Moslems invaded France, placing Charlemagne himself on the defensive. Bruhier was the leader of the Moslems, and was known far and wide as a great warrior. In fact, it was well known that no one could defeat him, except, perhaps, the knight called Ogier the Dane. Even as he surrounded the defeated army of Charlemagne in Rheims, Bruhier decided to test his might once again.

"Have your greatest knight face me." Bruhier cried out over the walls of Rheims, "And if he wins against me in hand to hand combat, I will return to the East. But if I win, all of this kingdom is mine."

Everyone in the land knew the only knight who could face a warhorse like Bruhier lay in the dungeon of the king.

---

[373] Ibid. p.273-275, from the ancient story of Ogier the Dane
[374] A Chinese proverb, attributed to Confucius

"Release Ogier," His advisors cried. "Even if you afterwards throw him in prison again! He is the only man who can defeat Bruhier!"

"I will not release him!" The king snapped. "Even if he is the only man who could save my kingdom."

Secretly, however, the king brooded, and could find no other solution. It was a tough choice. Either his kingdom must suffer or he must overlook the devastating hatred Ogier held for his son. He thought better of it at last and decided to let the old Dane go free. Better I suffer alone, than have my kingdom suffer, the king thought[375]. A noble solution.

Ogier, however, thought differently. He had raged away for seven years in the dungeon, and his horse had been sent off to pull stones for a cathedral. "I can hear the shouts even from my dungeon, that the King needs me. I will not fight for him, unless I am allowed to behead his son in return for the death of mine!"

Shocked by this, but determined to save his people, even at the cost of his only son, Charlemagne finally relented. "Better, sire, that one man die, than thousands". Ogier was free to face the powerful Bruhier. He gathered his horse and his armor, which bore the red eagle upon a black field, and rode through the gates to his destiny.

Bruhier himself stood a full head taller than the Dane, and powerful armor covered his great muscles. As he saw the knight, he laughed, "It would take ten knights to challenge such as I."

The two men jousted, and the Moslem hit the Dane so hard it killed Ogier's horse from under him. Enraged anew, the Dane jumped up and came on with his sword, and though Bruhier was physically stronger, Ogier had more finesse in his moves, so that the battle lasted for hours. Back and forth, the two men exchanged blows, until both were exhausted.

As happens sometimes in these strange bouts, the two men agreed to allow for a respite. "You are too powerful to follow this foolish king." Bruhier said. "Follow me and my religion, and I will allow you to marry my sister."

"You dare tempt me to treason and blasphemy!" Cried Ogier, and they renewed their terrible onslaughts. Bruhier felt himself weakening, and threw himself at the knight with his full force. Ogier sidestepped and sliced the Moslem's shield in half with such a blow it threw Bruhier to the ground. In desperation, Bruhier grabbed the knight's knees.

---

[375] Similar to King Arthur's prayer, see (White, 1958) pg. 171

"Spare me, and I will become a Christian." Bruhier cried. "Only spare my life."

Ogier sheathed his sword and threw down his shield, turning toward the city as if in surprise. The Moslem, however, raised a great stone over his head to hurl and crush the Dane's skull. A shout of warning from the city walls sent Ogier to the side just in time to avoid the stone. Spinning around, he drew his sword and stabbed Bruhier clean through the heart.

The city and all of France were saved. But now the Dane faced an even greater test. The final test of Mercy or Vengeance.

Charlot had placed his own head on the chopping block.

Ogier grabbed him by the hair and raised the sword, the sword even now that dripped with the blood of the Moslem leader. Here was the knave who had killed his only son; this was the spoiled ingrate that had destroyed Ogier's hopes forever.

The king, Charlemagne, hid his face.

The sword hung in the sky for long minutes while everyone held their breath. But as with all great men, suffering brings a kind of understanding. "Oh, King," Ogier said as he set the sword down gently, "I know what it is to lose a son. I give you back yours."

With that, he released Charlot, unharmed[376].

Richard LionHeart, knight and king, known for his brilliant and brutal exploits against Saladin and the Moslems during the 3rd Crusade, also could show mercy. This mighty warrior, after all the far-flung campaigns in the desperate deserts of the Middle East, finally found himself knocked down from a single arrow. But it festered, and the ensuing infection threatened to kill the Lion among men. Near death, he forgave the hand that had shot the arrow[377].

Courtesy

"The greater man, the greater courtesy"
—Alfred, Lord Tennyson[378]

---

[376] (Moncrieff, 1976) pg. 273-275 for Ogier's story from *The Romance of Chivalry*
[377] (Miller, 2001) pg. 109
[378] (Tennyson, 1983) from *Idylls of the King*, the Last Tournament, line 638

A true knight must always reflect the Earl of Warwick, of whom it was said that, if all Courtesy in the world was lost, it would be found again in him[379].

When the Cid's entourage saw the leper, his men turned their heads, for few can stand the horrible sight and stench of such a wretch. They urged the Cid to keep going as they looked for a place to rest for the night.

But just as Saint Francis would some five hundred years later, the Cid asked himself, "Is this poor thing not a man, even as I?"

The leper was stuck in a bog, and the Cid carried him out and placed him on the Cid's own horse. When they found a lodging, the Cid had the leper sit beside him, as an honored guest, allowed to eat out of the same bowl as the Cid, which was the custom of the time. Rodrigo's friends were appalled, for no one could even bear to touch a leper, or look at him, let alone sit and eat with such a one!

As if this was not enough, The Cid had the leper sleep in the warrior's own bed, another custom of the time for an honored guest[380].

Courtesy is an outward sign of great strength and self control. A knight can always be distinguished from a common warrior by this one small but important aspect[381]. Honorable men everywhere recognize each other by this mark.

This is how a knight shows his respect for all of GOD's creation, and even to his enemies, even to the lowest in a society. It is also keeping to a promise, all the way to the avoidance of interrupting a conversation. It is the honoring of a truce on the battlefield, to opening a door for a lady. It is allowing one's enemy to mourn and bury the dead, to avoiding the spread of rumor. It is the respect of property not one's own, to the return of borrowed money. It is the gentle use of words to refresh, invigorate, and even inspire, instead of the bludgeoning of hearts by a heavy and arrogant tongue[382].

As we have seen, King Arthur gave courtesy to the unknown wayfarer, Sir Gareth, and Sir Gareth gave it back again. Courtesy is the

---

[379] (Scudder, 1917) pg. 195
[380] (Matthews) pg.84
[381] (Lull, 2001), pg. 97, just as a knight was marked by his horse, more importantly he was marked by his courtesy
[382] Proverbs 16:24 the Revised English Bible

gift that is like giving and receiving at the same time. It harms no one, and honors everyone, the giver and the receiver. In this way, it is like Mercy[383]. The Practice of Courtesy is imitation of GOD, who is merciful and courteous to all[384].

In the Civil War, General Robert E. Lee was careful to never use an abusive epithet toward his adversary, the Northern Army. Even after both sides slaughtered each other for years, and the commandeering of his own homestead for a national cemetery as a planned affront, Lee never called his enemy anything else but "those people"[385].

Ronald Reagan and Tipp O'Neal were terrible enemies on either side of the political aisle in Washington D.C. They wrestled with each other's ideologies for years, sometimes with heated words and strategies. Yet, legend has it that, hanging in O'Neal's office was a plaque from Reagan which read "From one Irishman to another: top of the morning to you"[386].

At the end of the day, all men are brothers. We fight a common enemy, what we perceive to be evil in the world. The least we can do is treat each other with civility.

"Be wise as serpents and harmless as doves"[387]. "A word of courtesy turns away wrath, and settles many fights before they begin"[388]. Remember, as knights, we must choose our battles carefully, and reserve our strength for truly great affairs, not trivial matters that school children fight about.

A Second Question and Reliance on GOD

Just as there are three kinds of men[389] and three kinds of strength, there are three questions that are of utmost importance when considering strength.

The first question is "What is Strength?" As we have seen, it is the power to defeat evil outside, as well as inside, the soul. If taken in pieces,

---

[383] The Merchant of Venice Act IV, sc. i
[384] A quote from St. Francis pg. 19 of (Schroeder, 1984)
[385] According to Shelby Foote and others
[386] (O'Connell, 1987) and (Smith, 1983)
[387] Matt. 10:16 KJV
[388] Proverbs 15:1
[389] (Pascal, 1966) pg. 82

it is humility, patience, fortitude, long-suffering, diligence, self-control, discipline, justice, mercy, courtesy and temperance all at once.

The second question is "Where does it come from?" or "How is it derived?" or, most directly, "How does one acquire it?" We have seen that true and lasting strength springs from humility, grows in discipline, and finds its culmination in purity and self-control, with many tasks and obstacles along the way. Courtesy tests it, Justice aims it, and mercy and temperance restrains it. All through this journey, focus and discipline enables the knight to find it and use it.

Yet herein is the paradox. While true strength IS humility and fortitude, and patience, and discipline, and selflessness; to gain these things, strength itself is needed! Strength is required to gain strength! It can be said that strength is a man's will, but it is more than the will of man that makes true strength possible!

Therefore, there must be a source outside of the knight that compels him and propels him, draws him toward strength even as he uses it. This source of strength to gain strength is GOD and HIS will, and GOD HIMSELF is the ultimate well-spring of strength.

The knight gains strength from GOD in several ways. The first way is known as Grace[390].

GOD's Grace

> Amazing grace! How sweet the sound
> That saved a wretch like me!
> I once was lost, but now am found,
> Was blind, but now I see.
> > *Amazing Grace* by John Newton[391]

Grace is a kind of perfection on earth, where special things are possible through GOD[392]. It is GOD's presence. When spoken of in the sense of strength, GOD's Grace is a kind of strange power, a holy and unutterable connection with GOD which brings about unbelievable

---

[390] (Annotated Catechism, 1981) pg. 146, art.125
[391] Olney Hymns (1779)
[392] Ibid. pg.145

might[393]. Sometimes the strength is mental, moral, or spiritual, and sometimes it is very physical.

Grace that translated itself on earth in a very physical form could be seen in Samson. Samson's direct connection with GOD's will is seen in two ways, his Nazarite status and his long hair.

As long as his hair was long (a sign of GOD's Grace), he could defeat a hundred men, wrestle a lion's jaws apart, carry a huge city gate away on his back, or destroy a large temple made of stone with his bare hands (slaying thousands of evil-doers in the process)[394].

Grace can also be thought of as a desire to strive for goodness and holiness. The source of such desire is nothing earthly or worldly, but springs directly from GOD's hand. Without this holy desire, nothing truly good or strong is possible. A man must desire to be a knight before he can find the will to become one, and GOD gives such desire[395]. It is like the young Percival in the forest of his home. Suddenly he saw knights riding through his forest, and without knowing exactly what they were, he burned to become one[396].

Have you ever wondered why some people desire to be good and virtuous, while others never would dream of wanting such things? Why do some men desire to be truly and spiritually strong, while others only want to wallow in their weak desires? Some would answer "Upbringing!" or "Genetics!". But haven't you ever seen a good man spring from a horrible family situation, or an evil person come from well-meaning parents? Of course. The desire to be good and virtuous, to be strong and knightly, is a gift of grace. If it were not for GOD's grace bestowed upon me, I would be like any other criminal, trying to carve my foolish desires out of an equally foolish world.

A wise man stands on a curb as he sees a criminal carted away to jail. Under his breath he says "There, but for the grace of GOD, go I"[397].

---

[393] Many forms of Grace abound. See the Faith chapter for the State of Grace and other concepts

[394] Judges 13-16

[395] Phil 2:13, (Anthony Schraner, 1981) pg.146, art. 125

[396] (Moncrieff, 1976) pg.14-15

[397] From The Writings of John Bradford, the biographical notice in the Parker Society Edition, 1853

Reliance on GOD (The Leap of Faith)

"All things are possible with GOD"
> —Luke 1:37, from the King James Bible, becoming a
> seventeenth century proverb

He who created us without our help will not save us without our consent.

> —St. Augustine[398]

The second way a knight gains the strength to be truly strong is through reliance on GOD[399]. This translates as a kind of dependent relationship, where the knight consciously places his pride and worried care aside and asks GOD to aid him. When the knight can do this, he connects with the infinite and cosmic power of GOD, making himself a channel for the Force of GOD, making himself into the Weapon of GOD.

This is truly frightening, and is sometimes known as the **Leap of Faith**. The knight places aside his worries of the future; his concerns, whether practical or not, must be ignored for the moment. Fear and pain arc only feelings, and must be set aside and controlled.

Largesse can sometimes be seen as a type of this reliance. In Edmond Rostand's brilliant play "Cyrano De Bergerac", the title character, a honorable and flamboyant knight-like swordsman, delights in tossing his entire month's pension away to prove a point. Instead of complaining on his later hunger, he laughs as he "feasts" on a cookie, a grape, and a gulp of wine[400]. To him, his flamboyant honor was more important than money, and that is the point. Sometimes we must physically and very concretely show what is most important to us, by denying everything else.

To the outside world, the Leap of Faith seems an insane, even irresponsible way of acting. Many knights and saints throughout history have gone on quests and missions without sufficient food or a clear plan of action, simply because GOD told them to go. St. Francis gave over even the clothes on his back to his father before leaving on his mission of evangelization. Elijah camped in the desert with nothing to sustain him

---

[398] In Augustine's 169th sermon
[399] (Lull, 2001) pg. 68
[400] (Rostand, 1982) pg. 36-8

until the ravens brought him food[401]. The Knights of the Table Round set of in the quest for the Grail, without any idea where it was to be found, or even if it was possible to find it[402]!

"Then calling together the twelve apostles, he gave them power and authority over all the devils and to cure diseases. And he sent them to preach the kingdom of GOD and to heal the sick. And he said to them: Take nothing for your journey, neither staff, nor scrip, nor bread, nor money; neither take two coats. And whatsoever house you shall enter into, abide there and depart not from thence"[403].

Knights in this way, especially on quests, were forced to reside with whomever took pity upon them. Sometimes knights stayed with hermits or strangers Christian enough to open their homes. When such hospitality was not available, knights boiled pine cones to fill their empty stomachs and huddled alone beside lonely campfires, listening to the desolate wind[404].

This is not an invitation to always go on missions without an idea of self-preservation or plan of action. But eventually, somewhere along the line, a righteous person must take on a project without a clear idea of exactly how to do it, or even a clear hope of its fulfillment. The only thing known is that it must be attempted. If you feel convicted that GOD has asked you to do something, it must be tried. And, if GOD has asked you, you must with all strength and speed do everything in your power to make it happen. If GOD has truly asked you, HE will assist you. This assistance will come in different ways, but it will be powerfully felt. What you think the goal of the action is may not happen exactly as you envision it, but GOD will still be served. "Dieux le volt!"—GOD wills it[405]!

Washington's Reliance

Over the years I have heard unbelievers say that Reliance on GOD is simply an excuse, a crutch for those who cannot take care of everything.

---

[401] 1 Kings 17
[402] (Malory,1962) pg. 365-6, (Matarasso, 1969) pg. 44
[403] Luke 9:1-4 Douay-Rheims Bible
[404] (Moncrieff, 1976) pg.206
[405] The battle cry of the First Crusade (Gies, 1986) pg. 36, (Robinson, 1991) pg. 10, (Belloc, 1992) pg. 19

Thus are the foolish musings of those who do not understand the rigors of Reliance.

As a simple response to the unbelievers, no one can prepare for everything, and no one can control every contingency. Even Sun Tzu and Mei Yao-ch'en say this: "No one can control everything"[406]. Whatever we cannot control must be left up to GOD. We must have the courage to do this, to trust GOD.

But a leap of Faith does not demand GOD do our work for us. When relying on GOD, we dare not become lazy or stupid, but instead work as hard as humanly possible, even more so. Anything less would be "tempting GOD". My father would often quote St. Augustine, "Work as if everything depended on you, and pray as if everything depended on GOD (because it does)"[407].

Relying upon GOD demands great responsibility. First, we must work harder than we have ever worked in our lives. Second, we must retain our virtue, withstanding every temptation. Third, we must stay in some sort of communication with GOD, keeping our hearts, minds, and souls open to HIS direction. We must pray fervently, constantly, and the situation will probably be so terrifying that we are compelled to do this.

George Washington, during the Revolutionary War, matched these requirements[408].

Washington knew full well the power and might of the British Empire. Britain was THE great world power at the time, and it swung around to bring its full might smashing down upon the American upstarts sometimes called the United States. The Americans had a tiny, ragtag army made almost entirely of volunteers, while Britain had the largest, best trained army in the world. The Americans had some squirrel rifles, while Britain had the best equipment, guns, and cannonade. The British had the greatest navy on the planet. The Americans didn't even have a navy. The Americans did not have a chance.

Many believe that Washington had felt a calling to lead this impossible war. He saw the immense problems, prayed about his decision,

---

[406] (Griffith, 1971) pg. 85, this is an excellent translation of Sun Tzu's *Art of War*

[407] This has been attributed to both St. Ignatius and St. Augustine, and my father quoted it all the time

[408] First requirement: (Flexner, 1984) pg. 69, 77, 89, (Bennet, 2006) pg. 105; Second: (Wheeler, 1972) pg. 255; Third: (Hart, 1997) pg. 296

and then stood before the Continental Congress, wearing his old uniform from the French and Indian War. His intentions were obvious. No one else had his experience, and no one else even had a uniform.

He asked to lead the American forces, without pay[409].

The next years would be a kind of purgatory on Earth for Washington and his men. They suffered together through horrendously lopsided battles and even a mini-ice age, constantly working against time and disease, the enemy and death. While British officers took their ease in lavish hotels and towns, Washington and his men weathered the terrible cold and gnawing hunger. Their souls became like steel, beaten and scorched in the smithies of GOD, literally forged by the horrors of Valley Forge. But Washington never forgot his responsibilities to his men and to his GOD, constantly caring for even the lowest of privates[410], riding into battle alongside his men to inspire and lead, insisting upon treating even his enemies with courtesy and praying whenever possible[411], kneeling before the Bible or in the snow, at night and far from home.

Whenever someone suggests that Reliance on GOD is an excuse or an easy way out, even recourse to a kind of "deus ex machina", tell them about Washington.

And where was GOD in all this suffering? All the time, and behind the scenes, an invisible, spectral hand seemed behind events, slowly but surely leading towards an impossible American victory. Washington took long chances and narrow escapes, and always they seemed to pay off, as if the Continental Army had something in their favor, a mighty but unseen ally. Historians still marvel at the turn of events. Great generalship and sacrifice were not enough to explain this seemingly ethereal aid; GOD's hand moved in history[412].

The impossible American victory occurred. When the British surrendered at Yorktown, their band played the tune "The World Turned Upside Down", for no one would have believed the pip-squeak nation called America could ever beat the mighty power called Britain[413].

Washington had known. He had relied on GOD[414].

---

[409] (Flexner, 1984) pg. 59
[410] Ibid. pg. 110-111
[411] (Flexner, 1984) pg. 69, 93,100, (Hart, 1997) pg. 296
[412] (Hart, 1997) pg. 302, (Flexner, 1984) pg. 216
[413] (Bennet, 2006) pg. 102
[414] (Hart, 1997) pg. 279, 302

Not a hundred years earlier, another impossible battle against a thoroughly superior force, involved another man who relied on GOD. This battle became known as the Battle of Vienna[415].

Every two to four hundred years, it happens. Moslem extremists move against the West, with gigantic forces[416]. Kara Mustapha Pasha, commissioned by the Turkish Imam to lead hundreds of thousands of men. Heavily provisioned and armed, the Islamic Ottomans felt totally confident. They conquered all the way to Vienna, on the edge of Eastern Europe. The year: 1683.

Pasha's plan was to surround Vienna, this beautiful key to the West. The great walls of the city should not present a problem, they felt, for they had experienced sappers with them. Sappers were soldiers who dug under castle and city walls, and then used explosives to weaken the fortifications. Once the walls would fall from the sappers' efforts, Pasha had planned to send in the dreaded Janissaries, Islamic shock troops, to plunder, terrorize, and crush the Christian civilians within.

The attack began around 4 o'clock in the morning, and soon the sappers were hard at work, tunneling under the walls. The largest explosive placement, set to finally collapse the already weakened walls, was fused and lit, the sappers running out before they too were crushed.

Vienna counter-sappers, Christian men whose job it was to find and prevent the sapper's destruction, worked feverishly to stop the impending collapse of the walls. They came upon this massive tunnel and rushed in, one man throwing himself to the fuse, snuffing it out a mere second from detonation.

Frustrated by this set-back, Pasha and his men still felt it only a matter of time before they held the city. Around 300,000 strong, and with plenty of supplies, their eyes shone with avarice. Soon the city had to fall, opening the rest of Europe before them like a gleaming gift.

Jan Sabieski, commanding 3000 Polish Hussar knights, watched all this from a hill nearby. He was full of consternation, for he knew he was terribly outnumbered, but he must do something to stop this monstrous machine of destruction from flooding into Europe, destroying Christianity and culture, and everything Sabieski held dear.

---

[415] (Stoye, 2006)
[416] (Stoye, 2006) pg. 12-13, (Stark, 2009) pg. 9

At that monumental moment, solemn on that hill, Sabieski resolved to do everything he could do, unto his own death, and prayed for GOD's assistance. In the face of overwhelming odds, he would do his utmost, and rely on GOD for the rest.

Leading his men, with their strange reverberating wings rippling from their armor and making a ringing, thunderous sound, Sabieski galloped down at the head of his Christian soldiers, upon Pasha's Islamic invaders.

It was about 5 in the afternoon, and Pasha's forces were exhausted from their efforts to take the city. Suddenly attacked by fresh warriors, the spearhead of which sounded like a storm of swords, the Islamic Ottomans panicked and broke, pulling back from the battlefield and leaving Vienna behind. The city, and with it all of Christian Europe, was saved.

Against overwhelming odds, Sabieski had won the battle in three hours.

As he saw victory, he summed up the battle, and the true spirit of Reliance, when he said, "I came, I saw, and GOD conquered"[417].

Peace of GOD

A knight has peace at the center of his being, even though his life seems to be in turmoil. Even when terrible things happen, or threaten to happen, the knight has an inward calmness that is sometimes unnerving to his enemies[418]. Some of this is because of endless experience with and proximity to death and battle. But a big part of this peace is derived from reliance on GOD and the staunch belief that everything eventually works to fulfill GOD's ultimate plan[419].

This peace is actually what is referred to when Christ promises His peace to us[420]. He is not promising peace on Earth, nor is He promising that no one will rise against the righteous person. It is a quietness in the soul, unmoved by the illusion of the physical World. "Be still, and know that I am GOD"[421].

---

[417] (Stoye, 2006) pg. 174
[418] (Romer, 1988) pg. 152, (Ellsburg, 2001) pg. 181, also St. George's and St. Mercurius's martyr stories
[419] (Ciszek, 1973) pg. 79
[420] John 14:27
[421] Psalm 46:10 KJV

This Peace of GOD is reflected and channeled in the Courageous calmness that true knights exhibit on the battlefield and in trying times. It is also reflected in his great faith in the final Triumph of Virtue[422].

The Coolness of Battle

Emotions are a mark of humanity: necessary for empathy, appropriate in the witnessing of innocent suffering, essential in the confrontation of injustice and cruelty. But there comes a time when one must lose all conscious connection to the self and one's own desires, cool and dispassionate, to defeat an implacable foe. At this point, emotion gets in the way.

When preparing for battle, especially against the greatest enemies, a knight places aside his conscious self, "turns off" his desires and emotions, and purposefully makes himself a conduit for GOD and HIS power. Selfish emotions get in the way of GOD, and the knight is the weapon of GOD.

Emotions can be great fuel for powerful fires of industry and accomplishment, and just as fire is a good servant but a terrible master, so too are emotions grand servitors, but can never be allowed to master the knight's mind and will [423].

To serve Justice, a man must be impartial, and closed off to influence, even from his own feelings. To administer mercy, a man must push aside old hatreds. To forgive, a man must give up his rage.

Righteous rage drives powerful deeds, energizing the knight's right arm, but is not allowed to cloud his mind. Righteous fury can be used to silence the other emotions, turning the knight into a warrior made of cold steel.

But even rage and fury can wear down a man's resolve, because it burns a terrible energy. In the heat of battle, that energy must be used with great care, and no distraction.

A knight must know when to accept the presence of his clamoring emotions, and when to quiet them. When faced with battles of the spirit, the defense of the soul, and the presence of radical evil, the knight must

---

[422] (Kersten, 1990) pg. 63
[423] (Kierkegaard, 1956) pg.53, 55

set himself aside, and allow GOD to work through him[424]. When the knight needs GOD to fill him, he must be empty.

In such times of spiritual combat, the knight pushes aside his fear and anger, which can be used by the demonic opponent, and allows thoughts of GOD and prayer to flood his mind and soul[425]. The Knight must let GOD's peace fill him, and allow nothing else. For GOD's peace is the armor of the soul. The armor of GOD is GOD Himself.

When a true sacristan opens the Tabernacle to collect the Eucharist, he is not thinking of himself or of his own feelings or desires, he is only thinking of the Eucharist and the task at hand. The mantel of the Priest is upon his mind and heart. At that moment, he is unconcerned of his unworthiness, of the temptations in his past, even of worries of mistakes. The task is all. GOD is all[426]. Prayer goes through his mind as he carries out the instructions, and nothing else matters.

To accomplish this, the knight, like the saintly sacristan, focuses of GOD[427].

Focus on GOD (The Razor of the Mind)

> "GOD knows that I love you, but I cannot be with GOD and with men—a thousand and a thousand thousand angelic powers have one will, but men have many. Therefore I cannot send GOD from me and come and be with men."
>
> —Abbot Arsenius[428]

---

[424] (Ciszek F. W., 1973, 1995) pg. 79

[425] (Baglio, 2009) pg. 217, (Ciszek F. W., 1973, 1995) pg.77-81

[426] (Paul, Moments of Decision, Profiles of Great Men and Women, 1975) pg. 13

[427] (Spoto, 2002) pg. 65

[428] From the *Verba Seniorum*, (xvii, 5), by Pelagius the Deacon, who later becomes Pope Pelagius I

"A GOD-intoxicated man"[429]

Focus on GOD is the fourth way a knight derives the strength to be strong. This is the final key, because the other forms of reliance on GOD require a fourth component. A man may have grace before him and be totally blind to it. The entire universe is dependent on GOD for everything, but may not be aware of it. The knight derives his unique and special strength from his focus on GOD. This focus unlocks the infinite power of the universe.

A martial artist focuses on a place beyond the brick. He imagines his hand smashing through the brick and reaching that one place. For a moment, there is no brick, nor is there any resistance at all. There is only the hand reaching the one place. Suddenly it is done, and the hand smashes through any barrier to reach the one place.

It is not enough, however, simply to have focus on something. It is true that focus can give great benefits, but it is only focus coupled with the perfect subject of that focus, GOD, that will yield the best results. A martial artist focuses on his one point, or nothingness, to quiet his mind enough to perform great or dangerous feats in this universe, but the knight who focuses on GOD, he is capable of changing the universe itself, even going beyond it. The martial artist focuses and breaks through a brick; the knight focuses on GOD and breaks through the world.

For the knight, everything in life is done through the lens of GOD's shadow, or, to say it another way, while keeping the soul's eye on GOD, all things are done. Just as a martial artist performs his movements with focus, so too does the knight perform his daily tasks with focus on GOD.

The knight is GOD-intoxicated! All his thoughts are in some way or another connected to GOD. GOD haunts his every thought and every move. But even more than this, the knight's ultimate purpose in life is GOD-oriented, to do GOD's will, whatever the consequences or obstacles[430].

---

[429] Said of Baruch Spinoza, probably by Novalis, aka Georg Freiherr von Hardenberg

[430] (Gautier, 1989) pg. 30, (Green, 1984) pg. 60, (Kierkegaard, 1956) pg. 121, Deut. 6:5-9, (Ciszek F. W., 1973, 1995) pg. 79

St. Paul speaks of fighting the good fight, running the course, and keeping the faith[431], turning his world and life's work upside-down in order to follow GOD. Sir Warwick abandons everything he loves in order to better serve the LORD and do penance for his past deeds[432]. Outside the walls of Jerusalem, in his desperate struggle to aid the Crusader armies to take the holy city, Godfrey of Bouillon finds his thoughts totally dominated by a tranquil focus on GOD[433].

St. Antony of Egypt was the epitome of such focus. He considered everything in this world as a distraction from the true reality of GOD, even the welfare of his young sister and the demands of his own body[434].

First, he gave the care of his sister over to trusted nuns, then decided to ignore, or more exactly insult, the needs of desires of his body by living on a tall pillar for several years. Roman soldiers, who considered themselves stronger and tougher than any other soldiers on earth, would stand in amazement at St. Antony's feat of discipline and inner strength. Several of these warriors resolved to become Christians because "No one could be as strong as this man, and he is a Christian, therefore I will become one"[435]!

Such self-denial and discipline, however, was not enough for St. Antony. To remove any distractions from his focus on GOD, he next lived in a cemetery, and then finally retreated far into the desert, hoping to find a place that would allow him to focus completely and continuously on the Most High GOD.

Finally, this exhibition of true spiritual strength drew the attention of the ultimate opponent, the Evil One. The Devil himself came to tempt Antony on more than one occasion, and in many different ways, sometimes as an arrogant child (!), sometimes as a beautiful (but still arrogant) woman, and even sometimes as ferocious beasts. But each time, St. Antony rejected him with ease, sending the Evil One back to Hell, frustrated and confused[436].

---

[431] 2 Timothy 4:7 KJV
[432] (Moncrieff, 1976) p.226
[433] (Gautier, 1989) pg. 115-116
[434] (Athanasius, 1980) pg. 31-32
[435] (Trape', 1986) pg. 106, (Augustine S., 1961) pg. 167
[436] (Athanasius, 1980) pg. 62

St. Ignatius read the Lives of the Saints and, instead of dedicating his life to the service of a lady like many knights in his time[437], focused his laser-beam-like focus on Jesus Christ. He pushed all un-knightly and earthly thoughts from his mind and created the Society of Jesus, based on chivalrous, military, and Catholic principles[438]. This organization is now known as the Jesuit order of priests (loved and feared throughout the world).

St. Augustine, enraged at his own weakness in the face of worldly pleasures, swore them off in his conversion to pure Christianity, dedicating himself to constant study of GOD forever in asceticism[439]. Sir Hughes De Payns decided to leave all semblance of luxury and even safety behind, by dedicated himself to the protection of Christian pilgrims in newly conquered Palestine, even using the Rule of Augustine to organize his new Order of the Knights Templar[440].

After his earlier mistakes, Sir Lancelot found his focus on GOD and was able to climb the many stairs of Castle Carbonek, even past the massive twin lions, to glimpse the Holy Grail[441].

All abandoned their earthly lives to pursue GOD and set their sights on HIM. All true saints and knights focus on GOD like a laser beam, and never turn away.

Some would ask, "I will never go into the desert or risk life and limb in pursuit of some saintly undertaking. I have great responsibility right here. My life is ordinary. How can I be "GOD-intoxicated", when I am unable to pursue such heroic undertakings?"

People misunderstand. To be "GOD-Intoxicated" is not to do anything necessarily superhuman, nor does it mean to go to church every day nor sink to one's knees every second. It simply means to constantly think about GOD, to constantly wonder and be in wonder of HIM.

Baruch Spinoza, for whom the phrase "GOD-intoxicated" was first coined, neither went to church nor ever went on Crusade. He was originally a Jewish philosopher who spent his days quietly working (he

---

[437] (Caraman, 1990) pg. 29-30, (Mottola, 1964) pg. 17, (Ganss, 1992) pg. 16
[438] (Caraman, 1990) pg. 41
[439] (Wills, 1999) pg. 49, (Trape', 1986) pg.119, 128
[440] (Addison, 2001) pg. 4, (Read, 1999) pg. 91
[441] (Malory, 1497) pg. 420-425, (Matarasso, 1969) pg. 260-1

was a lens grinder) and his nights constantly thinking and writing about his philosophies of the nature of GOD and the Universe[442].

The key is that he constantly thought of and was enraptured by thoughts of GOD's nature [443]. He even turned down lucrative careers so that he might have more time quietly conceptualizing GOD. He realized that all things were not good enough compared to philosophy and contemplation of the nature of GOD. One's belief in GOD may drive one to do many brave things, but focus on GOD simply means to think on HIM constantly[444], and to care more about one's understanding and relationship to HIM than anything else in the world.

But, Spinoza needed to take the next step.

Focus Becomes Purity of Heart, Mind, and Soul

> "Who shall ascend the hill of the Lord? And who shall stand in His holy place? He who has clean hands and a pure heart, who does not focus his mind on what is false and does not swear deceitfully."
> —Psalm 24:3-4, The Revised English Bible

> "My strength is as the strength of ten, because my heart is pure."
> —from *Sir Galahad*, by Alfred, Lord Tennyson

To focus on GOD in the way of St. Antony and St. Ignatius, is to reach a state of grace and purity. The desert and long trials and tribulations burn away any weakness of the knight, making his stare focused on GOD alone. Even his memories fade, the quest stripping his mind of anything that is illusion, leaving only that which is Honor and GOD. Such is purity.

Many people, when they think of purity, think only of chastity. This is understandable, but only partially true. Chastity is only part of Purity; a consequence of the focus on GOD that is Purity. Just as a solid block

---

[442] (Stewart, 2006) pg. 54-58
[443] Ibid. pg. 159-60, 54-58
[444] Psalm 1:2

of gold or silver is not filled with anything else and is thus pure, so is the pure mind and heart and will filled with and focused on nothing but thoughts of GOD. As Kierkegaard says "Purity of heart is to will one thing"[445]. If a man or knight focuses his entire mind, will, heart, and soul on GOD, the purest of all things, his heart grows to be pure, also.

No one can be pure like GOD, but the knight's soul reflects GOD's purity as a mirror may reflect the sun! It is not our purity, but GOD's purity flowing through us.

If one is pure and has GOD filling him, he cannot be filled with himself[446]. Thus a pure man is selfless, emptied of himself. If emptied of himself, his desires are wiped clean, placed there by GOD directly. The pure man wants what GOD wants.

This purity of heart is a singularity of purpose in action. Galahad does not fight for women's charms, wealth, gold, fame, or pleasure; he fights for one purpose, the greater glory of GOD and HIS justice. He wants GOD's will, and nothing else. This is purity of intention.

This purity, gained by focusing completely on GOD, can forge the knight into a powerful force.

> "Even in war it is the "elan vital" that counts. "Fervour," Said Napoleon, "counts against numbers on the field of battle as three to one". But there is something which when the human heart possesses it, more than trebles that ratio. It is the pure heart, flaming with a lofty ideal, and conscious of the righteousness of its cause. Nothing in this world can compare with the impetuous valour of men thus possessed."
>
> —James Burns,
> *Sir Galahad: A Call to the Heroic*[447]

But a knight is more than purity of intention. His purity is not only in heart, but in soul and in body. Knights like Galahad couple this purity of intention with a purity of body, disciplining his body until it is a machine with obedience only to his pure heart, his pure heart obedient to his soul, and his soul obedient only to GOD. His mind focuses only

---

[445] (Kierkegaard, 1956) ch.3,4
[446] Ibid. ch.6
[447] (Burns, 1915, 2013) pg. 3

on how to win in an honorable way for GOD, continuously finding the strategies necessary for such victory of Virtue. The purity of mind, body, heart, and soul, is purity of intention, discipline, focus, and strategy. A disciplined body, a strategic mind, a spirit of purity with purpose combines to make a man incredibly strong, a veritable lion against the foes of the Good.

"My strength is the strength of ten," Tennyson's Galahad proclaimed, "Because my heart is pure"[448]. "And at the flash of his sword the legions of darkness role back, for no cohorts, however consolidated, can stand against the impetuous rush of those whose hearts are set on fire by GOD, who have seen the Vision, and whose spears are leveled against iniquity"[449].

With GOD's help and grace, such a man is unstoppable, capable of things far beyond the normal realm. Such is the case of St. Antony or the allegorical Sir Galahad.

The Siege Perilous (The Seat of Peril)

When the round table was constructed by Merlin for the knights of King Arthur, it was circular to show that all knights are brothers and of equal importance[450].

But there was one chair at that table that always went unoccupied. No one dared to touch that seat. Each knight's place at the table was marked with a plaque showing their name, but marked on the untouched seat was a message that read "Only for the Greatest knight, and the Purist". "And Merlin called it 'The Siege Perilous,' perilous for good and ill; 'For there,' he said, 'No man could sit but he should lose himself . . ."[451].

The knights knew that if anyone not absolutely pure sat there, they would be destroyed, perhaps in a sudden blaze of fire, or in a terrible freak accident. When it first appeared, the knights debated for whom

---

[448] From Tennyson's poem—*Sir Galahad*
[449] (Burns, 1915, 2013) pg.3
[450] (Scudder, 1917) pg.44
[451] (Alfred, Idylls of the King, edited by J.M. Gray, 1983) chapter of the Holy Grail, v.173-174

it was placed, but each searched his heart and privately knew it was not he. It was no laughing matter, and all the knights sat humble and sincere around such a place.

They knew, as all knights do, that an impure heart is full of "self", filled to the brim and crowded with selfish desires, wants, lusts, and worldly ambitions. There is no focus or purity of intention and the will is scattered among a thousand demands. There is no room for GOD in such a heart. Even if there were the tiniest selfishness in an otherwise clean heart, it would still mark the person as if they were the most unclean. Any impurity at all is enough to make one impure and such a person can only fear when they sit in the Seat of Death.

For who can say that they are pure enough to reflect GOD? What knight can know his heart is as pure as the driven snow?

Then one day an old man led a young knight into King Arthur's castle. "This be Sir Galahad." Said the old man. "And he is Sir Lancelot's son, as well as a descendent of Joseph of Arimathea. He it is who shall sit at the Siege Perilous."

Of course this drew gasps, not only because of the identity of the knight but also of his "intrepidity at sitting in the Siege Perilous".[452] But when he was told of the doom of anyone who sat there, that they would lose themselves, Galahad cried, "If I lose myself, I save myself"[453]!

Galahad is absolutely pure; he loses himself intentionally, emptying himself, making himself free of selfish desires and worldly ambition. He keeps his eyes on GOD; he has no ambition but to fulfill GOD's wishes, no wish but to do the righteous thing, thus his heart is pure. He is as pure as a white, blank page or the white shield he later wins. He is an empty vessel, allowing room to be filled with GOD's grace and GOD's holy direction. And when he took his rightful place, everyone knew that it was the will of GOD.

Once he claims the Perilous Seat, his next mission is Holy Grail itself. While in the pursuit of this, he encounters many evil men and demons. But no one and nothing can stand in his way. Whether it be seven men at once, or evil spirits from Hell, none can withstand his righteous fury and his absolute purity.

---

[452] (Malory, 1962) pg. 362

[453] (Alfred, Idylls of the King, edited by J.M. Gray, 1983) chapter of the Holy Grail, v.178, see Luke 17:33

In his quest for the Holy Grail, he soon came to an enormous castle that was well protected by moats and high walls. He was told that this castle was known as the Maiden's castle.

Some years before, seven powerful brothers raided the castle and took over the lands that the castle protected. They killed the Duke of the castle, and when his daughter prophesied that they would be overthrown by a single knight, they took up the habit of killing every knight who came along, and raping every maiden.

Galahad's eyes narrowed. Even though on a quest, he lived for GOD and HIS justice, and could not let such a vicious and licentious group of men go unpunished.

He promptly rode up to the castle. He knew he would be challenged by the brothers. Sure enough, they sent a messenger to ask what he wanted.

"To have the men inside change their habits." Galahad said.

The gate was opened, and as Galahad rode into the courtyard, the seven brothers appeared, all on horses and with full armor. "Defend yourself knight, for we promise to kill you!" They cried and pointed their spears.

"Do you intend to challenge me all at once?!?" Galahad demanded. But he already knew the answer and prepared himself.

They rushed at him with their spears like a forest of knifes. Galahad struck the leader with his lance, catapulting that brother from his horse, while the others broke their spears on his armor. As the six left came around again, Galahad unsheathed his brilliant sword and beat them so fiercely they soon fled like the pigs they were. Seven against one, but still not enough for the pure Sir Galahad!

This reflects Sir Ramon Lull's motto: "He that lives by the life (of Christ), cannot die"[454]. It is said that on one occasion, the Cid single-handedly defeated more than a score of men, sending the survivors running as from a fire. The Cid fought like Galahad on that day. "The man who knows how to live need not fear death. He can walk without fear of rhino or tiger. He will not be overcome in battle. In him, the rhino's horn can find no place to pierce, the tiger's claws no place to tear. And weapons, no place to cut. For a man who knows how to live has no place for Death to enter"[455].

---

[454] (Zwemer, 1902) pg. 76-77
[455] Lao-Tzu, *I-Ching*, 50

Evil is no match for Galahad. All the robber knights and wicked men he encounters are thrown back and enfeebled or destroyed by his sword and spear. At an abbey he visits, his mere presence defeats the demon that had cursed the place for years. His touch brings healing to several wounded men, including a king, who recognizes him as the "Lily of purity". He defeats whole kingdoms, bringing entire cities under the sway of Christianity. Time after time and place after place, where ever Galahad goes, he purifies the region, defeats the evil, and wins the glory for GOD[456].

But the greatest victory for Galahad, or course, is the Grail itself: the most sublime symbol of Christ, the purist of the pure. Only Galahad, with his mighty and worthy friends Sir Bors and Sir Percival beside him, achieve the Grail, and only Galahad can grasp it in its entirety.

"Blessed are the pure of heart, for they shall see GOD"[457].

Only by emptying oneself as Galahad has, making oneself ready to be filled by GOD can one receive GOD, sit in the Siege Perilous, defeat the evil one, survive the valley of the shadow of Death, climb the holy mountain, and gain the wisdom and strength to find and win the Holy Grail[458]. "My strength is as the strength of ten," Galahad said, "Because my heart is pure."

Grappling with Purity

Purity is not simply Chastity. Purity is the tree and Chastity is only one of the many fruits of Purity. Absolute Focus on GOD, true Purity, brings forth many gifts and powers, making a knight or saint unstoppable, undeniable, holy, full of grace, and "with the strength of ten".

When people hear of the amazing feats of many saints and knights, they cannot believe. People find such things hard to believe because they have been surrounded all their lives by people who are not focused on GOD in the knightly way.

---

[456] We shall explore Galahad's adventures and techniques more fully in Book II

[457] Matthew 5:8, KJV

[458] Psalm 24: 3-4, (Alfred, *Idylls of the King*, edited by J.M. Gray, 1983), (Malory, 1962), (Matarasso, 1969)

But how does one know if he or she is totally focused on GOD? For one thing, their lives would mirror those of the saints and knights already mentioned.

For another, they would realize the true nature of the world. Remember, as Galahad did, how transitory is this world, as opposed to the Next[459].

But also, as Kierkegaard says in his famous book about purity, "If a man shall will the good in truth, then he must be willing to do all for the good, or be willing to suffer all for the good"[460]. If a man be truly focused completely on GOD, GOD becomes all important to him. Such a man would sacrifice anything and everything, because all things in the world are only distractions compared to the Truth of the Most High. The true knight, the man totally focused on GOD, would even face Hell itself if it be for the greater glory of GOD. Such a man is, as we have discussed before, "GOD-intoxicated".

Such laser focus, which brings on purity of heart, mind, and soul, is difficult to maintain. Many times, the mundane worries and cares of the world break in to the knight's mind. But he continues to struggle to keep such focus and purity for as long as possible. Especially when he faces his greatest tests and challenges, he calls forth this focus, ridding his mind of all impurities, and keeping his eyes set on GOD.

The focus I mean has two aspects, the mental and spiritual. The mental focus is thoughtful, but the spiritual focus delves into morality and the purity of Chastity. A true knight keeps both, mental and spiritual focus, meaning his mind is filled, as much as possible, with GOD, while his morality reflects this and GOD's grace, giving him the power to maintain Chastity. When done properly, both types of focus work well together.

Let us not forget the father of Modern Scientific thought, who, like Galahad, believed in the concept of virginity as a path to ultimate purity of thought and thus clarity of mental vision[461]. His full title was **Sir** Isaac Newton. Nikola Tesla also shared this opinion.

A true knight cares little for chasing after beautiful bodies in lust, or money, or fame. His mind, heart, and will are focused only on one thing, GOD. No one else is in his mind; not wife, not children, not family, not

---

459 (Malory, 1962) pg. 431
460 (Kierkegaard, 1956) pg.121
461 (Leshem, 2003) pg. 206-207

friends, not enemies, not even himself. "No one is worthy of me who cares more for father and mother than for me; no one is worthy of me who cares more for son or daughter; no one is worthy of me who does not take up his cross and follow me. Whoever gains his life shall lose it; whosoever loses his life for my sake will gain it"[462].

People might object to the image of a pure knight because it excludes a wife. Yes, it certainly seems to, although purity can be applied to love in this way: a knight who loves and desires his wife to the exclusion of all others is purely focused on one thing, his wife. Such is honorable and true, romantic love.

This loyalty and purity of thought must translate into loyalty and purity of thought containing GOD[463]. The wife can be a sort of practice for loyalty to GOD. St. Augustine speaks of "using" all the experiences on earth in order to reach a better understanding of GOD[464], and if one understands and fulfills his obligations and loyalties to his wife, he has a good picture of what it is to be loyal to an ideal or to GOD.

And loyalty to GOD can be a precursor to marital fidelity in body and mind. A man who understands and follows loyalty to GOD cannot be disloyal to his wife. To "cheat" on his wife is to go against the laws of Honor and GOD; no true and loyal knight goes against these[465].

But it would seem that pure focus cannot hold two aims; pure focus must only have one subject, in the end[466]. So, does this mean that loyalty to a human and loyalty to GOD are mutually exclusive? I believe it is possible to love purely GOD and a wife. But, to be totally pure of thought to GOD, a man cannot be fair to his wife, since his thoughts are only on GOD, and a wife has many needs. You might say, to serve GOD is to conduct your life in such a way that the wife would be treated well. This may be so, but the pure man of GOD must eventually do things, such as quests, that will aggravate the wife, and even make her second. Just as warriors always leave behind their families to better focus on battle, Sir Warwick forced himself to leave behind his wife and his world, to better serve and focus on GOD. St. Antony of Egypt placed his little

---

462   Matt 10:37-40 The Revised English Bible

463   (Malory, 1962) pg. 458—First a man must love GOD his creator, and then, if he is to be ennobled, he must love a woman.

464   (Deane, 1963) pg. 43

465   (Malory, 1962) pg. 458

466   (Kierkegaard, 1956) ch.3

sister in a convent, so that he may focus only on GOD. Sir Ramon Lull had himself declared legally dead when he entered holy orders so that his wife could collect his wealth and allow him to leave the material world.

So what must a knight do? Must a knight reject ever having a wife in order to better focus on GOD? Catholic priests do this, partly because they know that a wife and a family would only eventually split apart their focus between too many things. Most knights do marry, but are forced to create a hierarchy (mentioned in the Code and Obedience chapter) to help them keep their priorities. Whatever the case, it was a common Medieval idea, as spoken through Sir Lancelot[467], that a knight of absolute purity, with no wife nor lover, nor even licentious thought, is far stronger than a knight with these. And through Sir Galahad, we find that a knight absolutely pure is ten times more powerful than any other warrior.

If purity is so important, does it come before humility, or after? It is an unpopular idea, but purity does not come naturally and must be worked at. One needs humility to realize one is not pure or not pure enough[468].

Because of the nature of purity, humility must come first in most cases[469]. Purity is the focus on what is pure and good, namely GOD, and thus one must be humble enough to focus on something besides one's self and one's selfish desires and needs. One who is not humble can never be pure in this chivalrous way because a proud man's focus is on himself.

But our spiritual progress is many times not linear.

Also remember that all these virtues and words and explanations are simple labels for something ineffable. In the end, all true strength, as well as everything else in the universe, depends on the grace of GOD. To focus on GOD, to make GOD the center of your thoughts and being— to be the GOD-intoxicated man—is to reach the apex of true strength, and to tap into the infinite power that breathed the universe into life.

Finally, humility is needed to reach this apex, because humility is the answer to the final question about true strength.

---

[467] (Steinbeck, 1976) pg. 263
[468] (Epictetus, 1937) II, 17, (Gautier, 1989) pg. 32, (Augustine, 1986) pg. 12, (Clairveaux, 1977) pg. 150
[469] (Augustine, 1986) pg.12, Letter 118, 22

At the end of the Strength Chapter

> Why did you go into the wilderness, to hear the wind in the reeds?[470]
>
> —Luke 7:24

To have strength is not enough to impress GOD, nor win our way into the shadow of the LORD. We must know what to do with strength, as well as what not to do. This is the third question about strength. "What is the purpose of strength? What is it used for?"

There are two parts to the answer.

In reality, a man truly strong does little to further his own personal ends.[471] His concern is only with what GOD wants him to do. The knight "slays" his will, bow his intense will before the LORD; the knight controls himself. He keeps his emotions and desires under strict control. Even more, he molds his desires, so that he wants what GOD wants.

True strength is for the purpose of protecting the good, the Church, and the innocent, and the weak, to defeat the knight's selfish self, to save himself from himself and the Evil One[472]. The knight must right all wrongs, ensure justice tempered with mercy, and be the voice of the voiceless. The knight also uses his strength, not against others, but against the dark aspects of his own nature, as in the seven deadly sins. Such a purpose is to defeat the very enemies of GOD, to face whole armies with a laugh and a sword, to beat down the animal instincts in our own hearts, to push through illusion to find the truth, to force life itself to conform to the laws of Chivalry, to offer ourselves up in a single glorious sacrifice of pain, fire, and purity!

All this is strength!

But this is not all.

The Cid understood.

What if you were offered one of the most beautiful and important kingdoms in all the world? Would you take it? Would you claim the prize for yourself? The Cid, Rodrigo De Bivar, faced this question.

---

[470] Luke 7:24, this phrase is echoed by Sir Bedivere when King Arthur asks what he saw in Tennyson's *The Passing of Arthur*, v. 238 and 285

[471] (Kierkegaard, 1956) Ch.4, Ch.6

[472] (Gautier, 1989) pg. 38, 42-43

After terrible and agonizing combat with the Moors, he finally defeated them and rode with his army into Valencia, one of the greatest cities of that time. Cheering crowds and adoring throngs who loved him dearly, surrounded him, saw him as a demi-god, and expected, as he neared the palace and center of kingdom, to take their city for himself. They waited as he mounted the stairs to receive the crown of Valencia, which was his by hard battle and the shedding of his own blood.

Valencia! The jewel of Spain! What an awesome prize, fit for an awesome knight!

He lifted the beautiful, gold crown for the whole of the city to see. The crowd cheered "Cid! Cid!"

The Cid faced them. "I claim this crown of Valencia, for my lord Alfonso, King of Spain!"

The crowd was stunned, but then they realized. "What a noble vassal!" They cried. Who but the Cid could fight so hard for others instead of himself? Who, but one of the greatest knights of all time, could do such a selfless and noble thing[473]?

Sir Godfrey of Bouillon understood. Sir Godfrey had fought alongside thousands of other knights, through terrible long months of heat, miserable supplies, brutal enemies, and the implacable desert to finish the First Crusade and stand triumphant in the center of Jerusalem.

The crown of Jerusalem, the holiest of holy cities, was presented to him. The army and the people thronged and cheered around him. They had voted and decided to name him king! What an honor and what glory, to be crowned the King of the Center of the World! What power! What Glory!

He turned away. "I cannot wear a crown of gold," He said, "where my Lord wore a crown of thorns"[474].

George Washington understood. At the end of the Revolutionary War, his soldiers turned to him because they were disgusted with the Continental Congress. Who could blame them? They had not been paid sufficiently in years while they had endangered their own lives for this fledgling country. Only Washington had spoken for them, only Washington had believed in them, only Washington had fought alongside

---

[473] (Merwin, 1959) pg. 39, canto 1 stanza 3, (Gerritsen and Melle, 1998) pg.80, 84
[474] (Pernoud, 1963) pg. 84, this is probably one of the most famous quotes in the annals of Chivalry

them, and now, they trusted only him. They came to him one night with an offer.

"We will give up this democracy, with its slow decisions and quick arguments, and we will make you king." They told him.

He looked at them with those powerful but gentle eyes. "We have fought and suffered for our new country, you and I, all these years, suffering together, and in one fell move you wish to throw it all away?" He turned his back on their offer, refusing anything to do with talk of making kings. "If he [Washington] did that," George III said, "He is the greatest man in the world"[475].

To hold absolute, bludgeoning, and deafening power, but not to abandon oneself to its glow or glory; to use great power to strike at the very foundations of evil, but not to use it for one's own selfish ends; to have the whole earth in one's hands, and to use it for others, then turn away as if one had never tasted this power, this is true strength.

What if you had the greatest, most powerful weapon in the world; what would you do with it? Sir Bedivere faced this very question.

The final battle of the Round Table was over. King Arthur and his knights had slain the evil Mordred and his wicked army, but at a terrible cost. King Arthur himself lay dying from a wound to the head, and scattered all around him lay the dead and wounded.

Only Sir Bedivere survived. Now, this loyal knight stood before his bloody king, asking what next could be done.

"Take Excalibur" King Arthur managed, "and go to a nearby lake of pure water. Throw Excalibur into this water, and then return to my side"[476].

Bedivere took the mighty, magical sword and sought out a body of water. But as he stood upon the shore, he found he could not bring himself to throw Excalibur into the murky depths. He hid Excalibur and went back to his horse.

He rode back to the king's side, thankfully finding him still alive.

"Tell me what you saw when you threw the sword." Arthur asked.

"I saw nothing but the wind and the water in the reeds." Answered Bedivere.

---

[475] (Bennet, 2006) pg. 105
[476] (Malory, 1962) pg. 500

Arthur's face grew dark. "You did not do as I asked. Now go and throw Excalibur into the water."

With a heavy heart, Bedivere returned to the place where he hid Excalibur. He cocked back his arm, ready to hurl the sword far out over the lake, but still his heart would not let him. Could not this great sword be used for great good and to rebuild mighty nations, he asked himself. Why throw it away?

Once again, he rode back to his ailing king.

"When you threw the sword," The king said, barely whispering. "What did you see?"

"I saw nothing but a splash, and the wind in the reeds." Sir Bedivere said[477].

King Arthur's anger rose, and he pulled himself to standing. "I thought you loved me as your king, and you could do this simple task for me. Throw the sword into the water!"

"But why?" Bedivere cried, exasperated. "Could not the most powerful sword ever made still be used for good? While must it be thrown away, as if it is but a symbol of all the Chivalry that was your kingdom, now dissolved."

King Arthur's face grew sad now. "The kings and princes of this world would finally be corrupted by the power of this sword. GOD works in many ways, and all things must pass, least one good custom corrupt the world. Now go"[478].

Bedivere rode away one more time. His heart ached within him, but he took the blade, closed his eyes, and with a mighty heave, threw it far out over the water. Suddenly a beautiful and graceful woman's hand reached up from the depths, grasping Excalibur's handle, and then plunged back beneath the lake[479].

Sir Bedivere jumped upon his horse and traveled to tell his king what had transpired, but he feared that the king would not be able to hear him.

The final lesson of knightly power and strength is to not have power or strength as the final goal. Power and strength are only tools, not the prize. Such is the means, not the end. One must have the humility to

---

[477] (Alfred, Idylls of the King, edited by J.M. Gray, 1983) pg. 294-5, line 238-9, 284-5, (Malory, 1962) pg. 500

[478] (Alfred, Idylls of the King, edited by J.M. Gray, 1983) pg 299, line 410 of the *Passing of Arthur*

[479] (Malory, 1962) pg. 500

turn away, because the power is not ours[480]. The strength does not come from ourselves, nor is it meant for ourselves. Strength and power are not for their own sake, but for the good and GOD's ultimate plan[481].

All true strength, the real strength, the knightly strength of GOD, is properly aimed at accomplishing GOD's Will, not ours.

Jesus Christ had the power of GOD behind Him and could have destroyed His enemies with a nod. He could have called an army of angels to sweep the world clean of anyone who refused to listen to Him. Those who spit upon Him, He could have blasted to Perdition. Those who mocked Him, He might have ground them into powder. Those who hurt Him, He could have erased their existence. But this was not Christ's mission[482]. His goal was to present a better path in life and to forge a road to GOD, salvation itself, not to beat and manhandle everyone into submission. And so, even with all His power, He did not use it for His own sake. Christ turned the hammer of strength on itself and exploded His heart to save the world and pay the price of Justice[483]. Might for Right[484].

For this reason, for His very Humility[485], for His self-abasing absolute Strength, Christ embodies the ultimate Honor, the ultimate place, and the ultimate power, to conquer death itself and return one day as the ultimate Judge of the world. And on *that* day, He will no longer be the Lamb, but the Lion. The Great Lion of the Tribe of Judah. The Lion of GOD[486].

---

480 (Augustine, 1986) Letter 118, 22

481 (Kierkegaard, 1956) ch.6

482 Matt 26:53

483 1 Peter 3:18, Col. 1:22, Hebrews 9:14, 9:18, 10:10

484 (White, 1958) pg. 237, (Steinbeck, 1976) pg. 2, (Matthews, 1998) pg. 149, (Gautier, 1989) pg. 7, (Clairvaux, 1977) pg. 129-130, (Lull, 2001) pg. 48, 84-90

485 Phil. 2:6

486 Rev. 5:5

STRENGTH CHAPTER APPENDIX: SOME STEPS TO STRENGTH

Most modern self-help books tell you to be good or strong, but do not tell you how. As I peruse over this chapter, I realize my words might be vague on how to develop strength; therefore I will be very specific, and in a very American sort of way, I will be direct.

We will speak of some basic strategies of strength that the ancients truly used. We may use the wisdom of saints and pagans, but we will dispense with the silly droning of modern "feel-good" gurus and emotion-mongers. We will discuss how to truly be strong, both inwardly, and outwardly. We will discuss how a true knight may increase his physical, mental, and spiritual power, one step at a time. These listed below can be a beginning.

[Because all kinds of strength are so essential, this section will not exhaust every strategy, not come close. We will discuss more strategies in Book II: *Beat the Devil*.]

Humility—The first step to any true strength

❖ **Walk through a graveyard frequently**. Look at the graves and know that all of the people there had hopes and dreams, aspirations and strengths, weaknesses and faults. Their fate is ours. There is only GOD and the Angel of Death—and then only GOD.

❖ **Surround yourself with difficult images**, images of death, of somber tones and serious things. As Epictetus instructs, place fearful images on the walls to remind you of nearness of death. This reminds men that they are not gods. As the samurai does, imagine all the ways that violent death can fall upon you—stabbing, falling, being crushed by rocks, decapitation, punctured by arrows—and imagine this every single day.

❖ **Perform some menial task every day that others might see as beneath them.** Traditionally, knights trained as servants before becoming warriors. Gareth served others at table and in the kitchen, while traditional martial artists cleaned the floor of the dojo. Help unclog toilets and clean them. Water trees and feed various animals. Pick up trash and leave everywhere better than how you found it. Consider that Christ, the Messiah Himself, washed the feet of His disciples. "He that would be first among you must be your servant".

❖ **When someone compliments you about anything**, do not sheepishly shy away or perform anything of false modesty. Accept the compliment, but then say something to the effect of: "Thank you, but I must continue to work harder all the time, and improve." And mean it when you say this.

❖ **Decide today that you are ugly and undesirable**. This will free you from worry over such things. Never spend more than a few seconds in front of a mirror. It is not a crime to look good, but it is a crime to be vain, and it is the worst of crimes against the soul to consider the outer appearance more important than the inner shine. All deep religions agree on this.

❖ **When thoughts** of how great and advanced you have become occur to you spontaneously, immediately greet them with thoughts of your errors and mistakes, and how far you have to go. When thoughts of your mistakes and stupidities come to your mind spontaneously, immediately greet them with acknowledgments of your successes and victories. This is Saint Ignatius's method of dealing with vanity and despondency, alike. Humility is not focusing on your defeats all the time, but on your true appearance before GOD.

❖ On a given topic, you must be open to the possibility of being wrong as much as the possibility you are right. Be willing to admit mistakes. Question yourself as well as the other man. Augustine says to hear the opponent's argument, and he constantly questioned everything. But question the Zeitgeist most of all.

❖ **In the evening, look over your day and discover the mistakes you have made,** then resolve to fix them. Also find at least one victory everyday that you can offer to GOD.

❖ **Thank GOD every single day,** in the morning and at night, for all your blessings and even for your pains and sufferings. St. Francis thanked GOD for the sun, the moon, brother Fire, and sister Death.

❖ **Eat last.** After honored guests, the women, children, and even the animals. Guillaume d'Orange (Sir and Saint William of Gellone) always fed his horse first, before he allowed himself to eat.

❖ **Do not think you are powerful enough to accomplish these virtues immediately, or all at once.** Work on them one or several at a time. Remember how Benjamin Franklin approached his 13 virtues.

Fortitude

❖ **You have heard it said "that which does not kill you makes you stronger". This is not true.** It is how you react to suffering and pain that makes you stronger or weaker. If you use pain and suffering to make yourself closer to GOD, to focus yourself on excellence, and to purge your soul, you grow stronger. If you become a bitter and cynical fool because of what you have suffering, you slide backwards—you grow weaker.

❖ **"Thank GOD—every morning** when you get up—that you have something to do which must be done, whether you like it or not. Being forced to work, and forced to do your best, will breed in you a hundred virtues which the idle never know."—Charles Kingsley

❖ **Practice some form of martial arts every day,** especially brutal or vigorous training. By that I mean something that is especially grim or painful. This might manifest as a hundred push-ups done on the knuckles for one person, or long and lonely shadow-fighting in a forest for another. Even if you go on a trip, and must perform calisthenics in a tiny room, or isometrics in a chair, do not neglect this activity. Such practice, done every day, will make you used to pain and struggle, mental stress and purposeful discipline. They will become your treasured companions.

❖ **Read stories about people who have suffered tremendously** but have come through it all with honor. Research your family tree to find the people who have suffered much and who have done much, and then know that their blood flows through yours. If you can't find anyone in your lineage who is worthy, adopt some honorable person who suffered much and achieved much. Make them your family.

This is the true use for pride. Not arrogance, which is the bloating of one's ego, but an understanding that one must live up to one's capabilities and one's ancestors. Anything less is worthy of nothing but shame.

Control of Emotions

❖ **Begin this by controlling the simpler emotions and feelings.** Hunger is a good place to start. Simply refuse to eat a meal when you are hungry. For one afternoon, try this. Then try one whole day, as long as your physical health is good and fasting will not over-burden you.

❖ Choose another emotion to tackle. **Wrestle with fear**, by constantly placing yourself in a fearful situation. Spend the night in a graveyard if you have a lively imagination. If you have a fear of spiders, place your hand in a garden spider's web. When you come away unscathed, you will discover how the irrational has such control over us, and yet has no substance.

❖ **Consider yourself when you get angry.** Ask yourself, what makes me angry and why. What is the real reason for your anger in this or that situation? Anger is a secondary emotion, the first emotion is pain. Something pained you, or frightened you, but you only experienced the anger, because the pain or fear hid, even from yourself. In a thousand years, will this situation matter? Consider the grave. Think about GOD and HIS peace. **There is only GOD.** All other things, including you and I, the human race, the planet earth, and the universe itself, will pass away to dust. Remember what St. Teresa of Avila said.

❖ **Anger is a common emotion** over-wrought in this modern age. For men, to dwell on anger and discuss it does little good. Instead, do something useful, and try to fix the situation if possible. If not, do not curse or scream, for that simply gives energy to the anger, and fixes nothing. Use that rage to crush a punching bag or wield a practice sword. Turn such energy into something positive.

❖ **Meditation can quiet the emotions**. Meditating on breathing is an excellent way to quiet the clamoring of fear, anger, worry, and the other emotions which burden the human race.

❖ **Do not allow yourself to dwell on worries in the middle of the night**. You are most vulnerable then to mental and spiritual attack, for your energies are at a low-ebb, worries seem to expand, and you feel weakness most acutely. This is a time for prayer.

❖ **Most all the Deadly Sins use emotion as their weapon**. We will discuss how to tackle them more fully in Book II, *Beat the Devil*.

Courtesy

❖ **Plan to show courtesy to a stranger at least once a day**. Look for the opportunity and get into this habit. Do not forget your friends or your enemies. Make sure you have shown courtesy, generosity, and magnanimity to both friend and foe every day. Eventually, the goal is to show courtesy all the time, to everyone.

❖ **Begin with the small courtesies**. Opening a door for someone, etc. Even the small courtesies will force you to consider the needs of others.

❖ **There should be no cursing around women**. Many moderns assume this prohibition signifies a kind of weakness on the part of the woman, as if the knight is worried the cursing will harm the woman's sensitive ears. How silly. I do not curse in front of my parents or superiors, or even in polite company. Does this mean I consider my parents, superiors, or polite company somehow too weak?

If you are showing an honored guest your house, do you first take them to the garbage-disposal, or offer to open the garbage can? No. Thus, one should not curse in front of others, especially women. (Cursing is a habit that draws one's mind into laziness, and stifles the imagination. I have known people who can no longer speak without a curse word sprinkled into every sentence, as if they are addicted to this habit.)

❖ **It is best to avoid bodily functions around women** and honored guests as well. All these small observances teach reverence and self-discipline along with courtesy.

❖ **Greet people with respect, even if you do not enjoy their company.** Learn everyone's title, if not their name.

Focus on GOD

❖ **Set aside time to pray every day.** This seems so simple and basic, but to set aside time is to struggle against the daily demands and trifles of the world to focus on GOD. If you must, use a timer, but insist on your time with GOD. Think about, as you pray, how the LORD of the universe is listening to you. Focus on thoughts of HIM, and when other thoughts try to barge in, and they will, gently push these imposter thoughts aside, meditating on the word of GOD, or the image of GOD in your mind.

❖ **Dedicate what you do to GOD**, whether it is work, driving, practicing martial arts, playing a game, drawing a picture, etc. Everything is done through GOD and in GOD.

❖ **Continuously ask yourself, what will bring greater glory to GOD?** What can I do to help GOD's kingdom on Earth? This is the quest of St. Ignatius himself. Read his *Spiritual Exercises*, which is a brilliant work by one of the greatest of spiritual masters.

❖ **Do something for GOD every day.** Going to church is not done for GOD. Praying is not done for GOD. These things do not help GOD, but us. Nor is the Kingdom of GOD on earth much advanced by taco or cake sales. Ask seriously, what can I do to help GOD's kingdom today?

❖ **Consider yourself a stranger**, outside the world of humans.

❖ **Wear something that will always remind you of your commitment to GOD.** Whether it is a ring, a necklace, even a tattoo. Experiment with ways to remind yourself of GOD every day.

Grappling with Purity

❖ **The proper incentive** for Chastity is necessary, because for so many men, it is very difficult. Consider that one is neither chaste to please a grandmother, nor even to reach Heaven (as Sir Joinville and Kierkegaard point out). A true knight is chaste and pure in mind, body, and spirit, in order to walk ever closer to the presence of GOD, to avoid the traps that lead one away from HIM, and to continue to fight for HIM with all available energy and skill.

❖ **We should endeavor to surround ourselves with friends who are good, honorable, and decent people**. If our friends indulge in indecent activities, it will tempt us to do so as well. St. Augustine points out that the choice of one's friends is very important.

❖ St. Teresa of Avila and Father Scupoli both insist on the **importance of avoiding opportunities and situations that may lead to unchaste thoughts and actions**. Scupoli describes sexual temptation as a fire that could engulf a man as easily as a bale of straw. Do not get too near. We should know our limitations. Avoid images, conversations, entertainments, places, internet sites, or people that might tempt us toward dishonor.

❖ **Resolute focus on GOD** can keep one from the disaster of unchaste thoughts and actions. Keeping guard over our thoughts, night and day, and gently chasing out anything that does not help our quest for focus on GOD will strengthen us. Light focused becomes a laser beam strong enough to cut steel. Light defused is weak and cannot make a jewel sparkle properly.

❖ St. Paul reminds us that we always have **the option of marriage**. Not everyone can be a priest or a Galahad. Know your limitations, and make wise choices.

❖ **Within marriage**, many do not escape the temptation of infidelity. The key here is to guard against even a fleeting thought of infidelity. Marriage is holy, and held by the knight as the highest type of vow and promise. Know better than to place yourself in situations where you will be tempted, find friends that are faithful to their spouses and take it very seriously, and keep important work before you at all times. These will help avoid such a despicable and loathsome trap.

❖ **Prayer cannot be over-emphasized**. Whether the enemy comes with thoughts, or physical temptations, prayer is a great shield and weapon. Focus on the suffering Christ, who suffered for all of mankind, and hide in His wounds.

❖ Because we are human, we are susceptible to failure. When we fail, whether in pursuit of purity or any other virtue, confession helps us climb back into the battle. Think and determine how the enemy got to you. **Analyze your weaknesses and strengths**. And then try again. Thank GOD that HE is merciful.

❖ The Ascetics knew that even **small pains of the body can distract from temptations**. Monks all over the world still place stress on the body through waking up early, fasting, praying at odd hours, strenuous exercise, and work to ease the clamor of temptation.

❖ **Refuse to listen to voices of weakness**. I mean the voices that insist that somehow you are too weak to resist. Such voices are only fearful that you will win success where they failed. Taking on sexual temptation is like fighting a true dragon, if you take weak advice, you risk your life and soul.

❖ **Never laugh at sin**. Never think to yourself that chastity, purity, and sexual temptation are small things, of little import. If you do laugh at these important concerns, like so many do in our world, eventually sin will be laughing at you while its foot is on your neck.

❖ As always, **find heroes and role models who are chaste and strong**. Look for heroes who find power in their self-control, who even revel in their emotional strength and focus. Emulate them, and not the emotionally-crippled pygmies that seem to populate the globe.

❖ **The libido is a great store of energy**. There must be a way to harness this energy for positive means, instead of sexual temptation. Great and strenuous missions, diverse activities, even hobbies can help channel this energy into the river of self-discipline.

❖ **Death is, in many ways, the opposite of sexual thoughts**. As Epictetus always recommends, keep Death and sobering images always before you. Upon waking every morning, and before going to bed, the samurai would imagine and force themselves to envision the thousand ways they could experience death. Every cut, every drop of blood, every bruise, every gasp, they would see in their minds, from mortal sword duels to falling off a cliff.

❖ **Two kinds of sexual temptation exist, physical and mental**. After even some training, the knight should be able to resist the physical temptation of a questionable woman with ease. It is the thoughts, the sexual temptations that flow through the heart, that are much more sneaky, disastrous, and difficult to guard against. This deserves careful consideration.

THE SECOND PILLAR OF HONOR

COURAGE

Burn from my brain and from my breast
Sloth, and the cowardice that clings,
And stiffness and the soul's arrest:
And feed my brain with better things.
—Gilbert Keith Chesterton, *A Ballad of a Book Reviewer*

To know what is right and not do it, is the worst cowardice.
　　　　　　　—Confucius, Analects, bk 2, ch. 24

The fear of the Lord is the beginning of wisdom.
　　—Proverbs 1:7, 9:10, Job 28:28, Psalms 111:10 in the
　　KJV, (with Psalm 110:10 in the Douay-Rheims Bible)

The fear of the Lord is the beginning of love . . . and he
who fears the Lord will tremble at nothing.
—Ecclesiasticus 25:16, 34:16, of the *Douay-Rheims* Bible

You will not fear the terror of the night,
Nor the arrow that flies by day,
Nor the pestilence that stalks in darkness,
Nor the destruction that wastes at noonday.
A thousand may fall at your side,
Ten thousand at your right hand,
But it will not come near you."
　　　　　　—Psalms 91:5-7 of the World English Bible

> I have a rendezvous with Death
> At some disputed barricade . . . .
> At midnight in some flaming town
> When Spring trips north again this year,
> And I to my pledged word am true,
> I shall not fail that rendezvous.
> —Alan Seeger, *I have a rendezvous with Death*

> He that knows how to live, need not fear Death.
> —Lao-Tzu, *I-Ching*, 50

> In telling a lie, the spirit commits treason against itself.
> —Martin Buber, *Good and Evil*, pg. 7

Courage Itself

Just as there are three kinds of strength, so are there three kinds of courage. There is physical courage, as in a child finally confronting a bully, or a warrior standing against a hundred foes. There is moral courage, such as a righteous priest facing down an evil mob, or a man deciding to do the right thing against selfishness and ridicule[487]. Then there is spiritual courage, which has its anchor in Faith, as when a man ponders the grave honestly, or a saint faces a demon[488]. All of these types of courage become one in the heart of the knight[489].

The Battle of Rhodes

The year was 1480. The knights of the Order of St. John had fought their best for four centuries against two enemies. One foe being suffering, for the knights took care of the poor and weak, feeding 2000 of the hungry a day from their great hospital (hence their name "Hospitallers"). The other enemy being the Saracen, as the knights called them, who were the Arabs and Turks under the banner of Islam. At this time, the knights

---

[487] (Stalker, 1902) pg.42,43,44
[488] Ibid.pg.46-49, (Athanasius, 1980) pg. 64
[489] (Lull, 2001) pg. 48, (Holmes, originally 1980, electronically 2002) pg. 37

and most Christians were convinced that the Islamists were the arm of the Devil himself.

Now the knights of St. John looked over their surrounded fortress on the island of Rhodes, their last outpost in the Mediterranean Sea. This is what they saw:

In the first line of attack, coming up the beach from the booming ocean, were the Bisha-Bazouks, mercenary soldiers whose sole occupation was rape and pillage. Behind them were the Ottoman officers of Mehmet II, who were to drive the Bisha-Bazouks before them, allowing none to turn back on pain of death. Behind them, marching with steel nerve, came the Janissaries, Islamic marines trained from infancy to kill and destroy with fanatic intensity. After them marched the main army of Mehmet II, some 70,000 strong, outnumbering the Rhodes knights 100 to one. And behind them, nearly seventeen feet of iron, the "Basilisks", cannons that thundered loud enough to be heard hundreds of miles away, and firing an iron ball seven feet in circumference. And behind these, the Turkish armada, sporting the pride and force of the Islamic navy. All of these with the concentrated aim of destroying the Knights of St. John[490].

The knights were literally caught between the devil and the sea. Being only about 600, with about 2000 paid troops, the knights might have been forgiven to consider surrender. The odds were mightily against them, and many historians find it amazing that they decided to defend their island against so many. But these knights were Hospitallers, and like the Knights Templar, were sworn to never surrender before the enemy[491]. In their eyes, that would be like giving in to the Evil One. They had fortified their little island as best they could, and under the leadership of their commander, Pierre d'Aubusson, they prayed and prepared for victory or death.

A constant bombardment of cannon and Greek fire had swarmed down upon the defenders of Rhodes for weeks, until the walls of the city defenses were little more than rubble. But d'Aubusson and his knights had prepared well, and they waited on walkways along the ruined walls for the waves of warriors to storm in a violent sea of hand-to-hand combat. Perhaps an impossible fight, yet this was the time when an

---

[490] (Bradford, 1972) pg. 90-95
[491] (Reston, 2001) pg. 37-39, (Howarth, 1982) pg. 114, (Gautier, 1989) pg. 26

individual man, with courage, backed up by skill and armor, might be able to turn the tide and beat the odds, as long as his bravery held[492].

Hope began to fail the knights, however, when the defense towers surrounding the city fell one by one, and finally the entire island looked to one bastion left, the tower of Italy. Here the Bisha-bazouks swarmed over the walls and along the parapets, until they had smashed everything and thundered toward where d'Aubusson and some twelve knights raised their massive swords to meet them.

How many battles have been turned by the guts and sheer courage of a leader who is willing to put himself in harms way for the sake of his men!? D'Aubusson and his knights crushed all who ran against them, until a spear cut through d'Aubusson's breast plate and punctured his lung. Their great leader fell, mortally wounded, and so did their hope, but the knights steeled themselves and refused to give in as hundreds of Bisha-bazouks and Janissaries strove to fill in the gaps left by their fellow attackers[493].

Here, the chroniclers disagree. Some say a huge, burning cross spread across the sky above the tower, totally disrupting the Turks. Others say that the very flags of the Hospitaller order, with images of St. John the Baptist and the Virgin Mary across them, seemed like terrifying spirits to the Bisha-bazouks, unfamiliar as they were with any picture or image. Others would say that the Bisha-bazouks simply overcrowded themselves on the parapets, finding themselves crushed between the fanatical Janissaries on one side and the small band of armored, fanatical knights on the other, and panicked. But all the historians agree on one thing, the Ottomans' courage shattered against the knights' will, and they fell off the parapets to their doom or pushed away from the defenders, scattering backward out of the city and into defeat[494].

The Island of Rhodes was saved by the implacable courage of the Knights of St. John, and this set off a string of victories and stalemates against the Islamists lasting for nearly a hundred years.

Forty years later, the Islamic Ottomans tried to take Rhodes again with a force considered to be 200,000 strong. Many historians think that medieval observers exaggerate troop numbers, but even if the above

---

[492] (Bradford, 1972) pg. 96, 97, (Barclay, Gospel of Matthew volume 2, revised edition, 1975) pg. 76, (Vauchez, 1993) pg. 60-61, (Matthews, 1998) pg. 68

[493] (Bradford, 1972) pg. 96

[494] Ibid. pg. 97

number is hyperbole, half that number would have still meant the knights were outnumbered more than 100 to one again! L'Isle Adam, leader of the Hospitallers at this time, again refused to surrender and held up a terrific defense for eight incredible months. Finally, the Rhodian townspeople themselves could stand no more onslaught and surrendered from beneath the knights' feet! But the knights' valor had won great respect from the Moslems, and the Sultan Suleiman gave the knights peaceful and honorable passage, even providing ships for the knights if theirs were too badly damaged[495].

Courage, in these examples, is the deciding factor. If one can keep his courage longer than his enemies, one can expect victory or a glorious death.

Heroes of True Courage

Many are shocked by the brutality of stories such as these, in their minds the violence in these pages reflecting animalistic viciousness. They say that even an animal can have personal courage in facing death and pain. Even an animal may demonstrate amazing bravery battling difficult foes or overwhelming odds, for the sake of self-defense, or defense of a loved one.

Are these stories truly "animalistic viciousness"? Brutal examples have confused them, for the bravery of animals in self defense and the pursuit of survival is called ferocity[496], and Courage shines above it like the sun above the moon. True courage is illuminated by Wisdom and discernment, aimed at the fulfillment of Honor and right, not selfish goals. Careful inspection reveals the goals of the Hospitaller knights to be far more than simple self-preservation. And thus dwells the difference.

The Hospitaller knights were not just fighting for their lives. They could have surrendered and perhaps saved themselves. No, they fought for the sake of Christianity and the West, keeping the Moslems from gaining a foothold upon Christian ground, holding back another wave of the Saracen horde. In their minds and hearts, they were standing against the onslaught of evil incarnate. For the knights on those fateful

---

[495] (Bradford, 1972) pg. 113-119
[496] (Stalker, 1902) pg. 36

days at Rhodes, Malta, Lepanto, and every battlefield for all time, they were fighting for the preservation of their religion, their beliefs, and their sacred honor.

[It is appropriate that all the battles to protect Christianity emphasize the involvement of knights: the Crusades, the battles of Jan Sobieski and Charles Martel, El Cid and at Lepanto, each protecting the entirety of Christian Europe from the advance of Islamic domination and Moslem tyranny.]

In a wider sense, knights show courage and face death for righteousness, face destruction for holiness, face pain to protect the innocent, face annihilation simply for what they understood as good and right. No obstacle is too great. The knight's courage is a hammer, smashing every barrier in pursuit of honor[497].

The enemies may change. They may be physical, mental, or spiritual. The battle fields, the tactics, the obstacles will fluctuate, but the goals remain the same. The greatest knightly battles are fought for righteousness, justice, and Honor, no matter the horror, the pain, or the humiliation. Physical courage becomes a branch of moral courage, and moral courage a branch of the spiritual. Courage, true courage, then is that which the knight uses to reach through pain and hardship in the pursuit of righteousness[498].

This requires a hero. A hero with every courage. Such a hero is, and must always be for all time, a knight. The blending of physical and moral courage happens over and over again in the life of true knights and saints.

Moral Courage

"To know what is right and not do it is the worst cowardice."
—Confucius[499]

The most difficult kind of courage is known the world over as Moral Courage. Beyond physical courage, Moral Courage demands the strength to stand up for what is right and true, in the face of all resistance, peer

---

[497] Ibid. pg. 34-36
[498] (Stalker, 1902) pg. 44-47,
[499] *Analects*, bk.2, ch.24

pressure, ridicule, persecution, torture, and death. Unlike in this modern age, when goodness and righteousness are somehow seen as effeminate, the ancients identified Courage and Virtue together, so that the very roots of the word Virtue is tied to Manliness and Courage[500].

True Courage and virtue, indeed, are brothers, and cannot be found without the other[501]. Ramon Lull, in his great treatise on Chivalry states "Then if all you find is nobility of Courage, ask of it faith, hope, charity, Justice, strength, temperance, loyalty, and other noble virtues. For in them is the nobility of Courage; by them is defeated the heart of the noble knight from wickedness, from treachery, and from the enemies of chivalry"[502].

The mixture of virtue and valor, absolute courage and the purest of missions, unselfish devotion in the face of death, all of these knightly traits find their culmination and apex in the life and struggle of one man. This man, whom the whole history of the world revolves around, is the model used by every true knight, and the ultimate symbol of Moral Courage. This man is Christ Jesus.

The Moral Courage of Christ

"What made me respect Jesus greatly," one atheist admitted to me, "is that he knew what was going to happen, and he still went through with it. He still chose to follow through with his mission. That is impressive. That makes me want to be a Christian more than any preaching, singing, Bible thumping, or other argument."

Even an atheist, an outsider to religion, can recognize moral courage in the mission of Jesus, if they are willing to honestly analyze it. For the true Messianic mission to save the world comes with a terrifying personal price.

Anyone raised in full Jewish tradition, as Jesus, was well aware of prophesies of the Messiah and how this Messiah would save the world,

---

[500] (Stalker, 1902) pg. 18-19, 37-39, 44- 47

[501] "Courage is not simply one of the virtues, but the form of every virtue at the testing point"—C.S. Lewis, *The Screwtape Letters*, Letter 29, February 1942

[502] (Lull, 2001) pg.48

but would have to be a "man of sorrows, well acquainted with grief"[503]. Jesus would have been well aware of the Law of Moses and the story of Abraham, and how there is no remission of sins without the shedding of blood[504]. The Messiah was to be a lamb of GOD, led to the slaughter. According to Scripture and Church teaching, Jesus not only knew the torture and death that was coming for him, but knew the details of each horror in depth. Not only because he was taught these prophesies from a young age, but also because he was the focal point and the center of the plan of Creation[505].

The plan, all along, was for the Son of Man to suffer and die for the sins of the world, for the lamb to take upon himself the sins of humankind, even as the sacrifices in the Temple, even as the lambs die for someone else's sins, to redeem the whole world[506].

Being divinity, he understood this plan very well, and, being a man, he also suffered from its anticipation, feeling emotions as other men.

What would it have been like, for Jesus Christ to know, even as a boy, the kind of death he would face? To feel ghosts of the nails in his hands and feet, the as yet ethereal crown of thorns, the whisper of the flagrum, the weight of the Cross, as he went about his daily life, year after year. Did he feel the holes in his hands as he worked with his father? Did he feel the spear in his side when he breathed? When he touched the wood of any carpenter's trade, did he envision the rough wood of the Cross, which would eventually tear at his back?

In his 30th year, Christ journeyed into the desert[507] to prepare his mind and body for his mission of the Gospel, even then knowing where it would lead. The desert, a mirror of the wilderness after the Exodus from Egypt, was traditionally known as a place of introspection and focusing, elimination of distractions[508], and penance, but also a dwelling place of Evil spirits[509]. In Jesus's case, he journeyed into particularly brutal northern portion of the desert of Judea. "Other deserts may be

---

[503] Isaiah 53:3

[504] Hebrews 9:22, Deut. 21:9

[505] Ernest Renan: "The whole of Creation is inconceivable without the Christ." (Barclay, Gospel of Matthew volume 2, revised edition, 1975) pg.76

[506] John 3:14-15, (Sheen A. F., 1990) pg. 73, (Anthony Schraner, 1981) pg. 172

[507] Matthew 4:1, Mark 1:12

[508] (Barclay, 1975) pg. 63, (Bonaventure, 1978) pg. 134

[509] (Talbot, 2005) pg. 15, 17, (Athanasius, 1980) pg. 7, (France, 1997) pg. 20, the veil is thin in the desert

like a deserted cemetery, over whose tombstones the traveler steps without horror," Fr. Maas observes, "but this country offers a perpetual death-bed scene, life always struggling against death without decided victory on either side"[510]. In this lonely, terrible place, as Christ was finishing 40 days of disciplined meditations, the Evil One came to him.

There was no shock of such an appearance, no real surprise. Christ and Satan met as two old adversaries. No greetings were exchanged, no silly salutations. Both of them knew why they had come.

Always looking for a weakness, the Devil began his temptations.

"These stones around here look like bread. You're hungry; why don't you turn them to bread and eat." Already, the Ancient Foe was attempting to move Christ away from the rigors of the spiritual life, away from disciplines and asceticism, and away from the ultimate pain of the Cross[511]. The Devil failed miserably, for the Son of Man knew full well the importance of self-control and self denial, hallmarks of the Cross.

Christ said, "Scripture says, man is not to live on bread alone, but by the Word of GOD"[512].

Then the Evil One turned to more subtle matters. He brought Christ Jesus to a tall mountain, perhaps the one Fr. Maas identifies as Quarantania, which rises almost perpendicularly 1,300 feet out of the desert floor[513], and is located on the road from Jericho to Jordan in the desert of Judea.

The Devil gestured to the vast lands visible from this vantage point. "The whole world is mine and I can give it to whoever I choose. Follow me, give homage to me, and the whole world will be yours." The Devil aimed his comment directly at Christ's mission—to conquer the world, to seemingly win it for GOD—but the Evil One offers an alternate route to avoid the Cross. "Imagine the good you could do", Satan might have said, "If you control the world now, without waiting for the Cross. Give homage to me and the world is yours now, without the pain."

"Scripture says, you shall give homage and worship the Lord, your GOD, alone." Christ responded, unshaken in his focus[514].

---

[510] (Rev. A.J. Maas, 1952) pg. 52, footnote
[511] (Sheen A. F., 1990) pg. 61
[512] Matt. 4:4, Christ is quoting Deuteronomy 8:3
[513] (Rev. A. J. Maas, 1952) pg.52, footnote
[514] Matt. 4:10, Christ is quoting Exodus 23:25 and Deuteronomy 6:13

Nonplused, the Devil suggested another way to avoid the Cross, this time daring to use Scripture to summarize the plan.

"If you are the true Son of GOD, throw yourself down from here, and the Angels will save you." This taunt would echo the jeers of the onlookers 3 years later, when Christ hung on the Cross, his mission nearly complete. "If he is the Son of GOD, why doesn't he save himself and come down from the Cross. Why doesn't GOD or the angels save him?"

Satan, in an indirect way, was suggesting another escape from the Cross, this time by exercise of Divine power. The Cross was a hard road, brutal and slow, compared to the working of wonders and miracles that would wash the world in astonishment, and would certainly win the flippant human race, at least temporarily.

"The angels won't even let you smash your foot on a stone." The Devil reminded him. "They won't let anything happen to you, if you only command them!"

"Scripture says not to tempt the Lord, your GOD." Christ said[515].

The Devil left Him then, as Luke says, "but bidding his time". For the Evil One would return, in time to try one last temptation[516].

Many modern religious people, as well as non-religious, forget that Christ was a man and GOD, not an automaton, nor a robot; He could have chosen not to suffer the Cross. Not only did Christ suffer as a man, he had free will as a man, coupled with the intellect of GOD, thus he knew full well the other options open to him besides death on the Cross. He could have side-stepped all the pain of crucifixion and instead blasted all his enemies, even brought an army of angels to wipe all evil-doers from the Earth. "My kingdom does not belong to this world. If it did, armies of angels would be fighting to keep me from the clutches of evil men"[517]. But this, as Christ knew, was not the Father's will. While Christ's intellect showed him all the actions possible, it also reminded him that there could be no redemption without blood, no redemption for the world without the Cross.

As Calvary drew closer, even as Christ walked to Jerusalem with his disciples, the tension and terrible anticipation of the Cross wore on

---

[515] Matt 4:7, Luke 4:12, Christ is quoting Deuteronomy 6:16
[516] Luke 4:1-13
[517] John 18:36

Christ's mind. He revealed something of this to the apostles, especially to Peter.

Peter was horrified. "You can't allow this to happen! You should not go to your death!"

Jesus rebuked his sternly. "Get behind me, Satan!"[518]

Without knowing it, Peter had echoed the sentiments, if not the words, of the Devil himself, spoken 3 years ago in the desert.

Jesus was truly alone, even now, for not even his disciples completely understood his mission, or what he had actually set out to do. Christ, from the very beginning, had planned to suffer and die for all Mankind.

Now, at Gethsemane, the Mount of Olives, the place where olives would be gathered and then crushed to make oil, Christ Himself would be harvested and crushed, if he allowed it. He was being offered a cup of terrible pain, where if He chose it, he would have to drink of suffering and death unto the dregs.

Even Christ's friends seemed to abandon him. The Disciples, Peter among them, were to pray near-by, but, unaware of the great danger, they kept falling asleep[519]. Their lack of vigilance and inability to understand Christ's mission separated them from their master, as if by continents and worlds. Christ was alone with his agony.

Christ, as the Son of GOD, had the power to be obedient to GOD's will and plan, or choose another way. Once again, the Tempter, Satan, emphasized the other ways[520]. Once again, Christ felt very much like a mere man, with fears and pains. He saw the terrible suffering of the Cross that was coming, and He shuddered.

The Devil may have supposed victory was near.

Scripture says the tension and terror was so great that night in Gethsemane, Christ sweated blood[521]. Some have considered this to be hyperbole on Luke's part, to emphasize Christ's human suffering. But many doctors, including Dr. Pierre Barbet, in his marvelous book, *A Doctor at Calvary*, testify to the very distinct, though rare, possibility, of this phenomenon. Called haematidrosis, extreme stress causes an "intense vasodilatation" of the capillaries directly below the skin, bursting when

---

[518] Matt. 16:23

[519] Luke 22:39-45

[520] (Rev. A.J. Maas, 1952) pg. 55, Fr. Maas suggests that the Devil returned in Gethsemane for a final test

[521] Luke 22:44

they come against sweat glands in the tissues. These flood the sweat glands with blood, and the sweat and blood join to bead upon the skin, giving the impression of literally sweating blood[522].

More than the dread of coming physical agony and death, the Cross meant not only a torturous demise, but the taking on the sins of the whole world. Neither is this some metaphysical hyperbole or melodramatic metaphor. By taking the Cross, Christ would suffer inhuman and unfathomable spiritual punishment for such a burden, the entirety of justice and punishment meant for the whole human race and for an eternity of blackened sin. Pascal writes "This is a suffering from no human, but an almighty hand, for he must be almighty to bear it . . . . And thus, Jesus is left alone to the wrath of GOD"[523].

Christ's agony drove him to his knees. Only once, says Pascal, does he complain. Only once does he pray for things to be different. "Father, if it be your will, take this cup from me." Then, twice, he prays "Yet not my will, but yours be done, Father."

From the pit dug by the sin of all humankind, Christ's courage erupted like an inescapable and penetrating beacon of Holy Fire. Christ reached for the Cup of the Cross. He acknowledged, even through his dread, that this terrifying Cross was the only way to defeat sin and the Devil, and save mankind, all other ways being illusion. The Cross was the Will of GOD, and no pain, no horror, no terror, no power could tame the bravery and valor of the Son of the Living GOD. Christ grasped the Cup of Death, with the grip of absolute conviction and absolute courage. He chose the Cross and destroyed the Devil's hold on the world forever.

Thus, through His absolute moral courage, Christ is forever known as the GOD Hero, the Savior of all Mankind[524].

Courage in Every Place and At All Times

In the footsteps of Christ, a knight is always in greatest glory when he fights for others, especially for a victim of some injustice, even if it is

---

[522] (Barbet, 1953) pg.70

[523] (Pascal, 1966) pg. 312-313, *The Mystery of Christ* from the fragments of *Recuel Original*

[524] Isaiah 9:6 from the New American Bible, revised edition, sometimes translated as "mighty GOD"

a stranger. Sir Bors does not hesitate to defend a woman from a rapist[525], Saint George gallops to the aid of a city brutalized by a dragon[526], St. Max Kolbe dies a torturous death to defend a father of a family he will never meet[527], and St. Joan suffers humiliation and a burning pyre to free a nation from foreign domination[528].

Inside or outside of battle, the knight must possess the highest moral courage[529] to struggle for others. It is common that even without imminent bloodshed, a knight or saint, in the footsteps of Christ, must still face prejudice, peer pressure, public scorn, hatred, all sorts of calumny, torture, and persecution for his belief, for his insistence on Honor, and for his persistence in what is right, wholesome, and good.

St. Martin[530] and St. Patrick[531] risk slavery and death to rescue whole populations from ignorance and superstition, while Sir Beckett and Sir More labor under sovereign displeasure and receive martyrdom to save religion from manipulation by the crown.

St. Francis and the Hospitallers make themselves servants of the poor and sick, while St. Aquinas perserveres on a mission that brings scorn and ridicule from his own family[532].

Sir Ramon Lull turns himself into an intellectual weapon to free Moslems from their mental chains. When he left his beloved home to preach the Gospel across the sea, he purposefully sailed directly for the Moslem world, and certain death. He knew the Moslems could not stand such a mission, and would eventually kill him, even though he carried no sword[533]. His Moral Courage overcame his fear, and their hatred.

His men were shocked and horrified when Sir Rodrigo De Bivar, El Cid, offered a seat at their table to a leper. How can he demean himself, some of them must have thought, to give your seat, your water, your food, and even your room to a beggar whose skin would soon fall to pieces? El Cid not only did all these things, but did it proudly, as if he gave this

---

[525] (Malory, 1962) pg. 400
[526] (Morgan, 2006) pg. 45
[527] (Ellsburg R., 2001) pg. 351
[528] (Spoto, 2007) pg. 18 of intro
[529] (Lull, 2001) pg. 48
[530] (Daniel-Rops, 2002) pg. 26-27
[531] (Patrick, 1998) pg. 24
[532] (Barron, 2008) pg. 17
[533] (Zwemer, 1902) pg. 29-30, 33,36-37, (Ellsburg R., 2001) pg. 384-385

respect to a king[534]. And he was right. For Christ always said that to do a good turn for the least of His brothers, is to do it for Him, the King of Heaven and Earth.

Saint and Pope Leo knew that no army on Earth could stop Attila the Hun and his terrifying hordes from attacking Christian Rome. Therefore Leo decided to stop Attila by himself, and, without weapons or any feasible defense, armed only with righteousness and GOD's own grace, marched up to Attila's tent, demanding the warlord to spare the great city[535].

Centuries earlier, a group of Roman soldiers from Agaunum decided that it was not right to punish people in their region for being Christian, nor did they think it right to sacrifice to pagan gods, being Christian themselves. The commander of their legion insisted. The soldiers refused. The legion surrounded them and threatened with their swords. The group of soldiers still refused, but offered no physical resistance. Known as the Martyrs of Agaunum, they refused to back down and were hacked to death[536].

Perhaps the most maligned knight in literature, Don Quixote, himself on an impossible quest, captures Chivalry in its shine of Moral Courage in a sentence when he sings "To fight for the right, without question or pause, to be willing to march into Hell for a Heavenly Cause"[537]!

Never in the history of the world was there such a list of men and women as the knight and saints, devoted to Moral Courage, to righteousness for its own sake, to charity for all, even in the face of every storm.

The Truth is that even without physical battle, Moral Courage demands terrifying mental and spiritual struggle. With or without the shedding of blood, the knight and saint must wage terrible resistance within themselves and against the world. A knight who faces the terrors of such ethereal battle must summon the same iron courage and will as the knight who stands and fights monstrous foes in the flesh.

But must courage always take the shape of a strong, powerful knight? Young Agnes, a little girl of twelve, decided to risk torture and death instead of selling her virginity. For this, she was stabbed in the neck, a traditional form of execution in the Roman world at that time. She later became known as Saint Agnes. If this tiny girl can show superhuman

---

[534] (Matthews, 1998) pg. 84
[535] (Jones, 1994) pg. 159
[536] (John, 1995) pg.29
[537] (Darian, 1972) from Dale Wasserman's musical *Man from La Mancha*

courage in the face of terror for what she believes, how much more can we, powerful men, show great courage in the face of what we fear, fighting for what we know is right[538]?

No Excuses

Courage remains a difficult road. But if a child of twelve can show such an excruciating shine of courage, then we must do no less. And what of the elderly, and infirm, what is expected of them?

In 1565, after the Order of St. John had moved to the island of Malta, the Islamic Sultan of the Ottoman Empire again threw a force of between 30,000 and 40,000 crack troops against the knight's mere 540. La Valette, leader of the knights, also had command of around 4,000 militia men, but even he worried at the prospects, because the Sultan also was amassing an equal number of Iayalars, who might be compared to today's suicide terrorists, so much did they seek death[539].

At one point, when all seemed lost and a huge portion of the defending wall was blasted away, La Valette, now seventy years old, jumped into the battle with barely any armor and his sword, holding back the tide of attackers until his men could fill the breach. When reinforcements finally came, the Islamic Ottomans had already lost heart, and news of a relief force only gave them an excuse to pull out[540].

This Battle of Malta, considered by some one of the most famous battles ever[541], was more amazing than even the Rhodes battles. And it had been won by the sheer daring of a seventy-year-old man who had left his breastplate behind[542].

And the lame? The crippled? Can they grasp courage as well? King Baldwin IV took up the sword for his home and his faith even when leprosy stole his eyesight and made it difficult to close his fingers on

---

[538] (John, 1995) pg.29
[539] (Bradford, 1972) pg. 145
[540] Ibid. pg. 164
[541] (House, 2010-2013)
[542] (Bradford, 1972) pg. 163, (House, 2010-2013)—House considers La Valette to be Washington, Churchill, Robert E. Lee and Cromwell all rolled into one man!

the handle[543]. He secured his hand to the sword with a rag and leading 500 men along-side the Templars, totally trounced and routed the great Moslem leader Saladin at the battle of Montgisard[544] during the Crusades. Saladin only escaped with his life because he had a faster camel than most of his men.

The battle of Lepanto, involving both the Spanish and the Knights from Malta, effectively destroyed the Turkish maritime power in the Mediterranean Sea[545], and established the knights as legendary figures. Here too, another knight, Miguel Cervantes, would suffer two shots to the chest and another nearly destroying his left hand, but he fought bravely against impossible odds, and would later write the first novel in history, *Don Quixote De La Mancha*[546].

When asked if it was worth it, to lose a hand for the preservation of his world and his faith, Sir Cervantes replied, "I lost the movement of the left hand for the glory of the right"[547].

The Bloodless Warrior

Must one spill blood to be brave?

Most knights are great warriors against any foe, but at least one knight decided to wage war only against spiritual enemies, refusing to raise any weapon against another man. His main target became the pagan gods of wood, earth, and stone. And one day he became a great and pacifistic saint in the roll-call of the Medieval Church.

Even in this modern day, one might find a picture of St. Martin of Tours, above the entrance of many houses. My martial arts master had a picture of Martin, full in Roman regalia, above the entrance of the *dojo*, or training hall. A Roman soldier by profession in the years around

---

[543] (Read, 1999) pg. 152
[544] (Howarth, 1982) pg. 132-133
[545] (Hickman, 2013), (Dougherty, 2012) pg. 70-71
[546] (The New Encyclopedia Britannica in 30 volumes, Macropedia, volume 3, 1982) pg. 1183, article by William C. Atkinson
[547] (Kelly, 1913) pg. 22, note 1

337AD[548], Martin had been trained as any other warrior of the time, brutal and precise, completely capable of killing in the wars of the Roman Legions.

A change came about when, after hearing the Christian message, he began to treat the slaves of the Roman army with great respect. The traditional picture shows Saint Martin, on his horse and in armor, cutting his cloak in half with a short sword to share it with a beggar.

Even though his fellow soldiers insisted he was insane for doing this, he continued to treat even slaves well[549]. They made fun of his new-found "hobby" of respecting and helping beggars and the poor, unable to understand why a soldier of the most powerful country in the world would want to bother with the "trash" of humanity.

The next turn of Martin's character did not make his friends and officers laugh. They did not even smile when he announced he would not again raise a weapon against a human being. In the tradition of Justin Martyr, Tertullian, and Origen, Martin was laying down his arms forever[550].

"Coward!" Sneered his fellow soldiers, and the emperor at the time, Julian the Apostate.

"I have as much courage as any of the greatest warriors!" Martin exclaimed. "Place me in front of the army of the enemy, with no weapon, and I will face them all. But, even as they run to kill me I will not raise my weapon against them. How many of the Roman Legions are brave enough to do the same?"[551]

Not satisfied with courage against human assailants, Martin turned his attention to the gods. Pagan gods littered the landscape, sometimes as statues in temples, and other times as sacred trees. These trees were worshiped by the Druids, and many other mystery religions of the time. So venerated were these groves, they were even the recipients of human sacrifice. Martin decided to face these god-trees as well.

One day he appeared with a mighty ax, and people gasped as they saw him walk up to the holy tree.

---

[548] (Jones, 1994) pg. 172
[549] (Daniel-Rops, 2002) pg.29
[550] (Gautier, 1989) pg. 5
[551] (Daniel-Rops, 2002) pg. 30, (Encyclopedia Britannica, volume 6, 1982, micropedia) pg. 653

"You cannot possibly mean this!" The people cried. "The gods will punish you!"

Is it possible that Martin feared these trees for a moment? In those ancient times, many believed that there were many gods, and although GOD might be the greatest, other gods could inhabit the world and bring disaster upon people. Martin did not flinch, and whether he believed in the possibility of nature spirits or not, he raised the ax.

"Wait!" Some people cried. "Before you strike! Pit yourself against the god in the tree. Place yourself under the tree as it falls and stop it with your own hands. If you can catch the tree without it hurting you, then we will believe your GOD is greater than the spirits of nature."

Martin looked at the huge tree before him. "Very well. I will show you that GOD is greater than any tree."

So Martin chopped away at the sacred wood, and then placed himself in the path of the groaning giant. Incredibly, his courageous hands easily stopped the tree as it fell. He lowered it to the ground, himself unharmed, but the cult of the trees fell irreparably harmed forever

In today's politically correct world, attacking pagan beliefs and splitting god-trees would be seen as great sacrilege. But for Martin, it was war. A war as real and dangerous as any armed conflict. He waged his most holy GOD against the ignorant ravings of a fierce people who sacrificed humans to plants.

Although I do not agree with total pacifism, one cannot deny the terrifying moral courage of this man.

This courage confirmed the Catholic Church in pacifism for 600 years, until Alexander II and Urban II realized a holy warrior[552], in the shape of the virtuous knight, was called for at last to battle the rising tide of Islam and the corrupting force of villainy across the world.

The Battle from Within

Before a knight and saint can face the external foes of this world and the next, he must face himself. Moral courage is internal fortitude and character, the courage to do what is right, in the face of all pain, all

---

[552] (Vauchez, 1993) pg. 71

disaster, all trial, and even against one's own self. The greatest foes come at us from within[553].

It is difficult to face hardened enemies or death by torture. But to have the courage to face one's own internal enemies, that is even greater[554], and perhaps even more awesomely surprising. These enemies I speak of, these internal foes, are known as moral weakness, lack of self-control, lack of character, loss of temper, self pity, the lure of dishonesty, the temptation of lust, the glamour of greed, the lies of evil, and unadulterated Selfishness, all the illicit desires and unreasoning fears that human nature is heir to. These are great and implacable enemies of the saintly knight and hero, and require the greatest courage to defeat because they reside within, and use our own drives and energies against us.

With this courage, the knight combines the hero and the saint, defeating all opponents, ignoring fear of death and loss, while gaining total self-control, discipline, personal integrity, and self-lessness. The true knight uses these saintly traits to battle the inherent flaws of his own humanity, even as he uses physical courage to combat physical enemies.

Such Courage is doubly difficult because many times it remains unseen, hidden within the mind, will, soul, and emotions of a man. The battle between two men is obvious, the battle between armies, un-ignorable, but the battle within a man? The war he wages upon himself to restrain himself, to force himself to instead do what he desires not to do, this goes unnoticed. A man wins neither fame nor praise for the struggle within himself. No fanfare heralds him and no trumpets announce him, no battle fields speak of his glory, yet his inner power is the well-spring from which all great actions flow.

Courage and Calmness

Another aspect of this inner well-spring of courage is the ability to control panic. The knight does not allow terrible circumstances or

---

[553] "The History of the Renowned Don Quixote de la Mancha, Volume: 2 (1743) by Miguel de Cervantes Saavedra; Chapter: VIII, Page 75; Sir Thomas Browne, *Religio Medici*—"Every man is his own greatest enemy, and as it were his own executioner."

[554] (Scupoli, 1945 edition) pg. 6

changes of fortune to trouble him to the point of hysterics, as the faithless might[555]. He accepts what GOD has sent[556].

Rodrigo de Bivar, El Cid, was to be exiled several times, sent from his home and family because of the jealous and wrathful schemes of lesser men who had the ear of the Spanish king. As Rodrigo looked back at his empty home, he nearly wept. "My enemies have done this," he said, but added "GOD be praised for all things"[557].

As Saint Augustine watched the whole world seemed to crumble around him, surrounded by heretical enemies and the sureness of helpless death, he quoted the Psalms, and then Plotinus, "No great man is he, who thinks it a great thing that bricks and bridges fall and men die"[558].

As Saint Francis felt his body finally fail him and his spirit slipping away, he welcomed his "sister" death, and composed one of the most beautiful and poetic prayers ever devised[559].

Courage on the Road

Morality is the battle between the two sides of a man, the side that knows what is right and wishes to do it, and the side that either ignores what is right or wishes to do wrong.

Moral Courage is choosing the right side. But fears, desires, and instincts get in the way, not to mention the social and cultural confusions that drift up in every time and society.

For Saint Francis, one of his first tastes of this battle occurred on the dusty road of Assisi[560]. As a youth of 17, he had been filled with the Crusading spirit and the drive to be a knight[561], but his hopes of winning glory for GOD and himself on the field of battle had been crushed by a reoccurring illness that left him physically delicate and weak[562]. Now, in an attempt to rest his body and to ease the incessant swarming of ideas in

---

[555] Ibid. pg.14
[556] Job 1:21
[557] (Matthews, 1998) pg.86
[558] (St. Augustine, The Giants of Philosophy, produced by Carmichael and Carmichael, Inc., 1990)
[559] (Brady, 1983) pg. 22, (Spoto, 2002) pg. 199-201
[560] (Chesterton, 1989) pg. 42-43
[561] Ibid. pg. 41
[562] (Spoto, 2002) pg. 41

his head, Francis roamed the quiet paths of his boyhood home in solitude. The sound of a small bell came to his ears. He stiffened, because he knew what the bell meant.

A leper, complete with his warning bell, approached.

In St. Francis's time, Leprosy was a true horror that stalked the land. Without any warning or apparent cause, a person could be struck by this grotesque and disgusting disease. Victims would first suffer the numbing efforts in their limbs, and then these limbs would eventually blacken, decay, rot, and fall off, disfiguring the victim for life. Finally, the disease robbed him of necessary blood, an almost guaranteed death sentence.

Worse was how the victims were treated. Everywhere they went, they were labeled as things of terror, disease carriers, and cursed of GOD. Once someone showed any sign of the disease, they were ostracized from society and forced to wander the roads as beggars, their bodies slowly putrefying and falling apart as they walked toward their doom. Lepers were expected to ring a bell as they wandered, or were obliged to call out warnings, so that no one came too close. They were forbidden to enter a town, drink from a public well, or even venture to touch another person. Theirs was a lonely and disgusting death[563].

A great fear filled the boy Francis, but just as suddenly it occurred to him that Christ would have helped the leper in any way he could. Should he flee the leper, following his instincts and ride away, or should he welcome the leper as an unfortunate child of GOD? The battle within Francis was joined[564]. Presented with a moral choice, did he have the courage to make it? Knowing what was right, would he be brave enough to choose it?

Spontaneously, Francis ran toward the leper, embracing him as a long lost brother, sharing with him some kind words, and giving him a drink from his own supply. The leper broke into trembling sobs, while Francis, expecting the strangling smell of rot that always surrounded lepers, instead was greeted by the most aromatic smell of roses[565]. He would dedicate large amount of his time from then on to administering to the Leprous: begging for food for them, cleaning their wounds, being

---

[563] Ibid. pg 58
[564] (Chesterton, 1989) pg.42
[565] (Brewer, 1891) pg. 682, the Odour of Sanctity is similar to this

human to them. Such is a true Christian. Such is a true knight. Such is true Honor[566].

Francis had spent his youth desiring the inner strength and courage to be a knight. He found the courage to become one of the most influential saints of all time, and the Knight of GOD[567].

The Ox against the Prostitute

Courage on the battlefield or against terrible diseases is obvious, but such a trait is required by anyone who must engage opposition, whether physical, mental, or spiritual. Especially a man who sets for himself a moral or spiritual goal will find himself needing all his moral courage to achieve it.

One would think that in a life of solitary study, courage would not be necessary. But in his quest to rejoin reason and revelation, Thomas Aquinas had to muster the terrifying courage to resist one of the greatest enemies, the lusts of the world[568].

He always seemed the opposite of what people expected him to be. Thomas Aquinas was a bull of a man, called "the dumb ox" by his fellow students because of his sheer size[569] but quiet manner, and he did not have the ambition that such a large man might usually be expected to have. His family wasn't happy about that. They wanted their huge eighth son to be a powerhouse of politics, but he insisted, in his quiet way, upon being a preacher and beggar for the Catholic order of Dominicans.

His family sneered. Who could imagine this giant of a man as a beggar on the street! Besides, he came from a very influential family, and that family required him to bring power and influence to the family name, just as his other siblings had done.

---

[566] (Spoto, 2002) pg. 58, 60

[567] (Chesterton, 1989) pg. 16

[568] (Scupoli, 1945 edition) pg. 53—Lust requires greater defense and preparation to defeat

[569] (Chesterton, Saint Thomas Aquinas, The Dumb Ox, 2001) pg. 50, (Crawley, 2009)—Albertus Magnus, Aquinas's teacher, remarks "We call him the dumb ox, but in his teaching he will one day produce such a bellowing that it will be heard throughout the world."

His brothers, sick of his constant, if quiet, refusals, decided to take matters in their own hands. They vowed to put an end to all Thomas's foolish talk about being a worker for GOD and giving his life over to the service of the Church.

They kidnapped him and imprisoned him in a castle for two years[570], but when he still insisted upon being a Dominican, they hit on an even earthier plan. They agreed that what he needed to snap him out of all this spiritual "nonsense" was to get him a girlfriend.

When entering spiritual life, one reason why a knight or saint needs courage is how others will react. People will look down upon them, think them crazy, attack them physically and mentally, or, in this case, decide the honest impulse to higher things is a symptom of un-indulged libido. How demeaning, demoralizing, and insulting!

A lady of the night, his brothers thought pathetically, would take Thomas's mind off his spiritual focus and set him down to the earth, in a way that would convince him to begin an ambitious, earthly life of power and prestige.

One night, they sent a pretty, young prostitute up into the tower where Thomas resided. "Go on," They might have said. "He is strong but quiet and will not hurt you. All you have to do is seduce him and be on your way."

The girl, for her part, might have thought that since many men could be seduced easily with her charms, that this one would be no different.

Thomas sat in a room at the top of the tower, scouring tirelessly over stacks of books that he constantly surrounded himself with. He looked up from his studies when the knock came on his door.

He was surprised to find a pretty girl waiting for him on the other side, but when he discovered her mission, he became uncharacteristically angry[571] at the insult against his spiritual goals[572].

"Get out of here!" He bellowed, frightening the girl with the sheer volume of his voice and the power of his presence.

She had been paid to be persistent, but the Ox would have none of it. "Begone!" He bellowed again, and grabbing a hot poker from the fire,

---

[570] (Chesterton, Saint Thomas Aquinas, The Dumb Ox, 2001) pg. 39

[571] Ibid. pg. 44, Although St. Aquinas was usually quiet, this is clear example of Righteous Fury, as discussed in the Strength chapter.

[572] (Chesterton, Saint Thomas Aquinas, The Dumb Ox, 2001) pg. 43

waved it about and scared her out of the room, finally throwing the poker in her direction and embedding the metal into the wall.

Had St. Aquinas felt temptation? Perhaps he did, but he crushed it. Further, he prayed for more strength to defeat, once and for all, any lust that might try to invade his inner peace, his fortress of contemplation and solitude.

Nothing would impede Aquinas's mission to understand and be closer to GOD, not the wishes of his family, nor imprisonment, nor even the weaknesses of the flesh.

Moral Courage and the Rise of the West

A deep aspect of Moral Courage surrounds the ability to trust in the Truth.

As the Middle Ages wore on, more works of Aristotle found their way to Medieval Europe. Intellectual monks and clerics began translating and working on the great system of logic and science created by Aristotle, and many of them soon came to the conclusion that his system was the pinnacle of human thought concerning the physical universe up to that time[573]. His system seemingly contained every tool and concept necessary to understand the entire material universe, and the Medieval minds were greatly amazed and impressed.

There was only one problem. Aristotle's system seemed to contradict the Bible and Christian thought at several points. Many monks and clerics were distraught, fearing that they would have to choose between the greatest spiritual guidance and the greatest scientific system in creation. Some decided to totally abandon Aristotle, leaving him in the dustbin of the Church because of these seeming contradictions, choosing spiritual truth over corporeal understandings. Others decided to separate their understanding of truth, literally living in two worlds—Aristotle's for the factual world, and Christ's for the allegorical[574]. A few could not abandon the Philosopher, and chose him over their faith of Christianity,

---

[573] (Copleston, 1961) pg. 100-101, (Durant, 1953) pg. 82
[574] (Copleston, 1961) pg. 103, (Gilson, 1938) pg. 80

choosing science over religion in effect, seeing no way to bring into agreement the Master of the Greeks and the Master of Heaven[575].

Saint Thomas Aquinas, possibly the greatest thinker of all time, decided on a different route. He believed fervently, and with every atom of his being, that all Truth came from GOD, so there could not be any contradiction between physical truth and spiritual truth, there could be no battle between the great scientist and the great GOD— Hero[576]. Truth was the truth, because it had the same source[577], whether physical or spiritual. If Aristotle had the physical truth, and Christianity the spiritual truth, they had to be complimentary. Anything less was either a misunderstanding, or a miscalculation. Aquinas set out to prove these convictions, and his faith. He set out to make Aristotle's thoughts harmonious to Christian thought, without changing or compromising either[578]. He set out to make them into a beautiful, perfect whole.

Great courage was necessary, for the danger seemed very real. Some thought Aristotle's work could never be corresponded to religion, and anyone who tried was in danger of perhaps proving Christianity lacking. Other great thinkers in other traditions, as in Avicenna and Averroes from Islamic thought, had grappled with Aristotle as well, but suffered such a loss of their faith that they survived only with a sort of pseudo belief, bowing in defeated subjugation before the Philosopher[579]. Could the same fate await Aquinas, since he dared challenge the greatest Philosopher of the Ancient world? Could a man, intellectually honest with himself, science, philosophy, and Christianity, see the harmony in all four? Aquinas mustered his considerable courage, his open-minded unbiased intellect[580], and his confidence in his GOD as the origin of Truth, and proceeded where other great thinkers and even angels might fear to tread[581].

---

[575] (Copleston, 1961) pg. 104-105

[576] (Knowles, 1962) pg. 261-263

[577] (Chesterton, Saint Thomas Aquinas, The Dumb Ox, 2001) pg. 66, (Gilson, 1938) pg. 84, (Knowles, 1962) pg. 261-262

[578] (Chesterton, Saint Thomas Aquinas, The Dumb Ox, 2001) pg. 64-65

[579] (Copleston, 1961) pg. 66

[580] (Knowles, 1962) pg. 256-257

[581] Alexander Pope's original phrase, *An Essay on Criticism*, 1709

Years went by of toil and sweat, of mental effort and anguish, with Aquinas working fervently at his wooden desk in his tiny cell. Night and day flowed by, and the outer world began to take on an air of illusion. All that mattered was the task; all that was real was the work at hand[582].

That tiny cell, lighted with a miserable candle, might as well have been as big as the universe, lighted with the brightness of a thousand super novas, for when Aquinas emerged, he held in his hands the synthesis of science and spirit, the connection between Aristotle's logic and the love of the Almighty GOD. Aquinas had done what no other mind could. He had corresponded Aristotle to Christ, science to theology, writing enormous books that the Catholic Church still uses, nearly a thousand years later, as the bedrock of its understanding of Creation itself[583].

This brilliance and courage might have had an unintended and unforeseen consequence. Aquinas had assured the study of the material world and of science to be a very acceptable and appropriate practice for Christian learned men. In Christiandom, then, all the fruits of science, such as technology, could be found and accepted as long as they were used appropriately[584].

Other traditions did not fare so well. Because Avicenna and Averroes could not find the connection between Aristotle and the faith of the Koran, between the science of the day and their belief, their failure created a rift between the religious learned men and science, causing a pall to spread across scientific inquiry in Islamic lands[585]. Philosophy and science became enemies in many parts of the Islamic world, and their shining tradition of scientific advancement suddenly began to fade.

Aquinas's moral courage, bolstered by his trust in the truth of the Christianity, paved the way for the eventual technological superiority of the West[586].

---

[582] Aquinas's focus and ability were legendary, requiring several assistants taking dictation at once

[583] (Knowles, 1962) pg. 256

[584] Ibid. pg. 257

[585] (Gilson, 1938) pg. 84

[586] (Woods, 2005) pg. 64-66

Moral Courage in Dark Times

Compared to these mighty men, I am simply a petty complainer, a man whose concerns lean toward selfish luxury, a man whose courage wanes when troubles wax. Because of my moral weakness, when the day is not going as I would like, when I am in a foul mood, Moral Courage and treating others with kindness and respect seem even more difficult than usual. When I feel myself surly enough to ignore others in need, I remember St. Blaise.

St. Blaise lived in little more than a cave in a ditch, away from the common lives of men, but somehow he also worked as the Bishop of Sebaste in Rome during the year 316 AD. People who wished advice or assistance would travel to his little hermitage, and be pleasantly surprised by this old man's hospitality, dirt poor as he was. Everyone knew him as a kindly, pious physician, capable of curing people by medicine or miracle and his popularity soon attracted the deadly attention of the Roman Emperor Licinius[587]. The law of the Emperors said that no man could be a Christian in public, but here this man was not only a Christian, but living a life of honored asceticism and faith, winning converts and helping people in bold disregard for the law.

The Emperor sent a team of soldiers to capture this unusual and kindly man. They found him sitting outside his tiny cave, surrounded by animals that seemed to have come to him to be cared for, since each had a little wound or condition that the saint attended to[588]. Truth be known, the soldiers were frightened. Some of the animals were dangerous beasts, lions and hawks, and the soldiers hesitated.

"We've hunted all through these parts for days." The soldiers said to each other. "We didn't even see any animal during all that time. How is it that he has all these beasts?"

They shook their heads and went on with the arrest. "You there, old man, come out from among those creatures! The Emperor wishes to speak with you."

---

[587] Some say Diocletian, as in (Voragine, 1275, 1483)

[588] (Voragine, The Golden Legend, Readings on the Saints, translated by William Granger Ryan, 2012) pg. 151

"My sons, be welcome." Blaise said. "Do not fear the beasts, they will not harm you. As for me, I will go with you"[589].

Blaise knew these men were escorting him to torture and death, and yet, he greeted them with gentleness. He also knew, even now, even as he walked to his doom, that people would come from all over to ask for favors, even miracles.

Sure enough, as the soldiers led him, surrounded with spears, on the road to the Emperor, a woman ran up to them carrying a small child in her arms. "Help me!" She cried. "He swallowed a bone and now he can't breathe!"

With the bravery of a woman in dire need, she pushed through the soldiers and laid the child at the saint's feet. Blaise looked down at the boy whose face held the tortures of desperate choking, his eyes glazing, his skin turning blue.

"We don't have time for this!" Growled the lead soldier. "We have an appointment with the Emperor!"

Blaise bent down and raised his right hand over the boy's throat, touched him there, and then made the sign of the cross. Immediately, the boy breathed, his eyes fluttering open, the obstruction somehow cleared[590]. The woman screamed for joy, and hugged her son to her chest as the soldiers hesitated. What was it they had just seen? But without another word, they led the saint forward.

Not long after, another woman ran up, pulling her hair out of her skull. "My last pig!" She was crying. "My last pig is gone, carried off by wolves! What will I feed my family! My husband is dead and I have no one to help me!"

"Go back home." Blaise said gently. "I will talk to my friends the wolves. Your pig will be returned to you, I promise."

When the woman went home, not sure what to expect, she saw a huge wolf, with her pig in his mouth, carrying the swine like a mother cat might carry a kitten. The wolf brought the pig right up to the door of her home, dropping it there as if in delivery[591].

Never did Saint Blaze ask for a respite from these requests, even though his own life was in danger, and his freedom was at an end. Never

---

[589] (Voragine, The Golden Legend or Lives of the Saints, translated by William caxton, edited by F.S. Ellis, 1483)
[590] Ibid.
[591] Ibid.

did he ask for a reward or a returned favor from anyone, not even a "thank you", and it was his day to die. Never did he complain of helping others, while he went to his death.

But legend does tell of a favor returned for the saint. When the widow with the pig found out that Blaise would be imprisoned and then tortured, she slaughtered the pig and brought the best parts for him to eat. She also brought a candle to cheer him in his dark cell. For this kindness, Blaise told her to always bring a candle to church and light it, and she would receive blessings from Heaven. To this day, across the world, Catholics honor St. Blaise with a blessing of throats between two candles, on his feast day.

The knight who took on the Nazis

To face the terrors of starvation, the agonizing and constant grind of the stomach, and the slow deterioration of the body and brain for a higher cause, such would qualify as the pinnacle of courage. And to volunteer for it? Such was the power of St. Max Kolbe, the Knight of the Immaculate.

Once Kolbe was ordained as a Franciscan Catholic Priest, he immediately set about creating an organization called the Knights of Mary Immaculate, involving himself in everything from creating the largest religious community of friars in the world in Poland, to writing journals that spread the Catholic faith, to helping orphans in need[592].

When the Nazis invaded Poland in 1939, Kolbe knew what was coming. Many told him to escape, and happily offered him several routes, but Kolbe refused to leave. No knight or saint leaves orphans or friends behind to die, and he said he was determined to "suffer and die in a knightly manner, even to the shedding of the last drop of my blood . . ."[593].

As he knew would happen, he was arrested and sent to Auschwitz, one of the most infamous Nazi concentration camps. For three months, hard labor and hardly any food battered him and he suffered a relapse of Tuberculosis as he struggled in the camp. How hard it must have been to remain full of courage and consolation, when all around him death and

---

[592] St. Augustine, as bishop, also refused to leave his congregation in the face of Visigoth invasion

[593] (Ellsburg R., 2001) pg.351

pain held dominion. But he never lost his faith, and instead became a shining example to his fellow prisoners[594]. He continuously uplifted their spirits with prayer and brave inspiration, dumbfounding the Nazi officers.

But things were to get worse. When another prisoner escaped, the Nazis decided to punish the escapee's cell block and chose ten men for a terrible, slow death. These ten were to spend the rest of their days in an underground, cement bunker, without food or water or light, to slowly starve to death as the camp went about some semblance of life just meters above. It would be a premature burial—buried alive.

Ten prisoners were chosen at random, lined up and prepared to descend into the living tomb. One screamed out that he would never see his family again, weeping and inconsolable.

Kolbe stepped forward.

"Let me take that man's place." Kolbe said.

"Don't you know what is to become of these men, Priest?" The Nazis must have asked the saint. "Don't you know what is to become of you if you join them?"

Indeed, Kolbe did know. He knew the suffering he had experienced up to that point was nothing to what he would encounter in the bunker. He had suffered from Tuberculosis as a child, so he knew what such wasting of health could be like, but this was to be far more acute, with no hope of life and no ceasing of agony until the last rattling of his poor breath would escape the final desolation that would be his body. He had no illusions. He was prepared.

The Nazi commandant and the man he relieved looked at him with disbelief, but Kolbe insisted. He was simply fulfilling his courageous ambition, to die as a knight would, suffering for others and saving lives, no matter the cost.

Within the bunker, he and the others suffered for 14 days in semi-darkness, with the gnawing of every present hunger, thirst, and misery. He helped the other prisoners to pray and kept watch over them as they slowly died, one by one, until, when the Nazis came to kill who was left with injections of Carbonic acid, they found him still sitting up and peacefully praying. Three others were still alive, in and out of consciousness, surrounding him on the ground. Kolbe made sure that he was the last to receive oblivion, the last to be relieved of the pain[595].

---

[594] Ibid.
[595] (Ellsburg R., 2001) pg. 351

The Leper King

And what of the courage it takes to face the life of disease, and one's own personal horror and fear?

The story books paint young kings as typically looking forward to a wonderful life of ease, wealth, and peace, away from troubles that demand self-control and Moral Courage. But the kingdom of Jerusalem was no fairy-tale kingdom, and Baldwin the IV was no fairy-tale prince. When he was nine, his tutor and chronicler, William of Tyre, noticed that the boy-king did not flinch when his companions played rough games with him, pinching violently his arms to see who could take the most pain[596]. Indeed, Baldwin did not have pain at all in his arms, and William realized this was no indication of an incredibly high pain threshold; this was a sign of the most dreaded of diseases: leprosy[597].

Other boys might have given up, retreating into a fantasy world by occupying his mind with the pompous joys of wealth and privilege, ignoring impending death and duty, but Baldwin knew he could do no such thing. The Kingdom of Jerusalem was not only a kingdom, but a symbol for all Christendom everywhere, and it was Baldwin's singular responsibility to lead that kingdom through one of its most difficult times, surrounded and hounded by powerful enemies on every side. The weight of proper kingship fell heavy upon his cadaverous shoulders, but he accepted it wholeheartedly and completely[598], regardless of the leprosy that ate away his body, bit by bit. In the Medieval world, a leper was seen as an outcast, a pariah, but King Baldwin's indomitable spirit awed and unified those in his kingdom, and they accepted him naturally as their king.

The Islamists, with their powerful leader, Saladin, on the other hand, referred to this strange and regal man as "the pig"[599], identifying him with the filthiest animal in their culture. Despite their taunts, Baldwin IV would not let the disease or the enemies of Jerusalem eat up his spirit, or his courage.

---

[596] (Howarth, 1982) pg. 130

[597] Ibid.

[598] (Howarth, 1982) pg. 132

[599] So it is said in Roland Broadhurst's translation of *The Travels of Ibn Jubair*, pg. 316

It was not long before he would need all that courage. Saladin was on the move again, and, after consolidating his power in Egypt and overrunning three other Christian strongholds, the great Moslem leader turned his eyes on Montigisard, the next step in the attack on Jerusalem itself. Thinking he had King Baldwin barricaded at Ascalon, he felt nothing could stand between him and conquest of all the Christian lands of the Middle East.

King Baldwin bound up his right arm, now useless from leprosy, and gripped his sword with his left hand. Even crippled, he would meet Saladin in open battle.

The Christian forces surprised Saladin not far from Montigisard, King Baldwin leading his men as they attacked Saladin's plunder-weary army. The Christians were outnumbered nearly six to one, but still they drove the Moslems from the field in a terrible rout; Saladin himself only escaping capture because he rode a racing camel[600]. By the time Saladin arrived in far-off Cairo, he had lost most of his men.

Disease and stress continued to take their toll upon King Baldwin. Forced by his ailments to give up his active leadership of Jerusalem, he reluctantly handed over regency power to Reynard of Chantillon. Baldwin hoped against hope that his kingdom, divided as it was with in-fighting and fraternal bickering, would remain in peace.

After such a terrible defeat at Montigisard, it took some time before Saladin was ready to try again. This time he attacked the incredibly fortified Templar castle called Kerak, an almost-impregnable structure in Moab. Once again, the capture of this fortress could be used to springboard a full invasion of the kingdom of Christian Jerusalem.

King Baldwin, now almost totally crippled, would not let the most important Christian kingdom of the East fall on his watch. Struck lame and completely blind by leprosy, he now engineered a chance to defeat the great Islamic General yet again, and perhaps for good. He knew that Regent Reynard was residing in Kerak at this very moment, and if he could gain Reynard's assistance, he could smash Saladin's forces between his knights and the great walls of the castle, literally catching Saladin between a rock and a hard place. Unable even to rein his horse, King Baldwin demanded someone lead him into this last battle, for even near

---

[600] (Howarth, 1982) pg. 133

death and almost paralyzed, he would not avoid battle with the enemy of his kingdom and Christ[601].

Outside the walls of Kerak, even as his men attacked, throwing themselves against the castle walls and attempting to scale them, Saladin gave a small chivalrous flourish. Learning that a wedding was being celebrated, he told his catapults not to hammer at the tower that contained the ceremony, but instead to fire away at other targets. For this, he was sent a slice of the wedding cake. As he munched on dessert, Saladin planned the sacking of the castle and the slaughter of its knights, savoring this beginning to the main course of his war, the capture of Jerusalem.

Suddenly, King Baldwin and his men charged to the rescue, effectively pinning Saladin and his forces in the plain beside the castle. Very effective but outnumbered, King Baldwin only needed Reynard of Chantillon to aid him, and they would smash Saladin once and for all here, in the shadow of Kerak. But Reynard was moved by other ambitions, rendering Baldwin's forces too small to press his advantage. Saladin slipped away, limping home to prepare another attack[602].

This is not only the story of courage for King Baldwin, but a study in the lack of moral courage in many other men at the time. Soon after the battle of Kerak, Baldwin's tortured body finally gave out. Christian Jerusalem fell not long after his death, the city a victim more of petty squabbles and lack of vision than to Saladin[603]. Unknown but decidedly different would be the fate of Jerusalem if King Baldwin had lived a longer life. But the life he did have he used to its fullest effect, showing greater inner courage than most men with full health and full opportunity. Sad to say, many other men charged with protecting this great city were more concerned with their own welfare.

How can a knight, or even a king, triumph if he is surrounded by duplicity, back-stabbing, and deception?

As the story of King Baldwin indicates, all battles begin with a steadfast and courageous control of one's self, weaknesses, and fears. We cannot begin to win for others if we do not first confront ourselves and take responsibility for our actions, regardless of our faults. One of the most important inner battles with ourselves will be the battle of honesty

---

[601] (Pernoud, 1963) pg. 136
[602] (Pernoud, 1963) pg. 136-137
[603] (Pernoud, 1963) pg. 137

within. Regardless of what others do around us, we cannot triumph until we are honest with ourselves, destroying all self-deceptions.

Such inner honesty, pure and brutal vision, is at the heart of moral courage.

Honesty

> I hope I shall possess firmness and virtue enough to maintain what I consider the most enviable of all titles, the character of an honest man.
>
> —George Washington[604]

Moral Courage, in everyday life, is simply Honesty; honesty with others, honesty with yourself, honesty with GOD, and Honesty in action. It is the power to face the truth, in all its forms, even within oneself, and to embrace it. Paul forced himself to look at the truth when he learned of his grave mistake, and accepted it. Moses told Pharaoh exactly what would happen if he refused to cooperate with GOD, a kind of honesty that could have killed the prophet. King Baldwin accepted his condition, and simply refused to let self-pity stop him, knowing that the fate of Jerusalem rested in his crippled hands, regardless of the circumstances. It takes great courage to be this honest.

Thus, lying is dishonorable and cowardly. When we lie, we are "fearful towards men and arrogant towards GOD"[605], since we conveniently forget GOD's law in order to avoid pain.

Generally, only two reasons to be dishonest surface: to avoid losing something or someone, or to avoid a hurt of some kind. But this is simply fear, fear of loss or pain, fear of ridicule, even fear of the loss of pleasure or peace of mind. People lie because they fear the consequences if they don't. To lie then is to go against Courage. To lie is to be a coward.

Many ancients connect cowardice with a kind of inner death. Shakespeare said that the coward dies a thousand deaths, the brave man only once[606]. The real death of the body is what faces the brave man, but

---

[604] In his *Letter to Alexander Hamilton*, August 28, 1788
[605] Proverbs 14:16
[606] From his play *Julius Caesar*, Act 2, Scene 2, and one of my mother's favorite sayings

the coward, through his own lies, deceptions, and avoiding destruction and pain, suffers a thousand "little" deaths. In his fear of death, the coward loses his Honor.

A knight fears nothing but GOD. He fears no man, no punishment, no ridicule, no torture, no loss. A knight is honest, because he fears only GOD. And he is totally honest because he is totally courageous.

As a knight then, always tell the truth, to everyone. To do less is to spit at GOD and Honor and to fear men instead. In the movie Excalibur, Merlin was asked what aspect of knighthood was the most important. "Honesty," He responded, "Yes, honesty, when a knight lies, he murders a part of the world"[607]. The "part of the world" he means could be a piece of the knight's soul, or literally a piece of mankind, since the knight is the pinnacle and moral compass of all earthly men. If such a compass sways or does not point true, how can the rest of the world hope?

The Legend of Sir Gawain and the Pledge Word

While everyone else was feasting and merrymaking for Christmas, Sir Gawain risked freezing to death as he cooked pine cones, the only thing he could find to eat, in a small kettle in the middle of nowhere. If the cold or hunger did not kill him, he was determined to keep to an appointment with his executioner.

Why would he do such a thing, even as the other knights were staying warm by the fire and exchanging gifts? He was keeping his pledge word.

The pledge word is the Chivalrous equivalent of keeping a promise. It is often said that a man is only as good as his word. A knight's honesty, and thus his Honor, hinges on how well he can keep his "pledge word"[608].

Sir Gawain, in this legendary tale, is the height of Chivalry[609]. He knew well the value of his word, and placed his promise over his comfort and even his life, as all knights should.

---

[607] (Boorman, 1981), see also (Buber, 1953) pg. 12—those who lie go down into nothingness
[608] (Gautier, 1989) pg. 67
[609] (Borroff, 1967) line 630-635, (Gerritsen and Melle, 1998) pg. 116

The Round Table company had just settled down for a feast when the front doors blew open and the Green Knight entered on a towering horse. A true giant of a man, and obviously a magical creature, being over seven feet high and completely covered with the color green, even his lips, hair, and skin. He held a gigantic battle-axe, also green and very sharp, in his massive, muscular hand[610].

"I have heard of the strength and courage of the Round Table Knights," He said loudly from his horse. "I have come to test this bravery and power. I challenge you, King Arthur, to a match, a game. I will allow you one strike at me with my axe. Make it a good and strong strike, for if I live, you must promise to allow me the same strike! Let us see how brave and strong you really are!"

It has been suggested that this "game" was a test of strength often used between two powerful warriors as a way to "feel" out each other's ability. Each would take a turn striking at the other with "no hold's barred" ferocity. But only one strike was allowed, and if this strike did not lay low the opponent, the opponent would then be free to attack in his turn with the same viciousness. A brutal game indeed, often leading to death.

Before King Arthur could speak, Gawain jumped to his feet. "I will accept this crude challenge which my king is too great to notice," Cried Gawain, "And I will give you a good hit, befitting the rude way you have treated my king and this court. And if you survive my strike, you may have your axe back and take your best swing."

The young knight took the axe from the giant's hand and waited as the Green Knight stepped down from his horse. Then with one clean strike, Gawain struck off the Green Knight's hairy head.

Gawain turned and started walking to his seat, assured the "game" was over. But he stopped as the audience groaned. The Green Knight still stood, and leaning down to pick up his own severed head, placed it back again squarely on his broad shoulders[611].

No one moved as the Green Knight gained his horse. The giant pointed at Gawain with the blood-smeared hand. "Remember your word," The Green Knight said. "You agreed to the rules of my game. You have agreed to receive a strike from me as terrible as the strike I received from you. But not today. I command you to visit me at my chapel, a year

---

[610] (Borroff, 1967) line 145-215
[611] (Moncrieff, 1976) pg. 204

and a day from now. And bring the Axe. There, in one year and one day, we will truly finish this game"[612].

With that, the Green Knight turned his mighty steed and rode out of the court, and into the misty forest beyond.

Sir Gawain could have done many things. He could have said magic was involved and thus any promise was forfeit. He could even have pleaded lack of sense brought on by temper or lack of years, or a host of other lame excuses.

He did none of these. He hefted the axe in his hand and set off to find the "chapel of the Green Knight", so that he might keep his promise. But everyone knew, he most of all, that his neck did not have the regenerative powers that the Green Knight possessed. Gawain had no magic to save him from the edge of the axe. When he left to find the chapel, he was riding toward certain death.

Gawain searched for a year and a day, and on the anniversary of his fateful strike, he placed his own head on the Green Knight's chopping block. A knight's word is his bond, and when he gives it, he will keep his word to the bitter end[613].

Because of this, it is important to promise only those things which you intent to carry out. Never give frivolous promises, or promise to anything that is impossible, or promise against the Code and GOD's law. If you make a promise that cannot be kept, you will be proven a fool, and if you make a stupid or dishonorable promise, you must fulfill it and suffer[614].

Honesty with Yourself

It is exceedingly difficult to be honest all the time, especially when the world constantly wants you to agree with it. But as torturous as honesty with others may be, the most difficult form of honesty is with yourself[615].

---

[612] Ibid. pg. 204
[613] (Lull, 2001) pg. 42, 71, (Moncrieff, 1976) pg. 428, 430,
[614] Proverbs 6:1-5
[615] Miguel Cervantes, "Make it thy business to know thyself, which is the most difficult lesson in the world", *Don Quixote*, Part II, bk. iv, ch. xiii

Here to, as we look at ourselves, there are fears to overcome. Paul of Tarsus knew them well. Fear of ridicule, fear of guilt, fear of the unknown, fear of simply being wrong. This is one of the things that made Saint Paul so great, he had the courage to face the fact that he had made a terrible mistake.

This courage, Moral Courage, is the rarest and most humble of all. I have known men who would fight any man or beast, risk death over trivial matters, but who didn't dare the moral thing because they feared someone would laugh at them. Worst of all, for these men, was admitting that they were wrong.

These men can't accept the blame for even the smallest error. But Paul's error wasn't small.

Who can tell the horrid struggle that must have raged within him? All his schooling, all his life had led him to his actions against the Christians, and now he had to face the fact that he was totally wrong. Men had died for his mistake, innocent men. No one had erred more than he, for Paul had warred against the GOD of his fathers, the GOD whom he loved. He had killed GOD's children. How could he live with himself now?

A weaker man would not have been able to face it, and would have ended his life or gone insane. But Paul had great courage, and he decided to use it by repairing the damage he had done to GOD's house. From then on, he went in to the world, preaching the very Gospel that he had rallied against before, until he stood, like Gawain, facing death, at the foot of a Roman chopping block[616].

He could have lied to himself, or denied the whole thing. Yet he had the raw courage to face himself and admit his sin. He looked himself strait in the eye.

Whenever we make a mistake and debate about covering it up, we should remember the honesty and courage of Saint Paul.

Another man who refused to lie to himself, and suffered greatly for it, was Johannes Kepler.

---

[616] Ignatius of Antioch, letter to the Ephesians, chapter XII

The Cosmic Mystery

Can we be honest with ourselves? If we look clearly, will we see clearly? If we strive for objectivity, can we actually gain it? Is it possible to be objective, even though everything around us is subjective?

It can be done. It has been done.

The year was 1595. Without knowing it, Johannes Kepler stood at the meeting of puritanical religious conviction and precise astronomical measurement[617]. He was an astronomer and a mathematician, firm in his belief in objective reality and trusting in actual observation and fact, but he lived in a time when even the fundamentals of scientific thought were yet to be formed. He was also a deeply religious man, firm in his understanding of GOD as foundation of all Truth and reality, but the world around him constantly tortured itself in mistrust and religious turmoil.

As many scientists today, Kepler was convinced that GOD had created the universe using exact geometric laws[618]. Even as a child, Kepler felt that GOD's thought must be serene and beautifully symmetrical, and all that HE created must contain the stamp of Euclidean wholeness[619]. Just like all astronomers and mathematicians before him, he believed even the orbits of the planets should draw out perfectly geometric patterns, have beautifully harmonious and steady motions in these patterns, and the most perfect geometric pattern in existence was the circle.

As a math teacher, Kepler stumbled upon a concept that was to influence his dreams for the rest of his life. While drawing the orbits of the six known planets of the time, and the five spaces between them, he suddenly wondered if these had anything to do with the five known "perfect solids" handed down from Pythagoras. It seemed that there was a connection, and why not? Didn't GOD think in geometric perfection? GOD was the ultimate geometer[620], and so, the orbits must fit inside of each other, just as the five perfect solids should fit inside of each other! "Kepler thought the two numbers were connected, that the reason there

[617] (Sagan, 1980) pg. 56, (The New Encyclopedia Britannica in 30 volumes, Macropedia, volume 16, 1982) pg. 369, by Jerome R. Ravetz, (Koestler, 1963) pg. 255, 258
[618] (Sagan, 1980) pg. 56
[619] (DiLiscia, 2011)
[620] (Sagan, 1980). pg. 57

were only six planets was because there were only five regular solids, and that these solids, inscribed or nested one within another, would specify the distances of the planets from the sun"[621]. He called this the "Cosmic Mystery"[622].

While he worked on his theories, shifting from job to job, avoiding religious persecution and war, he sheltered and nurtured these concepts, hoping that one day he would be able to prove them. They were really all he had. His wife did not understand his work and she resented him for it. The world around him kept exploding in terror and violence, several times running him and his family out of town after town.

He longed to understand the universe and see it as he believed it must be: a perfect and harmonious creation of a peaceful GOD.

He collected observations of the planets, studied and mapped out their orbits. But no matter how much he worked, he couldn't seem to make the orbits fit inside each other as in his "Cosmic Mystery".

Shaken, Kepler decided at first the observations had to be wrong, so he traveled to collect the most exact observations available in that time, from an astronomer named Tycho Brahe. To gain Tycho's observations took many months, because Tycho jealously guarded his information from what he saw as rival astronomers. Finally, Kepler was given the observations, but his elation evaporated when he discovered these more precise observations did not confirm his theories. What was worse, Tycho's observations of the orbits didn't seem to draw out perfect circles.

Most of the orbits were regular and harmonious, but the orbit of Mars seemed strange, non-circular, and given to weird movements. Kepler spent years trying to conform the Martian orbit to what he and generations of astronomers and mathematicians believed had to be right: circular perfection in a simple steady motion. But Mars revolted from a circular, simple motion by as much as eight minutes of arc[623].

Carl Sagan explains in his book, *Cosmos*, how small eight minutes of arc really are. "Now, there are 60 minutes of arc in an angular degree, and 90 degrees, a right angle, from the horizon to the zenith. So a few minutes of arc is a very small quantity to measure-especially without a

---

[621] Ibid., (Koestler, 1963) pg. 249

[622] (Sagan, 1980) pg. 57, (Koestler, 1963) pg. 247

[623] (Fowler, 1996), (The New Encyclopedia Britannica in 30 volumes, Macropedia, volume 11, 1982) pg. 519 by Michael J. Belton, and Micropedia Vol. 5, pg. 766

telescope"[624]. Some historians say the shape Kepler measured for the orbit of Mars was about .004 percent different than the circle, about half of one percent of a difference[625]!

To Kepler, eight or .004 might as well be a thousand. "If I had believed we could ignore these eight minutes, I would have patched up my hypothesis accordingly. But, since it was not permissible to ignore, those eight minutes pointed the road to a complete reformation of Astronomy"[626].

But for Kepler, it was a terrible blow. He had based his entire life's work on his theories of the "Cosmic Mystery", steady motions, and circular orbits, and now he watched them slipping away. After abandoning his dreams of a perfect, harmonious, circular orbital system, he described what was left as "only a single cartful of dung"[627].

Weaker men might have doctored the observations, quietly covering any discrepancies in order to keep themselves in the right. But Kepler refused[628]. He had the total courage to be totally honest, with the world and himself, even at the expense of his own dearest, lifelong dreams. He saw the truth as more important than anything else. A true knight must do the same.

Kepler did not lose his faith, he simply realized he was seeing creation in the wrong light, and that GOD had the right to create the universe as HE wished. GOD had formed the universe, not using simple Euclidian lines, but a more complex, intricate, and supple geometry much more delicate than formerly thought.

Kepler went on to establish the fact of elliptical planetary orbits and to develop three rules that lay the foundation of modern Astronomy, redefining and completely revising that science forever. Long after Kepler's death, and the other planets were discovered, scientists could see that Kepler's laws applied to these "new" planets as well.

In his very faith and devote imaginations, Kepler helped to form what we moderns see as science. With his original theory of the "Cosmic Mystery", he publicly defended with outspoken force, the Copernican

---

[624] (Sagan, 1980) pg. 61

[625] (Fowler, 1996)

[626] (Sagan, 1980) pg. 62,

[627] Ibid., (Fowler, 1996)

[628] (DiLiscia, 2011), (Fowler, 1996)

system[629]. In struggling with inaccurate data and forming the proper ability to discern accurate observations, some say that Kepler, 400 years ago, had a hand in perfecting the Scientific Method itself[630]. When secular humanists laugh at the much attacked "Intelligent Design" system, in their arrogance and ignorance, they do not realize that Kepler brought forth the very concept of science from his vision of the placid, serene logic of the Creator GOD[631].

Many believe that learning will somehow contradict GOD and the more we know, the less we will believe in GOD. Kepler's experience, as well as my own, has shown and proved that GOD is not contradictory to the facts, but essential to reality. GOD and true reason go hand in hand. GOD used logic and reason to create the universe, and thus humans can use logic and reason to understand creation.

When we have the courage to "look clearly", we will see "clearly", and serve GOD and the truth in ways perhaps unseen before. Courage and honesty go hand-in-hand with GOD's plan[632].

(Indeed. When someone asked why I wrote about Johannes Kepler, when he was no knight or even a warrior, I pointed out that his ideas had found a knightly friend in the world at the time: The Jesuits[633]. Kepler pursued truth like a knight, and other knightly men recognized this.)

To Search For Truth

Carl Sagan, in his book *Cosmos*, had a profound influence on my understanding of Johannes Kepler and his work; but Sagan, a confirmed atheist, insisted that Kepler's courage came from his scientific search for truth in the face of any superstition, whether his or the age in which he lived. Sagan did not realize that Kepler's courage was not in the search for truth in spite of belief (what Sagan calls "superstition"), but in the search for truth *because* of his belief. How brave would it have been for Kepler to ask questions without any belief whatsoever? Any child can ask a million questions without fear, simply because the child has no emotional or

---

[629] (Fowler, 1996), (DiLiscia, 2011)
[630] (Fowler, 1996), (DiLiscia, 2011), (Koestler, 1963) pg. 255
[631] (DiLiscia, 2011), (Koestler, 1963) pg. 261
[632] (Lull, 2001) pg. 42
[633] (Koestler, 1963) pg. 279

intellectual stock in the answers. But the man who faces the possible nullifying of his devout belief over answers to questions? The search for truth, in that case, requires a steel nerve.

There seems to be a kind of tension, easily discernable in today's world, between faith and the search for truth. Sometimes it is seen in religious faith. A man may be afraid to study science for fear that it may force him to question his beliefs.

In almost the same way, a political worker may find himself afraid to research a particular issue for fear that he might find his side proven wrong. By the same token, scientific atheists may sincerely dread religious discussion, since real theology, spoken from a real theologian, is a formidable and awesome opponent.

But I say to you, if your faith is in something real and true, you cannot allow yourself to fear knowledge. If we believe in something that is reality, then the facts and the knowledge we gain in our studies will eventually show that reality. In my experience, every time I felt information might attack my belief in GOD, I discovered that my fears were foolish, and my belief became strengthened through knowledge, not depleted by it. Whether it was through the study of science, philosophy, or comparative religions, my faith and, indeed, my knowledge of GOD, has grown. Surprising to some, my faith in GOD reflects the ancient saints and biblical heroes more now, after all my study, than when I started!

If our faith is real, then we should not fear knowledge. Kepler's faith was real, and at the end of his studies and at the end of all his disappointments, he discovered his GOD to be the Great Artist, perhaps not as the world saw HIM at that time, but how He truly was. "I am the Truth,"[634] said Christ, "And the Truth shall set you free"[635].

Yet, a search for truth on the scale of Kepler's, or my own on Chivalry, requires constant vigilance and exhaustive research. I constantly inundate my own views with questions, constantly flooding myself with new inquiries. Only the truth can survive infinite observation and questioning. Only the truth can survive total intellectual honesty.

---

[634] John 14:6
[635] John 8:32, the Revised English Bible

Intellectual Honesty

It is possible to want something too much.

A knight must not fall into this trap. He must avoid lying to himself, be totally and brutally honest with himself, see things the way they are and not the way he wants them to be. "To know thyself, which is the most difficult lesson in the world"[636]. This is the most difficult honesty[637], and the most difficult courage, of all, for "Lying to ourselves is more deeply ingrained than lying to others"[638]. Inner honesty is sometimes called Intellectual Honesty. It is ultimate honesty with yourself.

My father told a story about how, when he was young, many liberals in the medical profession seemed "just a bit more ethical than the rest of us". They seemed to "possess the higher ground". What was more, all the statistics and reports seemed to substantiate their theories.

But one day he attended a meeting for one of the most prestigious colleges in North America. The chairman of the meeting, an imminent doctor who always used references and research that backed his liberal views perfectly, and thinking he was in the company of only friends and liberals like himself, divulged an interesting secret. "Oh, I am not as prepared as it seems. When I need research or statistics to back my ideas, and none are at hand, I simply make them up. I know that no one will check on them, or verify them."

From that time forward, my father's views on the liberal, "progressive" community in his profession changed dramatically. He knew that when the facts disagreed with them, many of them could simply ignore the truth, sometimes twisting and even making up reports and research to fit whatever their views were. They "do not enter the kingdom themselves, nor allow others to enter"[639].

When I heard this story, I was not surprised, because I knew the philosophy of many of these "progressives"[640]. What does surprise me is that such people who make up research and statistics to "prove" their

---

[636] Cervantes, *Don Quixote De La Mancha*, Part ii, Book iv, Chap. Xlii

[637] (Barron, 2008) pg. 128, also Augustine's sermon 137, 4 (Augustine, 1986) pg. 148

[638] Quoted from Fyodor Dostoevsky

[639] Matt 23:13-14

[640] The "progressive" stance here is "Post-modernism", which teaches there is no objective truth

theories, lying intentionally and willingly, still believe in their theories! It is amazing they can sleep at night and live with their intellectual deceptions! My question is always this: if one must falsify research and reports to back up one's theories, why even support those theories at all? If you have to lie to back up your ideas, why do you believe them in the first place? And what is worse, how can you defend such ideas before others, intentionally steering other people from the truth, when you know you are wrong?!?

If you can do such a thing, you want something too much. You desire to force something to seem the truth, even when it is not. A lie can never be the truth, but if such illogic is used, we risk not only death, but a stupid death. We not only risk bodily demise, but the destruction of the soul[641].

Thus uncovered is the "post-modern" view of the Truth. "Post-moderns" believe that if they push an agenda long enough, hard enough, and back it up with enough "facts" loud enough, long enough, their ideas will become reality. Perhaps, if they wish hard enough, or if enough people believe it strongly enough, or if they rewrite history enough, or pass enough laws, their version of the "Truth" will come true. They will have molded the "Truth" to fit their claims. To them, "Truth" is plastic, and not real. "Truth" to them is in the eye of the beholder, without objective reality, so it can be molded to fit[642].

A knight knows the Truth to be the Truth. Reality cannot be altered by wishes or demands or ideas, no matter how eloquent or pleasing. The knight knows to search for and accept the Truth, no matter how disturbing or aggravating. Just as Johannes Kepler, a knight must choose the truth over his fondest dream[643].

I have struggled with this many times. But because I deal in reality and in the hard steel of Chivalry, deadly matters, and spiritual obstacles, I cannot ignore the real facts or close my eyes to the Truth. If I favor a sword because of its appearance, ignoring an inferior make, it will break in battle and my life will be threatened! If I proclaim a ward against devils, and have not tested it again and again, I am placing my soul and

---

[641] (Buber, 1953) pg. 7, a lie is the spirit's treason against itself, see Emerson, *Essays*, first series, 1841

[642] Not everyone who agrees with "progressive" views purposefully lie, but one must be careful

[643] (Sagan, 1980) pg. 67

the souls of others at risk! My soul and my knighthood, as well as my life, rests on my search for the purist Truth possible, wherever it may take me.

Which leads me back to Sir Gawain and the Green Knight. The story does not end with Gawain embarking on his long quest for the Green Knight's chapel and quite a lot happens before he arrives. At first, I intended to show Sir Gawain as a perfectly honest knight. It seemed to me, when I was younger, that his story did exemplify total honesty in the face of death, but as I read again all the versions of the story, I realized a problem.

All the versions have Sir Gawain resting from his journey for three days in a castle of a most generous warlord[644]. This lord loved to hunt and desired to have Gawain accompany him, but since the knight was nearly dead from his travels, starvation, and cold, he asked to rest during the lord's hunting trips. The lord agreed, as long as the knight agreed to a small game. The game consisted of the knight and lord exchanging whatever they had "caught" that day[645]. The knight was too tired to argue, although one must wonder what one would "catch" sleeping inside a castle room.

On the first day, as the lord went hunting, his wife came to spend the day talking to Gawain. The woman was beautiful and it soon became clear her intentions were less than honorable; yet Gawain, true to his knighthood, refused her advances. Instead, the wife gave him a quick kiss.

When the lord returned with a deer, Sir Gawain could only give him a quick peck on the cheek in return. This strange exchange went on for three days. After a while it becomes obvious that some sort of test is going on in this castle, and the listeners are supposed to realize it is similar to the "game" challenge of the Green Knight. But it is no game to Gawain. Just like Joseph in the Old Testament, the good Sir Gawain resists the amorous temptations of the wife and insists upon honoring her status as wife of his host[646].

It is on the last day that the wife presents a twist. After Gawain resists an especially long temptation, filled with seemingly logical arguments for adultery, the wife produces a special belt. She tells the knight that

---

[644] (Moncrieff, 1976) pg. 206

[645] Ibid. pg. 207

[646] Genesis 39:7-8, (Moncrieff, 1976) pg. 208-209, adultery and betraying a host were twin sins in the Ancient and Medieval world,

the belt is magical and can save him from all manner of death, especially a cut, as from a sword or axe. Now, the wife knows of the upcoming execution that Gawain faces, and she must be well aware of the salvation this belt may hold. She asks the knight to accept the belt as a token of her "unreturned love".

To my skeptical mind, such a belt would hardly seem tempting, since I know that such magic cannot exist. But for Sir Gawain, the implications are clear.

In one version of the story, Gawain feels somewhat abashed at refusing a lordly lady and accepts the belt to save her feelings, although he is doubtful of any saving power it may possess. In this version, he simply thinks the belt is too little of a trifle to swap with the lord's catch. Yet, in all the other versions, including the original version, Gawain accepts it as a short-cut from his troubles. With a magic belt, he can take the strike the Green Knight intends for him, and actually walk away, just as the Green Knight did, from certain death [647].

And this is the key, for in order to keep this belt, Gawain must use deception, pretending to have only received kisses, when the lord returns with a fox pelt. Thus Sir Gawain still breaks his word in the end, failing to reveal his final "catch" and concealing from the lord that which by rights is his. He uses deception, albeit a seeming small one, to escape the Green Knight's chopping block.

Marie Borroff, in her 1967 translation of the ancient story, offers an excuse for Gawain, saying "the most dangerous temptation is that which presents itself unexpectedly, as a side issue, while we are busy resisting another"[648]. But we, as knights, know too well that we can never excuse cowardice or dishonesty, even when we are caught off-guard. Sir Gawain knows this too, and must face the terrible fact when he is chastised by the Green Knight.

As a writer of a book on Chivalry, this is not the way I wanted it to be. I wanted Gawain to soar above all reproach, to face the Green Knight squarely and without subterfuge, to prove that his courage and honesty can face down death itself. I struggled long and hard with this story, turning it over for years in my mind, striving to see how I could *make it say what I wanted to hear*. I looked for hidden meanings and alternate interpretations to make the tale prove what I wanted it to prove.

---

[647] (Moncrieff, 1976) pg. 209, (Borroff, 1967) line 1955-7
[648] (Borroff, 1967) introduction, p.ix

I squeezed it, elongated it, shortened it, kicked it around until I was thoroughly convinced I was almost right. But "almost" is not enough.

I must present the truth to you. Truth is the mark of the knight[649]. I am no "post-modern progressive", to force the Truth to say what is not true. The truth is the truth, no matter what I want it to be. Christ says "I was born for one purpose, to bear witness to the Truth. All who can bear the Truth, hear my voice"[650].

Gawain, with the magic belt tucked under his armor, found the Green Chapel the next day.

It was not far from the castle, in a little grotto a bit removed from a small path. As Sir Gawain approached, he felt the weight of the axe on his hip. Fear must have hung over him like a shadow of death. Not a fear of the unknown, but a fear of the very known, for he knew what awaited him.

He entered the grotto and saw the chapel, and in front of the door he saw a chopping block made from a stump. Next to this, stood the mighty and gigantic Green Knight.

"My heart sings to see you," Said the Green Knight. "Now we can finish our little game."

"I wish I could say the same," Sir Gawain replied. "I have brought your axe, as we agreed." He uncovered the green blade, handed it to the giant, and knelt before him, placing his head and neck upon the chopping block.

The Green Knight hefted the axe and took aim. Gawain closed his eyes as he saw the giant swing up the axe. When the blade came down, it thudded into the block, having missed Gawain's neck.

"Aim better," Gawain hissed as he looked up. "I am right here."

The giant said nothing, lifted the axe and chopped down again. Amazingly, the huge axe smashed into the wood, but missed by an inch.

Gawain roared, "Cut straight! Stop playing games and get this over with!"

"Most assuredly," said the giant, and lifted again the great axe. It fell like a tall tree, cutting deep into the block, but only drawing a small cut across the side of Gawain's neck. Only a tiny nick.

---

[649] (Lull, 2001) pg. 42, 84, (Gautier, 1989) pg. 67
[650] John 18:37

Gawain touched the cut and looked at the blood. He jumped up and unsheathed his sword, "You struck at me as I had struck at you, and you have drawn blood, but still I live! The rules of your game are satisfied, so now let us fight unhindered!"

The giant laughed and raised his open hands. "Peace! Peace, my dear knight! I wanted to test the courage and strength of the Knights of the Round Table. I have tested you. I am satisfied. You are as brave and true as I have heard.

"You have traveled to set your head on my chopping block because you said you would. You have risked your life because you promised. And you have loyally placed yourself in this position to protect your king. Be at peace, for I will not fight you any more. I instead honor you and rejoice in your Round Table knights! Surely the greatest and most brave and honorable knights in the world!

"But I will reveal to you a mystery. I have been in disguise. I was the lord of the castle that you just left. It was I who played the exchange game with you as you enjoyed my hospitality. You honored me and refused the feigned advances of my wife, in honor of your knighthood and myself. Twice you did this and returned to me what you had won in your chamber. But on the third time, although you resisted my wife's advances, you did not surrender to me the belt you had won. In this small way, you have broken your word. That is why I spared you two strikes, and then cut you barely on the third strike. I could have killed you for that small offense of withholding your prize, but I know you were simply grasping at any chance to save your life. This is understandable, but return to your Round Table knowing that, although you were truly great, you must be greater. You are human, but to be a true knight, you must be more. A knight is stronger than iron and truer than steel."[651].

Gawain does return and explains the entire adventure to the amazed King Arthur and his court. In shame and humility, Gawain forever after wears a green sash around his waist, testifying to his struggle and small defeat.

Such a story still emphasizes the importance of honesty, even to oneself, and even to the point of analyzing motives and inner dialogues, but it ended slightly differently than I would have wished. I was looking for paragons of honesty in the world of Romance fiction, but found only

---

[651] (Borroff, 1967) line 2360-2368, this is why Excalibur is wielded only by the truest knights. Its name means "Cut steel".

a fallible man. But where Gawain may have failed in a small way, he is victorious in gaining Humility, even as we are victorious in seeing the truth as it is, instead of forcing the story to be what it was never meant to be.

Beware of lying to yourself, which is the easiest deception[652]. Beware of justifying your actions and being too easy on yourself. Many otherwise good men have failed because of their self deception.

Initiative and Courage

Courage is required everywhere in a true knight's life. In some men, the greatest battle and thus the greatest need for courage may be their own struggle with honesty, yet it seems small and hidden away, invisible to most people's eyes, as it occurs in the heart.

Other, seemingly small things require bravery, also hidden in the folds of one's character, only apparent to one who pays attention. One such knightly character trait that seems to receive little recognition is called Initiative.

I find the word initiative in almost no place, except an occasional reference in a career ethics pamphlet. Sometimes it is mentioned as something an employee needs to be successful and defined as the desire to solve problems. How diminutive, how un-inspiring. Yet every knight who ever achieved anything has exuded initiative from their pores. They almost never wait for problems to come to them—they go looking for problems to solve with the zeal of a bloodthirsty dragon-slayer. Saint George charges forward, demanding to question the conscience of an emperor and, in the mean time, wastes no time in killing a murderous monster. He does not even wait for request or permission. Sir Lancelot comes across a battle, and rides to defend the smaller side. When Sir Galahad hears of a castle spilling forth criminals that ravage the country-side, he steps up to the front door and demands combat! Sir Bors sees a woman being attacked, and rides to save her. When Gawain realized that no one dared take on the Green Knight's challenge, he perceives the problem of shame descending upon Arthur's court, and immediately

---

652 (Scupoli, 1945 edition) pg. 8,9, 21, Cervantes and others warn that self deception is of utmost easiness

raises his sword to rectify the situation. Saint Joan could have kept to her chores and childhood friends, but when she hears the call of the Angels, she happily answers. Even the Crusades began when Pope Urban II's attention fell upon the plight of Constantinople, being attacked by the Turks. When a problem is sighted, suddenly the courage and fiery strength of the knight is ignited!

Call it reckless, call it short-sighted, call it a fool-hardy rush to find adventure and pain, but the knight finds himself invigorated by the challenge! Bring on the storms, he shouts, let them come! Better yet, he laughs, I will go forth to meet them!

Sure, these are important things, life-and-death struggles, glorious contests. But the initiative needed to take on the world begins as a desire, indeed, to solve problems, even small ones. All aspects of courage begin small, and must be built up. In today's world, I am confounded by what I see, the absolute lack of desire to solve anything, to use any energy in the hearts of young men, unless it is to shout and bark at sports games, brothels, or attempts to gain beer. Even there, modern men give up rather easily, once confronted by a problem. How pathetic, the youth of today reduced to nothing more than monkeys, pawing the ground for scraps of pleasure.

I remember a time, staying at a house of a friend of mine. The brother lived there, with his common-law wife and several kids. He had not been able to secure a job in some time, and since I too was looking for a job, I assumed times were hard for everyone.

One day, after coming back from a job interview, I noticed the smoke alarms chirping, as they do when they need a changed battery. I, full of my concerns for the future, put it out of my mind, and continued with my job search. But every day, as I returned from a long day of job searches, with more diverse interviews every time, that infernal chirping still came to my ears.

It has been a week, I asked my friend's brother, doesn't that chirping bother you? He, engrossed in his TV watching and popcorn, shook his head. Chirp! And he put the volume louder on the TV. I, for my part, considered myself only a guest, and perhaps it was not my place to do anything. But after a few more days, I had had enough.

Guest or not, I resolved to solve the problem. Finding a ladder in the garage (where I actually slept), I climbed up to take a look at the chirping thing.

It was a new smoke alarm, one like I had never seen before, since I was used to the old type that simply sat on screws in the wall and could be easily removed. This device seemed much more complicated. No matter, I inspected it carefully, as my father had taught me when confronted by a new gizmo that needed fixing, and I discovered how to unscrew it, detach the wires, pop open the casing, and retrieve the offending battery. I then replaced the spent battery with a new one that I had purchased. Locating the other alarm, I replaced the battery on that one as well. In about eight minutes, the problem was solved.

The mother and sister of the house spend more time congratulating me than it took me to fix it. I looked over at the brother, still on the couch. Why did he not fix this himself? Was he simply lazy? Did he somehow fear the tiny challenge of the smoke alarm? Most likely he was never taught initiative. Not long after, I found a job that could allow me to have my own place. The brother spent the rest of his days, bouncing from place to place, content to sit on the couch and sometimes find a temporary job that paid for beer and diapers. I suppose I should be happy for his family that he did even this.

Thus is a simple, modern example of initiative, or lack of it, and the effects. Are there guarantees? No. But a story of a would-be knight that refuses to get off the couch to save the world, or a woman, even his wife and children, is a story that begins with a man unwilling to fix something small around the house.

Where exists the fire that burns within a man? What drives a person to greatness, or petty despair? Does initiative buttress courage, or does courage enflame initiative? Whatever the case, they support each other. Initiative must be infused in the man of courage before he is to be a knight.

Dragons! Great and Small

I have been careful to discuss types and shades of courage that not only deal with war and violence, but also courage in peace-time, because the use of courage is required everywhere[653]. A fool believes that bravery is seen only on the battlefield. Every man must have courage, if he is to be

---

[653] (Lull, 2001) pg. 70

considered a real man. Indeed, courage is required especially in a religious person's[654] everyday life. Facing the world, day after day, year after year, requires great courage, because this world wears at any person's strength like an insidious but powerful foe. Worries and concerns can choke a person just as surely as any torture. As my father always said, "The real battle is the every-day grind".

"Great Dragons" and wars, however, do occur. Rest assured, if you are a knight or any kind of true believer, eventually they will find you[655]. In fact, the more you reach for GOD, the more the demons will fight you, for they fear such a man[656].

One such "Great Dragon", persecution, faced the early Christians. Simply admitting to love Christ in the pagan Roman world was to risk true torture and horrendous death. Saint Peter was thrown in prison time after time for preaching the word of GOD. Finally, exasperated by this man who refused to bow before human authority, the Roman Empire threatened to crucify him, just as they had crucified Christ.

"I will not cease preaching the truth," Peter said. "Destroy me if you must, but I do not deserve the same death that my great LORD suffered."

The Romans honored this wish and crucified Peter upside-down[657].

For many centuries, it was customary for knights to go on Crusade. This "dragon" could take any form, from a physical call of battle to a spiritual call of pilgrimage[658]. This wasn't just leaving your home, it was to risk your life in a totally alien environment of deserts and spiraling towers, battling exotic warriors (whether physical or spiritual) with even stranger weapons and tactics. For all knights, the Crusades meant leaving the familiar to face the unknown, and very possibly face a painful end, bleeding to death in a sandy wasteland.

Our experiences may not be exactly as these were, but one day, in one fateful hour, we will be asked to choose between GOD and this

---

[654] (Stalker, 1902) pg. 44-47

[655] (Baglio, 2009) pg. 175, My father used to say that demons seek out the good, for they already have the other people

[656] (Sheen, 2003) pg. 192

[657] (Eusebius, 1989) pg. 65, (The New Encyclopedia Britannica in 30 volumes, Macropedia, volume 14, 1982) pg. 156, 157 by Daniel William O'Conner

[658] (Pernoud, 1963) pg. 40-41

world[659]. We must pray for the courage to choose GOD, even in the face of laughter, persecution, or the sword.

Battle, torture, and even execution may await us tomorrow. Thus we must prepare for physical violence and brutal engagements of all kinds today. Courage and valor are essential to this preparation. But we must also prepare for the inner battles that assail us continuously, even in the throes of everyday life, using honesty, initiative, and humility.

Such courage as we have seen, both physical and moral, comes from an ironic place: absolute fear! Courage begins with the fear of GOD[660].

True Fear of the Lord

"Fear of the Lord is the beginning of wisdom."
—Psalm 110:10

Modern Christians, and many modern people for that matter, are taught that GOD is love, and, to them, love seems sweet and syrupy, so it is therefore difficult to quite understand the concept of "fear" of GOD. Why would one fear love? Is not love completely good, even to the point of being "mushy". To many people, the phrase "Fear GOD" seems like saying "Fear the little baby angels that fly around, singing sweet nothings".

Such musings are a complete misunderstanding of two things— GOD and real Love. For GOD is more than love[661], and true Love can be like iron.

Fear of the Lord GOD is the realization that GOD is all-powerful, all knowing, all seeing, eternal, and perfectly just. It is one thing to say such phrases, it is another thing to actually comprehend these powers, to grasp them in their fullest meaning. GOD is ultimately terrifying. There is no way to fight or even avoid HIM. If HIS righteous wrath sets upon you, you will know unimaginable suffering, and if HE neglects to think about you even for a moment, you will cease to exist; even memories

---

[659] Matthew 6:33, Luke 12:31, Matthew 10:37-39
[660] Ecclesiasticus 34:16 of the Douay-Rheims Bible, 34:14 of the Revised English Bible
[661] Isaiah 30:18, Psalms 50:6, GOD is justice as well as mercy, the GOD of all things,

of you will evaporate like smoke. "It is a fearsome thing to fall into the hands of the Living GOD"[662].

Nothing on Earth can compare to the glory of GOD. No leader of men can come close to HIM, no army or weapon is as powerful or all-consuming as the LORD. The horrors of the universe disappear compared to the anger of GOD. The LORD is the creator and the destroyer of the entire cosmos.

Every great prophet fears the LORD, because they have experienced, or seen, a part of HIS awesome power. Some, like Ezekiel, experience GOD in strange visions that leave them breathless. Prophets like Moses are given a glimpse of GOD's limitless powers, as the Pillar of Fire, or rivers of blood. Wayward saints like Paul are treated to a small taste of GOD's wrath, and barely emerge sane.[663]

All the true prophets, without exception, fall to their knees before the horrifying might of the LORD GOD. From then on, they are changed forever. From that moment forward, they fear nothing but the LORD.

What a strange thing and how ironic, for the greatest courage to be based on the greatest fear!

This is the beginning of wisdom.

This is the beginning of courage.

The Burning Bush

> "He that feareth the Lord shall tremble at nothing and shall not be afraid"
> —Ecclesiasticus 34:16 of the Douay-Rheims Bible

Once you have experienced even a fraction of the LORD's power, everything else will seem diminished by comparison. All other fears pale; all other disasters evaporate. Fear of the LORD is the beginning of courage.

When Moses came across the Burning Bush and saw that it wasn't consumed even as it blazed, he realized he witnessed a piece of the power

---

[662] Hebrews 10:31
[663] Acts, 9: 1-6, Psalm 25:14 Psalm 33:8 and Matthew 10:28 of KJV

of the LORD. He fell down on his face, terrified. He was in the presence of the Living GOD[664].

GOD told him to go to the Pharaoh of Egypt, who had enslaved the people of Israel, and demand that Pharaoh set them free.

Pharaoh was, at that time, the most powerful man in the world. Pharaoh had the best chariots and the strongest armies. A literal pantheon of gods supported him, and his kingdom stood strongest and most brilliant among the earth. A look from his eye, a sneer from his lips, could mean certain death to any who dared demand of him.

Moses knew this well, but had seen the power of GOD. After that, facing the most powerful man in the world seemed as nothing. Who cares what the Pharaoh said or did? Moses had stood in the presence of the terrifying King of Kings! GOD is more awesome and frightening than anything in existence, and coming before him "face to face"[665], changed Moses' perception of everything. Moses feared nothing, but GOD[666].

Great Lion of GOD

> "Was Grace that taught my heart to fear, and Grace my
> fears relieved."
>
> —John Newton[667]

But how can Absolute Fear, even Fear of GOD, give someone perfect Courage?

No one knows about the Fear of the LORD more than Saul Paulus of Tarsus. Early in his life, no one deserved to fear GOD more.

Trained as a Pharisee, Saul lived in the time right after Christ, and the world was hostile to the new religion of Christianity. Saul considered it a plague upon the Jewish nation. He took responsibility of the martyrdom of several Christians, personally supervising the stoning to death of the first Christian martyr, Stephen. Innocent blood dripped

---

[664] Exodus 3:2
[665] 2 Corinthians 3:7 also, Exodus 33:11
[666] (Bangley, 2007) pg. 334, Moses prays before GOD
[667] Olney Hymns (1779)

from his hands, but he truly thought he did the right thing. He truly believed he was cleansing Israel of the disease called Christianity.

He pursued Christians relentlessly, and started on the road to Damascus to oversee more executions. Almost at the city gates, a terrible light suddenly blinded him. His horsed reared and he fell, stunned and terrified by the overwhelming shining that engulfed him.

Saul knew it to be GOD, and as he groveled there in his terror, the light spoke to him. "Why are you persecuting me?"[668] Saul then knew the horror that outweighed everything else. He realized the people he was killing, the very "disease" he worked to stamp out, was the Gospel of GOD HIMSELF! He had found himself at war with GOD[669].

The light left him utterly blind, with strange "scales" covering his eyes. Saul wandered alone to Damascus, where he lay in darkness for many days. He had much time to weep for his fate and his mistakes, and to ponder the true nature of the MOST HIGH.

This is where the secret happens: how Fear of the LORD truly brings absolute Bravery. There is more to the "Fear of the LORD" than fear. The Psalmist says that the Fear of the Lord is *the beginning* of wisdom"[670]. The beginning only, not the entirety.

GOD sent a holy man to heal Saul's blindness. GOD was giving Saul a second chance. Saul had been, up to that point, an arrogant killer of Christians, a persecutor of innocent people. Everlasting Hell would have awaited Paul if GOD wasn't a forgiving GOD. Saul had every reason to fear, but the mercy he received from GOD showed him Love.

He went out into the desert, thinking and studying about what had happened, contemplating his mistakes, the mercy of GOD, and GOD's Love

Traditionally, when a child does something stupid, the child fears the father because he is the one who doles out harsh punishment, as Saul was punished on the road to Damascus. But as the child grows, he or she becomes more aware of a good father's reasons and motives, just as when we mature spiritually, we become more aware of GOD's will in the world and more understanding of His actions. We still feel puny compared to the awesome power of GOD, but we see that HE is all good and truth.

---

[668] Acts 26:13-14
[669] Acts 5: 33-39
[670] Proverbs 9:10, Psalm 111:10

We see that he cares for us deeper than we care for ourselves, and even suffered on the Cross to save us from our own disgusting ways. The punishments and commands, which seemed so frightening, become the source for our improvement, our strengthening, our enrichment, if we let them.

We realize that GOD is the source of all good things in the world, and HIS power, at first terrifying, is in truth totally beautiful and pure. We feel we have been lead from a dark room into the light. First the light hurts our eyes, but then we become accustomed to it and for the first time, see things beyond shadow and void[671]. Just as the matured person understands the lessons he or she had to learn, so we also see GOD's wisdom in our lives. We learn to love GOD not through fear, but understanding.

Paul feared on that road in the desert perfectly, but this brought knowledge of GOD's mercy, and this lead to the love of GOD. He realized while fear is the beginning of wisdom, Loving GOD truly is the culmination of wisdom, complete and whole.

GOD's love is the final key to ultimate courage[672].

Saul went from town to town, continent to continent, preaching Christianity so fervently that he made thousands of converts. Saul feared nothing, and risking imprisonment, disease, snake bite, torture, enslavement, and assassination, brought the Gospel to every place he could find. He even preached to the Roman Emperor himself, once again the most powerful man in the world at that time and violently opposed to Christianity. In the end, Saul would be known as the greatest apostle, only sharing the spotlight with Peter. Some even called Saul "the most important man in the world".

This man, Saul, who changed his name to Paul and tried to convert the entire world, became known as the Great Lion of GOD[673].

The love of GOD filled Paul's heart and pushed all fear away. It is the love of GOD, ultimately, that drove Paul to sacrifice himself in the name of the Most High. Fear is the beginning, and love the fulfillment, of

---

[671] Just as in Plato's cave
[672] Ecclesiasticus 34:16 of the Douay-Rheims Bible
[673] Taylor Caldwell's book and name for Saint Paul

courage. When our hearts overflow with this love, fear of worldly things can find no resting place there.

The Road to Damascus

"The fear of the Lord is the beginning of His love."
—Ecclesiasticus 25:16 of the Douay-Rheims Bible

For most of us, *fear* must be the beginning of *our* wisdom. Moses has to go through the fear of facing the Burning Bush before he can find the one True GOD[674], just as Abraham must endure the "dread and great darkness" before he can make the covenant with the LORD[675]. Paul faces the terrible light on the road to Damascus, and St. Ignatius makes a mental trip to Hell the first stop in his *Spiritual Exercises*[676].

Most human beings cannot accept, or understand GOD's love without a jarring upset, a life-changing trial, and blistering spiritual experience. I think this is because most people can only be reached by fear. We are so stubborn, cynical, callous, or arrogant, that only a huge injection of absolute terror can wake us out of our earthly dream.

Most people live completely surrounded by fear. Fear of death, fear of loss, fear of reprisal, fear of abandonment, fear of so many things. Yet only GOD can truly harm us, so these fears must be for another purpose than simply to warn us of impending doom. We are to use these fears to grow stronger, just as GOD uses our fear of HIM to bring us into the light of HIS Love.

But most people stay with earthly fears, not daring to acknowledge the truer terror of GOD's wrath, that light on the road to Damascus. If only they would let go of their earthly fears and experience the unearthly fear of GOD, then they could come into the greater light of GOD's love.

The knight must travel through every fear until he comes to GOD's love. GOD demands the knight to perform all manner of terrifying things, regardless of how the knight feels, regardless of his fear. The knight thus commits actions from loyalty, duty, and love, and though he suffers from fear, is not a slave to it. The knight is then free from the

---

[674] Exodus 3:2
[675] Gen.15:12
[676] (Mottola, 1964) pg. 59, this is part of the first week, as an examination of sin

control of fear, since he has lived and battled through it to reach for GOD, in obedience to GOD, and in service of GOD. The knight does not reject sin because of fear of Hell, but because he can see GOD's love[677]. It is within reach.

The knight learns to control his fears and emotions instead of them controlling him, and he is truly free. This is what is meant by the phrase "the truth will set you free"[678]. If one follows the Truth, Christ, one will be free from the control of fear, and all other earthly constraints.

And in the end, it is the love of GOD that makes all the difference.

Love of GOD vs. Fear of Death

Now let us see if this Love of GOD, which begins with the fear of GOD, can truly conquer all fear, even the fear of cruel death.

I can think of no greater test than the trials of the Christians during the Roman imperial persecution. Let us make it an even tougher test, and let the victim be a woman (for supposedly women have a more difficult time finding courage).

Irene of Thessalonia's "crime" was of hiding Holy Scripture from Roman soldiers who would burn them, and of course, of being a Christian.

The governor of Macedonia captured her, but after burning her sisters to death, decided to be "generous" to Irene. All she had to do to escape the same fate was eat a little meat involved in sacrifices to Roman gods, something understood as denouncing Christ.

"My answer is NO", said Irene, "by the omnipotent GOD who created Heaven and Earth, the sea and all things that exist. The dreadful punishment of eternal fire is especially reserved for those who have denied Jesus, the Word of GOD"[679].

Irene certainly knew what to fear.

The judge asked her why she had kept the scriptures in her house. Irene said, "It was GOD, who required us to love HIM even unto death

---

[677] (Kierkegaard, 1956) ch.5, (Joinville, 1963) pg. 274, Augustine's *Sermon on 1 John 9, 5*

[678] John 8:32

[679] (Ricciotti G., 1992) pg. 125

and to allow ourselves to be burned to death rather than hand them (the scriptures) over"[680].

She was burned alive, as her sisters before her. Her love of GOD easily conquered any fear of horrid death. This occurred probably in April, 304, in Thrace[681].

Another martyr at this time, Euplius, showed how his love overcame any fear as well. He was tortured for making the sign of the Cross and admitted he read the Holy Scriptures despite the imperial orders.

The judge suspended the torture and demanded Euplius to worship Roman gods.

Euplius replied, "I adore the Father and the Son and the Holy Ghost. I adore the Trinity and outside of these Three Persons, there is no god. I am a Christian"[682].

He was again tortured, but Euplius prayed continuously for strength until he could no longer speak aloud. As he was taken to the place of his beheading, a herald went before him calling "Euplius the Christian, the enemy of the gods and of the emperors". Every time this was proclaimed, Euplius was able to reply in a hoarse but happy whisper, "Thanks be to Christ my GOD"[683].

To these accounts of love conquering fear and indeed death itself, any true historian must add the story of Polycarp. He was Bishop of Smyrna, somewhere between the years of 155AD and 167AD, and his story is considered one of the earliest accounts of Christian martyrdom under the Pagan Roman Emperors. He preached the good news of the Gospel and did charitable works wherever he could, helping the poor and needy, and converting untold numbers by his sheer humble kindness. Even so, he knew that the Roman soldiers would eventually come to take him to a terrible execution that a vision told him would involve fire, and when they did, he was ready[684].

At the time, fashion demanded that Christians be fed to ferocious animals, and the Pagan crowds would drive themselves to unparalleled levels of blood-lusting fury. One day, after watching a particularly courageous Christian actually drag the beast's jaws to his chest, the crowd

---

[680] Ibid.
[681] Ibid. pg. 126
[682] Ibid. pg. 147
[683] (Ricciotti G., 1992) pg.147
[684] For the whole story see (Eusebius, 1989) pg. 118-123

yelled "Away with the godless! Go get Polycarp!" and the soldiers were dispatched.

After torturing a few farmhands, the soldiers came to the place the poor wretches had instructed them to go. What they saw must have been strange to them. Polycarp, now well over eighty years old, came down from an upper room to meet them, greeting them with real kindness and courtesy, offering them a meal spread on the dinner table. In return for the sumptuous repast, he asked for one hour to pray. Somewhat caught off-guard, the soldiers allowed this, and Polycarp stood up and prayed with such beautiful fervor and heart-felt humanity that the soldiers could not help but question their mission and why anyone would want to kill such a man. After an hour, as promised, the old Christian allowed himself to be escorted to the arena, where the animals and crowds awaited him.

The noise from the bestial games was so loud that it could be heard from quite far away. Still, nobles and important people came to Polycarp before he entered the arena, begging him to simply denounce his faith, so that he would be spared. Polycarp ignored their kind but misled advice, and entered the arena, to the heightened cheers and blood-mad screams of the crowd.

"Are you Polycarp?" Demanded the Proconsul loudly, and then more quietly, he said, "Respect your years, and say 'away with the godless!'"

Polycarp turned toward the crowd, waved a hand at them, *indicating them*, and said "Away with the godless!"

"You must turn your back on this Christ!" The Proconsul said. "Do this now so I can spare you from the beasts!"

"For 86 years, my lord Christ has never turned his back on me. For all this time, with me as his servant, he has never done me wrong. How can I blaspheme my King who saved me?"

The crowds became incensed, screaming to feed him to the lions. But the games had been closed already, and so, such animal spectacles were now illegal until the games were opened again. The crowd then screamed out "Burn him! To the fire with him!"

Right there in the center of the arena, a pyre was quickly built, and Polycarp did not hesitate to step into the wood construction. The builders of the pyre knew that Polycarp would not flee the flames, and so they did not pin him to the lumber, only left him standing in the pyre.

When the flames went up, the crowd gasped, for the pyre seemed to become a "vaulted room"[685], a chamber made of fire, with the walls bellowing out like a sail caught by the wind, glowing all around the saint at the center, his skin gold and shining, itself like a refining furnace. Frightened by this, the crowd called for someone to kill the bishop, and a man leaned into the flames with his sword, stabbing Polycarp so that the blood flowed freely down the wooden planks, completely quenching the fire. All was still.

Everyone became silent, awed by such a strange apparition, and it was said that even the Heathen, to this day, remember the death of the man Polycarp[686].

These are just three examples of the thousands of Christian martyrs who died in the Roman era, with praise on their lips for the GOD they loved over all else, even life. Accused and condemned for simply following Christ, they did not face their doom sheepishly or with defeat. They glowed with a fiery love that could not be dimmed, even with the closeness of looming destruction. They loved Christ so much, they ignored the fear of death and even laughed at it. Their love conquered their fear. Or more precisely, the love of GOD in their hearts left no room for fear of death.

What woman wouldn't be jealous of such love, love which embraces every kind of death and pain to avoid betrayal? What man wouldn't shout for joy, to have such a brother-in-arms? What mother wouldn't find the utmost pride in a son who exhibited such love? What father wouldn't wish for such a son, with such mighty courage in his heart? What a king wouldn't give for a group of such men, who would stop at nothing for sheer loyalty?

And still, the martyrs endured. Eusebius, the ancient church historian, tells us of a man named John the Lector, who, after all the terrible persecution of the Christians for almost 300 years, stood up at a meeting and read from the sacred scriptures. Eusebius was struck by the love, the sheer adoration in the man's voice, and tried to get closer, to see what kind of man this was who could read with such feeling and truth. He assumed that John was reading from a written text, as any typical lector might. But as he approached he realized that this lector

---

[685] (Eusebius, 1989) pg.122
[686] (Eusebius, 1989) pg. 123

had suffered everything for Christ—his left leg shattered and ruined by Roman soldiers, his right eye gauged out and cauterized with a red-hot iron, so that only a ragged, gaping hole now gazed down at his empty hands. For John the Lector was blind, and the scripture he read was written on his heart, memorized by the terrifying, pure, total love of a humble man of GOD[687].

"Who shall separate us from the love of Christ? Shall tribulation, or distress, or persecution, or famine, or nakedness, or peril, or sword? . . . No, in all these things we are more than conquerors through HIM that loved us. For I am sure that neither death, nor life, nor angels, nor principalities, nor things present, nor things to come, nor powers, nor height, nor depth, nor anything else in creation, will be able to separate us from the love of GOD in Christ Jesus Our Lord"[688].

Love as Courage

Love creates courage. And perfect Love creates Perfect Courage.

As Sir Gawain approached the mystical castle, he felt trepidation grip his heart. The fortress seemed dark and otherworldly, and even seemed to float in the air, surrounded as it was with a curtain of mist.

He knelt and held his shield so that his eyes beheld the painting on the inside: the five glorious mysteries of the Virgin Mary[689]. Every time he beheld this, he was reminded of his love for the Great Lady, and how she was the perfect mirror of the perfect love of Christ. With these thoughts in his heart, he could advance toward his destiny.

Medieval romances are filled with the allegorical tales of Knights focusing on their ladies and their love for them, to fill them with undauntable courage and daring. Knights from Sir Guy of Warwick to Sir Percival are driven by this unquenchable passion. But Romantic love is a pale reflection and only a step toward the knight's love for Christ and GOD. Both become a powerful impetus, but the love of GOD is purer.

---

[687]   (Ricciotti G., 1992) pg. 82
[688]   Romans 9:35-39
[689]   (Scudder, 1917), (Loomis, 1951) pg. 343

Pure Love is a seething drive, an awesome, unstoppable engine frightening to foes and inspiring to friends. Pure Love turns a man into a juggernaut.

Without Courage, there can be no Love.

Even when one studies human relationships, it becomes obvious that Courage is required for romantic and true love. One might fear the possibility of having one's heart broken, crushed by the spurning or betrayal of one's love interest. How many times have I heard it? Someone says, "I am afraid to fall in love again, I have been hurt before."

When one ponders the purer love the soul should feel for GOD and Christ, another fear often sets in—the fear of losing one's self to such overpowering love. When one studies the reasons for a person not loving GOD, one finds people generally fearful of losing creature comforts or of being seen as naive, or foolish. They fear the disapproval of their friends, or the being proven wrong. They may even fear to discover that everything they previously held dear pales to the glory of GOD. It can be a fearful thing to discover your life and everything in it is nothing to the Infinite grandeur of GOD. And some are afraid to find they themselves are **not** the center of the universe.

It is always a fearful thing to surrender to Love[690]. When one loves truly and deeply, it opens the heart to pain, perhaps even a loss of autonomy. To care for someone means an attachment, and one is no longer able to simply go about one's own selfish business. Some would prefer to live without love, for they feel that they are unworthy, and cannot bear the thought of having value in the eyes of anyone, even GOD.

What is Courage for?

As one reads through these chapters, it will be difficult to determine which pillar of Honor is actually most important. Some say Strength is most important, as strength of will is needed to perform the feats

---

[690] Hebrews 10:31

of knighthood and reach the other pillars. Some, as Robert Howard, creator of Conan, would say that Courage is the most important; Howard comparing Courage to a kind of spiritual power, at least equal with Faith and Strength [691]. Sir Ramon Lull himself said that the Noblesse of Courage was the source of all honorable action[692]. Opinions differ, but what is certain is that Modern man only recognizes Strength and Courage as actual virtues, denying the others as mere phantasms of religious or Medieval minds.

Courage is especially valued among all nations and cultures[693]. What separates the knightly view of courage from other views, however, is the reasons behind that courage.

Many people, especially in the modern world, feel "courageous" because they are selfish, which is just another word for being afraid of loss. Some fear losing the things they possess, or the relationships they have somehow managed to gain, and so they show "courage" as a dog may snarl to protect a bone. This is not courage, but only ferocity[694]v. They may even fear ridicule, and consequently hurtle themselves into outrageous situations, pretending courage. Amazingly enough, some do not think enough to be afraid—they are simply driven by lack of perceived danger. Some of them even believe themselves, whether unconsciously or not, to be invulnerable and incapable of dying. Stupid courage is not courage.

The knight is no fool, and understands how close death hovers. He has two reasons, both almost totally alien to the modern mind, why he seeks and uses courage.

First, the knight's love for GOD commands, nurtures, and convinces the knight to risk everything for the sake of Right, Truth, and good men everywhere. GOD says we must do what is just and good in the face of all adversity[695], and the knight accepts the challenge with complete knowledge of what may happen. We must fulfill all righteousness[696].

Secondly, the knight has decided that the world should be something more than it is, and has also decided it is partially up to him to change

---

[691] (Howard, 1998) pg. 321
[692] (Lull, 2001) pg. 48
[693] (Stalker, 1902) pg. 37-39
[694] Ibid. pg. 36
[695] Mark 13:13
[696] Matt. 3:15

it, to protect it, to mend it. If the knight or saint will not lay his life and blood on the line to better the world and the fate of humanity, who will? Even more, since a knight or saint is particularly well-suited (through all his virtues) to make right the wrongs in the world, then it is his duty to try, no matter the consequences. The knight also wishes, out of sheer humanitarian feeling, to share the light of justice and truth with all people, since it is the height of joy. Knightly courage is connected to a sense of justice and moral right, over any desperation. Behold, Lull's Noblesse of Courage[697].

To do what is right, to follow GOD, and to change the world, all require courage. As a knight, you will find yourself drawing upon your courage in battlefields of the body, mind, heart, and soul; from the bloodied wastelands of war and carnage, to the haunted shores of the Spirit world, to the agonizing small hours of the night, when no one is awake but you and your concerns. Your greatest tests in these fields will always demand the greatest courage. No one has more courage than the sainted knight, and no one exercises that courage more.

---

[697] (Lull, 2001) pg. 48

THE THIRD PILLAR OF HONOR

SACRIFICE

Shall I abandon, O King of mysteries, the soft comforts of home? Shall I turn my back on my native land, and my face towards the sea? . . . . Shall I take my tiny coracle across the wide sparkling ocean? O King of the glorious Heaven, shall I go of my own choice upon the sea?
O Christ, will you help me on the wild waves?
    —An old Celtic Prayer, probably by Brendan, c. 400

Lord of all things, I offer myself to you. I offer not only my labour, but also my affections and emotions. I am willing to defy my own sensitivities and desires in your service, with your grace and favour. I make this offering in the presence of your infinite Goodness, and of your glorious Mother, and of all the holy men and women in your heavenly court. I wish to imitate you in bearing all injuries and insults, and in enduring material and spiritual poverty, in order to serve and praise you. I beg you to receive my offering, and to show me how to imitate you.
    —St. Ignatius of Loyola, one of his many prayers

You have no delight in the sacrifice of animals; if I were to bring a whole-offering
You would not accept it. GOD, my sacrifice is a broken spirit; You, GOD, will not despise a chastened heart.
    —Psalms 51:16-17

Let me finish what I have been permitted to begin.
Let me give all without any assurance of increase.
The pride of the cup is in the drink, its humility in the serving.
What, then do its defects matter?
—Dag Hammarskjold, *Markings* 1954: 1, 95

I have nothing to offer but blood, toil, tears, and sweat.
—Sir Winston Churchill, his first statement as prime minister, to the House of Commons, May 13, 1940

Without struggle, there is no success.
—Frederick Douglas, *Narrative of the life of Frederick Douglas, An American Slave and Essays*

Greater love than this hath no man, than to give his life for his friends.
—John 15:13 KJV

Sacrifice

The first two pillars of Honor, Strength and Courage, are lauded by many around the world in this modern time, and many modern men are comfortable with them as words of encouragement. They speak openly of Strength and Courage as something worthwhile to have, and even indispensable. They are correct, but they conveniently leave out another important aspect of Honor, Sacrifice.

Sacrifice is not mentioned often because it is, simply said, suffering in the cause of righteousness. No one enjoys suffering. There is no way to make suffering appealing to the casual glance. It is why the Cross is despised by the world[698], because it represents sacrifice and suffering, and the romantic visions one may have of Holiness and Honor quickly disappear when confronted by the personal terror that is pain and agony.

Even by the majority of religious, Sacrifice is left out of modern plans and lectures, especially in America. The stresses and strains of marriage,

---

[698] Matt 24:9—The world hates the idea of sacrifice for GOD's glory, (Sheen, 1990) pg. 118, also John 15:19, Proverbs 29:27

child-rearing, career building, and the everyday work of the world are seen as vastly enough troubles to deal with, and such concepts as purposeful sacrifice for GOD is left out as an antiquated afterthought. Sacrifice, especially in the West, has become the domain of story-book saints and biblical heroes, unsuited for the practical modern Christian. Spiritualism, feelings without the call for true sacrifice, has replaced religion which demands pain and inconvenience.

Yet, Sacrifice is needed to follow GOD at any level, whether it is in extreme cases as in the death of martyrs, or simply to go to church, which requires the tiny sacrifice of one hour a week. It cannot be avoided. From Cain and Abel, to Abraham, to Christ, Peter and Paul, and to the martyrs, saints and knights, sacrifice stands as the final way to Honor, and the gateway to GOD HIMSELF.

The Forty Martyrs

Licinius, ruler of Eastern Rome in 320 AD, betrayed Constantine's edict of Milan, and ordered all soldiers of his realm to bow down and worship idols. Forty men of the XII Legion, the Thundering Legion of Sebaste, refused. These forty soldiers, referring to themselves as *Miles Christi*, Soldiers of Christ[699], would not submit before pagan gods[700]. "There is only one GOD," They said. "And we will serve HIM alone."

All of them were young, probably no more than 20, but all of them were fettered together in a long chain and imprisoned. This was only the beginning.

After sitting in prison and tortured, the soldiers of Christ heard their sentence: to die exposed on a frozen lake, naked in the middle of winter[701].

So they gathered, huddling and unprotected, freezing slowly in the center of a huge slab of ice. To further torture them, their executioners made sure the martyrs could see a hot springs bath, set on the other side of the lake, with steam and light streaming from the doors. "For the martyrs this was a dreadful sight; a few steps would have taken them out

---

[699] A title many of the martyrs gave themselves at this time
[700] (Kirsch, 1909)
[701] (Ricciotti G., 1992) pg. 212

of their sufferings and allowed them to grasp the life which was leaving their bodies moment by moment"[702].

Yet, as the hours painfully ticked by, none of the doomed men left the ice. It must have looked like the lowest pit of Dante's Inferno, the frozen lake of the damned, with half-frozen corpses cast here and there. But these were not the damned; they were good men who did not deserve to die.

Sometime in the night, the resolve of one of the men cracked, and he dragged himself toward the light and heat and steam of the baths. The sudden temperature change killed him instantly[703].

Guards stationed along the edge of the lake were ordered not to offer assistance, nor prevent any of the prisoners to crawl toward the baths. Some accounts say that most of the guards fell asleep; all but one. First he saw the one deserter crawl and die. Then a strange light seemed to shine above the thirty-nine still on the ice. The shining seemed to be a ring of brilliant crowns, descending over the remaining men[704]. This lone guard suddenly stripped his clothes, proclaimed himself a Christian, and took his place among the freezing martyrs. The number of the prisoners on the ice returned to forty[705].

When the dawn came, many of the men were found to be still alive, clinging to whatever tiny spark still existed within their frozen bodies. The guards were ordered to torture the men, shattering their legs with hammers until their souls finally departed.

The last one to remain alive was the youngest of the group. His mother cried when she saw her son so long tortured, and she gripped him to herself. He died in her arms[706].

This is the ultimate, the pinnacle. Such is Mortal Sacrifice. Somewhere, someplace, there is a long, narrow path[707] that stretches from this earth to the Presence of the Most High, but it crosses this frozen, pitiless lake. Few ever come this way, and there is little, if any, traffic. To travel this lonely path will prove to be the most difficult task, for it is called "Sacrifice", the road to it is called "Discipline", and the toll charge

---

702 Ibid.
703 Ibid.
704 (In Memory of the 40 holy Martyrs of Sebaste, 2013)
705 (Kirsch, 1909)
706 (Ricciotti G., 1992) pg.213
707 Matt 7:14, also see Isaiah 35:8, Proverbs 16:17

is called "pain". These forty men have already traveled the path and have entered the small, narrow gate at its end. They wait for you.

To Purchase Honor with Blood

Mortal Sacrifice is Martyrdom. This is considered the "crown" of Christian living; the apex of a glorious life that ends in a glorious death for GOD[708]. It is often called the Red Crown, because of its high cost of blood.

There are two sides to this terrifying crown. A Christian may reach Martyrdom after exhausting all means of honorable struggle against the enemies of the Lord[709], and finding himself faced with the choice of death or the revoking of Christ, he chooses death. As did the Forty Martyrs, they sacrifice their lives for GOD and Jesus.

The other side is Martyrdom in battle. A knight or warrior, hurling himself against the soldiers opposed to GOD, placing his life and body on the line in the name of Christ and for the victory of Christ, achieves Martyrdom if he is killed[710]. A knight or warrior might do this by defending the Church and the faithful against the enemies of GOD anywhere, but those who chose to fight for Christ in the Holy Land, on the way to Jerusalem, were called Crusaders and their struggle was known by many as "taking up the Cross"[711].

To go to Jerusalem on peaceful, unarmed pilgrimage, or to go on purpose looking for an honorable fight, were both considered a very probable and respectable way of meeting one's martyrdom. The Middle East was full of Moslems who varied from tolerating Christianity to mass murder. Either by finding oneself in the midst of bloodthirsty unbelievers, or taking arms against pagans, simply taking the trip was placing oneself in true peril. Nonviolent pilgrims and warriors alike sewed small crosses to their garments to broadcast their intentions.

In today's world, people confuse the honorable title of Martyrdom with the terrorists of Islam, with their suicide bombers, attacking

---

[708] (Gautier, 1989) pg. 36, (Chadwick, 1993) pg. 177
[709] (Steinbeck, 1976) pg. 243
[710] (Gautier, 1989) pg. 10, (Clairvaux, 1977) pg. 130
[711] (Pernoud, 1963) pg. 40-41

innocent civilians. This is a cruel and diabolic aping of the Christian Martyr. In stark contrast, Christian Martyrs never attack the innocent, but instead offer their own bodies to be destroyed in the name of Christ[712].

Sacrifice—The Bloody Way

One of the things that makes Sacrifice so difficult to accept is it seems to throw away everything protected by Strength and Courage. Strength and Courage battle to keep life, to continue fighting, to never surrender before the enemy[713]. Lions certainly understand these aspects of Honor. Yet Sacrifice seems to stop and even destroy the knight, to force the knight to give up life and liberty. Lions do not die willingly.

Death may occur in the process of sacrifice, but death is not the final goal. In reality, Sacrifice is the ultimate weapon against the knight's spiritual enemies. For men like the Forty Martyrs, St. George, and St. Louis, the real battle field was not of this earth, but instead the landscape of their own souls. Through their sacrifice, they proved their ultimate loyalty to GOD beyond all questioning, defeating the temptations of the Evil One, and even inspired others to become Christians as well.

Even in this world, sacrifice by Godly men has the peculiar ability to confront the actions of evil men, transform them, and somehow bring forth goodness and eventual victory. In the following accounts, we also see that evil and misfortune are countered, out-maneuvered, and even destroyed by Sacrifices of heroes.

But whether Sacrifice accomplishes anything visible, it brings us closer to Christ by familiarizing us with suffering[714]. As we learn to undergo pain with Christ, we take part in HIS death and Ultimate resurrection, and thus we join with HIM in HIS conquest of the world, the Devil, and the flesh[715]. Through Sacrifice, ultimate victory is ours.

---

[712] (Clairvaux, 1977) pg. 131
[713] (Stalker, 1902) pg. 37-39
[714] Matt 16:24
[715] (Bonaventure, 1978) pg. 159

The GOD-Hero's Own Way

We know that suffering and sacrifice is the best way to Christ, because Christ himself suffered and sacrificed so much, making sacrifice almost exclusively a Christian way to salvation.

As it should be, much of the emphasis of Christ's suffering and death is placed on the Resurrection. So much emphasis has gone there, in fact, that many have lost sight of exactly what Christ suffered before that glorious Sunday morning. Even many clergy and religious, while understanding the mental trials and moral courageousness of Christ, know little of the physical agonies[716].

Incredibly, it is possible that children go to Sunday school without the least knowledge of the horrors that Christ endured for them. They have no idea of what it was to be Christ, and therefore they know little of what it will take to be a true Christian.

To educate both children and adults, the movie *Passion of the Christ* was released some years ago. Many people were grateful, but others were stunned by the graphic violence portrayed, and shunned the film as not fit for Christian consumption. Incredibly, many will refuse to see the truth, so caught up in their own versions of religion, the nature of the world, and GOD.

People have always found it difficult to look at the Suffering Christ. The first Christians did not look for or wear a cross, but instead used the Ichthus fish symbol as their sign[717]. Many artists in the early Middle Ages would portray Christ Triumphant: Jesus on the cross, but not suffering nor nailed there, instead in a rising gesture and dressed as a king[718]. They wanted to show Christ's resurrection and victory, even on the cross. Admirable, but still not a clear picture of what Christ suffered to redeem us all.

Knights, saints, and heroes, while celebrating the glory of Christ's resurrection, cannot afford to turn away from Christ's suffering. It is the knight's duty, as well as the habit of thousands of knights throughout history, to meditate on those holy wounds[719]. Perhaps it is no accident that

---

[716] (Barbet, 1953) pg. 8
[717] (Matthews B., 1986) pg. 77, (Julien, 1996) pg. 153
[718] (Barbet, 1953) pg.61
[719] (Loomis, 1951) pg. 343, (Borroff, 1967) pg.14, lines 645-650

one of the most precise renderings of Christ's crucifixion, complete with nails driven through the wrists, was presented by the Hospitaller Knights to Pope Pius XI [720].

We have already discussed Christ's moral and mental sufferings to some extent in the Courage Chapter, leading to his sweating of blood in the Garden of Gethsemane, but we will now focus more on His physical sufferings. A precise and medical rendering of the Messiah's passion is presented in the excellent book *A Doctor at Calvary*, providing information by experienced surgeons using Biblical accounts, the Shroud of Turin, and their own extensive anatomical knowledge.

After the ordeal at the Garden, Jesus Christ was led by a mob to the High Priest's residence, and then to the Praetorium. He may have received plenty of ill treatment along the way, but at the Praetorium, Christ was struck many times, beginning probably with a stick, around the head and face [721]. Then the scourging began.

For Scourging, Roman soldiers typically used a Flagrum, something like a "Cat-o-nine-tails", each leather strap fitted with two small leaden balls and one tiny sheep bone[722]. These fittings on the whips would have caused severe lacerations, on top of the cutting and bruising that the whip would have done by itself. The Hebrews believed in Moses' law, indicating that only 40 stripes should be given at such punishments. Barbet points out that the Romans would have had "no such limitations", and figures that Christ would have been struck at least sixty times, but probably much more, with his face to the column and his arms tied above his head. This treatment would have left a network of open, bloody, and raw strips of flesh across Christ's back and legs, especially tender now for the carrying of the Cross[723].

Not satisfied with the torture, the Roman soldiers decided to place a "crown" of thorns on Christ's head. Barbet reasons that these thorns might have come from the *Zizyphus Spina Christi*, a tree common in those parts with huge thorns[724]. Barbet also reasons that the branches of this tree were woven into a full cap, not just a crown, and then beaten

---

[720] (Barbet, 1953) pg. 92

[721] Ibid. pg. 83

[722] Ibid. pg.48

[723] Ibid. pg. 83

[724] Ibid. pg. 85

into Christ's scalp and forehead with a stick, causing severe lacerations and bleeding across Christ's whole head[725].

Anyone carrying a huge beam of wood in this condition and with such a cap would receive continuous scraping across the already lacerated back and legs, as well as constant smashing of the wood into the "crown" of thorns[726]. According to tradition Christ's fell three times, slamming the wood into various areas of his body, probably smashed his dominant knee into stones and dirt[727].

The whole traumatic experience, including the beatings and lashings, leading up to the crucifixion would have wounded the heart incredibly, causing serious pericarditis, a condition which includes "dreadful pains in the region of the heart, oppression, anguish, rigor, fever, and finally intense difficulty in breathing"[728]. Another symptom, hydropericardium, fluid flooding in around the heart, would have produced, as seen by St. John after Christ had died and the spear pierced his chest, what appeared to be blood and water flowing out of Christ's side [729]. This severe condition literally held his heart captive, and it is no wonder that Christ had difficulty carrying the cross along the Dolorous Way.

Nails, perhaps similar to railroad tie nails, were driven into Christ's wrists. While many artists favor portraying the hands as receiving the nails, Barbet points out that the wrists were much more logical to carry the weight of the body upon the cross, as well as corresponding to the ancient world's view of the wrists being a part of the hands. (The Knights Templar, perhaps because of their close proximity to the Shroud of Turin, were another of the first groups to portray this fact of Christ's wrists pierced, in art[730].) In fact, according to Barbet, the nails would have been driven directly through the median nerve of the wrists, twisting the thumbs inward. While there is little blood in this procedure, the pain is beyond comprehending.

Barbet explains: "(T)he median nerves are not merely the motor nerves, they are also the great sensory nerves. When they were injured and stretched out on the nails, in those extended arms, like strings of

---

[725] Ibid.

[726] Ibid. pg. 90

[727] (Barbet, 1953) pg. 90

[728] (Barbet, 1953) pg.123

[729] Ibid. pg. 122, scene in John 19:34

[730] (Meacham, June 1983), (Kannon, 2007) pg. 170

a violin on their bridge, they must have caused the most horrible pain. Those who have seen, during the war, something of the wounds of the nervous trunks, know that it is one of the worst tortures imaginable; so bad is it that its prolongation would not be compatible with life, without some sort of suspension of the normal functions; this most frequently takes the form of a feinting fit"[731].

But Christ did not allow himself the luxury of fainting. He was determined to suffer all, so that all would be forgiven. His incredible, indomitable will continued to persist, very conscious, and even speaking to those around him.

Then Christ's feet would have been nailed, either together or separately, most likely through the second intermetatarsal space[732]. Although many paintings and statures include a little ledge upon which Christ's feet would have balanced, Barbet shows that this was probably not present at the real crucifixion. Christ's legs and ankles would have been forcibly bent so that his feet lay flush on the wood of the base of the cross. Christ's whole body would have been balanced mercilessly on one or two nails[733]. These nails would be the point on which Christ would have to push up from, placing all of his weight upon the nerves and flesh torn asunder in his feet, and the splintered median nerves of his hands, in order to breath.

For breath, as much as the blood, is where life, and subsequently death, dwells. The cross is an instrument of death, not simply from the torture, but from the fact that it slowly suffocates its victim. The arms, spread as they are, tire the diaphragm muscles, and the victim finds it harder and harder to expel the used air from his lungs. In order to rest his diaphragm muscles slightly to breath out, he must place all his weight on his tortured feet to push his chest up. Then, when he can no longer sustain this position, he falls back, pulling afresh on the median nerve of his wrists, sending his bodies into new universes of pain.

Few instruments are more fiendishly cruel[734], than this monstrous device used to torture the only sinless man who ever lived. And to think, that this perfect man, with perfect will and perfect moral courage, chose this way of terrible death.

---

[731] (Barbet, 1953) pg. 105

[732] Ibid. pg. 110

[733] Ibid.

[734] (Barbet, 1953) pg. 72

"(W)ith what serene self control, with what supreme dignity He dominated this passion which was foreseen and willed by Himself. He died because he willed it, when He was able to say to himself in a state of full consciousness:—"it is consummated."—My task is accomplished."[735] He died in the way that He willed"[736].

This is how Christ defeated Death, and the Devil himself[737]. This is how Christ conquered the World[738].

We are not worthy to superimpose ourselves upon Christ's suffering, but from His lesson, we learn that we must suffer to follow Him. As St. Francis said, we must take up our own cross, and follow He who bears the Cross[739].

Sacrifice is not only the royal, yet bloody, road to GOD; it is the road to service of GOD. A road that is all pain. And there are many ways to walk this road, but all of them require the Cross.

Sacrifice to Grow Closer to GOD

Every religion in the world deals with death roughly the same. Suffering, however, is seen very differently depending on the religion[740]. Some religions say only the sinful and ungodly suffer. Islam insists that Allah, their supreme being, would never allow the righteous to suffer any pain at all. While they see Jesus Christ as a great prophet, they do not believe He died on the cross, since GOD, to them, would never allow such a righteous man as Christ to feel such agony[741].

Christians, on the other hand, understand that a righteous man suffers profoundly. Just as Jesus Christ suffered for all humanity, so too must the godly man take up his cross and suffer, in imitation of the GOD-Hero himself[742]. What remains to be seen is how suffering and

---

[735] John 19:30 It is finished.

[736] (Barbet, 1953) pg. 80

[737] (Bonaventure, 1978) pg.159

[738] John 16:33

[739] (Bonaventure, 1978) pg.189

[740] (Lewis, 1996) pg. 102-103, (Zacharias, 2001) pg. 27

[741] (Read, 1999) pg. 48

[742] Matthew 16:24

pain will unfold in each man's life, and which cross he will bear for the greater glory of GOD. "And I myself will show him everything he is to suffer"[743].

For many Christians of ancient and medieval times, suffering and sacrifice were seen as the royal and exact way of connecting oneself to Christ, imitating Him to become like Him as much as possible, sharing in His sacrifice and thus sharing in His final glory. This terrifying voluntary suffering had two main branches, Martyrdom and Asceticism.[744] Both infused into lives of some of the greatest knights of all time.

Martyrdom we have already visited briefly. What remains is the far more lengthy sacrifice, called Asceticism.

Asceticism: The Meat of Sacrifice

Basically, a sacrifice is the giving up of something one doesn't want to give. A giving that hurts. The most powerful sacrifices, Martyrdom and Asceticism, are given "up" to GOD. Sacrifices that are deadly or lead to death are called "mortal", and have Martyrdom as their pinnacle. Ascetic sacrifices, sometimes called austerities, are generally not deadly, but involve varying levels of pain and discomfort, and the same spirit of sacrifice as Martyrdom[745]. True knights engage in all of them.

One mistake often made is the assumption that sacrifice of life and limb, mortal sacrifice or martyrdom, is the only sacrifice required of knights, saints, and heroes. Sacrifice, on the contrary, can be an on-going process. No less terrifying as martyrdom are the many great Ascetic sacrifices that insist the sacrificer to continue to live. Father Agostino Trape' states that those who tolerate death for GOD are honored as martyrs, but many are asked to "tolerate" a painful but enduring life for GOD, and these are to be honored too[746]. Sacrifice is a way of life.

They call it the White Crown. Saints and knights know the value of asceticism, suffering in the name of GOD, and the denial of oneself. Knights such as Ramon Lull and Saints such as Ignatius Loyola gave up

---

[743] Acts 9:16
[744] (Chadwick, 1993) pg. 177
[745] Ibid.
[746] (Trape', 1986) pg.360

all vestiges of their former, worldly lives, all the wealth and everything they had, to go on terrifying, self-denying missions for GOD, dressed in nothing but rags. Templar and Hospitaller knights took on a monk's lifestyle, giving up individual ownership of goods, freedoms, autonomy, and intimacy with women[747]. Similarly, knights like Guy of Warwick and William of Gellone would surrender contact with the world itself, making themselves hermits and adopting a saintly existence in the far corners of the world[748].

The Red Crown tends to be quick and terrifying, while the White Crown tends to be long and grueling. Neither are for the weak of heart. Both require intense strength and courage. Both have one main purpose, the service of GOD. The Red has two sides, while the White has many.

We will now explore the many sides and purposes of the White Crown of Sacrifice, asceticism.

Moral Sacrifice

Almost exclusively to Christianity, the path of GOD demands self-denying pain and sacrifice. In Christianity as well, the path of GOD involves helping other people.

When a man sacrifices greatly to exclusively help others in need, especially at risk or suffering to himself, we call this "moral" sacrifice. Although every sacrifice serves GOD and humanity in some way, these sacrifices stand out especially. Christ's passion is the ultimate example, and has changed the universe, but most moral sacrifices only affect a few at a time, and go un-recorded, committed every day by great men who are forgotten to history, and unrecognized by their neighbors.

I remember one man, though he did not stand out from the crowd, mostly quiet and unassuming. When I was a boy, I heard pieces of stories connected with him, though I only met him once. His name was Hilary, and he worked as other men, kept a home as other men, but while others would return to their wives and children when the day was done, the fruits of their labors and relations, Hilary returned to his brother. Hilary's brother was autistic or somehow mentally retarded, unable to care for

---

[747]   (Kannon, 2007) pg. 93
[748]   (Gerritsen and Melle, 1998) pg. 134, (Moncrieff, 1976) pg. 239, (Malory, 1962) pg. 505

himself, and Hilary spent most of 60 years, all his spare time, and any vestige of a normal life taking care of him, making sure all was well.

I also remember, with my boyish ways, unable to filter anything and consuming all whispers and fragments that came to me, that he was never to marry or have a family of his own. Some of the women of the clan had conspired to make sure of this, and to this day I don't remember how I heard the whispers, but I am sure I heard them. Hilary never complained or showed resentment, but simply did his duty, holding up his brother's world like Atlas at the edge of the earth.

After he and his brother had passed away, I was taken to his house. I wandered into the brother's room, and stood there for a moment. I imagined the many hours and days and years Hilary had spent there, with the various chores of taking care of an invalid. Hilary loved his brother, but I also imagined how difficult things might have been sometimes, with him knowing that he would never have a life separate from his responsibilities. The space, the blankness, the weight, the enormity of those years bore down on me in that little room, as I thought of one man doomed to a life contained within it, and his brother who deigned to share that doom. I became aware of the clock in the room. The ticking of that fateful clock!

Unknown and lost in time, but what can I tell you about the terrible pain and discipline that such sacrifices demand?

And some such sacrifices are so terrifying and bewildering that even the world stands up and takes notice.

In 1865, the beautiful landscape of Hawaii suffered marring by the outbreak of that greatly feared scourge of the Middle Ages, Leprosy. This disease flared like a sore across the land, threatening to destroy the entire Hawaiian population, until the king decided to quarantine large numbers of the infected, banishing them to a piece of Molokai island, separated from the haunts of regular men by a giant cliff wall.

These poor sufferers had been sent away to die a slow, horrifying death, abandoned by their people and by humanity itself[749].

When men lose hope, they tend to descend down into the pit of animalistic cruelty and selfishness, and this leper colony grew to become more than a physical horror. The Catholic Church became aware of

---

[749] (Fulkerson, 2010)

the situation. Who would come to help these starving souls find their humanity again?

Several missionaries and attempts were made to help these poor souls, but with little effect. In 1873, a Hawaiian newspaper published an appeal: "If a noble Christian priest, preacher or sister should be inspired to go and sacrifice a life to console these poor wretches, that would be a royal soul to shine forever on the throne reared by human love"[750].

A priest stepped forward. He would go by many names: Joseph de Veuster, Makua Kamiano[751], Knight Commander, but most would know him as Father Damien. He had just been ordained, and when the Bishop expressed worry over whether Damien understood the difficulties before him, Damien assured him that he was prepared to "bury himself alive" upon the island of dread[752]. It is rare that a man volunteers to journey into such a horrid field of battle.

He was a course, rough, stubborn man with a child-like faith, difficult to deal with and tough as nails[753]. But any man would have been put to the test the moment he arrived at the colony. Suddenly surrounded by an army of forms, some barely human, some whose faces were literally falling apart, all demanding aid or just a tiny hope to continue existence, and permeated by the stench of rotting flesh—the hallmark of Leprosy[754]. But Father Damien was determined to stay. He reported that it took two weeks for him to overcome the stench, and this mainly by taking up a smoking habit, purging his clothes and the air with pungent tobacco[755].

A strong physical component exists with most moral sacrifices. When Father Damien saw the deplorable conditions where they lived, he immediately set about building decent, hospitable homes, he himself sleeping out under a tree with the scorpions and other insects, until all the inhabitants had clean, proper quarters. He constantly cleaned wounds, bathed dirty skin, fed hungry mouths, and even amputated destroyed limbs, all with the loving and gracious care of a man tending honored flowers[756]. He discovered they had little training in the basic

---

[750] Ibid.
[751] (Daniel-Rops, 2002) pg. 190
[752] (Fulkerson, 2010)
[753] (Stevenson, 1890)
[754] Ibid.
[755] (Fulkerson, 2010)
[756] Ibid.

necessities of living in an isolated community and set about teaching them how to farm, build serviceable houses, and even construct the simple coffins that were needed every day. He insisted on a cemetery for the dead, so that they would no longer be discarded like trash on a rubbish heap, and soon he had pure water flowing to the inhabitants from mountain springs nearby[757].

Often overlooked, the spiritual component is essential in any moral endeavor. Father Damien performed the usual services of a priest with zeal, boundless fortitude, and energy, fighting the depression and black malaise of living with such a terrible disease. He preached against despair, and against the weird pagan rituals that threatened to absorb the community in superstition. He also found it necessary to patrol the island, watching for abuse and plunder of the dying[758], and indecent ceremonies where even children were attacked and molested. On these trips, he carried a trusty walking cane[759].

All this tending of and living with the sick led to the inevitable result: after 11 years among his tattered flock, Father Damien acquired leprosy[760]. He did not let this slow him down, and instead, felt a strange exhilaration, for now the lepers could truly accept him as one of their own. He kept working with incredible power and fierceness even in the face of the disease. Slowly but surely, his right arm failed him and had to be secured in a sling, one of his legs trailed behind, almost useless, his left hand and face covered with bloated sores, but he refused to stop. One eyewitness, visiting a few months before the priest died, said that he saw Damien helping to repair the roof of the church on the island, recently damaged by a storm, even though his leprosy was far advanced[761]. But Damien was not barking out orders from some safe cot, he was literally on the roof, repairing the shingles himself.

The people of Belgium voted Father Damien one of the greatest Belgians of all time, and a German newspaper said that anyone passing by the cliffs of Molokai should "bow low"[762]. Mahatma Gandhi, moved by Damien's powerful sacrifice to continue his own Indian social

---

[757] (Daniel-Rops, 2002) pg. 187
[758] (Daniel-Rops, 2002) pg. 186
[759] (Fulkerson, 2010)
[760] (Daniel-Rops, 2002) pg.190
[761] (Fulkerson, 2010)
[762] (Daniel-Rops, 2002) pg. 192

campaigns, said that whatever it is in the Catholic Church that could produce thousands of saintly men like this priest ought to be studied and imitated[763]. The King of Hawaii dubbed Damien "Knight Commander of the Royal Order of Kalakaua", and when the Princess Lydia Liliuokalani came to Molokai to bestow on Damien the award, she broke down and wept in the presence of his steadfast love and selflessness in the wake of so much pain[764].

After 16 years in Molokai, Father Damien died, his last wish to be buried under the same tree where he spent his first nights in the colony[765]. Just as there are still scorpions crawling there, rumors still lurk about the poor priest. For even in this labor of suffering, when a man is victorious, he creates enemies of the envious. Robert Louis Stevenson, the famous author, took it upon himself to debunk these rumors. He said that Father Damien would stand for all eternity as a far better man, a more honorable man than any of his ridiculous detractors[766]. Father Damien, in imitation of Christ, had dared to entomb himself with the living dead, under the altar of Sacrifice.

Spiritual Sacrifice

And now we have come nearly full circle. Some serve others and serve GOD in the process, while others serve GOD and serve others in the process.

I give these Southwestern Texas people I live with some credit. For the most part, barring the occasional licentious idiot, these people are hard workers and understand, however vaguely, various types of sacrifice. They have sacrificed time, energy, and the pain of work to support their families, so they understand physical, even moral sacrifice. Perhaps an occasional ambitious dream has energized some of them to enter into mental sacrifice, exercising their powers of self-denial to study and write

---

[763] (Volder, 2010) pg. 167
[764] (Representatives, 2009), (Aiona, 2009)
[765] (Daniel-Rops, 2002) pg. 193
[766] (Stevenson, 1890)

in the service of their love of kin or material success. They understand sacrifice grounded on this earth, close to the soil and heart of men.

But, again, we approach a true terror: one that is beyond the sacrifice of practicality, mental gymnastics, or even self-denial in the name of Christian charity. This next kind of sacrifice is unintelligible to the practical, down-to-earth nature of the Texan, unaccustomed as they are with mysticism. Protestants cannot grasp it because it seemingly has no practical applications in helping the community or proselytizing. Atheists find it bewildering and ridiculous, because they do not fathom even the aim of such sacrifice, let alone its rigors.

Edward Gibbon, skeptical author of the classic *Rise and Fall of the Roman Empire*, considered the spiritual sacrifice of martyrs and ascetics as dangerously insane, blaming their spiritual aspirations and neglect of worldly concerns as two reasons for the fall of the Roman world[767]. Who can explain the mysteries of GOD to an unbeliever? It would be like speaking of color to a blind man, or taste to a man without a tongue. Spiritual sacrifice is well beyond the concerns and thus the senses of this world.

Indeed, only two types of men can truly understand and approach true spiritual sacrifice, who Kierkegaard called the Knight of Infinite Resignation and the Knight of Faith[768]. These have left all attachment behind, and have only one goal—GOD[769]. They stand, willing to give away all and in terrible pain, with no material gain or advantage possible, and all things given up and denied, simply to become close to GOD.

And these knights do so willingly, and with their whole heart. In the tradition of Ascetics like John the Baptist, Psuedo-Dionysius, and John Cassian, they grasp that GOD alone is reality, only GOD is real, only GOD is worthy of attention. In sacrificing everything, they reach for everything within GOD HIMSELF.

Simeon Stylites

Spiritual sacrifice is the most demanding, and sometimes the most spectacular, giving of one's self. Many times it goes unnoticed by the

---

[767] (Gibbon, 1781) vol 3, Ch.37, part II, para.72-72
[768] (Kierkegaard, 1983) pg. 37, 38, 42-50
[769] Ibid. pg. 43

world of men, sometimes even they are stunned by its power. It combines the many types of sacrifice, blending the moral with the mortal, ascetics with fiery adoration, requiring triple the discipline because it combines all the sacrifices together.

Simeon Stylites began life as a shepherd, and one day stumbled into a church. The priest there was giving a sermon on the "Pure of Heart shall see GOD", and Simeon was instantly riveted. He wished to have this ability, this "purity to see GOD", and he was told that joining a monastery remained a good way to find it[770].

Apparently the Monastic life proved not ascetic enough for him, and after several years, he set off alone, into the mountains, to embrace a life of even more self-denial by restricting his living space. At one point, he chained himself to an area roughly twenty feet in diameter[771]. While he limited his traveling, others took it up to ask him questions and implore him for prayers. His holy example and asceticism became so powerful and well known that it brought constant visitors, and he was unable to complete his prayers, which he felt should be continuous.

He had a vision where he was told to build a structure, several feet high, something looking like an altar. After several years of living in pits and caves, gathering various asceticisms from other holy men, he went back to this structure, and began spending his days on top of it. When crowds began to come more and more, seeking healing miracles, exorcisms, and advice, he built his pillar higher and higher, so as to gain some sort of control of the endless flow of people.

Finally, even Roman soldiers sat in stunned silence, watching Simeon stand vigil, praying unceasingly on top of a 60-foot-pillar in Syria, near Antioch[772]. They realized the power and strength of this man, and crowds from miles around came to ask his advice and his insight.

And with Simeon, he always stood, kneeled, or bowed, never allowing himself the luxury of sitting or reclining, forever praying in a posture of attention[773]. No roof rested his sun-burned and tired skin, or shaded the squinting of his eyes. No walls defended him from the hot winds during the day, or the dry cold at night. Sometimes the flesh of his feet split from the strain, or the muscles of his stomach gave out form

---

[770] (Visser, 1996)
[771] (Thurston, 2009)
[772] (Visser, 1996)
[773] (Lent, 1915) para 576-578

bowing, or his back went out of joint, but he simply continued to pray[774], tying himself to a stake secured to the pillar[775]. He would sleep in short intervals before dawn, and that too standing up, again tied to the stake behind him[776].

Several times, his eyes failed and he was blind for long periods of time, but he continued his vigils and his speeches to the crowds, only his attendants realizing his maladies[777]. All his meals were raised to him by two admirers taking turns; questions and requests for prayers were shouted to him from a scaling ladder.

And there he stayed, praying ceaselessly, standing like a human church steeple, unmoved and unmoving for 36 years[778].

Why live atop a column, instead of some other austerity, with no shade and no relief from the elements, constantly exposed to surveillance for one's entire life? An obviously holy and ascetic man of Simeon's caliber had always attracted crowds of admirers and even detractors, and once Simeon had tried to avoid them by traveling long distances, he finally avoided them vertically by building taller and taller pillars[779]. Watching the sun rise and fall, and the turning of Ursa Minor at night in its tireless trek around Polaris, the North Star, Simeon had left behind the mundane world and approached, in a very concrete way, the silent spheres of Heaven[780]. In every way, he had left the world behind, in search of GOD.

But by doing this, by constructing for himself a giant vertical podium, he perhaps inadvertently created the ultimate stage for missionary work. At once, his presence could command a large field, and everyone could hear him. He would lecture twice a day from this incredible sounding board, and thousands, otherwise insensate to other sermons, would listen intently. Persians and Armenians were converted in large numbers, and especially Arabs, totally unwilling to listen to the preaching of other Christians, were awed and convinced by this man's

---

[774] (Lent, 1915) para 574-576

[775] (Thurston, 2009)

[776] (Visser, 1996)

[777] (Lent, 1915) para 576

[778] (Thurston, 2009), (Visser, 1996) says 37 years

[779] (Thurston, 2009), (Visser, 1996)

[780] (Visser, 1996)

obvious determination to reach GOD, and by his calm words from the pillar[781].

(In this way, lone and ascetic spiritual searches often create abundant fruit, gathering souls for GOD. In a world where churches feel an irresistible pull to be more modern, earthy, and "hip", Simeon's unearthly and purposefully ascetic example is enlightening. If a religion wishes to gain recruits, perhaps instead of becoming more lax and conforming, the best way is to show a stark, disciplined alternative to the world.)

An honest man, either religious or atheistic, when confronted by true Spiritual Sacrifice, is caught in awe. Even Gibbon, a scoffer at martyrs and saints, himself was taken aback a moment by the authentically disciplined example of Simeon[782]. The amount of discipline necessary to accomplish this feat, the total dedication and the iron resolve, are enough to impress the harshest of critics.

Gibbon could not conceive how this absolute devotion and embracing of pain could lead to anything else but stress and bitterness. Any man, Gibbon thought, torturing himself to this extent must finally succumb to hatred of life and thus hatred of fellow man[783]. But Simeon, far from hating others, seemed always brimming with warmth and concern. Even though he wished to escape constant distraction from visitors, he constantly prayed for them, and set up a sermon schedule twice a day for his visitor's edification. Not only were the crowds at the foot of the pillar exposed every day to excellent advice and true compassion, miracles appeared.

People almost immediately came to this holy man for cures and heavenly help. One man came, whose legs were so deformed that his thighs adhered to his sheens, and could not be separated[784]. A noble came, constantly hemorrhaging blood from a strange fever[785]. A woman came who continuously lost so much blood from her mouth that it was thought a demon possessed her. The entire village of Telneshe came with tumors all over their bodies[786]. A heathen man came whose muscles were locked in such a way that he could not lift his head from his chest.

---

[781]   (Crake, 1873) pg. 492
[782]   (Gibbon, 1781) Vol. 3, Ch. 37, part II, para. 71-72
[783]   (Gibbon, 1781) Vol. 3, Ch.37 part II, para.72
[784]   (Lent, 1915) para. 550
[785]   (Lent, 1915) para 551
[786]   Ibid. para 550

Whole communities came, suffering from drought and famine. Seven children came, poor things tortured by paralysis since the day they were born[787]. People came with leprosy, with bizarre maladies of the brain, with myriad terrible diseases, coming for themselves or for their loved ones. All of these begged the holy man, pleaded with him and cried to him to have mercy, so that Simeon looked down from his pillar with profound empathy.

"I am nothing." He said to them, "And my hands are nothing compared to the hands of your Bishops. But I will prayer for you so that the hands of GOD, if HE so wishes, will come down upon you and bring blessings upon you, so that you may be healed"[788]. All the sick who came to him were cured almost immediately, and those who came for some assistance were helped mightily, and more crowds came with more pleadings and concerns. Even those who could not come across the many miles to see the Holy One, as he was called, might expect aid. One man, paralyzed completely so he could not walk or speak for years, languished as the four men who carried him across many miles wearied and could not continue. Simeon had a vision of them, and sent an assistant with the means to cure him, so that the paralyzed man could walk and speak before he ever saw Simeon's pillar[789].

Why would a man who suffered so much be so compassionate to others? Would it not be as Gibbon thought, that anyone sacrificing so much must finally succumb to bitterness and hatred for the others around him? Perhaps Gibbon did not understand the inspiration to sacrifice in this way, the motivation behind sacrificing.

Finally, only two motivations exist in life: Love and Fear. If a man sacrifices out of fear, he may eventually grow to hate that which he sacrifices for, because fear has driven him to absorb much pain. But Love, as the motivation, is different. With complete Love shining in a man's heart, all sacrifice seems as nothing if he can serve such love, and his heart will seem even happy, through every pain and suffering.

Simeon Stylites, and so many other saints, sacrificed out of Love for GOD. Everyone must fear the power of GOD, but our love must be greater than even that fear.

---

[787] (Lent, 1915) para 552,553, 554

[788] Ibid. para 553

[789] Ibid. para 566

And still the Saint stood, day after day, year after year, a beacon to the lost and suffering throughout the world. It seemed that the more Simeon suffered, the more GOD's cure and help came to poor souls who beseeched him. When his skin would split from the strain of constantly standing or exposure, and his sores would fester with maggots and puss, until even his life was ready to flow away, he would not pray for himself. "GOD will do with me what he will," He told his followers on these occasions, "If he wishes to cure me, he will, otherwise, my soul will go to Him"[790]. Many times he was healed, but there came one last time.

The human body, no matter how great the spirit, can only take so much. Gibbon says it may have been a large ulcer in Simeon's thigh, burst by the continuous exposure and strain of standing, that eventually helped end this saint's life[791]. When Simeon's acolytes noticed he had not spoken for several days, they ascended the pillar to find his soul had gone. His body was still in the attitude of prayer, bowing forever, but his spirit had finally joined completely with GOD[792].

These are extreme examples to be sure, but the knight and saint mirror each other with the intense pain and strength in their various modes of sacrifice. While the saints, spiritual knights as they are, tend to have a monopoly on moral and spiritual asceticism, saintly knights tend to make their sacrifice ring with a decidedly martial sound. But all asceticism has the first aim of Sacrifice: service to the LORD.

Whatever the type, whether venial or mortal, and whatever the arena, moral, spiritual or physical, true sacrifice can prove to be agonizing indeed. Terrible, icy sacrifices that bode only ill for the body, heart, and senses. It never ends, and lo! Always another sacrifice looms for the true knight. The knight continues down that path of giving until there is nothing left. No one, at least looking with materialist eyes, can say the knight gains anything from these great sufferings. Chivalry, through sacrifice, strips everything from the knight, until he stands in rags[793].

---

[790] (Lent, 1915) para 579
[791] (Gibbon, 1871) ch. 37, part 2
[792] (Shea, 1894) vol.1
[793] (Spoto, 2002) pg. 60, 55, 63

The Ragged Man in Ragged Clothes

When people ask my opinion on who the greatest knight was, I say, "Barring Lancelot and Galahad, the greatest knight in the world was Sir Guy of Warwick. Not because of his strength, which was truly great, but because of his sacrifice. Worldly happiness and all his dreams lay within his grasp, but he gave them up for GOD in one bold gesture."

Guy of Warwick started out as the son of a servant in the court of Earl Rohand in Warwick, England[794]. While helping his father serve the royalty their meals, he fell in love with the Earl's daughter, Phelis. It was that terrible, wasting kind of love that you read of in romances.

Phelis felt it ridiculous for a mere servant to love her, and she spurned him. But the young man burned with the highest passion, the most noble obsession, and wouldn't leave her alone until she revealed how he could win her heart.

"If you become a knight and win great deeds, then I will deem you lovable," Phelis told him truthfully.

Guy trained night and day until he became one of the strongest knights in the land, then set off to distant places to test that training and prove his mettle with knightly deeds. Years went by, and he battled giants and armies of evil until his name became practically a "household" word. He did it all for love.

He returned a world-famous knight, and found Phelis true to her word. She would marry him now, and his would be one of the most beautiful women in the world, along with the wealth and lands of the Earl.

But Sir Guy of Warwick's travels had made him a wise man. On the days after the wedding, when he should have been preoccupied with wedding bliss, he climbed the tower of the castle while a strange sadness hung over him. He looked over all the richness he would inherit. He thought of the stunning woman who was his wife. He had obtained his wildest dream, even from a lowly birth, he had won the woman of his heart and literally gained a kingdom. He had risked his life a thousand times for these things, but now he felt as if something was wrong. In the

---

[794] (Moncrieff, 1976) pg. 226

rush to win the princess and the fame and fortune, he had forgotten his GOD.

He went down to where Phelis waited for him and stood before her. "My princess, I love you more than anything in this world. I must go to the Holy Land and ask my GOD forgiveness."

Phelis blinked at him. She was speechless. How could he abandon her now, after he had pursued her for so many years?

Yet Guy of Warwick set off for his pilgrimage. He gave everything he owned to the poor and spent his time trying to help everyone around him. Many adventures he experienced walking through the world, fighting evil and rescuing anyone who needed him, so many that not all could be contained in the annals of Chivalry. Finally in Jerusalem, he understood that he had spent the first part of his life and talents for selfish reasons as he saw them, since everything he did was to win the hand of the woman he loved. The only way to set that straight was to spend at least an equal portion of his life living for the GOD he loved. Seven years.

At first, Guy assumed he would wander as a pilgrim, far and wide, well away from the concerns of warriors and knight-errantry, but he soon found out that this was wrong. Everywhere he went, he found devastating problems that only he as knight could solve, terrible enemies that only he as knight could fight.

Kings constantly asked him for assistance, Princesses begged him for help, peasants beseeched him for succor, and no matter how much he tried to avoid it, he always seemed the only one who could come to their aid[795]. He could not turn his back on them for he felt obligated to aid the oppressed, the needy, the innocent. To help these was to do the work of GOD. So be it, he would say, and humbly ask to borrow armor and weapons, since his was long at home in far off Warwickshire.

In these later adventures, Guy keeps his identity a secret, never accepting fame nor reward for the great and impossible feats he accomplishes. Whether against giants, dragons, evil warriors, or wizards, he risks his life and suffers terrible pain, hunger, self-induced exile, and crushing loneliness for a higher cause. His goal is no longer a spectacular

---

[795] (Moncrieff, 1976) pg. 238

name to impress the beautiful Phelis; he now only fights for the greater glory of GOD[796].

Two of Guy's most famous battles are legendary, and both involve giants. One, the Dun Cow, he battles near the beginning of his adventures; the other, Colbrand, when he returns to England after his pilgrimage. Both are still remembered in Children's stories[797]. But I often wonder, when children read about Guy of Warwick, if they realize he is on a mission of penance; do they attend to his anonymity, or his refusal of all reward? Most stories of Guy only emphasize the battle with the massive giants. But we know the true combat is with the crushing pain of self-denial, and the sacrifice which shattered his mighty heart.

When he returned to England, he did not go back to Rohand's Castle and his beloved Phelis, but instead set up a domicile nearby as a hermit. He sat among the other old, pious men of the town, and heard their tales of the generosity and piety of the Countess of Warwick. He resolved to see for himself. Every day, in a disguise, he would beg at the door of the great castle that he once owned, so he might steal a glimpse of his princess and test her charity[798].

On Phelis's part, the sorrow had changed her as well. Every morning, the gorgeous and pious lady would grant charity to each hermit with her traditional statement, "All pilgrims are welcome here, for the sake of one"[799]. She would hand out the baskets of foot at the door herself, and sometimes bring her young son. When Guy saw him for the first time, he almost lost his composure. Careful to keep his hood over his face, but reaching out his robed hand to the boy, he gasped "May the Lord give you the Grace to do what is pleasing in HIS eyes"[800]!

Phelis turned to him and said, "Kind and gentle man, please pray for us." This was the extent of his life with her: she as his princess from afar, he as a beggar at her door.

To this day, Sir Guy of Warwick, along with Sir William of Gellone, Sir Ramon Lull, and the two originators of the Knights Templar, Sirs Hugues de Payens and Geoffrey de St. Omer, stand as the exemplars of

---

[796] Ibid. pg. 238, thus is the original motto of the Jesuits, and all true knights
[797] (Marshall, 2000-2012)
[798] (Marshall, 2000-2012), (Moncrieff, 1976) pg. 238-239
[799] (Moncrieff, 1976) pg. 239
[800] Ibid. pg. 239

men who spent the greater part of their decidedly knightly lives in saintly service, choosing the path of discipline, penance, poverty, and piety to crown their roles as warriors for GOD.

Even though he was a warrior, Warwick's life is exactly as the monk Schellenberger said, "This is no life. But it is not meant to be a life—a safe, solid, certain, cozy condition. This is precisely the burden and the cross of the prophet's calling: not to lead a "normal", satisfied, quiet life, but to be a wanderer, a fugitive, a pilgrim, a stranger . . . Strictly speaking, it is an impossible life—because it is geared to HIM who is to come"[801]. The knight lives an "impossible life" for his GOD[802].

Sacrifice to fight for GOD—Monk and Knight combined

Many ascetic knights took the greatest characteristics of knighthood and combined them with the greatest characteristics of monastic life, creating a hybrid form of hero called "warrior-monk". Perhaps the greatest group of such "warrior-monks" was known as the Order of the Temple of the Poor Knights in Jerusalem, better known as the Templars.

Circa 1119, after the first Crusade, Sirs Hugues de Payens and Geoffrey de St. Omer saw a glaring problem. Jerusalem, the aim of hundreds of thousands of pilgrims, sat firmly under the control of the Christians again, making the city itself a fairly safe place to visit the holiest sites, but the road leading to Jerusalem was still full of thieves and cutthroats, primarily Moslem tribes. De Payens and De St. Omer decided to solve this problem like many had done before them in Europe. In a world without organized police nor consistent law, and the roads and woods dense with robbers and thieves, brotherhoods of knights would join together and drive out or crush the criminals[803]. Churches

---

[801] (Schellenberger, 1981) pg. 29-33

[802] Miguel De Cervantes - In order to attain the impossible, one must attempt the absurd. From "Galatea" (1903) Book: III (page: 135).

[803] (Kannon, 2007) pg. 66

and monasteries, also, depended on bands of knights sworn to protect them[804].

Naming themselves the Poor Knights of Christ, these two knights shed any vestige of their former lives besides their armor, weapons and Honor, and took on the severe vows of Augustinian Monks, that of poverty, chastity, and obedience. With nothing in this world to hold them back, they set about defending and saving the pilgrims who traveled the dangerous roads of the Middle East[805]. This was completely voluntary, "No church or brotherhood had asked this of them—it was a sacrifice to their faith that they made of their own free will"[806].

Soon, seven other knights joined them in this austere quest. Imagine how lonely and difficult those years must have been. Without help and without material gain, these nine knights patrolled the howling wastelands and risked their lives thousands of times with nothing to comfort them but the sharpness of their deadly swords, the brightness of their confirmed belief, and the righteousness of their actions. No crowds cheered them, no women pleaded for them, no treasures waited for them, only the breathless heat, the deafening stillness, and the constant threat of death. They modeled themselves after John the Baptist, complete with abject poverty, total zeal, total reliance on GOD, and lonesome survival in the desert [807].

Yet, despite the terror and asceticism, between 1119 and 1125 the small band of brothers grew so that Hugues de Payens considered himself justified when he set sail for France to seek help, both in contributions and men, to further the incredible service he offered freely throughout the realm of Jerusalem. The Pope recognized them as a holy order, and gave them permission to function where-ever necessary.

Before he and de St. Omer were done, they created one of the most respected and feared organizations of all time, built on the twin concepts of righteous war and monastic holiness[808]. Soon, castles and keeps dedicated to the Poor Knights sprung up everywhere across the Outremer and Europe, all harboring the same commitment to protect Christians

---

[804] (Nicolle, 2005) pg. 140
[805] (Kannon, 2007) pg. 13, (Read, 1999) pg. 91-92
[806] (Kannon, 2007) pg.67
[807] (Kannon, 2007) pg.70
[808] (Read, 1999) pg. 105, (Clairvaux, 1977) pg.140

and Christianity from their enemies, while maintaining help and charity for their members.

Baldwin the Second, king of Jerusalem, became so impressed by these heroes that he gave them the Temple Mount in Jerusalem as their head-quarters, the site of the once great Temple of Solomon. Thus these Poor Knights became known as the "Order of the Temple of the Poor Knights of Jerusalem", the "Templars".

The Templars lived as both monks and knights. Monks in the sense that, individually, they owned nothing, and kept watch over their minds and hearts with a code or set of 72 regulations established by St. Bernard of Clairvaux, and later augmented by the Cistercians, that governed everything: when to sleep, when and what to eat, when to pray, and what to wear[809]. Theirs was "extreme monastic asceticism"[810]. Knights in the sense that they were expected to give their lives in battle; everything they did had to do with fighting for GOD, even to the elimination of "horseplay" or visits from family[811]. I seem to remember that hunting even was restricted, unless it was for the most dangerous of all prey, the Lion[812]. Grim and serious business. This was no romp at a tournament or a festive, occasional battle for fun, but a sacrificial preparation for a showdown with the Devil, on earth and at high noon.

Other knights and men, impressed by this example, began to create similar orders of Warrior Monks. The Hospitallers, who spent most of their time in Jerusalem tending to the needs of pilgrims and the poor, decided to make themselves into a Military order as well, dedicated to the same discipline and sacrifice as the Templars[813]. Other orders, such as the Teutonic knights, followed soon after.

Because of the Templar and Hospitaller's extreme dedication to their vows and the Knight code, totally willing to sacrifice everything in service of their beliefs, the Moslems soon came to see them as implacable and unnerving foes, arming castles that seemed impregnable, and

---

[809] (Kannon, 2007) pg. 68, 74, 89

[810] Ibid. pg. 87, and all of Chapter 4

[811] Ibid. pg. 74

[812] (Pernoud, 1963) pg. 105, The lion carried double duty in symbolism; it could represent GOD, as in Hosea 5:14 or Revelations 5:5, or, in this case, the devil, as in 1 Peter 5:8

[813] (Bradford, 1972) pg. 33

forming terrifying lines of armored cavalry that could bear down on the Islamic armies like the thunder and wrath of GOD.

The Hospitallers and Templars were so willing to sacrifice, that many of the Moslem groups simply gave up fighting them. The Old Man in the Mountain, as he was called by the natives, ran a feared secret society of Moslem assassins from a secret mountain base. They struck terror in the hearts of kings and sultans across the Middle East and even in Europe, because they wielded power by assassinating leaders in the night. But even the Old Man gave up trying to frighten the Hospitallers and the Templars. These knights were the only group that did not pay tribute to the Old Man, but the Old Man paid tribute *to them*[814].

The Templars were great adversaries of the Moslems, so much so that Moslems saw them with particular dread and knew them to be undauntable. This is why, as far as the Moslems were concerned, they could not allow Templar or Hospitaller knights to survive when captured[815]. Other Christian warriors might be offered conversion to Islam in exchange for life, but the Templars and Hospitallers were always offered nothing but a bloody death. Such a foe, the Moslems knew, who refused to surrender or retreat, totally dedicated to discipline and martial belief, had to be destroyed completely whenever possible simply because they posed too much of a threat to Islam. When a knight became a Templar or Hospitaller, he knew that he would eventually spend his life as a sacrifice, in extreme prayer, training, and dedication, or would die as a sacrifice, far from home and at the end of a Saracen blade.

Although the Templars and their brethren had many victories, their defeats, when they came, were studies in nightmare. The Templars faced these defeats with dignified resignation, for they were accustomed to sacrifice.

One of the most horrific defeats in Templar history was the battle at the Horns of Hattin, a desolate and hilly stretch of desert about four kilometers from the Sea of Galilee, known as the Oven of the Devil[816]. It was here, where the temperatures can easily reach 130 degrees Fahrenheit, that the Templars, along with other knights and foot soldiers, made an ill-planned stand against a strategically and numerically superior force of Moslem warriors under Saladin. The Christian force, without water for

---

[814] (Joinville, 1963) pg.277

[815] (Addison, 2001) pg. 127, (Robinson, 1991) pg. 148-149, (Belloc, 1992) pg. 241, (Nicolle, 2005) pg. 72

[816] (Robinson, 1991) pg. 148-149

days and completely exhausted, was surrounded and finally overwhelmed. Usually a magnanimous man, Saladin demanded that each of the surviving Templars and Hospitaller knights be beheaded[817].

The knights lost for lack of planning by their leaders, but not for lack of discipline or willingness to sacrifice.

The knights lined up, one by one, without being forced, and even gently shouldered each other out of the way, willing to be first. One by one, they bared their necks for the blade, without complaint[818]. As Saint Paul, John the Baptist, and a thousand other saintly martyrs before them, they met their demise squarely. This is what was expected. These men understood sacrifice, and died as true knights. It was July 4, 1187, and the Third Crusade would soon begin.

Thus, from the Forty Martyrs to Sir Warwick, the Knights of the Round Table to the Knights Templar, we have seen the species of sacrifice a knight must make in service of his GOD, from life to death. His existence, because of the sacrifices he makes, becomes a painful denial of everything other people work for in life.

The Calmness of Sacrifice

Through the terrors of sacrifice, a true warrior, saint, and knight remains calm[819]. He may worry and even tremble at the thought before the time comes, but when the moment of truth arrives, he is strangely composed, even serene[820].

When the Pagan Roman Emperor Decius ordered Saint Mercurius, called the saint of the two swords, to be beaten with nail-tipped whips, then slowly skinned and roasted over an open flame, the saint remained calm and patient. While Mercurius went through the tortures as if they were no more than the tauntings of small children, Decius became the one enraged and unhinged by this powerful saint[821].

---

[817] (Addison, 2001) pg. 127
[818] (Read, 1999) pg. 160, (Addison, 2001) pg. 128
[819] (Scupoli, 1945 edition) pg. 80
[820] (Athanasius, 1980) pg. 70
[821] (Woods, 1999) section 11-13

Calmness in adversity is not only a trait of saints, but all great warriors everywhere.

The story of Thermopylae is another scene of this calmness. There, 300 Greek Spartans prepared to hold off an army of over a million Persian warriors. A Persian spy observed the Spartans and then ran back to tell Xerxes, the Persian king, what they were doing on the eve of the lope-sided battle.

"They are just combing their hair and exercising!" The spy said. "As if nothing were to happen on the morrow!"

An advisor who knew the Spartans well told the king: "This is the very way they face death, as if it was simply another day. Now, oh king, you are face to face with the bravest men of Hellas"[822].

These Spartans stood their ground and resisted the advance of the Persians, even though the Persians out-numbered them by more than a thousand to one. At the end of the battle, all the Spartans were slain, but the Persians had suffered terrible losses in the battle, and were soon forced to retreat. They would never conquer the Greeks.

Men of great discipline treat an obstacle or misfortune as if "it were simply another day". They do not complain, even in the face of overwhelming odds and hardship.

This great calmness finds its way to Spiritual warriors as well. When Rabbi Akeeva was captured by the Romans, they tore his flesh off with combs of iron. But the Rabbi did not complain or even cry out. Instead, he sat there calmly.

His torturers, young and pagan Romans, were visibly shaken by the Rabbi's stern calmness. One cried out, "Oh, man! How is it that you can do this?"

"Calm yourselves." The Rabbi said. "I have just realized an interpretation of a prayer that I had not thought of before"[823].

Christ himself, as he stood before Pontius Pilate, and even as he suffered upon the cross, had complete presence of mind and control of his reactions. Unmoved by the taunting of the unbelieving thief and the crowd around him, even as he bled and fought to breath, he showed kindness to the thief who asked his mercy. He made sure John took care of his mother Mary, and had Mary accept John as a member of the

---

[822] (Macgregor, 2000-2012)
[823] (Romer, 1988) pg. 152-153

family. Even nailed to a cross, Christ's concern was for others, and he held his quiet dignity till the last.

He cried out once, but only as the weight of the world's sins settled upon his purest soul, and his cry was a quote from the Scriptures: Psalm 22[824]. Even in death and utmost agony, he was quoting the Psalms.

This almost unearthly calmness in the face of pain, desolation, and death brings into high relief the incredible self-discipline of Sacrifice.

Sacrifice as Discipline, and its limits

Sacrifice in this manner is a terrifying power. It is the ability to give up something lesser for something greater. The Saints and holy knights sacrificed to save their souls and the souls of others. Christ gave his suffering so that through Him, the whole universe could be saved.

How should a man gain for himself this terrifying power, that he may offer his body to be burned or destroyed, and yet stay calm, selfless, and quiet even unto certain torture? There are many ways of Sacrifice, just as there are many ways to serve GOD. One road is ultimate Martyrdom, while another is Asceticism and Austerities, crusades, pilgrimages, and quests. Sometimes these ways of sacrifice converge, and others never cross. But all the ways demand one essential knightly trait.

The road of Sacrifice, on which all instincts and desires are corrected and focused or ignored and burned away, requires Discipline. "Discipline" is a terrifying word to many, for it brings to mind the frightful crucible of ultimate pain, self-denial, starvation of all pleasure, and iron resolve in the face of every imaginable torture. Yet, as you now know, Discipline is used in every aspect of knighthood, especially Sacrifice. This kind of sacrifice leads to Strength—True Strength.

True knights practice limited sacrifice, through discipline and self-denial, as a way of strengthening the will, soul, body, and mind[825]. It is surprising how limited sacrifice through discipline, when properly focused, can generate great strength. But be aware. Certain sacrifices are not recommended for knights. Not because the asceticism may prove

---

[824] Matt 27:46, also Mark 15:34,—Christ, in his incredible suffering on the cross, is quoting Psalm 22:1

[825] (Lull, 2001) pg. 77-94, (Clairvaux, 1977) pg. 138-140

too difficult; it is a matter of goal. While the monks or saints of old had the goal of spiritual and moral victory, the knight must have victory in all arenas, physical and mental, as well as spiritual. Some austerities obstruct the way to physical victory in combat, even mental victory. Lull says not to give everything away so that one may maintain his ability to fight evil[826]. "Bread and water" knights, knights that fasted too much or ate only bread and never ate protein, were despised by Hospitallers and Templars because their diets wore away their muscles, making such a man too weak to fight effectively. A balance of asceticism, the golden mean, must be established so that physical, mental, and spiritual goals can all be achieved. A knight must be an effective knight, sacrificing and yet retaining the ability to fight evil in all arenas[827].

Sacrifice and talent

In this modern America, as in Rome under Constantine, no one is obligated to die for Christ. For the time being, at least, no one is howling for the persecution of Christians, no Nero is hunting them down as scapegoats, no mob wishes to lynch them. For the knight or intense man of action, that glorious path to GOD, the red martyrdom, dying for GOD, is no longer an option, and perhaps such a knight feels a small pang of disappointment. There remains the white.

In Augustine's time, as in ours, the way of sacrifice is a bloodless one, the white martyrdom. There, a righteous person may choose detachment from the world, a life of asceticism, or using one's talents to bring greater glory to GOD. All are noble and awe-inspiring. But although the last one seems easy and obvious, it remains neglected.

GOD gave each of us talents and abilities that seem unique and call us out of the masses. This man shows brilliant moves in sports, that woman has incredible business sense, this man writes words that burn the soul, and that woman plays the violin to charm the world. These talents and abilities, the small and the more glorious, can all be used to bring glory to GOD.

No blood and no violence, but no less a sacrifice. The developing of ability is difficult work. Talents are like seeds that must be nurtured

---

[826] (Lull, 2001) pg. 71, 73, (Martin, 2010) pg. 187
[827] (Lull, 2001) Ibid

before they grow into saplings, and pruned before they can grow into massive Oaks. They require time and practice, work and struggle, painful decisions and focus. The knight, as well as any man or woman, should always push to improve themselves in body, mind, and soul[828].

Then, once we have harnessed our abilities and sharpened them, the world makes claim on our talents, tempting us to use them only for ourselves, only for our selfish wants, only for our own glory and satisfaction. We have been given these gifts freely, but we have to say no to ourselves and control our emotions, otherwise we will run away with them, painting our world with successes without giving thanks to the One responsible, without paying back the One who authored our abilities.

Even worse than misuse is ingratitude heaped on ignorance. Many people complain to GOD and anyone who will listen, forgetting the vast store of skills and powers waiting to be harnessed, never using the facilities lent to them to solve their own problems. In my daily conversations with students, the vast majority are either totally unaware that they have talents, or shrug un-interested when I ask about their aptitudes. Some would rather play video games or chase the opposite sex, suck down beer all day or discuss sports. How boring and how typical. Where is the fire to pursue glory? Where is the gratitude for the sheer joy of using talent or discovering an ability? What could possible cause a young person's soul to seem so dead?

Even more bewildering are those who know their talents and have refined them, avoided the traps of the world and laziness, only to stop cold, throwing down their abilities and skills in the dust. They tell me, "GOD wants me to do something else, to give this up so that I may join a prayer group and work for Church or help the poor, or something like that."

Join the prayer group, turn your back on the world, help the poor— but use the talents GOD gave you to do these things in a glorious way! Instead of throwing GOD's gifts in the trash, use them to follow HIS spirit! Why else would HE have given these abilities to you? All that is required is an imagination to discover how to use these gifts to help the

---

[828] (Vauchez, 1993) pg.61

poor, or pray to GOD. Sacrifice means to give up selfishness, not to give up GOD's gifts!

Often, we may feel a pull in opposite directions like this, opposing forces suggest denying our talents, marking them as only part of "this world" and foreign to GOD. These conflicting feelings come from a well-meaning church, perhaps over-zealous in limiting how GOD should be served.

St. Augustine had conquered himself and his doubts, settling down to a life of quiet reflection and contemplation. Many had noticed the saintliness of the man, and it wasn't long until the local authorities were pounding on his door. They wanted Augustine to be Bishop of Hippo Regius.

Augustine hesitated. He wished to serve the Church and the people, but he felt that GOD was also calling him to a life of writing and reading, praying and fasting. Especially the writing and reading. He possessed a deep desire to continue gathering wisdom, then to write about how this wisdom related to GOD, and he was good at it. The ordinary duties of a bishop would hamper the contemplative studies that he had so looked forward to. Both were good and holy pursuits. Augustine felt caught in an unanswerable quandary. Was he being selfish by wanting to read and write holy works? Should he turn his back on what obviously were gifts from GOD, so that he may answer the will of the people who needed his leadership?

Augustine eventually figured a way to accomplish both, becoming a good bishop and creating a vast library that would rival the most prolific authors. He fed the Church's thirst for scholarship, and astounded the religious and secular world alike with the power of his writings. Augustine did not turn his back on the Church or his GOD-given talents. He used one to fulfill the obligations of the other.

Our talents shine as gifts from GOD, glorious tools by which we may build a better world in HIS light. We must take hold of them and use them in HIS name, thanking HIM all the way. Anything else is a waste and an insult.

Discipline and Success

Discipline and limited sacrifice can strengthen anyone. Bartholomew Roberts started his strange life as a Puritan, but found himself captured by pirates and forced to become one. He said to himself, "If I must be a pirate, I will become the best there is"[829]. He knew, because of his religious studies, that a man cannot accomplish anything without discipline and he thus realized that the drinking, carousing, and womanizing of most pirates were sabotaging any other goal they might have. He decided not to make the same mistake.

Roberts invested in a little self-denial. He insisted that no member of his crew drink alcohol while aboard ship, nor cavort with prostitutes, nor harm women[830].

The result of this extra discipline made him one of the richest pirates of all time[831].

Such is the illumination of a pirate: that discipline can make or break a man. Discipline, that great tool of the will, can help a man avoid pitfalls of life, or the lack of it can destroy him, no matter his physical strength. No matter the goal, a man can use this small sacrifice and discipline to postpone or deny the pleasures of the present, to help win the desires of the future.

But discipline, even as a tool, is not fulfilled in such a life as a pirate's, selfishly striving for material wealth. Its other uses are far more powerful.

Charles Martel used discipline to make his men into the ultimate strategic fighting force, saving all of Europe from imminent invasion. This required of his men to sacrifice their various pleasures, to ignore their emotions, and to avoid the drag of their weaknesses. Every general and every knight must use this lesson to harden himself, to protect the Church, all of civilization, and even himself from every enemy. When discipline is discarded, only disaster can result. Sadly, many would-be knights have discovered this, especially when they refuse to heed a disciplined order in favor of individual pride and personal glory[832].

Still, physical battle is not the zenith of self-control. Discipline finds its ultimate culmination in the pursuit of spiritual wealth, spiritual life

---

[829] (Cawthorne, 2003) pg. 210-211
[830] See the Pirate Articles in the index of honor codes
[831] (Cawthorne, 2003) pg. 210
[832] (Barber, 1995) pg. 229, (Clairvaux, 1977) pg. 138, 132- 133

itself, through sacrifice, which is the highest, most glorious, but most difficult and awe-inspiring of all. At this height of discipline, everything, even physical and mental ability, is given away.

St. George, the 40 martyrs, Mercurius, and thousands like them embrace this final sacrifice. Here, a true knight becomes a saint, using discipline to sacrifice everything, but for others instead of himself, and for the greater Glory of GOD[833].

Discipline and the Sacrifice of Training

How does one gain discipline of sacrifice, so that one may better serve GOD, battle the devil, or achieve the military miracles of Charles Martel, or a thousand other skilled and hardened knights, heroes, and warriors? Save for Grace, training is the only way.

Sir Ramon Lull stresses that a knight should train constantly, whether with the body, as in violent sports that mimic battle and danger, or with the spirit, involving the constant practice of all the knightly virtues and morals[834].

Training is much overlooked in the modern world simply because the media only broadcasts the end result of the training. A great athlete hurtles the javelin, runs the race, wrestles his opponent, or makes the basket and touchdown on a huge screen, but the training that gets him there is largely overlooked. It is not glamorous. Good training is arduous, thorough, realistic, carefully planned, researched, driving the student to his utmost endurance, and beyond.

Extensive training, of a rigorous and even brutal sort is always required to produce the best discipline, a discipline that demands sacrifice and self-denial, a discipline that leads to victory. Knightly training requires even more, requiring a kind of austerity and asceticism, sometimes brutal to behold, always grueling to practice.

Charles Martel, as we have seen before, created a great and almost unbeatable army by instilling in his men an unconquerable discipline. This was done by months and years of extensive and continuous training. Sts. George, Mercurius, and the 40 martyrs were all soldiers, and knew this type of disciplined training well.

---

[833] (Gautier, 1989) pg. 36, 38, 40, (Clairvaux, 1977) pg. 130
[834] (Lull, 2001) pg. 30, see also (Clairvaux, 1977) pg. 138-140

In the Middle Ages, a young man destined to be knighted, at the tender age of seven, was whisked away from his own home and boarded at a patron's manor, sometimes an uncle, but always a male. Far away from the comforts of home and the attentions of his mother, and required to serve as a waiter and a cutter of meat at the table and other basic duties, he could not dwell on his loneliness. Called pages, or valets, such boys were also trained to wrestle, hunt, joust (tilting), and horsemanship[835].

At fourteen, everything became harder. They were required to cross streams, run across fields, and climb walls with a full suit of armor. The page would train with swords, and maces, showing incredible endurance, while being required to hold a battle axe out strait in front of his body for set lengths of time. Every conceivable fighting move would be performed on foot and on horseback for hours at a time, with the helmet and visor holes constricting his breathing[836]. Mock battles that were nearly as deadly as the real ones were fought until someone fell from exhaustion or death. Even though dulled swords and spears were used, many still died from the concussion, and many more were crippled for life.

This brutal training, full of practical exercises, painful disciplines, and realistic combat, can be seen in Steinbeck's treatment of the story of the young Sir Ewain, which Steinbeck adapted from Sir Malory's famous book. In this story, Steinbeck places within a Lady Lyne thoroughly practical and deadly advice, and makes Ewain the stereotypical inexperienced young knight, full of wrong concepts and glorious dreams without the skill and knowledge to make them happen. The mysterious Lady Lyne shows herself a master trainer as she molds and hammers the young Ewain into a fighting machine.

"(H)is training began—hour upon weary hour with a lance, while the lady stood and watched and caustically described the errors and found little good. And after a time, when the spearhead could find the mark, she set the target dancing on a rope, and crowed with triumph when the spearhead missed. And after the lance work, hours with a sword weighted with lead to tear and mold the muscles, and not against an opponent but chopping work on an upright log, with every angle of cut inspected and criticized. The feeding was as rough as the work—porridge boiled with mutton and cold, bracken-flavored water—and struck the dark, Ewain stumbled bleary eyed to his sleep skin in a corner and sometimes pushed

835 (Bulfinch, 1962) pg.41
836 Ibid. pg.41

a goose aside to make room for himself. Heavy sleep fell, until a rough boot stirred in the dark for a new day. And two more months and two more. Ewain was gaunt and lean and as muscled as a yew tree. He did not long for death in the evening any more or dread the toe in his ribs that awakened him if he did not rise first. Now he found his own errors and tried to correct them, and no longer did he slink away to sleep on the heels of his dismissal . . ."[837].

Artistically presented, this vignette accurately portrays how true knights often trained and how they should train in order to be the best and the most consummate warriors.

As all knights, Ewain learns that pleasure and easy living makes a man soft and simple to defeat. All the knight's accoutrements must enhance skill, not attract women or cause others to admire him. The knight's horse, the knight's partner in battle, must be looked to first, and is fed even before the knight himself dines. Underhanded fighting, which is grouped with and symbolized by magic[838], is condemned. One of the most important lessons, that a knight must be humble enough and intelligent enough to accept criticism in order to become better, is coupled with the idea that stern discipline and perpetual training, first forced and then self-imposed, is the only life for a true knight[839].

Priming the Body, Molding the Brain

Behavior molds the brain just as much as the brain molds behavior[840].

For many years, people assumed the opposite. Take this strange but important example. Many progressive-minded researchers, sociologists, and psychologists assumed that because the typical serial killer may have a differently formed brain than the average, this one detail was the reason for his terrible actions, e.g. murdering people.

Further research and study showed, however, that the very shape and form of the serial-killer brain was **affected by** his actions. The actions came first, and then the structure of the brain changed to accommodate

---

[837] (Steinbeck, 1976) pg 181-183

[838] (Steinbeck, 1976) pg. 179, 241-243, various other stories normally have the villain using magic, a form of cheating

[839] (Steinbeck, 1976) pg.174

[840] (Schueler, 1997), (Anji, 2013), my father, the psychiatrist, would say this often

the actions. The actions of the serial killer mold his brain, just as much as, if not more than, the structure of his brain will affect his actions. Actions molding the shape of the brain, and then the shape of the brain perpetuating behavior, has been found to be true in every kind of person.

One's behavior hardwires the brain, predisposing the brain to these behaviors. One's actions thus have a tremendous effect on one's future deeds, and even on how one thinks. That is why we train ourselves in anything we wish to be excellent in. Serial killers, while having some experience or problem that initially sends them on the path of wrong, train themselves to be more evil. Knights and heroes train themselves to be good, and to stop the serial killers.

Training makes one skilled at something, and more training makes one better. Even if one has a talent, this talent can be enhanced by continuous and carefully planned training. No matter how courageous one feels, how angry one becomes, how capable one seems, how physically strong one is, one needs focused, disciplined training to become good enough to be a hero and knight.

Some of this training may take the form of coincidental preparation, as in someone who is exposed to a language at an early age might more quickly develop a marked ability for that language as opposed to someone who was not exposed early. Such early accidental exposure can mold the brain in such a way that the brain is more apt to learn that material. But almost all training must be purposeful and regular, continuous and requiring a commitment. A knight trains always, and in every situation.

All of this is true for moral and spiritual strength and discipline, as well as physical ability. Few are born with the innate ability to make the correct moral decisions, to make shrewd judgments, or battle demonic forces. If one wants to be a more moral person, one has to act like it and train for this ability[841]. If one wants to think better and more precisely, one has to continuously try to think in this way and train[842]. Even to

---

[841] (Scupoli, 1945 edition) pg. 6-7, 26, 34, 49, also Attributed to Heraclitus—
"Good character is not formed in a week or a month. It is created little by little, day by day. Protracted and patient effort is needed to develop good character." (Luck, 2008) pg. 59, (Durant, 1953) pg. 61, Durant, in his excellent treatment of Aristotle, comments that we are what we repeatedly do, and thus excellence is not an act, but a habit.

[842] (Scupoli, 1945 edition) pg. 19, Leonardo Davinci understood, saying, "Iron rusts from disuse; stagnant water loses its purity and in cold weather becomes frozen; even so does inaction stay the vigor of the mind."

battle demons, one must prepare and train for the day when demons attack[843].

To Begin

If a man wishes to prepare himself for great battles, he must start training in small ways, slowly building up his ability and strength. The sacrifices and discipline necessary in the terrifying and brilliant struggles against evil are born within tiny beginnings.

Like a muscle, his discipline grows, through greater and harsher sacrifice, until he can accomplish the great sacrifices of legendary saints and heroes. Step by step, asceticism by asceticism, self-denial by self-denial, he forges his discipline like a sword in the furnace, until nothing can stand in his way.

Asceticism can start small. As a part of their disciplined training, knights often engaged in small limited sacrifices that seem equally strange to the decadent times we live in today, such as sleeping on the floor or ground instead of a bed, sleeping in one's armor, drinking only water, abstaining from food at certain times and for prolonged periods, withstanding cold or heat beyond necessity, and wearing aggravating and even painful material such as hair-shirts[844].

Made famous by John the Baptist, hair-shirts were worn by knights from Sir Lancelot and Sir Bors, to Charlemagne and Saint Francis[845], disciplining the body in a truly itchy mass of prickly hair, camel or otherwise, worn next to the skin, usually in secret[846]. This sort of austerity does not impede training or drain physical ability, and can be very secretive, for it can be covered by other cloths. These aspects of hair-shirts made them very useful in the disciplined and austere training of a knight.

Austerities like hair-shirts and fasting were part of discipline training for many chivalries around the world[847], but for the Christian Knight,

---

[843] (Baglio, 2009) pg.47, (Scupoli, 1945 edition) pg. 19, 46-50, St. Basil, Homily 8—pg.979 in the World Treasury of Religious Quotations

[844] A penance that dates from Biblical times - (Alston, 1910)

[845] (Chesterton, 1989) pg. 48

[846] (Alston, 1910)

[847] (Spoto, 2002) pg. 65

they were also part of other important reasons for Sacrifice: service, penance, and spiritual warfare. The shirt not only corporealized their sadness for sin, but helped him resist temptation by aggravating the body and flesh, distracting him from even the most alluring enticements[848].

These sacrifices accomplish three things: gaining ruler-ship over one's body and desires, pious imitation of Christ, and Penance. Knights and saints throughout time have excelled in these disciplines, using them to purify their bodies and souls. (Imitation of Christ, besides dying for GOD's causes, includes his embracing of poverty, ascetic fasting, intense prayer and wandering by oneself. Penance may involve these same things, and can include pilgrimages. All such austerities require an iron control over the flesh.)

Another type of austerity requires no physical component at all. "Time," said Theophrastus, "is the most valuable thing a man can spend"[849]. To become a saint, takes a lifetime of quiet work and prayer. To train as a knight requires many years, years that could have been used for something more worldly satisfying. While the saint is praying and the knight is training, others may amass fortunes, or have some other profitable endeavor. On the trivial side, parties, entertainments, even television programs populate the lives of others, while the knight and saint engages in grueling practice and contemplation. Just like saints, many knights would often spend whole evenings in prayer, on their knees, in quiet agitation of spirit, waiting for a sign of worthiness.

Some saints and knights that practiced some form of Asceticism:

-Sir Ramon Lull
-St. Antony of Egypt
-Sir William of Gellone
-St. Ignatius of Loyola
-St. Augustine
-St. Aquinas
-Hospitaller Knights
-Templar Knights
-St. Francis of Assissi

[848] (Alston, 1910)
[849] Theophrastus, student of Plato, then Aristotle. He was placed next as the head of the Lyceum

-Sir and Saint Thomas Beckett
-Sir and Saint Thomas More
-Sir Guy of Warwick
-Sir and Saint Louis
-Simon Stylites

All of these knights and saints started with small ascetic practices, and then moved on to more heroic ones. Even the smaller asceticisms can bring discipline and focus. They help separate oneself from the world and its fleshy pleasures and thus grow more focused and closer to GOD by severing slowly one's physical ties and needs of the world.

Mental training—Preparing for Mental Ordeals

How hard must a person train the mind and study to be worthy of knighthood and its total sacrifice? Imagine you must defeat the dragons of ignorance and deceit, darkness and imbecility, their claws and fangs hovering over you, their eyes shining with lust to drown you in falsehood and error, just as they have done so many others. There is only one way to defeat them—study, understand, inquire, focus, and push yourself beyond your own endurance.

Charlemagne understood. As emperor of the Holy Roman Empire, he did not need formal education to rise up in the ranks of the world. He was already "at the top". Instead, he valued education for itself. Deep into the night, his crown resting on his bed, he studied. Never easy for him, he refused to quit and sweated through his studies, even as king, insisting on learning as much as he could[850].

With deep respect for mental prowess and the force of will needed to obtain it, he searched through his kingdom, finding the hardest working and most deserving of his subjects, regardless of their rank in society, and made sure they received the education to match their potential[851].

The Catholic Church has continued this tradition, searching out pupils willing to train their minds and place themselves under strict discipline for the sake of the intellect. These students must be ready to

---

[850] (Einhard N. t., 1969) pg. 79, from Einhard himself
[851] Ibid. pg. 94-95, from Notker the Stammerer

sacrifice other pursuits and periodic pleasures to make time and room for study and the gathering of knowledge. Then, more time and effort is required to development the wisdom to use that knowledge. The mind is a difficult weapon to sharpen properly. And the dragons are always hungry for fools.

My father always battled the dragons of ignorance with gusto.

When I was a boy, my father never talked too much about how well he did in Catholic boarding school. Trained by various brothers and Jesuit priests, he mainly spoke of their intelligence and not his, their skill and not his own, and how they never allowed radios or TV within the school, demanding the students study deep into the night in absolute silence, even on Saturday and Sunday. Day to day, he lived with the old priests, slowly but surely influenced by their quiet, tough, and disciplined ways. While his friends laughed on their way to regular school, he worked odd jobs, earning his keep and education by the endless pealing of potatoes and the occasionally battle with villainous rats in the ancient cellars. He chuckled when he spoke of the tests, which sometimes included whole scholarly books, 400 pages or more. The brother would give the students a copy of a paragraph from anywhere in the book, and the students would be required to find the purposefully omitted sentences, and replace them, word for word, from memory.

He went on to study medicine and Psychiatry at Georgetown University, another Catholic institution, the sculptor of presidents and princes. There too, the incredible discipline of the Jesuits permeated any serious student's life and being. After long years there and in Medical school, he won honors as a psychiatrist for adults and children, a decorated flight surgeon and a full Colonel in the U.S. Air force, trusted with top secret security clearances, administered to secret agents in the field while they spied on the Soviet Union, and then designed houses and built decks in his spare time. Offered a generalship, he declined it, remarking that it would take him away from patients and into more paperwork.

It was not until some years into my own high school studies that I found some of his text books. They had strange messages on the first pages, messages like—"99, for I never give 100 averages in this class". Cleaning out a closet in the garage, I found a trophy, covered with dust, awarded to my dad for achieving the highest scores of any student for the year. When I asked my grandmother about these things, she simply said, "Any time we went to see him, we could never find him anywhere else but in the library. The Librarian would say 'Sure, I know exactly where he is. We've given him his own chair he studies here so often—the one with the high back over there'. They called him a stack of books, with legs."

No wonder Dad could find mistakes in the dictionary from time to time, or a misquote in an encyclopedia, and then dismiss it with a joke. No wonder he knew a thousand philosophers, quoted them in several languages, and discerned the strengths and weaknesses of their arguments as he ate an evening meal. He had un-told numbers of scholarly books, all which he read, studied, annotated and consumed into his ever-growing repertoire of knowledge. He could wake up at any needed hour, kill a snake that had invaded the house with his bare hand, give an appropriate soliloquy from Shakespeare, design brilliant houses for his family, work well into the night, and never complain of long hours, or less-than-glorious working conditions. Simply stated, he is the most brilliant, effective, and disciplined man I have ever known.

When I asked him about these things, and related what I had discovered of his honored ability and acumen, he simply said, "It is still not enough. A man can never learn too much."

Aquinas and Augustine, Charlemagne, Anselm, the Cid, and Sir Ramon Lull would have whole-heartedly agreed.

A man must continuously learn, because he is not and can never be perfect, so susceptible to error and self-deception if he is not supremely careful and open to Grace[852]. Finally, only GOD is perfect, and only GOD can be totally relied upon[853]. And yet, a man must learn all he can to properly serve GOD[854].

Within his stories of campus life, Dad would relate the need for extreme focus and almost hypnotic meditation on his studies, requiring a disciplined silence and regimen. In the Catholic Church, focused intellectual study of any subject is called "Meditation", and unlike the Eastern version of that word, it is about filling the mind with knowledge and careful thinking. Careful reading of the Scriptures, sincerely and

---

[852] (Cavanaugh, 1952) pg. 5
[853] (Knowles, 1962) pg. 263, Deut. 32:4, 2 Samuel 22:31, Psalm 18:30
[854] (Scupoli, 1945 edition) pg. 19, (Illingworth, 1903) pg. 25-26, 27-28, 29

thoughtfully, is in itself a time-honored Christian asceticism[855]. The opposite would be "Contemplation", a much better reflection of the Eastern ways of meditating, is the emptying of the mind to everything but thoughts of GOD. Mental training requires both intellectual study and contemplative prayer. Both require a laser-like focus. Everything requires brutal discipline.

All are needed to defeat the dragons of ignorance and error. Such Knightly training brings mental anguish, sweat, and tears, and although the struggle is in the mind, it is very real. Other students may be dating, eating, or watching TV, but you must set aside these things and put yourself through a rigorous training schedule, ignoring the desires and weaknesses of your body, battling the constant distractions of the flesh, weariness, boredom, and drudgery—hour after hour, night after night.

The willingness to sacrifice and the valuing of mental prowess over temporary pleasures can place you in the level of Charles Martel, Charlemagne, and St. Louis—king of all you survey, and, what is more, ruler of yourself.

There are those who would not believe me, who would laugh at their idea of the rough and brutal knight actually taking time to study. Thus stood the attitude of Agrican, the Tartar king who fought the great Roland, mightiest of Charlemagne's Paladins[856].

In this legendary story, they met as enemies on the battlefield and fought all day, until the evening came on and dusk began to take hold. "You are the best fighter I have ever met." Agrican said, "Let us take a rest awhile under that pine tree, and renew our battle in the morning."

Roland, ever the courteous one, agreed, and the two warriors, one Moslem and the other Christian, sat under the tree and watched the stars.

Roland spoke: "Look at that canopy of the Heavens. No greater argument for GOD exists than that."

"Ah, you talk of Faith and learning," Laughed the Tartar. "I will tell you at once that I never could learn anything when I was a boy, and I finally broke the head of the teacher who tried to teach me. What is the good of a gentleman pouring over books day and night[857]? Learning I left to other men. For me, there is only fighting and women."

---

[855] (Eusebius, 1989) pg. 51
[856] This story can be found in (Bulfinch, 1962) pg. 405- 415, The Siege of Albracca
[857] (Bulfinch, 1962) pg. 412-413

"I agree that fighting and women are important to a knight," Roland said, "But learning does no one dishonor. Learning is as much a crowning of a man's ability as the beautiful flowers crown this meadow. And the man without knowledge of GOD is like one who might as well be a stone or a beast"[858].

At midnight, Agrican decided to renew the fight, and Roland could not help but defend himself. For five hours and more they fought, 'til the sun came and Roland's mighty sword Durendal[859] finally sunk deep into the Tartar king's breastplate. Agrican fell nearly dead, and, remembering their conversation, asked to be allowed into such a religion that made men both wise and formidable, learned and strong.

Moral Training

Even a future saint must practice.

In moral training, as well as all other types, one begins with small disciplines, slowly forging a soul of steel. St. Joan saved all of France, but she began simply as a young girl who would visit the sick, pray for the hurting and lonely, and on occasion, invite homeless people to board the night in her warm room, while she slept on the porch of the house[860]. Saint Maximilian Kolbe, long before taking his final, brutalizing walk to martyrdom, spent his young life in the service of orphans and the poor. Even while held in several Nazi prison camps, he went about comforting others, sharing his food, and even placing his own blanket on the shivering of strangers[861]. Such practices were almost a habit. As Joan, and so many other saints and knights, Kolbe's incredible final sacrifice was a culmination of a lifetime of training. His "was a life trained in self-giving and striving for sanctity"[862].

Far from simply doing "acts of random kindness", saints and knights must consistently and deliberately train themselves to become who they should be.

---

[858] Ibid.
[859] (Sayers, 1984) pg. 38
[860] (Spoto D., 2007) pg. 6
[861] (Faccenda, 1999) pg. 22
[862] (Faccenda, 1999) first page of the introduction, pg.11,

Maybe because of Rousseau, people assume children are born good and thus need no fine-tuning in the moral arena[863]. Somehow, in this progressive and modern way of thinking, children are always and by nature cute and cuddly, and everything they do is deemed fine, until they are corrupted by society.

This corruption may happen, but the knightly and Christian concept of Original Sin, also called the Fall of Man, indicated that children are barely above animals, and any "cute" or "cuddly" actions they make are totally coincidental, having nothing much to do with their fundamentally flawed nature. Even a quick study of children will show this. They are greedy and demanding things, using force when they can, and when they can't, they use manipulation and trickery. Children are not evil, but their instincts have free rein if they are not trained and formed to be good, moral people.

These instincts carry over to adults, and the basic human nature of people, warped by Original sin, still function and rule, unless reined in, restrained, or molded by persistent training. A man who is not trained with discipline and selfless love will not be able to sacrifice without direct intercession from Heaven.

If children are to grow into responsible moral adults, they must be trained to be moral, responsible beings.

This requires excellent and disciplined role models. The family of Joseph de Veuster (the future Father Damien) exposed him to exceptional moral and spiritual guides. His mother and father were pious, hard workers. His sisters became nuns who sacrificed to tend to the sick, and his brother became a disciplined and kind priest[864]. But many families may be too wayward, unruly, fractured, or simply too spoiled to serve as a training ground for a young knight or saint.

As we have seen before, in Medieval times, a young man had to leave his mother and safe, comfortable existence of his former home, and travel to the cold, unfamiliar castle of an uncle or other such relative. There, he served a knight as a page and squire, doing chores and menial tasks, while the knight taught him right from wrong and the proper knightly ways. He served the knight and others at table to become humble and

---

[863] Rousseau's comment: "Man is born free, and everywhere he is in chains", *The Social Contract*, I, Ch.1, 1762

[864] (Volder, 2010) pg. 7

understand what it is to be a servant[865]. The young squire was also expected to serve and fight for, in tournaments, a female in the castle and love her from afar, without touching or even seeing her closely[866] as a metaphor for serving the church without any reward.

Once the knight matures, how does he continue to restrain his human nature, bind it within the cords of conscience like rings of steel? By using self-discipline, discernment, and continuous struggle against temptation, (not to mention Grace).

Temptations come at us every day. Such is life, and temptation itself is no sin. Mostly, temptations of the flesh tend to be a by-product of having a body, and temptations of the mind, like jealousy and greed, come from our warped natures. But we must resist every time, for such resistance builds our moral and spiritual strength aided by Grace.

Begin with small disciplines to slowly build up your moral strength and courage. If you find you are distracted by thoughts of lust, put a pebble in your shoe to aggravate you all day, or a hairshirt next to your skin—reminding you that your body is not for your own pleasure. If you find petty jealousies confounding you, force yourself to do some small courtesy or favor for that person who has made you envious. If greed and ambition restrain you, give something small away, or when you are in a hurry, give your place in line to someone else, or deliberately fail to take credit for any great thing you do.

If you find that anger and wrath threaten to steal your temper in small things, force yourself to think of the stupid little errors we all do, and that we deserve the aggravations we suffer. Take the seven deadly sins when they are small, and crush them with equally small disciplines, the little tokens of the seven contrary virtues.

Prepare yourself for discipline and sacrifice by making sure your readings, exercises, hobbies, and past-times harden your heart against the fear of death[867]. Remind yourself of the plight of others around the world, by wearing a large cross under your shirt, and every day, when you touch it, think of those less fortunate than you, or place posters on your walls that remind you of every virtue you should emulate, or ever hardship you must overcome. Concern yourself with stories, and even movies that focus

---

[865] (Lull, 2001) pg. 21, (Bulfinch, 1962) pg. 41
[866] (Fife, 1991) pg. 111, (Barber, 1995) 83, 87-88, 90, Barber analyses the idea of aloof courtship well
[867] (Epictetus, 1937) pg. 166

or elucidate all that is strong, wise, and moral, filling your mind with the stories of strong, virtuous heroes. Avoid dwelling too long on the stories of weak-willed, wicked men, or the rumors spread by envious minds.

Even the smallest entertainments, stories that are told to children, must be aimed at the highest ideals. When he was a child, Joseph de Veuster loved the stories his mother read to him from the Lives of the Saints. He especially noted the diligence of an ancient Saint Damien and his brother from the year 303, who worked without rest to bring healing to the suffering. Inspired, Joseph poured himself into his chores and work, a dynamo of activity. It is no coincidence that, as an adult, he took the name Damien, when he adopted the missionary work of a priest as his field of endeavor[868]. From childhood, he had been prepared to spend his life helping the Lepers in Hawaii at Molokai.

The knight trains himself this way, every day, all the time, in small ways, almost unnoticeable ways, until he can face the larger challenges of evils full grown.

At first glance, any immoral pleasure a knight avoids may seem as sacrifice. The difference is that such "sacrificing" or giving up immoral behavior is not a sacrifice, it is a duty, requiring great discipline and sometimes asceticism, but not sacrifice in the traditional sense. A man does not throw his wantonness onto the altar of sacrifice, he must give up his wickedness **in order to** sacrifice.

Wickedness, which is moral weakness, will attempt at every turn to block sacrifice. Wickedness tends to use personal desires and weaknesses. The discipline of sacrifice sidesteps, destroys, or totally ignores much of personal feeling, desire, and weakness, making it a perfect weapon against the evil which resides inside everyone.

Spiritual Training

There is a battle within each man[869], though usually far beneath his consciousness. It begins with the petty pushes of selfishness and tiny temptations, slowly growing, until the cravings of childhood blossom into the full-force greeds of adulthood. Finally it blooms into

---

[868] (Volder, 2010) pg. 6
[869] (Scupoli, 1945 edition) Pg. 46, 87, 184

the titanic struggle between good and evil, between a man's higher calling, honorable intentions, faith, dogmatic beliefs, and Angelic communications, and his dark drives, vices, skepticisms, fallen nature, and Demonic prodding.

The war goes on his entire life[870], one side or another dominating for a time, only ending at his death. Then, the Angels and the Demons themselves wage war to claim him[871].

Unless the Grace of GOD comes down upon a person, endowing this person with supernatural knowledge and skill (which seems to happen in various saintly examples), he cannot succeed against the Devil. Even so, every person must prepare and train themselves for this spiritual warfare, for Grace must be coupled with human effort.

Grace joins with the Knight's use of discipline to build his resistance to the devil and the ability to battle Him. This spiritual discipline is also achieved by training.

Begin with prayer. Even as a young man, Simeon Stylites began his many disciplines by memorizing the Psalms and praying with them continuously.

The most important spiritual training involves prayer. This seems simple, but deceptively so. Since most of modern life is busy, we might think it enough to pray on the road or while we are doing something else, but prayer in the light of spiritual strength must be extremely focused[872], and should be conducted in a quiet place just for the purpose of prayer. We might have to begin with small chunks of prayer, for a few minutes at a time, everyday, focusing on Christ and His passion[873]. Even such a short time can constitute as "sacrifice" to many, because of their busy lifestyles or their addiction to entertainment. As you go about the rest of your day, try to keep GOD in your mind, thinking about GOD continuously, constantly trying to keep oneself attached to him in this way, for piety towards GOD is thinking of HIM always[874]. Without prayer, spirituality or religious living means little.

---

[870] (Scupoli, 1945 edition) pg. 197

[871] (Scupoli, 1945 edition) pg. 33, 184, 186, (Bangley, 2007) pg. 145, 265, a concept of Medieval times

[872] (Bangley, 2007) pg. 101

[873] (Scupoli, 1945 edition) pg. 57, 69, 80

[874] (Epictetus, 1937) pg. 167, 175

As you go about other business, thinking about GOD and praying to HIM, any difficulties or suffering that come your way can be seen as training from the great Trainer Himself, GOD[875]. Be aware that even this move toward disciplined spirituality may attract the attention of demonic forces who wish to stop any piety[876].

Be warned, any sacrifice, especially connected with prayer, is a direct assault on the evil in the world and demons. "Demons understand that prayer is a path to GOD. They will do anything to hinder this journey. Prayer is like fighting a war."[877]

Even before climbing unto his pillar, Simeon Stylites wrestled with strange visions of the Devil. Sometimes the Evil one appeared as a roaring lion, spitting flames, or as mysterious people with intent to harm him, or even as a huge black snake spewing smoke[878]. All of these manifested in order to distract Simeon from his prayers and austerities, so the Saint turned his back on the creatures and kept praying and training, just like St. Ignatius would many years later.

Spiritual training involves a component of physical discipline. The body must be disciplined before the spirit can be strengthened. Many saints, including Simon Stylites, Ignatius and Antony, commonly used fasting. One may start with small fasts and then work up to larger ones. The main idea is to be able to control the instincts of the body, so that they no longer hamper the workings of the spirit. (It is interesting to note that moderns use severe fasting to lose weight, but balk when presented with mild fasting for spiritual health).

One of Simeon Stylites's signature methods of disciplining his body involved control of his sleep, long before he took up standing on a pillar. While others slept, he forced himself to stay awake by hanging a stone around his neck and staying on his feet, or by standing on a rounded stone that required his staying awake to keep balance[879]. This prepared him later for his long vigils on the pillar, where he would tie himself standing to a stake, even while he took small cat naps.

---

[875] (Epictetus, 1937) pg. 173-174
[876] (Cruz, 1999) pg. 164
[877] (Bangley, 2007) pg. 68, so says Agathon
[878] (Lent, 1915) para. 535-7, para. 529, on pages 125 and 130
[879] (Lent, 1915) para 520, on page 119

One of Saint Damien's first austerities as a boy was a board, instead of a mattress, to sleep on[880].

Modern people may take up this example by forcing themselves to get up earlier or go to bed later than they are accustomed, simply refusing the body to have the last say. All these techniques can be used without harm to health or other training, as long as used wisely. Slowly build up one's discipline and austerities from small to larger, easier to difficult. Start small, with small things, taking time out for brief periods to think and pray—even this will be difficult for moderns at first, who have to be entertained or engaged every moment. Try this by memorizing prayers and watch how your earthly heart and mind struggle, even at such a small task. We have grown that weak!

This training requires the same discipline and discernment as Moral training, for when the Evil One attacks us, it is usually through our own desires and weaknesses, as reflected in the seven deadly sins. Temptations and wicked desires may happen naturally, but the Devil can use them, just like spies behind enemy lines, within our own minds, hearts, and souls.

We must have discernment to identify the wickedness within ourselves, and then the self-discipline to refuse. Day after day, hour after hour, when temptations come, we naturally strengthen our souls and spirit by refusing them[881]. It is important to resist every time, for each time we are successful, we grow stronger. But each time we relent and give in to the temptation, we grow weaker.

Sometimes we can feel miserable when resisting temptation. We may even feel cheated of enjoying whatever indulgences the rest of the world is experiencing. We may feel like some Olympic athlete, who, having to wake up early and train everyday in endless and grueling exercises, never gets to relax. We should remember that GOD is worth more than whatever we are missing[882], and, that relaxing does not make us stronger, just as giving in to temptation renders us spiritually flaccid.

[880] (Volder, 2010) pg. 7
[881] (Baglio, 2009) pg. 47
[882] (Epictetus, 1937) pg. 163

Exercise makes muscles and heart stronger, studying and contemplation strengthens the mind, and resisting temptation empowers the soul[883].

Knightly training of the soul, as all good training, resembles the disciplined training and focus of a stern and serious athlete, who, with his eyes on victory, takes all sacrifice and pain in preparation for his moment of truth[884]. This spiritual athlete, similar to the physical one, must train extensively, but this discipline hammers and strengthens his soul even more than his body, making him a greater foe of the Devil, and even a greater sacrifice if martyrdom comes. His discipline, while hardening and strengthening him now, can be preparation for the ultimate offering, the martyr's crown of heavenly glory and the Gates of Honor, far more than the crown of laurels or earthly reward.

Such training can take the form of long, arduous journeys[885] into the self, reflected by the long, arduous knightly journey called the Quest. Sirs Bors and Percival go through many austerities and terrible experiences that burn away their imperfections and perfect their spirits, enabling them to share in the feast of the Holy Grail, Christ's last supper. Even the perfect Galahad's quest becomes an allegory for the strengthening of the soul on the way to GOD, as he gathers perfect weapons and armor on the trail of the Grail.

Remember, the most important spiritual training involves prayer. One should begin by having 5 minutes of personal prayer in a quiet place. Prayer is absolutely essential, and to take even a little time every day is to grow closer to GOD's presence, and spit in the face of the Devil[886].

Epictetus warns to prepare and weigh carefully one's desire to begin such spiritual training, for it is long and terrible, just like the training of athletes in the Olympics[887]. His point is well taken Make sure you are able to complete the training, going all out, before you begin, otherwise, you may find it too much and fail or quit, bringing dishonor down upon yourself[888]. Before one goes on this great spiritual journey, one must test

---

[883] St. Basil, Homily 8, as shown in *World Treasury of Religious Quotations*, pg. 979

[884] (Epictetus, 1937) pg. 155, St. Paul and Justin Martyr use similar language

[885] (Augustine, 1986) pg. 83, commentary on Psalm 36(2), 16

[886] (Bangley, 2007) pg. 101, 145, (Scupoli, 1945 edition) pg. 7

[887] (Epictetus, 1937) pg. 155

[888] Luke 14:28

oneself and see if one proves worthy, hence the vigil a knight takes before he is dubbed "knight".

Whether the training is spiritual, physical, or mental and moral, the discipline and self denial a knight or saint uses to train himself to fight for GOD is the same discipline used in every kind of Sacrifice. The discipline and austerities of brutal training, although to hammer and strengthen the body and soul, can also be a kind of prayer, a kind of offering to GOD involving the agony of selflessness and sacrifice, especially when the knight or saint suffers in his training to win for GOD and the holy cause.

Martial Arts Training as a kind of Sacrifice

The martial artist wakes up early, with the world still asleep, and throws himself into push-ups, sit-ups, and stretches. Then he runs in place and performs all manner of kicks and punches, careening his limbs into a heavy bag. Or, as difficult, he rises in the night, the whole world still asleep, and finds a place to practice in the dark[889]. After 200 kicks and 4 hundred punches, he starts again. His body covered with sweat, his eyes brutal, clear, and focused. In his mind, he combats every known villain and terror, punishing them with his fists, knees, and feet. Then he takes up the sword, or a pair of Sai, and continues his onslaught against imagined foes, the pains in his body ignored and suppressed. His muscles scream, his joints groan, but he continues on in pursuit of perfection in every movement, absolute focus in every thought. Practice makes perfect, and perfect practice makes for victory[890].

Just like all forms of physical asceticism, a traditional martial arts regimen involves plenty of grueling, even agonizing practice for long periods of time, which could sometimes easily lead to wounds or death. When one makes a lifestyle out of this training, it molds the mind and tempers the spirit similar to the way Medieval religious disciplines shape character. Such training is usually not listed as an ascetic practice in the

---

[889] This regimen reminds me of the Bhagavad-Gita's second teaching, v. 69, (Miller, 1986) pg. 38

[890] Paraphrased from Vince Lombardi, and often quoted by my martial arts master

Western World, although the East has embraced it for many years as a sacrifice worthy of any saint.

The difference is found in one minor aim. The hermits and saints of old committed asceticisms, the disciplining the body and its desires, in order to get closer to Christ. Such disciplines also left the body completely behind. Martial arts also discipline the body, but not to abandon it entirely. Martial disciplines shape and purge the body, not to destroy it, but to commandeer the body as an ally in defeating enemies, dangers, and evil. This becomes a very chivalrous process, joining the body with the mind and spirit, as mutual weapons in the Army of GOD.

Both activities give glory to GOD, when used properly.

In the modern world, people might engage in martial arts training for many reasons, some as mundane as entertainment, or "slimming the figure", others as profane as inflicting fear or dominance. None of these were the original aspirations of such training—the modern world warps everything.

What often drives men to practice such arts? Fear of loss? Love of power? It doesn't matter. What matters is the channeling of all desire into one desire. The desire to follow GOD, to glorify Him by the disciplining of oneself.

It is true that I have a love of martial arts, but the practice is still agonizing and difficult, requiring vast quantities of time and concentration. Often it is the single most arduous part of my day, demanding every bit of discipline I have simply to engage in it, worn out as I am from long hours at work. I often dread my training, but then I push myself through it anyway in a frenzy of pain. A love of the arts alone would not cause me to endure this. My obsession for GOD exceeds all other desires in my life, and drives my practice on as my desire for martial skill is dwarfed by my desire to defeat the enemies of GOD. Thus I use even physical training to augment my spiritual and mental training, for they all flow into one river of discipline, all with the same goal.

There are few weapons I would not use to fight the Devil and Glorify GOD.

The various "why's of sacrifice"

As a Mighty Weapon (against the Devil, the World, and the Flesh)

A warrior always needs weapons, especially in the Arena of the Soul, as well as discipline and training to use them[891]. The stakes are much higher than life itself, for life goes on, whether in Paradise or Hell.

The knight, when confronting the spiritual enemy, must use weapons just as he would against a physical attacker. These weapons are very different than the material sword or shield, but their effect in the spiritual world is the same.

In spiritual warfare, one works with prayer, asceticism, sacrifice, purity, faith, courage, kindness, righteousness, obedience to GOD, and even martyrdom, and although they are different than other disciplines and austerities, they are the deepest and most profound disciplines of all[892]. Properly sharpened within the soul, they become weapons as surely as a sword[893] or a gun are weapons; they become strategies as surely as the strategies of a great general.

"For with Strength a man with a noble heart vanquish all vices"[894].

These spiritual disciplines and weapons can become the goal, or they may have a much higher goal than all others: To walk in the Shadow of GOD[895]. It is sometimes difficult to think of holy things like righteousness and purity as powerful weapons in an arsenal. Realize this is a way of seeing concepts and realities that only partially touch our limited understanding. The knight allies himself with the liege lord Christ, disciplines himself, chooses his weapons carefully, and goes to battle against a foe far beyond this earthly realm or human comprehension.

Meditation on Christ's Passion[896] remains one of the most powerful weapons against the Evil One, for it is by Christ's Passion that the Devil

---

[891] See Zech 4:6, Hosea 6:5, 2 Samuel 22:36, Isaiah 59:17, (Scupoli, 1945 edition) pg. 6, 7

[892] (Scupoli, 1945 edition) pg. 46-47

[893] Sword of the spirit, Ephesians 6:17, Hebrews 4:12

[894] (Lull, 2001) pg. 86

[895] (Scupoli, 1945 edition) pg. 17

[896] Ibid. pg. 57

was completely defeated. All kinds of prayer, especially the "Our Father", exorcisms, prayers that incorporate Bible passages, and prayers made with great yearning of the heart always are great and terrible weapons against the Devil. But the greatest weapons are those where the warrior for GOD commits virtuous actions, prays, and does austerities with absolute faith[897].

Christ says to defeat and drive out the worst of demons, fasting and prayer are essential[898]. St. Antony of Egypt and St. John the Baptist with their courage, prayers, austerities, penances and donations of all their material possessions[899] made them such a terror to demons that the Devil himself feared their activities[900]. When one voluntarily suffers in the name of GOD, doing the work of GOD, one makes oneself a mighty warrior in the realms of the spirit.

After years of austerities, penances, and battling demons, St. Antony of Egypt, became such a powerful presence, and inspired so many monks to adopt asceticism in his desert that the Devil Himself came to complain.

"I no longer have a place—no weapon—no city." The Devil sighed. "There are Christians everywhere, and even the desert has filled with monks."[901].

"Marveling at the Grace of GOD, I (Antony) said to him, "Even though you are always a liar, and never tell the truth, nevertheless this time, although you did not intend to, you have spoken truly. For Christ in His coming has reduced you to weakness and after throwing you down He left you defenseless"[902].

At hearing the very name of Christ, the Devil disappeared.

It is not what the saint and knight do that is so powerful in itself, nor the personalities of these heroes, it is the working of GOD through them and their activities. Asceticism and sacrifice in GOD's name, when done with the right knowledge, Grace, and promptings by the Holy Spirit,

---

897 Mark 9:29, Matt 17:21, KJV and the Douay-Rheims Bible
898 Ibid.
899 St. Thomas More, Dialogue of Comfort, 1535, Charity is a firebrand in the Devil's face
900 (Athanasius, 1980) pg. 70, 7, Matt.3:4, Mark 1:6
901 (Athanasius, 1980) pg. 62
902 (Athanasius, 1980) Pg. 62

bring one closer to GOD, and allows one to become a conduit for GOD's power.

Martyrs, such as St. George and St. John the Baptist, because of their great sacrifice, become very powerful in the spirit world, possessing as they do great reciprocal affection from GOD and His special rewards for their services. Even saints who were not put to death, but who lived their humble life in Christ, such as Simeon Stylites and Antony of Egypt, take on great power in Heaven. Catholics all around the world still ask for saintly intercession when confronted by devilish obstacles and possible demonic activity[903].

The aid of Angels is also much sought after in the battle against the unseen forces of the dark. Angels are messengers of GOD and are much of GOD's Grace and protection come through these intermediaries. While praying for intercession from these spirits, Catholics are taught to commit some act of asceticism, such as kneeling in front of a painting of St. Michael, or some other small austerity[904].

Sacrifice as Penance—A Weapon Against Sin

Lancelot's Penance

Sir Lancelot is one of my favorite knights. Whether or not he exists, so many writers and commentators have written and debated about him over the years that he almost seems to be a person of history[905]. John Steinbeck and T. H. White have created some of my favorite versions of Lancelot. Whatever the case, Lancelot is a reflection of the trials and triumphs that every knight may face.

By all accounts, Lancelot was a great and good man, a powerful warrior, but with great courtesy and gentleness. He was known as the best of all knights of this earth. Some may scoff that Lancelot committed a terrible sin, adultery with Guinevere, King Arthur's wife. As for me, I

---

[903] As in the Prayer of St. Michael
[904] (Bourdon, 1948), pg. 21 see actual prayers in the book *Devotions to the Angels*
[905] (Goodrich, 1989) pg. 33, 216 and others, Goodrich certainly thinks Lancelot existed

269

note that he only had one sin, similar to King David. I, as well as most other people, have many sins.

Lancelot had struggled with his one sin for many years, and when Guinevere and King Arthur finally died in the passage of time, Lancelot set himself to do penance. He prayed on his knees over the king and queen's grave for hours at a time every day, and spent the rest of his life at a monastery, fasting and weeping over his terrible sin.

After some years of constant penance, he became deathly sick, and his friends, knights and monks of renown, came to pray with him and attempt to make him feel better. Sir Bors and Sir Percival especially came, along with the Bishop of Camelot, and they all stayed with the ailing Lancelot for many days, as he slowly grew worse.

One night, the Bishop had a beautiful dream. He saw the bed of Lancelot surrounded by angels, all chanting hymns of joy, and the Bishop awoke suddenly, laughing. He ran to Bors and Percival, saying "Surely this is good news! Let's go to Lancelot's room, because I feel that this dream is a good omen, and that Lancelot must surely be healed!"

But when they burst into the room, expecting to find a rejuvenated Lancelot, they found his body, cold and dead. The Bishop noticed, as the others prayed or wept silently, that there hung in the room a most beautiful aroma. He took this to mean that Lancelot had been finally forgiven. The Angels had come—not to heal him, but to take him to Heaven.

This story can be found in the classic Sir Thomas Malory's *L'Morte d'Arthur*, and Walter Map's *Prose Lancelot*, as well as several other versions of the King Arthur mythos. Many stories of saints and holy men also bear witness to an odor or aroma of GOD's grace. It has been said, when a holy man dies, there is no smell of decay, but instead this beautiful aroma[906].

Penance discussed

One of the most misunderstood reasons for sacrifice is Penance. Even though it is still used by some in the modern religious community, it has

---

[906] (Underhill, 1990) pg. 268, (Brewer, 1891) pg. 682

lost much of its popularity, if such a thing ever had popularity, and the entire concept confuses the modern mind.

Simply said, Penance is the voluntary suffering of an individual taken on for the express purpose of showing sadness, longing for forgiveness, and paying reparations for sin or fault[907]. Usually, no physical product other than suffering in the individual is produced. It is an understanding between GOD and man. "I will do this penance, this suffering" says the penitent man, "to prove my sadness for my sins, to more strongly feel the shame and pain of the damage I have caused through these sins, and to seek some way of recompense for them." It can be seen as a way of lifting a small amount of suffering from Christ's back, and placing it on our own shoulders, taking full responsibility for our own faults. Though we can never repay for the towering injustice and sacrilege our sins represent, penance can offer a sign of the healing and reconciliation, as far as is possible for humans to accomplish.

Many Christians would take offense at even the way I have described Penance here. They would say, perhaps rightly, that "no man can pay for the sins of himself or others; only GOD, in Christ Jesus, could repair and repay such a rift in the universe represented by our grievance sins." As I have tried to show, Penance is not to replace Jesus' saving sacrifice or His saving Grace. Penance is simply an attempt, feeble as it may be, for a person to come to grips with his sin and to make some kind of repayment and apology for his own failings. Through Penance, we may join together with Christ, carrying our cross—following Him.

For the knight, Penance was a powerful expression of his continuing relationship with GOD, and the attempt to stay within HIS shadow, even with all the corruptions and failings of the human heart. It was the attempt to take upon one's own shoulders some of the weight of Christ's cross, even as Simon of Cyrene did, and to connect with Christ's suffering in a very real and concrete expression. If we are to live as Christ, should we not take upon ourselves the cross of the world, the punishment for our sins, just as Christ took upon himself the suffering for sins of the world[908]? And is it not right, that we should suffer for our sins, since we committed them?

Some have said that Penance is proof to GOD that we are sorry for our sins. But GOD, as any knight, theologian, or Bible reader would tell

---

[907] (Anthony Schraner, 1981) pg. 217
[908] (Anthony Schraner, 1981) pg. 216, 1 John 2:2, 2 Corinthian 5:19, Galatians 1:4

you, already knows what is in our hearts. Penance, more precisely, *is proof to ourselves* of our sadness for our transgressions—a confirmation of the sometimes illusive reality within us. It is a way to truly know one's self.

It is one thing to feel sorrow or repentant, it is another to have such a true penitent heart that we become capable of the most painful and aggravating austerities and actually perform them. This is the difference between thinking we are something and being that something. Barring hypocrisy, we may actually believe we are sorry enough, but the depth of our sorrow may not be sufficient or even proper, and such a state could be without our knowledge. It is easy to lie to ourselves[909] and believe we are repentant, when we would rather feel a moment of sadness, feel satisfied with a tear or two, and then move on, serene in our assurance that we are sorrowful enough for our sins. Penance reveals to ourselves how we truly feel. Penance reveals what is truly important to our inner selves, and how serious sin is to us.

Tears are one thing, but deciding to walk to Jerusalem, in rags and barefoot, like Saint Ignatius, Ramon Lull, and many others, is a quite convincing penance. Lancelot's hair-shirt, an itchy thing sometimes climbing with lice after years of continuous wear, is more assuring than saying "sorry". Sir Bors proved his sorrow over his sin by giving up meat, and accepting only water, on his quest for the Grail. St. Louis, risking his reign and his entire fortune, not to mention his life, by personally leading an army to free the Holy Land in the Pilgrimage called the Seventh Crusade, speaks volumes over a simple condolence.

Penance is obviously a very personally thing, part of the communication between ourselves and GOD. True knights performed penance secretly, or made very little show of it. This is why Sir Guy of Warwick never revealed himself to his wife as a beggar until after his death, and why Lancelot never wears his hairshirt where anyone can see it, but underneath his other garments and armor[910]. Pilgrimage or Crusade can be a more public penance, but this is because some penances are communal in nature, taken on not only for the individual but for the community as a whole or because a sin was committed against the community. Other penances, by their very nature, cannot be hidden well, but a true knight never makes a spectacle of them. Unless ordered by a

---

[909] Miguel De Cervantes—"Make it thy business to know thyself, which is the most difficult lesson in the world", Don Quixote, Part ii, Book iv, Chap. Xlii

[910] Matt 6:2, Matt 6:16

priest to make a public penance, such activity should almost always be very discreet.

Penance can have other purposes besides taking on pain to pay for sin. Many saints and knights do penance in order to purify themselves or the community, taking upon themselves the weight of certain sins, imitating Christ, burning themselves with pain like a goldsmith might purge and purify gold. This is often used to clean one's conscience in preparation for battle with demons: consider Christ's instruction to fast before the battle with certain types of devils[911]. St Louis, the ultimate Crusader King, made his penance not only for himself, but to free the Holy Land.

A knight can make a sacrifice into a battle for GOD's greater glory, a penance that not only brings the soul closer to GOD, but the mind and the body, and even the world into closer contact with GOD.

As off-shoots of this we have quest, crusade, and pilgrimage, all have physical, mental, and spiritual aspects, as well as a link to events in the world.

Sacrifice as a way of Freedom

What is freedom? To be slaves to animalistic desires and drives? To be forced to rut in the dirt of a thousand hungers, never satiated, never satisfied? How can any of that be freedom[912]? No, freedom is the ability to turn one's back on such demands and desires, so that one may see the glory, the beauty, and the peace that is GOD.

Moderns think that the soul of a man is somehow the primal, earthy emotions and instincts that burn to be unrestrained and unchecked. Predictably, to the modern mind, to "set the soul free" is to then wallow in these unrestrained drives and instincts.

These are not the soul, but instead simply the body's instincts, created and sustained by chemicals in the brain induced by thousands of years of conditioning. Indeed, such instincts and desires are the opposite of the soul, since the soul is spirit. (The songs and Bible say that the world

---

[911] Mark 9:29
[912] Galatians 5:13, Romans 6:22, John 8:32, Romans 6, (Brown, 2001) pg. 50-51

despises the Cross, that the Cross is a scandal, because the world despises sacrifice and suffering, which the cross represents.)

To a Christian, and to anyone with any clear concept of spirit, to "set the soul free" is to discipline the mind, heart, and body so that all instincts, feelings, and drives have no control or influence on them. Such is one goal of the Christian ascetic: to train his mind, heart, and even the nerve endings of the body itself to ignore the demands of the body and stomach and instinct, until the body and all else within him is completely under the control of his soul[913], and not the other way around. Instead of his experience mastering his soul, his soul becomes the master of his experience. He masters himself, in other words.

Once this is accomplished, he is now free to focus on GOD. All else in the world has only been a stepping stone or an illusion, because the final goal is to rest in GOD, free from the petty distractions that are, finally, all other things[914].

GOD's love

The ultimate reason why a man sacrifices is Love. The True knight sacrifices not out of fear of losing Heaven or gaining Hell, but out of love for his Lord and Master, Christ Jesus[915].

Sacrifice as a Weapon in the World

Before the great and terrible battle of Badon, Arthur bore a heavy cross on his shoulders for 3 days, to ensure his victory[916]. We have seen how Sacrifice is the royal road to GOD, the mark of discipline, the core of penance, and the sword of spiritual weaponry, but how does Sacrifice become a weapon in this world? Is it not clear enough, after seeing the Templars and Hospitallers, after seeing Jan Sobieski, after seeing Charles

---

[913] (Scupoli, 1945 edition) pg. 26-27
[914] (Epictetus, 1937) LXXI, pg. 142-143, (Aquinas, 2002) pg. 117, Ecclesiastes 12:13
[915] (Joinville, 1963) pg. 274
[916] (Dunning, 1998) pg. 24, (Hopkins, 2001) pg. 6

Martel and his phalanx soldiers, after seeing all the suffering saints and Christ HIMSELF, with their enormous impact on this world?

Each true knight thinks it a matter of course to risk his life for the Glory of GOD and for the well-being of others[917]. Such a focus, such a singleness of mind that ignores pain and possible death for the sake of Honor, molds the knight into a powerful engine, without obstacle and without hesitation, aimed at the betterment of the World and the destruction of evil. To find such a focus in oneself is to make oneself nearly invincible and to strike terror in the hearts of the enemy, and to find such focus in an opponent is cause for great concern.

The medieval story-tellers tried to communicate the power of this focus and willingness to suffer in many tales, including those of Sir Lancelot. When it comes to formidable, physical opponents, no one can dispute the power of Lancelot. But it is not only his strength and courage, but his willingness to sacrifice, that makes him an implacable and unstoppable knight.

Lancelot felt the familiar focus fall upon him as he looked at the situation at hand. In this legend, Guinevere, the Queen, and Sir Kay, her brother-in-law and foster brother to King Arthur Himself, had been recently kidnapped and carried away to a foreboding and strange land. Sir Gawain and Lancelot had risen to the challenge of bringing them back. They had ridden all day to the border of the land of the kidnappers only to find their way impeded by a strange obstacle.

Apparently, there were only two avenues into the land, either by a strange underwater bridge, the only path through a waterway of incredible currents, or by an equally strange sword bridge, which consisted of literally a great sword stretched across an impassible river[918].

"There is no way to cross alive." Gawain raged. "Either we will drown on one bridge or be cut to pieces on the other, even as we cross!"

Lancelot agreed, but there was nothing else to do. Somewhere, on the other side of those bridges, Guinevere and Kay needed rescue. Both men chose their bridges, and fell to the terrible task of crossing them, most likely to their dooms.

---

[917] (Gautier, 1989) pg. 39, 43-44—The knight has a twin aim . . . , Matthew 22:38, Mark 12:29, James 2:8

[918] (Scudder, 1917) pg.59

Each of these bizarre tests represent great obstacles, typical in their occurrence, but terrible in their power. Water, this time, represents death, and the sword, violence.

Gawain chose the underwater bridge, and simply stepped off into the water, moving jerkily as his armor struggled with the waves.

Lancelot gingerly set on his arms and knees, crawling across the razor sharp blade that served as the bridge itself. Every step cut him, every slip lacerated him until he was bleeding from a thousand cuts, but he continued on[919]. Finally, trembling, nearly comatose and struggling to keep his head up, Lancelot reached the other side and collapsed. After some time, he found his strength again and proceeded to a distant castle in that land, where he was to open his wounds again in rescuing Guinevere and Sir Kay.

On the way back, they were able to rescue Gawain as he still persisted in attempting the underwater bridge.

For anyone who knows the stories of Sir Lancelot, although the circumstances may be fantastical, this type of suffering for others was not unusual.

True History is full of even greater examples of how Sacrifice is a powerful weapon in this world. The sacrifice made by the Alamo defenders and the 400 at Goliad, seemed at first glance to have accomplished little. Yes, Sam Houston and the Texians had gained time to create a new government for Texas, but Santa Anna, dictator of Mexico, was certain he would track and kill all the rebellious Texians before long. He called the Alamo "But a small affair"[920].

The Texians thought otherwise. So enraged were they by the wanton killing of so many brave men at the Alamo and Goliad, Sam Houston could barely control his army as he prepared for battle against Santa Anna. "We can't wait any more!" They shouted. "We must attack now! Remember the Alamo! Remember Goliad"[921]!

In 17 minutes, Santa Anna's men were completed routed and Santa Anna himself soon captured. This battle was one of the shortest in history[922]. Brave men are inspired tremendously by the sacrifice of other

---

[919] (Scudder, 1917) pg.64-65
[920] (Hardin, 1994) pg. 155
[921] Ibid. pg. 207-209, (Pohl, 1989) pg. 39
[922] (Hardin, 1994) pg. 213, (Pohl, 1989) pg. 43

brave men fighting for the same cause. It is very possible that without the initial deaths of so many brave men as impetus, the Texians may not have found the pure righteous fury to win against their better-trained and numerous Mexican counterparts. Without the Sacrifice of the Alamo and Goliad, history may have been vastly different.

As we have seen with the stories of El Cid, King Arthur, and others, when a true man and knight places together his strength, courage, faith, and sacrifice, combining it with the same of other true heroes, GOD HIMSELF listens[923]. The impossible can become the possible. And even the Sacrifice of one man can change the entire world.

Two thousand years ago when Paul of Tarsus told his friends that he wanted to preach in Rome[924], they told him that he was crazy. Yet a vision had informed him that a trip to Rome was GOD's plan, no matter the sacrifice[925].

"Don't you understand that Rome is not like these outskirts nations?" His friends might have said. "In Rome, they won't want to hear about your GOD of mercy, they will just put you to death when you refuse to worship their gods and their emperor."

"Even so." Paul said. "I will preach in Rome and I will preach to the Emperor Himself!"

Soon he found the way to do this. Brought before the governor of Jerusalem for the trumped-up crime of speaking against Rome, Paul called upon his legal right as a Roman citizen. "I appeal to Caesar"[926]! This appeal would bring him directly to the Emperor of Rome itself, Caesar Nero, and, so his friends were sure, death.

Indeed, Paul did get his chance to preach about Christ in Rome for two years[927]. And indeed, he was eventually put to death, as was Peter later. But soon, everyone was talking about the seeds these men had planted in Rome itself. It was these seeds that inspired thousands of martyrs to sacrifice their lives even as Paul and Peter had done, and finally, the whole of Rome began to pay attention and take notice to this strange fledgling religion that so many were willing to suffer and die for.

---

[923] With faith and sacrifice, as well as a repentant heart, GOD is more inclined to listen

[924] Acts 19:21

[925] Acts 23:11

[926] Acts 22:25

[927] Acts 28:30, 31

It took much blood and many years, but a miracle emerged. Some three hundred years later, Emperor Constantine announced that Christians were no longer to be persecuted. Rome Herself became Christian.

Today, Rome is the seat of the world-wide Christian vision, the Roman Catholic Church.

Sacrifice and Serving

Sacrifice is not only the communing with GOD through Christ, and the strengthening of discipline and the GODly army, but also to serve GOD, one's neighbor, even the whole human race. It is in the nature of the knight to sacrifice, because it is the goal of every true knight to serve GOD and HIS church. Modern man cannot see himself as a servant, but the knight accepts it as his duty. From the very beginning this was so, for just as Japanese Chivalry named its adherents Samurai, literally "to serve", the German origins of the word "Knight" reflects his ultimate station in life: "servant"[928].

Not to serve as a footman or house servant might, but as a warrior serves his lord by protecting the lord's people, lands, possessions, and ideals[929]. The knight places his own body and his very life in the path of anything that would threaten the peace and harmony of the lord's lands. The knight is the servant of the king (whether temporal or spiritual).

And when the knight is a king himself[930]? Then this royal knight is doubly-charged to serve! Not only must he serve the people and the land, his proper focus is on serving a King higher than himself[931]. Many times over, to serve Christ is to serve our fellow humans, and to serve either or both is to be Honorable[932].

This willingness to serve and sacrifice, whether through life, wealth, or blood, is the legacy of King Arthur.

Not much is known about the historical King Arthur, but through the puzzle pieces historians have gathered, they have constructed a picture of a British warlord in the fifth century AD, facing the fact that his

---

[928] (Barber, 1995) pg. 21-22

[929] (Lull, 2001) pg. 31

[930] (Lang M. A., 1912) on St. Louis

[931] (Joinville, 1963), (Barber, 1995) pg.332

[932] (Lull, 2001) pg.29, 31, 35

beloved country would be overrun by barbaric, undisciplined marauders and the rapid dissolution of all law, order, and civilization[933]. To prevent this, he gathered the best warriors he could find, had them vow to uphold GOD, Honor, justice, mercy, and country, even in the face of death, dedicating them all to the preservation of society itself[934].

Civilization as they knew it was indeed falling apart. The Roman Empire, which had literally been the center of civilization for the Western World for almost a thousand years[935], had been decimated by roving tribes of Barbarians, internal intrigue, and strife. The entire Western world looked to Rome for leadership, and now, with Rome itself fallen, the center of civilization became a gaping hole.

Everywhere else, civilization staggered; even in Britain. Arthur and his knights presented a wall upon which the colossal waves of chaos would strike and rage, but could not break[936]. Men are mortal, and this wall could not stand the assault for ever, but for a time, Arthur created an oasis in a world of despair, ignorance, and destruction. His spirit and leadership, built on the concepts of Honor, GOD, and Sacrifice, set up a kingdom and an example that would shine down the centuries.

This fight for civilization was not without its price. Their heroic service required a single-mindedness of action and attention, demanding almost every waking hour and every drop of blood and sweat. Nowhere could Arthur rest, or live a "normal" life. He could never simply live for himself and his family, nor could he spend his valuable time constructing domestic tranquility as so many others strive to do. As El Cid[937], and many other knights after him, King Arthur sacrificed any semblance of a "traditional" life in the service of mankind.

Wasn't there a great reward, you may ask, since Arthur and his knights are praised and known forever for their actions in the service of GOD and humanity? It is difficult to assuage yourself with the praise of future generations when your life of the present is constant warfare without respite. Servitude is difficult, tiresome, and deadly.

But that is the mark of a knight, to sacrifice for others.

---

[933] (Monmouth, 1982) pg. 188-195, (Goodrich, 1989) pg. 43, 44

[934] (Lull, 2001) pg.29

[935] (Matthews, The Elements of the Arthurian Tradition, 1989-1993) pg. 2

[936] (Goodrich, 1989) pg. 13, 43-44, (Fife, 1991) pg. 12-17

[937] (Matthews, Warriors of Christiandom, 1998) pg. 76, unceasing battle for at least 30 years

Some serve Christ directly, as in the saints. Others serve Christ indirectly, as many knights and heroes, fighting for Christ-worthy causes, as Justice and Peace, Freedom from Tyranny, or Goodness against Evil. Some start by serving persons, but eventually take on greater causes, as in Warwick's case. Whatever the cause, honorable serving will eventually lead to sacrifice. For that is what Honorable sacrifice is, to serve another, instead of one's self[938].

Such allows a knight to engage in true Loyalty.

Loyalty

That which drives the greatest of warriors to sacrifice himself upon the altar of Honor, the thing that causes a hero to hold himself as the holocaust, the burnt offering, and that which takes from the knight, and seemingly gives back nothing, is one of the greatest motivators at the heart of the knight and the very seat of Honor.

This demanding trait is called Loyalty, springing from the knight's heart overflowing with Love.

The Loyal Vassal

Every nation has a hero that stands out from all the rest. Usually a knight or a king, this hero's sacrifice in loyalty and strength brings together the country. For England, this hero is King Arthur, and for France, Charlemagne and Joan of Arc. For Spain, a country struggling to find common identity in the eleventh century, that hero was Sir Rodrigo De Bivar.

Rodrigo had two titles: "El Cid", and "Compeador". The latter literally means "Conquerer", for he won nearly every battle he engaged in. But Rodrigo never became king, although he conquered enough kingdoms to have ruled many times over[939]. He refused to be king unto himself[940]. Instead, he fought for and was forever loyal to the king whom

---

[938] John 3:30—He (Christ) must increase, while I must decrease.
[939] (Matthews, Warriors of Christiandom, 1998) pg. 70
[940] Ibid.

he felt was the rightful ruler of Spain: King Alphonso. Rodrigo dreamt of uniting all of Spain under one Christian king's banner[941], no matter how much pain or suffering it cost him personally, even if it meant he himself would always be a servant.

The Spain of Rodrigo's time lay fractured by the internal struggle of nobles and the strange balancing act between Moslem and Christian cities-states, for Spain was half Christian and half Moor. The Moslems had come some hundred years earlier, splitting the country into a mishmash of alliances, with constant invasions from African Moslems, Berbers under the fanatical Moslem, Yusef, who always endangering the tenuous balance.

Only a man like Rodrigo could pull this logistical and political nightmare into one cohesive country. In an age when one great fighting man could win the day, and with a steel arm and impressive tactical and leadership abilities, he forced city after city under the protectorate of the king of Spain. Soon, no one dared deny the might of the Compeador. His ability and loyalty would be put to the test.

Indeed, it was the Cid's zeal that would lead to trouble. When Toledo rebelled against the king, the Cid rushed off to quell the rebellion without asking for permission. The Beni-Gomez family, an enemy of the Cid and very probably connected with the rebellion, whispered to the king that Rodrigo meant to take Toledo for himself[942]. They pointed out that the Cid's personally army was almost as large as the king's own, and this could only mean, so they said, a future coup.

The king of Spain, Alphonzo, showed himself to be not as loyal as his vassal. Incredibly, he sent the Cid into exile[943]. But, after sending his family to the safe monastery of Cardena, the Cid then continued to unify Spain. After a long campaign, he negotiated a treaty with Saragossa, an important caliphate, and made it a protectorate of Spain, after defeating its enemies. The Caliph of Saragossa offered him amazing gifts, but the Cid refused them all. The Cid instead asked for only one thing: for the Caliphate of Saragossa to swear allegiance to King Alphonso. Everything he did was for the king of Spain, even in exile.

---

[941] (Matthews, Warriors of Christiandom, 1998) pg. 66, 72
[942] (Matthews J., Warriors of Christiandom, 1998). pg. 65
[943] (Gerritsen and Melle, 1998) pg. 80

When the mighty Yusef threatened to overcome all of Spain with his fanatical and fundamentalist Moslem army, Alphonzo hesitated to call for his greatest vassal. How could he call upon someone who he had sent into exile? But when Yusef squashed his army, the king finally humbled himself and sent a cartload of treasure to the Cid for forgiveness and to ask for aid. The Cid gave back the treasure. "If the king needs me," the Cid said, "all he need do is ask"[944].

When Yusef suddenly departed back to Africa, the Cid quickly raised an army to recapture much of the land lost to the Moslems. This worried Alphonzo again, for so many men wished to join under the Cid. It must have been almost like Saul's jealousy of David[945]. When Yusef attacked again, and the Cid was not able to join Alphonzo on the battlefield fast enough, the king sent the greatest vassal into exile again!

This time the king demanded the family of the Cid, his wife and twin daughters, be put into prison! Such action enraged the Cid, and he asked for a trial by combat to prove his innocence[946].

When this was not forthcoming, the Cid turned his wrath to Spain's aid instead[947], attacking and conquering the rogue caliphate Valencia, which was truly a magnificent city. All the people assumed he would take it for himself, and he did govern it, but only as a steward might govern, keeping himself under the law of the land[948].

According to one story, the Cid had one of his men take the Valencia crown itself and offer it to Alphonso[949]. Alvar-Fanez Minaya, a close friend of the Cid, solemnly walked to the throne, bowed before King Alphonso, and said "My King, the Cid sends you the crown of Valencia"[950].

The king must have been flabbergasted. "Did he not know I have had his family thrown into prison? His wife, his children?"

"He knew." Alvar-Fanez said simply.

"He wants something!" The King fumed. "What does he want?!"

---

[944] (Matthews J., Warriors of Christiandom, 1998) pg.68

[945] 1 Samuel 18:29

[946] (Matthews, Warriors of Christiandom, 1998) pg. 69

[947] Another excellent example of the Chivalrous use of righteous rage

[948] (Matthews, Warriors of Christiandom, 1998) pg. 87

[949] (Gerritsen and Melle, 1998) pg. 84

[950] (Gerritsen and Melle, 1998) pg. 84, this is reflected in the famous movie with Charlton Heston

"My Lord the Cid asks for nothing." Alvar-Fanez said. "But I ask for him! Who has done more for you and for Spain! WHO!"

The king still would not bring the Cid out of exile, even though the Cid now was the real power in Spain. But when Granada, a great Spanish city was attacked, one letter from the Queen of Spain brought the Cid to his king's side once more[951].

Over and over again this same scene played, with many armies, but always the Cid being victorious, constantly fighting to unify Spain. Rodrigo fought for nearly forty years straight, injured badly, given up for dead—twice—, allowing himself little time to rest, giving himself nothing of a normal life or domestic peace, and losing his one son in battle along side the king. Servitude is indeed difficult.

According to legend, the Cid did not even allow his body to rest after death. When King Bucar and a huge army of Moors swept Spain, bringing with him thirty six kings and even an army of Amazon-like warrior-women, the Cid answered the call. The battle waxed horribly, and the Cid died from an illness brought on by prolonged exposure and blood loss, but he had ordered his body mummified with rose-water and strapped to his horse, so that he looked ready for battle as on the first day of his campaigns[952]. With his armor gleaming and his arm raised by a contraption under his cape, he led his army out against Bucar and totally trounced the invader.

Bucar and his men were convinced that the Cid had risen from the dead to fight, sending Bucar and what was left of his army away forever[953].

Even in death, the Cid served his beloved Spain, one last time.

It is certainly not unseemingly for an honorable man to sacrifice and remain loyal to his country, no matter the consequence[954]. Thousands of knights and heroes throughout history have remained loyal to their country even in the face of death, as the Cid, William of Gellone[955], Joan of Arc, and even Socrates.

---

[951] (Merwin, 1959) El Poema de la Cid, intro
[952] Ibid, xxv-xxviii
[953] (Matthews, Warriors of Christiandom, 1998) pg.94
[954] Socrates, also (Sheen, 1990) pg. 111, even Rousseau
[955] (Ferrante, 2001) pg. 33

Jeremiah Denton, prisoner of war for eight years during the Vietnam War, and author of the incredible book, *When Hell Was in Session*, is a living example of loyalty to country in the face of terrible torture.

He writes of George Coker, who feared torture might weaken his resolve enough to write damaging letters in favor of the North Vietnamese. To avoid this, Coker purposefully smashed his hand to a pulp with a heavy desk in the very torture room, so that no matter what, he would not write the letter. George Mcknight was under the same pressure to write what would be excellent propaganda for the North Vietnamese. He instead purposefully aggravated a pulmonary condition by inhaling dust from his blanket, making himself too sick to write anything[956].

Whether the cause is friends, freedom, country, or GOD, the final price of loyalty is sacrifice. The true Knight, the man of Honor, the real Christian, holds fast to loyalty. Loyalty forever! Loyalty unto the last!

Loyalty, the fuel of Sacrifice (Loyalty and Friendship)

How may a man prove his loyalty? One may as well ask: how may a man prove his love? Are words enough? Are deeds enough[957]? What sacrifice is worthy to prove ultimate love and loyalty? Like the Cid, a hero may offer his life as proof, or his death. In the end, the ultimate knight and the ultimate hero offers both, and everything he has.

Knights are well known for their loyalty to king and country, and especially toward their women. But one of the most prized loyalties in the Middle Ages was among friends. King Arthur built the legendary round table to accommodate his knights, having them sit together in a circle of equal friends. Gawain and Lancelot, as well as Bors, Galahad, and Percival, shared great friendships born out of shared hardship, mission, and danger. One of Gawain's five points of knighthood was fellowship. "An example of the highest kind of friendship is what existed between Charlemagne and each of his peers [paladins], and among the peers

---

956 (Denton, 1982) pg. 140
957 (Steinbeck, 1976) pg. 220, (Sheen, 1990) pg. 61

themselves"[958]. Throughout time, Friendship has always been at the heart of Chivalry, and a great source of willing sacrifice.

"Greater love hath no man," Christ said, "Than to give his life for a friend"[959]. The True Knight was a mirror of such love.

The gates of the Alamo opened, and James Butler Bonham drove his horse through the enemy lines and into the unknown.

Sent with an urgent message to General Fannin in Goliad, Bonham rode his spirited horse to the breaking point. The Alamo was surrounded by nearly three thousand enemy troops under the dictator Santa Anna, and the only hope for the 187 men inside was reinforcements. Fannin possessed those reinforcements, one hundred miles away.

"There is nothing I can do." Fannin said, the next day. "The Alamo is doomed. But I can offer you shelter here, Bonham. Stay with us, for you know if you return to the Alamo, you will die."

"I will report the results of my mission," Bonham replied. "Or die in the attempt"[960].

On the long journey back, Bonham had time to rue his flamboyant words. He went to Gonzales and other towns along the way, but found only empty streets and deserted houses. The echoes of his calls for aid seemed to mock him.

He must have thought, "Is there no one left? Is there no one at all to help us?" He knew what was coming. He knew that he sealed his fate with that ride.

Retracing his way with a heavy heart, he intercepted a courier riding back from the Alamo. "If you're going to the Alamo," The Courier said, "Forget it. So many enemy troops surround it now, no one can get through the lines. Only a dead man would even try it"[961].

Bonham grinned without mirth. He patted the neck of his cream-colored horse.

With astounding speed, so fast the Mexican soldiers were stunned and had no time to aim, he burst upon their lines[962]. Bullets flying

---

[958] (Sayers, 1984) pg. 30
[959] John 15:13
[960] (Guerra, 2001), (Tinkle, 1985) pg. 170
[961] (Tinkle, 1985) pg. 169
[962] (Tinkle, 1985) pg. 169-170

around him, he thundered through. As the gates swung closed behind him, legend says he cried out, "My friends, we die together!"

With Bonham's message, all the defenders of the Alamo knew what would happen on the last day[963]. They resolved to meet death. General Houston needed them to hold back Santa Anna long enough so that he and the rest of the Texian congress could ratify their independence and a new government. The Alamo stood for 13 days against Santa Anna. The men of the Alamo paid for that time with their lives.

To commemorate the sacrifice of these men, flags representing their home states and nations are displayed for all time. If you visit the Alamo Chapel today, even at this very hour, you will find Bonham's native flag of South Carolina. The Cid's flag of Spain is also there, with its thousand-year-old symbols of Castille and Leon. Among the other banners that decorate its hall, you will find one that seems even older. Upon this flag rests green and white colors with a strangely thin, red dragon. The flag of Wales, it is also the traditional symbol of King Arthur. How fitting to find these flags once again, in yet another hall of Honor, Heroism, Loyalty, and Sacrifice.

The Commodity of Loyalty

Loyalty is a precious commodity. Especially the loyalty and sacrifice a knight exudes. Many governments and leaders in today's world strive to win, or coerce, such loyalty.

The knight is wary of giving his incredible loyalty to just anyone, and he must research and study carefully before he bestows it on anything but GOD.

The knight looks around. Is any earthly leader worthy of his love? And who is beside the knight, showing the same level of commitment to a cause? Who is willing to join the knight in true sacrifice and unselfish serving?

---

[963] (Hardin, 1994) pg. 135

The "Would-Be" Sacrifice

The most prized warriors in history were always those who were the most loyal[964], and who were willing to sacrifice for a cause or leader. It makes sense then that many in today's world would want to imitate this. But it is one thing to imitate, and then another to truly be a loyal warrior, willing to sacrifice.

Many wish to sacrifice, or at least appear to, but many more do not understand the definition of sacrifice. You have seen plenty of them. Yes, the performers, celebrities, and famous people on Television. They show off their supposed charity by holding fund-raising events. I suppose this is better than nothing, but then they try to compare themselves to knights and saints of old!

If I own a bank, should I brag when I give away a dollar? A true, great sacrifice, showing true honor, is giving until it hurts, as in giving away much when you don't have much. The giving of one penny to the poor is a great sacrifice when you only have one penny. Christ said that the poor woman who gave two pennies sacrificed more than the wealthy who gave huge donations[965]. Indeed, a wealthy person, to truly compare himself with this poor woman, would have to give away half or more of his estate, or dedicate his riches to the protection of the poor and innocent, or other worthy cause[966].

And what constitutes a worthy cause? If a man is loyal to himself, and gives up small pleasures so that he may have bigger pleasures later, this is common sense, but hardly equals the sacrifices of saints and heroes. And what if a man or woman is loyal to a stupid cause? Can they be called heroes? Can they be equal to someone who suffers for a great cause?

Misplaced Loyalties vs. Discernment

I am always amazed when I encounter people who wish to be loyal and even suffer for irrelevant or stupid causes, and the modern world abounds with these.

---

[964] (Barber, 1995) pg. 52

[965] Mark 12:42

[966] Bonaventure says that a godly man always has two pennies to give: his body and time

287

Many adolescent boys allow themselves to be punished so they may wear what I call "half-mast" pants, their jeans sagging and their underwear exposed. Girls insist upon remaining loyal to cruel and unfaithful boyfriends, these so-called "players" bent upon showing their "prowess" by bedding as many girls as they can. Then there are hundreds of young people, claiming to be willing to die for their "gang" affiliations, even though these gangs exist only to inflict crime and pain upon others, preying on the poor, the destitute, and the ignorant. But there are even worse and misguided loyalties than these, as we shall see in a moment.

So many people want to be loyal to ridiculous slogans and groups, prejudices and misconceptions, illusions and weaknesses, that I am almost convinced the human race is willing to suffer and sacrifice for anything, and if not a good cause, then a self-destructive and evil cause.

It is a shame that I must mention these idiotic causes in the same book as the great cause of Chivalry. But for the modern person to understand the difference, I must compare and contrast, as with the sacred and the profane. Even worse, when I bring up in conversation the great and knightly sacrifice spurred by loyalty, many people, in their modern, misconceiving way, immediately mention suicide bombers of Radical Islamic movements, evoking an extreme example of misplaced loyalty and sacrifice.

It is typical of modern people to be unable to discern the difference between honorable sacrifices and stupid, even selfish sacrifices, just as it is typical that they are unable to tell between right and wrong. Many cannot understand the vast differences between knightly sacrifice and suicide bombers, simply because both actions have violence. These modern observers lack discernment. So do many who seek to give their loyalty and sacrifice.

Discernment, that great knightly skill, is needed to determine where one's ultimate loyalties may rest, and thus for what cause one should sacrifice. Discernment as an art rose to its fullest height in that knightly saint, Ignatius of Loyola[967].

As a great saint, his power, loyalty, and ability to sacrifice were at the ready to perform for a great cause. Not only did this attract angels and the blessings of GOD, but also the attention of demons. Whenever Ignatius prayed, and visions appeared to him, he would have to be able to

---

[967] (Green, 1984) pg. 14

determine which visions were from GOD, and which might be from the Evil One. His loyalty and his work were at stake, but also his eternal soul. One must be able to discern which path to take, which voice to heed, which cause to take, if one wishes to truly serve GOD[968].

One night, as Ignatius prayed fervently, a strange and beautiful vision came to him. A swirling array of colors, that he described as almost like the multi-colored scales of a huge, glowing serpent, twisted and sparkled before him. At first he thought it must be from Heaven because of its beauty. Then he realized it was distracting him from prayer. If it distracted him from prayer, which is in GOD's name, how can this vision be from GOD? Why would GOD wish to take him from prayer?

Although beautiful and seemingly heaven-sent, Ignatius determined this vision diabolical in nature. Ignatius ignored the vision, and continued to pray[969].

When we are not sure of the right path or who and what to follow, Ignatius is a great model. Ignore all else and keep praying.

Many things on earth seem honorable, beautiful, heaven sent, or worthy of loyalty and sacrifice, but are illusions and can be even evil distractions from the true things worthy of loyalty. With many who wish to sacrifice for selfish causes or movements, they are simply and obviously distracted by their own desires and whims of the flesh. With the above mentioned suicide bombers, they may believe they are killing for a higher cause, when it is a trick of the most vile, demonic type.

Many of these bombers, once they blow themselves up, know that their families will be paid a handsome sum by some political and malignant benefactor. Others are focused on the supposed "seventy-two virgins" and sundry rewards awaiting them in their Islamic heaven[970]. Still others want to harm those they see as infidels, their goal to inflict pain and terror much more than save souls. The most suicide bombings are done by communists, trying to inflict their tyrannical and antireligious politics on others, exposing the lie that such terrors are only made in the name of religion.

Sir Joinville understood the temptations of zealousness, as well as the more subtle motivations of selfishness hidden within feigned religiosity. He knew a man must not struggle, sacrifice, or battle for fear of Hell,

---

[968] Ibid. pg. 91
[969] (Loyola, 2004) pg. 21, 27
[970] (Spencer, 2005) pg. 101, 104

nor for a desire for the delights of Heaven[971], even a heaven on earth. For anyone to do so is actually selfishness in disguise[972].

What then is worthy of loyalty, what then is worthy of true sacrifice? How may one know if a sacrifice is valuable or not, truly selflessness or hidden selfishness? Hosea, a minor prophet of the Old Testament, states clearly that love and loyalty to GOD is more important than sacrifice[973]. The sacrifice by itself is nothing without faith and love of GOD to qualify it. When we sacrifice for a great and noble cause beyond ourselves, to give greater glory to GOD or to uphold HIS ways and HIS kingdom, and for love of Him, then it is a good sacrifice[974]. Within and reflected by this loyalty and love can also be the love of one's friends, for Christ himself said that no greater love has he, than to lay down his life for his friends.

And how does one know if one has this love and loyalty to GOD? One who loves GOD truly, follows HIS commandments, and treats others as he would want to be treated. One who loves GOD respects GOD's creation, never placing it, themselves, or others in danger unless absolutely necessary. One who loves GOD, imitates His Son, Christ Jesus, and follows in His footsteps.

Without loyalty and love for GOD, even sacrifice means nothing[975]. Love and loyalty drive to true sacrifice, so if one is missing the love and loyalty, the sacrifice will be hollow. A "stupid" sacrifice would then be one devoid of love and loyalty. If a man sacrifices simply to attempt to bribe GOD, or sacrifices to gain other than GOD's will, such an action is hollow and will achieve nothing, no matter the vigor or cost of the sacrifice. Even mortal sacrifice that is aimed against GOD's will is no sacrifice at all, but nihilistic suicide.

---

[971] (Joinville, 1963) ch.11, p.274, Penguin Classics
[972] (Kierkegaard, Purity of Heart is to Will One Thing, translated by Douglas V. Steere, 1956) ch.4, 5
[973] Hosea 6:6, Mark 12:33
[974] (Joinville, 1963) ch.11, p.274, Penguin Classics
[975] 1 Corinthians 13:3

Sacrifice and Suicide

The kingdom of Heaven cannot and will never be established with murder, wanton and whole-sale killing, dishonor and terror[976]. But because the modern person many times cannot tell the violence of self-defense and defense of others from the violence of needless destruction, they become confused.

From a modern perspective, the sacrifices of warriors and saints, because of the violence of their passing, might resemble the intense zealousness of Radical Islamic suicide bombers. True discernment would plainly show that the sacrifices of knights and saints follow the ways of GOD and the love of GOD. Suicide bombers, in their zeal to serve perceived holy purpose, have been deceived, either by leaders bent on political success, misconceptions of religion, or even subconscious motivations. They have fallen horribly victim to their lack of discernment, the illusions and feigned holiness confusing them and leading them away from what otherwise might have been sincere belief. The suicide bomber dies for hate, the knight and saint dies for love.

If this is not clear to the modern reader, if the hugely disparate motives are not obvious, then the difference of means will suffice. A knight fights to defend the innocent and weak against terror; the suicide bomber purposefully targets the innocent and weak to inflict the most terror. A knight aims his attacks at other warriors and those who can battle him openly, proving his bravery and skill; the suicide bomber stays clear of soldiers unless he can kill them with deception and cruel cowardice. The knight avoids killing unless it is necessary; the suicide bomber's entire aim is murder and deals in killing as many as possible. The knight shows mercy when possible, willing to win a friend; the suicide bomber must avoid mercy, for his victims are the very ones a good man would protect.

And what of suicide warriors such as the Kamikaze during World War II? They attacked warriors such as they, attempting to inflict maximum damage on their enemy's military. Such may seem different from the ways and means of the modern suicide bomber.

Simple suicide is not condoned by Chivalry. Steinbeck, in his *The Acts of King Arthur and His Noble Knights*, explained best the difference

---

[976] Matthew 5:9 also, Luke 6:35, James 3:17

between Kamikaze and Western Chivalry. "Perhaps he (Lancelot) must die, but if he must the code (of Chivalry) required that he approach his death as though it were a part of life, and if any chink appeared in the inevitable, he must seize it instantly and with all of his strength . . . . A man could accept death with a good heart and gaily if he had exhausted every honorable means to avoid it . . . . It was his duty under chivalry to accept whatever GOD might send, but also even GOD expected him to use what endowments he had . . . . At least it was worth a try, and a try—a headlong try—was all the rules of chivalry required"[977]. A knight has an obligation to himself and to the GOD that created him, to strive to fight Evil and protect the Good, but also in preserving his life if honorably possible. Death in battle is highly prized, but a knight aims first for Victory in battle, accepting death as a real, but secondary, possibility.

But if all honorable avenues have been exhausted? We have already seen this, with the 40 Martyrs of Sebaste, with Polycarp, with Joan of Arc. Christ Himself knew that he would accept the Crucifixion *only* after his preaching was done, and only as the culmination of His mission.

Samson too, knew his time was over, and stretched his arms out as if to accept crucifixion as well.

Samson was a judge of Israel, but also a strange man with many inconsistencies. Possessing unbelievable strength, he was a Nazarite, consecrated to GOD and sworn to uphold HIS Law, but a man who also found it hard to resist women. He was sworn never to cut his hair, as a sign of his consecration, nor to drink wine[978], but one day he became intoxicated by the beauty of Delilah, her own hands shearing his head. Without his hair, Samson was bereft of his connection with GOD, and he was helpless[979].

Delilah was a Philistine[980]. The Philistines were an ancient people who had migrated from Crete to the shores of Modern Israel and Palestine. They had warred with the ancient Israelites for many years, and now had the great protector of Israel in their grasp. The Philistines had

---

[977] (Steinbeck, 1976) pg. 243-244
[978] Judges 13:5, Judges 13:4-5
[979] Judges 16:17
[980] Judges 16:4

always hated Samson most of all, the entire race of them complicit in his abduction and torture.

They burned his eyes out with a red-hot iron rod and tied him to a mill to grind grain, treating him like a beast of burden. After some time, they decided to make use of poor Samson as entertainment during the Festival for Dagon, one of their chief gods[981]. They stood Samson up in the temple of Dagon, chaining the once invincible man between two tall pillars that supported the temple. They did not notice that his hair had grown back.

It hardly seemed to matter. Even if he could break the chains, he could not see to make his way from the midst of his enemies. There was no escape, and thus no way to protect himself or his people from the continuous onslaught of the Philistines. The Philistines laughed at him, and jeered at his sightless visage—the ruined, gaping holes in his face and his useless, knotted muscles. The whole of the crowd scoffed at him and mocked him as they celebrated their victory. Delilah and all who had plotted his demise were there.

But Samson cried out to the Lord. "Oh GOD, remember me this day! Give me strength one more time, to avenge my two eyes. Oh GOD, let me die with the Philistines![982]"

He wrapped his arms around the pillars and pulled with all his might, bringing the very temple down upon the rulers of the Philistines and their subjects, so "the dead whom he killed at his death were more than those he had killed in his life"[983].

Samson only accepted death when no other honorable way was possible. And when he struck, he struck at those responsible.

For the knight and saint, the end never justifies the means. For a suicide bomber or kamikaze pilot, the means do not matter, as long as the end is reached. For many communists and political parties as well, their means and actions are wiped clean by success, at least in their eyes. But not in GOD's eyes. This has made them the enemy of all knights and saints everywhere.

---

[981] Judges 16:25
[982] Judges 16:28-30
[983] Judges 16:30

The Slaying of the Will

That is the final aspect of true sacrifice, and Honor: it doesn't serve us. It was never meant to serve our desires or our needs. Whether we live or die in our sacrifice, we do so for GOD's will, not our own.

When we sacrifice as knights, we do not do so to achieve pleasure, fame, wealth, vitality, or praise. The sacrifices we face make these supposed "rewards" seem as dust. True sacrifice rarely brings these things and nothing can equal the pain we must endure. Honor was known in the Middle Ages as the "skull word", indicating that Honor most likely brings pain and death. Not even Heaven can be our goal when we sacrifice[984], for Heaven is unknowable and unsearchable[985].

Indeed, when we sacrifice as knights, we exercise something called "Slaying of the Will". This is not the destruction of will power, but it is the destruction or at least the holding back of our selfish desires, self-preservation, and self-perpetuation. Slaying of the Will is doing what GOD wants, obeying what GOD demands, instead of what we want or wish.

All the heroes we have discussed have subordinated their own wills and wishes to the will of GOD. They did not want to suffer or die, but they knew these things were necessary to accomplish GOD's will. They "killed" their own wills. They knew themselves to be only small dots in the great fabric of the universe.

Many would-be heroes in history fall short because they convince themselves that their own desires are the true good in the universe. They fail because they subordinate GOD's plan to their plan. They make their wishes equal, in their own eyes, to GOD's wishes. Their wishes thus become their god.

This is why feminists, homosexuals, secular humanists, and racists never live up to knightly standards. Such concerns as these individualized aspects of human society are dwarfed by Justice, Life and Death, Good and Evil. I'm not saying human interests are not worth anything, I am saying that GOD and Honor are worth more.

If we wish to be knights, we should not drag other, personal goals into the pursuit. For the knight, there is only service of GOD. There is

---

[984] (Kierkegaard, Purity of Heart is to Will One Thing, translated by Douglas V. Steere, 1956) ch.6

[985] (Barron, 2008) pg. 25-26, 32, 37, 61, 68

no room for political motivations, earthly power, or ambition. Desire to capture another's heart has no place. Hate for other races has no purpose. Lust for money or gold has no meaning. "You cannot serve two masters . . ."[986].

All our dreams must be subordinated to the quest for Honor. There will come a day when we must choose between those dreams and knighthood. On that day, our choice will determine the rest of our lives: the life of a true knight, or a "knight wanna-be".

Expect your heart to be broken by the Honor code, or by your search for Honor. Better yet, break your heart yourself, now, and get it over with. My heart has been broken long ago by Honor, and every so often I still step on the pieces in my continuous pursuit, grinding them into the dirt.

It takes ultimate strength, courage, humility, and honesty to "slay" our wills. Honesty and humility tell us when our desires are not GOD's plan[987]. Strength and courage help us ignore these desires, to go past them and into the Truth[988].

> "I have slain my will,
> And yet I live.
> I bleed my bones,
> My marrow to bestow
> Upon that GOD who knows
> What I would know."
>
> —Theodore Roethke[989]

Why is Sacrifice the Way?

Thus it is for the knight as it was for John the Baptist. He denied himself and became "the voice in the wilderness"[990], fighting against sin, the desires of the flesh, and political and social pressure, paving the

---

[986] Matthew 6:24, Luke 16:13
[987] (Green, 1984)
[988] (Stalker, 1902) pg. 51-53, (Lull, 2001) pg. 48
[989] From his poem *The Marrow*
[990] John 1:23, Mark 1:3, Luke 3:4, Matthew 3:3 also, Isaiah 40:3

way for Christ Jesus[991]. And then, when he is at his peak, so that he can actually recognize the true Messiah, he must relinquish all glory, all power, even his freedom, and finally his life. He accepts it willingly, saying "He must increase, as I must decrease"[992].

Must it always be this way? Must the knight rise with great achievements and overflowing compassion, the shining example and strongest and most deserving, only to win nothing but death in a silent grave? Must it always end the same?

GOD made everything, and the Bible says GOD made everything good, but why must we eventually sacrifice things of this world?

The world, and all of creation, is not opposed to GOD. In fact, it would point us to GOD if we had the wisdom to see truly[993].

But we are blind and tend to see the world, not as GOD intended, but as we wish it to be. Our greed and selfishness wish to mold the world into a place where we can abuse every pleasure and misuse every gift, until the world is unrecognizable. What is more, our faulty minds, corrupted by original sin, become enamored of the world and worship it instead of GOD[994]. Place these together, and you have the world forced and molded by humans becoming the god instead of GOD.

I do not mean this in an environmental sense, for that is seeing things in only one dimension. I mean that when we only pay attention to creation, we lose sight of the creator. When we forget why we were given the world, we end up using it for selfish reasons.

To cure ourselves of blindness to GOD and the greed that is the ignorance of GOD, we must turn our backs on the world, even the pleasure and beauty of it[995]. Just as we might turn off the porch light to better see the stars, we must blot out the world's treasures in order to better see GOD. There is nothing inherently wrong with the porch light, and it can be a good thing, but its brightness gets in the way of a more precious glow.

The world is good, since GOD made it, and is in harmony with HIM. But we, sinful creatures, aren't in harmony with anything and thus we must sacrifice to grasp GOD and better understand HIM.

---

[991] John 3:28

[992] John 3:30

[993] (Augustine S., 1961) pg. 212, (Barron, 2008) pg. 122

[994] (Augustine S., 1961) pg. 213

[995] Matthew 10:37 also, James 4:4, John 15:19, 1 John 2:15

GOD's Gift of GOD

We have seen that a knight gives away, in his sacrifice, the lesser good to grasp the greater good, and the knights, saints, and heroes show us that the more pain we encounter as we sacrifice, the better it is.

Therefore, the greatest sacrifice is the most painful, and the best sacrifice wins nothing of this world. The ultimate sacrifice is the giving away of oneself.

In a way, every sacrifice is simply giving back to GOD what once GOD gave us. Even our lives are not truly our own, since GOD made us and breathed life into us. We owe GOD everything good in life, and so it is right to offer it back to HIM. It is HIS, anyway. GOD made everything, and thus everything is GOD's, by right.

Is it not rude, however, to give back to GOD the gifts he gave us?

We humans tend to forget that GOD gave all gifts. We start thinking that the gift is simply ours and has always been ours. Many times we mistreat a gift, as many mistreat their bodies; or even worship a gift, as many worship the world.

So GOD gave us one final gift more precious than the others, because HE suffered so much to give it—HIS only son, Jesus Christ, who is GOD. GOD's greatest gift to us is thus HIMSELF.

When we come for that gift, we see that all the other gifts were simply copies or things to tide us over until we obtain this real gift. We surrender the other gifts, because GOD's final gift means more than all the others combined. It is like comparing a store-bought painting to one that has been suffered over and signed by a true artist.

To grasp this final gift, Christ, we cannot have our hands full. We must put down the temporary gifts in order to embrace this last, greatest one.

When we finally have GOD's greatest gift with us, we will look back and see that the other gifts have disappeared. They were never truly there in the first place. At least that is what it will seem, after we behold Christ face to face. Nothing else will matter. For now everything we ever wanted, or ever needed is in Christ. All things, all gifts, all beauty, all love, all true joy is in Christ. We realize that Christ is what we wanted and needed after all. We have given everything, only to receive GOD in return.

Yes, it must always end the same. We lay down in the dust with the crucified Christ. And then we rise with HIM on the third day.

At the End of Sacrifice:

The Dark Throne of Care

Cyrano de Bergerac awaits grinning death with his last thin coat and a lonely heart. King Arthur orders his beloved sword Excalibur to be thrown in a lake, as he himself lies dying. Sir Lancelot kneels at the grave of King Arthur, knowing that the same fate awaits him as well. Sir William of Gellone cradles the head of his best friend, dead from terrible wounds. Sir Warwick grimly gives up his kingdom and his wife for a beggar bowl and a cold death in a rotten shed. Christ himself, even as he breathes raggedly on the cross in anguish, surrenders everything—all comfort, friends, mother, blood, and finally, life.

Every knight must eventually come to this absolute place, this crushing pain and desolation. As Alexander Pushkin, the Russian poet, said of his great, poor knight, "Silent, sad, bereft of reason, in his solitude he died"[996].

Why be a knight then? Is Loyalty so important, is Honor so prized that pain, aggravation, and a lonely death should be tolerated, even embraced, for them?

I should not have to explain, or convince you that knighthood and Honor is worthwhile. If you do not understand now, you will never understand. A true knight, a true saint, a true man, a true hero, automatically understands the worth of sacrificing for a higher cause. "A man does not fight only to win"[997].

But if I were to put this into words, I could possibly explain it this way. Honor, through sacrifice, cuts away everything in life and provides pain, yes, but if done for love, it is beautiful. It is like the practice of ballet dancers to dance on their toes, even though it slowly destroys their feet. Knighthood is a captivating art that finally costs the world, and

---

[996] Alexander Pushkin's poem, *The Poor Knight;* behind the knight is the dark throne of care
[997] (Rostand, 1982) pg.195

leaves the knight with nothing except Honor and GOD. Indeed, Chivalry demands everything without reward, as Holiness did Moses and the Levites, because their portion was GOD HIMSELF. You cannot receive something in your hand until your hand is empty, and then GOD fills it with the universe and HIS Presence.

The Chivalrous way to GOD, in fact the only way to the LORD, is through suffering. We must suffer and reach a point of total emptiness in our hearts, when every thing else is stripped away, so that GOD can then fill us. "How else but through a broken heart may Lord Christ enter in?"[998]

Suffering allows us to imitate Christ, and, in a sense, join Him on the cross. Uniting ourselves with the suffering Christ in His ultimate act of love, binds us to Him and that ultimate love, and guarantees our rising from the dead and reigning with Him.

Today we may face the frozen lake of sacrifice, or the terrible burning pillar, but tomorrow—tomorrow we ride with our King!

---

[998] (Oscar Wilde, The Ballad of Reading Gaol (1898) pt. 5, st. 14).

THE FOURTH PILLAR OF HONOR

FAITH

What people don't realize is how much religion costs. They think faith is a big electric blanket, when of course it is the Cross. It is much harder to believe than not to believe. If you feel you can't believe, you must at least do this: keep an open mind. Keep it open toward faith, keep wanting it, keep asking for it, and leave the rest to GOD."

> Flannery O'Connor, *The Habit of Being: Letters of Flannery O'Connor*

For prayer is nothing else than being on terms of friendship with GOD.

> —Saint Teresa of Avila, *Life of Prayer*, ch. 3

In Homeric times, people and things had two names: the one given to them by men, and the one given by the gods. I wonder what GOD calls me?

> —Miguel Unamuno, *Mist*, 1914

And now I take upon me the adventures of holy things, I see and understand that my old sin hinders me, so that I could not move nor speak when the Holy Graal passed by.

> —Spoken by Sir Lancelot, from *King Arthur, Tales of the Round Table*, edited by Andrew Lang, pg. 79

Atheists. What grounds have they for saying that no one can rise from the dead? Which is harder, to be born or to rise again? That what has never been should be, or that what has been should be once more? Is it harder to come into existence than to come back? Habit makes us find the one easy, while lack of habit makes us find the other impossible.

—Blaise Pascal, *Pensees*

Across the threshold I had been afraid to cross, things suddenly seemed so very simple. There was but a single vision, GOD, who was all in all; . . . Nothing could separate me from Him, because He was in all things. No danger could threaten me, no fear could shake me, except the fear of losing sight of Him.

—Father Walter Ciszek, S.J., *He Leadeth Me*, pg. 79

Kill therefore with the sword of wisdom the doubt born of ignorance that lies in thy heart.

—Bhagavad-Gita, 4:42

Faith

Faith is the most mysterious key to Honor, and perhaps the most important. Faith in GOD is the reason a knight is honorable, and without Faith, everything a knight does seems only an exercise in futility. Even Love for GOD cannot exist without Faith in GOD. Strength, Courage, Sacrifice, and Obedience are the "how" of Chivalry, while Love, Loyalty, and Faith in GOD are the "why". The knight, using his strength and courage, lifts the cross of Honor and lays down his life in sacrifice, because he BELIEVES.

The Maiden of Faith

Imagine GOD told you to fight the greatest military force in the world. Would you have the faith to do it? What if there were thousands in that enemy army? What if you had no proof GOD had spoken to you and no one believed you? What if you were only a peasant girl, barely 16 years old?

Thus was the situation for the young Joan of Arc, shining with faith and courage within, but surrounded by doubt from others. Her actions, based on faith, would make her a saint, hero, and one of the first female knights[999].

Joan had always been an extremely pious and church-going little girl, as many in her hometown of Domremy, France, in 1424, remembered[1000]. She particularly loved the church bells of her town, visited sick children, and sometimes prayed and went to church so earnestly and so often that the boys of her town would laugh at her[1001]. But in that year, as a 13-year-old, a voice came to her that identified itself as St. Michael the Archangel, and soon St. Catherine of Alexandria, St. Margaret of Antioch, and St. Denis, joined him. At first, they simply told her to continue to be pious and go to church, but as she grew older, the voices began to tell her that, as GOD had pitied the Israelites in Egypt, so too did HE pity the French in their plight against the English.

France, as an independent country, was almost gone. The British had taken by force or intrigue all the major cities, and were slowly squeezing the life out of the French government, having surrounded the prince-elect of France in Bourges-en-Berri. Paris itself had been occupied by British troops since 1418. Joan's little town of Domremy was in their path, and nothing of consequence stood in their way of more conquest.

The Prince of France, Charles the Seventh, was about to give up. His treasury was nearly exhausted, his troops vanishing, and even his mother had disowned him as illegitimate[1002]. He was losing faith in his own cause. There seemed to be no hope.

He went to his chamber window and whispered to GOD for aid in his dying cause, but if it could not be given, he asked to be punished alone, and his people be spared from further suffering[1003].

---

[999] (Gautier) pg. 57

[1000] (Williamson, Biography of joan of Arc (Jehanne Darc), 1999-2011) segment 1

[1001] Ibid.

[1002] (Williamson, Biography of joan of Arc (Jehanne Darc), 1999-2011) segment 2

[1003] Perhaps it reflected King David's prayer in 2 Samuel 24:17, Ibid, segment 4, see margin note 1. This is similar to King Arthur's prayer in T.H. White's *The Once and Future King*, (White, 1958) pg. 171.

He could not have foreseen how his prayer would be answered, or how a young girl would suffer in his stead, and in the stead of all France.

When Joan was 16, she resolved to act on the voices, whether anyone believed her or not. She was taken to the local commander, where she explained that she was petitioned by GOD and HIS angels to help lead the French in victory against the British.

The commander, unsure of his future but dead sure about the likelihood of a teenaged girl at the head of an army, sent her back with a laugh. A little girl leading him and France to victory, indeed!

About two months later, when Domremy was in the direct path of the British army, Joan tried again and this time explained in detail a forthcoming battle and its outcome. The commander nodded at her prediction but sent her home again.

He gulped when her prediction came true to the letter[1004]. "All right". He told her. "I will take you to see my superiors and you can explain yourself to them. But, on the way, as a precaution, we will dress you in boy's clothes as a way to prevent unwanted advances and other misadventures."

Joan agreed, donning a vest and pants set with ties and fastens all through it[1005].

The Prince heard of his strange visitor before she arrived and may have been advised to disguise himself to test this young seer from Domremy. Not only did she choose him out easily from the crowd and decoy prince, but quoted back, word for word, the prayer he had whispered from his window nearly a year before. The Prince felt convinced, but, very wary of any rumors about insanity from his court, and since his country had suffered from unstable leaders before, he had the poor girl examined for three weeks by religious, clerical, and priestly judges. They sent her back with a glowing report.

"But the true test will be if she can lead my army to victory." He said to his advisor and lords.

The army itself had its doubts, with this young girl in a boy's outfit, homemade banner, and borrowed sword, especially when Joan arrived and immediately began driving away all prostitutes and licentious

---

[1004] (Williamson, Biography of joan of Arc (Jehanne Darc), 1999-2011) segment 3
[1005] Ibid.

behavior[1006]. But when reports of a saint leading the army began to swell the ranks of Charles's force, and victories began to pour in, with this girl always at the head of the first charge, the spirits of the knights and foot soldiers soared. "Lead on, maiden!" They cried.

The first battle Joan took part in freed the city of Orleans from the clutches of the British. It had been a sizable gamble and many of the military advisors had warned against it, but Joan galloped in with one of the first assaults and soon the British fled the ancient town. Joan herself, though wounded in the shoulder, displayed such courage and fortitude that many of the army hailed her name and swore to follow her[1007] from then on.

The battle of Patay, with Joan again riding at the head of one of the frontal assaults, gave such a crushing blow to the English that many called it an "Agincourt in reverse". Half the British force fell in death, while the French received minimal loses[1008]. At the Battle of Jargeau, the Duke of Alecon, not a huge supporter of Joan, found himself crediting her with saving his life during the battle. The battles of La Carite-Sur Loire, Lagney-Sur-Marne, Meung-Sur-Loire, and Beaugency were also great successes. Many cities, as in Troyes, capitulated without a fight, bowing before the obvious power of the Maiden of France.

The tide was turning in France's favor, and Joan drove the spearhead-thrust of that tide. The impossible had happened. A young girl was changing history, all because she had faith, not in herself, but in GOD. Soon, all of France saw her as the very weapon of GOD[1009].

At first, few believed she knew great military strategy. She was after all, simply a young peasant girl. Many of the military advisors and leaders were wary of letting her plan actual attacks. But she was far from being a mere mascot, as some historians have tried to suggest. Both the group of theologians that first examined her and an archbishop decided that she should be in command of an army or at least a consultant to the leaders because her mind was so keen, sharp, and in their eyes, Heaven-sent. She

---

[1006] (Pernoud, 2007) pg.120

[1007] Ibid. pg.138

[1008] (Pernoud, 2007) pg.121, Thibault d'Armagnac, a knight, captain, and eye-witness of the battle, said that Joan promised few French casualties, and only one was killed.

[1009] Ibid. pg.127

constantly gave advice and ideas that turned out to be effective[1010], and constantly placed herself in physical danger to rally the troops in battle after battle, usually carrying only her banner of Christ and her armor, and soon the men simply would not fight without her[1011].

During several battles, Joan, unsupported by any official backing, spontaneously called and led full assaults with a small group of men, found immediate victory, much to the surprise of the soldiers around her, even her bodyguard[1012]. Many historians and chroniclers of the day stated clearly that any mistakes or disasters that came during her campaigns flowed from unfortunate or irresponsible Royal policies, not from anything Joan said or did. Several times she was given no aid or supplies from the Prince, but most of the time she gained success anyway.

She did, however, call for an attack that was doomed to failure. She had known for some time that soon she would have to suffer and be captured[1013]. She did not know which battle or how it would happen, but she knew it would come. The Duke of Burgundy, a British supporter, had besieged the town of Compiegne with a large Burgundian army. Joan refused to stand by and let this city fall, "which had showed such courage in its defiance"[1014]. She and her small group slipped past the siege and into the city to help in its defense. While attempting to push back the enemy Burgundian forces, a drawbridge was pulled up too quickly, and she found herself and her small force caught between the enemy and the river. Joan was captured.

The duke sent her to the English, who were more than happy to have this enemy weapon in their clutches. They engineered a trial to discredit and condemn her, but she had already accomplished her mission. The British forces in France had been effectively broken, and Charles VII was firmly established as the French King. A young girl with no military experience had stopped a world power in its tracks, with naught but Faith in the quiet voice of GOD.

[1010] Ibid. Pg. 121, D'Armagnac, among others, thought she was truly skilled as a military leader

[1011] (Spoto D., 2007) pg. 65

[1012] Ibid. pg. 97

[1013] (Thurston, 1910-2009), (Williamson, Joan of Arc, Brief Biography, 2010, 2002-2005)

[1014] (Williamson, Joan of Arc, Brief Biography, 2010, 2002-2005)

All was accomplished, except the bitter end. Joan waited patiently as a new set of examiner priests, this time assembled by the angry English, prepared to test her for any inkling of witchcraft, heresy, or insanity. As before, they found her answers to be bright, dogmatically perfect, and even frighteningly profound. They probed hard and skillfully, but the only crime they could find was an obscure reference that no woman should reside in the clothes of a man, a rule in no way meant for this case[1015], but they seized on it[1016].

Joan graciously surrendered the offending clothing, accepting a proper dress. This would have ended the matter, since even this so-called heresy was only a capital offence if it was persistently repeated[1017]. Ironically, some sources say that at this change of clothing, an English lord attempted to rape her in her cell, prompting Joan to demand back her boyish clothes[1018]. Another source suggests the English did not provide a change of clothes at all, forcing Joan to remain in her original attire.

Whatever the case, Joan had wittingly repeated an action expressly forbidden by canon law, and by inquisition law she was now subject to full punishment as a heretic. The spirit of the law was obviously being ignored, but the English-sponsored clerics moved quickly to condemn her to burning. In no way was this truly about clothing, the assembly was all about the execution of who they saw as an enemy of England.

At the stake, Joan asked for two priests to hold a crucifix in front of her pyre, so that she might look upon the cross until the very end[1019]. As the flames rose higher, she repeatedly screamed the name of Jesus, and thus she died.

Everyone who witnessed the execution was moved. The secretary of the English king himself returned from the execution exclaiming "We are all ruined, for a good and holy person was burned." The Cardinal of England and the bishop, who had been a brother to the man who

---

[1015] (Williamson, Joan of Arc, Brief Biography, 2010, 2002-2005)
[1016] (Spoto D., 2007) pg. 179
[1017] Ibid. pg. 183, 184
[1018] Ibid. pg. 185
[1019] Ibid. pg. 190

captured Joan, wept openly. Even the executioner confessed that he had murdered a saint[1020].

After the war was over, the Catholic Church began the long process of canonizing this remarkable and faithful girl, and, by 1920, both English and French soldiers alike were evoking her name and aid in their allied struggles of World War I[1021].

When the knight has faith, he or she possesses all the other pillars of Honor. True Faith bestows the Strength to battle the evils of the world, the Courage to attempt the impossible for GOD, the willingness to sacrifice for a higher cause and a higher world, and it brings the humility and reasoning behind obedience.

What is Faith?

Faith basically is trust in GOD, in the goodness of GOD, in the word of GOD, and in the final triumph of goodness through the workings of GOD. Faith is also a relationship with GOD that, as it grows in strength, mirrors the personal relationship[1022] between two close family members, or even a child and parent.

There are two styles to approach this belief[1023], trust, and relationship. One way is intellectual, using the logical and creative abilities of the human brain to grasp philosophies and concepts that help establish and bolster Faith and understanding in GOD. As we will discuss later, St. Augustine, scholastics as St. Anselm, and Blessed Ramon Lull, are advocates of this approach. They believed that Faith can be built[1024], partially at least, through reason, albeit a reason elevated by illumination from Heaven[1025].

[1020] (Williamson, Joan of Arc, Brief Biography, 2010, 2002-2005), (Spoto D., 2007) pg. 193

[1021] (Williamson, Joan of Arc, Brief Biography, 2010, 2002-2005), (Spoto D., 2007) pg. 204

[1022] (Doornik, 1953) pg. 396

[1023] (Gilson, 1938) pg. 8, 16

[1024] (Daniel, 2006) Pg. 3

[1025] (Zwemer, 1902), (Aquinas, 2002) pg. 118, (Barron, 2008) pg. 29, 30-32

The other approach, advocated by such as Tertullian and Blaise Pascal[1026], is infinitely simpler, and infinitely more difficult. It is based on Revelation: the direct GODly infusion of belief and even contact into the soul. Then it is nurtured and developed as a conviction. This revelation can come in a single burst, totally changing the life of an individual, as in the case of St. Paul, or in a more continuous supply of visions and events, as in the life of St. Joan or St. Peter. In the Revelation approach, one either receives Faith or one doesn't, and the reason of humanity is either totally inadequate, or provides a stumbling block to it.

It is often said that faith, at its most basic, is belief in something unseen or unproven[1027]. This is an understatement with Faith by Revelation, and even when Faith is supported by reason, human eyes and ears and sense often cannot find support for it. Faith can sometimes seem totally reasonable, but then as we have seen in the Saint Joan's story, Faith can seemingly contradict experience, logic, and sometimes, even common sense. Popular support will often turn against True Faith. Sometimes, scientific and empirical evidence can claim the opposite! But Faith doesn't care and doesn't move. Even when all supports are stripped away, True Faith is as strong and still as the center of the universe. True Faith must eventually stand alone.

Whether based on reason or not, true Faith is not simply a cold and sterile belief in something. It is not simply belief in a god; it is belief in a personal GOD who interacts with man on the deepest levels. It is not simply belief in some force of justice, it is faith in supreme and divine Justice, were all things are accounted for, from the smallest to the largest. It is not belief in some sugar-coated paradise, but in a supreme Truth, beyond all senses, feelings, emotions, and illusions.

Modern man has often assumed saints to be wide-eyed and naïve believers, certain they will never feel pain or defeat. True saints know better, for faith is a crucible, as well as a gift. True faith carries no guarantees your feelings or your life will be saved. To perform such great feats, as St. Joan, or any other saint and knight, requires a willingness to suffer—a willingness often answered with actual pain. One must be prepared. A true and good relationship often requires work, sweat, and tears. GOD may demand much from you. Christ is very specific about this. But at the end, all is balanced, all is revealed.

[1026] (Gilson, 1938) pg. 8, 16
[1027] St. Paul's definition—Hebrews 11:1

Faith as Relationship

When people think of GOD, they tend to think about what GOD can do for them, instead of what they can do for GOD. When we pray, many times we want something. But Christ said our Father knows what our needs are before we ask HIM, so it is better sometimes to just talk with GOD in our prayers, thank HIM for what HE has already given us, and try to be quiet in our minds long enough to listen to HIM[1028]. This is what real prayer is, a talk with GOD[1029].

People tend to use faith in the same way as they use prayer, as a way to get things from GOD. This is not true faith. Faith is not a way to improve your golf score, financial holdings, or emotional and physical health. True Faith is the relationship between GOD and man.

T.H. White said that Lancelot thought of GOD not as an aloof spirit, but as a personal friend and confidant as well as the Lord; he saw GOD as being as real and as approachable as anyone else in his life[1030]. This is not to say that GOD only speaks to us as a regular person might; He speaks through every sight and sound in the universe, even the very existence of the universe communicates the whispers of GOD's Grace, if we simply listen[1031]. And yet He is very close. We must strive to see GOD as a friend, mentor, confidant, teacher, partner, and master in the battle that is our existence, and see HIM all around us. Consider that Grace is the very presence of GOD. How else to cultivate that than to not only believe in GOD, but hold Him close as a friend[1032].

The ancient Hebrews worked directly with GOD in partnerships called covenants[1033]. Bible commentators stress that the Hebrews were unique from all other ancient peoples in the Middle East in that they believed the LORD interacted directly with them and their destinies[1034]. Other gods were mainly concerned with the vast cycles of nature, but the GOD of the Hebrews not only controlled these cycles, but made

---

[1028] (Corless, 1981) pg. 52,

[1029] (Barron, 2008) pg. 32-33,

[1030] (White, 1958) pg. 473

[1031] (Buber, 1958) pg. 136

[1032] James 2:23

[1033] Genesis 15, Exodus 24:6, Luke 22:19 also, 1 Corinthians 11:25, Hebrews 8:9, Jeremiah 31:32

[1034] (Romer, 1988) pg. 61, 91

agreements with men that directly influenced the lives of individual people[1035]. Faith and prayer provide a two-way communication for these covenants.

It is this relationship, this friendship, this covenant that the Saints and great men of history are most concerned with. Everything else, like miracles and Heavenly signs, are extra icing on the cake. For every incredible thing GOD performed through Moses, there were thousands of hours that Moses spoke with GOD on the mountain.

Daniel spent only one night with the lions, but untold numbers of nights in prayer. GOD came down and saved these men in their hours of need, but these men had faith and prayer all the time.

This requires spending time with GOD, developing our dialogue with HIM and cherishing this relationship[1036]. We will grow closer to HIM than anyone else in our lives. Gifts and signs and even miracles will come to us, but we will find our walk with GOD to be the most precious of all.

How to Recognize Faith

When we have faith, we encounter the events, relationships, and states of mind I have described in this book. We feel this friendship with GOD and an unexplained closeness with HIM.

Our hearts become set on GOD. We place GOD over all things, because we love him and understand something of HIS nature. It may be difficult, but we see that nothing is too great a sacrifice in becoming closer to GOD and walking with HIM and in HIS shadow.

True faith is marked by action on that faith. Just as with St. Joan of Arc, St. Ignatius, Sir Ramon Lull, St. Augustine, and so many others, a sure sign of faith is the willingness to act on it. It doesn't matter if the faith tells them to go to church, or if the faith tells them to risk their lives to save the world, they do so with willingness and clear vision.

Yet there is more. With faith, often we feel half in this world, and half in the spirit world. Many times we will be distracted from physical things, thinking of GOD and Honor instead of more material matters.

[1035] Ibid.

[1036] (Bangley, 2007) pg. 151, as in praying everyday, (Harvey, 1998) pg. 51, (Gautier, 1989) pg. 31-33

While others are concerned with money issues and political bureaucracy, we will ponder a favorite prayer or phrase from the Bible. While others are knee-deep in parties and celebrations, we will be puzzling over the nature of GOD, or working to further HIS work in the world.

No matter how exciting or pressing the pursuits of the World of Men, they will not be enough for us. We will constantly search for something deeper, something more real than what the world presents to us[1037]. The knight digs through the layers of reality, searching for glimpses of GOD.

Neither pleasure nor pain will distract the Man enraptured in GOD.

This intense eye on another world is often very calm. Geoffrey of Bouillon, although not an intellectual as Aquinas, still experienced this calm focus on the ethereal, even in battle. Wounded upon the walls of Jerusalem during the great siege, with fire and sword all around him, his mind kept going back to prayer and the calm presence of his GOD[1038]. His fellow crusaders found themselves in awe of Geoffrey's great spiritual serenity. He had complete faith in their victory, and in the overshadowing of GOD's Grace.

Whether faced with impossible battles or tortured by hideous devices and methods, saints and heroes of faith are calm, even serene, in a universe of fear and pain. Their faith is as a fortress of peace around their souls.

When others see disasters, we will see GOD's hand, showing an opportunity we were blind to before. When others see a fortunate event, we will see GOD's hand again. Even when others think GOD acts in anger, we will see beyond such personifications, understanding all things simply flow as GOD plans.

With the eyes of faith, the knight sees the hand of GOD in many things. Even with creations of humanity itself, the knight is never distracted or satisfied with the surface appearance. He looks for the worship of GOD, the glorification of GOD in every artwork, in every manuscript, in every structure made by man.

I have found hints of GOD's presence in the paintings of Michelangelo and Frank Frazetta, in the books of St. Augustine and Edgar Rice Burroughs, in the music of Handel and Iron Maiden, even in the comics of Creepy and Frank Miller. Everywhere that wonder, love,

---

[1037] (Sheen, 2001) pg. 91
[1038] (Gautier, 1989) pg. 115-116

Honor, pain, and dignity are somehow found, there we will see a glimmer of GOD also.

Nothing exists without some fingerprint of GOD, somehow hidden within it. We can't see this unless our hearts are blasted pure by GOD's fiery Grace[1039].

Even in works expressly opposed to GOD, like the atheistic volumes of Karl Marx, or the rabid ramblings and fate of Madalyn Murray O'Hare, GOD's hand can still be seen. Perhaps it is in the simple fact that these people wish to fight so terribly and so pathetically against what they call "nothing"; if GOD is nothing, why do they struggle so viciously against HIM[1040]? Could it be that they long and thirst for Righteousness and are angry at GOD for not revealing it immediately? And so many communists, secular humanists, and haters of GOD speak longingly of a social paradise, which is only a cheap and false imitation of Heaven. The Devil himself, in his howling opposition but longing aspiration, can only mimic and copy divinity[1041], with arrogant and undignified attempts at becoming GOD that flop and collapse when True Divinity shines.

The very act of creation which so many artists adore, Christian or not, is only the imperfect mirror of GOD's mighty creation. GOD CREATES; man or devil only mold from the crumbs of Genesis.

With the eyes of Faith, focused on GOD, it is simple to see GOD's hand moving all things. We will have the power to avoid discouragement and dismay, because we will see that nothing truly can say no to GOD's might; all things, in their way, serve GOD and bow before GOD. The planets move in their orbits to write the glories of GOD, the seas pound the shore in the rhythms of Heavenly song. The mating seasons of the animals even, all revolve around GOD's eternal clock.

All things serve GOD. The Gates of Hell serve GOD, as Dante reminds us. Posted over those terrible gates are these words: "The Portal to the town of Woe am I, . . . Mighty Power Divine, Supremest Wisdom and Primaeval established me"[1042]. Even the Evil One himself knows

---

[1039] (Barclay, The Gospel of Matthew Volume 1, revised edition, the Daily Study Bible Series, 1975) pg. 107-Matthew 5:8, Psalms 73:1

[1040] (Sheen F., 2000) pg. 68-69, (Wills, 1999) pg. XV

[1041] Augustine thus calls the Devil, the Ape of GOD, because the Devil so imitates

[1042] (Alighieri, 1954) Dante's Inferno, Canto III, lines 1-21

GOD[1043], and, like the serpent crawling in the dust, cannot help but fulfill GOD's ultimate plan[1044].

In Faith, this knowledge will be ours, and all manner of strange insights and delvings will find us. Knock, and the door will be answered. Ask, and you shall receive.

With True Faith, there will come times that we may "think as GOD thinks, not as men think"[1045]. Our minds, imperfect and finite as they are, will approach something of the thoughts of the Master. Like holding a mirror to the sun, we will catch a glimpse of GOD's fiery vision.

When Augustine reached True Faith, he received understandings of Good and Evil, why Evil exists (or seems to exist)[1046], why disasters must happen, why scorpions and other terrible things walk the earth, the nature of Original Sin, and other mysteries[1047].

While others stood there totally confused or incredulous of the whole question, Augustine understood. He saw that evil is no thing and actually exists only as the absence of Good, instead of the opposite of Good. He saw that Evil is simply a wrong choice in a world of two choices, that evil is simply the non-truth in a world aflame with Truth, existing simply so that GOD could give us Free Will.

We will know that time is like a stream, and Christ is like GOD's right hand placed in the stream, or like a rock the builders rejected, tossed in the water. Ripples expand from this in all directions, backwards and forwards, right and left. Everything in every time is affected by Christ, just some more than others, and this is why every religion reflects Christianity in small or large ways. Everywhere has a piece, if not the whole, of the Truth of Christ. Too bad Joseph Campbell missed this. He didn't have the light of Faith.

It is this focus on GOD and the subjects surrounding HIM that marks Truth Faith, not miracles, wonders, or signs. Such things may or

---

[1043] Job 1:6

[1044] Genesis 3:14, Micah 7:17

[1045] Mark 8:33

[1046] (Copleston, 1962) pg. 100-101 St. Augustine sees evil as a "negation" or lack of good, not a "thing"

[1047] (Burleigh, 1953) pg. 264 in the True Religion section of Augustine's Earlier Writings

may not follow the person of True Faith, but Focus is always there, as is the unseen presence of GOD.

Faith rises above experience

Many religions of the world, and especially modern spiritual pursuits, focus on experience of holy things. Buddhists look for elimination of suffering and an enduring peace; Taoists look for the experience of oneness with Tao, or the way of the universal law. Both sometimes relate these experiences as "becoming one with the void", or experiencing emptiness and a uniting with what they perceive as the non-personal force behind the universe. The Moslems, Jews, and many Christians look to the ultimate joy of Heaven, and the Born-Again Christians aspire to feel the Holy Spirit alight on their hearts in a fiery conversion experience on Earth.

But as I have shown, the path of the knight can possess many religious experiences, or none at all[1048]. Such does not have to have bearing on the knight's path. He is concerned mainly with the completion of his righteous duties and the preservation of his Honor and soul. In fact, in some ways, the knight's path is the ignoring of the pain or pleasure of experiences or feelings, making any "spiritual" experience like "inner peace" totally secondary to the working of GOD's Will. The knight cares not for what he experiences, as long as he carries out GOD's Law[1049]. Even his friendship with GOD is expressed by and revolves around his following of this Law and Will. Any wonder or experience should ultimately be secondary to the continuation of the knight's mission, the bringing of ultimate glory and Honor to GOD.

Remember St. Ignatius, and his vision of the flashing, snake-like thing? When he decided it was distracting him from praying, he ignored even this, something that seemed a vision from GOD. Ultimately, nothing holy will distract from the True GOD.

We as GOD's creation are always in contact with GOD in a very personal and intimate way, whether we are aware of it or not. Our very

---

[1048] (Wills, 1999) pg. 44
[1049] Ibid.

being and existence is directly connected to HIS thoughts of us and the universe around us. Indeed, we do feel closer to GOD when we are constantly vigilant in our actions and prayers, and this may be for our benefit. Thanks be to GOD that HE does answer prayer and grants personal experiences with HIM often.

Faith in the Triumph of Goodness

At times, every type of Faith must stand without support. Nowhere is this more true than with the Faith a knight or saint must have in the final triumph of GOD and goodness against the forces of Evil.

Noah stood alone. Just as in Saint Joan's time, everybody knows the story of Noah, and just as with Sir Joan, GOD directly gave Noah a disturbing message that would literally change the shape of the world, with special responsibility placed on Noah.

GOD said that the rains were coming, and with them a monstrous flood that would surge the destruction of all life. Noah, since he was the only righteous man on earth, was to build an ark to save a remnant of humanity[1050].

Not only was Noah ordered to build a gigantic ark that would take an enormous amount of time, energy, and materials, no cloud was in the sky. There was no threat of rain at all. Certainly not like the storm that GOD was talking about. And for years, some Biblical researches say 120 years, no giant flood occurred.

One cannot blame people too much for laughing at Noah. He was working hard, but no great storms came for generations. Could Noah have doubted at times? Could his sons have said, maybe Dad just had a dream, and that was all it was?

Who would think to build an ark with no sign of rain? It is absurd! Who would think a teenaged, peasant girl could lead an army and save a nation? It is absurd! Who would believe in a soul when it cannot be found? It is absurd! Who would believe in an after-life when no one has been back from the "undiscovered country" to tell the tale? It is absurd! And who would believe that a good and just GOD is in control and watches over this inane, violent, irreverent, and chaotic world? That seems

---

[1050] Genesis 6:17-18

the most absurd. While there is little evidence for either verdict on the soul or after-life, evidence abounds for an evil world. Perhaps humanity can survive a deluge, and maybe a girl can save a nation, but who could possibly believe that Justice and Fairness will win over terror and evil in the end?

The great Saint Augustine had direct experience with evidence of evil. As with Saint Joan, there were times when evil seemed to completely surround him. Such a time occurred in 430AD. Saint Augustine, 76, had faced many evils in his life, and had conquered them all, but as he approached death from old age, one last challenge confronted him like no other.

Even though he knew his bodily strength was ebbing away, he had written many letters and held many conferences in the last years to stem the growing power of Arianism, a heretical sect that not only threatened the Christian Church with blasphemous teachings, but marched upon the cities of the Christianized Roman world with thousands of armed and violent barbarians. Augustine had continuously encouraged a Baron Boniface to use his armies against the Arian Goths, but the Baron married an Arian princess, who, although she claimed to have become a Catholic, did so in name only and baptized many in the name of Arianism. Another army of barbarians, Vandal hordes, fighting under their Arian King, were squashing cities all across North Africa and would eventually sack Rome herself. Augustine's world and church faced double catastrophe, not only a physical, but a doctrinal and spiritual collapse.

The Barbarians swarmed everywhere, in libraries and churches, cities and country-sides, burning everything they did not cut and rape and pillage. Temples were left as burned out husks, holy priests and sisters tortured or put to the sword, until the whole of the land seemed empty of life or sound, without the bells of churches or the singing of hymns[1051].

Then, the Vandals surrounded Hippo, the city where Augustine lived. Even the Baron had fled there to avoid the barbarian hordes that now burned and ransacked the countryside. If Augustine survived the initial raids, he knew he would face torture and possible execution. But worse, as Trape' put it "the entire fruit of forty years of pastoral toil, for him and his colleagues, was suddenly and heartrendingly lost"[1052].

[1051] (Trape', 1986) pg. 325
[1052] (Trape', 1986) pg.325

Augustine must have looked out over the surrounding hordes that were destroying his world, even as his own life waned. A massive, daunting, and depressing sight. It probably seemed like the end of the World, as if the Apocalypse foreseen by John had come at last.

But Augustine is reported to have said to himself, "No great man is he, who thinks it a great affair, that bricks and bridges fall, and men die", a quote from Plotinus, the Neo-Platonist[1053]. Augustine refused to surrender within himself. His faith remained strong. Somehow, he believed that GOD would not let HIS church be consumed, nor would Augustine's work and love be for naught. Somehow, Augustine believed, GOD's Providence would prevail and even flourish through this time to end all times. Somehow, Augustine still had faith.

As death finally loomed over him in his bed, according to Trape', Augustine remembered a saying from his old friend Saint Ambrose, "My life is such that I need not be ashamed to live on among you; but neither do I fear death, for our Lord is a kindly Lord"[1054].

A "kindly" Lord? With such a fate, knowing, as you lay dying, that your world and your faith that you worked so hard to build was disappearing, alongside your people, would you say such a thing? And, as if this statement wasn't amazing enough, Augustine firmly believed that somehow, The Lord would use this terrible situation to further the cause of Christianity, right, and goodness. Augustine put his trust in GOD that everything he had done was not in vain. Only with True Faith, could we even dare to venture such a hopeful, trusting statement.

Then as now, such Faith does not come easy. Our world is a noxious mix of pain, bitterness, and betrayal, full of natural evils like malformed babies and human evils like serial killers, rapists, and pedophiles. Children are boiled alive by their own mothers, wild animals drink the blood of old women, supposed friends stab others in the back, an army rapes and pillages innocent civilians, scientists create still another chemical horror, and good men die. How can anyone come away with even a theory of goodness, after seeing all that?

We live in a world where enemies of righteousness seek to destroy everything. Dictators and thugs of every sort, some who rule through

---

[1053] (Trape', 1986) pg. 326, (St. Augustine, The Giants of Philosophy, produced by Carmichael and Carmichael, Inc., 1990), tape 2, side 2
[1054] (Trape', 1986) pg. 327

illogical laws and some who rule through drugs and violence, threaten the very fabric of society and sanity. China looms on the horizon, a Communist government not satisfied with the hollowing of its people, but with a growing power that will one day rule the world. It, or another nation, will strip my nation of everything, including the right to prayer and worship. Islamic extremists, with fervor hot enough to employ nuclear, biological, or chemical weapons, wish to see our loved ones and our temples burn in cancerous gray radiation. And if they are unable to ruin my home and my people, the very nation that I adore seeks to rend itself asunder, with "progressives" who want to reduce everything to Marxist theory and politically-correct babble, with rogue priests who preach sedition against their own church and politicians who shout hate in the guise of social justice. Homosexuals scream that my Church is bigoted because it refuses to recognize sodomy as a legitimate show of love and affection. Hollywood adds its own inane rhetoric, turning children into mindless drones of perversion and parents into helpless, infantile slaves.

In the face of all this, to believe in a deus ex machina that will save us seems the height of ridiculousness. To actually look forward to a day of justice, when all evils will be silenced forever and GOD's people may rejoice in salvation, seems to ignore every possible fact and speculation. To see a universal and personal GOD behind the suffering children and dying heroes seems a kind of insulting ignorance.

And, at the very limit of sanity, to think GOD could use a tool like me against the evil that now rises, seems to heap arrogance beyond absurdity, as if an insignificant particle of dust at the bottom of the ocean wished to help change the course of the universe. I am barely even an insect squeaking a lone dissent in the ear of a deaf rhinoceros, with the roar of a stampeding herd all around, rushing toward certain destruction. Against the tide of political pollution and brutal corruption, I do not register; I am invisible. I do not matter and my voice is nothing. Although I stand and rail against the destruction of the good, the sea that destroys my world can't even imagine my existence. Lately I could not even sustain a job to help my family, let alone save the world. I am defeated, browbeaten, and utterly hopeless[1055].

[1055] Dostoevsky, a greater champion of Faith said "my hosanna has passed through an enormous furnace of doubt", from his *Last Notebook*, 1880-1881

To continue to believe in my religion, the sanctity of the Scriptures, and the justice and mercy of my GOD in the face of all that I am and the world is coming to, such is true, unadulterated, breathless, desperate faith.

The Modern World calls this faith absurd. Absurd? Tertullian said, "I believe because it is absurd." A true believer will tell you, no matter what it seems now, that "GOD is not mocked"[1056] and He and everything that follows HIM will triumph in the end. Noah builds his ark under Blue Skies, Augustine keeps hope as he faces death for himself and his world, and the true Christian believes in goodness even under the tyranny of evil. Absurd, perhaps, but such is true Faith.

Somehow, Faith visits from Heaven like a lone cardinal[1057] alighting on your shoulder. Then it is gone so quickly, but you keep the memory of it hidden in your heart and your soul, dearer than the face of your first love. I have defended that faith against every terrible, bitter, cynical thought that has ever blistered through me like an Arctic wind. I have clutched it close while others have sacrificed theirs to the gods of greed, hopelessness, ignorance, pleasure, or self-preservation. Indeed, I sit vigil over its tiny glow, constantly blowing on it with the breaths of knowledge, trust, courage, and patience. Seemingly everything in the secular world has demanded my little spark of Faith as payment for entrance into its sumptuous realm, but I have refused, and remained outside.

Yes, this little spark will cost much. And people will laugh at you and even "pity" you, saying you are ignorant and naive for not abandoning your faith. They will tell you that you haven't learned enough, seen enough, or experienced enough yet, and that is why you have faith still.

Don't listen to them. I have seen many strange and terrible things, and yet still I have Faith. Many have suffered far worse, and they still believe. And our three heroes that we have discussed, Joan of Arc, Noah, and Augustine? Their faith has already been vindicated.

Just as Noah put the last finishes on the Ark, led his family and the animals inside, and closed the door on his laughing neighbors, the rains came. And they kept coming, until they covered the Earth and killed

---

[1056] Galatians 6:7

[1057] I have always seen these birds as symbols of the quiet presence of GOD. I used to listen to their soft peeping in the night hours of my childhood.

everyone. Everyone but Noah and his family. Noah's faith in his GOD saved him[1058], and through him, the future.

When total destruction and disaster threatened the world again in the time of Augustine, GOD gave him an ark as well, in the form of books and monasteries. Augustine's faith bestowed upon humanity incredible wisdom and an enormous library that has enlightened and strengthened Christians ever since, and has become something of a backbone for the Christian Church. His monasteries, founded on his idea of discipline and his own example, have been filled by righteous men and women for centuries. Fifteen hundred years after his death, Augustine is credited with not only helping to spread the Faith of GOD across the world and against all attackers, but is revered as a father and a doctor of that faith. In the face of all, Augustine had faith that GOD's word would spread and thrive, and Christianity, hardly dying with the Roman world, burst the bounds of that ancient kingdom and has conquered the world over, even in lands that Augustine could not have dreamed of. For over one millennia after his great life, the Western World turned to him as the final judge and jury, and for the past five hundred years, he has inspired untold numbers of thinkers and the devout, with more commentaries and discussions written about his works than any other religious writer[1059]. Saint Augustine was and is a true hero of a Church that survived and is still flourishing, almost 2000 years after his lonely death, partly because of his monumental vision and efforts.

And Joan of Arc? We have already seen how a girl, filled with faith in Divine Justice and the power of GOD, can conquer a nation and change the balance of the world. It is absurd, but it is obvious: a person with faith in an Impossible GOD can accomplish the impossible and more[1060].

Faith offers no warranty and no guarantee, but the knight, saint, and person of GOD must grasp that faith as surely as if it did. If we can do this, GOD will work through us, and give us the chance to save the world again.

[1058] Hebrews 11:7.

[1059] (Knowles, 1962) Evolution of Medieval Thought, pg. 32-33

[1060] "In order to attain the impossible, one must attempt the absurd."—Miguel De Cervantes "Galatea" (1903) by Miguel de Cervantes Saavedra; Book: III (page: 135).

Pieces of Faith

As customary for this book, we will divide True Faith into sections, so that we may better understand it and recognize it.

For the Medieval man, Faith came from GOD's Grace, and signs of this can be labeled *Focus on GOD* and *Reliance on GOD*, as well as the strange power that is essentially *Grace itself.* These are the lynchpins of the Knight's Faith. They are also at the heart of Chivalry, and as we have seen, the source of the knight's strength. Just as all the roads once led to Rome, all the knight's ways lead to these pieces of Faith.

Remember, as we have seen, the ability and willingness to sacrifice is also a mark of Faith enlivened by Grace. Faith is not a warm blanket; it is the Cross. In every story of Faith, there too is sacrifice. Faith, like Chivalry, breaks the earthly heart, but fills the soul to bursting!

Holy Focus

Saint Augustine knew the teachings of the book of Ecclesiastes that matched the Stoics and the Neo-Platonists[1061], and knew them to be true. Everything in the physical world, eventually, could be seen as a distraction, if it turned one's focus away from GOD[1062]. All the saints and true knights, in one way or the other, have complete focus on GOD, ignoring the world, its desires and pains, joys and sorrows, demands and attachments[1063].

To illustrate this, we turn to one of my favorite historical, eye-witness accounts of the Crusades, Sir Jean Joinville's. Regine Pernoud, in her beautiful book on the Crusades, said this about Joinville's account: "Its heroes seem to be familiar with the spiritual world to a degree that makes their outlook profoundly different than our own, and different too from any outlook that might have seemed normal in a less fervent or less generous atmosphere. There was, above all, that calm affirmation of their faith in the worst possible circumstances that earned them the admiration of the Moslems themselves"[1064].

[1061] (Trape', 1986) pg. 98-99
[1062] Ibid. pg. 103, also (Colliander, 1982) pg. 29
[1063] (Malory, 1962) pg. 431
[1064] (Pernoud R., The Crusaders, the Struggle for the Holy Land, 1963) pg. 308

As the king's seneschal, Joinville describes the Ninth Crusade, the attempt by Louis the IX, king and saint, to re-conquer Jerusalem from the Moslems. Any crusade was the deliberate leaving behind of the known world in a faithful attempt to win GOD's favor by risking life and limb to see Holy Jerusalem. This particular endeavor not only nearly killed the Saint and his friends, but placed his kingdom in jeopardy of seizure by hostile outside forces and nearly bankrupted his treasury, not to mention earning the severe irritation of his Queen. To all this, the humble Louis simply stated he was doing GOD's will.

At one point, Joinville was captured and threatened with religious persecution. Armed Moslems ran into the tent where Joinville was chained, bringing an old man with them who inevitably asked "if we believed in a GOD who had been taken prisoner for our sake, wounded and put to death for us and who on the third day had risen again[1065]. Knowing how Moslems viewed this belief of the Christians, and how Moslems punished any belief in a "son" of GOD, it is easy to predict the fate of Joinville and his companions in the hands of such people. But Joinville simply said that yes, he believed.

Expecting death, Joinville was amazed when he was allowed to live, but there were other trials. Typhoid killed many of Louis's army, and Joinville, as well as the king himself, soon came down with the terrible illness. Because of this and his wounds, Joinville took to his bed and stayed there until a priest came to give Mass in his tent.

The priest, too, suffered from Typhoid, and as the Consecration of the Mass came near, the priest stumbled and nearly fell. Forgetting his own hurts and jumping to his feet, Joinville held the priest up, whispering all the while that he "would not leave him"[1066]. The priest was able to finish once he was steadied, but Joinville quietly states the priest died soon afterward. Pernoud says "Our reaction if a priest feinted at the altar would be to fetch a doctor. For a thirteenth-century knight, the important thing was that the Mass was said and the sacrifice consummated"[1067].

Many saints have taken the extreme road to this total Focus. Saint John the Baptist and Saint Antony of Egypt came to see their possessions

---

[1065] (Joinville, 1963) pg. 247

[1066] (Pernoud R., The Crusaders, the Struggle for the Holy Land, 1963) pg. 309

[1067] Ibid.

and even their families as distractions, and left all such things behind. They went out into the desert, shunning all human contact, until their vision was consumed by the fiery light of GOD.

Other saints might retain a foot in the human world, still moving about humanity as if they are one of the crowd, but their eyes are trained elsewhere.

St. Aquinas had been invited to a sumptuous and extravagant dinner hosted by the King of France himself, but had barely noticed he was there, so caught up in thinking about GOD and related issues. I wager the saint would have rather declined the request, whether from a king or not, since he had been busy creating a theological and philosophical discourse against enemies of the Church. But, at the last moment, he had relented, and the saint sat at the huge dining table with the other guests. The noisy and jovial crowd did not seem to notice that Aquinas neither spoke nor ate, but remained motionless, staring at his plate. For the saint, he party became only a distant noise to the saint, like the squeak of a mouse in a giant church.

Sometime during the dinner, Aquinas, a huge ox of a man, smashed his fist into the table and cried, "That is it. That is how we will defeat them!" He then fell back into studied silence.

The other guests were stunned as Aquinas' shout echoed throughout the hall. "What was it he had said?" they asked each other. "What was he talking about? Why hadn't he eaten anything?"

But the king, Saint Louis the IX, understood. He stood a proper king and held feasts for his subjects, but his own saintly heart was always with GOD. A great king and a good administrator, he too found room in his heart for constant thought of GOD. Louis motioned a servant to him and pointed. "Go over there and copy down anything that man might say. He has been in silent deliberation all night, and I wager what he says will be important"[1068].

On the opposite side of distraction, St. Anselm lay on his deathbed, while his monks worried over the shadow of his demise. Anselm, although completely aware of his fragile mortality, asked for his pen and paper to be brought to him. Hardly worried about impending death less than a week away, he calmly explained to the brothers that he wished to write a book

---

[1068] (Chesterton, 2001) pg. 78

about the origin of the soul, a question he considered himself capable of answering more thoroughly than anyone else; Anselm only wondered if GOD meant to leave him on this earth long enough to finish it[1069].

Focus Leads To Action

These saints, Aquinas and Louis, are two sides of the same coin of holy and chivalrous focus. Both are focused on Heaven, but their work is on earth. While Aquinas is contemplative, harnessing his Godly focus to fight GOD's foes in the intellectual world, Louis ignores the pleasures and responsibilities of kingship to go on crusade, fighting for GOD in a very physical way. Both are moved to work for GOD, but in different ways.

Chivalry, while demanding holy focus, requires action. Focus, as well as Faith, means little unless it is wielded to help people and defeat evil. Knights, and many of the saints, coupled their heavenly obsession with a mission.

One knows when one is focused on GOD, because faith becomes the reason for all action. Everything the knight does is to achieve a closer union with GOD, to understand GOD more fully, to "see" GOD and to do GOD's work. We know we have the proper faith when we have Focus on GOD, and we use the Focus properly when we attempt to improve our world for GOD and HIS people.

Retreating into Focus

No one would have believed, viewing his early years, that Francis of Assisi could muster any such holy focus or mission. Like many young people of any time, he squandered his early years on parties and the various desires of the flesh[1070]. This life of undisciplined frivolity was easy to obtain for Francis, being the son of a wealthy and industrious merchant. Francis might have continued on his way, never thinking about

---

[1069] (Shannon, 1999) pg. 31
[1070] (Cunningham, 1994) pg. 8

GOD or pondering true religion, if he hadn't tried, around the age of 24, to be a knight[1071].

Dressed in armor, although never dubbed, Francis fought and was captured in the battle of Perugia in 1202. There, he witnessed terrible blood-letting, and while in prison for a year, viewed all the suffering that humanity is heir to. When he finally returned home, after being ransomed by his father, his small body was so racked by the horrors of his experience, he languished in convalescence for a year[1072].

How many heroes of faith have been created by an experience of horror? Francis emerged from his convalescence a distinctly changed individual. He left the habits of his earlier life, no longer partying or carousing, contented instead to walk the fields and roads, helping beggars, and thinking about GOD. He embraced a leper during one of this walks. He continuously gave away his fancy clothes and expensive possessions to anyone in need. He stopped often in the dilapidated and abandoned church of San Damiano[1073] to pray. One day, after praying in that silent church, he had a vision where the Crucifix seemed to speak to him. It told him to rebuild Christ's Church. In his typical way, Francis took the message literally and began to rebuild, by hand and stone by stone, the ruined and tiny church that surrounded him.

Imagine the reaction of his worldly and practical father, discovering his son wandering the countryside in a beggar's cloak, or repairing the walls of an abandoned church like some insane fool! Furious, the father demanded time and again for Francis to stop this lunacy and take up the family business.

Francis responded by selling the cloth from his father's business and giving the money to the poor. Almost out of his mind in fury, Francis's father dragged the young man before the Bishop of Assisi, demanding repayment for, in his eyes at least, the foolhardy waste of merchandise.

[1071] (Cunningham, 1994) pg. 8

[1072] Ibid. pg.8

[1073] This church was named for St. Damien, the same 3rd century saint who would later so inspire Joseph de Veuster, aka Father Damien, mentioned in the Sacrifice chapter.

Focus Blends into Reliance on GOD

Standing before the Bishop on that morning in 1206, hearing the anguished and angry shouting of his father, all manner of forces must have battled within Francis. All his life, up until only months ago, he had obeyed the customs of society, relying on them to direct him, just as he had always relied on his father to care for and clothe him. Yet now, his friends made fun of him for his abnormal behavior of late[1074], and his father threatened to remove his care and protection, throwing him into the cellar at one point, and demanding the return of the clothes Francis had "stolen" from his father's company[1075].

Francis was beginning to see that "When faith ceases to be a challenge to the standards of polite society, it is no longer, or has not yet become, faith"[1076].

Looking into the eyes of the worried Bishop Guido, Francis stepped forward. He agreed to return the clothing and everything else that was his father's. Quickly stepping out, he returned totally nude, and bearing the neat package of his clothes and his father's money.

"Until now", he said, "I have called Peter Bernardone my father. But because I have proposed to serve GOD, I return to him the money on account of which he was so upset, and also all the clothing which is his, and I want only to say from now on, 'Our Father, who art in Heaven,' and not 'My father, Peter Bernardone'"[1077].

Regardless of what moderns think of people in the Middle Ages, Francis' nudity did not shock the crowd watching all this[1078].

"That morning in the piazza, what did shock the Assisians was Francis' willingness to make a complete break with his family, its structure, its security, and its support. Nakedness was thus a powerful symbol of what Francis desired: freedom . . ."[1079]. Not simply from the requirements and responsibilities of his father and society, but freedom from the tyranny of attachments and "like a naked newborn, without the burden of worldly goods or privileges, without the pleasures and

---

[1074] (Galli, 1994) pg. 22
[1075] Ibid.
[1076] (Spoto, 2002) pg. 49
[1077] (Spoto, 2002) pg.54
[1078] Ibid. 55
[1079] (Spoto, 2002) pg. 55

responsibilities of possessions and fine clothes. However lost he had been until then, he had always kept the ties of attachment to his family's influence and money, but now he was throwing his lot with all those who had nothing—and in 1206, to have nothing meant literally to have nothing, not simply less"[1080].

With this grand and moving gesture, Francis had given his life, his well-being, his security, and his entire physical and spiritual reliance to GOD. A very frightening thing, indeed. "From that day, he would take his place with the disenfranchised, with the poor and with the Christ whom he had seen on the crucifix at San Damiano"[1081].

But when the bishop covered Francis's nakedness with his own splendid cloak, this too was a gesture full of import. Just as Christ sent his Apostles out into the world, admonishing them to take "no staff or cloak", so a true knight of faith must rely completely on GOD HIMSELF for protection and sustenance, and even for the tiniest things.

If a person can actually bring himself or herself to do this, to leave fate, chance, safety, the future, and needs in the Hand of GOD, then GOD Himself will provide! When Elijah and Elisha isolated themselves in the desert, as John the Baptist and St. Antony of Egypt would do so many years later, it is GOD who sends birds with their beaks full of bread for the men of faith. Through all manner of poverty and hunger, the slight and fragile Francis, with his reliance on GOD, was able to create a giant and renowned community of the faithful that would one day strive to convert the world.

Calling himself a Knight of GOD[1082], Francis continued to place this reliance into action by traveled to the Holy Land during the Crusades, with his hands empty and his spirit full, placing himself directly in mortal danger.

Outside the Egyptian town on Damietta, circa 1218, Francis and Brother Illuminato approached the camp of the Moslem army. Pernoud states that the Moslem guard must have assumed, as these two men approached them, that they were insane, for only insane Christians would surrender themselves after the Sultan of Egypt had ordered any Christians killed on sight[1083].

[1080] Ibid. pg.55
[1081] (Spoto, 2002) pg. 55
[1082] (Pernoud R., The Crusaders, the Struggle for the Holy Land, 1963) pg. 269
[1083] (Pernoud R., The Crusaders, the Struggle for the Holy Land, 1963) pg. 264

Indeed, when they walked up to the face of the guard, they stated clearly and definitely, "We are Christians; take us to your master." Amazingly, that is exactly what the guards did.

The Sultan, Malik Al-Kamil, most likely burned with rage against Christians. He was losing the defensive battle against John of Brienne, King of Jerusalem, and he certainly was not pleased to see two Christians trying to preach among his men[1084]. But "the wild beast was quietened by the sight of the man from GOD and [Al-Kamil] listened attentively to the sermons about Christ that he [Francis] preached for several days to him and his followers"[1085].

Though the Sultan listened, he was not quite convinced. Francis offered to walk through a fire with a "Moslem priest", an ordeal to prove which faith was the better. The "Moslem priest" who was there quickly left the room. One historian explains this as the "priest" reacting to what he might have thought of as "testing GOD". For Francis personally it would not have been, for GOD had already brought him through an array of frightening "fires"[1086].

The Sultan then offered Francis many gifts that the Knight of GOD refused[1087]. "Give them to your poor," The Sultan suggested. Alluding to Jesus' response to Judas at the woman's presentation of perfume, Francis answered with another negative, "affirming the Divine Providence looked after the needs of the poor"[1088].

Although completely convinced that these men were authentic and honorable[1089], the Sultan was, perhaps because of this, worried of the effect they may have on his men. He had them sent back to the Christian camp.

These two men of faith had walked and preached unharmed where no man armed to the teeth could have lived[1090].

[1084] (Spoto, 2002) pg. 161, Al Kamil's counselors demanded the two Christians be executed on the spot

[1085] (Pernoud R., The Crusaders, the Struggle for the Holy Land, 1963) pg. 267

[1086] Ibid. pg. 268

[1087] (Spoto, 2002) pg. 162

[1088] (Pernoud R., The Crusaders, the Struggle for the Holy Land, 1963) pg. 269

[1089] (Spoto, 2002) pg. 161

[1090] (Spoto, 2002) pg. 160, 161 admits that this meeting was unprecedented and highly dangerous

The Leap of Faith

Saint Francis and people like him consistently took what is called the "Leap of Faith". They trusted GOD exclusively and intensely enough to risk their lives, reputations, and even torturous fate in order to walk in HIS precepts. There was no misunderstanding, nor naïveté. Heroes of Faith know what is at stake and know that GOD is under no obligation to save them, but they place their lives and souls in HIS hands, focus their minds, and step forward into the fire.

In the Bible, Daniel and the King of Persia, Darius the Mede, knew each other well, and respected each other, but Daniel knew that Darius could be a difficult and arrogant man. So when Daniel was told that no one was allowed to worship any god or man except King Darius, and that any one caught worshipping any other god or man would be thrown into a pit full of hungry lions, Daniel believed it. He continued to pray to GOD three times a day[1091].

It was inevitable that someone would eventually report Daniel's actions back to the king. Daniel looked down into the pit, knowing this to be a very dramatic leap of Faith. But he trusted in GOD entirely. He did not deny the charges and simply stepped down into the den of roaring lions, and the king had a stone rolled over the top, trapping the weaponless and helpless man inside.

Helpless? When the king came the next day, he called out, even before the stone could be rolled away: "Daniel! Has the GOD whom you served so faithfully been able to save you from the lions?"[1092]

As the stone came away, Daniel's voice rang from inside. "Oh king, GOD has sent his angels and they have shut the mouths of the lions so they have done no harm to me."[1093]

When Daniel climbed forth, unharmed and totally intact, King Darius brought together the people who had accused Daniel and had them thrown in with the lions. The lions fed on their flesh, leaving nothing left[1094].

[1091] Daniel 6:13
[1092] Ibid. 6:20
[1093] Daniel 6:22
[1094] Ibid. 6:24

Shadrach, Meshach, and Abednego faced a similar situation, although the teeth of the lions were replaced with tongues of fire. Nebuchadnezzar, King of Babylon had ordered that everyone in his kingdom must bow down before a giant golden idol in the plains of Dura. Anyone who refused would be burned alive in a fiery furnace[1095].

"We may be officials of the kingdom of Babylon," One of them said, "But we are still sons of Israel and Abraham. We have never stopped praying to and serving our GOD. We cannot bow before an idol!"

When the three men refused to bow before the idol even in front of the king himself, Nebuchadnezzar had his guards stock a furnace full of wood, raising the fire within to an enormous bloom, and ordered the three thrown within.

"I want to see them consumed by the flames!" Nebuchadnezzar said. The guards warned him not to get too close, because the furnace was so hot it was burning the guards who stood beside it throwing Shadrach, Meshach, and Abednego within!

"Did we not throw three men into the furnace?" The king demanded, stunned. Because now he could see four men in the furnace, walking among the flames unharmed. "The fourth," He exclaimed, "seems to be a shining man"[1096]!

He called out to the men and had them stand before him. "You see how they are un-singed and unhurt, and do not even smell of smoke"[1097]!

These are very physical situations, were men face death as a bodily danger. But what of facing spiritual attack? What if the consequences involve the possible dissolution of the soul?

One of the most famous stories of extreme reliance and focus on GOD involves Saint Antony of Egypt, written about by another saint, Athanasius, around 365 AD. Antony did not face persecution by humans, but constantly fought the torturous actions of demonic spirits, and even the Devil Himself.

He prepared himself by constantly disciplining his body and ignoring its desires, as well as focusing on making himself the kind of man who could stand before GOD on the day of judgment and be counted among the righteous, "that is, pure of heart and prepared to obey his [GOD's]

[1095] Daniel 3:1-6
[1096] Daniel 3:25
[1097] Daniel 3:27

will, and no other"[1098]. He gave over his welfare to GOD and isolated himself from the world of men by first living in a tomb on the edge of a desert. The only human contact he had was with a friend who periodically brought him some scraps of bread.

Not long after, the Evil One became incensed by this behavior, apparently "apprehensive that Antony might before long fill the desert with the discipline"[1099]. Athanasius reports that the Evil One came with a horde of demons and whipped Antony with such force that he lay "on the earth, speechless from such tortures"[1100]. But GOD caused that morning to be the time when the friend decided to stop by with the bread, and, finding Antony beaten, carried him to a local church to be nursed back to health.

That same night, unwilling to quit his mission even for recuperation, Antony secretly had his friend carry him back to the tomb for a rematch between himself and the demons. "Here I am—Antony," He said out loud to the empty tomb and the haunted air. "I do not run from your blows, for even if you give me more, nothing can separate me from the love of Christ"[1101].

The Evil One came at him then with even more ferocity, filling the tomb and the area around it with demons that took the form or every kind of predator and dangerous animal, from lions to snakes, each taking its turn to harass and strike at Antony. Their attacks were exactly as those of actual animals, and Antony suffered from terrific bites, scratches, and stings.

Antony, wounded as he was, remained unimpressed and even goaded them on. As if to say "is this all you've got", Antony cried out "If you are able, and you did receive authority over me, do not hold back, but attack. But if you are unable, why, when it is vain, do you disturb me? For faith in Our Lord is for us a seal and a wall of protection"[1102].

Suddenly a ray of light shot somehow through the ceiling of the tomb, bathing all in eldritch glow. The demonic animals disappeared, as did the pain in Antony's body, and his wounds evaporated. The walls

---

[1098] (Athanasius S., 1995) pg. 37, Spiritual Classics of Western Civ. Version, but a smaller book

[1099] (Athanasius S., 1995) pg. 37

[1100] Ibid. pg. 37

[1101] (Athanasius S., 1995) pg. 38-Romans 8:38

[1102] (Athanasius S., 1995) pg. 39

of the tomb, burst by all the attacking animals, were restored. From the light, GOD said, "I was here, Antony"[1103].

Antony would face demons and other strange visions again and again, but never could they shake him or harm him in any significant way, for the Lord shielded him from every kind of attack, physical, mental, or spiritual.

These are incredible examples of GOD delivering people from harm who are loyal to HIM and rely on HIM. Does this always mean that those who are faithful to GOD are saved in such a dramatic way?

For those who scoff and say that these stories are from the distant, even mythical past, there are scores of modern day stories, easily confirmed, although mystifying.

Just a few years ago, a mentally disturbed man wandered into a church with a gun and walked up to the pulpit, shooting point blank at the preacher, emptying the revolver. The bullets struck the pulpit, the wall behind, and all around, but somehow missed the preacher entirely. The preacher in this story was John Hagee, a fire-and-brimstone preacher from San Antonio.

One news documentary show, famous for its investigative journalism, decided to investigate the alleged miraculous escapes from death performed by Arkansas faith healers. So-called "snake handlers", to prove their faith these non-denominational Christians regularly dance with poisonous snakes and drink Strychnine, a substance considered to be one of the most poisonous known to humans. The snakes were certainly poisonous and lively, and when the reporters had the Strychnine, drunk from jars, sent to a lab for examination, it was confirmed to be very pure and very deadly[1104].

In 2012, one such preacher, commonly engaged in snake-handling, was reported to have died from a poisonous snake bite. Many in the media scoffed or held up his story as an example of the foolishness of the faithful, presenting him as an unwashed ignorant Southerner who put faith in an empty idea. Many made fun of all religion through their laughing at this poor man's suffering. What they failed to wonder about

---

[1103] Ibid. pg. 39

[1104] I couldn't find this television report, but I saw this particular episode twice when I was younger.

was that this preacher had been handling poisonous snakes and even living with them loose in his house for more than thirty years[1105].

A very humble and dedicated deacon from the Saint Dominic's Catholic Church in San Antonio, whom I had met several times, was well known to have some sort of healing power. I have interviewed several people who swear that this man cured them of various deadly illnesses through the power of their faith. Although he never spoke of this "power", so many others have sworn by it that many of the sick would come to the church just to have him commit the "laying of hands" upon them.

Throughout history, there are as many stories of martyrs and holy deaths as there are tales of miraculous deliverances. It was the medieval and knightly belief that GOD would intervene on behalf of the truly faithful, protecting HIS own until their missions and purposes were done, but that every person must die one day as well, and GOD showed His favor by bestowing on many glorious deaths, befitting great men and women.

Be warned. Reliance on GOD does not mean to fly recklessly into the face of danger whenever one feels it, or at the request of arrogance or bravado. Francis and the others knew how to rely on GOD and did so at GOD's express request. "Readiness to suffer for faith, in his view, no longer meant a reckless disregard for one's own life, much less a rush toward suicide. A preacher had to be plain and direct, to be sure; he should also be prudent, gentle, and respectful—and the five friars in Morocco had shown none of these qualities"[1106].

Francis had sent these five friars to preach in the streets of Morocco to the Moslems. The pagans had indeed listened to the preachers for several days, but when the preaching turned to attacks on Mohammed as a liar, the friars were killed. Nothing was accomplished but the death of five men.

It is easy to assume that because we want something, GOD wants it also. Our Reliance on GOD must be free from personal ambition and the foolish advice of ungodly or myopic men. That is why focus on GOD

[1105] (Smith, 2012)
[1106] (Spoto, 2002) pg. 164

goes hand-in-hand with reliance on GOD. And even then, sometimes GOD says "no" to plans that are good, in favor of HIS Ultimate Plan, which is the best.

The knights, being tied to their duties as they are, leave the non-spiritual world in a special way: they follow the saints in spirit, mirroring the saint's attitudes, thoughts, and outlook, if not in location. A knight's body may be working in the world of men, but his mind is trained on GOD and Honor, rather than on politics, styles and fashion, intrigues and plots, even family and friends.

GRACE

These men of Faith walked where no others dare walk, literally strolling "where angels fear to tread"[1107]. They risked all, and performed actions that people still marvel over, while skeptics scoff but inwardly tremble and historians debate the meaning with theologians.

How does a person of Faith fight demons and walk across battlefields unscathed? How do knights of faith "see a thousand fall by their side"[1108] but somehow receive no wound, nor cut, nor scratch? How does the person of prayer triumph over "the pestilence by night and the noon-day devil" let alone "the arrow that flies by day"[1109]? This is not simply courage, for a man with courage may still die. This is a kind of power beyond understanding, where the angels and GOD Himself step in to shield the person of faith from harm and eventually work to bring about victory for Goodness and Right. This is a mark of Grace.

In 452 AD, Grace was the only weapon Pope Leo carried with him as he walked to the tent of the most feared and reviled barbarian in history, Attila the Hun. While Rome itself, and its pope, stood physically defenseless, Attila marched a giant army of blood-mad barbarian followers that usually left death, famine, and rape in their wake. Leo had come to ask Attila not to sack and burn the holy city of Rome.

[1107] Alexander Pope's *An Essay on Criticism*
[1108] Psalm 91:7
[1109] Psalm 91:5-6, from the Douay Rheims Bible

No one knows what this solemn pope told the pitiless barbarian leader. But the next day, Attila and his hordes packed up their tents and went home[1110].

Three years later, Genseric and the Vandals threatened to wipe Rome off the map. The Vandals were so destructive, their memory is still preserved in the word "vandal", usually reserved for the most irreverent, irresponsible, and violent of hoodlums to this day.

This time Genseric ignored Pope Leo's request and attacked the defenseless city anyway. But, although the place was ransacked, none of the beautiful buildings or homes were burned. Even though he had always demanded burning in the past, Genseric had promised Leo that no such devastation would occur in Rome[1111].

Attila, Genseric, and all the Barbarians are gone; the Church in Rome remains.

Grace, typified here by avoidance of death, usually comes with an <u>indescribable feeling of calm and inner peace.</u>

Both in success and failure, Leo "possessed throughout everything a quiet and unshakable belief in the doctrinal and spiritual supremacy of Rome and his example brought new respect and influence to the papacy"[1112]. This is why Leo is still called "The Great". He lived up to his name, Leo, which means "lion".

St. Ignatius, like many saints before him, was confronted by the enormous and almost insurmountable tasks of conquering the world and himself for Christ. Only a few years into his ministry, he became obsessed with the weight of his own guilt, and contemplated giving up his strenuous life of a poverty-stricken, traveling preacher, and even thought of suicide. Suddenly, after weeks of fervent prayer, he was visited with "a deep serenity and peace that never left him for the rest for his life"[1113].

This light, beaming into their lives, giving not only meaning and direction, but pure joy and serenity, is another aspect of Grace.

Still, Grace is more than unearthly calm and the ability to face dangers, it causes the possessor to have strange powers, see visions, and behold miracles. With Grace, Elijah and St. Paul pressed down on

---

[1110] (Bokenkotter, 1979) pg. 98, (Kirsch, 1910/2009),
[1111] Ibid.
[1112] (Jones, 1994) pg.159
[1113] (Caraman, 1990) pg.39

dead children, bringing them back to life, St. Patrick could escape the clutches of his enemies by appearing as deer to their eyes, St. Francis could tame wild and ravenous wolves, St. Martin could move huge trees with the wave of his arm, and St. Antony could wrestle demons and win arguments with the Devil. St. Francis heard Christ talking to him from the Crucifix in San Damiano and received the stigmata, St. Joan heard the voices of angels telling her the right path, while St. Ignatius and St. Aquinas beheld visions of such intellectual brilliance and beauty that they could not find words to describe them. The lives of the saints teem with such abilities and occurrences, in such diversity and abundance too wide to tell here.

The saints do not plan or create these abilities and events, they are direct gifts from GOD, and sometimes the people involved have no control or clue about the workings of a miraculous occurrence. This is one of the distinguishing aspects of Grace: divine events do not correspond to the plans or aspirations of human beings. GOD works in HIS own way and in HIS own time[1114].

Up to the age of 15, Sundar Singh hated Christianity so much he publicly burned a Bible to prove it. Not long after this egotistical challenge to GOD, in a conversion story similar to St. Paul's, Christ appeared to Sundar, and after that, nothing could hold the young man back from praising the very GOD he had wished to defy. He became a traveling holy man, dependent on the handouts of others, and preaching Christianity to all who would listen.

In 1906, he traveled from his homeland in Punjab to Tibet, where he encountered plenty of hostility from the reigning Tibetan religious, the Dalai Lama. So infuriated by the preaching of this traveling convert, the Lama had Sundar thrown into a dried well to starve to death. The top of the well was locked, and Sundar, at the dark bottom, could only wait for death among the decomposed bodies of the other victims.

Some three days later, a sound from above interrupted Sundar's prayer. It sounded like someone unlocking the top of the well. But only the Lama himself carried the key! Whatever the case, a rope descended to

---

[1114] This is the difference between "magic" and miracle. Magic is the human attempt to force the hand of the supernatural. Miracles are done by GOD, "before the face", regardless of human action—(Underhill, 1990) pg. 70-71, 156-157, see also Martin Buber's *I and Thou*, the section on GOD and the Spirit of Man.

Sundar and a voice told him to hang on. Once he was pulled forth into the fresh night, he turned to thank his liberators, but no one was there.

Not long after, Sundar was again dragged before the Lama for preaching Christianity. The Lama recognized the man as the same whom he had sent to death, but scoffed at Sundar's tale of liberation.

"Someone has stolen my key; that is all!" The Lama cried, but he found it exactly where it should be, tied to his waist.

Terrified at the implications, the Lama had Sundar kicked out of Tibet. To this day, no one can explain exactly what occurred or how Sundar had been freed. Sundar himself had decided that GOD had intervened, as when St. Peter was freed from his own prison[1115].

Knights and warriors too, when in the hold of Grace, could perform wonders beyond the reach of mere humanity. The Knights Hospitaller at the battle of Rhodes held on to their faith, and were visited with a mighty vision, helping them defeat a much larger force. King Baldwin the leper, faced with impossible odds, called upon Grace and defeated the enemy of his religion. Constantine, a thousand years before, painted the sign of Christ on his shield and the shields of his army, then rode on to defeat an evil enemy force much larger than his. St. Joan, let us not forget, was only 13 when she first hear St. Michael's call to arms, and by 16 was driving the great English army before her.

Forgiveness itself is a power that men of faith receive flowing from Grace. Father Walter Ciszek was able to forgive the tyranny of the Soviet Union, who held him in prison for 20 years simply for being a Catholic priest[1116]. Pope John Paul easily forgave the Soviet assassin who shot him, knowing full well that it was the Soviet Union, once again, who was truly at fault.

Special Wisdom descends upon many who have been touched by Grace. We have already spoken of St. Thomas Aquinas, who saved the world with his thoughts on Aristotle; Ramon Lull, whose logical ways of persuasion led to the first computers; and Johannes Kepler, who saw in the infinite night sky the hand of GOD the Geometer.

[1115] (Riley, 1988) p.357
[1116] See his amazing book, *With GOD in Russia*, (Ciszek, 1964)

Grace also bestows the power to <u>resist the irresistible temptation</u>. St. Aquinas, for instance, asked for and received the ability to ignore all sexual temptation forever. He had a dream that an Angel came to him with a shining cord that was tied around his waist, and after that, he lost no time in combating sexual sin, for the temptation did not even occur to him[1117].

Grace is a special power, given by GOD, that bestows Faith, miraculous powers, ability to forgive, and a kind of irresistible vigor and might that eventually culminates in victory for goodness.

How to Recognize the State of Grace

The young Sir Lancelot[1118] was certain, as long as he remained in a state of Grace, that he might be able to perform one miracle[1119]. The size and shape of this miracle did not matter to him; it was the fact that a man like himself, only a man, could have a strong enough relationship with GOD that he might walk with the saints, if only for a moment.

Others might have seen his prowess in arms as a miracle in itself, seeing that he was never defeated, but Lancelot felt his abilities as only terrestrial things, accomplished by anyone with enough practice (although he did think that a man totally focused on Honor and GOD, rather than having a paramour, was stronger in battle).

The state of Grace, so Lancelot held, was shown by two signs: purity in mind and in body. His thoughts were always on doing what was right, and his body had so far resisted falling into lust with a woman. He ignored many a beautiful lady's advance, because of his loyalty to GOD, of course, but also because he wished for his miracle more than anything

---

[1117] (Shea, 2013) based on Shea's *Little Pictoral lives of the Saints*, in 1894, which in turn is based on Butler's *Lives of the Saints*

[1118] This is before Lancelot committed his one sin.

[1119] (White, 1958) pg. 312, pg. 358 for the full story. See (Malory, 1962) pg. 470-471 for a similar miracle story, but one where Lancelot weeps because he knows GOD performed a miracle through him despite of his sins, as the lowest of the low, and in this way, Lancelot still shows himself to understand Grace and how far he had fallen from it. See Chretien de Troyes's *Knight of the Cart* for another type of miracle story with Lancelot.

else in this world. To him it would be a sign of GOD's friendship, something unexplainable, mysterious, and sublimely beautiful.

His chance finally came, without his knowledge. As he rode one day, in search of adventure, a crowd of people swarmed about him, begging him for assistance. Since the knight's duty is to help people, he readily agreed, but when they brought him to the task, he hesitated.

Before him stood a huge cauldron of churning water, boiling and fuming, with a huge fire burning beneath it. Within this monstrous vessel suffered a beautiful woman, slowly boiling to death. As Lancelot approached, he noticed that while the woman should be dead already, somehow her flesh was not falling away, nor were her eyes melted, nor did she show the other signs of someone being tortured. She only languished there, utterly hopeless.

"This is a wonder." Lancelot whispered.

"She is cursed to stay here in this living death forever, burning but not dying, until the Purist Knight in the World comes to rescue her and perform a miracle."

"Have you looked for this purist knight?" Lancelot asked them. "Surely he will be able to lift her out without being boiled himself."

The people looked at him as if stunned. "You are the Purist Knight in the World. You are Lancelot."

"You are wasting your time with me," Lancelot replied sincerely, "For surely I am not the one you seek. I am Sir Lancelot, but I am only Sir Lancelot."

"You are mistaken when you say you are not the purest!" The people shouted. "We have heard of your deeds! Who else could do this miracle?!"

"I will attempt to save the maiden, because it is my duty to help all in distress." Lancelot said tiredly. "But after I fail, be prepared to search for the man who will succeed."

At this, the knight prayed. "Oh Lord, may that I do what is right. Your will be done."

Lancelot reached across the cauldron for the hand of the maiden, all the time expecting the searing steam to burn his flesh. But even as he stretched out, the heat of the fire and the metal subsided, and, as his fingers closed around those of the maiden's, the steam turned to mist, the water grew tepid, and the maiden emerged from the scorching bath as one from baptism. As Lancelot wrapped her in his cloak, all could see that she remained unscarred and unblemished from the terrible trial. A miracle had been accomplished.

Lancelot remained the most surprised of all[1120], and wept like a child[1121].

Consider this story, with its inadvertent public display of GOD's friendship and Grace, a typical legend. Real miracles occur more often than you might think. But usually, more private settings are fitting for such miracles.

Deep in the night, long after all were asleep, a sacristan was making his rounds through the monastery where Anselm and many other monks lived. As he passed the chapter room, a place where large meetings were held during the day, he happened to look in. There stood Anselm, obviously in prayer, but surrounded by a miraculous ball of light and fire. Stunned, the sacristan backed up and ran without a sound.

Shouldn't the monk Anselm be in his bed this time of night? When he checked, Anselm's bed was empty. Returning to the chapter room, the sacristan found Anselm still standing there, praying as before, but the ball of fire had vanished[1122].

What the sacristan had accidently witnessed was a private display of St. Anselm's very real and very intimate relationship with GOD. This too was a sign of the state of Grace.

Is this state always illuminated by such signs and visions? Not always, but many times they are.

How to find the state of Grace

One cannot build Faith as Strength and Courage can be built. One cannot build within one's self GOD's Grace; one can only leave one's heart and soul open for GOD's presence. Too many times, people seem to think that if they go to church enough, or intone the proper prayers, or do some difficult thing in the name of GOD, they will be given a miracle, or Grace, or some incredible Faith. It takes more. A true believer must look and search. One must look for GOD as one looks for a long

---

[1120] (White, 1958) pg. 358

[1121] (Malory, 1962) pg. 470-471, it is Malory who writes of Lancelot's weeping after his miracle with Sir Urry.

[1122] (Shannon, 1999) pg. 31 This story is true, while Lancelot's miracle is legendary

lost friend. This is the knightly way. Reaching out to GOD as to a friend, a comrade of terrific battles long past, not to ask for favors or requests or gifts, but simply for the presence of the old, best friend of one's youth[1123].

Look with all your faith, and omit nothing in your striving to ask for forgiveness for any sins in your path. Do your utmost, go to confession[1124], submit to painful penance; even if the spirit drives you into the desert for years, whatever it takes. Above all, desire for your good friend to forgive you. No one is perfect, certainly not Sir Lancelot, and yet he found friendship with GOD. Abraham, Moses, all the great patriarchs had sinned at one time or another too. They went through their trials and sufferings, so should you, but only keep in mind your friend, as they did. Strive to be the best you can, just as Christ suffered so much to save you, and remember His face.

How does one search and seek like this?

This is how to be in a state of Grace. Keep your mind on GOD and Honor, and keep yourself as humble as the "Ill-Made Knight", doing good in the world and living for GOD. Just as important, think on GOD constantly, like St. Anselm, setting aside time to talk to Him in a quiet place. Do this alone, separate from any evangelization or public ministry. Make it a habit, because you are spending quiet time with GOD[1125].

If you can do this, holding your Lord in your heart and your mind, looking for HIM in sincerity and humility, you will find HIM. Behold, He is with you, til the end of time[1126].

Looking For Grace—The Hunting Habits of GOD

Blaise Pascal always said that in the end, only three kinds of men walked this world: men who search for GOD, men who find GOD, and those who neither search nor find[1127].

Notice how Pascal is careful to break up into groups those who seek and those who find. They are not necessarily the same. As in the Grail,

---

[1123] Jeremiah 3:4 also, Jeremiah 2:2, Hosea 2:15, Psalm 71:17
[1124] (Lang, 1967) pg. 88
[1125] (Shannon, 1999) pg. 43
[1126] Matthew 28:20
[1127] (Pascal, 1966) pg. 82, thought 160, in ch.xii, *Beginning*

it is not simply where one looks. It is the kind of person who does the looking, and what resides in their hearts and souls.

Indeed, those who find GOD, are often those who seek him. They search for Him diligently, in the lonely places of this world, and in the dark, sequestered chambers of their own hearts. Those who find GOD have longed for Him, like the parched deer longs for water[1128], like the good wolf, howling alone at the edge of the world. They truly seek him, with open heart and open mind, humble and sincere.

Sometimes, not all those who find him, have sought him. At the beginning of their careers, Sir Ramon Lull and Saint Ignatius had no desire to find GOD and actually actively fled Him, burying themselves in the pursuits and desires of the world, as the Prodigal Son. Perhaps, as many of us, they feared that if they gained GOD, they would lose everything else, failing to see that GOD contains everything real or worthwhile.

Some think they have sought him, resting on dreams and self-deceits, thinking they possessed Him fully. Saul of Tarsus rested like this, serene in his vision of himself as righteous, before he became St. Paul.

Suddenly, for both these groups, the true GOD comes upon them in terrifying visions that cannot be denied. They did not hunt for GOD; GOD was hunting for them!

> I FLED Him, down the nights and down the days;
> I fled Him, down the arches of the years;
> I fled Him, down the labyrinthine ways
> Of my own mind; and in the mist of tears
> I hid from Him, and under running laughter . . . 5
>
> those strong Feet that followed, followed after.
> But with unhurrying chase,[10]
> And unperturbèd pace,
> Deliberate speed, majestic instancy,
> They beat—and a Voice beat
> More instant than the Feet—
> 'All things betray thee, who betrayest Me.'

[1128] Psalm 42:1

GOD is traditionally referred to as a male. HE is a hunter[1129]. Whether we seek HIM or run, GOD "captures" us at HIS own time. We are at the mercy of GOD's will, and we must wait. "The moment when a person first becomes aware of a great Power is essentially passive: something happens to someone—it is not a matter of what one chooses to do or refuses to do. Nor does it involve thinking benevolent thoughts or being kind to others or planning for the future, although some of these events may follow in various forms during the process . . . . We cannot produce this experience at will by some arcane mystical methods. We can ask, we can seek, but essentially we must wait"[1130]. Search for HIM, yes, but know that *HE will find you.*

Many see Grace, or even conversion, as initiated by the person, but it is initiated by GOD[1131]. Notice that most religious experiences in the Bible are radical intrusions by GOD into the rather humdrum lives of various characters[1132]. Most were good and holy people who loved GOD with all their hearts, but they were not thinking of GOD at that moment. But GOD was thinking about them.

This is why setting aside quiet time, time to be alone, and time to be separate from all earthly activity is so essential. This is our "waiting time". One does not know when GOD will come calling. This is not so we will be in some "proper" quiet mood when GOD comes to us, as if GOD needed us to be in it, but so we will be prepared for such an event when it does come. We must be prepared to respond properly. And what if we miss it, because we were focused on something else! What if we weren't listening[1133]! That still, small voice[1134] sometimes comes so softly in our loud world. We must be careful. I say "wait", but that word seems to suggest a kind of sitting and doing nothing. On the contrary, this waiting is patient, but requires effort and looking, but we have to abide by GOD's time. We search for HIM, but we have to wait for HIM.

[1129] See *The Hound of Heaven* poem lines 1-15, by Francis Thompson

[1130] (Spoto, 2002) pg.48

[1131] (Anthony Schraner, 1981) ch.125, pg. 146, (Sheen A. F., 1990) pg. 94

[1132] Consider Samuel, St. Joseph, and St. Mary, visited by life-changing, world-changing holy visions, when they were engaged in something else

[1133] The polite part of talking to GOD is being still long enough to listen.—Edward Gloeggler

[1134] 1 Kings 19:12 KJV

And what will we find when we have waited? It may be that the very act of waiting is a kind of Grace. Could it be that the desire to search for GOD, the desire to understand GOD, to love GOD, is also a Grace, as powerful and important as any miracle? Could it be, that in the very act of desiring GOD so deeply, HE stood with us the whole time?

Then there are those who seem to seek HIM, but never find HIM. As the true hunter, GOD cannot be "captured" or even properly pursued by some supercilious, self-important, self-determined, willful, deliberate, and fully precocious person. Walking in darkness forever, they miss HIM at every turn. I remember a TV documentary where a troubled teen-ager, tired and disgusted with his ridiculous way of life, decided to pray in order to see if there was a god out there who could help him. He prayed this: "GOD, if you are out there, if you exist, give me a sign." This is not really a prayer[1135]; it is a demand, a demand for GOD to prove HIS very existence. When nothing happened, the child simply shrugged his shoulders and decided religion didn't "work" for him.

How arrogant of us, to demand that GOD prove HIMSELF by performing some "trick", as if GOD was some circus animal or side-show magician. Of course, one may wonder what "trick" is enough to satisfy us. Consider how different this selfish and churlish demand is from Lancelot's story, or St. Anselm's midnight vision. Demanding GOD to appear before you, to satisfy your whimsy, is not seeking, but stamping your feet in a temper tantrum. It produces nothing.

Finally, the saddest—those who truly never bother to seek, nor find. Sometimes, GOD Himself comes to them and asks for them, but they turn away. I cannot visit such a terrible place: the heart of one who has turned his back, intentionally, on a personal invitation from GOD's own spirit. Cain possessed one of these[1136]. Perhaps this is reality, that GOD, the mighty hunter, comes to all of us at one time or another, sometimes when we are not fully aware that it is HIS voice, calling our names, like HE did Samuel's, in the deep night. May the Lord grant that we hear HIM, at last.

[1135] All the saints advise to pray, to ask, even beg GOD for help, not signs. Also, turn away from sin.

[1136] Genesis 4:6-7

Faith Itself as Grace

Faith itself is a Grace from GOD. It is not inborn or taught[1137]. No human action can automatically produce Faith in an individual. Even witnessing an unexplainable miracle, with all the trappings and light and voices streaming from the sky can't ensure Faith.

Consider Judas Iscariot. He lived with Jesus Himself, along with the other disciples. He saw all the miracles and he must have felt the power emanating from the Word Made Flesh. But in the end, he still betrayed Christ[1138].

Many people say, "Well, if Jesus came up to me and talked to me, then I would do things differently". Really? Several people received direct invitations to follow Him from Christ's own lips, and still they declined. Jesus warns us in the parable of Lazarus that even if all the angels in Heaven were sent to warn people from their sinful ways, it would not be enough[1139].

The 3 Pieces Come Together

To become a true knight or a saint, to be a friend of GOD or have spiritual strength[1140], it is essential to gain Faith. But how? At first, the answer seems strait forward: through Focus on GOD, Reliance on GOD, and Grace. Although these are signs of Faith, and may lead to a stronger Faith, they also require Faith to enact them!

To simply read about the aspects of Faith and think about them is not enough to give us the Faith we need. Time and again we will see that becoming a saint, knight, or hero is not a linear process. We must understand how these pieces fit together, not just as concepts on a page, but how they come together in the soul of a person. The early life of a hero of Faith, Saint Augustine, can give us clues on how this is done.

Before we begin, however, there is the question of whether Faith can be earned or gained. Augustine later wondered if gaining Faith by one's own efforts might be impossible. Real, iron-clad Faith, he reasoned, came

---

[1137] (Doornik, 1953) pg. 394, (Copleston, 1962) pg. 98-99
[1138] It is no advantage to be near the light if your eyes are closed, says Augustine.
[1139] Luke 16:30-31
[1140] (Trape', 1986) pg.87

from GOD's direct interaction, because Faith is a type of Grace, freely given by GOD. From the beginning of Time, it seemed, GOD entrusted a certain select few with the Faith, through Grace, to reach HIM, with no special merit or action on their parts[1141].

Does this mean that we cannot grow faith?

Augustine's faith, if freely given to him by GOD, surely did not begin as very strong in his childhood. Any faith in the boy seemed completely imperceptible! His mother, Monica, had a strong faith, yes, but she could not seem to transmit it to her child, who felt ashamed at following the example of a woman in such matters, or in morality in general[1142].

Like the young Francis, the youthful Augustine was something of a "party animal". He enjoyed merry-making and women. He saw no reason to follow Faith at first, nor asceticism, nor give his life in the pursuit of Holy endeavors. He wished, at nineteen, to become a successful teacher and enjoy life: a material, worldly life.

But something very important eluded him. It haunted him, and whispered in the back of his mind so that he was never satisfied by his success or studies. He described it as simply "the name of Christ"[1143]. Even with his flippant lifestyle, he still knew somehow that Christ was important, but he kept this locked away in his innermost self. Could this tiny acknowledgment of GOD, deep in his psyche, be considered Faith? Certainly not the Faith that we see Augustine beaming with later, and certainly not the faith that can move mountains. This name, hidden within Augustine, rarely affected his actions at all, nor caused him to avoid sin, let alone become a Champion of Christianity. He did not even name this spark of a name within him "faith" so I can hardly bring myself to call it True Faith. But the name of Christ, like a dormant seed waiting for the right time to sprout, lay within him, none the less. Perhaps even this is Grace.

But this tiny seed needed more to become the Faith we need as knights. What happened to grow this seed into a tree of powerful Faith?

For Augustine, it began with the reading of *Hortensius*, by Cicero[1144]. A strange book to bring about Christian Faith, because it was written by a pagan. Cicero was a Roman philosopher who moved readers to fall in love

---

[1141] (Doornik, 1953) pg. 394, (Copleston, 1962) pg. 99

[1142] (Trape', 1986) pg.38

[1143] (Trape', 1986) pg. 44, (Augustine, 1961) book III, part 4, pg. 59

[1144] (Trape', 1986) pg. 42, (Augustine, 1961) book III, part 4, pg. 58

with Greek wisdom and philosophy. Nowhere did it mention Christ, but it sparked within Augustine an agonizing search that would culminate in the finding of Ultimate Wisdom.

Cicero taught the pursuit of the four cardinal virtues, and that no particular school of philosophy, but only philosophy itself, is worthy. Philosophy itself is the pursuit of the Truth, and Augustine knew that Truth would somehow have the name of Christ stamped upon it[1145].

Cicero also taught that the pleasures of the human world, especially bodily pleasures, were simply distractions from the Truth[1146]. Such distractions had to be ignored before one could see the Truth. Now that Augustine realized he loved Wisdom and Truth, for they were the only things deserving love[1147], he now wished to dedicate himself entirely to them, throwing away everything else. The young man would later find examples of this extreme Focus in the life of Antony, and other famous saints of the period[1148].

With this piece of the Faith puzzle, Augustine began to realize that his life did not match a true philosopher's life. His mind was not purely on Truth, yet. Sure, his mother had pointed that out to him time and again, but now men he respected were telling him the same thing, and showing him examples in their lives.

The persistent problem pressed him. The Name of Christ. He could not find it in Cicero, and he could not understand how GOD and Christ fit in with Wisdom and Truth. When he had read the Scriptures, especially the Old Testament, they seemed earth-bound and full of weird phrases that had no place with the intellectual thirst for wisdom in his mind[1149].

Following Cicero's lead, Augustine tried to solve the problem using philosophy. If he found the right philosophy or mix of philosophies, he reasoned, he would be able to understand the connection between Christ, GOD, and Truth, and also find the spiritual strength to focus his life on Wisdom, as he knew a true philosopher should.

[1145] (Trape', 1986) pg. 44, see Josiah Hotchkiss Gilbert's *Dictionary of Burning Words of Brilliant Writers* (1895) pg. 62, (Augustine, 1961) book III, part 4, pg. 59

[1146] (Trape', 1986) pg. 43, (Wills, 1999) pg.27

[1147] (Trape', 1986) pg. 27, (Wills, 1999) pg.84

[1148] (Trape', 1986) pg. 106, (Augustine, 1961) book 8, pg. 167

[1149] (Trape', 1986) pg. 52 and (Wills, 1999) pg. 28

He tried many philosophies: Manichaeism, skepticism, scholasticism, and so forth, but he discovered that he could destroy their arguments and reduce them to absurdity[1150] by the power of his own reason[1151]. Worse, none possessed the name of Christ nor gave him the power to focus his mind, body, and life on wisdom. He was still plagued by uncertainties, and the desires of the flesh distracted him no end.

He then came to the Neo-Platonists, especially the writer known as Plotinus. Plotinus and the others were not Christian, but they understood a very important piece of the puzzle, that GOD WAS the Truth[1152]. This idea exploded upon Augustine like a bombshell. Of course! GOD and Truth and Wisdom were not only connected, but the same!

Augustine saw the picture of Wisdom in its entirety, thanks to the Neo-Platonists. But they only admired Wisdom and GOD, without fully understanding how to reach them. They could only show a picture, not the path to it.

Augustine felt closer now, but still he was miles away from his goal. How could he reach GOD and Wisdom, and how could he obtain the focus he needed to be purely concentrated on GOD?

When he heard the preaching of Saint Ambrose, this understanding became further cemented. Ambrose explained how many of the Scriptures, what Augustine had seen as "earthy" before, could actually be understood in a different way[1153]. Ambrose re-interpreted the scriptures for Augustine, showing that they pointed to the same goal that Cicero and the Neo-Platonists did, GOD and the Truth. Augustine suddenly realized that Reason and logic did not have to be at odds with Faith. They should work together[1154]!

There was one monumental difference, however, between Ambrose's lessons and the Neo-Platonists. Platinus and the Neo-Platonists could admire the Truth from afar. The scriptures, Ambrose said, held the actually path to the Truth. The path was Christ, because the Truth was Christ.

[1150] Not Tertullian's version of absurd, but a true absurdity which fell apart under Augustine's stare

[1151] (Trape', 1986) pg. 85

[1152] (Trape', 1986) pg. 99, (Augustine, 1961) pg.61, in book III, see Augustine's *De Libero Arbitrio*

[1153] (Trape', 1986) pg. 82-83, (Wills, 1999) pg.57, 66

[1154] (Trape', 1986) pg. 119

Now, only one thing stood in his way: his own bodily desires. But no matter how he tried to bend his body to his will, these desires forced him back down.

"I can do so many things," He said to himself. "I can reason with the great thinkers, and command my body to move this way and that, but when it comes to commanding my own desires and wants, I seem to be utterly helpless"[1155]!

Indeed, it is always the self that is the hardest to conquer, and becomes the worse enemy[1156].

It must be understood that Augustine's life, even as "earthy" as he saw it, was about what is accepted now as normal, even Christian[1157]. He had a monogamist relationship, and he had an active life of faith. Anyone in this modern world would have thought him as being a good, decent man and full of moral values[1158]. But Augustine wanted to do and be more. Without knowing it, he was making himself a saint and a hero of faith[1159].

One day, after hearing stories of St. Antony's amazing discipline and asceticism, something in Augustine snapped. He could not stand his weaknesses any longer! In desperation, he ran into a garden. Spiritual discipline was the final weapon he needed to burst through the wall separating him from the presence of GOD and the lifestyle GOD wanted for him. But could he take it? Could he grasp this last piece? Could he make himself take the next step? Breathless, without full understanding of what he was doing, with tears streaming and anger at his weakness boiling over, he threw himself down on the ground, sobbing.

He heard a voice, "Take and read. Take and Read". There, near him rested the Scriptures. Augustine accepted this as a message from GOD, an angel's voice helping him do the right thing. He opened the book, letting the pages fall, seeming randomly, but with an awesome purpose straight from GOD.

[1155] Romans 7:19, (Wills, 1999) pg.47, (Augustine, 1961) 8.20, 8.27, pg. 171

[1156] Our greatest foes, and whom we must chiefly combat, are within.- Miguel de Cervantes, *The History of the Renowned Don Quixote de la Mancha* Volume: 2 (1743); Chapter: VIII, Page 75. See also, Sir Thomas Browne's *Religio Medici*

[1157] (Wills, 1999) pg. XVII, (Trape', 1986) pg. 102

[1158] Ibid.

[1159] (Wills, 1999) pg. 44

The verse was Romans 13:13, telling Augustine to live in chastity, and to put away the passions of this world. He suddenly was filled with the wisdom to know what GOD wanted him to do, and the Strength to do it.

From then on, Augustine found he possessed the discipline needed to leave his secular life behind forever, embracing fully his priestly asceticism and discipline. Somehow GOD had infused in him the power to finally corral and dominate his bodily desires. Because of his faith, GOD had given him the power to control himself.

For St. Augustine, the three pieces of faith had come together, at last.

Even with Faith the size of a "mustard seed", a faith so small it cannot be seen easily, a person may find the way to become a hero of GOD— with Faith growing so large, the birds of spiritual success and sainthood may find rest there[1160].

Devices of Providence

The Revelationists, like Tertullian and Pascal, insist that Faith comes upon one like a thief in the night, suddenly and with mystery, and without proper human understanding. This seems to be so, but can Faith come about in another way? May hard work, study, and constant prayer, even logic and philosophy bring Faith, even the size of a mustard seed? When we look at the testimony of St. Augustine, the answer seems to be an affirmative, at least to a degree[1161].

The life of Saint Augustine shows that strong Faith is not automatic, nor is it easy, but it can be done. GOD gives us the special Grace called the seed of Faith, but it must be nurtured with the sunlight of GOD's word, the water of good example, and special, almost hidden, devices of Providence. The Heroes of GOD, knights and saints, usually find these "devices of Providence" in the following activities, events, and struggles.

<u>Good Examples</u>: Augustine had his mother, Saint Monica, as an example of a tireless person of Faith. He scorned this example at first, but it could not help but have an effect on him, simply because she was

---

[1160] Matthew 17:20, Matthew 13:31, Luke 13:19, Luke 17:6
[1161] (Kersten, 1990) pg. 132

consistent, and, although not very educated, brimming with love. He also had good friends like Simplicanus, who, later in his life, would help him down the road of Christianity.

Such examples cannot be stressed enough, especially in one's youth. Where would Joan of Arc be without the priests and sisters who instructed her, so when the voices of Angels came, she knew what they were and how to react?

Can it be possible to grow up a hero of GOD without good examples? The masters of Faith, like Abraham and Noah, did not seem to have anyone around them that could demonstrate the life of a good, Faithful person. Abraham, the Bible suggests, was the first Monotheist, and Noah, the only man of his time who was good. How can we explain this? Only through Grace. GOD HIMSELF led these Masters of Faith.

GOD will continue to lead HIS specially chosen; but for the rest of us, we who are neither Abraham nor Noah, we must continue to use the other devices of Providence.

<u>Study of the Scriptures</u>: Many think it enough to read the Bible everyday to have Faith. It is not enough. One does not believe in Prince Valiant simply because his syndicated story is told from day to day in thousands of newspapers. More to the point, an eight-year-old can read plenty of things, even pieces of Plato's Republic, but this does not mean the youngster understands much of what is read.

It is important to read scripture everyday, yes, but it is more important to understand the scripture, even to struggle to understand, as well as hear different interpretations of it. Augustine had read the scriptures with full desire to believe, but at first had been lead totally astray by his own untrained understanding. He was disgusted by the "vulgar wording" of the Scriptures, since no one had taught him how to read and understand them properly. Only after hearing a sermon on the subject by Saint Ambrose did Augustine finally start understanding Scripture[1162]. To truly study the Scriptures, one also must read with one's heart, as well as one's mind—mind open, heart open[1163].

Another very important concept in studying Scripture is that one's understanding should grow along with one's maturity. If we went to Bible

---

[1162] (Trape', 1986) pg.80, (Wills, 1999) pg. 45
[1163] (Shannon, 1999) pg. 38-40, 44

School as children, we heard the various stories of the Bible, and this was enough. But as we grow older, it is essential to understand these stories in new ways, and see them as deeper truths, rather than simply subject material for coloring and pasting on Sunday letters to Mother. "When I was a child, I spake as a child, I understood as a child, I thought as a child: but when I became a man, I put away childish things"[1164].

This does not mean that a child's faith is wrong, the trust of a child is correct, but that our understanding must continue through adulthood, always growing deeper.

Study and Pursuit of Wisdom: Tertullian would have said that the study of the Scriptures is enough to have great understanding and powerful Faith[1165]. That may be true, but I think he thought this because his faith had been a gift from GOD, complete and whole. For the rest of us, who have to carefully nurture our faith so that it may grow, I think the more complete and successful route is Augustine's method, study of Scripture and philosophy.

True philosophy and Scripture complement each other. Justin Martyr, that great Christian "athlete" from the terrifying second century A.D., believed that there were pagan philosophers, like Cicero, Socrates, Plato, and Epictetus, who "partially knew Christ" and could be aids in understanding HIM and act as stepping-stones in understanding Scripture[1166]. Christianity, Justin knew, was a fulfillment of philosophy, not a negation[1167], just as the New Testament is a fulfillment, not a negation, of the Old. He went on to say that "Whatever things were rightly said among all men, are the property of us Christians"[1168].

It can be said that Augustine strove to pursue GOD when his desire for Wisdom was awakened by Cicero[1169], and perpetually fed by his studying of Plotinus. Perhaps others can find GOD and the true meaning of the Scriptures in a quicker way, but I believe that true understanding

---

[1164] 1 Corinthians 13:11
[1165] (Gilson, 1938) pg. 8-10, (Gilson, The History of Christian Philosophy in the Middle Ages, 1955) pg. 16
[1166] (Gilson, The History of Christian Philosophy in the Middle Ages, 1955) pg.11
[1167] Ibid
[1168] Ibid. pg.13
[1169] (Trape', 1986) pg.42

usually and naturally takes a more holistic approach. This may be because I need to understand as well as believe, as Augustine did[1170].

Studying Heroes of Faith: Similar to good examples are the study of Heroes. While good examples may be thrust upon us, it is our duty to search for and study heroes that we can emulate.

When the soldier and knight, Ignatius of Loyola, was wounded terribly in battle, he faced many months of idle waiting for health. He decided to read away the hours of boredom, but instead of chivalrous romances, which were his first choice, his hands found a book on the lives of the saints. Such books were common in the medieval world, but rarely were they used to their natural conclusion. Ignatius found his heart on fire for GOD when he read about these saints. They were heroes of GOD, and he desired to be one of them, fighting for the glory of GOD, instead of the glory of the world. When he was able to walk again, he vowed not to serve a prince or princess further, but to serve GOD as a Knight of Christ[1171].

Augustine was stunned when he heard about Saint Antony of Egypt[1172]. A friend relayed to him the story of this Saint, who was already well known in the West, but largely unknown in the East. Augustine had no idea that men could do such things, and he had especially never heard of someone trying it with the blessing of the Catholic Church. Two Roman soldiers, the friend pointed out, when they heard about Antony, were so on fire from Antony's example of brutal piety that they immediately went off to live a Christian monastic life. All of these stories sealed Augustine's conviction. He was ashamed of himself and his weakness, and vowed to become a similar man of faith[1173]. It was exactly then, right after his friend had left, that Augustine took his fateful trip to the garden[1174].

Think About GOD: To have true Faith, a true knight must find out, as far as is possible, whom the True GOD is. This takes infinite study and

---

[1170] (Gilson, 1938) pg.19
[1171] (Ellsburg, 2001) pg.327
[1172] (Augustine, 1961) pg. 167, bk 8
[1173] (Trape', 1986) pg.106
[1174] ibid

precise thinking. Indeed, before we can have faith or even love GOD, we must have an idea of who GOD is. We must first think about GOD. We must have questions, and burn for the answers[1175].

Justine Martyr said "it is truly the duty of the philosopher to investigate the Deity"[1176]. Augustine believed that good Philosophy, even Greek and pre-Christian, can help one reach a true vision of GOD. Neo-Platonist Greek philosophy was the primary type that Augustine worked with, and he acknowledged that it was only a help, not a sure path, to understand GOD; but still, Augustine emphatically pointed to philosophy and learning as an important step in reaching a better understanding of GOD, and this understanding can help Faith[1177].

At times, Faith may seem blind and absurd, but it is not stupid. Faith must be based on knowledge of GOD, diligent study of the saints, scholastics, and the sayings and lives of wise people. How can you love GOD if you do not think about GOD? Faith becomes an aid to Reason, and Reason an aid to Faith[1178]. Ramon Lull, the knightly philosopher, said it best: "Those who can understand, should understand"[1179].

Discipline of the Body: This piece proved to be a particularly difficult one for St. Augustine, but he had learned, as every religious person before him, that the demands of the body had to be controlled before the spirit could be reached. "Before the mind can be trained" Master Kan said in *Kung Fu*, "the body must be disciplined"[1180].

Isn't the young Augustine's struggle a reflection of what many of us struggle with today? So much emphasis is placed on physical pleasure in our culture that it is hard to see room for anything else, let alone spiritual growth. Augustine winced at the small failings of his early pursuit of asceticism, but our culture piles so many lusts, gluttonies and greeds upon our backs from media, peer pressure and culture that it is a wonder anyone thinks of spirituality at all. But the struggle must be taken up.

Discipline is connected to Faith in a number of ways. Faith in GOD is the "Why" of knightly Discipline, just as discipline is part of the

---

[1175] (Wills, 1999) pg. xi, "Augustine thinks in questions", according to Karl Jaspers.

[1176] (Gilson, The History of Christian Philosophy in the Middle Ages, 1955) pg. 11

[1177] (Gilson, 1938) pg. 16, (Trape', 1986) pg. 119

[1178] (Gilson, 1938) pg. 16, 26, (Illingworth, 1903) pg. 2-8

[1179] (Gilson, 1938)pg. 31

[1180] (Thorpe, 1972)

"How" of Faith. To be self-disciplined, one needs a particularly good reason to be so. GOD, the faith and love in HIM, makes for a very good reason to endure all the disciplines and pains necessary to pursue a greater faith, as well as the trials of a religious person in this society.

Reason and Revelation

"Not to act in accordance with reason is contrary to GOD's nature."

—*Pope Benedict XVI*[1181]

I have made much of Faith seeming to be absurd. But, obviously, it isn't "absurd" at all.

An ancient struggle between Reason and Revelation has roared forever, seemingly. In the ancient world, as in the Middle Ages, Revelation meant "revealed" information, directly from GOD. Information of this sort and caliber, as in prophesy and divinely inspired writing or oratory, is unavailable to the human mind alone. The Bible is all inspired, and comes through the authors by Revelation. Only a person "touched" by GOD can know this information, and many times it goes against logic and common sense.

Noah, for instance, knowing about the up-coming flood, or St. Joseph, knowing about the holy origins of Mary's pregnancy[1182], or Elijah, hearing the message in the "small, still voice"[1183]. Tertullian is a champion of Revelation as the only source of Christian theology or doctrine[1184].

Although Faith may seem irrational and otherworldly, there exists another side. Augustine, a man who shunned even the suggestion of superstition, despised irrationality and ignorance, and fought pseudo-intellectualism continually, found the reasonable teachings of Cicero, and let the logical Greeks lead him to the pursuit of the absolute Truth. This eventual led him to Christ. Augustine became the champion of

---

[1181] From Pope Benedict's speech at the University of Rugensberg, Spetember 12, 2006, taken originally from the comments of the Byzantine emperor Manuel II Paleologus in 1391

[1182] Matthew 1:20

[1183] 1 Kings 19:12

[1184] (Gilson, 1938) pg. 6-8

Reason coupled with Revelation[1185]. He would say that we must weigh all testimony with already known inspired material, philosophy, tradition, and already existing doctrine—as we understand it. Not only can a source falsely claim to be "inspired", but even true Revelations might be mis-interpreted. We must use reason to interpret revelation, good philosophy to interpret faith, and solid intellectual traditions to see mystical vision properly.

Saint Thomas Aquinas showed that even the works of the founder of Science, Aristotle, pointed to one GOD, fulfilled in the Christian vision and understanding. Incorporating the pure logic of the Great Philosopher and the revealed Religion of Christianity, Thomas's ideas became the foundation of the Church's understanding of physical reality and its relation to the invisible, the perfect marriage of body and soul, science and spirit[1186].

Sir Ramon Lull, using logic and syllogism, in the face of all contemporary expectation and doubt of his peers, created a device or machine that could prove GOD and the Truth of Christ. This device, paper wheels that lined up separate but related arguments, used pure logic in a relentless system that could not be denied, absolute reason agreeing with and even demonstrating Revelation[1187].

Still, Human reason is not the summation of Faith.

Lull's machine worked too well. The Catholic Church admired his zeal in proselytizing to the Moslems, but worried at his claims of "proving GOD". No man, taught the Church, could completely grasp GOD within reason alone[1188]. Lull disagreed, firing up his examples from the machine. The Church was steadfast, and even though Lull finally suffered martyrdom at the hands of Moslems for his preaching of the Gospel, he was never granted sainthood in the Roman Catholic Church. To this day he is known as Blessed Ramon Lull, the "blessed" title being one step away from sainthood. Lull, according to the Church, had overstepped the bounds of Human reason. He had gone too far.

[1185] (Gilson, 1938) pg. 16
[1186] Ibid. pg. 83-84
[1187] (Gilson, 1938) pg. 30-31, (Zwemer, 1902) pg. 69-71
[1188] (Zwemer, 1902) pg. 69-71, (Knowles, 1962) pg. 263, (Cavanaugh, 1952) pg. 5

Saint Aquinas, the mental powerhouse of the Church, came close to completing his *Summa Theologica*, the complete compendium of the heights of Human reason coupled with Revelation. As he set about the last chapters, he was struck with a vision from Heaven that left him breathless. He found he could not finish the Summa, and never was able to return to it. The beauty of that vision, which opened Heaven's understanding before him, made everything he had ever written or thought, although great and true, seem as "mere dross"[1189].

Augustine, with all his great powers of reasoning and careful logic, came up to great barrier. He found he could not believe in what he did not understand, and try as he might, he could not understand the beauty and greatness of GOD completely. He realized he must believe first, and then understand[1190]. Only with the power of faith behind him, could he ever hope to understand the mysteries shown to him by GOD.

What can we make of these seemingly opposing views? How can we bring together these seemingly opposite ideas? We must not fall into the trap of assuming these two poles of understanding Faith as simply two opinions or concepts that cannot be reconciled. Though Reason can never completely fulfill the demands of Faith and Revelation, there is a certain corresponding, a certain relationship, a certain agreement between the two worlds. They should be two touchstones, two poles of clarity, to understand GOD and the true Scriptures. The knight and the saint must use their minds to interpret and understand GOD's words and will. Faith may be blind at times, but not stupid or devoid of sense. Although Reason can never fathom Revelation, and Revelation can never completely make sense to Reason, they are compatible, because they are both true. They both come ultimately from the same GOD[1191].

Science, as the study of reality using fact, observation, logic and experimentation, cannot be the enemy of the true man of GOD. The supposed break between reason or Science and religion is not only artificial, it is an illusion, created by people perhaps afraid of both true reason and true religion[1192]. In the famous Sistine Chapel painting of the

---

[1189] (Barron, 2008) pg. 23

[1190] (Gilson, 1938) pg. 16-17, I must believe to understand

[1191] Aquinas—GOD is the source of all truth, (Gilson, 1938) pg. 84, and (Knowles, 1962) pg. 262

[1192] (Cavanaugh, 1952), for this one, 1961, 3rd edition, 4th printing, pg. 234, (Muggeridge, 1985) pg. 73-74

Creation by Michelangelo, Adam reaches up with his feeble hand to the powerful GOD who gestures down with HIS finger. Mankind must use his reason as a striving to find GOD, while GOD reaches down from the Heavens with Revelation. GOD has the greater ability, and thus the greater reach, but Adam must reach as well, to the best of his ability, though his vast knowledge is but chaff in the wind. GOD must reach down to us, or we can never hope to understand even the tiniest portion of HIM. And we must use all our powers of insight and reason, because GOD is reality itself.

Both Ramon Lull and Blaise Pascal had deep faith, but approached GOD and their religious practice in opposite ways. Pascal, the mathematician and inventor of the calculator who thought and prayed like a mystic, his vision of GOD a complete revelation, beyond the logic of mankind[1193]. Lull, the romantic poet and courtesan turned lettered knight and missionary, who built a logic machine to touch the mind of GOD. Both opposite kinds of men, but both found GOD. Both had extreme mystical experiences that shook and transformed their lives. Pascal felt an overwhelming and transcendent peace descend on him, filling his soul with complete joy and peace for over an hour[1194]. Lull saw a terrifying image of Christ on the cross, suspended before him as if Lull stood on the hill of Calvary itself[1195]. Whether working from logic or seeking mystical illumination, the sincere person, searching for GOD with true Faith, will not be disappointed.

If we search for GOD honestly and with all our heart, mind, and strength, HE will find us.

The Limit of Reason—(The edge of Human Reason)

But our minds have limits. Although we can reach some understanding of GOD, we cannot understand GOD's fullness, nor can we grasp, with human logic or science, the complexity and holiness of

---

[1193] (Pullen, 1966) pg. 205-206, Pascal's mystical experience beyond logic and science

[1194] (Krailsheimer, 1966, 1988) pg. 14, (Underhill, 1990) pg. 188-189, (Pullen, 1966) pg. 205

[1195] (Zwemer, 1902) pg. 27

GOD, nor HIS thoughts. We are finite beings, thus our understanding is finite.

Both Augustine and Tertullian knew this. If human understanding and human philosophy and human common sense could grasp the completeness of GOD and HIS thoughts, GOD HIMSELF would simply be a human concept, limited to human thought[1196]. But since GOD is infinitely more, HIS mind being above the human mind as Infinity is larger than any number, True Faith in GOD must not be based on human logic or understanding. But what is outside of all human logic and understanding? Seemingly, only the absurd. Tertullian thus said, "I believe because it is absurd."

He knew that the time always comes for every saint, and every hero of GOD, when no kind of philosophy or understanding can reach GOD's plateau[1197]. Up to this point, a trained and sharpened mind, wise in the ways of philosophy, is useful in finding the stair-steps to Faith; but, finally the true knight stands on a precipice. The edge of a place that is no place, where all theories and presuppositions about GOD and true reality, crutches all, fall away. The Dark Night of the Soul. On the other side of this vast and un-searchable darkness is the shining glory of a complete relationship with GOD and perfect Faith. We may try to find our way through this darkness, but to go any further using human wisdom or logic is impossible. We have now come to the limit of reason. For the rest of the way, we must walk with Faith, and only Faith.

Some call it walking with Faith. Some call it the Leap of Faith. And we may very well feel as if we are leaping off a precipice, because we will have to rely solely on GOD. This leap of faith was one of Augustine's most difficult barriers on his road to True Faith.

How to approach the Leap of Faith

When we are dealing with the leap of Faith, we must look with other eyes besides reason and logic. Even the lessons of experience have no meaning here. We must trust the quiet voice in our souls, instead of the

---

[1196] (Cavanaugh, 1952) pg. 51, (Knowles, 1962) pg. 258, 263, (Cavanaugh, 1952) pg. 5

[1197] (Underhill, 1990) pg. 383

loud voices of our eyes and mind and fears. Listen to the wind. Focus on GOD and not our thoughts or feelings. Take the leap.

A curious and singular story from Sir Thomas Malory's *L'Morte D'Arthur* echoes this truth. Lancelot climbed the hundreds of stairs to Castle Carbonic, where he knew the Holy Grail rested. About half-way up, he unsheathed his sword, for he came to a terrifying sight. Two huge lions stood before him, their burning eyes staring at him and their jaws and roars gaping for him. He prepared himself for a terrible battle against the two beasts.

Then he heard a voice. "Do you not trust me?!" It cried from nowhere, "Why do you need your sword instead of my grace? Put your sword away."

Lancelot knew the insanity of putting away his sword at this moment. Two huge lions were about to rend him apart! But Lancelot knew GOD was speaking to him through the voice. Which would Lancelot trust, his common sense and experience, or the word of GOD?

Lancelot set down his sword. He walked up to the lions, and amazingly, they let him by as if he was not there[1198]. Lancelot had relied on GOD alone, and he made a successful leap of Faith. This is why he captured, a few minutes later, his glimpse of the Grail.

Relying on Faith alone was difficult for Saint Augustine. He was an intellectual, and relinquishing his education and mental habits would have seemed similar to Lancelot's dropping his sword before a battle. Augustine wanted to believe in GOD completely and have a relationship with HIM, but he found it hard to do this on GOD's terms, through Faith alone[1199].

Questions constantly plagued Augustine, questions the intellectual side of him demanded answers to before he could dedicate himself to Faith. These questions screamed for answers. How is GOD eternal? How does one explain evil in the universe created by a Good GOD? Does GOD's perfect and total knowledge predestine the final fates of people? How did GOD become incarnate in the flesh of Jesus Christ, the Word Made Flesh? How can GOD be three beings in one? How can we come to know such a GOD, outside time and space?

[1198] (Malory, 1962) pg. 422 and (Matarasso, 1969) pg. 260 for the full story
[1199] (Trape', 1986) pg. 90, 92

These questions haunted Augustine no end, wrestling with him day and night, forcing him to search for answers in many philosophies and leaders of various religions. He listened to wise men and fools, Orthodox believers and heretics, but whenever he found someone who claimed to explain these questions and justify Faith, Augustine could dismantle their arguments. This went on for years.

Augustine's heart despaired. Without the answers, how could he sustain his Faith? He struggled to believe in a GOD he could not understand, in a Religion he could not grasp through reason. He desperately searched for the bridge between reason and revelation, the connection between mind and soul. A great paradox.

If this had been Augustine's only problem, he might have gone down in history as a great searcher, as in Nagarjuna, or Zeno, but there was more. Augustine knew that to reach GOD, one not only had to think rightly, but live rightly. Up to that time, Augustine struggled mightily with his own bodily passions. He needed his common-law wife badly, but everything indicated he would not be able to live for her and for GOD, both[1200].

Even if he sent her away, Augustine knew, he would end up living with another woman. It was a great weakness, and no philosophy seemed to give him the power to leave this behind.

Almost empty of hope, Augustine tried again reading the Apostle Paul. Something then happened in him that seems so obvious to us, but for a man steeped in human reason, it was nothing short of a miracle. Trape' called it a "spiritual experiment", where Augustine ascended step by step from the body, to the soul, and from within the soul, to an intellect "that is enlightened by the changeless light"[1201].

He was going about this the wrong way, he realized. Only the eyes of the soul could perceive GOD completely[1202]. Up to this point, Augustine had thought of GOD in admittedly physical, spatial, and logical terms, as if GOD was nothing more than a difficult mathematics problem to solve. The Scriptures had revealed to him that only through the grace of GOD, direct intervention of GOD, an infusion of Faith, could the mind understand

---

[1200] (Trape', 1986) pg. 102, (Wills, 1999) pg.49

[1201] (Trape', 1986) pg. 99

[1202] Ibid. pg. 98, (Augustine, 1961) pg.133-134, bk. VII

the mystery of GOD. Only with GOD's help, not simply by man's efforts alone, can a man see truth and live as he should[1203]. This is reliance on GOD: trust in the Lord. To trust like this is to take the leap of faith.

Augustine's fundamental obstacle had been based on the very philosophies that had sent him in the right direction. Cicero and Plotinus both assumed that the soul could reach GOD by its own reasoning, by its own exertions, by the force of its own will[1204]. The Greek philosophers tended to be "naturalists", believing that the ability to obtain true sight of GOD dwelt within the natural ability of man, as long as he did the right things and thought the right way. Augustine tried to do the right things and think the right way, but it wasn't enough. He still fell into his old, bad habits and the clear view of GOD seemed just outside of his reasoning grasp because he was only relying on reason[1205]. When Augustine made his faith like a child's[1206], that is, unlimited by human reasoning and full of trust, and took the leap of Faith, suddenly he understood answers to the questions that had so plagued him, and he received the Grace to leave his passions behind. He had gone beyond Reason, and reached the fulfillment of Reason at the same time. He had correctly knocked on the door of the Lord, and the door had been opened. He had taken the Leap, and landed firmly.

Augustine had gone from the dwelling of the Knight of Infinite Resignation, to the doorstep of the Knight of Faith. (According to Kierkegaard, the Knight of Faith has no trouble accepting the leap of faith, and does it often. The Knight of Infinite Resignation can never quite make it; he always accepts the possibility, but can never actually take the leap and land again. We will discuss the meaning of these terms shortly.)

[1203] (Trape', 1986) pg. 99, 105, 161, (Gilson, 1938) pg.16-20
[1204] (Trape', 1986) pg. 98-100, (Gilson, 1938) pg. 8-18
[1205] (Trape', 1986) pg. 99, 105
[1206] (Cavanaugh, 1952) pg. 5, (Shannon, 1999) pg. 84-86, to believe in order to understand, Augustine and Anselm's motto, (Gilson, Reason and Revelation in the Middle Ages, 1938) pg. 16-19, 21, 24, Matthew 18:3, Mark 10:15

Mysteries of Faith

Nothing can completely prepare us or guarantee us the successful taking of the Leap, but we may prepare ourselves nonetheless. Contemplation of the Mysteries of Faith is one way to prime ourselves for the Leap[1207].

Most people think of a mystery as something to be solved scientifically, as if the mystery's only value is in its solution. This is not true for the Mysteries of Faith. These mysteries cannot be "figured out" by logic or human reason, yet they mold our hearts and souls until we are closer to understanding GOD. We do not solve a mystery of Faith, we grow by it. The mystery solves us[1208].

A mystery may not have a solution, for a solution is an ending. But Godly mysteries do not have an ending. Understanding continues on. Understanding can be approached, just as Augustine learned to approach the mysteries that plagued his rational mind. As we think on the mystery, our grasp of the spirit world becomes stronger and sharper. We see and understand things we never could before.

Stranger still, the more we approach understanding, the bigger the mystery gets, and the more there is to understand. We will never come to the end of them, just as we can never come to the end of GOD's love.

A good example of a Mystery of Faith, one that haunted Augustine until his conversion opened his eyes, was the mystery of the Infinity of GOD. At first, the concept of GOD's infinity seems simple. GOD's power and presence go on forever. But, it is impossible to grasp forever or infinity, just as it is impossible to count to forever and come to a finished product. As high as you can go, there is always plus one. Forever doesn't have a numerical value.

Words are too flimsy and two-dimensional for these concepts, let alone the powers of the spirit. These mysteries can only be approached if experience, attitude, and preparation are correct, with Grace added; an occurrence that will fill us with joy and terror at the same time.

We cannot even think properly about forever or infinity. We have finite brains, and they cannot contain forever. But we can use special

---

[1207] (Scupoli, 1945 edition) pg. 152, (Pullen, 1966) pg. 205

[1208] This is one favored saying from Dad, see (Barron, 2008) pg. 61, (Gilson, Reason and Revelation in the Middle Ages, 1938) pg. 18-19

ways of thinking, to help us comprehend a part of it. Thoughts of outer space are a good place to begin.

Think about all the billions of stars, and always another zillion waiting behind these. But that is not all. Those stars have to exist in a space large enough to contain them and all the spaces between these stars; this is the universe.

Then there is the idea that each molecule in our universe, each atom of each star and each planet contains another universe, and in that universe there are untold numbers of molecules that contain their own universes. And those universes have molecules that contain their own universes and so on. That is why it is said, "When you pick a blade of grass, you destroy a universe"[1209].

But our universe then is inside a molecule that might sit in a portion of grass on some impossibly huge world. And that world is only part of a universe that resides in a molecule of a larger universe and so on. These are the universes of the very big and the very small.

Compared to this reality, a human being is a totally tiny, non-existent fly-speck on the toe of existence. The entire human race is just as tiny.

We are not finished yet. How about alternate realities? Let us say each decision one makes affects one's life, in effect creating separate lives, and other universes. In this universe one takes the left turn, in another universe one takes a right turn. Each is a separate reality, each with molecules that are universes and so on.

There's more. There are around five or six billion people making these decisions everyday, every hour, every minute. More alternate realities!

We haven't even discussed time, dimensional space, or the spirit world, yet! We haven't begun measuring the universe!

Remember the "foolish" medieval notion that the Earth is at the center of the universe? In such an infinite cosmos as ours, any place is the center. If you want to make Earth the center, it is just as much the center as any other place. One could also say there is no center. To be a center, there must be limits or sides. If there is none, every place and no place is the center[1210].

[1209] See William Blake's poem *Auguries of Innocence*, Alexander Pope's *Essay on Man*, line 87

[1210] (Lewis, 1970) pg 58, (Gleason, 1966) pg. 34, Pascal, from the <u>Misery of Man without GOD</u>, section 43

Where does GOD fit in all this? GOD "holds all this in HIS hand". GOD keeps all this in HIS mind and makes it work. GOD's mind is infinite and so HE can do this.

If this makes you feel totally unimportant, you're on the right track. Who would or could pay attention to a fly-speck on a fly-speck?

GOD. Even with a fantastically complex mutli-universe to run, GOD takes our lives and souls seriously enough to listen to us. GOD knows of every single blade of grass, every single person, on every single world, around every single star, in every single universe. HE knows them better than they know themselves. HE knows, as the Bible says, "the number of hairs on our heads"[1211]. HE knows, and cherishes all of us and all of creation.

When we consider the overwhelming task of this sort of love, and couple it with the truly personal nature of that love, we realize a part of GOD's incomprehensible and inexplicable love for us. And it makes our own love for HIM grow as well.

Our minds can only bring us to a certain point. From there we have to let go and learn to see with our souls, listen with our spirit. Here, Faith becomes our guide. Not that science and reasoning have no place; many stepping-stones to understanding GOD and HIS nature require them. But at the limit of our own minds[1212], we must trust on GOD to give us the rest of the equation. Each Mystery's correct answer always leads to a better relationship with GOD, and a greater love for HIM.

In the modern world, especially for minds that have constructed their own boundaries against religion, many ignore such Mysteries, or write them off as excuses, incomprehensible as they may seem. How ironic! Perhaps the people who have "liberated" their minds to "anything goes" orgies, see the idea of liberating their souls to the search for GOD as threatening and disturbing. They hide this, even from themselves. The very people that demand to "question everything", never question the things they should.

Even when one has a deep relationship with the Lord, and can grapple with these Mysteries of Faith, there comes a time in almost every saintly or knightly life, when the closeness of GOD can no longer be

---

[1211] Luke 12:7, Matthew 10:30, Luke 21:18

[1212] (Gleason, 1966), Pascal points out how limited we really are in the <u>Misery of Man Without GOD</u>

felt or perceived. A gulf seems to open between the knight and GOD, through no fault of his own, and the man feels utterly alone, even abandoned by GOD. This is called the Dark Night of the Soul. A truly terrifying time, and some have lost their faith in this spiritual wasteland, (although many of these eventually regain their faith). When the Dark Night comes, one knows he is about to take the leap of faith, or strangle in the desert of doubt for ever.

The Dark Night of the Soul

For all Heroes of Faith, there comes a time called the Dark Night of the Soul[1213]. For some, as for Saint Augustine, this Dark Night is the precipice that we spoke of earlier, when all reliance on human logic must be thrown away for a time, and the leap of Faith must occur. For others, perhaps those who did not rely on philosophy and logic as such, it comes at a different time and in a different way. But this dark time must come. It is a period where the soul is put through a particular, intense, terrible suffering, shaking the very foundations of their faith. Every Hero of Faith must go through this dark time, however, no matter whom and no matter how strong.

Some heroes and saints experience it as a strange spiritual solitude, where once they felt intense closeness with GOD. This is perhaps the most terrible of all. Although Jesus Christ was the Son of GOD, He had chosen to withstand the very depth of human suffering, and so even He had to endure the Dark Night. While dying on the cross, surrounded by scorn and ridicule, he quoted the Psalms: "Oh GOD, oh GOD, why have you forsaken me?" GOD was never far from Him, but the sense of GOD's presence had been withdrawn, so that the Son could no longer perceive it[1214].

Strange enough, this temporary separation from GOD is of GOD, sent by GOD as a kind of test[1215], which usually comes right before the union with GOD's Will. It is meant to ultimately strengthen the Faith, by blasting away all crutches, supports, and philosophical short cuts that

---

[1213] (Underhill, 1990) pg. 383
[1214] (Sheen F., 2000) pg. 53, (May, 2004) pg. 146
[1215] (May, 2004) pg. 95, 96

artificially buttress our all-too-human belief[1216]. Even Lancelot's sword can be of no use here. Our Faith must stand alone, unsupported by feelings, or even intellect, traditions, logic, or culture.

In the past, Americans have taken many things for granted that help Faith: books, churches, songs, a tolerant society, a Judeo-Christian culture, perhaps Christian parents and a Christian up-bringing, even theological schools and impressive philosophical reasoning. In an environment like this, it is relatively easy being a Christian, as opposed to a repressive regime like Ancient Rome. But in the Night of Faith, all this is turned on its head, and a hero of Faith must go forward without any such help from surroundings.

In the story of Abraham, the father of Faith, we see something of this. GOD first tells Abraham that he will father a great nation through his son Isaac, and the whole world will be blessed through his son[1217]. This is relatively easy to believe once the child is born. But soon after, GOD demands Abraham to literally kill the child as a burnt offering on top of Mt Moriah! The two utterances of GOD do not mesh or make sense with each other. But, worst of all, the Good Lord is demanding a death of an innocent child! This is completely unlike the honorable and loving GOD that Abraham had come to know. Abraham is faced with the paradox that no intellect, logic, common sense, or moral calculation can solve.

Abraham's mind and heart must have been completely befuddled and defeated as he rises in the morning to take his beloved son to the mountain, the place of sacrifice. Yet he goes. For three days they walk[1218]. Abraham must continue simply by faith, and only with pure faith can he resolve the task. Incredibly, deep within Abraham, he still believes GOD will accomplish everything HE promised. Even though the promise and the demand are mutual exclusive, somehow, even with the death of his son, his son will give rise to a mighty nation and bring great blessing upon the world[1219].

The engine of his Faith drives him along the path, even as his son asks "Father, I see the wood and the knife for the sacrifice. But where is

---

[1216] (May, 2004) pg. 67, 99, 149

[1217] Genesis 17:5

[1218] It is no coincidence that Abraham's journey takes 3 days, the time Christ lies in the tomb

[1219] (Kierkegaard, 1983) pg. 115

the animal to be used[1220]?" Abraham's eyes are blinded with tears, his ears hissing with terror, as he binds his own son and lays him on the pyre. His hands shake, his strength fails him, as he lifts the knife to plunge it into Isaac's heart.

Abraham wills to give up everything he loves, even the common sense of his culture, love of himself, the pleasure of his son's presence, the very love of his son, and the comfort found in his image of GOD, in order to follow his Faith. The knife gleams in the air, shaking slightly. He closes his eyes and prepares to bring the dagger down into the flesh of the son GOD promised to him. "May this sacrifice be acceptable to the Lord," he prays.

Suddenly, GOD says "Stop! Abraham, do not harm the boy!" And Abraham opens his eyes to see a ram with its horns caught in a bush[1221].

Who can understand this story, except as the ultimate test of Faith[1222]? Everything is sacrificed, including the supports of culture, reason, morality, decency, and common sense, to blast clean the pillar of Faith. The pillar stands alone, terrifying and pure.

In a brilliant poem by Wolfram Von Eschenbach, Parzival, the German form of Sir Percival, experiences a similar long, Dark Night of the Soul[1223].

All through his young adulthood, Parzival heeds the advice of his mother, and several old knights at King Arthur's court. But his understanding is terribly imprecise, and while he struggles to fulfill the letter of this advice, he drastically misses the spirit. But, so far, everything comes about as his mother said it would. As long as he follows the word of those he assumes know GOD, Truth, and knightly Honor, all is well with the world.

Until he comes to the Grail Castle, and then everything goes awry. In the castle, he sees a great banquet table set before a king on his throne. While the king was obviously once mighty, he now languishes in great pain. Parzival, still a boy at heart, aches to know what this scene is all about, and even more, wishes to address the king with a simple question,

---

[1220] Abraham answers, "The Lord himself will provide the lamb", which is a prefiguring of Christ, Gen.22:8

[1221] Genesis 22:13

[1222] (Kierkegaard, 1983) pg. 115, 101, 113, 121

[1223] (Hatto, 1980) pg. 414, 235, just like in Chretien de Troyes's story - (Loomis, 1951) pg. 4

"What ails you, my king?" Just a simple question, one that is full of human compassion[1224]. We understand that Parzival would do anything in his power to help the king, since it is his custom to help anyone in distress.

Yet Parzival remembers the advice of the worldly knights at the court: "Never ask questions." No one wants to answer boorish questions that should already be obvious, these worldly knights had assured him. Perhaps he did not want to seem stupid, embarrassed as he was that he seemed the only one ignorant of the answer to his unspoken question. With his naïve spirit against his conscience, Parzival remains silent. Although the mentor knights meant for him to be humble and compassionate[1225], Parzival, in his naiveté, fulfills the letter of the law, but misses all else.

The knight is given lodging for the night, but he can't shake the notion that he has failed somehow. He vows to approach the king again in the morning and find out the source of the monarch's pain. Yet when he awakens and moves about the castle, it is no longer a beautiful estate, but a ruin of age and disuse. The castle is deserted.

Parzival soon discovers that the king was suffering from a wound that could only be cured by the question, "What ails you?" A curse hangs over the king, the castle, and the kingdom itself, and until someone asks the question of compassion, the kingdom and king are doomed to suffer. Now, no matter how he wishes to, he cannot return to the castle again, this time to ask the question and break the spell. Parzival wanders far and wide, but to no avail, for the king and castle have disappeared.

His problem is common: his own understanding of great things failed him. Parzival is confused, then angry. He struggles with himself, and then GOD. How could GOD allow me to err so badly, he demands. How could GOD be so unfair? "I didn't know! I didn't know!" cries Parzival's heart.

He lashes out at GOD, wondering over how a good GOD could allow such things to happen: a tortured king, a knight helpless to aid him. His confusion and anger persist and he sinks into a long tirade against GOD's supposed unfairness, even throwing away his allegiance to GOD for a time. "Wherever, in church or minister, GOD's praise was sung, no eye has seen me since that day. I have cared for naught else but

---

[1224] (Hatto, 1980) pg. 241, Wolfram's *Parzival*
[1225] (Matthews, 1989-1993) pg. 65

fighting. Yes, and I bear great enmity towards GOD, for he has fathered my sorrows and made them mighty. My joy is buried alive. If GOD's power were ready to help, what an anchor my joy would have been! Now it has naught to hold to, grief sucks it down. If my hope is wounded past help, or if it survives the scar wherewith sorrow's sharp crown has branded my knightly prowess, each way I maintain, it is a shame of HIM Who has power to help, if all they say of His help be true, that He helps not me"[1226]? Thus he loses sight of the Grail[1227], and even the Grail castle, all disappearing.

After a long journey, his anger falls away and he meets a holy hermit, who explains what he must do to reach the Grail Castle once again. ". . . how a man should steadfastly serve HIM Who never wearies in giving help to sustain the soul . . . All false ways does HE abhor," Says the Hermit, "Think upon that: He can forsake no man.

Learn to do likewise, be on your guard and see you are true to Him"[1228]. Parzival's mind couldn't grasp the problem, nor his heart feel its way around it, nor his sword arm slash through it. The answer was only the faith to obey GOD through the hermit's words[1229].

Just as GOD provides the ram for the Abraham's sacrifice, GOD, through the Hermit, reveals how Parzival may return to the Grail Castle and cure the king and his kingdom. Finally, we must reach out to GOD, blindly and with humility, hands open to whatever GOD will give. This is the Leap of Faith, and the resolution to the Night of the Soul.

All those who think they know the ways of GOD will be stupefied in the dark night of the Soul. The way will become no way, the path muddled and obscure. The mind cannot go there; the heart cannot feel its way through. Only Faith can shine forth there. "There is no clear way to the hidden GOD"[1230]. All sense will fail, all pre-suppositions not fit. All assumptions are drained and destroyed. The impossibility of Faith laid bare, naked.

All of us, to reach GOD's side and to do GOD's work, must suffer this dark night of faith. It is a terrible obstacle, but it is a wall that can

---

[1226] (Barber, 1985) pg.102, this is his *Arthurian Legends*, in the section of *Parzival*
[1227] (Bailey, 2006) pg. 108-109
[1228] (Barber, 1985) pg.103, this is his *Arthurian Legends*, in the section of *Parzival*
[1229] (Loomis, 1951) pg. 82-87, (Hatto, 1980) pg. 231-255
[1230] (Cummins, 1991), pg.99

be climbed to Heaven. It is a dark pot, hiding a brilliant lamp. It is the shining light of GOD that is so powerful it blinds the unbroken heart. Its pain purifies us, but prepares us for GOD's presence. It is a difficult door, but it can open, and behind it is GOD. As St. John of the Cross said, it is the dark cloud that illuminates the night with its hidden rays[1231].

Here, only the Knight of Faith can stand. If we can stand strong, survive this stripping of all crutches and supports, our faith will shine forth like a star in the darkness, and be the strongest Faith of all.

Different Nights

For each saint and knight, the long dark night of the soul will be different, and will come at different times. Some, as St. Francis and Mother Teresa, will experience this night later in their lives, some, as St. Augustine and St. Ignatius Loyola, will experience it early in their struggle.

What is also confusing about the Dark Night is how it manifests itself within the psyche of each mind, therefore taking on different aspects and terrors. One man may find his struggle of Faith to involve the sacrifice of his son, another the seeming uselessness of his life, another the evils of the world, and another the very worries that surround him.

Thus was the case of Ignatius Loyola. Even after terrible physical pain and suffering, his dark night manifested itself not in the outer world, but within his own mind.

Ignatius's path to sainthood began with his reading of the Lives of the Saints while healing from a terrible leg wound. This injury, contracted from a battle in which his leg was spilt apart by shrapnel, was set on the battlefield and not properly done. His leg had to be broken again, involving intense physical pain. Ignatius withstood it without a word. It was discovered that the leg still hadn't healed properly, and the doctors not only broke his leg again, but even stretched his leg on the rack to make sure it set properly. For the rest of his life, this leg would give him enduring pain, especially as he walked throughout Europe[1232]. For some,

---

[1231] Ibid.
[1232] (Caraman, 1990) pg 25 - 26

this would be enough for them to question GOD's benevolence, but Ignatius only faced it as an inconvenient fact.

But later, as he prepared to become a "knight of GOD" and wonder the world converting people to the light of Christ, he discovered strange worries that constantly pestered him[1233]. These would become an even deeper night for him.

He vowed to roam as a completely poverty-stricken beggar, relying on GOD's providence to save him from famine and death. He decided also to live as his hero St. Honorifico, also known as St. Humphrey: sleeping on the floor, eating nothing but what was absolutely necessary to sustain his body, and taking no care for his physical appearance, similar to Sts. Francis and Dominic. None of this frightened him or stupefied his spirit, and for the first months, he seemed elated to suffer and travel, edifying the world of men.

But he began to wonder if he could keep up the terrible austerities that he had begun. Could he, for the rest of his life, forego the comforts of a normal life, the company of a mate, and the possessions that pepper the world of more materialistic men? Could he, as Honorifico and other saints before, live his entire life defying everything within his selfish self for the greater glory of GOD? Ignatius desperately wanted to say yes to this question, but could not be sure he had the strength to do it[1234]. It seemed a devastatingly and overwhelmingly depressing thought: to work 70 years in pain and hunger, asking nothing in return. (He had come to the length of 70 years because Honorifico had lived in the desert for 70 years, dressed only in his own hair and a breechcloth of leaves).

A second blow to his resolve was a grinding worry that he was somehow not worthy of his mission, and that he had not confessed his sins properly or completely, although he had confessed to Father Chanon for three solid and thoughtful days before his mission had begun[1235]. This worry, obsessive and very destructive to many, is called "Scruples". This perceived weight of sin dragged him down under a suffocating swamp of worry.

Amazingly, these twin thoughts constantly harassed him until he was reduced to thoughts of suicide. Thus, Ignatius's Dark Night had arrived.

[1233] (Caraman, 1990) pg. 41
[1234] (Loyola, 2004) pg. 23, (Caraman, 1990) pg. 38
[1235] (Caraman, 1990) pg. 38

His response was quick and characteristically severe, especially toward his own weakness. He resolved to fast continuously and pray, until he found a solution or until GOD sent him a sign as to how to proceed[1236]. Notable was that he did not ask for a cessation of any physical sufferings, nor did he ask to be set free of his chosen saintly life. He was asking for GOD's direct assistance in this terrible labyrinth of worry.

After about a week, his confessor forced him to stop fasting, since this austerity, compounded by his others, had hammered him to near death. Perhaps the confessor had realized that even Ignatius's love and devotion to austerities was somehow impeding his way to GOD. The desire and love for GOD must stand alone, the pinnacle of our hearts. Still worry and doubt assailed Ignatius, and he continued to pray fervently.

Then one day, he suddenly received illumination, sending his worries to oblivion. He realized now that his focus should be on GOD's greater glory, not pre-occupation with imagined sins and a laundry list of austerities. Serve GOD and fellow man; that was what GOD wanted him to do. He was given amazing insight into great mysteries of faith and for the rest of his life, the peace of GOD filled him[1237] as he gave glory to GOD.

He went on to preach and serve GOD in amazing acts of mercy and kindness to the poor, as well as create an order of priests that would become the "Marines" of the Catholic missionary world. The key of Ignatius's Dark Night was to continue to pray, rely on GOD for assistance, and never to give up.

The Knight of Faith

We, to become Knights of Faith, must revisit Abraham, as Soren Kierkegaard did. In his book, *Fear and Trembling*, Kierkegaard maps out, step by step, how to become the Knight of Faith and face what cannot be faced, endure what cannot be understood, and wrestle with the impossible.

First, we must become Knights of Infinite Resignation. We must understand that to walk with GOD, we must surrender everything that

---

[1236] Ibid. pg. 38
[1237] (Caraman, 1990) pg. 39

we love in the world. This love of worldly things cannot be a timid sort of love, allowing us to give up things easily[1238]. If we give them up easily, it was not a true sacrifice. If we sacrifice something and feel little about it because we felt it an illusion anyway, how is that a real sacrifice? Abraham loved Isaac more than anything else, and not just as a father loves his son. Abraham loved his son as his only son, as a son that took a hundred years to achieve, and as a son who would become the vehicle by which GOD would bless Abraham and the world forever[1239]. But "no sacrifice is too severe when GOD demands it"[1240].

If Abraham had deigned to sacrifice Isaac while giving up hope, resigning to the idea that all his love of GOD and GOD's promise was only dust in the wind, then he would not have been remembered as the Father of Faith. If Abraham became resigned in the knowledge that his lot in life is to suffer for GOD, that GOD requires him to sacrifice everything, and nothing is truly gained by it, than he would simply have despair.

This despairing action, this brutal breaking of all ties to the world, does not demand true Faith, according to Kierkegaard, only resignation[1241]. Abraham, as a true Knight of Faith, went far beyond this! And if we wish to survive the dark night of the Soul with our souls intact, we must do the same.

To go farther than infinite resignation, and step toward true Faith, we must let go of our previous understandings of GOD and goodness. If Abraham had listened to his culture, his wife, his feelings, or even his previous conceptions of what GOD is and what GOD wants, he would have failed in Faith, according to Kierkegaard[1242]. When Wolfram's Parzival listens to the voice of reason, "good taste", and courtly ethics from the mouths of worldly knights and his mother, he loses the Grail and his power to save the fisher king[1243].

[1238] (Kierkegaard, 1983) pg.20

[1239] Ibid. pg. 23

[1240] Ibid. pg.22

[1241] (Kierkegaard, 1983) pg. 35

[1242] (Kierkegaard, 1983) pg. 22, if so, it would have been here that Abraham doubted

[1243] (Hatto, 1980) pg. 226

We must become solitary, separate from society, a stranger[1244] to everything humans see as acceptable, for we have forsaken it in our sacrifice, especially the understanding of our fellows. We have become sojourners in this world. The things other men devote themselves to, we cannot, even the universal good and the culturally praised. "The true knight is always absolute isolation, the spurious knight is sectarian"[1245].

We must, as Abraham did on his journey, retain our focus. There are innumerous distractions in this world, everything trying constantly to take our focus from GOD[1246]. But our love and Focus on GOD must remain within us, regardless of the hopelessness in seeing HIM, and of understanding HIM, and seeing goodness triumph in *this* world[1247]. Humbly, we must approach GOD again with our minds and hearts open and penitent, willing to accept whatever GOD asks, just as Parzival humbles himself to the hermit, and is willing to accept the instructions of the hermit, whatever they might be[1248].

Also, the power of prayer is always essential to navigating the Dark Night. Whether it seems futile or dry, the relationship between GOD and man must be forever revived by continuous prayer[1249]. Fasting can also be an incredibly effective weapon against the despair of the Dark Night, as well as focusing our spiritual energies. Ignatius used both, especially constant prayer, to negotiate through his terrible Dark Night.

Finally, True Faith comes, actually is created, when Abraham not only knows that his son will die, nullifying all of GOD's promises, but believes that all the promises will still come true! We know the end of the story: that Isaac will be spared by GOD, but Abraham, on the road to Mt. Moriah, did not know. He believed anyway. This is not naiveté or the innocence of simple minds speaking, Kierkegaard explains[1250]. On that trip to the mountain, Abraham knew his son was to die, by his own hand, no less; there is no way that Abraham doesn't face the very brutal fact. Yet, Abraham firmly believes, without hesitation, that GOD will make it possible for Isaac to come back and fulfill all the promises

---

[1244] (Bangley, 2007) pg. 25, (Athanasius, 1980) pg. 31-32

[1245] (Kierkegaard, 1983) pg.79

[1246] (Kierkegaard, 1983) pg.43

[1247] Ibid. pg.44

[1248] (Hatto, 1980) pg. 233

[1249] (Bangley, 2007) pg. 15, 25 and (May, 2004) pg. 21

[1250] (Kierkegaard, 1983) pg.47

through the boy's life. The promises will become reality, regardless of what happens! Somehow, in Abraham's faith, he will sacrifice Isaac, and still have Isaac, alive and well[1251]! This is absurd, as Kierkegaard readily admits, but is exactly why it cannot be understood. "By virtue of the absurd, everything that is sacrificed is returned[1252]!"

Easily written on paper. But as we have seen, it is difficult to believe that any of our sufferings will have reward, beyond the sufferings themselves. Who can believe that our love for Honor and Goodness in the world will come to fruition and we will see Honor blossoming across the Globe, when we are surrounded everyday with scum of the earth and evil? True Faith is not simple belief in an afterlife, according to Kierkegaard[1253], but belief that GOD will show HIMSELF as Master in This Life, as well as the Next, and that we will see it with these eyes, one day, even though we die!

Yet, we believe! Christ died to the world, allowing Himself to die as a sacrifice, with full knowledge of a real death, and yet he knew GOD would bring Him back to take possession of the world, which is His by right.

We, as Knights of Faith, die with Christ, as well as rise with Him to take back the world in His name. We die, with full belief that we will never die; we give our lives, with full belief that we will see our lives returned. We sacrifice all, in order to gain all within GOD. Nothing is truly lost, because the world is within GOD, meaning nothing without HIM. Nothing is truly gained but the greatest gift, GOD HIMSELF, who contains all joy and all of creation within HIMSELF. And so, we come to the completion of Faith, past the Dark Night of the Soul.

Some thoughts on Abraham's Dark Night

Two thoughts keep me awake at night when I write about the Dark Night of the Soul. Honestly, I fear Rudyard Kipling's warning: "If you can bear to hear the truth you've spoken twisted by knaves to make a trap for fools, Or watch the things you gave your life to broken, And stoop

---

[1251] Ibid. pg.36

[1252] Ibid. pg.49—This echoes Tertullian, "I believe because it is absurd!"

[1253] Ibid. pg.20

and build 'em up with worn-out tools . . ."[1254]. I know that my writing is no match for the concepts I struggle to place on paper, and thus I worry sometimes over how people will take them. These two thoughts should be carefully considered:

1) Often, people think tests of Faith, as in the Dark Night, occur at the moment of crisis, but in reality, <u>Faith is forged beforehand</u>. Whether it be in GOD's own forge, deep within our souls, or by our exercising the Devices of Providence. With Abraham, the true test of Faith is **not** whether he will sacrifice his son literally on an altar. Both the Knight of Faith and the Knight of Infinite Resignation are capable of terrifying and dizzying sacrifices. Only the Knight of Faith could retain his belief in all the promises about the boy and yet still see him destroyed, though it shatter his heart. A Knight of Infinite Resignation would resign himself to the loss, but not believe the promises.

   This is what separates them, and why only the Knight of Faith can succeed through the Dark Night with his faith intact. Somehow, Abraham, as the first Knight of Faith, possessed that Faith from the beginning.

2) Because we live in this modern world, a modern man, after reading this, may turn to his friend and say: "You see, this crazy religious nut is saying we have to sacrifice our sons". As always, the modern misses the message completely, pointing at my allegorical descriptions in horror, and yet allowing one million abortions a year on the altar of Progressive Rights. No one, certainly not GOD, is saying "slaughter your children". What He is asking is "What is important to you and what do you have true faith in?"

Knights, Christians, and good people sacrifice by placing GOD's importance first, even over beloved families, friends, emotions, desires, and especially the self. Modern man would have us sacrifice others and GOD in favor of the self.

[1254] From Rudyard Kipling's poem called *If*

Faith in Chivalry

Another aspect of Faith very important to the knight is the belief in Chivalry. What is this belief? This is the idea that a man, through help from GOD, can be good, and moral, and honorable. Also, that GOD will help the honorable man, the knight, succeed eventually against evil, even if it is only the evil within his own soul.

The man who makes no error is an impossibility, of course, but too many people believe that no man is capable of anything good, or decent, or honorable at any time! These people believe that the stories one hears from time to time of honorable men are simple fabrications or deceptions. For whatever reason, through bitterness of terrible experiences with the evilness of some men, or even the failures of their own soul, these forlorn people have given up on Chivalry. They have lost their belief in goodness, and this loss can only hurt the cause of Righteousness in the world, as well as in their own lives.

Indeed, the belief in Chivalry is difficult to maintain at times of terrible trial, and can be as difficult as Faith in GOD. These two beliefs are intrinsically connected and one helps the other, and the lack of one diminishes the other[1255]. Ayn Rand's warning is well taken, "Kill Reverence, and you kill the hero in a man"[1256]. If the belief in Chivalry disappears, Faith in a good GOD soon fades, and a man loses the ability to even desire heroism. Even if you can't see the connection between these two faiths, belief in Goodness and Honor cannot be allowed to diminish. Without this desire to be honorable, to be good, all things fall into ruin: "The most important human endeavor is the striving for morality. Only morality can give beauty and dignity to life"[1257]. Without belief in Chivalry, the spirit of Honor, life itself becomes wooden and unreal, and the soul dies. "Mine Honor is my life, both grow in one. Take my Honor from me, and my life is done", Shakespeare said[1258].

Just as every saint must walk the dark night of the soul, so must every knight struggle to keep his faith in Chivalry and Honor. This struggle

---

[1255] (Gautier, 1989) pg. 30, (Lull, 2001) pg. 48, 54, 68

[1256] Ayn Rand places this as the villain's scheme to destroy the soul, in her book, *The Fountainhead*, pg. 669

[1257] From Albert Einstein's *The Human Side*, pg. 95, in a letter to a minister on Nov. 20, 1950

[1258] From Shakespeare's Richard II, Act I, scene I, lines 182-185

comes especially when the knight sees another fail, when he himself fails in a mission, or when the cause of Righteousness seems bleak or unsalvageable.

Another way many people stumble into this loss of faith is when they misunderstand the path of Honor and Chivalry. Even brave and decent people sometimes think that Honor and Chivalry must lead to fame, fortune, gratitude, and acceptance.

These well-meaning people assume that as long as they act honorably, bravely, or gallantly, they will receive a just reward on earth for their strivings and sufferings in the name of Honor. They forget that Honor is its own reward[1259], and thus miss the true way and find themselves on the other, darker path.

Sir Miguel Cervantes found himself on that dark road.

He did not expect it, for he had recently fought in one of the greatest battles of European history, the battle of Lepanto. Lepanto, 1571, was a terrible sea-battle against the European Christian's implacable enemy, the Moslem, and the prize was possession of the shipping routes of the Mediterranean Sea. "No battle was more famous than Malta", said Voltaire[1260], but he meant "except for Lepanto". To be in such a victorious battle against overwhelming odds was great, but to have fought valiantly as Cervantes had[1261], and to have come away terribly wounded in the cause of goodness and Right[1262], that was greater. Cervantes had been shot several times, one blast crippling forever his left hand, but he wore these wounds like badges of honor, calling himself proudly the "Cripple of Lepanto"[1263]. How could Cervantes expect that an even greater battle and a black defeat awaited him?

Cervantes had fought in several other sizable battles against the Saracen, including Navarino in 1572, Tunis in 1573, and La Goletta in 1574, but it was on his way home in 1575 when he encountered his first set-back. While sailing to Madrid with his brother, their ship was

[1259] Attributed to Cicero, Zeno, Ovid and Seneca, see (Stevenson, 1948) pg. 2434, also (James, 2012 (reprinted)) pg. 45
[1260] (House, 2010-2013)
[1261] (The New Encyclopedia Britannica in 30 volumes, Macropedia, volume 3, 1982) pg. 1183
[1262] (Brewer, 1891) pg. 982, this victory released 12,000 Christian slaves held by the Ottomans
[1263] (Konstam, 2003) pg. 81

captured by Barbary pirates and Cervantes taken prisoner. Because he possessed a letter from the King of Spain, the pirates thought him of great importance, and decided to hold him hostage far longer than his brother. A massive ransom was asked, and for five years, through terrible suffering and four unsuccessful escape attempts, Cervantes waited agonizingly for anyone from home to save him, or even remember him.

Finally, a group of priests raised enough money to ransom him and he returned, not as a far-flung hero, but a man of obscurity, in terrible debt (he had to pay the ransom back), without money and with no job to speak of. He had expected a decent post in the government of Spain as a gift of the king, for had he not served his country well, even sacrificing his left hand for Spain and Christian glory? But the king seemed not to remember his name, and only grudgingly threw him a small administrative post as a master throws a scrap to a dog. Even this was a hindrance, for the post was terribly underpaid and ill-staffed. Twice Cervantes was thrown into prison because of "fiscal irregularities" that historians now believe were caused by calculation mistakes, subordinate error, and even a banker running away with the money[1264].

Cervantes sat in the prison in Seville for months, a defeated and broken man surrounded by rats and poverty[1265]. It may have been here that he set out to write a story of a man who, though caught up in a fiery desire to live the life of a knight, becomes totally unhinged by the very knightly stories he wishes to emulate and pursues giants and monsters where only windmills and donkeys exist. The women whom he thinks are beautiful princesses are only prostitutes and dim peasants, and the knights he thinks he encounters are but shop-keepers and barbers. In his bitterness against his own ideals of honor and right, Cervantes made this story a mocking tragedy, where the one man who fights for goodness in the world is a mere laughingstock of the community, incapable of anything but to gallivant around in rusty armor, railing against a world that neither listens to or understands him. He wished to mock Chivalry and tear it down, to crush it as he himself was crushed, as Ayn Rand warned a man might do to destroy Reverence. This story became the first

---

[1264] (The New Encyclopedia Britannica in 30 volumes, Macropedia, volume 3, 1982) pg. 1184

[1265] Ibid.

novel, and the most famous book of Spanish literature: *Don Quixote de la Mancha*.

For three years after that fateful imprisonment, he faced continuous poverty and his futures prospects did not brighten. He continued to write. But Cervantes outdid himself, for, as he wrote about the hero, the saintly but deranged Don Quixote, a strange thing occurred. The more blinded by brilliance and dream the rusty knight grew, the more noble he seemed to become. Was Don Quixote truly insane, or did he see things the way they should be, whilst the people around him suffered from the paralysis of only seeing things the way that they are? Cervantes later wrote, "Too much sanity may be madness. And maddest of all, to see life as it is and not as it should be"[1266]!

As Cervantes continued to write about this strange hero, his faith in Chivalry began to return. As many read the novel, they could not help but admire a man who stands for justice and the Right against overwhelming odds, where even reason and reality are raging against him. When I read the book as one of my first books on knighthood, I found myself wishing to be like Don Quixote, for no one else in the story comes close to his brilliance and honor. Only this man is willing to fight for Truth with all his might, although he cannot see reality, fight for the nobleness of love with all his heart, though no one around him is worthy of love, strive for the honor in all things, though the world is a shameful farce! Yet, Don Quixote is covered with glory, even as the world mocks him, because he fights for Honor, finding its greatest and only reward within it. It is these interpretations of Don Quixote that drove Dale Wasserman to rewrite the epic into a play known as *Man from La Mancha*, celebrating Don Quixote's transforming power of goodness and chivalry.

"Don Quixote is an ancient character who is still relevant in today's time and situations—who has generated fascination across centuries and countries. It establishes the end of the period of literature based on realism and stands for everything that is gentle, pure and gallant," Said Javier Parrondo, cultural counselor of the embassy of Spain in 2005[1267].

[1266] "Essays on the periphery of the Quixote" (1991) by Anthony George Lo Ré; page: 112

[1267] Quote by BANASREE PURKAYASTHA, Financial Express, July 3, 2005), (Ellis, 1915) pg. 243

Finally, as if led by his own creation, Sir Miguel Cervantes leaves his bitterness behind, and once again embraces GOD's goodness and what seems through experience to be impossible[1268]. "I know how to write," He said, "But Don Quixote knows how to live."[1269]

Cervantes, in his dark cell, could not have guessed what his book would mean to the world, and how he would become famous the world over not only for writing the first novel, but for giving the world an implacable and noble character beloved for generations. He watched his selfish and worldly dreams of personal honor die, only to receive the wealth and wisdom of True Honor from the ashes.

Through his life and in his writing, Cervantes showed that life rarely flows exactly as it is portrayed in romantic knightly stories. Indeed, life is a struggle, not only to keep life and limb, but also to keep any semblance of humanity, Honor, or soul. Constantly and constantly, life simply keeps coming, with a seemingly infinite number of variations, seeming to mock Chivalry and everything else. "Until Death, it is all life". It is easy to lose hold of values, and become lost in a sea of broken hopes and ideals. In a world such as ours, it is easy to lose faith in Chivalry.

While in this dark night, hold on to belief and Chivalry, even though it seems to be empty, as if one is just "going through the motions". Pray even though the prayers feel dry and withered. Loss of Chivalry and Honor is terrible and cannot be allowed to happen within you. For a knight, Honor and Chivalry through GOD is the meaning of life. A man who has lost meaning in life is not waiting for death; he is dead[1270]. But is there a resurrection? Cervantes and Don Quixote proved there is.

The Knight of Faith and GOD's Gifts

I have met many people lately who have decided to sacrifice in pursuit of Faith. But, I was disturbed to find, they had decided to sacrifice GOD's gifts to them, not in the way of the Knight of Faith, but in the way of the Knight of Infinite Resignation.

[1268] (The New Encyclopedia Britannica in 30 volumes, Macropedia, volume 3, 1982) pg. 1185

[1269] Attributed to Cervantes, in his *Don Quixote*, Vol.2

[1270] A man without honor is worse than dead—Miguel de Cervantes, *Don Quixote*, Vol.2, part 1, chapter 33

One woman told me she loved jewelry, but she told me she was to throw away her jewelry business in order to "follow GOD". A great Karate master was going to stop teaching karate because he felt he had to spend more time with his family and church. Another man told me that since he had become a born-again Christian, he was going to give away his much-beloved sword collection.

These "sacrifices" are commendable, but misguided. Did Abraham go to Mount Moriah and stab his son to death, ignoring GOD's plea to spare him? Did Percival, once he lost the Fisher King's castle, give up his pursuit of the Grail? Did Saint Francis give up his possessions and inheritance to go sulk in a cave and do nothing? Did GOD give us great gifts and desires to simply burn them up on the altar, throw them away, or discard them?

People often think that to follow GOD is to destroy everything else that they love. This is partially true, and especially when the things they love are contrary to GOD or impede the pursuit of GOD's Grace. But when GOD gives us a gift, as in an appreciation for beautiful things, a great talent, or a unique possession, it is not only discourteous, but a sin as well to destroy it wantonly and without purpose.

GOD gives us a gift to use it, not for our petty or selfish needs, but for GOD and HIS greater purpose. It would be the height of folly, and a sin, to destroy the gift without using it in GOD's honor.

The knight of faith, as we have seen, sacrifices to GOD with the complete assurance that he will again receive the gift, only this time within GOD HIMSELF. Abraham raised the knife with the perfect intention of sacrificing his beloved son, but with the complete faith that GOD would restore his son, somehow. Why? Not because of the son himself, or even because of the Abraham's love for the son, but because the son was a gift from GOD. Abraham's son was not only for Abraham, but for the salvation of the world. From Abraham's son would come Israel, and from the line of Israel would come Christ. In Abraham's intended sacrifice of his son, he moves towards and is willing to sacrifice the whole world, and in GOD giving back his son, the whole world would bow in wonder and reverence at the act of Faith, calling Abraham the Father of Faith. Because of one man's willingness to sacrifice, GOD would give Christ as a gift to the world, and the sacrifice of Christ would save the world. Abraham's son emerging unscathed would prove the benevolence of GOD to the world, and Christ returning to life would guarantee our own eternal life.

GOD gives the gift of the appreciation of Jewelry so that the woman can somehow use it, not for herself, but for GOD's purpose. The sacrifice might be that she refuses to sell pagan or secular things, only choosing GODly shapes, and giving the money to the poor and charities. The Karate master may teach physical and mental discipline to his students, accentuating the positive elements of martial arts, instead of using tournaments and prestige to enhance his own image or the worship of power. Yes it will cost much time, but he will give many people a lifestyle that shows morality in the light of strength. The swordsman may sell most of his swords and give the money to the poor, but keep one sword, the truest, keenest, and straightest, as an example of the life of an honorable man: true, keen, and straight in deed and thought. When he and his children look upon the sword or practice with it, they may understand spiritual truths in a tangible way, gaining inspiration to reflect the spirit of the sword of Christ in their lives.

Through these actions, they sacrifice the worldly and material effects of GOD's gifts, while using the gifts to bring glory to GOD. They have given the gift back to GOD, only to receive them again within GOD.

Using GOD's gifts with wisdom, and through HIM, can eventually save the entirety of Creation.

Brutalized Faith—What is Faith really for?

A modern mantra shouts "Believe in yourself!"

Is "self" one's emotions and desires? If so, I know I cannot trust "self"[1271]. Discovering a diary from my former wife showed me how much she believed in her "love" for me at the time of the diary. A few years after the diary was written, she betrayed me in the worldly way. I am left knowing that my trust in her was ill-founded, and the trust she had placed in her feelings for me also proved foolish. When I look at the ragged hole in my heart caused by the betrayal, and see the dead love there, I know the trust I placed in my own feelings was unwise. How

---

[1271] (Scupoli, 1945 edition) pg. 7-8

many of us can remember when we were so certain of our "love" for another, and then later that "love" fell apart? Obviously, even strong emotions cannot be trusted or believed in.

Does this mean we cannot believe in love itself (another modern mantra)? The only human love I can believe in is Chivalrous Love, which is not based on emotion, but the concept of duty and Honor. True love is not emotion, but discipline. How many modern people share that concept? How many modern men even understand the words, let alone practice them? How many modern women are self-aware enough to question their actions on a day-to-day basis even to recognize loyalty or betrayal?

And what of other "trusts"? Can we always trust the leaders of our countries? The country I have the most trust and respect for elected a leader that could not even be loyal to his wife, let alone loyal to the Constitution or even the common welfare of the nation's members.

And the culture and beliefs of this country? I used to be able to walk among children and see some form of innocence and trust. Now, thanks to a flood of irresponsible media, pornography, foolish laws, and mindless parents, the children of this country have become slavish materialists who can't even understand the language of their fore-fathers, let alone the culture or morays of their own nation. These creatures will go on to rework the very face and thinking of the nation I used to recognize.

Supposedly moral organizations, set up to defend the vestiges of concepts of Justice and Fairness, as in the United Nations, are simply mobs of sweet-speaking amoralists, attempting to spread idiotic laws that further their own ends, and the ends of weird sociologists who refuse the meaning of Truth. If an organization does not believe in the existence of objective truth, how can that organization be trusted? Trust, fairness, and justice have no final meaning in minds without Truth.

Only GOD has this Truth. Therefore I place my trust in HIM. This is the final goal of Faith, to place it in something that is worthwhile and full of Truth. I cannot trust my feelings or the feelings of others, nor leaders, nor cultures, nor organizations, if they do not reflect GOD and Truth.

Joan of Arc did not fulfill her mission by believing in herself; Saint Augustine did not become a Father of the Church by leaning on his own plans or desires; and neither Noah nor Abraham, nor Sir Cervantes achieved anything by placing faith in this world. Only by placing their faith in GOD and Honor did they find victory.

Faith in GOD and Truth is the only Faith worthwhile. And to act on that Faith is a good definition of Honor.

Why have Faith?

A man of honest temperament and open heart will find it difficult to have faith in anything on this earth. So why believe in the ethereal, otherworldly, and invisible GOD?

A knight has faith in GOD for the same reason a mathematician has faith in 2+2=4. It is an obvious truth, at least for the knight and the mathematician. GOD and HIS grace seem to me as reasonable as math and logic. One might as well ask me if I believe my parents will be waiting for me when I come to visit. Yes, because I love them and they love me. This is why I have faith, for GOD loves me, and the entire human race. Every time I have depended on HIM, He has come through. It is a relationship, this faith, between two rational beings, one of course being infinite. How can I turn my back on Him now, when He has never turned His back on me? And, in the future, if it seems GOD has abandoned me, I know in my heart HE has not, it is only my perceptions that have strayed.

Then there is the "belief in an after-life" argument. Atheists always tell me that religious people have faith in GOD because of a wish to go to a paradise or Heaven after death. I always chuckle at this; first because it seems strange that an atheist would tell me why I do the religious things I do, without understanding religion or me, and second, because a paradise after death is only one aspect of the giant panorama that is true Christianity.

Another argument for the existence of faith often involves morals and ethics. Without faith in some supreme being, morality tends to wane. Of course, without a supreme good GOD, morality seems a construct of finite minds like yours and mine, in fact simply the creation of ordinary humans. The only real reason to follow a morality constructed by ordinary humans is when it is instigated by brutal force. Such a society, based on morality as only a construct of humanity has been tried at least 5 times in the last two centuries: Nazi Germany, Stalin's Soviet Union, Mao Tse-Tung's China, Mexico's 1920 Revolution, and the French Revolution.

All of these ended in immense bloodshed on an untold scale unheard of until our Modern, "more enlightened", times. Nazi Germany killed

20 million of its own people, Stalinist Russia and Mao's China over a hundred million. This was not in wars, mind you, but in concentrated attacks on political enemies within the country, or to force people to follow the humanly created government. A regime not informed by the Judeo-Christian ethic, or some form of otherworldly conscience, becomes a true Terror, as the French Revolution did.

Imagine the culmination of human reason without revelation, a bunch of wind-torn men and women screaming around a guillotine, chopping the heads off their enemies, and then their former friends and confidants, and finally everyone. Compare this to the culmination of Christianity, a quiet seat at the Last Supper. And what a host!

There is some weight to the need for the Judeo-Christian belief to keep humanity from becoming inhuman on a grand scale. Even the more placid governments, leaving their religious roots and traditions behind as each generation grows more stupefied and indolent, see themselves wasting away. Europe has less than a hundred years to live, and the streets of Chicago and Detroit carry the blood of a continuous war of the nation's youth against itself. But even this is to miss the point.

True Faith is not to gain Heaven or even a political paradise on earth, but to be friends with GOD, and even to fulfill our humanity, which is deeply connected to the One who made humanity. Real Faith is a relationship with GOD, such faith of true knights and saints, and can't be only to reach Heaven or build a paradise, because those with true faith are already experiencing the Kingdom of Heaven right now—death being simply the gateway to a deeper understanding of that kingdom[1272]. And to force others to partake in a paradise on earth would be impossible, for it can only be felt in the soul of the person open to such a relationship. A knight believes and serves GOD first, and lets the flight to paradise take care of itself.

"Thou hast formed us for Thyself, and our hearts are restless till they find rest in Thee"[1273].

"Question: What is the chief Goal of Man? Answer: Man's chief Goal is to glorify GOD and enjoy Him forever"[1274].

[1272] (France, 1997) pg. 23

[1273] (Augustine, 1961) pg. 21, *Confessions*, bk 1

[1274] (Tozer, 1948) ch. 3, question taken from the *Shorter Catechism*

But even with this relationship with GOD, faith can be difficult at times, even impossible. At these times, whether in the Valley of the Shadow of Death, or in deepest despair and depression, remember those who came before you on this road of Faith.

Faith 'til the End

As Christians, when we read about the events surrounding the Last Supper and the Passion, they do not seem very remarkable to us because we have grown up listening to them. But if we place ourselves in the shoes of the Disciples, it would seem very different.

Friday's night and Saturday's dawn came with great mourning, lamentation, utter confusion, and despair. The man whom the Disciples thought would save the world and defeat evil had been, himself, dragged down and defeated, literally nailed to an ignoble cross, the instrument of destruction for criminals and bottom-feeders

Some might have expected Christ to perform some miracle from the cross, perhaps an amazing display of righteous salvation or a calling down of Heavenly power. But nothing of the kind happened. Christ bled, suffered, cried out, and died. How could there be any hope left now? And it did not help to remember that Christ had said this event would come, nor did it bring consolation to think that their journey of three years had lead to this moment. All the miracles, tribulations, struggles, and great speeches had been for nothing, it seemed. Judas had the added knowledge that he betrayed Christ to the trial, and Peter scorned himself bitterly for having denied even knowing Christ three times. The disciples huddled together and wept, afraid to even leave their hideout.

Yes, afraid—terrified. Terrified that they would be next to be crucified. The Pharisees and leaders of the Sanhedrin still looked for the rest of Jesus' followers, to finish the job and crush this fledging religion once and for all.

All was lost. All was darkness and despair. How could the tiny spark of Faith stay alive in view of the crucified Lord? The Dark Night for the Disciples had arrived.

There were, as there are today, two responses. Judas showed his response by hanging himself in the Potter's field[1275].

Peter sat in the dark, weeping. Could the tiniest sparks of Faith still burn within him, absurd as it was, so small and so ridiculous that he dare not say a word to his fellow Disciples? He had remembered Christ's words, but did he still cling to them, even now, though they seemed dim, far away, and without weight?

On Sunday morning, the Disciples were so afraid they almost didn't answer when there came a knock on the door. Mary Magdalene, Mary mother of James, and another woman had been to the tomb of Jesus. They nearly shouted as they said the stone had been rolled away and two people stood within the tomb, and the two seemed to burn with a Heavenly light.

"And they said: Why do you look for the living among the dead?" Mary reported. "They said that the Master is alive!"

"That makes no sense." Some of the Disciples said. "The Master is dead. You saw him crucified. What is wrong with you?"

The women were hushed up and sent away. No report from half-hysterical women could shake the finality of certainty within the Disciples. They all settled back into their weeping and hiding.

Except for Peter. He slipped away and ran to the tomb[1276]. Trembling, he bent down to see what something within him knew he would see.

The impossible had taken place. The absurd had happened. Just as Noah believed in GOD's warning without a rain cloud in the sky, just as Joan of Arc trusted GOD's word when all around her thought it lost, just as Saint Augustine relied on GOD's plan even in the face of enemy hordes, just as all of their faith had been justified, Peter's faith had found vindication. Jesus Christ had risen in Glory from the dead.

[1275] Matt. 27:5, Acts 1:18
[1276] Luke 24:12, for the whole story see John 20, Luke 20, Mark 16:3, Matthew 27

THE FIFTH PILLAR OF HONOR

OBEDIENCE

Love and serve the Lord with all your heart, all your
soul, all your mind, and all your strength.
> —Mark 12:30, Luke 10:27, Deut. 6:5

One GOD, one law, one element,
And one far-off divine event,
To which the whole creation moves.
> —Alfred, Lord Tennyson, *The Two Voices*

Listen to my song . . . . You will learn how to suffer here
below to accomplish the law of GOD; that law which all
honest men obey. Essanplir la loi Deu.
> —Leon Gautier, *Chivalry* pg. 27

Now this is the Law of the Jungle—as old and as true
As the sky
And the Wolf that shall keep it may prosper, but the
Wolf that shall break it must die.
> —Rudyard Kipling, from *The Law of the Jungle*

Where law ends, Tyranny begins.
> —William Pitt, *Speech on the Case of Wilkes*,
> Jan. 9, 1770

To live without duties is obscene.
> —Ralph Waldo Emerson, from his lectures

Liberty means responsibility. That is why most men dread it.

—George Bernard Shaw, from *Man and Superman*

To the king, one must give his possessions and his life; but Honour is a possession of the soul, and the soul is only GOD's.

—Pedro Calderon de La Barca,
The Mayor of Zalamea, 1st day

Obedience

Obedience is a word accursed in today's society. The feminists tell me how horrible and unacceptable it is to obey their husbands. The atheists tell me how unintelligible it is to obey religious leaders. Teenagers tell me how degrading it is to obey their parents and teachers. When I asked them about obedience to GOD, the teenagers see a Heavenly parent, the atheists see a holy bureaucrat, and the feminists see a celestial patriarch. They shudder with distaste. And rules? Especially the dictates of Chivalry, I am told, are too hard to follow, or too foolish to understand. Thus it is unthinkable for the modern person to be obedient to anything.

What the modern person sees as degradation, the knight saw as a measure of loyalty and Honor. They strove to follow the third pillar of Christ's life: Obedience. In the tradition of St. Joan, St. Louis, Sir Ramon Lull, and so many other knights and saints, a true knight dedicates his life to the obedience of GOD's law. The origin of the word "knight" was the Old English "cniht", which simply means "servant"[1277], similar to the Japanese word, "Samurai", which means "to serve".

But what does it mean to have Obedience? Obedience is similar to loyalty; yet as loyalty can be to a king, country, or deity, obedience is deference paid to a law, code, or rule, uttered by these authorities. The knight's loyalty is to GOD and the Code of Honor established to glorify GOD, and thus the knight obeys the law of GOD and the Code of Honor[1278] as if they were one and the same.

[1277] (Barber, 1995) pg. 22, (Coss, 1996) pg. 13
[1278] John 14:15 and (Gautier, 1989) pg. 26, 27, 29-30,

Knightly Obedience does not detract from maintaining individualism or self-rule, it is simply the decision, backed by the stern self-will, to be authentic, truth-seeking, and truly in touch with GOD. If one loves GOD, one will follow HIS statutes and obey HIS commands[1279]. If one loves the Truth, he will search for Truth and follow it when he finds it.

The knight's obedience finds its highest level in his obeying the will of GOD. This is usually illuminated by the Code of Honor, but can have other manifestations and duties. A knight may also have obedience to a king, country, and host while maintaining loyalty to friend, or wife, and, although these are at a lower level than his obedience to GOD and the Code, the knight considers these other duties as considerably important, higher than his own life and limb.

In this chapter, we will explore all the knight's obediences, and the codes from around the world that were created to list such duties. We will also explore the hierarchy that a knight has for his observances, so that no duty may impede the next higher observance, and that no demand may overshadow his duty to GOD[1280].

Sir Ramon Lull and the Mission of Obedience

In many ways, Sir Ramon Lull reflected the modern mind-set toward Obedience. He was extremely stubborn and truly obstinate when it came to considering opinions that did not match his own. Indeed, he possessed a myopic mind, driven and determined, completely self-assured of its own reasoning, ability, and mental prowess[1281]. (As we shall see, he was well justified in this belief).

Only one thing separated him from his modern doppleganger: when GOD called him to an impossible task, Ramon obeyed. And this made all the difference.

It was the height of the Middle Ages, circa AD 1260.

[1279] Ibid. and 1 John 5:3, 1 John 2:5, Deut, 11:13, Deut 11:1, Deut 30:16, Joshua 22:5

[1280] (Gautier, 1989) pg. 61

[1281] (Zwemer, 1902) pg. 24-25, the most popular poet of his time in Spain, possible founder of Catalonian poetry

In his twenties and as a courtier under King James of Spain, Ramon engaged in many of the indulgences of contemporary court life, including the chasing of women not his wife[1282]. Even then, however, he had felt a strange dissatisfaction with this flippant life-style, a thirst for something distinctly detached from the worldly life he had found himself sunk in[1283]. A voice decidedly otherworldly called him beyond the vacant princes, heads of state, arrogant lords, and decadent women that surrounded him[1284].

Perhaps this is because a man who was dubbed a knight cannot completely escape the Chivalrous impulse that should be within every heart. One night, while composing a poem to a mistress, a vision came to him of Christ on the Cross, completely real and bloody, three different times[1285], Christ's eyes regarding him with plaintive disapproval[1286]. Ramon found himself burning to serve GOD for some higher purpose, although a purpose he could not at the time guess at. His chivalrous soul burned for a holy mission beyond the customs of the time and he knew GOD wished him to use his knightly skill, determination, and great courage for something[1287]. But what? What did GOD wish him to do?

Ramon made arrangements for his wife and family to be taken care of as if he himself were dead, and became a tertiary of St. Francis. This involved him to have largesse in a flamboyant way that must have pleased him as a knight: he gave away everything he owned. Heroic as such an act might have been, Ramon felt that GOD had called him for something more than even this renouncement.

One bright day he climbed a hill in Majorca. It is a familiar scene in Biblical history: a man, climbing to a high place, to ask direction and illumination from GOD. Moses, Abraham, Elijah, and many other great and holy men have done this. And now a knight would follow in their footsteps. He closed his eyes, opened his mind and heart, and waited for GOD to show him the next step.

And it came to him, as bright and big as the sky. He saw the whole shining world before him, and from this he gathered that all the world

---

[1282] (Ellsburg, 2001) pg. 384, (Barber, 1995) pg. 135

[1283] (Zwemer, 1902) pg. 25-26

[1284] (Barber, 1995) pg. 135

[1285] (Zwemer, 1902) pg.41

[1286] (Barclay, 1975) pg. 82, Letter to the Corinthians edition

[1287] (Daniel-Rops, 2002) pg. 47

had not yet been evangelized[1288]. Far from it. The Moslems especially had not heard sufficiently the word of Christ. His mission was to spread the gospel to the most anti-Christian people in the world, the Islamists[1289], just as St. Francis had tried to do some years earlier. Whole countries full of often violent people, fresh from two hundred years of wars with Christians and still wary or down-right militant against the Christian faith. He envisioned a new crusade, but using reason and revelation, instead of the sword. St. Francis himself had nearly died several times in the attempt, and could point to very little finally accomplished among the Moslems[1290]. How could Ramon hope for any greater success?

It did not matter. GOD had showed him the mission, and Ramon readied himself. As Francis before him, Ramon vowed himself a Knight of GOD, obedient to the end.

He prepared himself, as all knights should, with familiarizing himself with the "enemy"[1291]. He spent ten years learning Islamic language like a native, and studying the philosophy and ins and outs of Islam so well that he could argue into a corner any imam that dare challenge him to a verbal duel[1292].

He did not presume that GOD meant for him to do all this alone. Ramon set up a school for missionaries at Miramar, one of the first of its kind: a school expressly dedicated to train men to convert foreign countries, using theological argument, logical debate, and intellectual as well as faithful ability[1293]. Several times, Ramon discussed his vision of armies of missionaries with the Pope and the Spanish king, but both were more concerned with conversions closer to home, rather than half-way around the world. They helped with advice and funds, but Ramon realized that if he was to actually follow through with GOD's will for him, he would be on his own. It was one man against the entire Moslem world.

Finally he was ready for the first attempt. He had himself taken to Tunisia where he preached in the streets and discussed Christ with

---

[1288] (Daniel-Rops, 2002) pg. 49
[1289] (Zwemer, 1902) pg. 40, 41
[1290] (Spoto, 2002) pg. 161
[1291] (Zwemer, 1902) pg. 38-39
[1292] (Daniel-Rops, 2002) pg. 46
[1293] (Zwemer, 1902) pg.40

anyone who would listen, even sometimes in Moslem theological schools themselves[1294]. At first, many people listened to this obviously holy and honorable man, but when his words turned to the abandonment of Mohammed and the worship of Christ Jesus, the Moslems gasped and grumbled against him.

It is not that Moslems do not recognize Christ as a prophet, but they consider it blasphemy to say that Christ is greater than Mohammed, and they consider it doubly sacrilegious to say that GOD has a son. Lull's Christian preaching was alone enough to enrage the average Moslem, but as if that was not riotous enough, he preached Christ's sovereignty and GOD-hood in ways that made perfect, logical sense to the Moslem mind, for he had studied their ways of thinking. This was too much for many Moslems, and they came after him with threats of imprisonment and death.

One morning as he preached, he was hustled off the streets and thrown in chains, then tried in an Arab court for blasphemy, and sentenced to death quickly. As he waited in the damp, dark cell for his final minutes, he wondered if his martyrdom had come too easily. Then a guard rushed him outside, whipped him soundly, and threw him on a ship for Majorca, dripping blood and sweat. A prominent Tunisian citizen who had heard him preach had pulled strings to save his life.

Others might have been relieved that they had escaped alive. But the mission was not to escape. The mission was to evangelize. Ramon, determined and even cheerful, with knightly courage and fortitude, waited for nightfall, and dropped over the side of the ship. Still bleeding and stinging from a thousand cuts, he swam back to Tunisia to try again[1295].

He would return again and again to various parts of the Moslem world, spending 38 years enduring scorn and conflict for his obedience to GOD. He would be thrown into prison again, only to write still another book arguing against Islam, then to be kicked out of another country, on ships in storms where he lost everything to return again, then again to be kicked out, beaten, or threatened with more imprisonments, all to spread the word of the Gospels to the unwilling ears of the Moslems.

[1294] (Daniel-Rops, 2002) pg. 54
[1295] (Daniel-Rops, 2002) pg. 55

Finally, when he was almost 78, he climbed aboard another ship for what he knew would be his last attempt. This time, he quested to the far-flung coast of Africa, to the very lands of St. Augustine, where six centuries before, the Moslems had swept through and conquered. It was a good place to make a last stand. He smiled and clenched his fist.

Amazingly, he was able to preach for a full year, in the streets[1296] and without protection from the elements or the scorn of crowds. Finally, a mob of Arabs, incensed by the bravery of this old man, picked up stones and beat him in the center of the street, leaving him for dead. Sailors found him and tended his wounds, and he came to consciousness when the ship was already at sea. They meant to bring him home, but he died of his wounds, even as Majorca came into view[1297].

Sir Ramon Lull would have wanted it this way: to die, not in the safety of home, but in pursuit of the most glorious mission, the most shining obedience.

Some question the point of this obedient mission. Why would GOD send Ramon Lull on such a quest and not guarantee his success? This is a misunderstanding of the nature of Ramon's work. Every soul has the responsibility to accept or reject the Gospel; Ramon's task was simply to give as many Moslems as possible that definite opportunity. He spent more than half his life in this beautiful dedication. His mission to make the Gospel heard was a success; it only remains for the Moslem world to respond.

The First Obedience

Sir Lull is an example of the first and most important obedience a knight or a saint has: Obedience to GOD and HIS laws.

Sir Ramon Lull was obedient to GOD by following what he took to be a direct order from GOD HIMSELF. Most people do not have this sudden divine illumination, but must discover GOD's laws and GOD's will by a more mundane route, if one could call it "mundane".

[1296] Ibid. pg. 57
[1297] Ibid. pg. 58

This route includes the study of scripture, which focuses on the Ten Commandments, as well as the Golden Rule.

The Old Testament heroes, Noah, Abraham, Moses, Joshua, David, Solomon, and the rest, continuously and emphatically stress the importance of Obedience to GOD by following the Ten Commandments, and GOD's direct commands to them, in the face of unpopularity, terrible trial by fire, ostracism, persecution, and the wrath of pagan nations. Daniel's famous ordeal of the Lion's Den, and the literal trial by fire of Shadrach, Meshach, and Abednego, come about because of their superhuman obedience to GOD's requirements, in this case the ironclad law of the First Commandment, worshipping the one True GOD alone. [As a whole, when the Hebrew people and their leaders were obedient and loyal to GOD, they succeeded in everything; when they strayed from GOD and the truth, they faltered and became enslaved. Joshua's meticulous observance of GOD's instructions as to Jericho is the true reason why Jericho falls to the Hebrews. The wandering in the desert, the destruction of Sodom, and the petrifying of Lot's wife, stem from disobedience to GOD's express requests[1298].]

The New Testament, John the Baptist, Peter, Paul, Stephen and the rest, emphasize obedience to GOD's divine law in the midst of personal sacrifice, pain of death, and torture. The GOD-HERO, Christ Jesus, walks forth from the New Testament as the physical embodiment of the willing Obedience, even in the shadow of the brutal Cross. Christ is not only a teacher and master of the Law of Moses, but is GOD's law itself[1299].

In the first centuries after the New Testament, as the world shuddered in the death throws of the pagan Rome and the birth-pains of the fledgling Church, Christians continuously proved their holy obedience against the horror of state-organized persecution. These Christians continuously butted heads against state-sanctioned sin, refusing to sacrifice to idols, to murder in the Gladiator games, to share wives or husbands, to look greedily on the possessions of others or the possessions of other nations. They refused to fight for twisted ideals in the military, or to betray their god-fearing parents to the authorities, honoring them as much as possible. And they struggled to be ever faithful to the letter and spirit of the Scriptures, sacrificing their bodies to defend

---

[1298] Genesis 19:24-26, Exodus 14:3, Deut. 29:23, Revelations 14:10
[1299] (Rev. A.J. Maas, 1952) pg. 496, (Aquinas, 2002) pg. 39

their faith, the teachings of Christ, and even the physical parchment of the Holy Writ[1300].

In their pursuit of loyalty to GOD and purity within HIS law, followers of Christ (Like St. Paul, Justin Martyr, Ignatius, and Polycarp) developed the discipline of the greatest athletes, the most powerful ascetics, with the self-control, interior training, and inner power resembling the strongest competitors in the Olympic Arena[1301]. As a contender in the games challenges himself and his opponent in grueling contests, the Christian Athlete faced down the lion's jaws and every sort of agony "as being a perfect athlete [in the Christian life]: where the labour is great, the gain is all the more"[1302].

As the Early Christian Athlete became the Medieval Christian Warrior, knights and heroes continued recognizing and studiously honoring the demands of Obedience to GOD[1303]. "Be watchful, possessing a sleepless spirit. Speak to every man separately, as GOD enables you . . . . Be sober as an athlete of GOD: the prize set before you is immortality and eternal life . . . Please Him under whom you fight, and from whom you receive your wages. Let none of you be found a deserter. Let your baptism endure as your arms; your faith as your helmet; your love as your spear; your patience as a complete panoply[1304].

Knights and kings traveled on Crusade to free the Holy Land from the grip of Moslem robbers, sparking the rise of the Templar and Hospitaller orders. These orders of knighthood not only defended the newly Christianized Jerusalem and surrounding kingdoms, but constructed massive hospitals and other charitable organizations, some caring for and feeding 2000 poor and pilgrims a day, honoring Christ's command to "care for His flock". These knights, feared and respected by their Moslem enemies, lived as warrior-monks, swearing poverty, chastity, and obedience to GOD and the Pope alone.

When the Middle Ages came to a close and St. Ignatius of Loyola instituted the Jesuit order of Priests, they continued in this stalwart tradition, traveling over the whole world as missionaries and spiritual

---

[1300] (Ricciotti, 1992) pg. 124-125
[1301] (Donaldson, 2009), (Nyssa, 2010), (Talbot, 2005) pg. 20, 2Timothy 2:5, 1 Corinthians 9:27, and 9:25
[1302] (Antioch, 1885, 2009) ch.1
[1303] (Gautier, 1989) pg. 26, 29, 30
[1304] (Antioch, 1885, 2009), ch. 1, 2 and 6 from St. Ignatius of Antioch Epistles

Marines of the Catholic Church. Where others feared to tread, they went gladly, even to the farthest reaches of the Earth, obeying Christ's great request, to preach to all nations[1305].

From the beginning, a knight's strength, courage, and faith were continuously tested, hardened, increased, and sharpened by single-minded obsession and focus on obedience to the Everlasting GOD, reflected in a most sublime and all-encompassing list of rules called simply the Code of Chivalry. To obey the code of Chivalry is to obey GOD[1306].

Such an overwhelming importance placed on laws and commandments may seem strange to many today. Modern Christians place much importance on Faith, sometimes forgetting how much Faith is proved and strengthened by works and obedience. True Faith and Obedience cannot be separated and remain intact.

The following list of rules, known as the Code of Chivalry, might seem even stranger to a modern Christian. What use have we, they might say, for such an old code? Remember that the Ten Commandments itself is also an old "Code", a simple list of rules reflecting the Laws of GOD.

The Demands of Chivalry: Obedience to the Code

Chivalry from around the world may belong to different religions, but every Chivalry obeys a code, or list of rules.

Every great man instinctively knows there are rules that he must discipline himself by, rules that will help him and keep him in good stead, even make him a leader among leaders. "Our first president was in many ways an ordinary man who, though singular self-discipline, rose to greatness. But his progress was no accident. As biographer Richard Brookhiser explains, "Washington was fastidious about hewing to a strict code of conduct, courtesy, and honor. Clearly, it was this deliberate, disciplined way of approaching life's difficulties that vaulted Washington ahead of his luminous peers—intellectual giants like Jefferson, Franklin, and Hamilton—and into a position of leadership" [1307].

[1305] The Great Commission, Matthew 28:19, Mark 16:15, (Martin, 1988) pg. 162
[1306] (Lull, 2001) pg. 42, "GOD and Chivalry concord together"
[1307] (Brookhiser, 1997), front flap

Washington's rules came from a list originally collected by Jesuit priests[1308]. No Chivalry allows men to arbitrarily decide the path of Honor; the way of Righteousness and Honor rests in a handful of specific requirements, thought to be not only divinely inspired, but obvious, a priori, and handed down faithfully from generation to generation.

The Christian knight's Code of Chivalry consisted of laws similar to the Ten Commandments in importance and value. Indeed, the knight's prowess at arms balanced against the weight of two sets of responsibilities to GOD and Honor: the Ten Commandments of the Old Testament, and the ten demands of Chivalry[1309]. A knight disobeyed the Code of Chivalry at the cost of his knighthood and Honor, and even the smallest infraction or mistake appeared as a sin. While other Christians were required to obey the Ten Commandments, the Knight saw himself unworthy unless he followed both the Ten Commandments and the Code of Chivalry[1310].

Hugh of Tabarie said, "On that day when I was received into that sacred order [of knighthood], I vowed to hold honor dearer than life and he who doubts our good faith knows little of Christian Chivalry.'"

"'I would know more of this order and its vows" said the Sultan[1311].

This exacting Code came to perhaps its most polished form around 1100 and reflects the terrifying rigors of the Crusades. Compiled by Leon Gautier in his famous *Chivalry*, this version of the knight's rules, labeled the "Decalogue", or "Ten", is possibly the most popular and widely noted[1312].

The Decalogue[1313]

I.   Thou shalt believe all that the Church teaches, and shall observe all it's directions.

II. Thou shalt defend the Church.

[1308] Ibid. pg. 4
[1309] (Gautier, 1989) pg. 18, 23, 26, the "eighth sacrament"
[1310] (Lull, 2001), pg. 57
[1311] (Moncrieff, 1976) pg. 429
[1312] (Gautier, 1989) pg. 25-26
[1313] (Gautier, 1989) pg. 25-26

III.   Thou shalt respect all weaknesses and shall constitute thyself defender of them.
IV.   Thou shalt love the country in which thou was born.
V.   Thou shalt not recoil before thine enemy.
VI.   Thou shalt make war against the infidel without cessation, and without mercy.
VII.   Thou shalt perform scrupulously thy feudal duties, if they be not contrary to the laws of GOD.
VIII. Thou shalt never lie, and shalt remain loyal to the pledge word.
IX.   Thou shalt be generous, and give largesse to everyone.
X.   Thou shalt be everywhere and always the champion of the right and the good against injustice and evil.

I.   Thou shalt believe all that the Church teaches, and shalt observe all its directions.

Christian knights firmly believed in the doctrines of the Church and in the readings of the Bible. "They delighted to recall the miracles of the Old and New Testament . . . Our heroes considered it always necessary to affirm distinctly their faith in all these miracles"[1314].

At the time that this Code was formulated, the only Christian church of note in Europe was the Catholic Church. Knights consistently observed the rules and requirements of the Catholic Church, baptism being the first absolute essential requirement of any Christian knight. Attending Mass every morning, making confession before every battle or duel, following the traditional sacraments as other Christians, and relying on a priest, deacon, or monk as spiritual advisors became the mainstays of knightly life[1315].

The Templar and Hospitaller Orders of knighthood went further, adopting the Augustinian Rule, the oldest Catholic rule for monastic life, swearing poverty, chastity, and obedience. In the spirit of the Church's rules and teachings, the Hospitallers accepted eight rules that are known as "aspirations" or "obligations", more firmly defining and refining Christian knighthood. These eight aspirations, symbolized in the eight points of the Hospitaller cross, ignited a standard that would shine like a beacon for all knights everywhere: Live in Truth, have faith, repent of

---

[1314] (Gautier, 1989) pg. 32
[1315] Ibid. pg. 26, 33

sins, give proof of humility, love justice, be merciful, be sincere and whole hearted, and endure persecution[1316].

In the *L'Ordene de Chevalerie*, a Moslem prince named Saladin asks his prisoner, Hugh de Taberie, to explain how knights are made. The Moslem insists that the knight explain everything, and also insists that he, Saladin himself, wishes to go through the necessary ceremonies[1317]. Hugh de Taberie decides to lead this strange class, and at one point gives Saladin excellent advice about how always to preserve Honor. The first two pieces of advice are to never make deals with traitors and always treat women with respect. The other two obligations to retain Honor concern the Church: "the third obligation is piously to observe all fast days and days of abstinence; and finally, to hear mass every day and make an offering at the monastery"[1318].

No matter how brutal or warlike knights had been, they were continuously infused with more and more of the Catholic Church and Christianity, until even the dubbing ceremony itself was no longer simply a military rite, but a religious experience. "However irreligious, however brutal, however much of a soldier the knight might have been who admitted the aspirant, he could no longer content himself with saying 'be a valiant knight'; he was constrained to say, he was compelled to recognize the Christian spirit, and say to the novice: 'Be thou a soldier of Jesus Christ'"[1319].

By the time of St. Louis, a Bishop conducted the benediction and dubbing of knights[1320]. At the end of the dubbing ceremony, as the Bishop blessed the new knight and handed over his sword, the Bishop would command "Be thou a soldier—peaceful, courageous, faithful, devoted to GOD." The Bishop would raise his hand to the new knight's face, not to strike him hard against cheek or neck, as was done in past ceremonies, but to touch him gently on the face as if to wake him. "Awake from dull sleep, and rise to the Honor and Faith of Christ"[1321]!

[1316] (The Military Order of Malta, http://flagspot.net/flags/smom, pg. 2, 2/5/2005).

[1317] (Moncrieff, 1976) or the *Ordene* itself - (Lull, 2001) pg. 110

[1318] (Gautier, 1989) pg. 250

[1319] (Gautier, 1989) pg. 259

[1320] Ibid. pg. 254

[1321] (Gautier, 1989) pg. 257

"Amongst the obligations which belonged to this first commandment of chivalry, is another, the last, "to die in the faith and for the Faith"[1322].

II. Thou Shalt Defend the Church

Charlemagne's most famous knight, Roland, was called "the falcon of Christianity"[1323]. Charles Martel was called the "Hammer of GOD". Knights were referred to as Miles Christi, "soldiers of Christ". Some have dared to even call the knight a "military priest"[1324], and a priest, a "spiritual knight"[1325].

When the Bishop blessed a new knight's sword, he would first say "Bless this sword so that Thy servant may in the future be in opposition to the cruelty of heretics and pagans; the defender of the Church, and of widows and orphans, and all those who fear GOD"[1326]. The Pontifical says to the knight, when receiving his sword, "Receive this sword in the name of the Father, and the Son, and the Holy Ghost, use it for your own defense and that of the Church of GOD, and for the confusion of the enemies of the Cross of Christ"[1327].

"Chivalry has never been, is not, and never will be anything other than armed force in the defense of unarmed truth"[1328]. "Wherever the Church was, there the knight also was to be found to accompany and protect this holy mother . . ."[1329]. Often, knights found themselves on the edge of a vast sea of enemies, who wished not only the destruction of Christian countries, but the annihilation of Christianity within all of Europe and the world!

In the 600's, Mohammed began one of the largest and most long-lasting and continuous assaults on the Christian Church, and indeed against any religion not of Islamic faith. This was the "Jihad", or "Holy War" which has labored on, periodically, for nearly 14 centuries.

[1322] Ibid. pg. 36
[1323] Ibid. pg. 175
[1324] Ibid. pg. 223, (Meller, 2002) pg. 10, (Fife, 1991) pg. 58
[1325] (Lull, 2001) pg. 60
[1326] (Gautier, 1989) pg. 225
[1327] (Gautier, 1989) pg. 38
[1328] Ibid.
[1329] (Gautier), pg. 39, (Lull, 2001), pg. 25

Moslems, or Saracens as the knights called them, invaded everywhere from Egypt all the way to modern day Spain, France, Russia, and Italy, including Rome, the eternal city, in wave after wave of alternating attacks[1330], some intense, some slow and stealth-like[1331].

In these battles for world domination, the knight stood forever as the champion of Christianity; the muscle, sword, shield, armor, and teeth of the Church against Moslem aggression. Time and time again, knights were called not only to defend the weak and the innocent, but also the Church and Christianity itself from annihilation.

In 732, Charles Martel literally hammered the Moslems in a place called Tours in France, beating them back with heavy infantry and brilliant strategy that set the standard for medieval campaigns and fighting for centuries to come. Rodrigo De Bivar, known as El Cid, fought Moslems already in Spain and the invading Moslem North Africans until the invading commander Yusef fled. Again in France, Charlemagne and his twelve Paladins beat the Saracen out of the Rhine and then fought a tug-of-war battle until they finally crushed the Saracen after the tragic and terrible battle of Roncesvalles. "It was thus in obedience to the call of duty that Roland died . . . ."[1332]. In 1095, Byzantium, center of the Eastern Orthodox Church and very much aware of another growing Moslem threat, sounded the alarm and the Catholic knights answered, touching off the Crusades and bringing the battle to the enemy for eight long and grueling campaigns. When Moslem control of Mediterranean trading and shipping threatened to capsize European Christianity, Sir Cervantes and his many knightly brethren, under various flags but one Christian standard, crushed the Islamists at Lepanto and re-established Christian influence on the Mediterranean Sea[1333]. In the 1600's, a desperate but disciplined dash by Jan Sobieski and his 3000 Polish lancers stopped another invasion of Europe by hundreds of thousands of Moslems during the battle of Vienna[1334]. Although pursued by many different Islamic countries and groups, and in different settings, one may call these clashes a thousand-year Jihad. And for a

---

[1330] (Belloc, 1992) pg. 9, (Babinger, 1978) pg. 494

[1331] (Karsh, 2007) pg. 5, 93 and (Spencer, 2005) pg. 157

[1332] (Gautier) pg.37

[1333] (Hickman, 2013), (Encyclopedia Britannica, Micropedia, volume 6, 1982) pg. 157

[1334] (Belloc, 1992) pg. 247

millennium and more, the knights have always provided an unparalleled and successful defense with Strength, Courage, Faith, and blood.

Even Sir Ferdinand Magellan, after sailing around the entire world and finally nearing his homeland, discovered in the Philippines a battle between Christian natives and Moslem interlopers. Although from a different culture and land, Magellan threw himself into the fray, saying that one Christian should always help another. After a journey of a million miles and in a far-flung and foreign land, the greatest explorer of his time gave his life in defense of friends he had just met, simply because they had converted to Christianity[1335]. Of course. Magellan was a knight.

III. Thou shalt respect all weaknesses, and thou shalt constitute thyself defender of them.

All Christian Knights everywhere were held to the obligation of defending anyone who might need protection from the powerful, the oppressor, the bully, the criminal. Especially women, widows, orphans, and the poor could expect protection from the true knight, but anyone who was harassed or oppressed by Evil[1336].

"If anyone injures those little ones or their land, here is my sword that shall cut off the head of any such traitor or robber!" Shouted Sir William of Gellone, with his blade held high[1337].

The knight was bound to help everyone whenever he could, especially the poor, the diseased, and the innocent children, and this obligation went far beyond the physical defense of their charges. Many people assume that the Templar and Hospitaller Orders of knighthood were constructed to win the Crusades. In actuality, these orders were established to protect and care for the poor in general[1338], and, in particular, the pilgrims coming to pray in Jerusalem. Christians taking the journey to the Holy City were required to travel unarmed, and bandits, most of them Islamic, often robed and killed the defenseless pilgrims. The Templars and Hospitallers not only protected the pilgrims,

---

[1335] (Thomas, 2005)
[1336] (Gautier, 1989) pg.43, (Lull, 2001) pg. 35
[1337] (Gautier, 1989) pg.43
[1338] (Miller D., 2001) pg. 52-63

but took care of their wounds and illnesses in gigantic hospitals rivaling the size of hospitals today[1339].

Knights have always been the champion of the weak and poor.

Even at a disadvantage and in dire straits, the True Knight always found a way to help the down-trodden around him.

Rodrigo De Bivar, unjustly exiled from his home and wealth, did not become obsessed with his own misfortune. An old woman, obviously poverty stricken, stood near the door as Rodrigo walked from his home for perhaps the last time. He turned to her and said, "Go in and take what-ever you would like"[1340].

One night, as the Cid and his loyal followers looked for a place to simply rest themselves and their exhausted horses, hopefully with a mouthful of well-water to drink, they spied a small, out-of-the-way farm that might present shelter in the form of a barn.

A young girl, no more than ten approached the small band. "I beg you," Pleaded the girl, "You cannot rest here. The king has ordered that anyone who gives aid to the Cid will be stripped of their belongings in shame. Have mercy on my poor family."

Rodrigo and his men pushed wearily on[1341].

The Cid and St. Francis's incredibly tender treatment of lepers, the lowest outcasts of society at the time, are now legendary.

Sir Guy of Warwick, after gaining an entire dukedom, gave away his enormous wealth to the beggars along the streets, the blind, and the lame, until he himself lived among them and tended to them as best he could[1342].

Saint George, patron saint of knights, risked his life to save the daughter of the king of a city. When the king showered him with gold for the great task he completed, Sir George explained to the king that a knight protects his honor by giving to the poor. He gave away all the treasure to the people as he rode away[1343].

[1339] (Woods T. E., 2005) pg. 178
[1340] (Matthews, 1998) pg.86
[1341] (Gerritsen and Melle, 1998) pg. 84
[1342] (Moncrieff, 1976) pg. 239
[1343] (Morgan, 2006) pg. 47

IV. Thou shalt love thy country in which thou was born

The legendary Roland, the most undauntable of all of Charlemagne's Paladin knights, turned to face the impossible army of Moslems advancing toward him up the cragged hill. He and his men were badly outnumbered, nearly one hundred to one, but he raised his sword Durandel and prepared to hold his ground.

He had three reasons. The first was his duty, charged by Charlemagne, to protect the rear guard of the army against all foes, especially Saracen Moslems. The second: Roland was one of the twelve paladins, the most powerful and courageous knights of France. The third reason, in his mind as valuable as any: he felt these enemies wished to destroy and conquer his beloved France[1344].

Roland's eyes blazed with a terrible inward fire. The army had battled the invading Moslems and had finally pushed them out of the neighboring country of Spain, and now as it returned home, Charlemagne placed Roland as the leader of the rear guard. This rear guard, populated by Paladins and sent to protect and patrol the back of the homebound army, only contained a small group[1345]. Knowing this, and having some clandestine foreknowledge of their position, the Moslems had launched a surprise attack on the rear-guard, and effectively cut them off from the rest of the army. Charlemagne was not aware that the rear was under fire. This was the battle of Roncesvaux.

"We should call for reinforcements!" Cried his Paladin friend Oliver, standing nearby. "Use the horn that the King gave you!"

"No." Roland spoke slowly and with brutal purpose. "One of us is worth a thousand of these pigs! We are sons of France!"

And he was almost right. Thousands of men rushed the hill, but only a few at a time could advance on Roland and his fellows, standing on the hill as they were.

"We cannot allow their feet to sully our beloved land!" cried Roland as he chopped into one invader after another.

The morning turned to day, and still Roland and Oliver held the hill against the thousands of Islamic foes. Their friend, Arch Bishop Turpin, himself wielding a mace and smashing his share of heathen heads, worked

---

[1344] (Gerritsen and Melle, 1998) pg. 234, (Sayers, 1984) pg. 7
[1345] (Sayers, 1984) pg. 7, 21, 96, (Einhard, 1969) pg. 64-85, (Matthews, 1998) pg. 31, 149

nearby. But every minute there were fewer of their fellow Frenchman, every moment there were less Christian swords on the hill. The Moslems, thousands strong, still came on without ceasing.

Mid-day brought a small lull in the battle. The Moslems, frustrated by their inability to sweep away this small amount of men and move on to further surprise attacks on the army of Charlemagne, set back to determine a strategy.

Roland and Oliver had time to lean on their huge swords and rest, letting the whistling and gulping of their breath return to normal.

"Call the king." Oliver pleaded. "We are strong, but we cannot hold them off forever. We endanger the whole of the army by not warning them of this attack."

Roland was of a different train of thought than his friend, but he looked down at the horn at his belt, an immense horn made out of wood and bone. Simply by blowing this ornate trumpet-like device, Roland could send a loud blast across the country-side, alerting anyone for miles around. It had been a gift of King Charlemagne, but for obvious reasons, he was not to blow it unless terrible and imminent danger was afoot, danger that the redoubtable Roland could not handle on his own. If Charlemagne heard this horn, he would come to their aid, bringing the entire army with him.

It is difficult to imagine today, but Roland refused Oliver's request. "If I were to blow the horn, what would they think of us in France? That we could not hold back these ruffians ourselves? I will not allow France to be shamed because of me. I will not have the reputation of France sullied because of me! We fight on"[1346]!

The Islamists rushed up the hill again, redoubling their efforts to storm this tiny natural fort, and Roland and Oliver fought and hacked and parried hour after hour, blood and sweat dripping from their armor, a thousand bodies of the foe spread around them in a bizarre and gory half circle.

Oliver, Roland's mighty friend, fell to the ground. Arch Bishop Turpin, himself a great warrior beside his priestly abilities, received several mortal wounds[1347]. Roland still stood, his armor in shreds as well as his skin, but that frightening and flashing sword, Durandel, rose and hacked, rose and hacked.

[1346] (Gautier, 1989) pg. 51
[1347] (Sayers, 1984) pg. 18-19

"Call the king!" Cried the Archbishop as his blood pooled around him to join the red of the slaughtered enemy. "Blow the horn now, I beg of you!"

Roland looked at his friend, even as he chopped down another Saracen. He saw his comrades dying or dead, slumped in the little corners of their final stands, piles of bodies surrounding them; he saw Oliver, broken and still.

He severed the head of the Saracen coming at him, and in one motion released the horn from its strap. "Oh France! May I never bring disgrace to you," He whispered as he placed the horn to his lips[1348].

The blast of sound was enough to startle the Islamists around him. It rolled through the hills like thunder.

But Roland knew that the head of the army would be many miles away, and so again, he raised and blew the horn. The sound, like Gideon's trumpet, reverberated and seemed to vibrate the earth with earthquake force. The Saracen, still stunned, eyes wide, stared at the device.

Sir Roland looked at his dead friends once again, tears in his burning eyes. Even as the Saracens recovered and came at him again, he blew the horn with a terrific blast so powerful he ruptured his lips and tongue, blood spewing forth from his mouth, and the wave of sound seemed to split the sky like spears of lightning.

"You will never see my beautiful land!" He cried through bloody teeth as he fought the remaining foe. "You will never sully my country!" He shouted with cracking voice as he cut and slashed. "France Forever"[1349]!

Charlemagne and his men found Roland near the top of the hill, his body bloodied and bruised almost beyond recognition. All around him and throughout the area, the bodies of the Saracen lay thick, and, interspersed with them, rested the bodies of Oliver, and the remainder of the rear guard. Curiously, not far from Roland's body, they found his sword, Durandel, bent against a boulder.

"To prevent any Saracen from finding it and using such a weapon later against France or GOD's people." Turpin knew. "He would not allow harm or shame to fall upon them, even in death"[1350].

[1348] (Gautier, 1989) pg.51
[1349] (Gautier, 1989) pg. 51
[1350] (Sayers, 1984) pg. 141

"No nation can", Gautier wrote, "even in this latest age of ours, offer such a type, a more glorious ideal of the love of country"[1351].

Although proud and reckless in the *Song of Roland,* which greatly mythologizes the real battle of Roncesvaux that occurred on August 15, 778 in the Pyrenees, this Paladin will always be remembered as a symbol of Honor, Justice, and Nationalism. From El Cid in Spain, to Roland in France, to Arthur in England, to George Washington in the United States, to Ignatio Zaragosa in Mexico, it is the honor and tradition of knights to uphold their countries, bring glory to them, and set them up as bastions of hope and courage.

V. Thou shalt not recoil before thine enemy

Brother James of Mailly, Marshall of the Templars in 1187, knew the trials and tribulations of obedience better than anyone. He stood with his leader, Gerard of Ridfort, Master of the Templars, and one hundred and twenty other knights as they looked down from a cliff onto a gathering of 7000 Islamic soldiers, the Saracen, the traditional enemy of the Templars[1352]. There was no misunderstanding. The knights were outnumbered more than 53 to one.

The Moslems were unaware of the knights looking upon them. They were traveling through Tiberius, a tiny kingdom in the Middle East ruled by Raymond of Tripoli. Although this was Christian land, they had permission to transverse it for one day.

For the knights, this was unallowable.

Brother James frowned at the odds. He turned to his master. "There is no way we, with our few numbers, can take them. We should go back."

"Have you forgotten our sacred oaths!?" Demanded Gerard. "We are to be the first to attack, and the last to retreat!" Not only were the Templar Knights dedicated to this deadly vow, it also echoed the command of the Decalogue, the ten general rules of Chivalry: "Thou shalt never retreat before the enemy".

[1351] (Gautier, 1989) pg. 52
[1352] (Read, 1999) pg. 157-158, (Robinson, 1991) pg. 144

James Reston, in his book *Warriors of GOD* says that Gerard shouted "Remember your fathers the Maccabees! Their duty was to fight for the Church, the Law, and for the inheritance of the Crucified One"[1353]!

Gerard then galloped down into the Saracen, waving his sword. Brother James remembered his oaths very well: Poverty, Chastity, and Obedience. He spurred his horse down the same trail after Gerard, joining him as thousands of Islamists parted to allow this tiny band of attackers a path to their doom.

Brother James soon found himself surrounded by spears, menaced on all sides by literally thousands of the enemy, but his brave sword cut such a wake through them that, according to Reston, it was said the amazed Islamists pleaded with him to surrender, awestruck by his courage[1354]. Brother James refused, rather dying a knight than living as a traitor. Finally, they overwhelmed him with multitudes of javelins, projectiles, and stones, but not until he had ringed himself with piles of the dead. For the Templars, Reston reports, "It was sweet for a man to die thus, himself in the center, surrounded by the unbelievers whom his brave arm had slaughtered"[1355]. As for the Moslems, his power and courage amazed them so, he seemed superhuman, to have been sent by GOD himself; they thought he was the Christian Saint George, in the flesh[1356].

Somehow, Gerard and four of his men were able to hack their way through the enemy army and, though badly wounded, they arrived in Nazareth that evening[1357].

Some historians called the attack "foolish"[1358]. But to the Templars, everything hinged on fulfilling duty by obeying a sacred and ancient law. Whether it meant facing certain death or terrible pain, and no matter the cost or the impracticality, obedience to the Code of Chivalry stood as paramount in the Templar's mind. So it is for all true knights.

Every man must eventually die. This is a law of life. The choice is to die like a man or die like a dog. If a man dies in the pursuit of a glorious and selfless duty, his death will indeed be glorious and divine, marking

---

[1353] (Reston, 2001) pg.38
[1354] Ibid. pg.39
[1355] Ibid. pg. 40
[1356] (Howarth, 1982) pg. 148
[1357] (Reston, 2001) pg. 39
[1358] (Reston, 2001) pg. 38

his life as touched by GOD. And imagine dying so gloriously as to be mistaken for a Warrior Angel of GOD, even St. George himself[1359]! But if a man deems to go the other way, following not a code or a supreme law, but following the selfish demands of his impure heart, he will perish as any animal, unworthy of even a burial place. Your choice: glorious angel or lowly dog.

Another man who made a worthy choice was Ulrich Baier, a Teutonic Knight, who remembered this rule, even in the very lap of death in 1281[1360]. Fighting Prussians and mortally wounded in Brescia, so that he could no longer stand, he insisted that his head be propped up by a large stone, so that even mortally wounded, he faced the enemy, and would never turn his back on them. Sir Roland had done the same.

VI. Thou shalt make war against the infidel without cessation and without mercy.

As the Crusaders made ready to take Jerusalem from the Moslems in 1099, they cried, "Were the walls of Jerusalem of steel, were they of steel, we would tear them with our teeth"[1361]. To me and many knights of later years, this burning rage against pagans seems overly harsh and brutal. War against the Moslem invaders, yes, and even Crusade, it can be argued, were defensive measures against the formidable Moslem presence in the Holy Land. But to say "without Mercy"? We have already shown that it is an ideal of knighthood, from the Hospitallers, who were Crusaders themselves, to Rodrigo De Bivar, El Cid, that mercy be extended whenever possible.

We must remember, as Gautier reminds us, that the Moslems for 1400 years have been a constant threat to the West and Christianity, Israelis and Buddhists, Hindus and Bahai, Coptics and Zorasters. Without Charlemagne, Charles Martel, Jan Sobieski, the likes of Godfrey be Bouillon and Miguel Cervantes driving back the invading hordes of the Mohammedan again and again, the West would have long ago been destroyed or enslaved. The Moslems have relentlessly conquered most of Africa and half of Spain, conquered all the way to Poitiers and

---

[1359] (Howarth, 1982) pg. 148
[1360] (Meller, 2002) pg 60
[1361] (Gautier, 1989) pg.60

Toulouse[1362], and with the Moslem Brotherhood, even assisted Hitler in the 1940's[1363], until today, releasing upon the world the staggering brutality of suicide bombings and every form of terrorism. The Crusader knights saw their war with Islamists as a war of self-defense against a tide of death, for culture and religion, as well as the body[1364].

To solve this controversy, the knight must have two hearts. One, full of mercy and compassion, the other for battling evil[1365]. Many of the knight's enemies can receive mercy if they can accept it, but those who align with evil must be destroyed.

VII. Thou shalt perform scrupulously thy feudal duties, if they be not contrary to the laws of GOD

In the middle ages, a knight's life was dictated by a sometimes enormous collection of obligations. At least, a knight might have the obligation to assist the Church, as well as the obligation to his nation as a whole, his king, his wife, his family, his father, and the men who worked his lands[1366].

But one of the most outstanding obligations a knight had, beside his loyalty to GOD and the Code, was his feudal obligations, which were generally his assistance to the king[1367].

A messenger from King Louis of France came to a church. This church glowed and resounded with the pomp and circumstance of a wedding in progress. The vows were even then being exchanged. It was the long-awaited wedding of Sir William of Gellone, already a famous knight for his honor and gallantry, so the ceremony was beautiful and sumptuously decorated and attended.

But the messenger did not stop at any of the guests. He came directly to the altar, where the priest waited to pour his blessing over the gorgeously attired knight and lady. He stood directly behind the knight, even as William reached for the ring to place on his beautiful bride's

---

[1362] Ibid., (Barber, The Knight and Chivalry, Revised Edition, 1995) pg. 49
[1363] (staff, 2011)
[1364] (Belloc, 1992) pg. 16-17
[1365] (Gies, 1986) pg. 96, (Corley, 1989) pg. 55, (Lull, 2001) pg. 36
[1366] (Lull, 2001) pg.31
[1367] (Lull, 2001) pg. 28, 31, (Barber, The Knight and Chivalry, Revised Edition, 1995) pg. 52, 64

finger. Against his will, the knight turned from the vision of his veiled wife-to-be and to the sad visage of the horseman.

"My king!" William cried out. "In danger"[1368]!

In that terrible moment, a decision had to be made. How many times must a knight decline all his wishes and dreams in a small but agonizing moment? How many times must he turn his back on everything he loves and everything he desires in order to fulfill his knightly obligation? A thousand and a thousand times over[1369], "quitting his place at the altar, the priest, and his pale-faced bride on whom he would not look and whom he would never see again, leaving the happiness of which he would not think—"[1370]. It has been said, a knight's heart will be shattered again and again by Honor, and it would be better if the knight shatters it himself.

The Cid, Sir Rodrigo De Bivar, found himself in a similar situation. He had been sent into exile a second time by the spoiled and undisciplined King of Spain. But to further bring home the punishment, the king had not only sent the Cid away from his only home, but had taken his wife and children captive.

What man could bring himself to follow such a ridiculous lord whose temper continuously overpowered kingly magnanimity? The Cid burned with the rage of righteous indignation. His wife! His children! Held in a stinking and rotten dungeon and he himself unable to help them!

But, as with William, a messenger arrived, riding hard and fast. This man presented Rodrigo a letter, carefully wrapped, contained by a regal perfume.

"No," waved Rodrigo. "Not now. Do not bring me a message now." Not only did he have his family concerning him, but at the moment, he was waging a battle against the Moorish city of Leira, on his continuing campaign to unify Spain. This fortified city was about to crack before the might of the Cid[1371]!

"From the Queen." The messenger said.

The Cid's face, once of stone, now softened with concern. "What event could be so terrible that the queen herself should send a message instead of the king?" He thought to himself.

[1368] (Gautier, 1989) pg. 65, (Ferrante, 2001) pg. 102, XXXIII of the Coronation of Louis

[1369] Matt. 18:21-22

[1370] (Gautier, 1989) pg. 65

[1371] (Matthews, 1998) pg. 68-72

In the letter, the queen begged the Cid to personally aid the king, since the royal sovereign waged a bitter campaign against Granada, a great city and bastion of Moorish Spain. Even with all that had gone before, she pleaded, the Cid must remember his loyalty, for king and for Spain.

Rodrigo did not hesitate. He ignored the city of Leira, ready to surrender before him. He ignored the stunned complaints of his men. He ignored the bitter anguish in his heart[1372].

"Tomorrow, we ride with our king!" He told them.

VIII. Thou shalt never lie, and shall remain faithful to the pledged word.

> "The code of the medieval knight was founded on respect for his engagements, which led him to loath a lie. It mattered not whether his oath was given on the book of Evangels or relics of the saints, or sworn to with his bare, uplifted hand."

—Paul LaCroix and Walter Clifford Meller[1373]

The Ten Commandments simply state that a Godly man should not bear false witness against his neighbor. The Decalogue of Chivalry takes this obvious meaning a step further[1374], stating that a Christian knight should never lie in any place and for any reason[1375]. This is reminiscent of Christ's fulfillment of the law[1376], as in his direction to not only avoid adultery, but to avoid even looking at a neighbor's wife with lust[1377], and to not only avoid murder, but to avoid even cursing or getting angry at one's neighbor[1378]. The Code of Chivalry, like Christ, brings out the spirit as well as the letter of the law. And to the end, this spirit and letter of the Law would exemplify the knight as the man of Truth who hates all lies[1379].

[1372] (Matthews, 1998) pg. 72, (Barber, The Knight and Chivalry, Revised Edition, 1995) pg. 64

[1373] (Meller, The Medieval Warrior, 2002) pg. 52

[1374] (Lull, 2001), pg.42

[1375] (Gautier, 1989), pg. 68

[1376] Matthew 5:17

[1377] Matthew 5:27-28

[1378] Matthew 5:21-22

[1379] (Lull, 2001) 64,

This should be obvious! For, the ancient poets used one phrase to separate the knight's GOD from all other gods. They called HIM, "The GOD who never lies"[1380]. And the knight, whose greatest loyalty, obligation, and obedience is to this GOD of gods and KING of kings, it is fitting that he should follow such an example, honoring GOD and Christ by always keeping Truth before him. Chivalry, reflecting GOD's glory like a mirror[1381], only deals in Truth.

Always, when the knight is victorious over himself and the vices of the world, he is truthful, and when any knight fails in the truth, he brings great destruction with him, not only for himself but for those around him as well[1382]. The Crusades were lost because of broken promises, and no knight should forget[1383]. A man who lies, and deludes others in his lie, pulls many down with him into nothingness[1384].

From time to time, knights have fallen into weakness, as in the one episode of Sir Gawain, when, while keeping a terrifying promise that would lead to his beheading, he could not quite keep a tiny promise to the lord of the house and thus lied. He paid the price for the rest of his life, wearing a green sash to indicate to the world that he had failed, even though only once. He let everyone know that he had dishonored himself, as a lesson to all others not to fall into the same trap. He knew, as all true knights, that Truth is everything, even above life[1385].

We have seen how Saladin, that leader of the Moslem world during the Crusades, had a legendary conversation with Sir Hugh de Tabarie, where the Sultan asked for an explanation of the Code of Honor. How did such a conversation come to pass?

Sir Hugh had been found nearly dead from loss of blood, with a ring of slain Islamic Warriors around him. He was brought to the Mighty Sultan Saladin to receive judgment.

"Why did you come all this way to die," Saladin demanded, "When you could have stayed at home in comfort, and lived?"

[1380] (Gautier, 1989) pg. 68, Numbers 23:19
[1381] (Lull, 2001) pg. 42
[1382] (Lull, 2001) pg. 64
[1383] (Stark, 2009) pg. 127
[1384] (Buber, 1953) pg. 12, (Alter, 2007) pg. 292—Even a small injustice can lead to the destruction
[1385] (Lull, 2001) pg. 39

"I am no cow, that I should not seek honor." Hugh explained roughly. "I have come to free the holy land form the grip of pagans."

"Ah, you speak of Honor," Smiled Saladin. "And I am sure you know much about it."

"I belong to a set of warriors who live and die by a Code of Honor, which none of us ever relinquish. This code guides us in every aspect of life as a warrior for Christ."

"Well, you have come on a fool's errand. And now you will pay for your impertinence. Your ransom will stand at 100,000 bezants or you will pay with your head."

"Even if I sold all my lands and holdings, I could not produce such a sum," Hugh said. "So be it. I am ready to die."

The Sultan liked the bravery in this man, and so came up with an alternative.

"Suppose I let you travel back to your homeland, to ask all of your neighboring lords and ladies to help you in raising your ransom. Would you promise to return to me on a set day, even if you did not gather all the money, to face your doom squarely?"

Sir Hugh was taken aback a bit. "That is an honorable offer. I will promise to return, even if I do not have the proper funds."

"How can I know I can trust you to return?" Saladin smiled thinly.

"A knight's word is stronger than iron chain,"[1386] Hugh responded.

And so, Hugh of Tabarie traveled among his fellow Christians, but no one could aid him with the amount Saladin had asked for. As the appointed day approached, he said a final farewell to his wife and children, and made the grim trek back to the camp of Saladin.

Saladin looked him in the eye. "Many a man would have worried more over his own safety than to honor his promise to me."

Sir Hugh looked him back, square in the face. "I am a man of honor, who lives by a Code which demands complete loyalty to the pledge word."

"And to die by this code?" Saladin demanded.

"I am ready," Hugh said, "as that first day we met."

Saladin stood. "I would know more of such a man, and such a code that brings forth such loyalty and honor. I would know more of this Code of Honor you speak of, this Code of Chivalry."

[1386] (Moncrieff, 1976) pg. 428, for the full story, see pg. 427-431,

And so Saladin spared the life of Sir Hugh, and in return, the knight shared with the Sultan that mighty Code and way of life that had so impressed them both[1387].

"Not to tell lies, and to keep one's promise, are, to this day, the two chief traits in the character of a gentleman"[1388].

IX. Thou shalt be generous, and to give largesse to everyone.

Sir Godfrey of Bouillon, called "The Brother to the Poor"[1389], because he shared his wealth to anyone he found less fortunate. Knights often gave away everything they owned in pursuit of Asceticism and imitation of Christ's advice to the wealthy man. Sir Guy of Warwick, Sir William of Gellone, Hugo of Bordeaux, and Sir Ramon Lull were among these.

At the beginning of his chivalrous classic *Perceval, or the Story of the Grail*, Chretien de Troyes illustrates the importance of Charity in the mind of the knight. "According to the text [the Bible], GOD is charity, and whoever lives in charity-St. Paul says it and I have read it-abides in GOD and GOD in him"[1390].

De Troyes praises his patron, Count Phillip of Flanders, above other men, even Alexander the Great, because of the count's great charity and Largesse. Largesse, for knights, was a kind of spontaneous generosity, unconnected to reciprocation, recognition, or reward, "for he gives without hypocrisy and without guile, according to the Gospel, which says: "Let not thy left hand know what thy right hand doeth . . . The left hand, according to the story means vainglory, which comes from false hypocrisy. What does the right hand mean? Charity, which does not boast of its good works but rather covers them up so that no one knows of them save HIM who is called both GOD and charity"[1391].

[1387] This is based on the ancient poem *L'Ordene De Chivalerie*

[1388] (Gautier, 1989) pg.67

[1389] (Meller, 2002) pg. 52

[1390] (Loomis, 1951) pg. 8

[1391] (Loomis, 1951) pg. 8

X. Thou shalt be everywhere and always the champion of the Right and the Good against Injustice and Evil.

> "Loyalty, courtesy, liberality, and justice were the virtues essential in the estimation of mankind to the character of the knight in the days of Chivalry. A more splendid virtue than all others demanded of the young aspirant for knighthood, both before and after initiation, was the pursuit of Good, the detestation of evil, not solely when found in his own soul but also in that of the world".
> —From *The Medieval Warrior*, by Paul LaCroix and Walter Clifford Meller[1392]

The Code as the Conquest of Self

When modern man looks at this code and these stories, he says to himself, "This does not apply to me. I am not a man with a sword and armor, riding on a horse, nor am I trained to do this. Should I take up a sword and hack someone's ear off every time someone insults the Church? How can I fulfill feudal duties when the feudal system no longer exists? How can I wage war on the infidel and fight crime when, in this modern age, I am obliged not to take the law into my own hands? How can I follow a king or lord when there are hardly any left in the whole world? How can I be loyal to my country when my country no longer has an identity? How can I be a champion of Right and Good against injustice and Evil when I would be thrown in jail for drawing a sword anywhere in public? Must I become a vigilante? Must I become a criminal to save society from itself? The code and these stories of the knight are for a by-gone era, when the actions of the warrior might have improved things, but now it would only make things worse and get me in jail or dead."

An old Chinese saying, "when the wise man points at the moon, the fool looks at his finger." Are we so blind we cannot see that the Code of Chivalry is not so much for the world to change, as for ourselves to be better? Are we so deaf as to think the letter of the law more important than the spirit of the law? The Code can apply to any age, place, or

---

[1392] (Meller, 2002) pg. 52

person, especially when it is aimed not at controlling others or the state of the world, but controlling ourselves first. The Code may have been originally meant to help knights fight the infidel and other foes, but the Modern knight can turn the code into a battle against one's self and against one's unjust or immoral desires, a way of purification and eternal discipline.

Such internalization of a code is not new. It has come down to us from millennia of practice, in many religions.

When the Buddha, in the 5th century BC, decided to try and stop the suffering in this world, he took the Hindu Warrior's code, called the Dharma Conquest, and turned it inwards, not against the evils of others, but against the evils within his own soul, mind, and heart. He determined that all real evil, all real suffering came from within. Therefore, instead of taking arms against the wrongs of the outside world, he stared instead at the wrongs inside[1393].

What wrongs, lurking in the human heart, mind, and soul, are these? As terrible and powerful as any dragon or army, these inner enemies have names like Lust, Discontent, Hunger and Thirst, Desire, Sloth and Drowsiness, Cowardice, Doubt, Hypocrisy and Stupor[1394]. These inner tumultuous opponents warrant a full scale war against oneself, using a brutal warrior code. To conquer them, would be the greatest of victories, the greatest of glories.

"If one man conquers in battle a thousand times a thousand men, and if another man conquers himself, he is the greatest of warriors" stated the Buddha[1395]. Indeed, all great religions encourage self-discipline[1396]—a rule or ethic used to discipline the self, and the internal wayward vices. Such discipline takes up arms against the monsters of the soul.

Rule Codes have been used in the Judeo-Christian ethic to curb interior, selfish desires since the beginning. Some 1500 years before Buddha, Judaism saw that a relationship with GOD depended on strict morality-based and rule-driven battles against the selfish desires of the human ego. The story of Cain and Abel, for example, hints at the violent interior struggle of ethereal virtue. "If you do what is right, will you not be accepted (by GOD)? But if you do not, sin is crouching at your door;

[1393] (Fields R., 1991) pg. 94-95
[1394] (Fields R., 1991) pg. 94-95
[1395] Dhammapada ch. 8:4-5
[1396] (Spoto, 2002) pg. 63-65

it desires to have you, but you must master it"[1397]. Stories such as this illustrated the Law of GOD used to defend one's soul against both the evil from within and temptation from without.

Other religions at this ancient time valued only worship, and considered little the ethical or moral side of mankind. But the Jewish vision of friendship with GOD demanded a strict ethic, and culminated in the Ten Commandments[1398].

The martial imagery of King David's psalms and the wise advice of Solomon's proverbs bring this most famous of rule codes into high relief and practical exercise. One avoids the snares of sin, beating the Devil and his minions, by adhering to this Decalogue.

But an expressly military code, used to defeat the vices and flaws of the soul with the weapons of the spirit, mirroring the regimen of ethical warriors of iron, begins soon after Christ. Saint Paul, reflecting his Roman citizenship, hints at the Roman battle tactics with his description of the true Christian: "Take on the full armor of GOD"[1399]. The armor and weapons of a real Christian warrior are virtues, the ethereal arms of the spiritual soldier of Christ.

Around 392 AD, Prudentius, a Roman Christian, devised poetry that taught the use of the seven virtues as a means to battle the seven deadly sins, all within the battlefield of the individual soul. "With many headed vice to wage eternal war, with pious Rage, for till the Spirit does subdue the wild ungovernable crew of monstrous Vices that infest with Ravage dire the human breast . . ."[1400]

By the 10th Century, the Judeo-Christian ethic, the Ten Commandments, and the warrior conscience had come together to produce the Western World's answer to Buddha's use of the Hindu Code: an internal, personal martial law blessed by the saints and sanctioned by the Church, designed to make the ultimate warrior a servant of GOD, and master of himself.

This is how the code of the Ballad of Eustache Deschamp, circa 1200, reads: "You who would take upon you the order of knighthood, it is fitting that you should lead a new life, devoutly watching in prayer, fleeing from sin, pride, and villainy. The Church you will defend and

---

[1397] Genesis 4:7
[1398] Deuteronomy 11:22-23, Psalm 119:30
[1399] Ephesians 6:11-13
[1400] (Prudentius, 1743) pg. 2

succor the widow and orphan; be bold and guard the people; loyal and valiant knights taking naught from others, THUS, SHOULD THE KNIGHT RULE HIMSELF"[1401].

Let us, for a moment, consider such a leap of spirit. If the Code of Chivalry were to be used, not only against the evils in others, but especially against the evils in ourselves; to not only use the sword against dragons, devils, and murderous criminals, but to use the blade of discipline and faith against the hideous impulses within our own minds; to fight doggedly against not only what is amiss in the world, but especially to crush the faults within our deepest selves, we would be fulfilling the mightiest quest, the greatest mission of Honor. Thus is the true Spirit of the Knight-Errantry. Thus is the true spirit of Chivalrous Law. "The man who conquers himself is greater than he who conquers cities" or countries, or worlds[1402].

Indeed, all Religions and philosophies of any worth attempt to build a better person and a better world by disciplining the self, using a set code to guide one's actions, internally and externally. But the code of the Judeo-Christian knight is different in several ways.

In Buddhism, during the successful battle against all internal passions and vices, the ultimate aim is the elimination of the self entirely. Such annihilation is "Nirvana". In Christian Chivalry, challenging the passions may eliminate them, but more precisely it transforms them into what they were meant to be, making the knight more himself, fulfilling the individual rather than destroying the individual—making him more fully human[1403]. Galahad, in Tennyson's version, does not cheer to "lose himself" only, but instead to "lose himself to gain himself"—to lose the selfish desires in order to gain his capacity to commune with GOD: a sharing of thought between two individuals, a relationship.

With this comes a gift which no Buddhist can expect. The knight is not alone against his vices and selfish passions. He has the Grace of GOD to aid him[1404].

When a knight internalizes the Code in this way, the Code becomes the inner road and training arena through which the knight reaches closer contact with GOD. The Code becomes the hard path, the path of

---

[1401] (Meller, 2002) pg. 52

[1402] Proverbs 16:32

[1403] (Zacharias, 2001) pg. 71-73

[1404] (Doornik, 1953) pg. 215

most resistance, the little-used path that leads to the Narrow Gate[1405]. The Code becomes the surrogate heart of the knight and trains him to keep his eyes on GOD. The Code becomes the knight's cross, his very life of discipline. It not only brings him in closer union with GOD, but makes him a better person, and strong enough to resist the world[1406]. It is his way of obedience to GOD's will.

Father Dom Lorenzo Scupoli published in 1589 a book that very specifically spells out the use of internal weapons as the way to serve the ultimate LORD by subordinating one's selfish desires. "The soldier of Christ must prepare early for the battle . . . . Consider yourself on the field of battle, facing the enemy and bound by the iron-clad law— either Fight or Die . . . . Begin to fight immediately in the name of the Lord, armed with the distrust of yourself, with confidence in GOD, in prayer, and with the correct use of the faculties of your soul . . . With these weapons, attack the enemy, that predominant passion you wish to conquer, either by courageous resistance, repeated acts of contrary virtue, or any means that Heaven gives you to drive it out of your heart. Do not rest until it is conquered. Your endurance will be rewarded by the Supreme Judge, Who, with the entire Church Triumphant, has witnessed your behavior. To repeat—you must not become tired of this war. Everyone must serve and please GOD"[1407].

If a knight can use the internal code to improve himself and win GOD's favor in a titanic battle with his instincts and human nature, might he also use the same weapons to improve the outside world? Indeed, King Arthur and his noble knights did not see themselves as simply warriors against their own selfish desires, but as emissaries of goodness and Christ to the whole world[1408].

Sir Ramon Lull, St. Ignatius, St. Francis, and countless others, showed how the Chivalry could be interpreted not as a physical battle against pagans, but as a battle of intellect, discussion, and strength of faith, the sword of the mind and soul. These weapons were first to be used against the evils within ourselves, and then, just as important, against the evils that threatened every soul around the world[1409].

[1405] Matt. 7:13, Luke 13:24, 1 John 5:4, Isaiah 35:8

[1406] (Augustine, 1986) pg. 46

[1407] (Scupoli, 1945 edition) pg. 46-47

[1408] (Fife, 1991) pg. 43, 58

[1409] (Augustine, 1986) pg.139, (Martin, 1988) pg 159-160

When the sword of the mind is sharpened, and used with the rules of Chivalry, a knight may go out into the world and spread the truth by the "sword of his mouth"[1410]. He uses facts, arguments, and logic, as well as example, to influence and convince people of the right path[1411]. Sir Lull studied long and hard his own religion and theology, and learning the language and philosophy of the people he wished to convert[1412], and laying out his life as well, he aimed to bring them over to his side. As a physical warrior trains his body to conquer a physical foe, so too a mental warrior trains his mind to conquer ignorance and the arguments of his various opponents[1413].

Leon Gautier, author of *Chivalry, the everyday life of the medieval knight*, understood that many in his time and ours would not be able to take the leap from the ancient, very physical Code of the sword to a more spiritualized Code of the soul by themselves. He wrote his book not only to bask in the glory of a by-gone age, "But we conceived of another idea, which may appear more daring still: this was to enlarge the mind, to check the mercantile spirit which abases, and the egotism which is killing it,: to convey to it some of the enthusiasm for the Beautiful, which is menaced; and for the Truth, which seems to us to be dying out. There is more than one kind of Chivalry, and lance thrusts are not everything! In default of the sword, we have the pen; failing the pen, speech : and in default of speech, honour, in our lives!"[1414].

The knight, using the Code of Chivalry, prepares his soul for the greatest combat. "The soul becomes the warrior[1415]" and faces the wickedness on earth, in his own heart, and the Devil Himself[1416].

[1410] Isaiah 49:2

[1411] (Barber, 1995) pg. 135

[1412] (Ellsburg, 2001) pg. 385

[1413] (Vauchez, 1993) pg. 98, (Lull, 2001) pg. 72, 34, (Martyr, 2001-2013) ch. 2, (Bangley, 2007) pg. 101, 277, (Scupoli, 1945 edition) pg. 19-20

[1414] (Gautier, 1989) preface

[1415] (Thorpe, 1972) from episode 5, *The Soul is the Warrior*, teleplay by Ron Bishop

[1416] (Holmes, originally 1980, electronically 2002) pg. 37-38, (Digby, 1829) pg. 70

The Spirit of the Code

Taking the lessons and stories found in the Bible and turning them into a practical lifestyle is called Theological Reflection. It is a necessary skill for any Bible-based Christian. Similarly, the modern knight takes the histories, codes, and legends of knight-errantry and Chivalry, translating them into a useful discipline to confront the worldly evils of Today.

We will take the ten rules listed above as a guideline, and, while combining them with other legitimate Chivalry codes and historically accurate knightly understandings, create a collection of strong Chivalrous rules that can be followed within any society. While reflecting the true spirit of Chivalrous law, this inner code will avoid express physical violence, concentrating on the evils within. The arm and sword of the knight will still be called upon from time to time, but only in the face of physical danger and armed conflict.

Why this focus on the inner battles, rather than the outer, physical battles? The modern perception sees knighthood and Chivalry as primarily a material affect, swords and shields and armored men on horseback, actions done in this world only. Certainly, the physical, worldly battles and wars seem more exciting and glorious[1417]. But the true battles, the awesome and terrible conflicts of the mind and spirit are unseen and unheard by history and by one's fellow man. Imagine, battling against selfishness or lust, greed, or hate! What kind of dragon would the incarnation of Gluttony look like, or Avarice, or Prejudice? Then imagine taking up the sword of the soul against the Evil One Himself! A true knight does this every day[1418].

The Code of Chivalry, as in every aspect of the knight, must include the three arenas: the physical, mental and spiritual worlds, and deal with them. The true knight obeys the code in all worlds, fighting titanic battles in all three. For a knight, in fact, the spiritual and mental battles are first and foremost, and make the physical battles seem as nothing in comparison[1419]. "And therefore the knight who uses the things that pertain to the order of Chivalry as touching his body, and has none of the

---

[1417] (John, 1995) pg. 249
[1418] (Lull, 2001) pg. 85
[1419] (Zwemer, 1902) pg. 39- 40 for Lull's example of this very battle, (Barber, 1995) pg. 136

virtues that pertain to Chivalry as touching the soul is not the friend of the order of knighthood"[1420].

In true knightly fashion, we will simply focus more on the mental and spiritual battles than some codes did in the past. In this way, and in all ways, we honor the First Commandment, "Love the Lord your GOD with all your heart, mind, soul, and strength". The knight turns his mind, heart, soul, and body into a disciplined weapon for the LORD.

A Modern but Chivalrous Code

1. Believe what the True Church of Christ teaches:

We live in a confused world. Modern philosophies, cults and "religions" swarm today, stuffing the media and their followers with bizarre and un-Christian concepts: Communistic anti-religious rants, New-age ideas, Radical Feminist Earth-Goddess worship, revelries around the May Pole and Thor's hammer, not to mention the Atheistic craze of a universe bumped into existence by un-provable alternate universes.

Only a solid understanding of what it is to be a Christian, discernment, can steer the knight correctly through this bog of fuzzy thinking. But today, most people, including many Christians, do not know what Christian churches in general teach. Before one can take the first step of knighthood, fulfill even the first command of our code, one must know what it means to believe the Christian way.

For the knight of the 1100's, there was only one way. THE Church, the Catholic Church. To follow her doctrine was the official and only path for the knight. Today, there are many "branches of Christianity", but they all follow the same basic tenets. The official list of what Christians have believed for nearly two thousand years is compiled in what is known as the Nicene Creed.

[1420] (Lull, 2001) pg. 30

The Nicene Creed

We believe in one GOD
The Father, The Almighty,
The Maker of Heaven and Earth,
Of all that is seen and unseen

We believe in one lord Jesus Christ,
The only Son of GOD
Eternally begotten of the Father,
GOD from GOD, light from light,
Begotten, not made
One in being with the Father
Through him, all things were made
For us men and for our salvation
He came down from Heaven
By the power of the Holy Spirit
He was born of the Virgin Mary
And became Man.

For Our sake he was crucified under Pontius Pilate
He suffered, died, and was buried.
On the third day, he rose from the dead
And is seated at the right hand of the Father
He will come again in glory to judge the living and the dead
And his kingdom will have no end.

We believe in the Holy Spirit
The Lord, the giver of life
Who proceeds from the Father and Son.
With the Father and the Son He is worshipped and glorified.
He has spoken through the prophets.
We believe in one holy, catholic, and apostolic Church.
We acknowledge one baptism for the forgiveness of sins.
We look for the resurrection of the dead,
And the life of the world to come. Amen.

(This is the Catholic version. The only real difference between this and the other denomination versions consists in the capitalization of the word "church".)

Belief in the words of this creed, and in the Scriptures that it reflects, are the core of any truly Christian church. If this creed seems incredulous and difficult, it is because we have been polluted by the imposing array of non-Christian influences that abound in our modern world.

The churches themselves are constantly invaded by alien or modern concepts that may appear sound, but deep within are contrary to Christ and His mission[1421]. It takes true discernment to carefully analyze and identify what is real and what is false in many of our modern churches. We should pray for wisdom.

With prayer as our bedrock, we then read and study our faith, striving to understand it better and more fully every day. While others are experts in only one field, we excel in them all, especially in the study of our own religion. While others waste their time in sports statistics and cooking shows, we invest in the contemplation of GOD and His law. Even the honorable responsibility of work turns shallow in comparison to such time spent.

2. Defend the Church

In the Middle Ages, the knights protected the entirety of Christianity against the Saracen Hordes, known today as the Moslems. From Spanish fields, to French country-sides, to islands in the Mediterranean, like Malta, knights gave their lives to keep even the physical structure of the Church from falling beneath fire and sword. At times, it seemed Christianity itself would be completely swallowed in a wave of invaders, and only the knight's courage and blood, driven by the Holy Spirit, saved her.

In today's world, the Christian Church, in all its "branches", is still under attack by a thousand enemies; some on the outside, some on the inside. In some countries, Christians are systematically slaughtered,

---

[1421] Many modern concepts are false to even logical reasoning, let alone religious doctrine

hunted down and executed, and in my own country, sentiment is building against anything that resembles pious Christianity[1422].

Perhaps I can understand why people in foreign lands might misunderstand or misperceive the Christian mission. But in the United States, there is no excuse for misperception. Yet, Homosexuals claim they are persecuted, when it is Christians who are not allowed to speak against them; Atheists claim they are brow-beaten, when it is Christians who are not allowed to utter the name of GOD in a school or football game or even show a cross in a public place; and Liberals claim that conservative Christians hold all authority, when the Ten commandments are not allowed on Government property and abortion on demand is still the law after forty years.

Other enemies lurk in the shadows, with names like modernization, greed, selfishness, relativism, complacency, decadence, ignorance, and prejudice. These are the enemies of the inside, and they lurk within the human heart and mind, and must be crushed like any disease.

Molesters, masquerading as church men, have been especially heinous. Many investigators have said these creatures placed themselves in churches on purpose, many especially to destroy the Church from the inside!

In many ways, these attacks are more destructive and fiendish than any Saracen invasion.

Some might ask: "Does not GOD defend the Church?" Why does the Church need knights or anyone else to defend her? It is a Chivalrous belief that GOD acts through men. Let us be those men. Let us be the ones that GOD uses to defend the Church. Let us ride forth against all enemies of Christianity.

But how? How will we fight these enemies? When they are mental enemies, the knight engages them in the mental realm, with the mental weapons of his intellectual arsenal. When the Church is attacked spiritually, the knight wields the spiritual sword alongside the true priests.

[1422] (Sexton, 2013) About two-thirds of all countries in the world have persecution, discrimination, and harassment against Christians, and across the world, most religious persecution, up to 70%, is against Christians. (Convention, 2014) Around 170,000 Christians are martyred every year, and around 200 million Christians are persecuted worldwide.

Knights and Saints like Sir Ramon Lull, St. Augustine, St. Aquinas, and St. Francis have already shown us how.

When the physical enemies come, and they will, whether they be Islamic Terrorists or Communists or whoever, it is of course the knight's duty to fight them physically, to stand and defend the Church against all who would wish to kill Christians and burn churches and Bibles. This is a defensive measure, for no knight would attack the enemies of the Church in this way unless her foes were already on the march. Even the Crusades were initiated to defend Christian pilgrims, the Byzantine Church, Church of the Holy Sepulcher, and Jerusalem, the Holy City, from the continuing degradation of Islamic slavery[1423].

In the meantime, let us conduct ourselves as Christians, true Christians, and this will defend our belief as well as any sword, and trumpet our cause better than any campaign.

3. Defend the weak, the innocent, and the poor

One of the most touching definitions of a knight was Victor Hugo's description: "He listened always if one called to him for help"[1424]. "That is to wit," said Sir Lull, "to help and to aid those who are weeping, who require the knight's aid and mercy, and who in the knight have their hope"[1425].

The knight will be confronted, as everyone is from time to time, by situations in which someone is bullying, oppressing, or viciously attacking another. In these individual situations, the knight has every right and responsibility in the world to stand up for the person in need.

When the Nazis, the ultimate oppressors, were threatening to imprison and kill orphans under his care, Sir and Saint Maximilian Kolbe was told he could leave in safety if he hurried and snuck out of the country. Kolbe refused. "How can I leave them behind while I go on to safety? I will stay with these children as long as I can and care for them"[1426]. Because of this and the fact he was a priest, Kolbe himself was placed in a concentration camp.

[1423] (Belloc, 1992) pg. 16-17

[1424] (Gautier, 1989) pg.73

[1425] (Lull, 2001) pg. 36

[1426] (Faccenda, 1999)

As we have seen, the knight has set himself specifically as a defender of anyone who is weak or innocent against any who would oppress them. This shows not only the knight's mercy, but his courage, for his charges are especially those who are targeted by criminals, evil doers, and tyrants.

This rule is not only a warning to those who would oppress others, but to the knight in order to control himself. It is a matter of history, that the stronger feel indeed tempted to use such strength to manipulate the weaker. The knight must guard himself against such temptation. "The wicked knight who loves not the order of Chivalry defeats the knight within himself"[1427].

But who are these people who are given specific protection? Throughout history, knights have been primarily concerned with five groups of the weak and innocent, religious persons, women, children, the handicapped, and the poor[1428]. Traditionally, these five groups have been the special targets of criminals and evil, so the knight has specifically chosen them as charges of protection.

The innocent were seen by the knights as those who were without stain of mortal sin. They could be anyone who generally led a lawful life, even though none are truly sinless. Also, anyone who could not engage in the terrible inward and outward struggle against evil, and thus were somehow sheltered from it, was considered an innocent. Children, who do not have the ability to perceive good and evil clearly yet, and thus whose sins are more excusable, are generally considered innocent. A tiny child or baby especially, or someone without the full mental facilities to perceive the difference between good and evil fall within this category. The Innocent and the good are given first protection, no matter who they are.

The next group afforded protection is known anciently as "the weak". When Lancelot came across two groups in mortal combat, since he could not determine which group was actually in the right or "innocent", he determined the weaker group and rode to help them[1429].

But compared to a trained and focused knight, almost anyone is weak. Civilized people, for instance, who spend their lives worrying over jobs and families, while building webs of possessions, have not honed their warrior instincts and can be classified as weak. The traditional

---

[1427] (Lull, 2001), pg. 35
[1428] (Lull, 2001) pg. 35
[1429] (Matarasso, 1969) pg.156, (Malory, 1497) pg. 391

lifestyles of priests and other religious persons, namely concentration on the spiritual, generally make them not as physically capable in physical battle, so they can be placed in the category of needing protection. Children and the mentally deficient, are obvious candidates for protection against those who would abuse or exploit them. Women, seen as physically weaker than men in general, and depressingly, a specific and persistent target of criminals, are traditional recipients of the knight's protection.

Even as late as the 1920's, many men were still focused on the protection of women in dangerous situations, even unto death. While the Titanic was sinking, Benjamin Guggenheim gave up his seat on a life boat to a female stranger. "No woman," He said, "shall be left aboard this ship because Benjamin Guggenheim was a coward"[1430]!

Thomas Andrews, managing director and shipbuilder for the company responsible for building the Titanic, deciding to give his seat to a woman and go down with the ship he had helped to build. He was 39, one of the youngest managing directors in his field, with a fortune and a great future ahead of him. But he saw the Honor of saving a woman's life, even a stranger's, as more glorious than any other fate[1431].

In recent years, some women have chaffed at the idea of being called "weak". As I have often said, when compared to the trained knight, especially with armor and weaponry and mounted on an unstoppable charger, almost anyone would be considered weak. It is not an insult. Some women have even balked at being called "innocent", suspecting within this title some weird license to consider them "chattel" or "empty-minded". The truth is, almost any non-combatant would be considered an innocent in the knight's mind, as non-combatant civilians are considered today.

These protective attitudes toward women, the young, and the mentally deficient have prevailed even into our time, where these groups are given special attention and deference in courts, cases, and public sympathy.

With these definitions in mind, one can easily see the horror a knight may experience when encountering a child or women actively engaged in evil. Even more confusing are the cases of persons with mental challenges who have committed atrocities. In such situations, the knight must

---

[1430] I saw this quote at the Titanic Museum in Branson, Missouri
[1431] (Biography, 2012)

consider the safety of those around them. No matter who is engaging in an evil action, others must be protected against this evil.

The poor are given great deference in the area of knightly protection. The code from the 1200's that we have used above does not specifically name the poor, but almost every other code of the Knight, used across the centuries, normally speaks of them by name.

Who are the Poor? It is difficult to ask this question without bringing up a myriad of images that vary from person to person, country to country. The Knight specifically thinks of the poor as those who are especially dependent on others, as in widows, orphans, and the handicapped. The best definition comes from Christ himself: the poor are those who *cannot* repay whatever kindness shown them; they are the crippled, the lame, the blind, the absolutely abandoned of society, with no one to speak for them[1432]. The poor are those who cannot help themselves, **not** those who refuse to work or decline to help themselves.

The great king Charlemagne, on his death bed now, called his son. What advice would the monarch impart, for this terrible time would only allow a message of most importance. He pulled his son close and "bade his son to humiliate himself before the poor. 'Before them be of no reputation. Give them help and counsel'"[1433].

As Charlemagne suggests, to truly help the poor, one treats them with respect and helps them in matters of counsel and education, not just by giving hand-outs.

Many in our confused modern world have understood this rule to promote heavy taxes, or even Socialism and Communism, since these systems pretend to help the poor by lowering everyone to the same economic level. Historically, such exercises benefit only tyrants or elitist governments. A large non-representative government forcing individuals or organizations, on pain of severe penalty or even death, to hand over treasure, savings, or money to said government is theft, Tyranny, and oppression on a grand scale, not Chivalry. Such abuse of power is exactly what the knight must fight against. Only if the wealthy person or organization has achieved wealth from subterfuge or ill-will should the

[1432] Luke 14:12-14
[1433] (Gautier, 1989) pg. 43, (Ferrante, 2001) pg. 68

knight fight against them, even take from them to give to the poor, as in the acts of Robin Hood.

Among these five groups who are especially deserving of the knight's care, there is a hierarchy. The innocent are always protected first, then the weak, then women, children, and the poor in general.

But why a hierarchy? Why should we make a hierarchy of these groups? Because discernment is needed to determine who should truly be protected from whom.

One may find a man who is innocent of any crime, but who is hunted by a group of deranged women. Because the man is innocent, he is to be protected. A wealthy giant, who has helped others with his wealth, can still be attacked by those who do not believe in a good man who is wealthy. He might be more deserving than the masses. A dirty, mud-smeared child can still be the one in the right, and the well-bathed children taunting her may need to be quieted. An outcast of society, chased and harassed by the well-dressed and respected, may be more righteous than all of civilization.

Nowhere can a knight assume anything. Even grandmas, seemingly sweet, old ladies, of any race, can turn out desperately wicked. Recently, the story surfaced of a man falsely accused of sexual abuse of his five-year-old relative. The grandma had convinced the child to blame this man, and he had sat in prison for 14 years, languishing under a charge created exclusively in the mind of a little, old lady[1434]! A knight, in this case, would find himself defending a man against a frail grandma.

Even an enemy may be protected, if he is hunted for a crime he did not commit. In the Conquest by Righteousness code of the warriors from India, circa 300BC, the eighth rule reads, "If entreated with joined hands, a warrior shall defend even his enemy"[1435].

In the final analysis, the knight protects all those who are good, but especially those who cannot defend themselves, against those who would oppress them wrongly. He must use discernment in how he accomplishes this defense, relying as much on his mind as on his strong arm.

The knight can do this in many ways, not just with a sword or his testimony. Giving others education, skill, and the ability to protect

---

[1434] (Kapitan, 2012)
[1435] (Fields R., 1991) pg. 86-87, see Appendix 2 for full code.

themselves in every way can multiply the knight's express protection a thousand fold.

As an example, understand this: General Robert Baden-Powell, in 1907, decided to create an organization which would train boys in the image of the King Arthur's knights of the Round Table. He called this organization the "Boy Scouts" and proclaimed their patron as St. George. For 106 years, the Scouts prepared boys to become honorable citizens and responsible defenders of Truth and liberty, decency and ethics[1436]. The knight must always teach Honor and inspire right action.

To shame evil-doers and make the world take notice, the knight must speak for those who cannot, even calling out the oppressors to answer for their crimes.

The knight is indeed the voice for the voiceless[1437]. This example will instruct and shine through many generations, and down the corridors of time.

Many have misinterpreted Christ's warning to avoid judgment as a command to never tell others when they are doing wrong. "If I do not warn you of your crimes against GOD and man, GOD will hold me responsible"[1438]! It is not only our duty to defend the weak and innocent among us, but to admonish those who oppress them. We do this not only for the sake of the innocent, but also for the sake of the oppressors. If we do not admonish the guilty, GOD HIMSELF will, using terrible suffering, in this world or the next.

4. Love your country

June 6, 1944. Hitler's Nazi armies had taken over most, if not all, of Europe. Italy, France, Spain, Poland, and Most of Russia had fallen to Germany's third Reich. Only England now could resist, but even this once great empire was bloodied and bruised, almost to death.

The president of the United States, FDR, and General Eisenhower joined forces with England, in a last effort to save Europe, and the world, from total destruction. The plan was called "Operation Overlord", and it required the landing of over a 100,000 men along the Normandy Beach area of Northern France. If American and British troops could gain and

---

[1436] (Morgan, 2006) pg. 112
[1437] (Gautier, 1989) pg. 42-44
[1438] Ezekiel 3:20

435

hold ground on this lonely stretch of beach, they might be able to slowly push back the tide of the Nazi war machine.

It was a desperate, almost suicidal gamble. The Nazis, fairly certain that some kind of attack loomed, had built up huge defenses along this area—machine gun nests, giant cannons that could blow away dozens of men at a time, tank traps that would stop even the toughest of armored vehicles, landmines—hidden bombs that would detonate when accidently stepped upon, and thousands of highly trained Nazi troops—waited behind high cliffs and fortresses of stone, all along Normandy Beach.

It was a death trap—everyone knew it—and that's why it just might work. No one would expect an attack at such a fortified place.

The water and wind blew chill that morning as Allied troops landed at Normandy, coming by parachute or boat—and many of them would never return. Hundreds of soldiers were shot even before they could clear the boats and get to the beach. Those who reached the sand met a wall of bullets. Soldiers threw themselves behind sand dunes and in pits dug out by cannon fire. But they knew if they stayed on the beach, they would die, so they pushed forward, directly into the teeth of the Nazis.

12,000 Allied troops died or were wounded, but more poured in— 155,000 Allied troops pushed forward and forced the Nazis to fall back, inch by inch, man by man, until finally the Americans and English had secured a large swath of beach, enough to launch another invasion, and to retake Europe. Months of fighting still lay ahead, but this was the beginning of the end for the Nazis, and World War II.

We would win. Thanks to those brave men who faced death on D-Day.

These men risked everything to preserve their countries and their freedom, and in so doing, avenged one of the worst crimes in history. Moderns mock on about the triteness of nationalism, and fools discuss how patriotism is for the ignorant. But the world owes its salvation to love of country.

What can we do to match the sacrifice of our forebears? Until our time comes, only a token. Every day, honor your country and its past. Working in a school, I make sure I pledge allegiance to the flag every day, in front of the students, as a sign of the honor I give the ideals of America. Even if they do not feel the same, I want them to see a man stand up for patriotism. I teach my country's history in a truthful and respectful way, highlighting its heroic ideals. I follow all the laws set down by the government, as long as they conform to the law of GOD; I want my country to benefit from my being in it, so I do what I can in civic duty and volunteering. Such, also, is the Code.

Some may scoff. They point at the flaws of my country, and there are some. Slavery, they cry. But what other country would split itself asunder, sacrificing thousands of her sons to cure herself of that disease? War, they shriek. But only America would go to battle for others, time and again, without any reward. Doubt me? Count the dead on Normandy beach.

And what of the other countries across the world? Is not there great examples in them, as well? Britain has King Arthur, Spain has the Cid, France has Joan of Arc, South Africa has Nelson Mandela. No wall stands for any patriot to find honor, whichever his country.

5. You shall never surrender before your enemy

There were 188 men guarding the Alamo, and over 3,000 Mexican troops attacking outside. The General Santa Anna did not offer terms, but demanded the surrender of the Alamo. "Surrender or Death!" The General said. Colonel Travis, commander of the Alamo, answered with a canon-shot over the general's head. "Victory or Death!" Travis replied.

The Alamo can be a metaphor for the soul of the knight. Every day, every hour, the soul of the Knight is attacked and surrounded by thousands of temptations, afflictions, and salvos of the True Enemy.

The true enemy is within, and is used by the Evil One[1439]. He knows human weakness and has had millions of years of practice in defeating humans. The Evil One uses every weapon against us imaginable: pain, worry, lust, greed, anger, thoughtlessness, weakness, selfish pleasure, guilt, cowardice, vice, and a thousand other stumbling blocks, some without name, all without mercy.

The knight must stand as a wall of iron and stone against this terrible storm, and not give an inch. To do so is surrender, which automatically equals death. Without honor in his soul, the knight knows he is dead[1440];

[1439] Our greatest foes, and whom we must chiefly combat, are within - The History of the Renowned Don Quixote de la Mancha, Volume: 2 (1743) by Miguel de Cervantes Saavedra; Chapter: VIII, Page 75.

[1440] A man without honor is worse than dead—Also in Cervantes's book, volume 1, part 1, chapter 33

not only dead but in everlasting darkness and death. Forever must he stand there, spitting in face of the Devil.

Neither can we surrender before pain or fear. Tyrants wish to control our hearts and silence our tongues through torture and subversion. Criminals wish to make us cower as we walk the streets or even sit in our homes. The bully in our neighborhood wants to make our blood turn cold when we hear him call our names.

But the knight calls the bully's name, defeats the criminal[1441], and forces the tyrant to worry on his throne. For the knight, fear and pain are no excuse for surrender.

True Surrender and True Victory begin in the soul. While upholding our beliefs and values, we are complete; without our beliefs and values, we are nothing. Without the Code, we will become an empty husk, blown away by the first breath of struggle. If we give in, if we surrender before evil, no force of arms and no good intention can save us.

Let there be no retreat in our hearts or our thoughts. Our inner-self is a country which we cannot allow to be invaded, because then there would be no hope. We must adhere to our beliefs, keep our values, uphold our Honor and Morals in the face of every opposition. Suffer all pains, withstand all torture, go through all shame and insult, and even die before we surrender our souls.

"But he who holds out until the end will be saved"[1442].

Victory or death[1443].

6. Make War on Evil, Without End and Without Mercy.

The phrase "without mercy" is shocking to me, because knighthood is immersed in mercy. A man may know which side is the blessed and good side, by how much mercy that side may show. There is only one place and in one battle where a knight has no mercy: the battle against Evil itself.

To the knight of the Middle Ages, the Islamic Saracen embodied Physical evil. This may seem like prejudice, but when we remember that the Saracen thought of Christianity as something to be beaten into

---

[1441] (Barber, The Knight and Chivalry, Revised Edition, 1995) pg. 137

[1442] Matthew 10:22 also, Mark 13:13. Luke 21:19

[1443] Col. William B. Travis's farewell phrase in his famous letter from the Alamo in 1836

submission and defeated, and then torturously converted, and that the Saracen conquered all the way to Southern France, the feelings of the medieval knight may be justified.

Still, to this day, a Moslem converting to Christianity is seen by other Islamists as the worst sin imaginable, worse than rape or murder, and is punishable by death. And what of the other side? The United States, long considered a Christian Nation, and hated by many Moslems, came to the aid of the Kurds during the Iraqi War. The U.S. captured Saddam Hussein, a tyrant who had massacred thousands of Kurds. Although many distrusted the American's actions, there was no mistaking the great service America had done for the Kurds, the people of Saladin. And who is Saladin? The leader of the Moslems during the 3rd Crusade, and one of Islam's greatest heroes.

No matter the past or the present, the knight cannot afford to see the Saracen as the greatest foe anymore. Even though the Islamists still teach, in many countries, that Christians and Jews are the greatest evil (especially Christian and Jewish Americans), the knight must look beyond to the truth. The religions of the world must join together to battle the true enemy, the Evil One himself.

This enemy is in every country, east and west, and in every human. Each man, woman, and child, must rise within themselves, and defend their souls against the onslaught of the Spirit of Evil and his lies. The three great monotheistic religions in the world believe in a Great GOD of Goodness and Truth, and through this they should be able to tolerate each other at least. Whatever the case, if we join together to fight evil, we may have a chance to help the world; if we fight amongst each other, the Evil One will simply move in over the ashes of our mutual destruction.

The knight stands ready to join hands with his former foe in an all-out campaign against the Devil, the true enemy. Just as Rodrigo De Bivar, The Cid, joined together with many Spanish Moors to defend Spain against the apocalyptic Yusef[1444]. My Moslem brethren, it is time to see where your true goals are, in the defeat of the Evil One, or in the destruction of the world.

But together or alone, the knight must continue to fight evil without rest, without cessation, and without mercy.

[1444] (Matthews, 1998) pg. 74

But many still have trouble with the idea of "without mercy". Evil may present itself in very physical terms, especially in the form of criminality. Imagine a criminal who has a record of violent crimes as long as your arm. Should we have mercy or pity upon him, since he stands before us with tears in his eyes, excuses, and sob-stories as lengthy as his criminal record? As a knight must, we should weigh in the balance this criminal's well-being with the rest of society. Who comes first?

For the knight, the well-being of innocents, the good, and society itself is always more important than the well-being of a hardened criminal. Is this pitiless? Is this without remorse or mercy?

So many times in the history of the United States, we have shown mercy on the criminal and allowed him to go free, even when he has proven himself an evil and unrepentant rapist or killer. This criminal then goes forth and commits even more heinous offenses. How was it merciful to let him free? We should show mercy upon the innocent and upon society, by removing that criminal from anyplace where he may inflict more damage. Mercy and pity for the criminal that continuously proves he cannot be trusted? No mercy for him!

And what about the child rapist, the gleeful murderer, the slave-trader, the drug-pusher, the torturer of animals, the panderer, the assassin, and the murderous tyrant? These people must be stopped at all costs. They kill and ruin lives of all around them, and poison the souls of everyone they touch and influence. No mercy for them!

Let these criminals and evil people fear the mailed fist that wields the sword of Justice!

But there is mercy, even here. The U.S. Justice system, borrowed from the Ancient Romans, allows for a jury made up of the suspect's peers. The modern knight must allow for the benefit of the doubt, if he has not seen the crime himself, or cannot use logic to discover the actual criminal. In other words, a person is innocent until proven guilty, and the modern knight defends a fair system to determine guilt, instead of becoming the judge and executioner himself. If this system is eliminated somehow, and the knight knows for sure the person is guilty, what the knight decides then is between him and his GOD.

And what of the mental enemies of the knight? The militant atheists and the secular humanists who spit upon the knight and Christianity, indeed every religion, and mock them with infinite materialistic arguments. What of these, who seem to become more obnoxious and cruel every year, made bold with their commentaries and lies? Some of these attacks border on evil, when their arguments keep people from a relationship with the Living GOD.

The knight shows even these mercy, by courtesy and respect. Though they spit on him, he never resorts to similar actions. Though they mock him, he never stoops to ad-hominem attacks. He comes at them with the mental charge of a runaway freight train or the stealthy strategies of a jaguar, but well within the laws of logic and fact, with respect deserved of an honored opponent. As long, of course, as the knight's enemies stay in the realm of the mental. Once they venture into physical attacks, against the knight, the innocent, or the church? What the knight does then is between him and his GOD—the GOD of Justice.

Is there always mercy in the Heart of the knight? Of course, even if he has to punish or stop evil people, he always looks for a chance to bestow mercy if Justice allows. But one place and time exists where a knight refuses mercy completely. Here there is no yielding:

In the eternal war against himself and his selfish drives[1445].

Remember, it is said that a knight has two hearts[1446], one soft, the other brutal. To his fellow humans, the knight has a heart of mercy. To his own sinful urges, his heart is a grey, merciless stone.

7. Perform All Duties to the Best of Your Ability

In the Middle Ages, the system of government in Europe consisted of a hierarchy of levels known as Feudalism. The king led the country, the lords and nobles ran the administration, the priests and monks prayed for everyone, the knights protected people and the law, and the peasants grew the food[1447]. Feudalism required everyone to do their stated role, or the whole system would fall apart. It was essential for the knights, especially, as the strong arm of the king's law, to uphold order and strictly perform their feudal duties.

Today, Feudalism is gone, and therefore no feudal duties exist. Our original seventh rule is no longer literally valid, but the spirit remains.

[1445] 2 Peter 1:6, Luke 21:19 also, Proverbs 25:28, 1 Corinthians 9:25
[1446] (Corley, 1989) pg. 55, (Gies, 1986) pg. 96
[1447] (Vauchez, 1993) pg. 124, (Coss, 1996) pg. 148

This spirit demands that we take our responsibilities seriously, and every duty we take upon ourselves, we must fulfill as best we can.

The duties to the nation, family, and career have replaced the knightly feudal duties and the knight should take on these duties with the same determination and gusto[1448]. Knights take care and defend their wives and children. Even when knights must go on quests or forsake the world for a closer walk with GOD, knights always make sure their families are cared for and their needs met.

A knight in today's world usually has a career where people depend on him at some level. The knight commits himself to doing the best job he can, and conscientiously takes his responsibilities seriously.

One aspect of Feudalism that has survived to this day is the idea that a man must pay for any goods and services he uses. A knight is required to exchange these goods and services for goods and services of his own. He need not pay immediately, but eventually he always pays his dues[1449].

When a man saves another's life, it becomes the divine responsibility and privilege of the recipient to find a way to repay such a service. It may even fall to the recipient's descendents to repay the benefactor. Whatever the case, no matter if across the ages, such a heroic act must be repaid.

In America's darkest hour, the French bestowed several gifts. In the 1770's, France gave the fledgling government of the United States a man named Lafayette, who assisted the General Washington during the Revolutionary War, and also a block-aid that assisted Washington's final battle against the British. Because of the block-aid, the United States was finally successful in its birth-pangs.

Since then, the U.S. was ever mindful of the fact that she owed France a great favor. But through the years, America never seemed able to pay the debt. Over a hundred years passed, and, honestly, there were those who thought that America had forgotten the debt, forgotten who had helped create the greatest country in the world. Cynics scoffed and said that nations, even the United States, would never help another nation to repay honor, for countries know only interests, not friends, quoting Lord Palmerston.

[1448] (Gautier, 1989) Preface
[1449] "Never stand begging for that which you have the power to earn." In Cervantes's book on Don Quixote, volume 1, chapter VI

Then, during World War I, the Germans threatened to overrun France. The United States answered the French call for help, and together with the French, turned the German tide.

Charles Stanton, chief disbursing officer of the American Expeditionary forces in France, stepped up to Lafayette's tomb.

In a strange footnote to history, Stanton spoke to the spirit of Lafayette. "What we have of blood and treasure are yours. In the presence of the illustrious dead, we pledge our hearts and our honor in carrying the war to a successful conclusion."

"Lafayette," He said, "we are here."[1450]

The Americans had come at last, paying the debt they owed from so many years before. Just like a knight would, the Americans always remembered their debt, returning again in World War II to liberate Europe from the Nazis.

8. Never lie, and always keep promises

Second only to the knight's battles for GOD and to protect the innocent, this rule of avoiding lies and broken promises is the most distinctive of Chivalrous traits. While the modern person might believe a knight is known by his sword and armor, the knight himself perceives he is known by the truth of his word and the binding of his promises. The word of the knight is stronger than iron chain[1451]. If you always tell the truth and keep your promises, you will stand out as clearly from the crowd of moderns, as if your forehead was branded with the truth[1452].

In the Middle Ages, the measure of a man was his ability to stand on his promises[1453]. The worse insult, far above individual insults or even having the family scandalized, was to be called a liar. Today, popular culture has shrunk the importance of promises to almost nothing. Movies even make fun of them. This is foolhardy, for all of society itself is build on the foundation of promises.

[1450] (Editors A. D., 2000) This comment was attributed to General Pershing

[1451] (Moncrieff, 1976) pg. 428

[1452] Ezekiel's mark, signifying a true follower of GOD, Ezekiel 9:4, St. Jerome says that it is the Tau, the last letter of the Hebrew alphabet, shaped like a cross, and St. Francis uses it as his personal mark. See the Douay-Rheims Bible (Challoner, 1941)

[1453] (Gautier, 1989) pg. 66-67

Few rules have more impact on society and life as this one. It touches every aspect of the modern world. Business men know the importance of this rule, and even movie moguls in Hollywood like to depend on a handshake and a verbal contract.

As a citizen, one has an implicit promise to keep the rules of the society one is a part of, and the society also promises the citizen certain rights and owes responsibilities to the common good. Without implicit or explicit promises, nothing within or without a society can be trusted. Without trust, all things in society deteriorate[1454].

This rule is at the center of marriage, as well as every single transaction between human beings. Recently, marriage vows have earned renewed scrutiny because of the gross abuses that many have visited upon marriage itself. Modern society scoffs at concerns when particular presidents or heads-of-state "cheat" on their spouses, but any knight or hero should pause. If a person can not keep their promises to a spouse, how can they be expected to keep their promises to a country, state, government, or ideal? And if they cannot keep their promises to any of the above, how can they be trusted to carry out even the smallest responsibility of office?

Some might say, "Well, marriage vows sure, but what of other promises, be they ever so small?" A knight should observe all promises and keep them as if they were precious jewels. Even the tiniest of promises reflects on one's strength of character and honor[1455]. They provide practice for the bigger promises, and create a positive reputation for anyone with the strength to keep them.

To be a modern knight, few rules of knighthood are easier to keep, but just as easy to break. One does not need a sword or even physical strength to keep a promise, and they can be as hidden as intentions or thoughts, but few things can wear more heavily upon the heart. The poorest or wealthiest man, both, will find promises easy to support and nourish, but just as destructive when made rashly or treated loosely.

Related to the promise is the rule of telling the truth. The rule does not mention or allow white lies to save feelings, or even important lies to save philosophies or state policies[1456]. To lie is to join oneself with

---

[1454] (Gracian, 1996) pg. 78, (Alter, 2007) pg. 292—Lying and Injustice are the first steps toward the apocalypse.

[1455] Luke 16:10

[1456] (Wills, 1999) pg.84-85, one may not do evil so that good may come from it

that which does not exist, that which has no being, and that which is truly nothing. The truth makes one strong, while lies make one weak and finally non-existent. St. Augustine said that evil itself is privation, nothingness[1457]. Therefore to lie is to align oneself to evil and meld oneself into death[1458].

Simply put, no knight may lie or break a promise, not in the past, now, or in the future. It would be better to die than dishonor oneself even in a trifle[1459].

But how, in this modern age may we, the willing, avoid lying and breaking promises, when all around us others lie and cheat every day?

The real question might be, how much is Honesty worth to you?

Such a question burned in the brain and heart of Ascension Franco Gonzales, a 23-year-old illegal alien living in Los Angeles, working as a dishwasher. He had been sitting at the bus stop, when an armored vehicle roared by, lurched, and expelled a bag of money[1460].

No one was around. Gonzales walked over to the clear bag, and could easily see the bundles of 20-dollar bills that filled it.

Worried that he might be seen with the money and killed for it on those crime-ridden streets, Gonzales quickly found an opaque sack out of a garbage can and stuffed in the bag[1461]. He admitted that he felt temptation to keep the money, but his conscience reminded him of several things: where he came from and what he wanted to be.

He had been raised by a poor but honest Catholic Family, in Hildalgo, the state of Mexico named for the famed warrior of humanitarian causes, Father Miguel Hildalgo. And he wanted, more than anything, to be an honest man.

This presented several problems. His friends would think him a fool for not keeping the money. And, wasn't he already breaking the law as an illegal? He had come to California to earn money to help his mother build a house back in Mexico, and here he earned $1300 a month, dishwashing. Why not use the money? Conditions back in his home

[1457] (Copleston, 1962) pg. 100
[1458] (Deane, 1963) pg. 40, (Buber, 1953) pg. 12
[1459] (Lull, 2001) pg. 42, 70, 71, (Gautier, 1989) pg. 83
[1460] (Becerra, 2001)
[1461] (Becerra, 2001) Ibid.

town gave him little choice about coming to America, but actually taking money that was not his[1462]?

He talked to his friends, who advised him to keep the money, and he thought about it all night long.

In the morning, he called the police, and turned all of the $203,000 dollars into the authorities. They were shocked by the sheer honesty of this poor man. And his mother cried tears of joy.

"GOD has placed him on the path of Honesty. We are very proud of him." She said.

"Yes, people criticize him," His father said. "But others congratulate us for having such a son." The ones who speak badly about him are shown the house that Gonzales would later build for his family, and "their mouth falls"[1463].

If an immigrant to the country, poor and barely scraping by, can be honest to this extent, no one else has an excuse to lie.

9. Largesse

Largesse has often been confused with charity, because the primary difference is small. Charity is primarily to those who need it, while Largesse could be to anyone, as in house guests, friends, or family. A knight, who usually had access to sums of wealth, either from inheritance, gifts, or the spoils of war, was expected to share this with his friends and the poor[1464].

Whatever the case, knights have a duty to avoid luxury and refrain from loading themselves down with materialism[1465]. Knights need certain things to fulfill their mission for good and against evil, but beyond that, wealth and luxury are to be given away, or used to do GOD's work.

This is a difficult thing to do, not only for the knights of old but especially in our time, when materialism and consumerism are everywhere. We are surrounded by advertisements and urgings to acquire more "stuff": furniture, clothes, accessories, status symbols, jewelry,

---

[1462] (Becerra H., 2002)
[1463] (Becerra H., 2002)
[1464] (Lull, 2001) pg. 19, 61, (Gautier, 1989) pg. 70
[1465] (Meller, 2002) pg. 48

electronics, etc. Consumerism isn't evil in itself, but it clouds the mind and shields the soul from what is truly important, the presence of GOD.

To guard against losing our way to GOD and Honor, the knight is asked to always give whatever he can, and to joyously do so.

If we cannot be charitable or at least show largesse, we will run the risk of the sin identified by the Legendary Saracen King Marsilus. Captured by Charlemagne, and brought to court, he looked over the people there. When he saw how fat the bishops and abbots were, and how emaciated the poor were in their presence, he cried out "and so that is the way in which you treat your poor, irreverently, and to the dishonor of HIM whose faith you profess! Well no, I shall not be baptized—I prefer death"[1466].

Many moderns like this rule, finding within it some reflection of their own concern over wealth and social justice. But they wish to flaunt their largresse, just like they flaunt their sexual license, in the street and loudly. They brag incessantly over their kind hearts and open wallets, even while they make others pay for their extravagant giving. The true knight tells no one when he gives, and is secretive to how much it costs him, while making sure it costs only him.

10. Thou shall always and everywhere be the champion of the Right and the Good against Injustice and Evil[1467]

The knight stands forever as the protector of good people and those around him. When he sees evil occur he must act, no matter where or when. This concept may prove as difficult as standing in front of the gates of Hell, for evil, brutality, and unfairness may be found everywhere.

Because of this responsibility, the true knight forges himself into a terrifying weapon in all three worlds of battle. Night and day, he pushes himself, trains himself, sharpens himself, defines himself, until he is as polished silver and purified gold. Never letting up, the knight constantly improves himself, growing stronger mentally, physically and spiritually.

Evil never sleeps. Therefore, the knight can never let down his guard. Being the champion of goodness and right means to stop evil everywhere and anywhere, regardless of the danger, or even the embarrassment, or even the inconvenience.

[1466] (Gautier, 1989) pg. 70
[1467] (Lull, 2001) pg. 38

In today's world, we do not engage in sword battles every hour, but there will be other confrontations. Small battles and struggles will come. Perhaps you hear noises in your neighbor's vacant home, or someone abusing a spouse. Perhaps you take up the cause of educating the ignorant, preventing the local bully from finding his victims, stopping drug deals on the street or anywhere, hampering the growth of violent gangs, obstructing an attack on an elderly person, shouting down the sneers of a bigot, defending a crippled man from the jeers of stupid children. You might even preach against the tyranny of an oppressive government, or speak for the voiceless in your community.

You have your choice of conflict, but Evil and injustice can attack you within your own mind and heart. Wrong desires of the heart will surround you, and selfish demands of the world will besiege you. You must stand up to them all, especially when you hear their complaints within your own head. The Evil One has many arenas and weapons, even in your home. Great saints can be attacked even when they are alone and in their rooms. Mother Teresa suffered from doubt, St. Francis suffered from exhaustion, and St. Ignatius worried of his own worthiness.

At the very end of things, I can promise you one thing. If you take on the mantel of knighthood and challenge the Devil as every knight must, you will know little rest. You will find plenty of battles to fight, and most of them will begin within your own fears and weaknesses. The only time you will find respite is within the presence of GOD.

So be it.

Hierarchy of Obedience—(Obedience, section 2)

There are many voices beside those of GOD and the Code.

In our lives, everything cries out for loyalty and obedience. Our GOD, our country, our conscience, our families, our bodies, our friends, our jobs, our political alliances, and even our indulgences, greeds, and ignorances. So many loyalties calling our names, how can a knight do what is right with so many demands on him, especially when they seem contradictory? Chivalry, in a disordered mind, can become a mishmash of loyalties and obediences. The knight, and indeed, any man who wishes to keep his sanity and honor, must be able to discern the most important between them, organizing them based on Justice.

Justice demands that the most deserving receives the most loyalty. GOD, from which all good things spring, thus receives the most loyalty and obedience. From GOD, comes Honor (reflected in the Code) and the life of the Soul, which is conscience. From these things, we learn what else must have priority. Many things are important, but some things are more important than others.

The knight has a rule that keeps his obediences and loyalties in the right order, so that he may govern and order his obedience in a way most pleasing to GOD. Knights call it their hierarchy of loyalties and obediences, Augustine called it *Ordo Amori*[1468], the Order of Love.

1. First is the knight's unswerving loyalty to GOD and Christ
2. Second is his unabashed observance of the CODE
3. Third is his alignment with his conscience
4. Fourth is his honorable service to his country or King
5. Fifth is his loving loyalty to his wife
6. Sixth is his defense of his fellows and the weak of the world
7. Seventh is the defense of himself

With such a hierarchy firmly in place in the soul, heart and mind of the knight, he then uses Reason and Revelation, strength and courage, to enforce them in his own teeming soul.

Obedience to Conscience

It has long been a tenet of the Catholic Church that a man must listen to his Conscience. This assumes that the Conscience is informed by the Holy Spirit, and is not blinded or clouded by the fog of human nature and weakness. It is placed here, halfway between the hierarchies of obedience, because Conscience can be greater than even the law of a country, but cannot be trusted if it goes against the Code or GOD's law.

[1468] (Cahall, 2005), (Copleston, 1962) pg. 100, The Love of GOD vs. the love of self

Alexander Hamilton received the letter he expected. It was a summons to a duel.

He remembered what he had told his son several years ago. His son had been challenged to a duel, and before the young man consented, he asked his father's advice. "A Christian man does not fire upon another Christian man," Hamilton said gravely.

His son took the advice, refused to shoot during the duel, and was killed by his opponent. Hamilton was devastated, quietly enduring the death of his son.

Now he faced the same situation. It is one thing to give advice; it is another to take one's own advice, especially when one has the knowledge of the inevitable culmination of that advice, and the destruction it has brought down upon loved ones.

Hamilton was required, by his day's standard, to accept the challenge to the duel. Any man, especially a statesman, who turned down a duel was instantly labeled a coward. Hamilton was no coward, but he knew that all the political and ethical ideas he had worked for would be eclipsed by this judgment if he declined the summons. He would have preferred to simply walk away, but his reputation and the reputation of his ideas for the country would be stained forever.

So the day came, and Hamilton chose his pistol as his opponent, Aaron Burr, chose his. They were to take twenty paces, turn, and fire. At this deadly range, even an attempt to "wing" Burr might have catastrophic results.

Both men made his paces, turned, aimed, and fired.

Dueling seconds, men required to witness the duel and ensure agreed upon rules, saw exactly what happened. They saw Aaron Burr take his paces, turn, and aiming directly at Hamilton, fire his pistol with deadly accuracy. They saw Hamilton at the same moment, turn and aim up at a branch over Burr's head. Both shots hit their mark[1469].

Men like Hamilton understood conscience, and were willing to obey its harsh commands.

For those who question Hamilton's actions, it remains a fact of History that Hamilton's impact on the United States is honored and

---

[1469] (Bennett, 2006), pg. 191

everlasting. Aaron Burr's entire impact is only measured by the fact that he took Hamilton away from his country.

The question remains: what is conscience? Emotions or moods of the individual cannot be the measure of this conscience. Such a limitation would be to greatly cheapen the concept of the conscience. Some conclude that it is a set of GOD-given concepts, almost like Grace[1470]. Whatever it is, a knight must always be careful of his own conscience. Is he serving his conscience, or just his inner feelings, or even worse, his inner selfishness? The final test is whether the conscience serves base desires, or GOD and Righteousness.

Obedience to Country and King

Obedience to a king or lord also stands as dogma in every kind of Chivalry, especially pagan Chivalry[1471]. Christian Chivalry itself gains its staunch Obedience to GOD from the more ancient Chivalry of Obedience to a lord or king, which the Christian Knight translated into obedience to the One LORD and KING, Christ Jesus[1472].

Since the dawn of time, every Chivalry automatically acknowledged the loyalty and obedience of knights to their kings and lords. Obedience was part of the Brotherhood of the Sword, the true way of warriors everywhere, and one of the main differences between the warrior and the violent brute. This translated into risking life and limb in aiding a lord in battle, sacrificing at the call of a lord, and donating land and money to the lord or king's cause. Chivalry demanded ultimate fealty.

Even in the most terrifying tests of Loyalty.

On Oct. 25, 1854, a strange and heroic event occurred that people all over the world consider as the symbol, the pinnacle of impossible heroism.

Consider the Crimean war—one of the innumerable conflicts between the Russians and the British. On one side of the battlefield, Lord Cardigan, British cavalry officer of the Light Brigade, with his 600 horsemen, faced—on the other side—a solid wall of Russian cannons.

[1470] (Anthony Schraner, 1981) pg. 286

[1471] (Caraman, 1990) pg. 27, (Gautier, 1989) pg. 30, 37, (Lull, 2001), pg. 29, consider also the famous *47 Ronin* story of Japan

[1472] (Anthony Schraner, 1981) pg. 286, section 272

Between them, a little more than a mile, or what was then called half a league. Cardigan's orders: charge at all costs. **Charge** directly into the mouth of the cannons, **push forward** directly into the fire, explosions, and death. The Charge of the Light Brigade.

For roughly 20 minutes, the 600 British horsemen were bombarded with hundreds of rounds of cannon shells fired directly at them as they galloped across the open field.

Alfred Lord Tennyson, the famous poet, described it like this:

> Half a league, half a league,
> Half a league onward,
> All in the valley of Death
> Rode the six hundred.
> 'Forward, the Light Brigade!
> Charge for the guns' he said:
> Into the valley of Death
> Rode the six hundred . . . .
>
> Theirs not to make reply,
> Theirs not to reason why,
> Theirs but to do and die:
> Into the valley of Death
> Rode the six hundred.
>
> Cannon to right of them,
> Cannon to left of them,
> Cannon in front of them
> Volley'd and thunder'd;
> Storm'd at with shot and shell,
> Boldly they rode and well,
> Into the jaws of Death,
> Into the mouth of Hell
> Rode the six hundred.

More than half of the 600 were blown away, many more wounded or missing. Incredibly, through the explosions and raking fire, the light brigade, with Lord Cardigan in the lead, broke through the Russian lines, chopping with their sabers until they were driven back by Russian reinforcements. When they returned, they looked around at what was left of their brothers. "I have lost my brigade," Cardigan said[1473].

He turned to his troops. "My men, someone has blundered in that order to charge".

"Never mind," The men replied. "If it is your command, we would gladly do it again."[1474]

Cardigan would have told you—sometimes it is not whether you survive or die, win or lose, it is fighting for what you believe in, country and loyalty, in the face of impossible odds, and in undeniable glory. Washington understood this, as did Roland, and the men on Normandy Beach on D-Day.

Another example, equally as terrifying, but you decide if it is more or less difficult.

"A traitor of the name Fromont one day murdered his lord and master, Girart de Blaines, and in his mad rage would have slain every member of the family . . . ."[1475]. One member was left, Girart's son Jourdain, a little boy only a few months old, left in the care of Girart's vassal Renier. Fromont demanded the infant be brought to him.

Renier refused, his wife reinforcing him with her wails. Fromont fumed that he would not rest until every single member of Girart's family was destroyed, especially the son, while Renier and his wife begged him to change his mind. Nothing melted the evil traitor's heart, and finally the baby was produced.

With one stroke, the baby's poor head careened down the stairs of the front of the castle. Renier and his wife nearly collapsed out of grief, but not for the death of their lord's son. They had secretly replaced Girart's infant with their own newborn[1476], and with restrained screams they had watched the death of their own child that day. But their lord's son lay safe.

And what of the liege lord, the master of the knights? Is he not held to the same exacting standard of loyalty and obedience to the Code?

[1473] (Britishbattles.com, 2002-2013)
[1474] As listed in Brewer's Historical Notebook, pg. 159, (Brewer, 1891)
[1475] (Gautier, 1989) pg. 64
[1476] (Gautier, 1989)pg. 64

As the true knight is known for his loyalty, a true king is known for his justice[1477].

King Arthur stood supreme as the ultimate embodiment of knightly loyalty to his subjects, and kingly obedience to his own sense of service to his country and its laws, which he himself established.

Well known throughout the land was the law that if anyone betrayed the king or the land itself, the traitor must be placed on trial, and if found guilty, put to death. Guinevere, Arthur's beloved but unfaithful wife, stood accused of infidelity. In England at the time, such sinful actions of a wife were considered traitorous to the husband, especially if the husband was the king. The people called for a trial. It was the law!

Arthur loved his wife, even with all her flaws. He walked the halls of his castle at midnight, striving to find a way out. How could he have his own wife placed on trial? How could he allow her to be carted off to the stake for burning, for that was the punishment for treason in those days? Could he not delay or cancel out such laws? Was he not the king?

Indeed, he was the king and a knight, and for that very reason he obeyed the law[1478].

Let us then look at one of the most famous debates between the individual prize of self-actualization and the demands of the Common good and societal rules. Consider the death of Socrates.

Socrates stood as one of the few philosophers who had also been a soldier, a literal "knight" of his native Greece. He understood the importance of the rule of Law, especially as represented by a benevolent Greek democracy. When that democracy started to fray, and faced with a conviction on a capital charge though innocent, he decided to respect the law and allow his own execution. "I have lived my entire life by the Democratic laws of Athens," He said. "Thus it is only fitting that I respect the law, even in death"[1479].

Socrates' allegiance was to Justice, a justice encapsulated in the laws of the land since his youth, Athens. Athens had protected him as a child, and he had benefitted from Athenian Law. Justice demanded that he give back to Athens the very life that he owed to Athens. Even though he could defy the men who ran the government, he could not and would not defy the Justice that the Law of that government represented. For now,

---

[1477] (Barber, The Knight and Chivalry, Revised Edition, 1995) pg. 52

[1478] (Gautier, 1989) pg. 19, (Lull, 2001) pg. 31-31, 99

[1479] (Jowett, 1969) pg. 40-43

the laws of his city seemed to him as the very hints of the will of GOD Himself[1480]. Even a pagan, albeit the philosopher prince of all pagans, understood the difference between the law of men, and the higher law of Justice.

Doubt of Obedience and the Justice of Kings[1481]

For obvious reasons, every leader, every warlord, and every king wishes to have strong, courageous, and honorable men such as knights working and fighting for them. Look at the stories of loyalty and obedience. Notice how loyal a knight can prove to be, and how extreme he can take his loyalty and obedience, to the point even of sacrificing himself and his loved ones, even his child, in order to fulfill orders or loyalty. What king or ruler wouldn't want that kind of loyalty and obedience? No wonder the company of knights is keenly sought. Loyalty of chivalry is the pinnacle of loyalty; one could not gain that kind of loyalty with bribes of gold or pleasure, nor even with the threat of death nor torture!

What could win the loyalty of such powerful and honest men?

King Arthur knew he had to search for and find the best men and fighters in the world in order to save his kingdom from darkness. When Arthur found them, he won their loyalty because he himself was an honorable, strong, and courageous leader. Because of this, he was able to lead his men into the very shadow of death and destruction, and they followed him. His men knew he was a great and honorable King, with a great and honorable mission, and they followed him to the gates of Hell itself. It mattered not whether they lived happily or died terribly; only the honor in the soul of their king mattered, and the nobleness of the mission[1482].

The Code of Chivalry demands this obedience[1483].

But not every king is an Arthur. When one looks at the fear modern men have of obedience, this fear is usually based on the idea that a

---

[1480] (Jowett, 1969) pg. 43
[1481] (Lull, 2001), pg. 99
[1482] (Scudder, 1917) pg. 32-34
[1483] (Gautier, 1989) pg. 61

leader, the one demanding obedience, is somehow deficient in morals, intelligence, or even basic humanity.

The Code of Chivalry was never meant to force good men to follow evil or even incompetent leaders[1484]. The Code is very specific, pointing to the hierarchy and the obedience to GOD first, and then the Code, and then, as last, the assorted duties and obligations a knight may have. GOD and the Code are always to be obeyed, for they are the standard by which everything is measured.

As the Decalogue implies, any loyalty or obedience to King, Lord, or country must now be secondary to the knight's obedience to GOD, the Code, and the knight's conscience.

❖ When good leaders make mistakes (Rebellion to Kill Dragons)

What do we do if a leader makes a mistake? What if the king or captain makes a rule against the higher law?

Legend says that a dragon of terrifying speed and power once lived on the Island of Rhodes[1485]. Frequently, it would roam into the countryside and even near towns, eating livestock and any hapless person that happened to cross its path. Many knights and would-be heroes attempted to kill this frightful thing, but none of them could contend with the swift and varied attacks of this creature, consisting of several corresponding lunges by its huge spiked tail on one side and a mouth full of jagged teeth on the other.

So many challengers died at the claws of this thing that the commander of the Hospitallers forbade anyone to search it out for battle. Any Hospitaller knight who wished to try his hand at killing this dragon would be disbarred from the order of Hospitallers, and would have all his awards and recognitions ripped away.

Theodore, a young Hospitaller, heard his commander and knew the price, if he even so much as looked for the dragon. But when he saw the suffering this creature continued to cause, he decided to disobey. His hatred of Evil overcame his obedience to his commander. His conscience and his understanding of his duty and the Code of Chivalry could not be

---

[1484] (Lull, 2001), pg. 99, (Gautier, 1989) pg. 61 - No one is forced to wage war against GOD

[1485] (Anderson, 1998) pg. 28-29, (Moncrieff, 1976) pg. 400 for the whole story of Theodore and the dragon of Rhodes

denied. A knight must be champion of the good in all places and at all times against the forces of evil[1486], even if it meant outright disregard of orders, the removal from his title of knighthood, and the destruction of his reputation.

Maybe not the most careful when it came to earning the love of his superiors, Theodore was certainly not a fool. He prepared extensively for the upcoming battle with the beast, training not only himself, but several dogs to wrestle with the thing's tail while he contended with its mighty jaws. He knew that no matter how many weapons and assistance he brought with him, he needed all the help he could get. His squire was told to wait, far from danger, but if the worst happened, to remove the knight's body for decent burial.

The fateful day came, and Theodore found the dragon fairly easily, wallowing in a pool of water. Theodore rode in for the charge, his spear at the ready. The beast's tail was so quick and powerful, swinging like a battering ram, Theodore's horse was immediately struck out from under him, and he had to fend off the beast's attacks on foot. As it moved on to dry ground, the thing heaved upward to crush Theodore, but the dogs leapt upon its deadly tail as Theodore thrust his sword into its unprotected chest, stabbing it clear through the heart.

In violent death throes, the thing twisted and contorted, falling full upon the knight, who barely could catch his breath under the weight and scales of the creature. Finally, Theodore found himself awash in its ichor and life-blood, caught beneath a dead monster with no way to pull himself out. It looked like the dragon, even deceased, would claim another victim.

Theodore's foresight saved him again and his squire appeared to pull him from the carcass. Together, they carried news of the battle to the commander of the Order, and the rough reception they expected.

True to his word, the commander stripped the heroic Theodore of all titles and awards, exiling him from the Order and Hospitaller lands. In typical Medieval fashion when punishing a wayward knight, his spurs were hacked from his ankles and his robe ripped away. Theodore knew this would happen. He had disobeyed a direct command, even though

---

[1486] Thus he remembered the Decalogue's rule #10 of the knight

he followed the code and his conscience, and now he quietly suffered the consequences.

Although this knight had done the right thing and his leader's order had been inappropriate, the knight did not complain or cry out when the sentence was made. We know his adventure was not reckless glory-hounding or childish disobedience, for he "opened not his mouth[1487]" when the Master of the Hospitallers called out his sentence, "To languish for the rest of his life, without glory, without honor, without even the title of knight. For he dared to disobey his master and disobey his allegiance and disobey his oath to forever obey."

Dismissed, Theodore turned and walked slowly away, his reputation and dignity hanging upon him as frayed and torn as his clothes and the remnants of his armor.

The master and commander of the Hospitallers watched this man leave the chamber, dejected and downcast. The master knew that this man had done nothing but attempt to save lives and destroy evil. He smiled.

"Look how he accepts even his sentence with perfect obedience and perfect humility. No one but a true knight of GOD could possibly be so perfectly obedient! Obedient to the will of GOD, whether to some whim of his master, and perfectly humble unto the end. Now hear me well, this man shall be reinstated as a knight Hospitaller, for no one is more deserving!"[1488]

The punishment had only been a test, to plumb the depths of the knight's true intentions and true loyalties. Theodore was taken back within the fold of the Hospitallers, given full honors and full awards, and embraced by his commander a true knight.

While a true knight understands the importance of obeying his commanders, he also understands that individual initiative to the call of Honor is sometimes more important. He is finally bound to his ultimate mission to GOD above and beyond all other allegiances, even as he resists arrogance to others, and accepts his lot humbly and as any sinner. After carefully weighing any strategic consequences, and understanding the

---

[1487] Isaiah 53:7, Acts 8:32
[1488] (Moncrieff, 1976) pg. 406

true expectations of GOD and the Code, sometimes it is better to beg for forgiveness than to ask for permission[1489].

The crossroads between obedience and courage highlights the knightly call of Initiative. Initiative is simply the courage to act, to do something to fix a problem instead of sitting around and complaining about it. In situations where obedience attempts to confound initiative, the knight always finds himself in a quandary. We must revisit Initiative another time.

❖ When Leaders fail to live up to themselves (Rebellion against a foolish king)

While, GOD cannot make mistakes, nor order something evil[1490], nor can the Code[1491], human kings and leaders are fallible. There are times when leaders simply make wrong decisions, human as they are, even though they may have good intentions. As any human, even the best of leaders can find themselves tempted by selfishness greed. The fear may be that the king or country or rule we serve is flawed. What then?

Rodrigo De Bivar, the Cid, feared such a thing. Rumors abounded that Alphonso, now king of Christian Spain, had obtained his position by covertly assassinating his brother Sancho. Now it is true that Alphonso did not use his own hands, but El Cid knew the rich and powerful very often have someone else do their dirty work. The Cid resolved to make sure his king was innocent, or as innocent as was possible, in the murder of his brother[1492].

In days of old, knights were not always the most careful or discreet in their dealings with royalty, and they tended to treat even kings as equals in certain cases. Sometimes this is seen as arrogance, but it can also be an understanding that everyone must obey the rules of Justice and fairness, even a king. Rodrigo decided to confront Alphonso on the very day of his coronation.

Legend has it, on that day, in the courtyard of the king, as everyone kneeled in preparation for the Prince Alphonso's coronation, one man did

---

[1489] This phrase is attributed to many, including the Jesuits, and is a dangerous phrase indeed.

[1490] (Copleston, 1962) pg. 99

[1491] (Gautier, 1989) pg. 73

[1492] (Matthews, 1998) pg. 64-65

not bow. Even as the bishop lifted the crown to place it on the prince, even as all those around him dared not look up at the scene, the Cid stood still and looked the prince in the eye.

"Why is it that the Cid does not bow before his king?" Alphonso asked.

"I must make sure you are truly my king." The Cid answered. "Everyone here knows that Sancho, your brother, was killed by an unknown hand in the dark. It is my contention that you are innocent of this, and any scheming that brought it about. But I must make sure before I bow before you as my king."

"How can this be accomplished," The king might have said. He could have easily have said, "How dare you!?"

"Swear upon the Bible that you had nothing to do with your brother's death, and I will be satisfied."

The holy book, nearby as it was for the solemn occasion of the coronation, was only a few feet from the prince's hand.

"Very well," Prince Alphonso said, and walked up to it. He placed his hand on the Bible. "I swear."

"Swear that you had no hand in the scheming of your brother's death!" Cried The Cid. "No one will follow a king far who is suspected of such wickedness!"

In obvious anger, the prince slammed down his hand. "I swear I had nothing to do with his death!"[1493]

If king or country does not live up to standards, it is the duty of the knight to force them to maintain honor. "No one is above the law, especially the king"[1494]. The price of a knight's obedience is the required Honor and Righteousness. The Cid is the model of knightly loyalty in the Sacrifice chapter, yet the CID is obedient to GOD and the Code first, forcing Alphonzo to take an oath of innocence upon holy relics.

Knights were loyal to their earthly lords, but also demanded righteousness from these lords as well. This sometimes lead to rebellion,

---

[1493] (Matthews, 1998) pg. 64-65, and other sources
[1494] (Lull, 2001) pg. 31-32, 99, (Gautier, 1989) pg. 19, all are GOD's men, including the king

for there are cases when the king or ruler becomes wicked. "Rebellion to Tyrants is Obedience to GOD"[1495].

When full rebellion is honorable

There are standards a king and government must live by. When these standards are not met, the knight's duty is correction. When these standards are continuously rejected with abandon, and spit upon by leaders, the knight's duty is rebellion[1496].

Count William of Gellone[1497], a powerful and honorable knight in many traditional stories, was very quick to judge rulers when they did not live up to chivalrous standards. In one tale, the son of Charlemagne, King Louis forgets his father's advice and decides to take from orphans and widows, thinking he can use their lands to pay William for his services.

"If you give me these lands, what is to become of the widows and orphans who live on them?" Demanded William.

According to Gautier, the king shrank back from the knight's rage, turning pale on his throne.

"If anyone injures those little ones or their land, here is my sword that will cut off the head of any such traitor or robber," Cried William[1498].

Because "An unfair law is no law at all"[1499].

In the middle of the Middle Ages, Sir Thomas Beckett found that he had to choose between his king and his Church. King Henry II and Beckett had been great friends, like brothers really, and were almost "of one mind" until Henry asked Beckett to become Archbishop of Canterbury.

Beckett took this appointment very seriously, and, with an eye on his vows to the office and the duties of a good bishop, his actions began to agitate the king. For one thing, Beckett's personal asceticism, strict

---

[1495] (Deane, 1963) pg. 147-148, the actual phrase is Ben Franklin's proposal for the Great Seal of the U.S.A

[1496] (Lull, 2001) pg. 31-32, a similar situation lead to the Declaration of Independence

[1497] Guillaume d'Orange, otherwise known as William of Gellone, another knight who became a saint.

[1498] (Gautier) pg. 43, quoted from Charroi de Nimes v.312, 322, 366-376

[1499] (Burleigh, 1953) pg. 118, Augustine's *On Free Will*, book 1, section V

before, became even more stringent, upsetting the king when he accepted an envoy from Rome barefoot and stripped of any lavish signs of his position.

But the terrible rift between the two men truly opened when Beckett refused to allow the Church to give donation to the royal treasury through the sheriff. This was supposed to be a "voluntary donation", but when Beckett openly refused, it became "the first recorded instance of any determined opposition to the king's arbitrary will in a matter of taxation"[1500].

Beckett continuously found his loyalties to the king and his loyalties to the Church confounding each other, and he continuously chose the Church's side, until the frustrated King Henry reputedly said, "Who will free me from this turbulent priest?!?"

Sadly, four French knights, hungry to obey their king, and forgetting their obligations to GOD and the Code, boldly came into the Canterbury Church, yelling "Where is the traitor?" Perhaps they truly believed Beckett to be a scoundrel in this sense.

Beckett stood at the altar, praying at Vespers. "Here I am." Beckett said. "No traitor, but Archbishop and a priest of GOD"[1501].

They tried to drag him from the church, but when they could not overwhelm this tough man bodily, they set upon him with weapons, slaying him with such violence that they shattered his skull and sprayed his brains on the floor.

Shocked by this event, King Henry apologized, doing public penance in front of Beckett's tomb.

Some 400 hundred years later, another Saint Thomas rebelled against another King Henry, when the king rebelled further against the Church. Sir and Saint Thomas More became famous for his moral courage when he informed King Henry VIII that the king was simply wrong. The king wanted to marry again and secure a divorce from the Pope, but when that was not forthcoming, King Henry went home and announced that he was getting a divorce anyway. Thomas, minister of the king, crossed his arms and refused to acknowledge this action, and when the king insisted Thomas recognize his new marriage on pain of death, Thomas accepted

---

[1500] (Thurston, St. Thomas Becket, 1912)
[1501] (Thurston, St. Thomas Becket, 1912)

the Tower of London and beheading instead. Thomas More knew the proper chain of command: GOD and the Pope first, and then the king.

Sir Thomas More became the patron saint of Religious Freedom.

For the last several hundred years, one of the most famous warriors from the Middle Ages, Robin Hood, has been connected with righteous rebellion. According to many modern stories, Prince John, brother of King Richard the Lionheart, had wantonly and illegally seized the throne while his brother was away on the 3rd Crusade. Robin Hood, not quite a knight, but almost, with a title of Yeoman and a knightly sword, spreads disorder through Prince John's tyranny, proving himself a thorn in the wicked despot's side, robbing from wealthy nobles and giving to peasants still loyal to King Richard.

One of the strangest stories of rebellion in the history of knighthood is the story of Philopater Mercurius, also known as Saint Mercurius[1502], the "the wielder of two swords", and sometimes called the "father of swords."

A powerful and brave Roman soldier in the third century A.D., Mercurius soon became recognized for his great bravery, skill in battle, and tactical ability. While Decius, the Roman Emperor, feared defeat during a battle with Berber tribes, Mercurius encouraged him, saying "my GOD will win this battle for us; you need not be afraid."

Mercurius himself then charged into battle, and during the days that followed, full of blood and sweat, the warrior had a vision in the midst of the fray. He saw the Archangel Michael, and the angel presented him with another sword, one of spiritual fire, compensating his physical sword of earthly power. Thus doubly armed and backed by an indomitable will, Mercurius drove the Berbers before him, and the Romans won.

The Emperor Decius, extremely pleased with his soldier, gave Mercurius rank and awards, but soon he heard rumors that threatened to change his mind. Just days before, ignoring the source of the Roman victory against the Berbers, Decius had decided to make a law that every Roman citizen must burn incense before Roman gods, worship and adore them in effect. He had then heard a Roman soldier's testimony that

---

[1502] (Woods, 1999)- See the Passion of St. Mercurius for the complete text of this interesting story

Mercurius refused to follow such orders. Under this shadow, Mercurius came before the Emperor.

"Haven't I been gracious to you and given you these awards and rank? And now I hear you refuse my orders?"

Mercurius stripped himself of his Roman cloak and ranking, throwing them upon the floor before the Emperor. "There is nothing on this earth I would exchange for the kingdom to come, and my allegiance to the true King."

The Emperor was shocked. He wanted this brave and excellent warrior to serve him and his gods, not the GOD of another religion. He gave Mercurius several chances, but when the hero refused them all, the emperor became angry.

"I will punish you for your disloyalty. If you do not raise incense to the gods here and now, I will tie you to four stakes and have you flogged with whips that have nails tied to them. You will suffer great agony!"

"Whatever you do," Mercurius shot back, "I wear the armor of GOD. Though you wound and kill me, I will not be harmed"[1503].

Enraged, the emperor did as he had promised. Mercurius was stretched out between four stakes, elevated so that it was easy to strike his bare flesh with lashes tied with nails.

Soon, Mercurius' body was a mass of quivering skin and exposed nerves and veins. "Where is you armor of GOD now?" The emperor laughed.

But Mercurius did not complain, nor cry out. The emperor then had a fire built beneath him, and his men were told to cut Mercurius' flesh with knives so to slowly burn and cut him to death at the same time. While they were doing this, the saint seemed patiently waiting, as if he suffered nothing at all, though his blood flowed profusely. Finally, the flames below him were doused by his blood and sweat.

The emperor, deciding that he wanted this upstart to suffer longer and die a more lingering death, sent him away to suffer in a prison cell, until his wounds and burns wasted him away.

The next day, Emperor Decius ordered the warrior saint to be brought before him. He gasped when he saw Mercurius without wounds at all, standing like a healthy man with a full night of sleep.

"How is this possible?!" Cried Decius.

[1503] (Woods, 1999) part 9

"My Lord Christ came to me in the night and healed my wounds," Mercurius said.

Almost out of his mind with fury, Decius ordered him to be tortured further.

"It does not matter what you do to my body." Mercurius told him matter-of-factly. "I do not fear you. I give you this advice: Do not fear he who can destroy the body, but fear HIM instead who can destroy the body and the soul in Hell"[1504].

Decius sent the saint to suffer several more tortures, including burning with white-hot irons, and being suspended upside-down with a boulder around his neck, but each time the saint seemed to heal immediately[1505]. Witnesses wept, converting and offering themselves up to GOD at the sight of this stoic and upright warrior for Christ. The emperor finally gave in, ordering the saint beheaded, rather than see more of his people converted[1506].

But Mercurius's rebellion was not over.

Roughly a hundred years later, yet another Roman emperor began persecuting yet other Christian saints. This time, Emperor Julian, called the Apostate, had threatened to destroy whole Christian towns and Christianity itself.

Saint Basil, concerned as he was with the future of Christianity, felt that everything they had worked so hard for was falling apart. When Emperor Julian first rose to the throne, everyone assumed he would continue to allow Christians to worship freely, as Constantine before him; but the new emperor had suddenly turned against the Empire's newest faith and forced out of office anyone who refused to burn incense before the old Roman gods. He discriminated against Christians in his appointments, and refused to allow any teachers in the Empire to be followers of Christ[1507].Thus Julian will forever be known as "the Apostate", since he had betrayed the wave of good will toward Christianity that Emperor Constantine had established.

At first, Julian avoided physical persecution of Christians, but when a newly built pagan temple, commissioned by Julian, burned to the

---

[1504] Matthew 10:28
[1505] (Woods, 1999) part 10 -11
[1506] (Irene, 2013), (Iskander, 2013)
[1507] (Chadwick, 1993) pg. 155-157

ground, Julian saw red[1508]. Although the fire had been accidently caused by a neglected candle, Julian blamed the followers of Christ[1509]. The tales of brutality against Christians, some at the order of Julian, others at the order of his administration, are studies in nightmare. Innumerable Christians throughout the empire were burned, dragged to death in the streets, and some even torn open to have pigs feed on their entrails[1510].

Saints Basil decided that such outrages, such arrogance toward GOD, must be stopped at all costs. He remembered St. Mercurius, and asked his intercession in this time of need[1511].

Legend has it that Mercurius appeared and said: "Worry not. For I, myself, will strike down this Julian for his crimes."

Emperor Julian was half a world away, battling Sassanid raiders, near Maranga. He had promised that when he returned, he would inflict more damage upon the Christians and stamp them out completely from his kingdom. On that day he had found the Sassanid enemy retreating and had rushed into battle without donning his armor.

Opinions conflict and many modern readers will scoff. But it is a historical fact that, on that day, June 26, 363, an anonymous rider suddenly broke from the battle and charged the emperor with a lance backed by a horse at full gallop. Emperor Julian was struck down and mortally wounded at the very moment of Saint Basil's vision. Julian had been killed in a way well known by medieval knights nearly a millennium later, because he neither wore his armor, nor the armor of GOD[1512].

This is why knights and honorable men are considered with worry and suspicion by so many elites in power. Knights do not follow with blind loyalty or out of fear, but instead insist upon righteousness for themselves and for any leader they acknowledge. Many moderns, as Friedrich Nietzsche, dismiss Morality and the concept of Honor as a way for leaders to control the masses. Nothing can be further from the truth, when it comes to true knights. Morality and ethics, backed by a chivalrous sword, can be a difficult problem for unscrupulous leaders.

[1508] Ibid. pg. 156, and many are the historic instances of martyrdom under Julian, see Pernoud and others

[1509] (Chadwick, 1993) Ibid.

[1510] (Fox, 2013), section called Persecution under Julian the Apostate

[1511] Some sources contain details that differ slightly, (Voragine, 2012) pg. 130

[1512] (Chadwick, 1993) pg. 158, (John, 1995) pg. 252, (Iskander, 2013)

To truly understand Honor is to see the knight autonomous, powerful, and an equal in a good government and a dangerous lion or loose cannon in an unethical government. The knight is constantly watching leaders, making sure they are worthy of the knight, and if not, it is the knight's duty to make them worthy[1513].

Obedience to Wedlock and obligation to Women

Even modern conceptions of knighthood reflect the near worship of women seen in the stories and songs of the Middle Ages. The very concept of Romance comes from these tales and poems, and numberless knights began their chivalrous careers with visions of serving and fighting for beautiful and virtuous women, peerless in their eyes. German and French knights were especially given to this mode of adoration[1514].

Out of all persons in the Medieval world, it was the knight who most likely would marry for love, against all convention. The Knight Code did not insist on his obedience to his wife, but many a knight found great solace in pleasing her and bringing her joy; many were the knights who ranged the world in honorable pursuits simply to bring happiness to their wives' hearts. Consider, for example, Guy of Warwick in the first half of his life, and how he journeyed to find terrifying adventures to win the hand of the beautiful and kindly Phelis. The knight wishes to please his wife; he is not required.

Where the code demanded action is when the wife was in danger or in pain. Here is where the knight's devotion takes on a special power, for his heart roars like a lion when his wife is in peril. Even when a female stranger was concerned, all knights understood their duty. In the *L'Ordene De Chevalerie*, when Saladin asked what made a man a true knight, Sir Hugh answered that, as one of the four most important rules, a knight must never lead women astray, nor allow pain to happen to them[1515].

Very seriously too did the knight take his vows to his wife. Never flippant or careless with his promises, the knight took special care to stay

---

[1513] (Gautier, 1989) pg. 19

[1514] (Tierney, 1978) pg. 37, (Headon, 1989) pg. 136, (Barber, The Reign of Chivalry, 1980) pg. 76, Ulrich's Credo

[1515] (Gautier), pg. 249, and the *L'Ordene* itself

467

loyal to his spouse, enshrining his Honor in the very vessel of marriage. Sir Willaim of Gellone refused to cut his hair while on Crusade as a sign of his Samson-like loyalty to his wife[1516]; Sir Percival would go into trances, enraptured by memories of his lady; Sir Ewayne of the Lion spent seven years to win forgiveness from his wife for once being late[1517]; and who can forget King Arthur, remaining steadfast and loyal to his wife, even in the teeth of her infamous treachery[1518]. Obviously, the true knight valued his wife over himself[1519]. The virtuous wife, loyal and loving, is, for the knight, one foretaste of the peace of Heaven[1520].

According to legend, Sir Hugh of Vaudemont, on Crusade and away from his beloved wife, suffered in an Islamic prison for sixteen years. Reports of his death came to his wife's ears, but she refused to remarry, sitting patiently day after day, and waiting for familiar footsteps[1521].

Finally, Hugh was released, and made the slow and agonizing trek back home, broken, beaten, and ashamed. But he had never given up, and neither had she.

If you go to the Musee des Monuments Francais, in Paris, France, you will see the 800-year-old sculpture of Hugh's return, carved out of stone, as a monument of their mutual grave. It is the ultimate 12th century symbol of a knight's loyalty to his wife, and hers to him. It stands to this day.

With such poignant stories of love and pain, it is no wonder that knights hold their loyalty to their wives stronger than death itself[1522].

True knights, however, are not blind to the practical reality of human nature, which is within women as well as men. Indeed, while a woman is "last and best of GOD's creation"[1523] according to Sir Malory, they can be hideous things undeserving of the title "Woman", and can bring about destruction[1524].

[1516] (Gautier), pg. 68
[1517] (Moncrieff, 1976) pg. 180, for the full story
[1518] Reminiscent of Hosea, the Biblical prophet called to be loyal to his prostitute wife
[1519] Ephesians 5:25
[1520] Proverbs 18:22
[1521] (Pernoud, 1963) pg. 125
[1522] Ephesians 5:25-28
[1523] (Malory, 1497) pg. 458
[1524] (Hatto, 1980) pg. 152, unwise love can lead to Hell (Steinbeck, 1976) pg. 288, Morgan Le Fey, see Barber

Love and consequently marriage are affairs of the heart, and thus one of the largest sources of pain, confusion, and difficulty for the knight. I remember one story where a young noble woman demanded to know if a knight, to prove his love for her, would hesitate to jump into a pit full of lions to retrieve a glove. To test him, she promptly threw the glove into the pit, watching the knight as he jumped in after it and barely escaped. He "rescued" the glove[1525], but this situation is the perfect metaphor for the deadly line a knight must walk where ladies are concerned.

The most famous discretionary tale of knightly relations with ladies is the story of Lancelot and Guinevere. In this story, Sir Lancelot, the best knight in the world, falls pitifully in love with King Arthur's young wife, Guinevere. Before this terrible occurrence, Lancelot is a model of saintly virtue and purity, but because of his heart he is dragged down to the point where he must choose between desire for his queen and loyalty to his king. Ultimately he makes the wrong choice and arguably the whole of Camelot is destroyed by the scandal[1526].

Modern writers and commentators, in their infinitely uncouth and insensitive renderings of such tales, usually like to focus on the lust and intrigue, but if one truly reads the old stories, one sees the terrible agony and travail of spirit that a man like Lancelot must have undergone in such a situation.

Sometimes I see this love triangle as an object lesson: Guinevere is a metaphor for the sinful world, with all its desires, dreams, and hopes, while King Arthur can signify duty and even loyalty to the Code and GOD. The knight, human as he is, caught in the middle, must choose.

In the Middle Ages, nobility often wed for political or monetary reasons, making many marriages without love. Scores of poets and song-writers portrayed married women as sensual targets for ambitious young knights, looking for status and affection. Partially because of this, the Cult of Romance sprang up in France. Started by Lady Eleanor of Aquitaine, the Romantic Movement drove the longings of the heart to a kind of religion, placing emotion and romantic love over everything else[1527], especially fealty to wedding vows. Lancelot's story reflects the emotion, beguilement, and danger, both moral and physical, of a young man blinded by such romantic yearnings. Of course, this sort of idolatry had

---

[1525] (Headon, 1989) pg. 136
[1526] (Malory, 1497) pg. 506, 472
[1527] (Hopkins A., 1999) pg. 52

been denounced by the Church, and seen by Gautier and other scholars as effeminate, selfish, and far from honorable[1528]. Placing anything before GOD and Honor must be avoided by true knights, and while they may borrow courtesies from time to time from the movement of Romance, they can never allow themselves to be blinded as Lancelot was.

On the other side of Lancelot stands Sir Guy of Warwick, more famous in England than anywhere else, and decidedly English, as Lancelot is French. Totally in love, Warwick performs his chivalrous duties and dangerous missions to win the hand of the beautiful daughter of the Duke of Warwick, Phelis. But once he does win her, he is suddenly visited with the realization that he has done everything for earthly reasons, and should have performed his duties for GOD. He chooses GOD over his wife, and spends the rest of his days as a hermit, in poverty and penance[1529].

Consistency and Loyalty

Having a set belief system or code, as a true knight does, demands that one is consistent in following and observing the tenets of this belief or code. In this way, obedience to dogma demands consistency. Otherwise, changing or ignoring the rules and tenets as one goes, one is nothing but a deceitful hypocrite and liar, especially to oneself— belonging to nothing, having no true beliefs, being less than no-one.

In the old days of Chivalry, when men still wore armor, the piece that protected the neck was called a gorget, preventing one from having his throat slit or stabbed. This piece represents the knight's loyal to his lord, as well as to the Order of Chivalry, and to its rules[1530]. If a knight decides to disobey a rule, "changing" that rule arbitrarily, as it were, one might as well allow his throat to be slit, for his loyalty to the Code has been compromised; his gorget has slipped off.

Back then, the reins not only led his horse, but represented the Code of Chivalry that led the knight. If a man were to suddenly not be consistent, deciding when to follow the obvious rules of Chivalry and

---

[1528] (Barber, The Knight and Chivalry, Revised Edition, 1995) pg. 90-91, (Lull, 2001) pg. 85

[1529] (Moncrieff, 1976) pg. 226-240

[1530] (Lull, 2001) pg. 67

when not to, it would be like the reins breaking and the horse leading the knight away from Honor[1531]. His spear also meant Truth, and a knight who intentionally lies to himself[1532], by not following the Code, or by telling himself reasons why the Code should be changed or ignored, would be like dropping the spear, and allowing any long range attack from the enemy.

The modern world, sad to say, abounds with examples of the fool who would open himself to attack and waywardness. One of the most blatant and shocking examples of lack of consistency, even on a basic level, is the example of one Episcopal "priest", recently reported about in the news[1533]. Child as she is of extremely liberal views, so much so that she was made a priest in the first place, she insists that she is a Christian and Moslem at the same time.

Any understanding of the basic tenets of these two religions indicates this to be impossible. Their creeds are mutually exclusive: one cannot say that one believes in Christ as GOD and the son of GOD, and that He died on the Cross to forgive our sins, then turn around and also say that Christ was only a prophet and did not die on the Cross and that sins cannot be forgiven!

A modern apologist for the Relativist Movement might say she is keeping an open mind, but, in her attempt to keep an open mind, she has betrayed the very religion she pretends to be a minister of, and both religions at once. This is not keeping an open mind; this is being ignorant of what one believes, or, even worse, lying about it and in truth believing something different from what one professes. One may keep an open mind, but one must also be intellectually honest. The purpose of an open mind is to finally close in on something real, true, and solid[1534]. Either this "priest" believes that Christ is the Son of GOD and GOD Himself, the definition of a Christian, or she believes that GOD has no son and Mohammed is greater than Christ, the view of the pious Moslem. Both beliefs are mutually exclusive. Not to mention the habit Moslems have of taking keen disgust over anyone who would call themselves Christian

---

[1531] Ibid. pg. 72

[1532] (Lull, 2001) pg. 64

[1533] I will not reward this stupidity by naming her, nor will I cause her pain by revealing her name.

[1534] G.K. Chesterton, from his book *Orthodoxy*

while they were Moslem. One wonders how she became an Episcopal priest in the first place.

The only way an honest person could possibly believe what she claims is by using the progressive and post-modern belief that all things are relative, saying "when I feel like being a Christian, I say I am; when I feel Moslem, I say I am". Both religions would find this intellectually dishonest, disrespectful, logically inconsistent, and even laughable. My view is that she is more a "priest" of Relativism than anything else.

"I wish you were either hot or cold"[1535]. A knight always adheres to the teachings of Christ and the Church, because the knight always believes that Christ is GOD and the Son of GOD. The knight is human, and thus susceptible to error, sin, and mistakes, but he strives to be true to these beliefs, and the implications of these beliefs, to the best of his ability. The true knight is loyal forever, in word and deed.

Sir Thomas More remained loyal to the Church and his beliefs, even in the face of the Tower of London and the chopping block. Sir Ramon Lull refused to convert to Islam and, instead, tried to convert the entire Islamic world to his religion. Saint and King Louis remained steadfast even in the face of the Bernicles, Greek Fire, and disease. Saint and Sir Joan of Arc refused to turn away from her beliefs, even when everyone laughed and scoffed at her. The apostles carried the Gospel across the world, in spite of hate, pain, suffering, and terror.

With no consistent loyalty to any creed and with an eye to popular opinion, people like the mentioned Episcopal "priest" have nothing to lose by stating their beliefs. Knights and heroes always know they have everything to lose if they adhere to their ideals and dogmas, but they remain loyal to them anyway[1536].

Why is Obedience to GOD and Code so difficult?

Obviously, if every human followed Honor, there would be no crime, nor cruelty, nor violence in the world. Every man would respect his neighbors and world, helping those in need.

[1535] Revelations 3:15-16
[1536] (Lull, 2001) pg. 72, Mark 13:13, Matthew 10:22

Then why don't people follow the Code and Honor?

People do not follow Honor for one main reason: Human Nature.

According to Medieval thought, at the beginning of the Human race, GOD created Human Nature. At this point, Human Nature contained all the drives necessary for the human being to survive, procreate, and pursue other activities, such as appreciating beauty and striving for a relationship with GOD. All drives and instincts were subservient to the human will at this point, and humans bowed to GOD[1537]. If Adam wished, he could tell his hunger to be quiet, or his lust to flair only for his wife. The man's instincts were servants to him. But human nature also contained free will[1538], and through this, Adam and Eve decided to break their agreements with GOD.

This decision led, not only to an estrangement from GOD, but also an estrangement from the goals that GOD gave Nature and creation itself, especially to a dissolving of the proper condition of Human Nature and its goals. It became demented and twisted. Every drive, instinct, emotion, and desire which had previously led to good goals, now led many times to selfish, egotistical, animalistic, and demented goals[1539]. The reflection of GOD's original creation still exists, but is fragmented, unfocused, and sullied by the Fall of Man.

Human nature is the instincts and emotions of our animal selves: selfish, defensive, many times abominable. Springing from what the Early Christians called the Fallen Soul, what the Greeks called the animal nature and the Ego, what Freud called the Id, and what the romantics call the darker part of the Human Heart; these powerful emotions do sometimes serve survival, but usually they are obstacles to our Honorable spirit[1540].

When we are confronted by rules set up by a higher power, even good and fair rules like GOD's, it is human nature to ignore them or rebel against them in some fashion. This does not depend on the merit of the rule or ruler, but on the selfish and rebellious nature of the human heart. It always helps to have reasonable, fair, and honorable rules, but even

---

[1537] (Aquinas, 2002) pg. 217-218

[1538] Ibid. pg. 72

[1539] Ibid. pg. 222

[1540] Romans 7:23

when we are given the greatest and best of rules, Human Nature will still find excuses to rebel or ignore. It feels good to follow emotions, and it feels torturous at times to deny the engines of feeling.

Incredibly, Human Nature is intricate enough to create seemingly valid reasons to rebel against anything, even against a reasonable GOD. The serpent gave Eve plenty of reasons to take a bite of the forbidden fruit, even though she knew it was wrong to do so. Adam didn't even argue, but like a stupid sheep, followed in Eve's footprints.

Human nature can establish conditions that seem to mimic obedience. There are some who have the desire to please others, to appear honorable, or who get caught in habitual and rigid systems of behavior which happen by circumstance. These are products of Human Nature, and do not reflect the Knightly Spirit of Obedience.

Because it is easier to follow our natures and emotions, than a difficult code, most of us fall by the wayside, never reaching complete obedience to GOD and the Code.

Simply put, our own desires are the Path of Least Resistance, and any animal could follow this. But the Code and GOD's law are the Path of Greatest Resistance, and only a few can find their way through this path, or to the small and narrow gate where it leads.

The Code of Honor fights human nature[1541], but also fulfills a part of it as well. Human nature is contrary, even to itself[1542]. There is an aspect of Human nature, divergent from the rebellious spirit mentioned before, which craves discipline and rules in order to be truly human. It is only through discipline and rules that our talents are sharpened and we reach our full potential. There is a desire within us to reach for these heights, and something within human nature understands that rules and hardship are necessary to do this. This is a residual piece of Grace, instilled by GOD, to be the best we can be and to hate weakness within ourselves[1543]. This too is human nature, reflecting a distant echo of GOD's original design, and thank GOD it is there.

[1541] Galatians 5:17

[1542] *Gaudium et spes* 13.2, Man is divided in himself. As a result, the whole life of men, both individual and social, shows itself to be a struggle, and a dramatic one, between good and evil, light and darkness.

[1543] (Copleston, 1962) pg. 98

This piece of our nature is only a sliver of its former self, and is often silenced by other aspects of human nature. Still, it exists deep down. Humans yet desire to go just a bit further in the long distance race, to push just a little harder when one is striving, to refuse to surrender when all things seem useless. It is the search for perfection—the search for GOD somewhere in our lives[1544]. After the Fall, after all the other glory fled humanity, this spark of light still remained at the bottom, like Hope in Pandora's box[1545].

Children, in their subconscious way, need rules and actively seek them out. Deep within them, although they fight against rules, they identify good and fair rules with parental love. If there are no rules, there is no love. Children may hoot and howl when unrestrained, but if their whole life is like that, they have an inner resentment lurking behind their consciousness. When an animal recognizes a weakness within itself, it hates that part of itself, and when a grown child realizes his talents are undiscovered and his strengths are undeveloped because of lack of discipline, he will despise himself, and those who allowed him to become that way. This may be hidden from the conscious mind, but it will have affects, self-destructive effects.

The Difficulty of Obedience and the Bane of Prejudice

It is easy to look back upon the horrors of history and say "I would never do such a thing. Those people back then must have been idiotic, evil, or both." Modern man thinks of ancient man in the same way: that ancient man, being supposedly lower on the evolutionary ladder, propagated all sorts of cruelties, greed, and violence because such men were ignorant, inferior, plain stupid, or evil. "I am superior." Says Modern man, "By the virtue of my evolutionary status and progressive intellect, I am incapable of such idiocy and evil."

[1544] (Augustine S., 1961) pg. 21, (Illingworth, 1903) pg. 3, 6, (Doornik, 1953) pg. 184

[1545] This restless desire for GOD, free will, and our capacity for intellect, seem to mark us as human beings. (Doornik, 1953) pg. 185, (Deane, 1963) pg. 15, (Tamburello, 2000) pg. 48, 50, Catechism of the Catholic Church, ch. 1, art. 1, 1701-1707

Beware. The Aztecs, guilty of ripping hearts out of humans and kicking the bodies down temple steps a thousand times a day, were not the lowest sort of native tribe. King Leopold and his Belgians, raping the Kongo for ivory tusks, were not a form of sub human. African tribes did not have the only corner of the cruelty market, selling their own brethren to European Slave traders, or because of their genocides in the Sudan. Americans are not below standard because of their institution of slavery. Turks are not the lowest sort of man because of their penchant for cutting necks. The Iroquois Natives in Canada were not the most animalistic because of their love of torture with the sharp edges of shells. The Kali Cult of India, the Thuggees, was not below human level because of its strangulation of strangers.

These studies in horror, like those in Conrad's *Heart of Darkness* or Golding's *Lord of the Flies*, are not stories of the evil in some men, nor the evils inside of Europeans, nor Africans, nor Americans, nor Danes. These are stories of the Evil within warped Human Nature itself, within every one of us. Evil lives within the Human Soul, and there, in that strange universe, any man or woman placed within certain situations, will find themselves tempted, and most, overcome, by terrible drives, evil concepts, and the darkest desires[1546], coupled with apathy, laziness, and a whole host of ordinary, pathetic sins.

The knight knows it is easy to assume that sinful, stupid, or destructive ideas and temptations are the property of others, whether other races, countries, governments, or organizations, or even other times[1547]. Instead, the knight understands evil to be within himself <u>and</u> everyone else, and this evil can only be defeated by constant obedience to GOD through discipline and the Rule of Chivalry, along with the aid of Grace[1548].

While all cultures, societies, and traditions must contend with the horrors inherent in Human Nature[1549], this does not mean all cultures are the same, for some cultures teach more self-control than others. The Judeo-Christian ethic, which enforces great self-control, has suffered murderers acting in its name from time to time. But compare the

---

[1546] (Oldridge, 2007) pg. 98, the subconscious is bestial; in my opinion, the origin of the werewolf legend.

[1547] Karl Jung, his *Synchronicity, An Acausal Connecting Principle*, 1960, p. 33

[1548] (Copleston, 1962) pg. 99

[1549] (Deane, 1963) pg. 57, 61

numbers of murders conducted in that tradition to the vast multitudes murdered in the name of Communism, Socialism, Nihilism, Tyranny, and Nazism, and one will see that while every belief must contend with horror, some are more successful in defeating that horror than others. Indeed, Christianity has Mother Teresa, Max Kolbe, Father Damien, Sir Ramon Lull, Simeon Stylites, and many others. What has the other side to show for itself?

Anything good in modern ideas, like mercy, forgiveness, good faith, were copied from the ancient Judeo-Christian ethic. All the best things of Humanity find their home with this, and especially in Chivalry.

Difficulty of Obedience and the Blight of Slavery

It is also natural, and a part of Human Nature, to despise enslavement[1550]. We sometimes forget that GOD created our hearts and Human Nature itself, originally to help us in our pursuit of Honor and His presence; but, because of the Fall of Humanity, this once divine Human Nature has become twisted and contorted by sin[1551]. It is right and proper not to want to be enslaved, and to not to want to enslave others. The drive to avoid slavery is a great and holy good. It is our perceptions, warped by Original Sin, that have confused us about Obedience, as well as our dimmed understanding of Morality, Honor, and the Law of GOD.

Because of these warped perceptions, the modern definition of slavery has been confused with the definition of Obedience. Slavery is not Obedience, and in fact their definitions are diametrically opposed. In order to be obedient or not, one has to choose. A slave cannot choose[1552].

Indeed, if we are not obedient to GOD, refusing to follow his law, we become slaves, in truth, to the various trivial things of this world: desires of the body and fallen human nature, materialism, etc[1553]. If we do not

---

[1550] It is natural to know that slavery of one's self is wrong; and thus Augustine's idea of Natural Law dictates all slavery is wrong. Sadly, it seems just as natural for humans to ignore such obvious law.

[1551] (Anthony Schraner, 1981) pg. 66-67

[1552] (Brown, 2001) pg. 100

[1553] Augustine's *City of GOD*, IV, 3—a good man is free, an evil man is forever a slave to his lusts and desires

follow GOD, we will follow instead the ways of the flesh, become slaves to them, and become subservient things; less than human, below them.

It was GOD who gave us freewill [1554], and obedience is a choice[1555]. But we have the option to be helplessly stupid if we truly wish it.

The Law of GOD is liberating, since it breaks the hold that untruth, error, falsehood, misperception, worldly desire, instinct, and the lie have on our poor souls. It is better to see and believe in the Truth, than to believe and cling to falsehood and nothingness, or to insist in error and void when the Truth of GOD is all around us. Nothing is more liberating than the Truth. "The Truth shall set you free[1556]." And GOD is Truth.

To be obedient to GOD is thus to serve the Truth and to be truly free. This is not the so-called "freedom" of slavery to our lusts and desires, not the license to do what we "want", but the freedom to do what is truly significant, the freedom to follow only the Truth, the freedom to avoid stupidity and sin, the freedom to reach our ultimate potential and be who we were originally meant to be[1557]. Imagine the freedom to resist the failings and errors of the world and the flesh and pursue instead ultimate Glory, ultimate Good, and ultimate Honor! Imagine being free to be truly human! This is true and glorious freedom! Freedom from the mistakes of sin and error.

Wrestling with GOD and Obedience

The fact that many in the modern world find *blind* obedience to other creatures stifling or distasteful is understandable, since human nature itself struggles and questions. GOD made us that way. A knight, saint, or religious person, as any other, is not made to be a mindless slave. GOD expects us to be obedient to HIM and the Truth, not to follow blindly, but to follow out of love and respect for ultimate reality.

[1554] (Deane, 1963) pg. 15, (Tamburello, 2000) pg. 48, 50

[1555] Chesterton Review 14: #3-4: 217

[1556] John 8:32

[1557] Dante Alighieri says, "Consider your origins", meaning the original origins of the Human Race before it fell from Grace, "You were not born to live like brutes, but to follow virtue and knowledge", *The Inferno*, Canto XXVI, lines 118-120, (Tamburello, 2000) pg. 48, 55

To this point, even arguing and struggling with GOD at times has become something of a religious tradition[1558].

GOD and Abraham stood upon a hill, looking down upon Sodom and Gomorrah. GOD informs Abraham that HE intends to destroy the entire area because of the absolute depravity of the inhabitants. Abraham, worrying over the life of his righteous brother, Lot, actually decides to question the Living GOD.

"Lord, what if there were 50 good men in those cities." Abraham asked. "Would you spare them for the sake of those 50?"

"I would spare the place for those 50." GOD said.

"Please forgive my audacity," Abraham pleaded. "But what if there are only 40 righteous men?"

"I would spare the area for those 40." GOD said.

Abraham continues his questioning, implicitly pointing to the righteousness of only one man in the two cities. GOD implicitly suggests that He will not destroy the area, if even one man could be found who was righteous in such a despicable place[1559]. He sends angels to escort Lot and his family out of the cities[1560]. The amazing thing is not GOD's mercy, but that Abraham would be so persistent in questioning the Master of the Universe.

While Abraham is considered the Father of Faith, Moses follows close behind in esteem among Jewish, Christian, and Muslim writers. Like Abraham, Moses looms a giant in the world of faith and obedience, but he also wrestled with GOD over his mission and the sense of his particular obedience.

GOD called Moses to bring the Jewish people out of Egypt and to demand directly to the Pharaoh their release.

"But Lord," Questions Moses, "The Hebrews will demand to know which GOD calls them out. Who should I say calls them?"

"Tell them it is the GOD of Abraham, Isaac, and Jacob that calls them. Tell them my name is "I Am who Am"[1561].

[1558] Genesis 32:28, Jacob struggles with an angel, and is renamed Israel, "Struggles with GOD".

[1559] Genesis 18:23-33

[1560] Genesis 18 and 19

[1561] Exodus 3:14

It is tradition, that at this moment, the entirety of the Universe, the birds and the beasts, the ground and the sky, the stars and the galaxies, all silently spoke in response, "Yes, LORD, Thou Are!"[1562]

Although moved, Moses still questioned. "The Children of Israel will not believe me that I am the spokesman for you. How can I convince them?"

GOD answers this practical objection with the granting of miraculous powers to Moses, as in the ability to create and cure leprosy at will, and turning water to blood.

Still, Moses objects again. "But Lord, I speak . . . . Slowly, surely I am not the right person for this mission, obviously a mission requires great oratory skills."

GOD might have sighed. "Then have your brother Aaron speak for you. But remember it is you that I want to lead my people"[1563].

Imagine, at the top of the mountain, even as GOD in all His glory speaks to you, that you struggle and question Him! As impertinent as it seems, Moses is not arrogant, he is simply being human. Humans always struggle with their requirements. Moses obeys, not blindly, but humanly.

In the final analysis, while the hero and the modern both struggle with GOD if they are honest, it is the hero who finally obeys, while the modern simply continues to struggle or eventually ignores GOD altogether[1564]. Which one are we? Are we to be the one who obeys GOD after great soul searching and struggle, or are we to be the one who pays lip service but denies GOD and the soul[1565]?

Why be obedient to GOD and the Code?

*The Need for Discipline

A man and a hero, especially the knight[1566], no matter how naturally strong or courageous he is, will finally need the discipline that obedience to a code of Honor can provide. A strong and courageous man, with

---

[1562] Christopher Smart's *A Song to David*, line 240

[1563] Exodus 3 and 4

[1564] (Krailsheimer, 1966, 1988) pg. 82

[1565] Matthew 21:28-32

[1566] The Christian and the Hero are inseparable—Samuel Johnson, *Rambler* 44

an honorable code of conduct, learns to discipline the dishonorable desires within himself, and uses the strength and courage for goodness, humanity, and GOD. The man who cannot follow rules designed to control dishonorable emotions will find himself a slave to them[1567], and he will follow these desires until they destroy him and the world with him.

History is full of people who, if only they had followed a Code of Honor, they would have avoided needless and despicable carnage. Consider Cortez and Pizarro, the brutal conquistadors who conquered the Aztecs and the Incas with impossible odds. Setting aside the greed and inhumanity, look at the courage, albeit ferocity, the plain sheer, terrible grit! If that sort of internal, animal power could be aimed for good, to help the world, what wonders could be accomplished? But neither of these men used their considerable power for the unselfish Right, and although they conquered these mighty empires and put a stop to human sacrifice, no one involved truly profited from their efforts. Whole civilizations suffered slavery anew and were crushed; at the end of their careers, Cortez died an embittered man, and Pizarro fell assassinated by his own men.

Just as a river, powerful, majestic, and useful when within its channels, becomes a slaughtering horror when it floods and escapes the confines of its own banks, the man who leaves behind the discipline of the Code becomes an all-destructive monster. Strength and Courage are the waters of the river, and the channels are the discipline of the Code.

What is more, if the river jumps its banks, it destroys at first, but soon loses its power, life, and identity, for there is nothing to channel or focus its force, and any unfocused force or power soon dissipates. Poetry is nothing without rhythm and meter; music is only noise unless it has beat and melody. Rhythm and meter, beat and melody are the rules, the special disciplines that make these arts what they are. Erase the rules, their codes, the discipline required to create them, and they become only mindless prattle or emotionless sound. So too, will a man lose his strength and edge if he has nothing to channel his bravery and energy. He will become nothing more than a destructive brute, soon shot down in the street like a dog. How many people have you known that started strong, full of verve and power, but who sooner or later become drunken sots or wasted ne'er-do-wells because they had no focus, discipline, or purpose in their lives? I have known many.

[1567] Augustine's *City of GOD*, IV, 3

There are just as many who used discipline to harness their potential. St. Augustine, St. Francis, and Sir Ramon Lull, as youths and full of intelligence, potential wisdom, and enormous energy would have wound up empty and ridiculous except for their discovery of a belief system that gave them discipline and control over their desires. George Washington and Abraham Lincoln refused to accept the easy path, found the road of discipline, ethics, and Honor, and saved their country. Heroes are made by discipline[1568], or are lost by the lack of it[1569].

The knight embraces the narrow road, the small gate, and leaves behind the path of least resistance. Only thus may he be a knight, withstand all evil, and enter the kingdom of Heaven.

The Need for Dogma

Many moderns, especially atheists and agnostics, scream of the "horrors" of dogma, basic set rules that are considered permanent and important to the observance of a religion. [They do not realize that Dogma, the laws of the Church, were not established by GOD to help GOD, nor to help HIM "lord it over" the universe. The Laws of GOD, the Dogma of the Church, were created to help protect humans from their own fallen natures and mistakes.]

One dogmatic rule in many religions, often considered a terrible burden to modern people, is chastity outside of marriage. In today's world, the complaints against this rule are loud and have no end. It is used as an example of how dogma, and thus most religions, are "unfeeling and tyrannical, unresponsive to modern needs and concerns".

The worst part of this rule and other dogma, claim many moderns, is the lack of freedom that they require. Yet most of the problems in the modern world, abused children, single-parent households, neglect, mistreatment of women, lack of knowledge of the past, debauchery, and so on, can be traced to lack of chastity and self discipline in the realm of relationships.

Anyone who understands human nature and the urgency of emotions understands the importance of dogma. Without some sort of set rule

---

[1568] (Clairvaux, 1977) pg. 166, and (Lull, 2001) pg. 71
[1569] (Barber, The Knight and Chivalry, Revised Edition, 1995) pg. 229

that is considered permanent and irrevocable, it is easy to allow violent emotion and the "heat of the moment" to control actions and events.

For example, a man is approached by a beautiful woman, and for that moment wrestles with the fact that he is married to another. His lusts and emotions are high, demanded he take the woman. If he has the dogmatic rule mentioned above, taught to him since childhood, he has an anchor to fight his irrational and unreasoning emotions and drives, for at that moment his heart will not easily listen to reason or mental argument. In the "heat of the moment", dogma may be the only thing that curbs his instinct.

Another man sees his wife with another man. For that moment he is filled with rage and murderous intent, his heart closed to any reasonable argument or restraint. Deep within his mind, so far back in his memory that it resides near the reptilian brain, he hears a voice reminding him of the rule not to murder. This important rule placed there by religion might be the only thing that keeps him from slaughtering. Often it is! What else is there to hold a man back at that blistering moment?

Dogma, as opposed to chaos, clears the way for reasonable and even free thinking, for it helps a human avoid consequences in the first place, and it allows society and civilization to exist. People need restraints, placed within them by careful religion, to control the beast that is human nature.

Dogma also sets the standard for groupings of religions and other beliefs. Without them, there is no point in belonging to this or that group, organization, or belief system.

The Need for Standards

Without rules and actions based on rules, no group, religion, or organization can differentiate itself from another nor last long. Imagine a church with atheists as members, or an atheist organization run by Christians. Such groupings would be irrational and would eventual tear themselves asunder. How silly is it for someone to say they are Christian, but not follow the Christian way of life. How meaningless is it to say one is atheist, but believing in GOD on the side. And once the standards of a group are meaningless, who would know if they belonged or not, even if such a group existed or not? How could one be sure without some way to judge members and non-members and what would be the point of having a group with no identity? Identity is based on rules and standards. Identity must equal the discipline to keep it.

Christ says we must be separate from the world[1570]. In other words, our actions should set us apart. If members of religions act as the ordinary world, or as people without religion, how could one say they are affected or impacted by their own beliefs? Why bother pretending? What is the point? Why even dare to call one's self a Christian?

And what happens to society and the Human Race in general if standards are erased?

Consider the French Revolution. At first it seems reasonable, and even trumpets the Reign of Reason and the upholding of Justice. Its mottos are difficult to argue against: Brotherhood, Liberty, Equality. But behind these nice sounding mottos was the erasing of standards, ethics, and traditions, so that nothing upheld the time-honored morals, the long-defended standards. The terrible reign of the selfish tyrants was over, perhaps, but the reign of the Terror had begun.

At first, only those suspected of aiding royalty were executed; but soon, at the taste of blood, the smell of total license, the guillotine slammed down on more and more, until everyone was under suspicion, and everyone went to the chopping block!

While things may seem calm, at any moment, people may panic and their normally calm reasoning may unravel. It is at these difficult times when standards are the most useful, even during the sinking of the Titanic[1571]. As the boat began to take on water, the men of the ship automatically started loading women and children on the life boats. The men had standards and traditional honor, ensuring the women and children were saved first, before the men.

Imagine the chaos and sickening cowardice during such a disaster, without this standard: men scrambling to escape their deaths in the icy waters by knocking aside women and children to save themselves in the life boats. A man named Ismay had snuck aboard one of the lifeboats dressed as a woman. A huge public outcry rose against him when his actions were reported in the press, and many threatening to hang him.

[1570] John 15: 19, John 17:16, 1 John 2:15, 1 Corinthians 7:31

[1571] In the modern world and without a code of conduct, people shamelessly panic and riot over less life-threatening situations, like losing a basketball game

His example shows that without standards, men would be reduced to nothing but selfish dogs, unfit for survival, but clawing for life like a wounded pig.

Without standards, other rules and obligations throughout the world begin to lose their meaning. If a demented individual reads the Golden Rule without any standard or normality to compare his experience, he may come to the conclusion that he may treat others dementedly, since he himself likes to be treated dementedly. Only by having standards and common rules, as in the Code, can one hold up a mirror to oneself, and be able to determine how the golden rule, or any other rule, should be applied.

Sad to say that there are people in this world who, on purpose and with definite aim, wish to erase away all standards, so that no one may stop them, chastise them, scold them, or hold them responsible for fiendish or disgusting actions[1572]. Some even do this to gain or hold power. They would set the whole world on a collision course with destruction, force the world to tolerate Hitlers, Stalins, and Khmer Rouges, terrible civil rights abuses, and twisted sexual practices, so that they could embrace their own twisted practices with impunity.

As a race and as individuals, we need to know that we are not the measure of all things[1573]. The minute a man or a group decides that they are the endpoint of all reasoning, then they feel they may commit the most intolerable crimes with impunity, and even smile with perfect peace of mind as they do it. They no longer doubt themselves[1574], and thus no crime is too vast for their egos. Hitler and Stalin thought they could do anything because they saw no higher authority than themselves, thus they became uncontrolled tyrants, murdering hundreds of millions. This is what will always happen, when people cease to recognize GOD, Honor, and Morality as constraining forces, and place themselves as god.

[1572] (Clairvaux, 1977) pg. 150, an arrogant man excuses himself, the humble accuses himself

[1573] (Runes, 1955) pg. 976, for Protagoras's phrase in the positive

[1574] (Scupoli, 1945 edition)—Total lack of doubt towards oneself is a sure step towards philosophical, mental, and spiritual error. Humility is the better, and more honorable, option.

The Need for Guidance

Are not people intelligent enough to make their own decisions without a code? Such a question might as well ask: do people have enough time in their lives to make all the mistakes over again? Why not learn from the past and from the mistakes of ancient peoples? All codes were made with a view to avoiding mistakes and pitfalls that ancient peoples learned about by hard experience.

My mother, a registered nurse of great experience with a master's degree, saw the old Jewish rules as not only for holiness, but for practical reasons. She would point out that the ancient peoples who ignored the Mosaic law against eating pork many times ended up with special diseases[1575]. A similar problem plagued many who neglected to circumcise their sons. In modern times, chronic infections of many boys' privates can be traced directly to the ignoring of the old Mosaic practice[1576]. These rules in the Old Testament, my mother would point out, were purposefully constructed to help avoid very physical, practical problems that ancient peoples needed to solve in order to survive.

Consider Monogamy. Many in the modern world see this as prudish, but if a man jumps from bed to bed, sexual encounters ad nausea, soon he finds himself swamped by paternity lawsuits, emotional wastelands, and the ravages of venereal disease. The woman involved in such encounters stands the same risk of disease and emotional scarring, let alone the possibility of raising children without help and without a male role model. This particular problem has caused so much contention, and so many have refused the obvious benefits of marriage and monogamy[1577], that governments have offered to "help" with patronizing policies, allowing the spectre of Huxley's *Brave New World* to loom around the corner. What a high price for lack of self-restraint!

Keeping an eye on the ancient and time-tested codes and ideas might help save our life and sanity, and more than once.

[1575] (Barclay, Gospel of Matthew volume 2, revised edition, 1975) pg. 102, 112

[1576] I have encountered many who substantiate this from their own experience.

[1577] Statistics indicate that, for women, marriage before children can almost guarantee monetary security, as opposed to having children out of wed-lock, which almost guarantees poverty.

The Need for Protection

In Ancient times, there were great and powerful warriors who called themselves knights. When these warriors followed the Code of Chivalry, they protected people, upheld the good, and sustained society. But, there were some who also called themselves "knight", but did not follow the knight code of Chivalry, and they became no more than glorified killers, destroying hope and whole communities, rupturing society like a disease.

Today, another group of people have the same power, but instead of wielding a sword, they wield the law. They also sign their names with the title "esquire", which means "knight in training". When they follow a good code of conduct, they protect people, uphold the good, and sustain society. But there are those within this group that do not follow any sort of code, except that of greed, and are no more than glorified tricksters, robbing society, and laughing at justice. We call both groups "lawyers".

Just like the warriors of old, the only difference between the good and the bad is the code of ethics, a code of Chivalry.

Only when lawyers change their ways and adopt the rules and laws of true knighthood, may they become true defenders of the people, and true "esquires"

Whenever a group of powerful people, whatever they are called, do not have rules that are placed higher than their whims, the innocent, the poor, the just, and society itself suffer. Anyone, especially with power, must be reined and fulfilled by a code that keeps them on the righteous way.

The Need to find Happiness

Without a code, without laws, a man loses much of the joy of life. Such a statement seems to go against all prevailing wisdom. Most modern people seem to assume that having no rules and allowing the whims and instincts of humanity free reign is to be happy[1578]. But the opposite is true. To have the blessings of discipline supplied by a code is to have more life, not less.

[1578] Consider the myriads of popular songs that shout the praises of "losing control", "no rules", "out of control", "insanity", "crazy", and total license.

Think of all the experiences that require the discipline of rules, even rules set up by ourselves. Victory in a race that required long days of practice and pain, achieving a difficult goal, arriving at a destination that only the dedicated and persevering could accomplish. These things cannot be experienced by an undisciplined rogue whose desires are all met by animalistic deeds. Without discipline, only the basest, the easiest, things are achieved. To achieve the greatest things, the most awesome things, the most difficult and unique and special things, even to appreciate such things, requires the habit of discipline.

Lack of discipline can be a punishment in and of itself[1579]. Those who live without discipline soon find their lives to be less than they wish. When Moses came down from Mt. Sinai with the Ten Commandments in his hands, he saw the Hebrews, already deep in their worshipping of a stupid, golden calf. Rage swept over him. Had they not seen the wonders of the Lord: the miracles in the desert! He knew the Word of GOD would bring them a higher happiness than they had ever known, and so when he found them performing such ignorance, he raised the stone tablets above his head and smashed them on the ground[1580]. His rebellious people did not deserve the law of GOD. Such a people, he decided, were unworthy of the law.

Think on that. To be unworthy of the law. To be unworthy of discipline.

My martial arts teacher of many years used to speak of a great lesson that I never forgot. While he trained with his masters, he noticed that some students were struck often with the Shinai[1581] of correction, while others, whose motions were just as lacking, receiving little correction.

This seemed unfair, and so he asked his masters about this.

The explanation came simply. "Being disciplined by the Shinai is only for those who have the capacity to learn and improve. The masters believe in them. The others, the ones who receive no correction, the masters can

---

[1579] (Augustine S., 1961) pg. 33, bk. 1-The punishment of every disordered mind is its own disorder

[1580] Exodus 32:19

[1581] A Shinai is a bamboo sword which hurts, but does not damage the bones, and is often used in traditional dojos, or training halls

already see that they will never listen or amount to much, and so he leaves them alone"[1582].

Why obey the Code when we have the Bible?

"Why all the concern over the code," some Christians demand. "Follow GOD, as Lull did in the beginning of your chapter." But, as one looks carefully at Lull's story, indeed, any knight's story, one sees that as they follow GOD, they do so by following the very tenets of the Code, whether unconsciously or consciously. They believe what Christ teaches, they defend that belief, they help the weak and the poor, they have no mercy upon the weakness and evil in themselves and do not refrain from chastising others who do not repent. And they see at the heart of the law is mercy. They find themselves champions of the right and the Truth in every place. This is the Code. The Code is the way to follow GOD. The Code is obedience to GOD. The code is the road to GOD as surely as the Ten Commandments. The Ten Commandments tell you how to be a good person, the Code tells you how to be a best warrior.

And Ramon Lull, as he dedicated his life to the Obedience of GOD, wrote the definitive book on Chivalry.

When in doubt, follow Christ's advice, "Love GOD with all your soul, heart and mind. And love your neighbor as yourself." All the rules of Chivalry are derived from these.

"Not everyone can be a priest. Religion is knight-errantry"[1583].

The Need to Judge Conscience

One man says his conscience demands this, another man says his conscience demands the opposite.

If every man who claimed to follow his conscience was right, Truth would be self-contradictory. Therefore, Conscience cannot be a completely trustworthy guide. Conscience must be weighed and

---

[1582] See Hebrews 12:5-7, 11-13
[1583] From Cervantes's *Don Quixote*, book 2, chapter 8

judged by a higher discernment[1584]. Obedience to a higher law is this discernment.

The Need for Honorable Men

When I look around, and listen to the average person on the street, I see and hear people wanting chivalrous behavior from men. They want men to be loyal to spouse, family, and community, as well as practice self-sacrifice and discipline. They want men to never abuse women or children, to help the elderly and weak, and to be ready to help people around them. They also want men to be gentle, and find rape abhorrent and killing wrong unless absolutely necessary.

In a word, they want men to be Chivalrous. They want men to have Chivalry in their hearts, minds, and souls.

Yet many popular interest groups stand against Chivalry, regardless of the effect this has on society. The same groups find men and fathers "expendable".

Those capitalists who refuse the Judeo-Christian ethic and wish to avoid helping others in need work to avoid Chivalry. They would rather sell exploitation and pander greed than grapple with Honor. Communists, though representing the opposite of capitalistic license, refuse the Truth of GOD and the glories of freedom, thus turning their backs on knighthood

Homosexuals curse at Chivalry, essentially Christian Chivalry, because they know it criticizes sodomy. Christian Chivalry is an aspect of the Judeo-Christian ethic, which further opposes Homosexuality as a viable lifestyle. The Homosexuals find themselves chanting against Chivalry, even though a knight is required to protect even them from bullies.

Modern Feminists, who should be the greatest proponents of Chivalry, deny it ever existed at all. To them, Chivalry patronizes them and, even worse in their eyes, expects them to live up to their full potential as honorable citizens of a decent society.

Racist groups yell and scream, and by their very nature ignore the justice of Chivalry.

[1584] (Anthony Schraner, 1981) pg. 287

Moderns are shocked by the Chivalrous ideas of objective truth and the sovereignty of moral law. They cannot allow Chivalry to grow, because if they did, then it would impede their schedule of reducing everything to multi-cultural pabulum, moral relevancy, and slack, cowardly platitudes.

Almost every modern political pressure group would deny Chivalry its right and duty to help our poor society. Chivalry is never convenient.

What of Chivalries that are dominated by other religions and cultures? Hindu Chivalry has the same problems, in modern eyes, as the Christian Chivalry, as does Islamic, Chinese, and Native American Chivalries. Even though Japanese Chivalry might at times allow Homosexuality, its record with Feminists, Pacifists, and Multi-culturalists is abysmal.

After a while, there is nothing left that will be allowed but a kind of white-washed, bleached out materialism, which has no set morality or standard, unless you count the modern "morality" of environmentalism, staying slim, and the pro-abortive superiority of the female. Except for the last aspect, the rest is exactly the same as the Nazi agenda of the 1930's. None of this encourages loyalty, nor spiritual concerns, nor kindness to all, nor nobility towards anyone.

As long as society raises its sons without concepts of Chivalry, there shall always be much disloyalty, much laziness, much debauchery, much abuse, much cruelty, and much dishonor.

The Need to Avoid a Deal with the Devil

In the movie, *The Devil and Daniel Webster*, the Devil, obviously a deceptive and creepy man, offers a young farmer gold in exchange for his soul. The audience can watch and lounge back in their chairs, saying to themselves "I would never be that stupid as to accept a bag of gold in exchange for my soul, especially with a guy that looks like that".

But Evil never appears obvious, at least not in the beginning, and it always starts small. The Devil often wears a clever disguise, covered with glamour to fool the eyes and senses. And his offer is more clever than a simple bag of gold, and it never seems to be in exchange for anything important. The deal will be much quieter, seemingly more sensible, and may not attract your suspicion at all. Indeed, the soul is un-understandable, not material, and thus modern people have concluded it to be immaterial (read as not important).

The Truth is also not material. A judge can rule for the truth, or for the side that will grant him a great reputation. The Nazis offer safety for the family in exchange for a sentence of information. The Communists will spare mother's life for a signed document. Turn your head and pay taxes without asking what the money is used for. Stand up for your spoiled son or daughter, even though what they are doing is wrong. Catching the coach in an embarrassing position with a student isn't enough to report him, is it? It is easy to slip into stupidity and evil!

In the end, it is all about priorities. The hierarchy in your heart is the key[1585]. What is most important to you? If it is not GOD and HIS Word, the Devil will get you to exchange a seemingly small favor to secure the most important thing in your life. And suddenly you have lost everything. How did it happen?

All these things, safety, family, friends, reputation, health, a good salary to support your kids, etc., are good in themselves. Only by seeing that the Best is better than the good, and the good, better than the average, can one see past the deal with the Devil. Only by understanding that GOD is most important, can one escape the tricks of the Devil.

The Last Reason

All the reasons we have listed above are excellent, but they are as nothing compared to the real reason a knight, saint, or hero obeys GOD and the Code.

The real reason a knight is obedient to GOD is to glorify GOD.

It is as St. Ignatius said: for the greater glory of GOD.

[1585] (Deane, 1963) pg. 41

Free will and Obedience

All these reasons above are powerful arguments to obey GOD's law, but arguments and good reasons are not enough for most. Few wish to abandon totally what they feel is Freewill. GOD understands this. HE is responsible for our freewill, and it was HIS plan to make sure we have it.

Free will is a gift from GOD[1586]. It is also a frightful test.

The Angels themselves were put to the test of Free Will[1587]. Indeed, according to St. Anselm, the angels had two wills, the will to do what is good, and the will to do what is good for one's self [1588]. Perhaps the Angels were refused total exposure to GOD's face, denied total knowledge of GOD, so that they could have Free Will. To see the face of GOD, to have full knowledge of GOD's power, is to choose GOD, for no other choice exists, when you see that all of reality is GOD. Like starring into the sun, nothing else can be seen. Perhaps, hiding a portion of Himself allowed the Angels a chance to make a decision[1589]. Choose GOD or not.

Lucifer, the greatest of the angels, could feel this gap, this holding back. Could this have convinced him to fall from Grace, simply because he felt that GOD was hiding something enormous from him? Perhaps he demanded to know this part of GOD held back from him. Whatever the case, Lucifer refused to choose GOD, instead choosing himself, choosing what seemed good for himself over what was good in itself. Origin says that Lucifer chose pride.

Then, when time began, Lucifer made sure Mankind received a similar test. A garden of absolute delight, but not with absolute freedom to choose. Adam and Eve had only to follow one rule, to avoid eating from the Tree of knowledge, the knowledge of good and evil. Once again, total knowledge is denied, because with complete knowledge there is no real choice. Only a fool would not choose the obvious choice. They only had to choose obedience or not. For whatever reason, whether greed, pride, or fear, they chose *not*.

[1586] (Deane, 1963) pg. 15, (Tamburello, 2000) pg. 48, 50
[1587] (Hopkins, 1972) pg. 144
[1588] (Hopkins, 1972) pg. 142-143
[1589] St. Anselm seems to suggest this

This choice, eating form the tree of knowledge, did give them knowledge, the knowledge of pain. Pain and suffering—the difference between good and evil, that there is evil and how it is different from good. They also gained the bitter knowledge of their absolute nakedness, piteousness, and shame compared to the Perfect GOD. Through one choice they lost their connection with GOD and gained all suffering.

Now GOD is far removed from us, and we seem to have complete ability to choose. GOD's presence would be like a beacon in a storm, and only a fool would not move toward that beacon. But where the beacon cannot be seen, any direction seems good. Our freedom seems complete, except we are blind. And suffering.

Why make us blind? Why take away our vision of reality, GOD's obvious presence in our lives? Why allow us to suffer so deeply? For all this allows for free will. And Free will allows for obedience. OR not. It is our choice. Suffering and blindness gives us one more chance to choose. Hopefully we choose wisely.

Such a terrible price for free will. But without that free will there is no obedience. GOD could force us by terror and absolute knowledge to bend us to HIS will, but that is slavery, not obedience. HE does not want the love of robots, for that is not love[1590]. GOD wishes us to freely choose. Freely, through the suffering and pain and terror, to choose HIM. FOR GOD, love and obedience are the same[1591]. GOD will not make us love HIM, nor will GOD make us obey HIM. GOD wishes us to come to HIM of our own free will, a conscious choice, to choose that which is absolute good, and to embrace HIM forever.

With our blindness and fractured perception, wounded reason and broken understanding, how can we find HIM? Who can see in this blindness without a beacon, without the slightest hint of the right way? Now, to complete our free will, and allow us to choose obedience, we need an alternative to our blindness. Something to give us an option to the darkness and pain that surrounds us. We must have something to choose besides the darkness, to really have a choice.

We need a beacon. A light in the darkness. The light of the world[1592].

[1590] (Anthony Schraner, 1981)pg. 138
[1591] 1 John 5:3, 1 John 2:5, Deut, 11:13, Deut 11:1, Deut 30:16, Joshua 22:5
[1592] John 8:12, John 9:5, John 12:46, John 11:9

Just as one man made a choice from untold ages that ruined the world, so too, one man must make a choice to save the world and make obedience possible. At a moment in time, in yet another garden, one man makes a choice with total freedom, while in absolute suffering.

The Last Obedience

The three pillars of Christ's life are Purity, Piety, and Obedience. Purity is Christ's perfect focus on GOD, giving him his incredible strength. Piety is Christ's love and relationship with GOD made into tangible action. These two are of utmost importance, but Obedience is the final key.

One can see this in culmination in the Garden of Gethsemane. Christ's blood joining with his sweat, pouring himself out, even then making himself the literal, figurative, and real Holy Grail, becoming the vessel of sacrifice and salvation for every man. Yet a pitiful sight, weeping, on his knees, a man especially terrified. But it is his finest hour, for here he takes his free will and makes his decision. While he allows himself to consider the alternative, he turns from it resolutely and forever, embracing completely Obedience to the Father's plan and will. "Not my will, but Yours be done, Father"[1593].

It is through the Obedience of Christ, the very acceptance of the Cross, that HE, and thus we, gain victory over sin, Hell, and the Devil[1594]. Through this Obedience, Christ allows himself to die to this world and death, but Resurrects to the Eternal World and Life. Through this one act of obedience, Christ defeats the most powerful enemies of mankind.

Obedience channels His great and terrifying power, showing Christ to be the ultimate weapon, the ultimate knight, the ultimate hero, the GOD-HERO[1595].

[1593] Luke 22:42
[1594] 1 Corinthians 15:57, 1 John 5:4, Micah 7:9
[1595] Isaiah 9:5-6, Zephaniah 3:17, 2 Samuel 23:1—GOD-hero is often translated as "Mighty GOD"

I pray you all gentlemen and gentlewomen that read this book of knights and saints, from the beginning to the ending, pray for me while I am alive, that GOD send me good deliverance from my sins and when I am dead, I ask you all pray for my soul. For this book was finished on the feast of the Epiphany of Christ, January 5th, in the year of Our Lord 2014, by Eric Robert Demski, a simple man, as GOD help him for his great might, as he is the servant of Christ both day and night[1596].

[1596] This is in imitation of Sir Thomas Malory's final request in his *Le Morte D'Arthur*

APPENDIX 2: SOME CHIVALRY CODES MENTIONED IN THE TEXT

The Decalogue (the knight code from the 1100's)
I.   Thou shalt believe all that the Church teaches, and shall observe all it's directions.
II.   Thou shalt defend the Church.
III.   Thou shalt respect all weaknesses and shall constitute thyself defender of them.
IV.   Thou shalt love the country in which thou were born.
V.   Thou shalt not recoil before thine enemy.
VI.   Thou shalt make war against the infidel without cessation, and without mercy.
VII.   Thou shalt perform scrupulously thy feudal duties, if they be not contrary to the laws of GOD.
VIII.   Thou shalt never lie, and shalt remain loyal to the pledge word.
IX.   Thou shalt be generous, and give largesse to everyone.
X.   Thou shalt be everywhere and always the champion of the right and the good against injustice and evil.

The Greek Warriors Unspoken Code (circa 400 BC.)
1. The worthy opponent must be treated with respect in death as well as in life.
2. Treaties, truces, and religious festivals will be respected.
3. The vanquished have the right to recover their dead and bury them properly.

4. Heralds, priests, and sacred ground shall not be harmed and shall remain inviolate.
5. The enemy's spirit must be crushed in open battle. Neither success nor victory shall be achieved with fraud or secrecy.
6. Secret or long-distance weaponry are an insult to the true warrior, and all decisive battles must occur through hand-to-hand combat.
7. Fleeing opponents are not to be pursued beyond the battlefield.

"Darkness belongs to robbers and waylayers. But my glory shall not be diminished by stealing a victory . . . . I am determined to attack openly by daylight; I prefer to regret my fortune than be ashamed of my victory."
—Alexander the Great

(Source: *The Code of the Warrior*, by Rick Fields, pg. 78)

The Dharma Conquest—"Conquest by Righteousness"
(India, circa 300 BC.)

1. Brahmans (ruler-priests of the Hindu) are exempt from battle unless they attack first.
2. "Only equals should fight each other".
3. Those who leave the ranks shall not be slain.
4. No attack shall be given without proper warning.
5. No one shall be struck who is confiding, unprepared, or panic stricken. (No one who is fatigued or frightened or refuses to fight shall be struck. No one who is engaged in battle with another, who has no armor, or whose weapon is rendered useless shall be struck. A woman, nor a weaponless man shall be attacked.)
6. No one who is ill or cries for quarter shall be struck, nor those who are aged or too tender of age.
7. Chariot drivers and draught animals, transporters of weapons and drummers and buglers shall not be attacked.
8. If entreated with joined hands, a Kshatriya (warrior) shall defend even his enemy.

"It is doubtful if any other ancient civilization set such humane ideals for warfare."
—A.L. Basham, Author of *The Wonder That Was India*

(Source: *The Code Of the Warrior*, by Rick Fields, pg. 86-87)

The Seven Contrary Virtues (circa 410 AD)
From *Psychomachia* "The Battle of the Soul", by Prudentius

1. Humility, against pride
2. Kindness, against envy
3. Abstinence, against gluttony
4. Chastity, against lust
5. Patience, against anger
6. Liberality, against greed
7. Diligence, against sloth

The Eight Obligations of the Knights of the Hospital of Saint John of Jerusalem (circa 1113)

Also called the **Hospitallers**, these knights were originally recognized as an order of monks by Pope Pascal II and were required to follow the *Augustinian Rule* of Chastity, Poverty, and Obedience. As knights, they continued the Rule, and besides the standard *Decalogue*, they were also required to follow these eight additional rules.

1. Live in truth
2. Have faith
3. Repent of sins
4. Give proof of humility
5. Love justice
6. Be merciful
7. Be sincere and whole-hearted
8. Endure persecution

These eight "obligations" or "aspirations" were often connected with the Maltese Cross, an eight pointed cross appearing like four arrowheads with their tips meeting at the center. There is some evidence to suggest the knights adopted this symbol in 1023, when they rebuilt their hospital in Jerusalem with donations from the merchants of the Republic of Amalfi (the republic having the arrow heads as their symbol).

St. George's Four Rules to Live By
From *The Golden Legend* of Jacobus de Voragine, 1266

1. To cherish the Church of the Lord
2. To attend Mass always
3. To honor the priests
4. To care for the poor

> "In the Name of GOD, St. Michael and St. George, I dub thee knight!"
> —Traditional proclamation of the dubbing of a knight, 1100's, Gautier, pg. 251

[Source of code: *St. George, Knight, Martyr, Patron Saint, and Dragon Slayer*, by Giles Morgan, pg. 47-48]

The Four Knightly Things of Sir Hugh de Tabarie
From the *L'Ordene De Chevalier* (anonymous, circa 1100's)

1. Never parley with traitors
2. Never lead astray dame nor damsel, but on the contrary respect them and defend them against injury.
3. Piously observe all feast days and days of abstinence
4. Hear Mass every day and make an offering at monastery.

> "Four things which a knight should observe all his life if he would preserves his honor untarnished."
> —Sir Hue De Tabarie in his lecture to Saladin

[Source: *Chivalry* by Leon Gautier, pg. 249]

The Unwritten Code of the Bushido

From *Bushido, The Soul of Japan* by Inazo Nitobe, 1905

1. Rectitude or Justice
2. Courage, the spirit of daring and bearing
3. Benevolence, the feeling of distress
4. Politeness
5. Veracity and Sincerity
6. Honor
7. The duty of Loyalty
8. Fortitude and Self Control

"There are, if I may say so, three powerful spirits, which have, from time to time, moved on the face of the waters, and given a predominate impulse to the moral sentiments and energies of mankind. These are the spirits of liberty, of religion, and of honor."

—from *Europe in the Middle Ages,*
by Henry Hallam, 1840

[source: *Bushido, the Soul of Japan*, by Inazo Nitobe]

"The Seven Vows of Knighthood"

As recorded by some medieval writers (circa 1400s):

1. Whenever he is on a quest or strange adventure, never to lighten himself of his arms, except to sleep at night.
2. Whenever in the pursuit of adventure, to never avoid perilous "passes" (like bridges or paths), nor to turn out of his way for fear of meeting powerful enemies, or from any dread of monsters, savage beasts or spirits, or anything which could only harm, or might be resisted by, the body of a man.
3. The knight was committed to defending a lady. He was rather to die than desert her, or suffer her to be offended.
4. He should be punctual to the day and hour in which he had been engaged to contend in arms with a brother knight.
5. Upon returning to court after having been about in quest of adventure, he should give an exact account of all he had

done, even if his actions should have been to his disgrace, his knighthood being the forfeit if he should disobey this ordinance.

6. Upon being taken prisoner at a tournament, he should, besides rendering up his arms and horse to the victor, not again contend without the special leave of the latter.

7. Finally, he should not, in company, fight against a solitary enemy, nor carry two swords, if he was unwilling to contend with two opponents. Arms, especially the destrier or warhorse, were rendered up to the victor as his right.

"Loyalty, courtesy, liberality, and justice were the virtues essential in the estimation of mankind to the character of the knight in the days of Chivalry. A more splendid virtue than all others demanded of the young aspirant for knighthood, both before and after initiation, was the pursuit of Good, the detestation of evil, not solely when found in his own soul but also in that of the world".
—From *The Medieval Warrior*, by Paul La Croix and
Walter Clifford Miller, pg.52

[source: *The Medieval Warrior*, by Paul La Croix and Walter Clifford Meller, pg.49]

The Five Virtues of Knighthood (14th Century)
According to the anonymous author of *Sir Gawain and the Green Knight*

1. Noble Generosity
2. Fellowship
3. Purity
4. Courtesy
5. Compassion

These virtues make up the five points of the Medieval Age's Star of Honesty, also called the Pentagram, often seen in today's pop culture but which has a long history. The Wiccans (circa 1960's) have hi-jacked it as one of their esoteric symbols, but Sir Gawain would have simply recognized it as a symbol of the above five virtues, as well as the five senses, and, most notably, the five wounds of Christ. The five pointed star appears on Sir Gawain's shield.

The five Virtues of Lancelot
(According to the Quest for the Holy Grail, pg. 141-3, anonymous, circa 1200)

1. *Virginity and Purity in mind, body, and soul*
2. Humility
3. Long-suffering
4. Rectitude
5. Charity

These Lancelot possessed before he fell from grace because of his affair with Guinevere.

The Cardinal Virtues
From ancient Greek Philosophy
1. Prudence
2. Temperance
3. Courage (or Fortitude)
4. Justice

These are from Plato's *Republic,* and later adopted by the Catholic Church as the Human Virtues

The Theological Virtues (1st Century AD)
From 1 Corinthians 13:13, by Saint Paul of Tarsus
1. Faith
2. Hope
3. Love (Agape), also called Charity

The Seven Heavenly Virtues combine the four Cardinal Virtues and the three Theological Virtues to complete the mystical number seven.

The Seven Corporal Works of Mercy
From the Catholic Church, based on the Christ's Sermon on the Mount
1. Feed the hungry
2. Give drink to the thirsty

3. Give shelter to strangers
4. Clothe the naked
5. Visit the sick
6. Minister to prisoners
7. Bury the dead

Thirteen Virtues of Ben Franklin (circa 1726)

1. "TEMPERANCE. Eat not to dullness; drink not to elevation."
2. "SILENCE. Speak not but what may benefit others or yourself; avoid trifling conversation."
3. "ORDER. Let all your things have their places; let each part of your business have its time."
4. "RESOLUTION. Resolve to perform what you ought; perform without fail what you resolve."
5. "FRUGALITY. Make no expense but to do good to others or yourself; i.e., waste nothing."
6. "INDUSTRY. Lose no time; be always employ'd in something useful; cut off all unnecessary actions."
7. "SINCERITY. Use no hurtful deceit; think innocently and justly, and, if you speak, speak accordingly."
8. "JUSTICE. Wrong none by doing injuries, or omitting the benefits that are your duty."
9. "MODERATION. Avoid extremes; forbear resenting injuries so much as you think they deserve."
10. "CLEANLINESS. Tolerate no uncleanliness in body, cloaths, or habitation."
11. "TRANQUILLITY. Be not disturbed at trifles, or at accidents common or unavoidable."
12. "CHASTITY. Rarely use venery but for health or offspring, never to dullness, weakness, or the injury of your own or another's peace or reputation."
13. "HUMILITY. Imitate Jesus and Socrates."

The Code of the Knight (circa 1360)
From the Ballad of Eustache Deschamps

You who would take upon you the order of knighthood,
It is fitting you should lead a new life;

Devoutly watching in prayer,
Fleeing from sin, pride, and villainy.
The Church you will defend and succor the widow and orphan;
Be bold and guard the people;
Loyal and valiant (knights) taking naught from others,
Thus, should a knight rule himself.

He should have a humble heart, should work always and follow deeds of Chivalry;
Loyal in war and a great traveler He should frequent tournaments and joust for his lady love.
He must keep honor with all so that he cannot be held to blame nor cowardice be found in his doings.
And Above all he should uphold the weak.
Thus, should a knight rule himself.

He should love his rightful lord and above all guard his domain,
Have generosity, be a faithful judge,
So seek the company of valiant knights,
Hearkening to their words and learning from them.

"The code of the medieval knight was founded on respect for his engagements, which led him to loathe a lie. It mattered not whether his oath was given on the book of Evangels or relics of the saints, or sworn to with his bare, uplifted hand."

(Source: *The Medieval Warrior*, by Paul LaCroix and Walter Clifford Miller, pg.52)

The Pirate Articles of Bartholomew Roberts (circa 1719)

1. Every man shall have an equal vote in affairs of moment. He shall have an equal title to the fresh provisions or strong liquors at any time seized, and shall use them at pleasure unless a scarcity may make it necessary for the common good that a retrenchment may be voted.

2. Every man shall be called fairly in turn by the list on board of prizes, because over and above their proper share, they are allowed a shift of clothes. But if they defraud the company to

the value of even one dollar in plate, jewels or money, they shall be marooned. If any man steals from another he shall have his nose and ears slit, and be put ashore where he shall be sure to encounter hardships.

3. None shall game for money either with dice or cards.

4. The lights and candles should be put out at eight at night, and if any of the crew desire to drink after that hour they shall sit upon the open deck without lights.

5. Each man shall keep his piece, cutlass and pistols at all times clean and ready for action.

6. No boy or woman to be allowed amongst them. If any man shall be found seducing any of the latter sex and carrying her to sea in disguise he shall suffer death.

7. He that shall desert the ship or his quarters in time of battle shall be punished by death or marooning.

8. None shall strike another on board the ship, but every man's quarrel shall be ended on shore by sword or pistol in this manner. At the word of command from the quartermaster, each man being previously placed back to back, shall turn and fire immediately. If any man does not, the quartermaster shall knock the piece out of his hand. If both miss their aim they shall take to their cutlasses, and he that draws first blood shall be declared the victor.

9. No man shall talk of breaking up their way of living till each has a share of 1,000. Every man who shall become a cripple or lose a limb in the service shall have 800 pieces of eight from the common stock and for lesser hurts proportionately.

10. The captain and the quartermaster shall each receive two shares of a prize, the master gunner and boatswain, one and one half shares, all other officers one and one quarter, and private gentlemen of fortune one share each

11. The musicians shall have rest on the Sabbath Day only by right. On all other days by favor only.

12. If a member of the crew were to rape a woman he would be put to death or be marooned.

Roberts and his men swore to these on a Bible, and went on to become some of the most successful pirates in history (Source: *The Pirates Realm.com*).

The Equestrian Order of The Holy Sepulchre of Jerusalem, Knight's Code of Honor (circa 2000)

My soul to GOD—by the full spiritual life;

My life to Christ the King;

My heart to our Blessed Lady; and

My own honor—the ineffable honor that comes to him who called the Church my Mother and to him who calls GOD, my Father and strives to live like His Son

Father Dom Lorenzo Scupoli's Four Weapons to obtain Spiritual Perfection (1589)

1. Distrust of self
2. Trust in GOD
3. Spiritual exercises; the proper use of the faculties of the mind and body)
4. Prayer

Source: Father Scupoli's *The Spiritual Combat*, (Scupoli, 1945 edition) pg. 7

APPENDIX 3: CLASSIFICATIONS OF CROSSES DISPLAYED IN THIS BOOK

<u>Title Page</u>

This is a form of the very standard Greek Cross, with a suggestion of the pate'e cross shown below, its "feet" slightly "splayed". This cross was used extensively in early Christianity, as well as in the Crusades. Around 900 years ago, many Crusaders carried this cross into battle, with various colors signifying different Orders of Knighthood. A red cross with a white field became connected with the Templar Knights, while the white cross with the red or black field became connected with the Knights Hospitaller. A grey cross on a black field (or reverse) typically announced the Teutonic Knights.

As the name suggests, it is now often seen as a cross of the Eastern Orthodox Church. It is also used by the international Red Cross organization.

Introduction

A form of the cross pate'e meaning "splayed feet", because the "feet" or arms of the cross "splay" out. This is also called a formee', but such is more a subset of pate'e. Also notice how the arms begin as perpendicular and straight lines, and the ends of the "feet" are flat.

Forms of this type of cross go back at least 1400 years, and are sometimes used with the Teutonic Knights, and rarely with the Knights Templar

'Prepare' Section

This remarkable cross is called the "Tau" Cross and is traditionally the mark of St. Antony of Egypt. It was also adopted by St. Francis of Assisi as his personal symbol.

Stretching back to antiquity, this cross is the last letter of the Hebrew alphabet translated into Greek, and is used to mark the foreheads of the good men in Ezekiel 9:4, as a kind of reverse of the mark of the Beast listed in Revelations 13:16. The Tau mark will save, while the mark of the Beast will damn.

Mental Attitude

This is another pate'e cross, called pate'e formee'.

A version of this cross is connected to St. George and is also called the Swedish Cross of St. George.

The more common Cross of St. George is the red cross on a white field, the horizontal bar twice as long as the vertical, as seen on the British and Canadian flags, as well as the Medieval kingdom of Georgia.

Strength Chapter

A form of the cross pate'e, but moving more towards a subset of that cross, called the Alisee formee'. In this subset, the "feet" are more rounded.

This is another Crusader cross, going back a thousand years.

Strength Chapter Appendix

The Cross of the Order of St. James. This is a fitched cross (having a sharp bottom) and is tipped with fleurs-de-lys. This knightly Spanish order was established in the 12th century to protect pilgrims along the Santiago Pilgrimage as well as drive Moslems from Spain. The Order had ties to the Templars, and mirrored them in their military style and Augustinian Rule.

Courage

This is the much-heralded Maltese Cross, used by the Hospitallers during their reign on the Island of Malta and still used today as the exclusive symbol of the Order. Several origins have been suggested, everywhere from four arrow tips coming together, to each corner of each arm representing an ideal to follow. The ideals are listed in the appendix on codes

One source contends that the Templar knights used this symbol as well; the eight edges of the arms representing the eight original Templars who helped Sir Hughes de Payens patrol the roads that led to Jerusalem.

Sacrifice

This is known as the Jerusalem Cross and is made up of four Greek crosses surrounding a "cross potent", which is a Greek cross capped with four Tau crosses, one on each arm.

This cross was often said to have been worn by pilgrims on their way to Jerusalem. More properly, it is the cross of the Crusader state of Jerusalem, signifying the Kingdom of Jerusalem controlled by the Christians after the First Crusade.

The cross can be considered five crosses, which can represent the five wounds of Christ, or the five major orders of knights that were created in the Holy Land: The Knights Templar, The Knights Hospitaller, the Teutonic Knights, the Knights of the Holy Sepulcher, and the Knights of St. Lazarus. It is now the official symbol of the Knights of the Holy Sepulcher.

<u>Faith</u>

This is the Cross Lorraine, which traditionally was considered St. Joan of Arc's cross. It is often confused with the Patriarchal Cross, which has arms crossing closer to the top. Lorraine was a Medieval kingdom along the Rhine river, now in modern-day, northeastern France.

A version of this cross was used by French freedom fighters during the Nazi occupation of France. It has a long, modern history, chosen by a vast assortment of groups to represent various ideals and purposes. Still, the real ideal and purpose was Christian, from more than 600 years ago.

Obedience

This cross echoes the pate'e formee' of the second, fourth, and fifth crosses mentioned above, on a shield. This very specifically calls to mind the Crusades, and the crusading knights that looked to this symbol as a source of inspiration, faith, courage, and strength.

BIBLIOGRAPHY

Addison, C. G. (2001). *The History of the Knights Templars, introduction by David Hatcher Childress.* Kempton, Illinois: Adventures Unlimited Press.

Aiona, L. G. (2009, October 10). *St. Damien Day Hawaii October 11.* (L. G. Aiona, Performer) Hawaii State Capital, in the Executive Chambers, posted on Hawaii Free Press October 10, 2009, Honolulu, Hawaii, U.S.A.

Alfred, L. T. (1983). *Idylls of the King, edited by J.M. Gray.* London: Penguin Group.

Alfred, L. T. (1923). *Idylls of the King, Intro and notes by H.W. Boynton, Academy Classics.* Boston, New York: Allyn and Bacon.

Alighieri, D. (1954). *The Divine Comedy, translated and edited by Thomas G. Bergin, Croft's Classics.* Arlington Hgts, Illinois: Harlan Davidson Inc.

Alston, G. (1910). *Hairshirt.* Retrieved August 1, 2013, from Tha Catholic Encyclopedia from New Advent: http://www.newadvent.org/cathen/07113b.htm

Alter, R. (2007). *The Book of Psalms,* translated by Robert Alter. London: W.W. Norton and Co.

Anderson, J. (1998). *Tales of Great Dragons.* Santa Barbara, California: Bellerophon Books.

Anji, A. (2013, January). *Discuss the Interaction Between Cognition and Physiology in Terms of Behavior.* Retrieved August 19, 2013, from Studymode.com: http://www.studymode.com/essays/Discuss-The-Interaction-Between-Cognition-And-1357138.html

Anthony Schraner, R. (1981). *St. Joseph Annotated Catechism.* New York: Catholic Book Publishing Co.

Antioch, S. I. (1885, 2009). *From Ante-Nicene Fathers, Vol. 1.* Translated by Alexander Roberts and James Donaldso, Edited by Alexander Roberts, James Donaldson, and A. Cleveland Coxe. The Epistle of Ignatius to Polycarp, 1885, Revised and edited for New Advent by Kevin Knight, 2009. Retrieved July 12, 2013, from Catholic Encyclopedia, New Advent: <http://www.newadvent.org/fathers/0110.htm>.

Aquinas, T. (2002). *The Shorter Summa Theologica.* Manchester, N.H.: Sophia Institute Press.

AssociatedPress. (2005-2011, May 21). Ethiopian Girl reportedly Guarded by Lions. *Associated Press*, p. 2011 The Associated Press.

Athanasius. (1980). *The Life of Antony and the Letter of Marcellinus, the Classics of Western Spirituality,* translated by Robert C. Greeg. New York: Paulist Press, the Missionary Society of St. Paul.

Athanasius, S. (1995). *St. Antony of the Desert.* Rockford, Illinois: Tan Books and Publishers.

Augustine. (1986). *Augustine, Day by Day,* compiled byJohn E. Rotelle O.S.A. New York: Catholic Book Publishing.

Augustine, S. (1961). *Confessions,* Penguin Classics, translated by R.S. Pine-Coffin. London : Penguin Book.

Babinger, F. (1978). *Mehmed the Conquerer and his times.* Princton, New Jersey: Princton University Press.

Bacon, R. S. (1919). *The Lay of the Cid.* Berkeley: On Line Medieval and Classical Library.

Baglio, M. (2009). *The Rite, making of a modern exorcist.* New York: Random House Inc. and Doubleday.

Bailey, M. A. (2006). *The Grail Code, Quest for the Real Presence.* Chicago: Loyola Press.

Bangley, B. (2007). *By Way of the Desert.* Brewster, MA: Paraclete Press.

Barber, R. (1985). *The Arthurian Legends, an illustrated anthology.* Yugoslavia: Dorset Press, a division of Marboro Books Corporation.

Barber, R. (1995). *The Knight and Chivalry, Revised Edition.* New York: Boydell Press.

Barber, R. (1980). *The Reign of Chivalry.* New York: St. Martins Press.

Barbet, D. P. (1953). *A Doctor at Calvary, The Passion of Our Lord Jesus Christ as Described by a Surgeon.* Fort Collins, CO: Roman Catholic Books.

Barclay, W. (1975). *Gospel of Matthew volume 2, revised edition.* Philadelphia: The Westminster Press.

Barclay, W. (1975). *Letters to the Corinthians, revised edition, the Daily Study Bible Series.* Philidelphia: Westminster Press.

Barclay, W. (1975). *The Gospel of Matthew Volume 1, revised edition, the Daily Study Bible Series.* Philidelphia: Westminster Press.

Barron, R. (2008). *Thomas Aquinas, Spiritual Master.* New York: The Crossroad Publishing Company.

Becerra, H. (2002, August 2). Ballad of the Poor Samaritan. *Los Angeles Times*, pp. A-1 edition.

Becerra, K. R. (2001, August 21). Man Has Honest Answer to a $203,000 Question. *Los Angeles Times*, p. The Nation section.

Belloc, H. (1992). *The Crusades, the World's Debate.* Rockford, Illinois, originally Milwaukee: Tan Books and Publishers, originally Bruce Publishing Co.

Bennet, W. (2006). *America, the Last Best Hope, Vol. 1.* USA: Nelson Curren (Thomas Nelson).

Bennett, B. (2006). *America, The Last Best Hope, Volume 1.* Nashville, Tennessee: Nelson Current, Thomas Nelson, Inc.

Bergin, T. G. (1955). *The Divine Comedy.* Harlan Davidson Inc.

Biography. (2012). *Thomas Andrews.* Retrieved July 29, 2012, from Biography.com: http://www.biography.com/people/thomas-andrews-283620

Bokenkotter, T. (1979). *A Concise History of the Catholic Church.* New York: Image Books, a division of Doubleday.

Bonaventure. (1978). *Bonaventure, The Soul's Journey into GOD, The Life of Saint Franics,* Translated by Ewert Cousins. Mahwah, New Jersey: Paulist Press.

Boorman, J. (Director). (1981). *Excalibur* [Motion Picture].

Borroff, M. (1967). *Sir Gawain and the Green Knight, a new verse translation.* New York: W.W. Norton and Co.

Bourdon, I. o. (1948). *Devotions to the Holy Angels.* Ireland: Apostolate of Christian Action.

Boyden, H. W. (1923). *Tennyson's Idylls of the King.* Boston: Allyn and Bacon, Norwood Press.

Bradford, E. (1972). *The Knights of the Order.* New York: Dorset Press.

Brady, I. (1983). *The Writings of Saint Francis of Assisi.* Santa Maria Degli Angeli: Edizioni Porziuncola ISBN 88-270-0060-7.

Brewer, Rev. E. C. (1891). *Historic Note-Book with an appendix of Battles.* London: Smith, Elder, and Co.

Brighenti, R. J. (2003). *Catholicism for Dummies.* Hoboken, New Jersey: Wiley Publishing, Inc.

Britishbattles.com. (2002-2013). *The Battle of Balaclava.* Retrieved August 8, 2013, from british battles.com: http://www.britishbattles.com/crimean-war/balaclava.htm

Brookhiser, R. (1997). *Rules of Civility, the 110 precepts that guided our first president in war and peace.* New York: The Free Press, a division of Simon and Schuster.

Brown, M. (2001). *The One Minute Philospher.* Manchester, N.H.: Sophia Institute Press.

Buber, M. (1953). *Good and Evil.* New York: Charles Scribner's Sons.

Buber, M. (1958). *I and Thou.* USA: Charles Scribner's Sons.

Buber, M. (1969). *Ontology, with Robert C. Wood, an analysis of I and Thou.* Evanston: Northwestern University Press.

Bulfinch, T. (1962). *Bulfinch's Mythology, The Age of Chivalry, The Legends of Charlemagne.* New York: Mentor Classics, The New American Library of World Literature.

Burleigh, E. J. (1953). *Augustine, Earlier Writings,* Library of Christian Classics Ichthus Edition. Philidelphia: Westminster Press.

Burns, J. (1915, 2013). *Sir Galahad: A Call to the Heroic,* originally published in 1915 by J. Clarke and Company. Retrieved July 26, 2013, from Sacred Texts.com: http://www.sacred-texts.com/neu/arthur/art040.htm

Butler, A. (1799). *Lives of the Primitive Fathers, in 12 volumes, vol. IX,* Edinburgh, printed by J. Moir

Cahall, P. (2005). The Value of Saint Augustine's Use / Enjoyment Distinction to Conjugal Love. *Logos: A Journal of Catholic Thought and Culture 8.1 (Volume 8, Number 1),* 117-128.

Caraman, P. (1990). *Ingatius Loyola, a Biography of the Founder of the Jesuits.* New York, San Francisco: Harper and Row.

Cavanaugh, J. H. (1952). *Evidence for Our Faith (Apologetics).* Notre Dame, Indiana: University of Notre Dame Press.

Cawthorne, N. (2003). *A History of Pirates, Blood and Thunder on the High Seas.* London, New Jersey: Chartwell Books.

Chadwick, H. (1993). *The Early Church, revised edition.* London: Penguin Books.

Challoner, B. (1941). *Douay Rheims Bible,* notes by Bishop Challoner, Letter on the study of Holy Scripture by Pope Leo XIII, Letter on

Biblical Studies by Pope Pius XII, and the preface by Rev. William McClellan, S.J., Francis L. Spellman (archbishop of New York)as Imprimatur. New York: Benzinger Brothers Inc., printers to the Holy Apostolic See.

Charbonneau-Lassay, L. (1991). *The Bestiary of Christ.* New York: Parabola Books.

Chesterton, G. (2001). *Saint Thomas Aquinas, The Dumb Ox.* New York: Image Doubleday.

Chesterton, G. (1989). *St. Francis of Assisi,* intro by Joseph Girzone. New York: Image Books Doubleday.

Chesterton, G. (2008). *The Everlasting Man.* San Francisco: Ignatius Press.

Ciszek, F. W. (1973, 1995). *He Leadeth Me, from the Author of With GOD in Russia,* with Fr. Daniel Flaherty, S.J. New York, San Francisco: Bantum/ Doubleday, Ignatius Press.

Ciszek, W. J. (1964). *With GOD in Russia,* with Daniel L. Flanerty. New York: McGraw Hill Book Company, The America Press.

Clairvaux, B. o. (1977). *Bernard of Clairvaux: Treatises III,* Cistercian Fathers series, translated by Conrad Greenia and Daniel O'donavan. Kalamazoo, Michigan: Cistercian Publications Inc.

Clairvaux, B. o. (1977). In praise of the New Knighthood, translated by Conrad Greenia. In B. o. Clairvaux, *Bernard of Clairvaux: Treatises III* (pp. 115-167). Kalamazoo, Michigan: Cistercian Publications.

Colliander, T. (1982). *Way of the Ascetics, The Ancient Tradition of Discipline and Inner Growth,* intro by Kenneth Leech, translated by Katherine Ferre. San Francisco, New York: Harper and Row Publishers.

Convention, T. E. (2014). *Persecution, Quick Facts: Reliable and Informative Snapshots of the Focus Issue.* Retrieved January 6, 2014, from The Ethics and Religious Liberty Commission, ERLC: http://erlc.com/issues/quick-facts/persecution/

Copleston, F. (1962). *A History of Philosophy Volume 2, Medieval Philosophy, Part 1, Augustine to Bonaventure.* Westminster, Maryland: Image Books and Newman Press.

Copleston, F. (1961). *Medieval philosophy.* New York: Harper Torchbooks, Harper and Brothers.

Corless, R. (1981). *Christian Alchemy.* New York: Paulist Press.

Corley, C. (1989). Lancelot of the Lake. In C. T. Corley, *Lancelot of the Lake,* The World's Classics, a new translation by Corin Corley. Oxford, New York: Oxford University Press.

Coss, P. (1996). *The Knight in Medieval England 1000-1400.* Gloucestershire: Alan Sutton Publishing Ltd.

Crake, A. D. (1873). *History of the Church under the Roman Empire AD. 30-476.* London, Oxford, Cambridge: Rivingtons.

Crawley, W. (2009, September 23). The Dumb Ox Still Bellows. *Will and Testament Blog,* p. 1.

Creasy, E. S. (1998). *Fifteen Decisive Battles of the World from Marathon to Waterloo.* Retrieved July 25, 2013, from standin: http://www. standin.se/fifteen.htm

Crossley, J. N. (2013). *Ramond Llull's Contributions to Computer Science.* Retrieved June 8, 2013, from Raimundus Lullus: http://www. raimunduslullus.eu/textos/crossley-llull-revised.pdf

Cruz, J. C. (1999). *Angels and Devils.* Rockford, IL: Tan Books and Publishers Inc.

Cummins, N. (1991). *Freedom to Rejoice, Understanding St. John of the Cross.* London: Harper Collins Publishers.

Cunningham, L. S. (1994, Issue 42, vol. XIII, No. 2). Tattered Treaure of Assisi. *Chritian History Magazine, Issue 42, Vol. XIII, No. 2,* pp. 8-17.

Dale Wasserman, J. D. (1972) *Man from La Mancha.* Theatrical play

Dales, D. (2004). *Alcuin, A Mind Intent on GOD.* Norwich, Norfolk: Canterbury Press.

Daniel, D. M. (2006). *Briefly, Aquinas' Summa Theologica 1.* Indianapolis/ Cambridge: Hacket Publishing Co.

Daniel-Rops, H. (2002). *Heroes of GOD.* Manchester, New Hampshire: Sophia Institute Press.

Darian, J. (1972). The Impossible Dream. *The Man From La Mancha* by Dale Wasserman.

Davis, E. W. (1912-1913). *Readings in Ancient History: Illustrative Extracts from the Sources, 2 Vols.* Boston: Allyn and Bacon, modernized by Dr. Jerome Arkenberg.

Deane, H. A. (1963). *The Political and Social Ideas of St. Augustine.* New York and London: Columbia University Press.

Denton, J. (1982). *When Hell Was in Session.* Mobile, Alabama: Traditional Press.

Deshields, C. T. (1935). The Battle of San Jacinto. *Tall Men and Long Rifles.*

Digby, K. H. (1829). *The Broadstone pf Honour, or the true sense and practice of Chivalry, book 1, Godefridus.* London: R. Gilbert, St. John's Square.

DiLiscia, D. A. (2011, Summer). *Johannes Kepler.* Retrieved July 29, 2013, from The Stanford Encyclopedia of Philosophy (Summer 2011 Edition): <http://plato.stanford.edu/archives/sum2011/entries/kepler/>.

Donaldson, A. R. (2009). *The Epistle of Ignatius to Polycarp, From Ante-Nicene Fathers, Vol. 1. Edited by Alexander Roberts, James Donaldson, and A. Cleveland Coxe. (Buffalo, NY: Christian Literature Publishing Co., 1885.) Revised and edited for New Advent by Kevin Knight.* Retrieved July 12, 2013, from New Advent, Catholic Encyclopedia,: <http://www.newadvent.org/fathers/0110.htm>.

Doornik, J. L. (1953). *A Handbook of the Catholic Faith, edited by Rev. John Greenwood.* USA: Newman Press Image Books.

Dougherty, M. J. (2012). *100 Battles, Decisive conflicts that shaped the world.* Bath, United kingdom: Parragon.

Dunning, R. (1998). *Arthur, the King in the West.* London: Grange Books.

Durant, W. (1953). *The Story of Philosophy.* New York: Simon and Schuster.

Editors, A. D. (2000, Summer). *One Example of Natural Diplomacy, Vol.5, No.3.* Retrieved August 7, 2013, from American Diplomacy: http://www.unc.edu/depts/diplomat/AD_Issues/amdipl_16/edit16_print.html

Einhard, N. t. (1969). *Two Lives of Charlemagne, translated with an intro by Lewis Thorpe.* London: Penguin Books.

Ellis, H. (1915). *The Soul of Spain.* Boston, New York: Houghton Mifflin Company.

Ellsburg, R. (2001). *All Saints, Daily Reflections on Saints, Prophets, and Witnesses of Our Times.* New York: Crossroad Publishing.

Epictetus. (1937). *The Golden Sayings of Epictetus, the Harvard Classics, as translated by Hastings Crossley.* New York: P.F. Collier and Son Corp.

Eschenbach, W. V. (1980). *Parzival. Pilgrim Classics,* edited by A.t. Hatto. New York: Penguin Books.

Eusebius. (1989). *The History of the Church from Christ to Constantine, Penguin Classics, translated by G.A. Williamson, intro by Andrew Louth.* New York, London: Penguin Books.

Faccenda, L. (1999). *A Heart Trained, Saint Maximilian Kolbe.* Krakow, Poland: Fr. Kolbe Missionaries of the Immaculata.

Ferrante, J. (2001). *Guillaume d'Orange, Four Twelfth-Century Classics.* New York: Coilumbia University Press.

Fields, R. (1991). *The Code of the Warrior, in History, Myth, and Everyday life.* New York: Harper Perennial, a division of HarperCollins Publishers.

Fife, G. (1991). *Arthur, the King, The Themes Behind the Legends.* New York: Sterling Publishing Co., Inc.

Filippo, S. N. (2007, April). *The Scriptual Roots of St. Augustine's Spirituality.* Retrieved January 1, 2014, from Ignatius Insight: http://www.ignatiusinsight.com/features2007/sfilippo_augustine_apr07.asp

Flexner, J. T. (1984). *Washington, the Indispensable man.* New York: Signet/Penguin Books.

Fordham. *Fordham University's Internet Medieval Source Book.* HYPERLINK "mailto:halsall@fordham.edu?subject=Medieval Sourcebook - Main Page"Paul Halsall, ORB sources editorLast Modified: Nov 4, 2011 [linked pages may have been updated more recently] The Internet Medieval Sourcebook is located at the HYPERLINK "http://www.fordham.edu/mvst/"Fordham University Center for Medieval Studies.

Fowler, M. (1996). *Johannes Kepler, Lectures 1 and 2.* Retrieved July 29, 2013, from Galileo and Einstein from the University of Virginia department of Physics: http://galileoandeinstein.physics.virginia.edu/1995/lectures/kepler.html

Fox, J. (2013, December 1). *Fox's Book of Martyrs.* Retrieved December 1, 2013, from www.biblestudytools.com: from http://www.biblestudytools.com/history/foxs-book-of-martyrs/persecution-under-julian-the-apostate.html

France, P. (1997). *Hermits, the insight of Solitude.* New York: St. Martin's Press.

Fulkerson, N. (2010, August 26). *May 10—Saint Damien: A Hero Who Died on the Battlefield of Honor.* Retrieved July 15, 2013, from The American Society for the Defencse of Tradition, Family and Property: http://www.tfp.org/tfp-home/articles/saint-damien-a-hero-who-died-on-the-battlefield-of-honor.html

Galli, M. (1994, Issue 42, Vol. XIII, No.2). Five Who Knew The Saint. *Christian History Magazine,* pp. 22-25.

Ganss, G. E. (1992). *Spiritual Exercises of Saint Ignatius.* Chicago: Loyola Press.

Gautier, l. (1989). *Chivalry.* New York: Bracken books.

Gerritsen and Melle, W. P. (1998). *A Dictionary of Medieval Heros.* New York: Boydell Press.

Ghezzi, B. (2000). *Voices of the Saints.* Chicago: Loyola Press.

Gibbon, E. (1781). *The History of the Decline and Fall of the Roman Empire, Vol. 3, by Edward Gibbon, [1781] Chapter XXXVII: Conversion Of The Barbarians To Christianity. Part II.* Retrieved September 12, 2012, from Sacred Texts: http://www.sacred-texts.com/cla/gibbon/03/daf03041.htm

Gies, F. (1986). *The Knight In History.* London: Robert Hale Limited.

Gilliam, R. R. (2011, August 3). The Genius of El Cid. *Military History Quarterly,* pp. Autumn 2011, Vol.24, No.1.

Gilson, E. (1938). *Reason and Revelation in the Middle Ages.* New York: Charles Scribner's Sons.

Gilson, E. (1955). *The History of Christian Philosophy in the Middle Ages.* New York: Random House.

Gleason, e. b. (1966). *The Essential Pascal, a new translation by G.F. Pullen.* New York and Toronto: A Mentor-Omega Group, New American Library.

Goodrich, N. L. (1989). *King Arthur.* New York: Harper and Row.

Gracian, B. (1996). *A Pocket Mirror for Heroes.* New York: Bantam Doubleday Dell Publishing Group Inc.

Green, T. H. (1984). *Weeds among the Wheat, Discernment, Where Prayer and Action Meet.* Notre Dame, Indiana: Ave maria Press.

Griffith, S. B. (1971). *Sun Tzu's The Art of War translated by Samuel B. Griffith.* Oxford, London, New York: Oxford University Press.

Guerra, H. (Composer). (2001). The Thirteen Days of the Alamo, produced by Matson Multi Media, Inc, 403 E. Ramsey Suite 101, 78216. [H. Guerra, Performer, & M. M. Media, Conductor] San Antonio, Texas, USA.

Harcourt, R. P. (2007). *The Catholic Sourcebook, Newly Revised.* Orlando, Florida: Harcourt Religion Publishers.

Hardin, S. L. (1994). *Texas Iliad, A Military History of the Texas Revolution.* Austin, TX: University of Texas Press.

Hart, B. (1997). *Faith and Freedom, Christian Roots of American History.* New York: Christian Defence Fund.

Harvey, A. (1998). *Teachings of the Christian Mystics, edited by Andrew Harvey.* Boston and Canada: Shambhalla Press.

Hatto, A. (1980). *Parzival by Wolfram Von Eschenbach.* New York: Penguin Group and Penguin Books.

Headon, J. H. (1982). *Knights.* New York: Schocken Books, Bellew and Higton Publishers LTD.

Hickman, K. (2013). *Muslim Invasions: Charles Martel.* Retrieved July 25, 2013, from militaryhistory.about.com: http://militaryhistory.about.com/od/army/p/martel.htm

Hickman, K. (2013). *The Holy League defeated the Ottomans at Lepanto on October 7, 1571.* Retrieved July 17, 2013, from Military History About.Com: http://militaryhistory.about.com/od/navalbattles14011600/p/lepanto.htm

Holmes, U. T. (originally 1980, electronically 2002). *A History of Christian Spirituality, An Analytical Introduction.* New York/ Harrisburg Penn.: Seabury Press/Morehose Publishing.

Hopkins, A. (2001). *Chronicles of King Arthur.* London, also printed in China: Barnes and Noble and L. Rex Printing Co. Ltd.

Hopkins, A. (1999). *Knights, the complete story of the age of Chivalry, from historical fact to tales of Romance and poetry.* London: Chancellor Press, Bounty Books, a division of Octupus Publishing Group.

Hopkins, J. (1972). *A Companion to the Study of St. Anselm.* Minneapolis: University of Minnesota Press.

House, B. (2010-2013). *The Great Siege, Then and Now.* Retrieved August 2, 2013, from Chalcedon: http://chalcedon.edu/research/articles/the-great-siege-then-and-now/

Howard, R. E. (1998). *The savage Tales of Solomon Kane.* New York: Del Rey/Ballantine Books.

Howarth, S. (1982). *The Knights Templar.* New York: Barnes and Noble Books.

Hugo Hoever, R. (1999). *Lives of the Saints Illustrated, St. Joseph edition.* New Jersey: Catholic Book Publishing Co.

Illingworth, J. (1903). *Reason and Revelation.* London: MacMillian and Co.

In Memory of the 40 holy Martyrs of Sebaste. (2013, July 7). Retrieved July 15, 2013, from Forty Holy Martyrs of Sebaste Orthodox Church: http://www.40martyrs.org/40martyrs.html

Irene, T. (2013, April 22). *Saint Mercurius.* Retrieved July 08, 2013, from Tamav Irene for All: from http://www.tamavireneforall.com/st_philopater_mercurius.htm

Iskander, E. (2013, June 18). *St. Philopatere Mercurius.* Retrieved July 08, 2013, from PHILOPATER.ORG: www.philopater.org

James, G. (2012 (reprinted)). *The History of Chivalry.* ebook, originally New York: Project Gutenberg, originally Harper and Brothers Publishers.

James, W. (1906). *The Letters of William James, to H.G. Wells.*

John, D. A. (1995). *The Penguin Dictionary of Saints, third edition.* London, New York: Penguin Books, Ltd.

Joinville, V. a. (1963). *Chronicles of the Crusades edited by E.V. Rieu and translated by M.R.B. Shaw.* Baltimore: Penguin Books.

Jones, A. (1994). *The Wordsworth Dictionary of Saints.* Ware, Hertfordshire: W. and R. Chambers.

Jowett, t. B. (1969). *The Apology, Phaedo, and Crito of Plato, the Harvard Classics edition, Charles W. Eliot editor.* New York: P.F. Collier and Son Corporation.

Julien, N. (1996). *The Mammoth Dictionary of Symbols.* London: Robinson Publishing.

Kannon, C. H. (2007). *The Templar Code for Dummies.* Hoboken, N.J.: Wiley Publishing.

Kapitan, C. (2012, Novmeber 3rd). After 13 Years in Prison, Ex-cop May Be Innocent. *San Antonio Express News,* p. My SA section.

Karsh, E. (2007). *Islamic Imperialism.* New York and London: Yale University Press.

Kelly, J. F. (1913). *Miguel de Cervantes Saavedra.* London/ New York: Oxford University Press.

Kersten, R. J. (1990). *The Bible, Day by Day, Minute Meditations for Every Day based on Selected Texts of the Holy Bible.* New York: Catholic Book Publishing Co.

Kierkegaard, S. (1983). *Fear and Trembling, Repetition, edited and translated by Howard and Edna Hong.* Princeton, New Jersey: Princeton University Press.

Kierkegaard, S. (1956). *Purity of Heart is to Will One Thing, translated by Douglas V. Steere.* New York: Harper Torchbook Edition, Harper and Row.

Kirsch, J. (1909). *40 Martyrs.* Retrieved July 24, 2012, from Catholic Encyclopedia at New Advent.org: http://www.newadvent.org/cathen/06153a.htm

Kirsch, J. P. (1910/2009). *Pope St. Leo (the Great).* Retrieved August 4, 2013, from The Catholic Encyclopedia, New Advent, copyright 2009 by Kevin Knight: http://www.newadvent.org/cathen/09154b.htm

Knowles, D. (1962). *The Evolution of Medieval Thought.* New York: Vintage Books, a division of Random House.

Koestler, A. (1963). *The Sleepwalkers, Grosset's Universal Library edition.* New York: Grosset and Dunlop, The Macmillan Company.

Konstam, A. (2003). *Lepanto 1571, The Greatest Naval Battle of the Renaissance.* Osprey Publishing.

Krailsheimer, A. (1966, 1988). *Pascal's Pensees.* London, New York: Penguin Books.

Kurth, G. (2008). *Charles Martel in the Catholic Encyclopedia.* Retrieved July 26, 2013, from New Advent: http://www.newadvent.org/cathen/03629a.htm

Lang, A. (1967). *King Arthur, Tales of the Round Table.* New York: Schocken Books.

Lang, M. A. (1912). *The Book of Saints and Heroes.* London: Longmans, Green, and Co.

Lent, F. (1915). The Life of Simeon Stylites. *Journal of the American Oriental Society 35,* 111-198.

Leshem, A. (2003). *Newton on Mathematics and Spiritual Purity.* Netherlands: Kluwer Academic Publishers.

Lewis, C. (1970). *The Discarded Image, an Intro to Medieval and Renaissance Literature.* London: Cambridge at the University Press.

Lewis, C. (1996). *The Problem of Pain.* New York: Harper Collins.

Library, J. V. (2013). *The Battle of Tours.* Retrieved July 25, 2013, from jewish virtual library: From http://www.jewishvirtuallibrary.org/jsource/History/Tours.html

Loomis, R. S. (1951). Medieval Romance. In R. s. Loomis, *Medieval Romances.* New York: The Modern Library.

Loyola, S. I. (2004). *Saint Ignatius of Loyola, Personal writings,* translation and intro by Joseph Munitiz and Philip Endean. London, New York: Penguin Books Ltd.

Luck, K. (2008). *Fight, Are you willing to pick a fight with Evil?* New York: Waterbrook Press, an imprint of Double Day, a Division of Random House Inc.

Lull, R. (2001). *The Book of Knighthood and Chivalry.* Chivalry Bookshelf.

Macgregor, M. (2000-2012). *The Story of Greece, from the Baldwin Project.* Retrieved August 1, 2013, from The Baldwin Project, Main Lesson: http://www.mainlesson.com/display.php?author=macgregor&book=greece&story=bravest

Malory, T. (1962). *Malory's L'Morte D'Arthur, Baines translation.* New York: Mentor, Signet, Penguin.

Marshall, H. E. (2000-2012). *Stories of Guy of Warwick Told to Children,.* Retrieved July 31, 2013, from The Baldwin Project, Main Lesson: http://www.mainlesson.com/display.php?author=marshall&book=guy&story=colbrand

Martin, J. (2010). *The Jesuit Guide to (Almost) Everything, A Spirituality for Real Life.* New York: HarperCollins Publishers.

Martin, M. (1988). *The Jesuits, the Society of Jesus and the Betrayal of the Catholic Church.* New York: Touchstone Publications, part of Simon and Schuster.

Martyr, S. J. (2001-2013). *St. Justin Martyr Dialogue with Trypho,* edited by Peter Kirby. Retrieved July 12, 2013, from Early Christian Writings.com: <http://www.earlychristianwritings.com/text/1clement-hoole.html>.

Matarasso, P. (1969). *Quest for the Holy Grail, anonymous.* England: Penguin.

Matthews, B. (1986). *The Herder Symbol Dictionary.* Wilmette, Illinois: Chiron Publications.

Matthews, J. (1989-1993). *The Elements of the Arthurian Tradition.* Dorset, Great Britain: Element.

Matthews, J. (1998). *Warriors of Christiandom.* London: Brockhampton Press, and member of the Hodder Headline PLC group.

May, G. G. (2004). *The Dark Night of the Soul, a Psychiatrist Explores the Connection Between Darkness and Spiritual Growth.* USA: Harper One, and Imprint of Harper Collins Publishers.

Meacham, W. (June 1983). The Authentication of the Turin Shroud: An Issue in Archaeological Epistemology. *Current Anthropology, Published by the University of Chicago Press,* Vol.24, #3.

Meller, P. L. (2002). *The Medieval Warrior*. New York: BCL Press and O.G. Publishing.

Merwin, W. (1959). *Poem of the Cid, Spain's great heroic Epic*. New York: Meridian, New American Library.

Michael Walsh, e. (1985). *Butler's Lives of the Saints, Concise Edition*. San Francisco: Harper and Row.

Miller, B. S. (1986). *The Bhagavad-Gita, A Bantum Classic*. New York: Bantum Books.

Miller, D. (2001). *Brassey's Book of the Crusade*. Dulles, Virginia: Pegasus Publishing Ltd.

Moncrieff, A. (1976). *The Romance of Chivalry (softcover)—Romance and Legend of Chivalry*. North Hollywood, Calif.: Newcastle Publishing Co.

Monmouth, G. o. (1982). *The History of the Kings of Britain, translated by Lewis Thorpe*. New York: Penguin Books.

Morgan, G. (2006). *St. George, Knight, Martyr, Patron Saint, and Dragonslayer*. New Jersey: Chartwell Books Inc.

Mottola, A. (1964). *Spiritual Exercises of Saint Ignatius*. New York: Double Day.

Muggeridge, M. (1985). *Vintage Muggeridge, edited by Geoffrey Barlow*. England: Angel Press.

Nicea, C. o. *Nicene Creed*.

Nicolle, D. H. (2005). *GOD's Warriors*. Westminster, MD: Osprey Publishers.

Nitobe, I. (1969). *Bushido, The Soul of Japan, The Classic Portrait of Samurai Martial Culture*. Tokyo; Rutland, Vermount; Singapore: Tuttle Publishing.

Nyssa, G. o. (2010, December 27). *Homily One: St. Gregory of Nyssa on St. Stephen the Protomartyr*. Retrieved July 12, 2013, from Mystagogy, by John Sanidopoulos: http://www.johnsanidopoulos.com/2010/12/homily-one-st-gregory-of-nyssa-on-st.html

O'Connell, S. (1987). Tip O'Neill, Irish American Representative Man. *Journal of American Public Policy*, 40.

Oldridge, D. (2007). *Strange Histories, The trial of a pig, the walking dead, and other matters of fact from the medieval and Renaissance worlds*. New York: Routledge, imprint of the Taylor and Francis Group.

Pascal, B. (1966). *Pensees, Penguin Classics, translated by A.J. Krailsheimer*. London: Penguin Books.

Patrick, S. (1998). *The Confession of St. Patrick, the classic text in new translation, translated by John Skinner, forward by John O'Donahue.* New York: Image books Doubleday.

Paul, D. o. (1975). *Moments of Decision, Profiles of Great Men and Women.* Boston: Daughters of St. Paul, St. Paul Editions.

Pernoud, R. (1963). *The Crusaders, the Struggle for the Holy Land.* New York: Ignatius Press.

Pernoud, R. (2007). *The Retrail of Joan of Arc.* San Francisco: Ignatius Press.

Pohl, J. (1989). *Battle of San Jacinto.* USA: Texas State Hisotrical Association.

Prudentius. (1743). *Psychomahia, The War of the Soul, or the Battle of the Virtues.* London: ECCO, Eighteenth Century Collection Online Print Editions, reproduction from a copy in the British Library.

Pullen, G. (1966). *The Essential Pascal.* New York and Toronto: Mentor Omega, New American Library.

Raffel, B. (2009). *The Song of the Cid, a dual language edition with parellel text, intro by Maria Rosa Menocal, the Penguin Classics.* New York: Penguin Group, Inc.

Rambaran-Olm, M. (2006). *The Dream of the Rood.* Electronic Edition.

Read, P. P. (1999). *The Templars, the Dramatic History of the Knights Templar, the Most Powerful Military order of the Crusades.* New York: St. Martin's Press, Griffin.

Representatives, S. O. (2009). House Resolution Declaring Oct. 11 A State holiday in Honor of Blessed Damien, H.R. 210. *House of Representatives 25th Legislature, State of Hawaii.*

Reston, J. (2001). *Warriors of GOD, Richard the Lionheart and Saladin in the Third Crusade.* New York: Doubleday.

Rev. A.J. Maas, S. (1952). *The Life of Jesus Christ according to Gospel History.* London: B.Herder Book Co.

Ricciotti, G. (1992). *The Age of Martyrs, translated by Rev. Anthony Bull.* New York: Barnes and Noble.

Riley, S. A. (1988). *Facts and Fallacies, edited and designed by Dorling Kindersley Ltd.* Pleasantville, New York/Montreal: The Reader's Digest Association Inc.

Robinson, J. J. (1991). *Dungeon, Fire, and Sword, the Knights Templar in the Crusades.* New York: M. Evans and Co. Inc.

Romer, J. (1988). *Testament, The Bible and History.* New York: Henry Holt and Co.

Rostand, E. (1982). *Cyrano De Bergerac, translated by Brian Hooker.* Toronto: Bantam Books.

Ruggerio, V. R. (1984). *The Art of Thinking, A guide to Critical and Creative thought.* New York: Harper and Row.

Runes, e. D. (1955). *Treasury of Philosophy.* New York: Philosophical Library, Inc.

Sagan, C. (1980). *Cosmos.* New York: Random House, Carl Sagan Productions.

Sales, T. (2013). *Lull as Computer Analyst, or Why Lull Was One of Us.* Retrieved June 8, 2013, from Ramon Lull: http://www.ramonlull.com

Sayers, T. D. (1984). *The Song of Roland.* New York: Penguin Books.

Schellenberger, B. (1981). *Nomad of the Spirit, Reflections of a young monastic.* New York: The Crossroad Publishing Company.

Schroeder, R. F. (1984). *Each Day is a Gift.* New York: Catholic Book Publishing Company.

Schueler, G. (1997). *Cognitive-Affective Bases of Behavior.* Retrieved August 19, 2013, from Schuelers.com: http://www.schuelers.com/psychology/HS812.htm

Scudder, V. D. (1917). *L'Morte D'Arthur and its sources.* New York, London: E.P. Dutton and Co, J.M. Dent and Sons.

Scupoli, L. (1945 edition). *The Spiritual Combat and a Treatise on Peace of the Soul, translation revised by William Lester nad Robert Rohan.* Rockford, Illinois: Tan Books and Publishers.

Senzaki, P. R. (1985). *Zen Flesh Zen bones.* Boston: Charles E. Tuttle Co., Inc.

Sexton, J. (2013, October 28). *Conversations, Conference Focuses on Christian Persecution Worldwide.* Retrieved January 6, 2014, from Breitbart: http://www.breitbart.com/InstaBlog/2013/10/28/Conference-Focuses-on-Christian-Persecution-Worldwide

Shannon, W. H. (1999). *Anselm, the Joy of Faith.* New York: Crossroad Publishing Company.

Shea, J. G. (1894). *Little Pictorial Lives of the Saints, a compilation based on Butler's Lives of the Saints.* New York: Benzinger Brothers.

Shea, J. G. (2013, July 13). *Lives of the Saints, Saint Thomas Aquinas.* Retrieved January 3, 2014, from Magnificat.ca: http://magnificat.ca/cal/en/saints/saint_thomas_aquinas.html

Sheen, A. F. (1990). *The Life of Christ.* New York: Image, Doubleday, Random House Inc.

Sheen, F. J. (2001). *The Seven Capital Sins*. New York: Alba House, Society of St. Paul.

Sheen, F. (2000). *The Cross and the Beatitudes*. Liguori, Missouri: Liguori/ Triumph.

Sheen, F. (2005). *Those Mysterious Priests*. New York: Society of St. Paul.

Sheen, F. (2003). *Throughout the Year with Fulton Sheen*. San Francisco: Ignatius Press.

Smith, E. T. (1963). *Philosophers Speak for Themselves, from Aristotle to Plotinus*. London: Phoenix Books.

Smith, H. (1983, March 17). Reagan and O'Neill: Each Other needs the other. *New York Times*.

Smith, V. (2012, May 31). Pastor Mark Wolford, Snake Handler, dies of Rattler Bite. *Associated Press*.

Spencer, R. (2005). *The Politically Incorrect Guide to Islam and the Crusades*. Washington D.C.: Regnery Publishing Inc.

Spoto. (2002). *Reluctant Saint, The Life of Francis of Assisi*. New York: Viking Compass, Penguin Putnam Inc.

Spoto, D. (2007). *Joan, The Mysterious Life of the Heretic who Became a Saint*. San Francisco: Harper San Francisco, Harper Collins Publishers.

Heston, C. (Performer). (1990). St. Augustine, The Giants of Philosophy, produced by Carmichael and Carmichael, Inc. Nashille, Tennessee, U.S.A. staff, e. n. (2011, January 31). *The Muslim Brotherhood—Nazi Connection*. Retrieved August 7, 2013, from Education News: http:// www.educationnews.org/breaking_news/106849.html

Stalker, J. (1902). *The Seven Cardinal Virtues*. New York: American Tract Society.

Stark, R. (2009). *GOD's Battalions, The Case for the Crusades*. New York: Harper One, Harper Collins Books.

Steinbeck, J. (1976). *The Acts of King Arthur and His Noble Knights, edited by Chase Horton*. New York: Farrar, Straus, and Giroux.

Stevenson, B. (1948). *The Macmillan Book of Proverbs, Maxims, and Famous Phrases*. New York, The Macmillan Company

Stevenson, R. L. (1890). *Father Damien*. Sydney: Robert Lewis Stevenson.

Stewart, M. (2006). *The Courtier and the Heretic, Leibniz, Spinoza, and the Fate of GOD in the Modern World*. New York: W.W. Norton and Company.

Stoye, J. (2006). *The Siege of Vienna, The Last Great Trial between Cross and Crescent.* New York: First Pegasus Books.

Talbot, J. M. (2005). *The Way of the Mystics, Ancient Wisdom for Experiencing GOD Today.* San Francisco: Jossey-Bass, a Wiley Company.

Talos124. (2008, December 22). *lion saves baby hippo.* Retrieved July 24, 2013, from youtube: http://www.youtube.com/watch?v=lrvu7P1Sp24

Tamburello, D. E. (2000). *Bernard of Clairvaux, Spiritual Master.* New York: The Crossroad Publishing Company.

Tennyson, A. L. (1983). *Idylls of the King, edited by J.M. Gray.* London, New York: Penguin Books, Penguin Classics.

The New Encyclopedia Britannica in 30 volumes, Macropedia, volume 3. (1982). U.S.A.: Encyclopedia Britannica Inc.

Thomas, H. (2005). *Rivers of Gold: The Rise of the Spanish Empire, from Columbus to Magellan.* New York: Random House.

Thorpe, J. (Director). (1972). *Kung Fu* [Motion Picture]. created by Ed Spielman, written by Herman Miller

Thurston, H. (1910-2009). *St. Joan of Arc.* Retrieved August 02, 2013, from The Catholic Encyclopedia/New Advent, edited by Kevin Knight: http://www.newadvent.org/cathen/08409c.htm

Thurston, H. (2009, August 16). *St. Simeon Stylites the Elder (1912) New York: Robert Appleton Company.* Retrieved December 15, 2012, from New Advent, the Catholic Encyclopedia: www.newadvent.org/cathen/13795a.htm

Thurston, H. (1912). *St. Thomas Becket.* Retrieved July 10, 2013, from New Advent, In The Catholic Encyclopedia. New York: Robert Appleton Company.: http://www.newadvent.org/cathen/14676a.htm

Tierney, B. (1978). *The Middle Ages, Volume 1, Sources of Medieval History.* New York: Alfred A. Knopf Inc.

Tinkle, L. (1985). *13 Days of Glory.* New York: McGraw-Hill Book Company, Inc.

Tozer, A. (1948). *The Pursuit of GOD, with intro by Samuel Zwemer, as listed on the World Invisible Library.* Chicago, Ill.: http://www.worldinvisible.com/library/tozer/5f00.0888/5f00.0888.c.htm.

Trape', A. (1986). *Saint Augustine, Man, Paster, Mystic.* New York City: Catholic Book Publishing Co.

Tuoti, F. X. (1999). *Why Not Be A Mystic?* New York: Crossroad Publishing Company.

Underhill, E. (1990). *Mysticism.* New York: Image Books, DoubleDay.

Vauchez, A. (1993). *The Spirituality of the Medieval West.* Kalamazoo, MI: Cistercian Publications.

Visser, M. (1996). *St. Simeon the Stylite, Volume 14 #2, He dug deeper and ended up higher.* Retrieved December 15, 2012, from Compass, A Jesuit Journal: http://gvanv.com/compass/comphome.html

Volder, J. d. (2010). *The Spirit of Father Damien.* San Francisco: Ignatius Press.

Voragine, J. d. (2012). *The Golden Legend, with an introduction by Eamon Duffy, translated by William Granger Ryan.* New Jersey: Princton University Press.

Voragine, J. d. (1275, 1483). *The Golden Legend or Lives of the Saints, translated by William Caxton, edited by F.S. Ellis.* Genoa : Temple Classics.

Wheeler, R. (1972). *Voices of 1776, the Story of the American Revolution in the words of those who were there.* New York: Meridan (Penguin).

White, T. (1958). *The Once and Future King.* New York: G.P. Putnam and Sons.

Williams, J. (2008, January 4). *The Virtue of the Sword.* Retricved January 4, 2008, from Bugei Trading Company: Bugei.com

Williamson, A. (1999-2011). *Biography of joan of Arc (Jehanne Darc).* Retrieved August 10, 2005, from arcgive.joan-of-arc.org: http://www.joan-of-arc.org/joanofarc_biography.html

Williamson, A. (2010, 2002-2005, March 30). *Joan of Arc, Brief Biography.* Retrieved August 2, 2013, from Archive Joan of Arc: http://archive.joan-of-arc.org/

Williamson, G. (1965). Eusebius. In e. b. G.A. Williamson translator, *Eusebius, the History of the Church from Christ to Constantine.* London: Penguin Books.

Wills, G. (1999). *Saint Augustine.* USA: Weidenfeld and Nicolson.

Woods, D. (1999, September). *The Passion of St. Mercurius.* Retrieved January 6, 2013

Woods, T. E. (2005). *How the Catholic Church Built Western Civilization.* Washington D.C.: Regnery Publishing.

Zacharias, R. (2001). *The Lotus and the Cross, Jesus Talks with Buddha, Great Conversations series.* Orlando, Florida: Multnomah Publishers Inc.

Zwemer, S. M. (1902). *Raymond Lull, First Missionary to the Moslems.* New York and London: Funk and Wagnalls.

Made in the USA
Middletown, DE
29 April 2021

38681290R00333